汽车综合故障诊断与修复

Automobile Integrated Fault Diagnosis and Repair

曹向红 主编

Edited by Xianghong Cao

化学工业出版社
Chemical Industry Press

·北京·
BeiJing

内 容 简 介

本书系统、全面地阐述了汽车故障诊断与修复过程、技术规范，共分14个学习项目，包括充电系统故障诊断与修复、润滑系统故障诊断与修复、冷却系统故障诊断与修复、汽车异响故障诊断与修复、发动机工作异常故障诊断与修复、传动系统故障诊断与修复、自动变速器故障诊断与修复、转向系统故障诊断与修复、制动系统故障诊断与修复、行驶系统故障诊断与修复、安全气囊系统故障诊断与修复、汽车空调系统故障诊断与修复、车身电器故障诊断与修复、汽车车载网络系统故障诊断与修复等。书中以项目导向、任务驱动和案例教学为载体，参照汽车维修企业的典型工作流程，依据凝练的汽车企业岗位工作核心内容和工作任务、岗位规范设计内容，突出实际应用。

本书可供汽车检测与维修技术等汽车类专业学习使用，也可用于汽车维修企业员工在岗培训。

图书在版编目（CIP）数据

汽车综合故障诊断与修复/曹向红主编. —北京：化学工业出版社，2022.7
ISBN 978-7-122-41825-8

Ⅰ.①汽… Ⅱ.①曹… Ⅲ.①汽车-故障诊断②汽车-故障修复 Ⅳ.①U472.4

中国版本图书馆 CIP 数据核字（2022）第 119602 号

责任编辑：韩庆利　　　　　　　　　　　　装帧设计：刘丽华
责任校对：杜杏然

出版发行：化学工业出版社（北京市东城区青年湖南街13号　邮政编码100011）
印　　装：大厂聚鑫印刷有限责任公司
787mm×1092mm　1/16　印张 24¾　字数 638 千字　2022 年 8 月北京第 1 版第 1 次印刷

购书咨询：010-64518888　　　　　　　　　　售后服务：010-64518899
网　　址：http://www.cip.com.cn

凡购买本书，如有缺损质量问题，本社销售中心负责调换。

定　　价：69.80 元　　　　　　　　　　　　　　　　　　版权所有　违者必究

前言

《汽车综合故障诊断与修复》为高等职业教育汽车类专业系列双语教材，是天津交通职业学院教师团队与一汽·大众汽车有限公司技术骨干合作开发的校企合作成果，是中国特色高水平高职学校和专业建设计划项目实施教材教法改革的成果，是天津率先实践的中外人文交流知名品牌——鲁班工坊的优质教学成果之一。

本书对接国际先进教育理念，以项目导向、任务驱动和案例教学为载体，以蕴含规范、安全、环保、服务、协作等要素和精益求精的工匠精神为引导，参照汽车维修企业的典型工作流程，依据凝练的汽车企业岗位工作核心内容和工作任务、岗位规范设计了14个学习项目和若干个学习任务，包括询问车主、试车与基本检查、检测与诊断、故障排除、检验交车等。每个学习任务通过车辆故障典型现象引出故障问题分析、诊断知识点和岗位素养要求，并加以系统、全面地阐述典型案例诊断与修复过程、技术规范。本书所附典型故障案例涵盖大众、丰田、奥迪等品牌车型。可适用于汽车检测与维修技术等汽车类专业学习，也适用于汽车维修企业员工在岗培训。

本书在编写体例上打破传统教材格式，每个学习项目设有学习目标、任务导入、任务实施、任务小结、任务报告单。每个任务配有工作手册式的任务报告单，支持以小组协作形式完成，有利于学生在学习态度、协作能力、实操能力等方面进行过程性量化评估和学习反馈。

本书由天津交通职业学院曹向红任主编，一汽·大众汽车有限公司天津分公司曾凯凯任副主编，天津交通职业学院刘新宇、刘冰月参编。其中，曹向红编写绪论、项目一～项目六、项目十四，曾凯凯编写项目八～项目十一，刘新宇编写项目十二、项目十三，刘冰月编写项目七。本书由天津中德应用技术大学关志伟教授主审，撰写过程中得到了天津市汽车工程学会及其部分会员单位和很多专业技术人员无私的帮助，在此深表感谢！

由于编者水平有限，书中难免有疏漏和不妥之处，敬请广大读者批评指正。

编　者
2022 年 5 月

目录

绪论　汽车故障诊断基础知识 …………………………………………………… 1

项目一　充电系统故障诊断与修复 ……………………………………………… 15

项目二　润滑系统故障诊断与修复 ……………………………………………… 18
    任务一　机油压力过低故障诊断与修复 ………………………………………… 18
    任务二　机油压力过高故障诊断与修复 ………………………………………… 21
    任务三　机油消耗过大故障诊断与修复 ………………………………………… 24
    任务四　机油变质故障诊断与修复 ……………………………………………… 28

项目三　冷却系统故障诊断与修复 ……………………………………………… 31

项目四　汽车异响故障诊断与修复 ……………………………………………… 35
    任务一　发动机异响故障诊断与修复 …………………………………………… 35
    任务二　底盘异响故障诊断与修复 ……………………………………………… 43

项目五　发动机工作异常故障诊断与修复 ……………………………………… 48
    任务一　发动机无法启动故障诊断与修复 ……………………………………… 48
    任务二　发动机有启动征兆，但不能启动故障诊断与修复 …………………… 55
    任务三　发动机启动困难故障诊断与修复 ……………………………………… 60
    任务四　发动机怠速不稳故障诊断与修复 ……………………………………… 65
    任务五　发动机动力不足故障诊断与修复 ……………………………………… 70

项目六　传动系统故障诊断与修复 ……………………………………………… 74
    任务一　离合器打滑故障诊断与修复 …………………………………………… 74
    任务二　手动变速器换挡困难故障诊断与修复 ………………………………… 77

项目七　自动变速器故障诊断与修复 …………………………………………… 81
    任务一　不能行驶故障诊断与修复 ……………………………………………… 81
    任务二　换挡冲击故障诊断与修复 ……………………………………………… 83

任务三	自动变速器异响故障诊断与修复	87
任务四	升挡迟滞故障诊断与修复	90
任务五	打滑故障诊断与修复	93

项目八　转向系统故障诊断与修复　　100

| 任务一 | 液压助力转向系统转向沉重故障诊断与修复 | 100 |
| 任务二 | 电子助力转向系统转向沉重故障诊断与修复 | 103 |

项目九　制动系统故障诊断与修复　　108

任务一	制动力不足故障诊断与修复	108
任务二	制动跑偏故障诊断与修复	111
任务三	ABS系统故障诊断与修复	114

项目十　行驶系统故障诊断与修复　　118

| 任务一 | 汽车行驶跑偏故障诊断与修复 | 118 |
| 任务二 | 轮胎异常磨损故障诊断与修复 | 122 |

项目十一　安全气囊系统故障诊断与修复　　125

项目十二　汽车空调系统故障诊断与修复　　130

任务一	空调系统不工作故障诊断与修复	130
任务二	空调系统制冷不足故障诊断与修复	134
任务三	空调易结冰故障诊断与修复	138

项目十三　车身电器故障诊断与修复　　141

任务一	中控门锁故障诊断与修复	141
任务二	电动玻璃升降器故障诊断与修复	145
任务三	汽车照明系统故障诊断与修复	149

项目十四　汽车车载网络系统故障诊断与修复　　154

参考文献　　159

绪论

汽车故障诊断基础知识

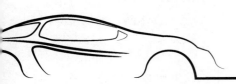

一、汽车故障诊断的基本概念

1. 基本术语和定义

（1）汽车技术状况：定量测得的表征某一时刻汽车外观和性能参数的总和。

（2）汽车检测：确定汽车技术状况和工作能力的检查。

（3）汽车故障：汽车部分或完全丧失工作能力的现象。

（4）汽车故障现象：汽车故障的具体表现。

（5）汽车诊断：在不解体或仅拆下个别小零件的条件下，确定汽车技术状况，查明故障部位及原因的检查。

（6）诊断参数：供诊断用的，表征汽车、总成及机构技术状况的参数。

（7）汽车维修：汽车维护和修理的泛称。

（8）汽车维护：为维持汽车完好技术状况或工作能力而进行的作业。

（9）汽车修复：为恢复汽车完好技术状况或工作能力和寿命而进行的作业。

2. 汽车检测与故障诊断的关系

汽车检测的目的是判断被测车辆的各项技术指标、性能指标是否符合规定，汽车检测是定性分析。

汽车故障诊断包含了"诊"和"断"两个环节，汽车故障诊断的过程就是由诊断技术人员从汽车的故障现象出发，熟练应用各种检测设备对汽车进行相应的检测，完成第一个"诊"的环节，同时结合对汽车原理与结构的深刻理解，对测试结果进行综合分析后对故障部位和原因做出确切的判断，完成第二个"断"的环节。

汽车故障诊断的目的是判断车辆的故障部位和原因，汽车检测是汽车故障诊断的依据。

二、汽车故障的分类

1. 按故障发生的部位分类

汽车故障可分为整体故障和局部故障。

（1）整体故障是指汽车达到设计寿命后，因整体老化导致的整体性能故障，表现为汽车动力性、安全性、经济性、可靠性、制动性、操纵性、环保性、平顺性等多种综合指标整体下降。

（2）局部故障是指汽车某部分出现的故障，这个部分的功能不能实现，但其他部分的功

能仍然完好。

2. 按故障发展过程分类

汽车故障可分为突发性故障和渐进性故障。

（1）突发性故障是指故障在发生前没有可以觉察到的征兆，故障现象是突然出现的，这是各种不利因素和偶然的外界影响共同作用的结果，这种作用超出了产品所能承受的限度，从而导致了突发性故障。

（2）渐进性故障是指故障现象的发生是循序渐进的，其程度是由弱到强逐渐形成的，通常与使用的时间相关联，随着使用时间的延长故障逐渐明显，这种故障发生的特点具有渐强性和必然性，具有明显的量变特征。渐进性故障可以在刚刚发生时就予以诊断，加以排除。

3. 按故障发生频次分类

汽车故障可分为偶发性故障和多发性故障。

（1）偶发性故障是指故障现象出现的概率非常低的故障，即发生次数极少的故障。例如：行驶中发动机突然熄火在很长时间内仅发生过一两次。

（2）多发性故障是指故障现象出现的概率比较高的故障，即经常发生的故障。

4. 按故障影响程度分类

汽车故障可分为部分故障和完全故障两种。

（1）部分故障是指汽车部分丧失工作能力的故障，即使用性能降低。例如：制动性能变差、加速性能不良、怠速不良等。

（2）完全故障是指汽车完全丧失工作能力的故障，即使用性能完全丧失。例如：完全没有制动、完全不能加速（一加速就熄火）、没有怠速等。

三、汽车故障诊断方法

1. 人工经验诊断法

人工经验诊断法是诊断人员凭借丰富的实践经验和一定的理论知识，在汽车不解体或局部解体的情况下，借助简单的检查手段，主要采用眼看、耳听、手摸、鼻嗅等手段，进行检查、试验、分析和确定汽车故障原因和部位的诊断方法。人工经验诊断法既是汽车故障诊断的传统方法，也是基本方法，即使在现代仪器诊断技术飞速发展的今天人工经验诊断方法也不可能被替代。

（1）"看" "看"主要通过直接用眼或借助放大镜、内窥镜等对汽车各部位进行观察，查看是否有异常现象，查找故障的蛛丝马迹。这是一种应用最多的、最基本的，也是比较有效的故障诊断法。

汽车故障诊断中可以"看"的项目及部位主要包括以下几个方面。

① 汽车故障指示灯的指示情况；汽车仪表及各报警灯、指示灯的显示情况。

② 有无漏气、漏水、漏油；液体流动性是否正常；机油、变速器油、制动液、冷却液等液体颜色与液面高度是否正常。

③ 发动机的排气颜色是否正常。

④ 各部件运动是否正常；连接部件有无松脱、裂纹、变形、断裂等现象。

⑤ 线路是否有破损、松脱、折断处；导线的接线端子是否存在锈蚀、变形等异常情况。

⑥ 油管及气管是否出现压瘪、弯曲、破损、裂纹等。

⑦ 各操纵杆、拉线、拉杆是否调整得当。

⑧ 进气管、进排气门处及气缸内有无结焦。

⑨ 轮胎气压及轮胎磨损是否正常；车架、车桥、车身及各总成外壳、护板等有无明显

变形，相关部位有无剐蹭痕迹等。

以上所列的观察项目及部位很多，但在实际故障诊断中所观察的是具体故障发生的区域，以及与故障相关联的部位或项目。

利用"看"进行故障诊断，类似于中医通过观察神、色、形、态、舌象等来测知病人的内脏病变。汽车故障诊断中的"看"，一方面可以将发生在汽车表面的故障查找到，避免走弯路；另一方面可以通过观察来获得汽车内部的故障信息，比如通过查看自动变速器油液的颜色及油中包含的物质即可大致了解变速器的故障原因。

（2）"摸" "摸"是通过人手去感受机件的温度、压力、振动等，以此来获得汽车的故障信息，就像中医切脉一样，这也是一种比较有效的故障诊断方法。

"摸"能够帮助进行诊断的故障及项目主要包括以下几个方面。

① 发动机水温异常；自动变速器油温异常。

② 空调系统的部分故障；汽车悬挂系统和减振器的部分故障。

③ 用手触摸可判断线路的插头及导线连接处是否松动，触摸线路连接处是否有不正常的高温，可判断该处是否存在接触不良。

④ 用手感受喷油器、各种电磁阀和电机等部件的振动情况，可以判断它们是否工作。

⑤ 用手触摸点火模块、点火线圈、继电器、电机等电器与电子元件的表面温度，可以判断它们是否正常工作。

⑥ 检查皮带的松紧度，可判断皮带是否存在打滑。

⑦ 用手触摸发电机、空调压缩机等部件判断是否存在连接松动。

⑧ 用手感觉机油、自动变速器油、齿轮油等的黏度，以及所含的杂质，可以判断油的品质及可能存在的故障。

⑨ 用手感觉冷却水管、燃油管的压力波动来了解冷却水循环情况及供油情况。

⑩ 检查摩擦面的磨损情况，检查摩擦副配合间隙，以及旋转部件的运转平顺性，判断这些部位是否存在故障。

⑪ 用手触摸离合器、制动鼓或制动盘，感知它们的温度，可以判断是否存在离合器打滑、制动拖滞故障。

比如当出现发动机水温高的故障时，用手摸一摸上下水管即可判断节温器是否能正常打开，用手触摸散热器表面感受各部分是否存在温度差即可获知散热器内部是否存在管路堵塞。

（3）"听" "听"主要直接通过耳朵的听觉或借助听诊器对汽车发出的声响进行监听，从而判断故障部位与类型，进而查找故障原因。这种方法主要用于查找汽车机械部分异响的部位及判断一些电气元件是否工作。

汽车故障诊断中涉及"听"的故障及项目主要包括以下几个方面。

① 进排气系统异响。

② 传动皮带打滑异响。

③ 发电机、空调压缩机等部件的异响。

④ 发动机的各种异响：气门异响、活塞销响、活塞敲缸响、曲轴轴承响、连杆轴承响等。机械传动部分异响：离合器响、变速器响、主减速器响等。

⑤ 点火系统高压线漏电。

⑥ 通过听继电器、喷油器、电磁阀等是否有接通的声音，以及电机、油泵等是否有运转声音来判断它们是否能工作。

⑦ 转向系统异响。

⑧ 制动系统异响。

⑨ 汽车悬架异响。
⑩ 车身、车轮在行驶中的异响。

通过"听"进行诊断时一定要注意方法和手段，比如在检查发动机异响故障时，一般是在停车状态下启动发动机，使发动机在不同的转速下运转，根据不同故障部位发出声音的不同，如连续性响与间断性响、脆响与闷响、有规则响与无规则响等，从而判断出响声的部位，有时还需要借助听诊器。对于传动系统的异响故障，往往需要通过路试的方法，围绕异响产生的条件进行行驶，从而确定异响部位。

（4）"嗅"　"嗅"主要通过鼻子的嗅觉感知汽车各部分产生的异常气味。通过"嗅"能够帮助进行诊断的故障或项目主要包括以下几个方面。

① 由发动机排放尾气的异味判断发动机工作情况，为故障诊断提供重要信息。
② 由发动机机油、自动变速器油等油液的异味判断油液的品质及相应系统的工作情况。
③ 由非金属材料焦煳味判断离合器打滑、制动拖滞等故障。
④ 由橡胶及塑料件过热后发出的橡胶塑料味来查找导线过热、线路短路等故障。

2. 仪器设备诊断法

仪器设备诊断法指诊断人员在汽车不进行部件拆卸或少拆卸的情况下，利用各种诊断与检测设备，对汽车各种诊断参数进行检测、试验、分析，以了解汽车各部分的技术状况，最终确定汽车故障原因和部位的诊断方法。用于车辆诊断与检测的设备很多，如万用表、燃油压力表、气缸压力表、真空表、示波器、故障诊断仪、正时灯等，这些设备都有各自的检测功能，在实际故障诊断中可以根据所需要的检测项目选择相应的设备，进行相应的检测。

比如，燃油系统可能存在故障时，通过使用燃油压力表检测燃油压力，可以确定燃油系统是否确实存在故障；当发动机进气歧管可能存在漏气时，通过真空表检测进气歧管真空度，可以确定进气歧管是否存在漏气故障。

3. 试验法

试验法即采用一定的方法和手段围绕故障进行相应试验，从而确定故障部位。

常用的试验方法主要包括如下几种。

（1）互换、替换对比试验

① 互换对比试验：指将同一台车上可能有故障的零部件与其他相同的零部件进行互换，若故障转移到另一处则说明被怀疑部件确实有故障。如单缸独立点火发动机2缸不工作，且故障很可能在该缸点火线圈时，就可以将该缸点火线圈与其他缸的进行互换，若故障转移到其他缸，则故障确实在2缸点火线圈。

② 替换对比试验：指将汽车上可能有故障的零部件用一个好的零部件替换，如果故障现象消失，证明故障就发生在这个零部件。这种方法特别适合在没有维修数据和资料，且配件充足的条件下使用。这种方法很简捷，不需要用检测设备进行检测，在有些故障的诊断中效率很高。

例如，当发动机出现加速不良故障时，若判断故障可能发生在空气流量计，则可以用一个好的空气流量计进行替换，如果替换后故障排除，即可确定故障发生在空气流量计。

（2）振动模拟试验　当振动可能是导致产生故障的主要原因时，就可以利用振动法进行检验。试验方法主要包括：在水平和垂直方向轻轻摆动连接器、线束、导线接头等；用手轻轻拍打传感器、执行器、继电器和开关等部件。在振动模拟试验时如果故障重新出现或故障消失，则说明被施加振动部件存在故障。

（3）加热模拟试验　当故障是由某些传感器或其他零部件受热所致时，可用电加热吹风机等加热工具对可能引起故障的零部件进行适当加热，如果故障重新出现，则说明被加热部

件存在故障。

（4）加湿模拟试验　当故障在雨天或湿度较大的条件下产生时，可进行喷淋加湿试验。试验时，将水喷洒在散热器前面或汽车顶部，如果故障再现，则重点检查易受潮部位的部件。

（5）分离（隔离）对比试验　这是将某些系统或部件进行分离（隔离），使其停止工作，通过故障现象是否变化来确定故障部位或范围的方法。

① 隔离电气元件或线路时故障消失，则故障在被隔离的部件或线路。如汽车发生短路故障并锁定某一区域时，将该区域的部件逐个隔离，当隔离到某一部件且故障消失时，则故障在该部件区域。

② 拆除机件时故障消失，则故障在该机件。如汽车有加速不良故障且故障可能由于空气滤清器堵塞引起时，可取下空气滤清器试车，若故障消失，则故障确实由空气滤清器引起。另外，在维修中常用的通过单缸断火试验检查发动机异响或怠速不稳故障也属于此方法。

③ 堵塞油气路，看故障现象是否变化。例如：掐住真空管路，若进气歧管真空度上升，则说明该真空管漏气；掐住燃油的回油管，若油压回升，则存在油压过低故障。

4. 故障自诊断法

故障自诊断法是使用汽车电脑故障诊断仪调取故障码，然后按照维修手册中提供的故障码诊断流程图表进行故障诊断的方法。故障自诊断法是仪器设备诊断法的一种特殊形式，它是以汽车电脑故障诊断仪调出的汽车电子控制系统故障码为切入点，进行汽车故障诊断的一种方法。汽车电脑故障诊断仪在自诊断分析中最重要的是故障码和数据流这两种显示方式，故障码可以定性地给出故障点的描述，数据流可以定量地给出批数据参数的显示，这些参数不仅能对电控单元输入输出信息进行多通路即时显示，还可以对电控单元控制过程的参数进行动态变化的显示。

四、汽车故障诊断基本流程

汽车故障诊断基本流程是汽车故障诊断中最基础的诊断过程，是对诊断内容的最一般的概括和总结，汽车故障诊断基本内容包括从故障症状出发，通过问诊试车（验证故障症状）、分析研究（分析结构原理）、推理假设（推出可能原因）、流程设计（提出诊断步骤）、测试确认（测试确认故障点）、修复验证（排除故障后验证），最后达到发现故障最终原因的目的。

汽车故障诊断的基本流程如图0-1所示。

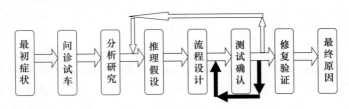

图0-1　汽车故障诊断基本流程

1. 最初症状

最初症状指的是需要维修的车辆所表现出的故障特征，对于维修人员来说，准确了解并描述故障现象非常重要，这关系到诊断的方向和效率。因为车主只能从车辆使用中的异常判断车辆出现故障，而维修人员需要根据车主的描述以及自身观察准确描述故障症状。

2. 问诊试车

问诊是通过对车主询问了解汽车故障症状的过程，试车则是对汽车故障症状实际验证进一步确认故障症状的过程。

（1）问诊　问诊是维修人员向车主询问汽车故障情况的过程，就像医生向就诊的病人询问病情一样。问诊应该是汽车故障诊断的第一步。问诊在汽车故障诊断中非常重要，把握好这个环节可以确定下一步故障诊断的方向、甚至可以锁定故障范围。

一般问诊应包括以下内容。

① 故障发生的状况。
- 初次故障发生的时间，汽车所处的状态。
- 故障是否还同时伴随着其他性能变化，故障发生之前有何征兆。
- 故障发生的频次：经常发生；有时发生；一定条件下发生；只发生一次。
- 故障发生后的变化程度：没有变化；越来越严重；迅速恶化。
- 故障发生的环境：故障发生时的气温、气候、道路情况等。

② 维修保养情况。
- 故障发生后是否进行过维修，进行了哪些维修，更换过哪些零部件。
- 故障发生前是否加装过设备，更改过线路或更换过零部件。
- 该车是否按时进行保养，是否在正规维修企业进行保养。

此外，在必要时还需要了解车主的驾驶习惯，经常行驶的道路条件及行驶车速、挡位情况，以及加注的燃油标号、品质及添加剂使用情况等。

注意，问诊一定要掌握技巧，询问故障症状发生时的情况时应尽量让车主多说，不要提示太多，否则会误导用户说出模棱两可的故障现象，增加诊断的难度。此外提问时要用车主熟悉的话语，使车主容易理解，尽量不要使用车主不懂的专业术语。

（2）试车　试车的目的在于再现车主所述的故障症状，以验证故障症状的真实性，同时试验故障症状再现时的特征、时间、地点、环境、条件、工况等客观状态，以便为进一步分析故障原因做准备。

在试车再现故障症状后，维修人员应该反复体会和观察故障症状出现时，各种状况、工况、环境、条件等细微过程，并且认真记录下来，确认故障症状。试车是维修人员感受汽车故障症状的过程，对于维修人员了解掌握故障症状特征具有非常重要的意义。完整的试车应该包括汽车各种性能的试验过程，即从发动机冷机启动、冷机高怠速，暖机到热机怠速、加速、急加速全过程的运行状况，以及仪表指示情况。此外还应该包括汽车起步、换挡、加速、减速、制动、转向等过程的行驶状况试验，根据车辆故障去选择检查汽车的动力性能、制动性能、行驶稳定性能、操纵可靠性能、振动摆动异响等状况，感受驾驶和操纵过程的各种反应，以便检查是否有车主未感觉到的汽车故障症状存在。

3. 分析研究

分析研究是在问诊试车后根据故障症状，对汽车结构和原理进行的深入研究分析，目的在于分析故障生成的机理，故障产生的条件和特点，为下一步找出故障原因做准备。分析研究首先要收集汽车发生故障部位的结构原理资料，了解汽车正常运行的条件和规律，并且与故障状态进行对比分析，分析研究的基础材料是车辆结构与原理方面的知识，以及所修汽车维修手册提供的机械与液压原理结构图、油路电路气路图、电子控制系统框图、控制原理图表、技术参数表、技术信息通报等重要信息。

4. 推理假设

在分析研究汽车故障部位的结构原理、查找对比汽车技术资料后，就应该根据逻辑分析和经验判断做出对故障可能原因的推理假设。推理假设是对故障原因的初步判断，它是基于理论和实践两个方面的。理论上是指根据结构原理知识，加上故障症状的表现，再从逻辑分析出发推出导致故障症状发生的可能原因，这个推导从原理上是能够成立的逻辑推理，这是基于理论

的逻辑推理。实践上是指根据以往故障诊断的经验，对相同或相似结构的类似故障做出的可能故障原因的经验推断，这个推断具有类比判断的性质，这就是基于实践的经验推断。

推理是根据工作原理和故障症状推出故障原理的过程，在这个环节中除了要对工作原理有深刻理解之外，还应该注意到故障症状所对应的故障本质。也就是说虽然我们还不知道是什么最终原因导致了故障症状的发生，还不知道故障点到底在哪里，但这时的故障发生机理应该已经基本明确。例如，发动机排放黑烟的故障症状，虽然不知道是哪个元器件损坏导致的，但从原理上讲一定是混合气浓造成的。假设是根据推理的结果进一步推断下一层故障原因的过程。例如，进一步分析导致混合气浓的原因，可以知道无非是两个，一个是燃油多，另一个是空气少。再进一步推理可知，燃油多可能有油压高和喷油时间长两个原因，而喷油时间长又可能有控制喷油时间不正常和喷油器关闭不严两个原因。空气少则可能有空气真少和假少两种情况，空气真少是由于进气系统堵塞导致的，空气假少则是由于空气流量计输出信号过高导致的。这就是一步步提出假设的过程。推理是推出导致故障症状发生的基本机理原因，假设是在推出的故障机理基础上进一步运用逻辑推理的方法向故障下一层纵深分析其原因得到的结果。很显然，上述例子中故障症状排放黑烟的故障原因机理是混合气过浓导致的，这个推断是被经验证实的，因此，这推理是经验判断的结果。如果故障症状是发生在应用新技术、新结构的汽车上，例如，混合动力车、柴油共轨喷射等系统中，那么故障症状的对应机理就无法从经验判断中直接得到了，此时必须对结构组成和工作原理进行深入分析之后，才能推出可能的故障机理原因的方向，进而做出深层原因的假设，这里就要用到逻辑推理的方法。

推理假设的过程是从大方向上寻找故障原因的过程，这个过程探究的是故障基本机理和基本方向。

5. 流程设计

流程设计是在推理假设环节之后，根据假设的可能故障原因，设计出实际应用的故障诊断流程。设计时要先确定应检测的项目，再确定分辨汽车各大组成部分或总成故障的检测方法，然后确定汽车各个系统和装置工作性能好坏的检测方法，最后才是部件和线路的测试方法。这些测试方法的应用目的在于逐渐缩小故障怀疑范围，最终锁定故障点。

6. 测试确认

测试确认是在故障诊断流程设计之后，按照流程设计的步骤通过测试的手段逐一测试各个项目。测试确认是在不解体或只拆卸少数零部件的前提下完成的对汽车整体性能、系统或总成性能、机电装置性能、管线路状态以及零部件性能的测试过程，它包含检测、试验、确认三个部分，这三个部分的内容是不一样的。检测主要指通过人工直观察看和设备仪器分析进行的检查和测量来完成的技术检查过程，试验主要指通过对系统的模拟实验和动态分析来完成的技术诊察过程。确认主要指通过对诊断流程的逻辑分析、对检测和试验结果的判断，最后确认故障发生点的部位。

7. 修复验证

修复验证是在测试确认最小故障点发生部位后，对故障点进行的修复以及对修复后的结果进行的验证。它分为修复方法的确定和修复后的验证两个部分。

（1）修复方法的确定　修复方法要依据故障点的故障表现模式来确定，故障点是导致故障发生的低端事件，是故障的最小单元，故障点所具有的不同表现模式，决定了修复中将采用的不同方法。

① 元件损坏、元件老化和元件错用等模式的故障，通常采用更换的方式进行修复。

② 安装松脱、装配错误和调整不当等模式的故障，通常采用重新安装调整的方式进行修复。

③ 润滑不良模式的故障，采用维护润滑的方式修复。

④ 密封不严模式的故障，通常对橡胶件采用更换，对机械部件采用表面修复工艺或更换的方式修复。

⑤ 油液亏缺模式的故障，通常采用添加的方式修复，但对于渗漏和不正常的消耗导致的亏缺，要对症下药找到根源给予修复。

⑥ 气液漏堵模式的故障，通常要采用疏通堵塞、封堵渗漏的方式修复。

⑦ 结焦结垢模式的故障，一般采用清洗除焦垢的方式修复。

⑧ 生锈氧化模式的故障，一般采取除锈清氧化的方式修复。

⑨ 运动干涉模式的故障，通常采用恢复形状、调整位置、加强紧固的方式修复。

⑩ 控制失调、进入紧急备用模式以及匹配不当模式的故障，采用重新调整、恢复归零以及重新匹配的方式修复。

⑪ 短路断路、线路损伤、虚焊烧蚀模式的故障，采用修理破损、清理烧蚀、重新焊接以及局部更换线路的方式修复。

⑫ 漏电击穿、接触不良的故障模式，采用更换或清理接触点的方式修复。

（2）修复后的验证　修复后的验证是指对修复后的车辆进行功能测试，如果故障现象完全消失，车辆功能恢复正常则可以确认车辆已经被完全修复。

8. 最终原因

在对前面环节中找到的最小故障点进行修复验证后，故障现象可能消除了，但是这时不能认为故障诊断工作到此可以结束了，因为导致这个最小故障点发生故障的最终原因还没有认定，如果不再继续追究下去，就此结束维修，让汽车出厂继续行驶，很有可能导致故障现象的再次发生。对故障点的最终故障原因进行分析，找到其产生的内部原因和外部原因，彻底消除故障发生的根本原因，杜绝故障再次发生，这就是汽车故障诊断基本流程最后一个环节的重要内容。

五、汽车常用故障检测与诊断设备

1. 试灯

试灯通常分为二极管试灯和普通灯泡试灯两种，如图 0-2 和图 0-3 所示。

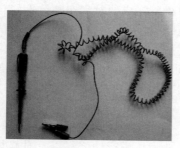

图 0-2　二极管试灯

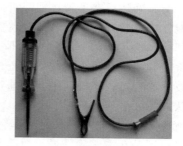

图 0-3　普通灯泡试灯

试灯使用简单、方便且直观，所以在汽车检测中应用广泛。但是要注意在检测与汽车电控单元相连接的线路时不能使用普通灯泡制作的试灯，而只能使用由发光二极管制作的试灯，否则会损伤汽车电子元件。

利用试灯可以检测线路是否带电。试灯的一端连接电瓶负极或者接地，另一端与被测部位连接，若试灯亮，说明线路有电，否则说明电路没电。

利用试灯可以检测一条线路是否存在断路。若用试灯检测电器电源电路中某一点有电，

但在电路的下一点检测没电，则说明该段线路存在断路。

利用试灯可以检测信号线路中是否有信号存在。如点火信号、霍尔式凸轮轴位置传感器等信号电路在用试灯检测时，试灯应有规律地闪烁，否则说明线路或者相关部件故障。

2. 万用表

汽车万用表如图 0-4 所示，它是汽车故障诊断中最常用的检测工具，一般具有测量电压、电阻和电流等功能，有些还可对占空比、温度、频率等项目进行检测。

注意，除非在测试过程中有特殊需要，否则不能用指针式万用表测试电脑和传感器，应使用高阻抗数字式万用表，万用表内阻应不低于 $10k\Omega$。

（1）电压检测　测量两个端子间或两条线路间的电压时，应将万用表（电压挡）的两个表笔与被测量的两个端子或两根导线接触。

测量某个端子或某条线路的电压时，应将万用表的正表笔与被测的端子或线路接触，将万用表的负表笔与地线接触。

（2）电阻检测　检查线路断路故障时，应先脱开电脑和相应传感器的连接器，然后测量连接器相应端子间的电阻，以确定是否有断路或接触不良故障。

检查线路搭铁短路故障时，应拆开线路两端的连接器，然后测量连接器被测端子与车身（搭铁）之间的电阻值。如果测得的电阻值很小或无电阻值，则可以判定导线与车身之间有短路搭铁故障。如果电阻值大于 $1M\Omega$，则为无故障。

检查端子、触点或导线等的导通性时，可用万用表（电阻挡）测量其电阻值，若导通则电阻值应很小或为零，若不导通则电阻值应为∞。

注意，电阻检测时需拆卸发动机电子控制系统线路，在此之前应首先切断电源，即将点火开关关闭。

（3）检测电流　首先将被测电路断开，然后根据所测的电流是交流还是直流，将万用表选好交流挡或直流挡，选择好量程，将万用表串接进线路中。红表笔应接在和电源正极相连的断点上，黑表笔应接在和电源负极相连的断点上。

（4）检测占空比　占空比是指在一个通电周期内通电时间与周期的比值。汽车上的许多信号都是占空比信号，如凸轮轴位置传感器、曲轴位置传感器、炭罐电磁阀等。

连接时，红表笔接信号电路，黑表笔接地或与蓄电池的负极连接。

3. 真空表

汽车诊断用真空表如图 0-5 所示，通过真空表检测真空度可以对多种故障原因及部位进行判断，它在汽车诊断中发挥着越来越大的作用。

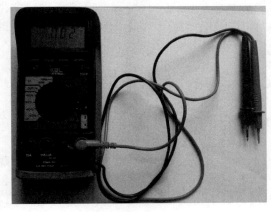

图 0-4　万用表

图 0-5　真空表

绪论　汽车故障诊断基础知识

发动机在不同工况下工作时，其进气管中的真空度是不同的。真空表连接在节气门后方的进气歧管上，利用真空表检测发动机在不同工况下的进气歧管内的真空度，可以帮助诊断发动机存在的各种故障。

(1) 启动工况检测　为了使测试结果精确，启动测试需要在发动机热机时进行。如发动机因故障无法启动，也可在冷机时测量，但精确度会降低。测量时要关闭节气门，断开喷油器插头，启动发动机，同时观察真空表数值。发动机各部分正常时，数值通常在 11～21kPa。如果低于 10kPa，则可能原因是：发动机转速过低，活塞环磨损，节气门卡滞或烧蚀，进气歧管漏气，怠速旁通气路开度过大等。

(2) 怠速工况检测　发动机在怠速工况下，进气歧管真空度通常在 50～70kPa（随发动机排量和压缩比的不同而不同）。若测量值不在此范围内，或者与正常值相比过大或过小，则说明发动机存在故障。

① 如果真空表数值有规律地下降 6～9kPa，数值稳定，则应检查初始点火正时、配气正时、气缸压力、曲轴箱强制通风阀和废气再循环系统、节气门的密封性和怠速旁通阀，以及检查是否有不工作的火花塞。

② 如果真空表数值不规则地下降 10～27kPa 时，则火花塞可能工作不良，或者存在气门卡滞、气门挺杆或液压挺杆卡滞，也可能凸轮轴严重磨损。

③ 如果真空表数值缓慢地在 27～34kPa 来回显示，则应检查混合气是否过浓（重点检查供油系统）和火花塞间隙是否太小。

④ 如果真空表数值很快地在 47～61kPa 来回变化，则应检查进气门挺杆与导管是否磨损、配合是否松旷。如果真空表数值在 34～76kPa 来回缓慢显示，并且随着发动机转速的升高数值变化加剧，则很可能是气门弹簧的弹力不足。

⑤ 如果真空表数值在 18～65kPa 大幅度来回变化，很可能是气缸衬垫漏气。

⑥ 如果发动机怠速转速过高，进气歧管真空度小于 40kPa，说明发动机节气门之后的进气歧管或总管漏气，漏气部位一般是进气歧管垫及与进气歧管相连接的诸多管路，如真空助力器气管等。

⑦ 如果发动机启动困难，并且保证不了稳定怠速运转，但发动机的进气歧管真空度在 50kPa 以上，就说明发动机的进气管路和气缸密封没有问题，故障主要在于电控系统造成的点火不良或喷油不良，如点火线圈异常等。

(3) 急加速和急减速工况检测　如果发动机各系统正常，急加速时真空表的数值应突然下降，急减速时真空表的数值将在原怠速时的位置大幅度上升。当迅速开启和关闭节气门时，真空表数值应随之起伏在 7～86kPa。如果活塞严重漏气，真空表数值的变化幅度将不大明显。真空表数值变化幅度越宽，表明发动机技术状况越好。如果怠速时真空表数值低于正常值，急加速时数值下降到 0 附近，节气门突然关闭时真空表数值也不能升高到 86kPa 左右，则说明活塞环、进气管或节气门体衬垫漏气。

(4) 排气系统阻塞的检测　若排气管时通时堵，则排气时的反压力增大，会使进气歧管的真空度降低。怠速时的真空度一般应为 50～70kPa。缓慢加速，使转速达到 2000～2500r/min，此时真空表数值应等于或接近怠速时的真空数值。使节气门快速回到怠速状态，此时真空表读数应先快速增加一个幅度（如 15～20kPa）然后又回落。

如果发动机在 2500r/min 时，真空表数值逐渐低于怠速数值或在从 2500r/min 猛然降到怠速时真空表数值没有增加，说明排气系统内背压过高，其排气阻力过大，很可能是三元催化转化器堵塞，或排气管与消声器堵塞。此时可以拆下排气管再试，若真空度恢复正常，即可确定排气管堵塞。

如果发动机不能启动时，真空度在 0 附近波动，甚至出现正压，就说明排气管或三元催化转化器堵死。

特别需要说明的是，因为发动机真空数值会随着海拔高度与空气密度的不同而不同，所以每一种发动机的标准数值会有所不同。

4. 油压表

油压表如图 0-6 所示，通过油压表进行油路压力检测可以对油路系统故障进行分析和判断。

（1）机油压力检测　拆下机油压力传感器或机油压力开关，选取合适的接头将油压表连接好，启动发动机并在怠速、加速、大负荷状态下读取机油压力值，与规定值对比，可以确定机油泵、机油压力传感器、机油压力表等是否有故障。

（2）燃油压力检测　首先断开燃油管路，然后选取合适的接头将油压表连接到燃油管路中。启动发动机并在怠速、加速、大负荷状态下读取燃油压力值，与规定值对比，可以确定燃油泵、油压调节器等是否有故障。关闭发动机，等待 10min 后观察压力表的压力值，通常应不低于 0.20MPa，否则为油泵单向阀故障。

（3）制动压力检测　首先断开连接总泵的油管，然后选取合适的接头将油压表连接到制动管路中。踩下制动踏板，观察油压值，与规定值对比。若油压值正常且能保持压力不变，则总泵无故障。若油压缓慢下降，则制动总泵的制动缸、活塞等磨损过大。

（4）自动变速器油压检测　首先拆下自动变速器测压孔上的螺母，然后选取合适的接头将油压表连接到测压孔上。启动发动机，在怠速及各挡位工况下观察油压值，并与规定值对比，若主油压不在规定范围，则说明油泵、油压调节器等有故障。若各挡油压不在规定范围，则说明各挡电磁阀、换挡阀等有故障。

5. 气缸压力表

气缸压力表如图 0-7 所示，用于检测发动机气缸压力，以此可以对发动机机械系统进行故障诊断。

图 0-6　油压表

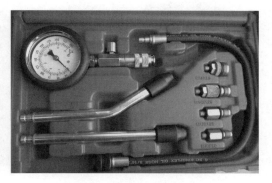

图 0-7　气缸压力表

气缸压力表可分为推入式和螺纹接口式 2 种。推入式气缸压力表用于汽油发动机的检测，螺纹接口式气缸压力表用于柴油发动机的检测。柴油机压缩力大，必须将压力表头严密地紧固在喷油器孔上才能测量。汽油机压缩力比较小，可用手握住压力表，直接顶在火花塞孔上进行测量。

气缸压力的检测与分析如下。

（1）检测条件　检测前，启动发动机并让其运转一段时间，进行预热，使水温升至 75～90℃，机油压力达到正常值后，再熄火进行测试。这是因为气缸的润滑状况对气缸压力

的影响仅次于曲轴转速，而气缸的润滑状况又与机油温度密切相关。测量时发动机的各种状态越接近实际工况，测量的结果越准确。对测得结果，还须结合使用与维修情况进行具体分析，以得出正确的结论。

（2）检测方法　发动机停机后，用压缩空气吹净火花塞或喷油器周围的灰尘和脏物，然后卸下全部火花塞（柴油机需拆下喷油器）并按气缸次序放置。将气缸压力表的橡胶接头插在被测缸的火花塞孔内，扶正压紧。将节气门位于全开位置，用启动机转动曲轴3～5s，待压力表头指针指示并保持最大压力后停止转动。取下气缸压力表，读取并记下读数，按下单向阀使压力表指针回零。按上述方法依次测量各缸，每缸测量次数不少于2次。就车检测柴油机气缸压力时，除应使用螺纹接头的气缸压力表外，其他检测条件和检测方法与汽油机相同。

（3）气缸压力检测结果分析　气缸压缩压力标准值一般由汽车制造厂提供。按照规定，在用汽车发动机各气缸压力应不小于原设计值的85%。每缸压力与各缸平均压力的差值，汽油机应不大于8%，柴油机应不大于10%。

测得结果如高于原设计规定，可能是由于燃烧室积炭过多、气缸衬垫过薄或缸体与缸盖结合平面经多次修理加工过甚造成的，这种情况一般较少出现。测得结果若低于原设计规定，可向该缸火花塞或喷油器孔内注入适量机油，然后用气缸压力表重测气缸压力，并进行分析。

① 第二次测出的压力比第一次高，接近标准压力，表明气缸、活塞环、活塞磨损过大，或活塞环对口、卡死、断裂及缸壁拉伤等原因造成气缸密封不严。

② 第二次测出压力与第一次略同，即仍比标准压力低，表明进、排气门或气缸垫不密封。

③ 两次检测结果均表明某相邻两缸压力都相当低，说明两缸相邻处的气缸垫烧损窜气。

6. 红外测温仪

图0-8　红外测温仪

红外测温仪如图0-8所示，通过该设备检测汽车部件的表面温度可以判断部件及相关系统是否正常工作。

红外测温仪进行检测时不需要接触被测物体表面。该仪器测量范围大，使用方便、简单，测量快速、准确而安全。

（1）发动机工作状况检测　检测发动机的排气温度，可以判断某缸是否工作或者工作是否正常。如果某缸排气温度明显低于其他缸，则该缸没有工作，如果该缸排气温度比其他缸相对低一些，说明该缸工作较差。

（2）冷却系统检测　若发动机水温过高，而冷却液量正常，不能直接判断出故障部位，则很可能是冷却系统内部管路堵塞、节温器、水泵等故障。

检测散热器进水管和出水管的温差应非常明显，检测散热器表面各部分温度应一致，否则说明散热器故障。

当发动机水温达到正常值时，检测发动机出水管的温度应明显升高，若温度升高不明显或者没有升高，说明节温器工作不良。

（3）检测发动机排气管温度　三元催化转换器出口端的温度应该比进口端温度高几十摄氏度，否则说明三元催化转换器工作不良。

7. 手动真空泵

手动真空泵如图0-9所示，通过该设备对被测部件施加真空，以真空度能否保持来判断该部件是否正常工作。

手动真空泵可以用于检测真空控制阀和气体控制电磁阀等，比如炭罐电磁阀、废气再循环阀等。检测时，选择合适的接头与软管，一端与真空泵相连，另一端与被测元件相连，如

图0-10所示,压几次泵杆,观察表的读数。阀在关闭时,表上显示的数值应保持不变,否则说明阀体关闭不严而漏气。

图0-9　手动真空泵

图0-10　手动真空泵检测炭罐电磁阀

8. 汽车故障诊断仪

汽车故障诊断仪分为通用型和专用型。如图0-11所示为一款通用型汽车故障诊断仪。通用型用于检测常用车型的汽车电控系统,而专用型用于检测某一车系的电控系统。

汽车故障诊断仪是维修中非常重要的工具,一般具有如下几项或全部的功能:

① 读取故障码。
② 清除故障码。
③ 读取电控系统动态数据流。
④ 示波功能。
⑤ 元件动作测试。
⑥ 匹配、设定和编码等功能。

使用故障诊断仪通常有以下几步。

① 在车上找到诊断座。
② 选用相应的诊断接头。
③ 根据车型,进入相应诊断系统即可进行相应检测和诊断。

图0-11　汽车故障诊断仪

利用故障诊断仪可以读取汽车上各电控单元中存储的故障码,如图0-12所示。维修人员可以通过故障码了解故障发生的部位和类型,故障码为故障诊断提供了诊断的方向。电控单元中存储的故障码可以通过故障诊断仪所发出的清除故障码指令予以清除。

读取动态数据流指的是读取汽车上各电控单元所收到的各种信号信息。电控单元能够将从传感器获取的直流、交流、串行数据等信号进行处理以实际值显示出来,如发动机水温传感器传输给发动机电控单元的电压是1.6V,对应发动机水温是70℃,则通过故障诊断仪读取的数据流即是70℃水温。

在进行故障诊断时,若遇到无故障码显示的情况,则可以查看数据流并与标准值对比来分析相关系统或部件是否存在故障。数据流如图0-13所示。

示波功能是很多故障诊断仪的重要功能,示波功能通常有单通道、双通道、三通道和四通道四种显示模式,比如双通道示波功能可以同时独立地显示两个不同的信号波形,可以选择相同的信号源也可以选择不同的信号源。示波器输入端有一个测试探头和一个接地的夹子,

绪论　汽车故障诊断基础知识

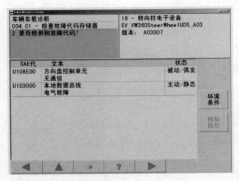
图 0-12　读取故障码

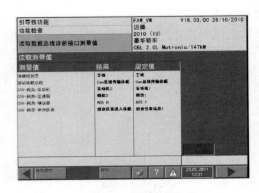
图 0-13　读取数据流

在测量时将夹子接地，探头放到需要测试的点即可，所测信号波形如图 0-14 所示。

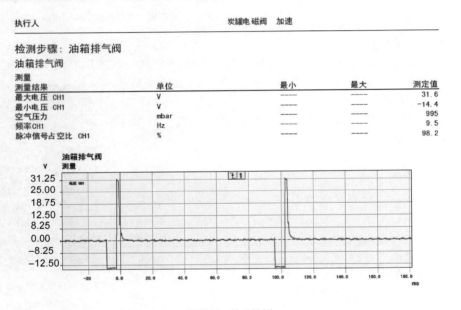
图 0-14　波形检测

诊断仪可以对信号波形的幅值和频率进行调整，使显示的波形清晰完整。通过波形可以了解信号的类型和信号变化的过程。检测出的波形与标准波形对比，即可分析出相关部件和线路是否有故障。

注意，测试点火高压线时，必须使用专用的电容探头，不能将示波器探头直接接入点火次级电路。

元件动作测试指的是由故障诊断仪向汽车电控单元发出指令，电控单元再控制汽车上的某个执行器（如喷油器、燃油泵、炭罐电磁阀）工作，通过判断元件是否响应来判断执行器及线路是否有故障。元件动作测试可以针对处于工作状态的元件，比如怠速电机，也可以针对非工作状态下的元件，比如燃油泵。

项目一 充电系统故障诊断与修复

充电系统故障有多方面,一方面有发电机及调节器故障;另一方面有充电系统线路及仪表显示部分故障,此外还有发电机传动皮带打滑、发电机固定不牢固等机械故障。充电系统常见故障主要有:发电机不发电、发电电压过低、发电电压过高、发电电压不稳等。

学习目标

1. 能根据报修车辆的故障现象确定问诊的方向及项目。
2. 能根据故障现象制定正确的故障诊断计划。
3. 能熟练查阅维修资料,能根据故障现象选用合适的检测与诊断设备并熟练使用。
4. 能根据诊断计划,运用合适的检修设备对充电系统故障进行检测。
5. 能对检测结果进行正确分析并确定充电系统的故障部位及原因。
6. 能对故障部位进行快速准确修复,并且消除故障隐患。
7. 能具有严谨细致的工作态度,提高安全意识。

任务导入

任务资料:一辆捷达轿车,行驶里程11万千米,用户反映车辆停放时间长会出现发动机不能启动,蓄电池电量不足的问题,蓄电池充电后启动正常,仪表充电指示灯显示未发现异常。

任务要求:根据该车辆的故障现象,查阅相关资料,并选用合适的检测与诊断设备进行故障诊断与修复,同时填写任务报告单。

一、故障分析

蓄电池电量不足有可能是蓄电池存在问题,也可能是充电系统故障,具体原因主要有以下几点:

(1) 蓄电池故障或老化会使蓄电池存电量不足。
(2) 电源线与蓄电池极柱接触不良。
(3) 发电机及其线路出现故障导致蓄电池充电不足。
(4) 发电机传动皮带打滑导致发电机发电电压低。

二、故障诊断

(1) 检查电源线与蓄电池极柱接触是否存在松动,若松动应进行紧固。
(2) 检查发电机接线插头是否连接良好,若存在异常应进行修复。

(3) 检查发电机传动皮带是否过松，若过松应进行紧固。
(4) 发动机启动后在蓄电池接线柱检测发电电压是否正常，正常应在14V左右。
(5) 发动机启动后在发电机发电输出端子检测发电机发电电压是否正常，正常应在14V左右。
(6) 检查发电机线路是否存在问题，若存在异常应进行修复。

三、任务实施

1. 询问车主

向车主了解出现故障的时间；发现故障后症状是否有变化，出现故障前是否有其他异常情况；车辆行驶的具体情况；车辆是否按时保养；故障发生后是否进行过其他维修。通过以上的问诊了解故障发生前后的情况及故障的具体信息，完成充电系统故障的初步诊断。

2. 试车与基本检查

进行试车，对故障进行确认。观察仪表充电指示灯显示正常。检查电源线与蓄电池极柱接触良好不存在松动问题，检查发电机接线插头连接良好。检查发电机传动皮带松紧度符合要求。此外要确定该车充电系统的结构特点和线路连接方式。

3. 检测与诊断

发动机启动后在发电机发电输出端子检测发电机发电电压，电压为14.2V，电压正常。
发动机启动后用万用表在蓄电池接线柱检测发电电压，电压为14.2V，电压正常。
电源线与蓄电池极柱重新紧固后，故障没有排除。
更换蓄电池后，故障依旧。
发动机启动后怠速运转，开启全车用电设备，再次用万用表在蓄电池接线柱检测发电电压，电压为13.5V，电压低于发电机输出端电压。
检查保险丝盒中充电线路中的保险，拔下后发现保险端子存在烧蚀现象。

4. 故障排除

对保险座进行处理并更换新的保险后，进行试车，故障消失。

5. 检验交车

故障检修完毕，同时没有其他症状，向车主交车。

四、任务小结

此故障是由于保险插接不牢固导致插接处电阻增大，在长时间有大电流流动后导致保险接线端角烧蚀，造成充电电流减小，使蓄电池充电不足，从而出现停车时间长启动困难的故障。在进行此类故障诊断时，除了检查一些常规项目，同时还应该在发电机负载较大时进行检测，从而获得更准确的检测结果，避免盲目拆装和更换。

五、任务报告单

专业		班级		姓名	
任务名称				学时	2
车型			发动机型号		
	考核项目	考核内容		分值	得分
任务完成过程	1. 故障症状描述			5	
	2. 故障可能的原因及分析			25	
	3. 检测与诊断过程			35	
	4. 故障排除			10	
	5. 故障诊断小结			10	
教师评价	作业质量、作业效率、作业安全等			15	
	总评分数			100	

六、知识拓展

【典型案例一】 桑塔纳 2000GSi 型轿车发电量不足。

故障描述：一辆桑塔纳 2000GSi 型轿车，蓄电池经常亏电，导致启动机运转无力，大灯灯光暗淡，每隔几天就需给蓄电池补充充电。

故障诊断与修复：检查蓄电池极桩固定良好，发电机皮带松紧度正常。通过与用户沟通获知蓄电池使用 2 年多，因此建议车主更换蓄电池，但更换新蓄电池后不久故障依旧。

启动发动机，用万用表检测发电机输出电压为 14.5V，充电电压正常，检查发电机线路，没有发现异常。

由于更换新的蓄电池，可以排除蓄电池故障，因此故障很可能在发电机内部。

启动发动机开启全车灯光，提高发动机转速到 2000r/min，检测发电机输出电流，电流值 1A，明显低于灯光所需的电流，因此判断故障在发电机内部。

更换相同型号的发电机后，故障消失。

故障诊断小结：因为发电机内部局部出现故障，比如电刷磨损、整流器局部故障、定子绕组故障等导致发电机在用电负载小时发电电压正常，但是在用电负载大时发电量不足导致蓄电池不能充足电。

【典型案例二】 全新迈腾轿车发电机发电电压太高导致组合仪表不工作。

故障描述：一辆全新迈腾轿车，行驶 3 万千米，发动机转速达到 3000r/min 以上时组合仪表不工作。

故障诊断与修复：用大众专用诊断仪 VAS6150 读取发动机控制单元和仪表控制单元故障码，发现无故障码。

检查组合仪表的供电保险没有问题，检查组合仪表搭铁线没有问题，更换新组合仪表故障依旧。

考虑到故障现象与发动机转速有关，连接 VAS6150 当发动机转速逐渐升至 3000r/min 左右故障再现时，读取车辆各电控系统基本运行状态。当读取发动机电控系统发电机充电电压时，发电电压随转速逐渐升高甚至达到 16V 以上，初步判断为发电机电压调节器故障。

在发电机发电输出端检测发电电压确实达到 16V 以上，判定发电机内部故障。

更换发电机后故障排除

故障诊断小结：此故障是由于发电机电压过高从而导致组合仪表故障。故障特点是与发动机转速有关，因此在查询故障时应该将发动机转速提高到故障发生状态，在此状态下查看有哪些异常的数据流，从而找到故障的方向。

项目二 润滑系统故障诊断与修复

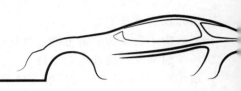

润滑系统故障主要分为两方面,一方面是润滑系统主要部件或者油路故障;另一方面是发动机故障导致机油压力过低、变质等故障。润滑系统常见故障有机油压力过低、机油压力过高、机油消耗过大、机油变质等。

任务一 机油压力过低故障诊断与修复

学习目标

1. 能根据报修车辆的故障现象确定问诊的方向及项目。
2. 能根据故障现象制定正确的故障诊断计划。
3. 能熟练查阅维修资料,能根据故障现象选用合适的检测与诊断设备并熟练使用。
4. 能根据诊断计划,运用合适的检修设备对机油压力过低故障进行检测。
5. 能对检测结果进行正确分析并确定机油压力过低的故障部位及原因。
6. 能对故障部位进行快速准确修复,并且消除故障隐患。
7. 能具有较强的责任心,良好的服务心态和意识。

任务导入

任务资料:一辆捷达汽车在行驶中通过一段坑洼路面后,机油压力报警灯闪亮。

任务要求:根据该车辆的故障现象,查阅相关资料,并选用合适的检测与诊断设备进行故障诊断与修复,同时填写任务报告单。

一、故障分析

机油压力过低故障指的是发动机在正常工作温度和转速下,机油压力低于规定值。此时发动机机油压力报警灯点亮或闪烁。

机油压力过低的故障原因主要有以下几点:
(1)机油压力表或机油压力传感器失准,传感器线路接触不良或有断路。

(2) 机油变质，黏度过低，机油中混入油、水。

(3) 机油油面过低。

(4) 机油泵磨损严重，供油能力下降。

(5) 机油集滤器、机油滤清器堵塞。

(6) 机油限压阀调整不当、关闭不严或弹簧折断。

(7) 机油管路有泄漏之处。

(8) 曲轴主轴承、连杆轴承或凸轮轴承磨损松旷、轴承松动、轴承合金脱落或烧损。

(9) 发动机过热。

二、故障诊断

(1) 检查机油油面是否过低，机油是否变质，黏度是否过低。

(2) 检查机油压力指示系统是否正常。先检查油压表与传感器的连接状况，若正常，拆下传感器导线，打开点火开关，使导线与机体搭铁。若油压表指针急速上升，说明油压表良好；若油压表指针不动或微动，说明油压表失效。

(3) 检查机油滤清器的滤芯、旁通阀是否堵塞，机油滤清器是否漏油等。

(4) 对于外装式限压阀，进行必要的检查和调整。

(5) 拆检机油泵，检查机油泵齿轮副的端面间隙、径向间隙和啮合间隙，并进行油压、泵油量等性能检测。

(6) 检查曲轴主轴承和连杆轴承、凸轮轴轴承等配合间隙。

三、任务实施

1. 询问车主

向车主了解出现故障的时间；出现故障前是否有异常情况；车辆行驶的路况；车辆是否按时保养；故障发生后是否进行过维修。通过以上的问诊了解故障发生前后的情况及故障的具体信息，完成机油压力过低的初步诊断。

2. 试车与基本检查

启动发动机，改变发动机转速，观察报警灯有无变化。此外，观察发动机外部机件是否有异常；观察是否存在漏油现象。

3. 检测与诊断

首先拔下机油尺，检查机油量和机油品质，发现机油面高于油尺上限位置，机油品质正常，此外发动机在急速运转时没有异响。据此判断机油润滑系统出现问题的可能性很小。此时怀疑机油压力报警开关或其电路有故障，于是用万用表检查机油压力报警开关及其电路，发现均正常，由此可以推断故障原因还是在机油压力系统。联想车主所说的该车在出现托底后出现了故障，同时结合机油油面升高这一现象，推断故障根本原因很可能在油底壳。于是将车辆举升检查油底壳，发现由于油底壳托底被撞进去一个大坑，并且坑的中心部位正好对着机油泵的进油口。

4. 故障排除

拆下油底壳并进行修复后，再进行试车故障排除。

5. 检验交车

故障检修完毕试车机油压力报警显示正常，同时没有其他症状，向车主交车。

四、任务小结

由于汽车行驶在坑洼路面，导致汽车托底油底壳变形，机油泵集滤器进油口受阻，进油不畅，造成机油压力过低，机油压力报警灯闪亮。

五、任务报告单

专业		班级		姓名	
任务名称				学时	2
车型			发动机型号		
	考核项目	考核内容		分值	得分
任务完成过程	1. 故障症状描述			5	
	2. 故障可能的原因及分析			25	
	3. 检测与诊断过程			35	
	4. 故障排除			10	
	5. 故障诊断小结			10	
教师评价	作业质量、作业效率、作业安全等			15	
	总评分数			100	

六、知识拓展

【典型案例一】 别克新世纪汽车机油压力报警灯常亮。

故障描述：一辆别克新世纪轿车进行大修更换了活塞等部件后，启动发动机，油压报警灯常亮。

故障诊断与修复：由于这是一辆别人修过的车，所以在诊断之前应先了解大修时都做了哪些维修和更换。通过了解得知发动机活塞、活塞环进行了更换，检查其他部件都正常，因此把所有的部件清洗干净之后进行了重新装复。

启动发动机仔细听发动机的声音，有一种金属的敲击声，而且机油压力指示灯被点亮。抽出机油尺检查液位及油的颜色均正常。机油压力报警灯点亮，说明机油压力低或者机油压力传感器线路有故障。而在打开点火开关做灯泡检测的时候，机油压力报警灯自动被点亮，然后熄灭，这证明故障不在线路上，问题还是在润滑系统上。

根据分析初步怀疑油道有堵塞的地方。于是拆下机油滤清器彻底放掉现有的机油。然后从机油滤清器处充入压缩空气，目的是清洁整个油路。这是在不分解发动机的情况下最简便的清洗方法。清洗之后重新加注新的机油至规定量，启动车后机油压力报警灯过一会儿又被点亮。于是进行机油压力的检测。检测发现机油压力较低。最后决定分解发动机做进一步的检查。分解发动机检查发动机曲轴、大小瓦、活塞、挺杆、推杆等部件基本正常。当拆下凸轮轴进行检查时，发现凸轮处有较大的磨损而且其轴承也磨损严重。更换凸轮轴和轴承，重新装配发动机后，故障排除。

故障诊断小结：该故障是因为凸轮轴磨损严重导致机油大量泄漏，使正常供给的机油压力降低，导致机油压力报警灯点亮。

【典型案例二】 速腾汽车发动机加速到 2000r/min 时机油压力报警。

故障描述：一辆 2011 款速腾汽车，该车在行驶中发现发动机加速到 2000r/min 时机油报警。

故障诊断与修复：询问用户最近的保养维修记录，获知最近一次保养没有在特约服务站保养，保养完之后行驶一段路就出现机油报警的现象。

于是用机油压力检测器 VAG1342 测量油压，怠速油压只有 40kPa，油压明显过低，提

高发动机转速油压能够继续上升，但压力始终偏低。发动机转速 2000r/min 时压力只有 160kPa，正常在 2000r/min 且机油油温为 80℃ 时油压应在 270～450kPa。因为机油报警后行驶了较长路程，所以拆下油底壳检查所有轴瓦及止推垫片的磨损情况，没有异常。在用户的要求下重新更换了机油滤清器，故障依旧，再次测量油压没有改善。更换机油泵也没有改善。在拆下机油滤清器底座时发现故障点。在机油滤清器底座中发现有异物卡在限压阀上，如图 2-1 所示。

将异物取出并检查限压阀无卡滞，重新安装后测量油压，怠速油压 400kPa。继续运转发动机至风扇工作，提高转速至 2000r/min 油压为 370kPa，符合 270～450kPa 的范围，不再报警，故障排除。

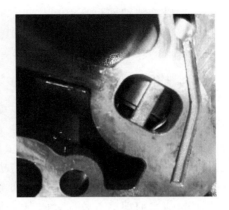

图 2-1　异物卡在机油滤底座中的限压阀上

故障诊断小结：机油滤清器底座的限压阀被异物卡住，导致关闭不严，而机油经此处流入油底壳，造成油压偏低。在车辆维修过程中，与用户的沟通非常重要，应了解车辆是否在正规服务站维修保养，在非正规地点保养后出现故障，应重点检查是否是因为不合格备件或不规范操作而导致的故障。

任务二　机油压力过高故障诊断与修复

学习目标

1. 能根据报修车辆的故障现象确定问诊的方向及项目。
2. 能根据故障现象制定正确的故障诊断计划。
3. 能熟练查阅维修资料，能根据故障现象选用合适的检测与诊断设备并熟练使用。
4. 能根据诊断计划，运用合适的检修设备对机油压力过高故障进行检测。
5. 能对检测结果进行正确分析并确定机油压力过高的故障部位及原因。
6. 能对故障部位进行快速准确修复，并且消除故障隐患。

任务导入

任务资料：一辆大众 POLO1.4L 汽车，装备 BCC 发动机，发动机在运转时有严重的气门异响，并在怠速运转时存在严重抖动现象，行驶时发动机动力明显不足。

任务要求：根据该车辆的故障现象，查阅相关资料，并选用合适的检测与诊断设备进行故障诊断与修复，同时填写任务报告单。

一、故障分析

机油压力过高故障现象是发动机在正常工作温度和转速下，机油压力高于规定值。机油压力过高通常易出现机油滤清器密封垫损坏、漏机油现象。

机油压力过高故障的原因主要有以下几点。

（1）机油压力表或机油压力传感器失准，传感器线路有故障。
（2）机油滤清器滤芯堵塞且限压阀卡滞或调整不当。

(3) 机油池油面过高。
(4) 机油变稀或新换机油黏度过大。
(5) 机油道内有堵塞或大修后发动机主轴承、连杆轴承、凸轮轴承等间隙过小。

二、故障诊断

(1) 检查油面是否过高，机油黏度是否过大，机油牌号是否符合要求。
(2) 检查油压指示装置有无故障。若接通点火开关就有压力指示，则说明油压表或传感器有故障。
(3) 检查、调整限压阀，对于与机油泵一体的限压阀，则应拆检机油泵。
(4) 拆检发动机，检查、清洗润滑油道，并用压缩空气吹通；同时检查曲轴主轴承、连杆轴承和凸轮轴轴承等各配合间隙是否过小。

三、任务实施

1. 询问车主

向车主了解出现故障的时间；出现故障前是否有异常情况；车辆行驶的路况；车辆是否按时保养；故障发生后是否进行过维修。通过以上的问诊了解故障发生前后的情况及故障的具体信息，完成机油压力过高的初步诊断。

2. 试车与基本检查

启动发动机，观察发动机运转情况，了解机油压力报警灯是否正常显示；改变发动机转速，观察有无变化。此外，观察发动机外部机件是否有异常；观察是否存在漏油现象。

3. 检测与诊断

拔下机油尺，检查机油量和机油品质完全正常。经初步检查判断造成气门异响的原因为液压气门挺杆损坏，故先对液压气门挺杆进行更换。在更换时发现气门室盖罩内淤积有大量的机油油泥沉积物，并且机油很脏。更换液压气门挺杆后，对气门室盖罩内的油泥进行清理，并更换了机油及机油滤芯。装复试车，在刚启动的约 30s 时间里，发动机运行十分安静平稳，而 30s 过后，发动机又开始严重抖动，并有动力不足现象，但气门响的故障消失。由于该车搭载的 BCC 型发动机缸盖结构较为特殊（凸轮轴安装在气门室罩盖上，气门、液压挺杆等元件则安装在缸盖部分），按照由简至繁的原则，用故障诊断仪 1552 对发动机电控系统进行检测，未发现有故障码。逐一拔下喷油器插头对各缸进行断缸试验，发现各个缸的工作都不是很理想，尤其第 2 缸最差，随后又更换了火花塞、点火线圈、喷油器，故障依旧。用气缸压力表检查了各缸的缸压情况，结果各缸压力显示均正常，因此认为气缸压力足够。随后对进气歧管进行检查，没有发现漏气现象，从而判定是油路或点火控制方面出现了问题。于是继续检查油路及控制系统，检测汽油压力也正常，检查各个缸的点火信号、喷油信号，均正常。又调换了点火线圈、火花塞及喷油器等部件，没有发现任何问题。怀疑配气正时错误，又拆装了两次气门室盖，反复检查配气正时，未发现异常。但发现一个现象：每次拆装气门室盖后都是在刚启动的约 30s 时间内，发动机运行平稳，大约 30s 过后，就开始严重抖动。

通过上述步骤的检修，确定正时和控制部分都没有问题。所有和气缸燃烧做功相关的条件都正常，发动机却出现明显的抖动，问题究竟出现在哪里呢？针对此故障，重新进行分析。发动机抖动和做功不良应从机械部分和控制部分入手。既然已经调换过点火线圈、火花塞及喷油器等执行元件，又检查了点火、喷油和油路，且没有发现问题（因为这些都能做出直观的判断），那么就应该重新检查机械部分。经过测量，气缸压力显示正常，似乎可以排除机械部分的问题。

在没有明确诊断方向的情况下检测机油压力,却发现机油压力很高,怠速时油压达到了300kPa(大大高于规定值)。于是这次连气缸盖一起拆下进行了解体检查,顺便查找机油压力过高的原因。在拆下气门时,发现气门密封不是很严。正常气门的气门口处应该有一圈光亮的环带,基本能够看到金属的颜色,而此车所有气门口在环带上都有局部轻微发黑现象(其中第2缸最为明显),说明气门口有轻微的漏气现象。通过仔细检查还发现气门摇臂上部的油道孔已经被机油油泥堵死,导致液压气门挺杆内的机油无法正常喷油,油压过高的原因与此有关。经彻底清理和疏通气门摇臂上部的油道孔后装复试车,发动机抖动现象大幅好转,但还是存在抖动。再次测量怠速时的机油压力,虽已下降至220kPa,但仍高于规定值。随后对机油泵进行检查,发现油底壳内也有很厚的机油油泥,推断机油泵内部也有大量的油泥,在油压过高时不能正常泄油。

4. 故障排除

更换了机油泵,并对油底壳和机油油道进行了清理,装复后,启动发动机,抖动消失,运转平稳,上路试车加速有力,故障彻底排除。

5. 检验交车

故障检修完毕,同时没有其他症状,向车主交车。

四、任务小结

该车辆由于摇臂上部的油道孔被油泥完全堵死,机油无法正常泄油,造成油压不断升高。约30s后,由于机油压力过高造成气门液压挺杆伸展过度,再加上缸内燃烧做功的压力,这样本来就很脆弱的密封就被破坏,从而导致发动机在刚启动的约30s时间内运行平稳,约30s过后开始严重抖动的奇怪现象。

五、任务报告单

	专业		班级		姓名	
	任务名称				学时	2
	车型		发动机型号			
	考核项目	考核内容			分值	得分
任务完成过程	1. 故障症状描述				5	
	2. 故障可能的原因及分析				25	
	3. 检测与诊断过程				35	
	4. 故障排除				10	
	5. 故障诊断小结				10	
教师评价	作业质量、作业效率、作业安全等				15	
	总评分数				100	

六、知识拓展

【典型案例】 一辆东风EQ1091型汽车发动机大修后机油压力高。

故障描述: 一辆东风EQ1091型汽车,其机油压力过高以致机油粗滤清器滤芯在发动机大修后的1周内损坏了3个,并且曾两次出现烧轴瓦的情况。

故障诊断与修复: 原承修该汽车发动机的修理人员认为机油压力高不是故障,是轴瓦与轴颈的配合稍紧,在这种情况下发动机的使用寿命较长。只要勤检查机油量,在发动机磨合后机油压力就会正常。在承修该车后首先检查机油压力表的指示,当把点火开关置于点火位置而发动机不运转时,机油压力显示为250kPa,当发动机怠速运转时机油压力为700kPa。这表明

机油压力传感器已失准。在更换机油压力传感器后重新检查机油压力,结果是当发动机怠速运转时机油压力表指示机油压力为600kPa,机油压力确实过高。在拆解机油粗滤清器时发现其滤芯的上端面已呈半球形,并不停地滴机油。在检查机油泵时发现,在其限压阀弹簧的一端垫有1只螺杆和3只弹簧垫片(总厚度达8mm),而弹簧的长度已明显不足。车主说,它们是在发动机大修前因机油压力过低而被垫入的,在发动机大修时未将它们拆下。考虑到弹簧长度的不足,修理员将螺杆和2只弹簧垫片拆下后(尚留1只弹簧垫片)装复了机油泵,然后进行试车。这时,机油压力恢复正常,并且机油粗滤清器滤芯也不再漏油。由于原机油粗滤清器滤芯已被损伤,所以更换了新的机油粗滤清器滤芯,故障排除。

故障诊断小结:从上述故障排除的过程中可以得到两点启示,即:要纠正"机油压力高一些有益而无害"的观点;机油压力过高无助于改善零件的润滑条件和延长发动机的使用寿命,相反,会使机油的泄漏增加导致机油的消耗量增加和机油粗滤清器滤芯损坏,甚至会引发事故。

任务三 机油消耗过大故障诊断与修复

学习目标

1. 能根据报修车辆的故障现象确定问诊的方向及项目。
2. 能根据故障现象制定正确的故障诊断计划。
3. 能熟练查阅维修资料,能根据故障现象选用合适的检测与诊断设备并熟练使用。
4. 能根据诊断计划,运用合适的检修设备对机油消耗过大故障进行检测。
5. 能对检测结果进行正确分析并确定机油消耗过大的故障部位及原因。
6. 能对故障部位进行快速准确修复,并且消除故障隐患。

任务导入

任务资料:一辆上海大众帕萨特1.8T手动挡轿车,行驶里程为20.1万千米,发动机在大修后行驶1.2万千米后,机油消耗量增大,并且高速时排气管有时排出蓝烟。

任务要求:根据该车辆的故障现象,查阅相关资料,并选用合适的检测与诊断设备进行故障诊断与修复,同时填写任务报告单。

一、故障分析

国标GB/T 19055—2003规定,在全速满负荷试验过程中,机油、燃油消耗百分比应小于0.3%,符合这一标准的发动机和车辆,其机油消耗量属于正常水平。

发动机机油消耗量过大的故障原因主要有两个方面:一方面是发动机"烧机油";另一方面是发动机"漏机油"。"烧机油"的故障从发动机的排气上能明显地反映出来,如果发动机排气管冒蓝烟,则说明发动机烧机油。"漏机油"的故障主要应从各个密封面及润滑系统管路的接头处来检查,漏机油处会有比较明显的机油污渍。

发动机"烧机油"主要有以下10个方面原因:
(1) 机油加注量过多导致烧机油。
(2) 发动机气缸"拉缸"导致烧机油。
(3) 发动机气缸垫烧蚀,机油进入燃烧室。
(4) 活塞与气缸壁间的间隙过大。

（5）活塞环的开口没有错开。
（6）活塞环粘环。
（7）活塞环的弹力不足。
（8）活塞环的"三隙"过大。
（9）活塞环装配错误。
（10）气门杆油封损坏及气门导管磨损过甚。

发动机"漏机油"的部位主要有以下几处：
（1）发动机前、后曲轴油封处，正时齿轮室，曲轴箱与油底壳的结合面处，凸轮轴后端油封处。
（2）气门油封处密封不良、气门杆与气门导管间的间隙较大。
（3）废气涡轮增压器漏油。
（4）发动机润滑系统各零部件的外漏。

二、故障诊断

针对机油消耗过大故障，首先应确定机油加注量是否正常，然后再去区分故障是由于发动机烧机油还是漏机油，最后再根据故障类型查找故障的具体部位和原因。

1. "烧机油"的诊断方法

（1）若排气管明显冒蓝烟，则可以确定机油消耗过大是由发动机烧机油造成的。当发动机大负荷、高速运转时，排气管大量冒蓝烟，拔下机油尺，从机油加注口也可以看到向外冒蓝烟，则为活塞、活塞环与气缸壁磨损过甚，或活塞环的端隙、侧隙、背隙过大，多个活塞环对口、粘环、扭曲环或锥面环装反等，使机油窜入燃烧室。此类故障应更换活塞、活塞环。

（2）若发动机大负荷运转时，排气管冒大量蓝烟，但机油加注口不冒烟，而气缸盖罩内却向外窜烟，则为气门杆油封损坏，气门导管磨损过大，机油被吸入燃烧室烧掉。此类故障应更换气门杆油封或气门导管。

（3）若发动机启动后排气管即冒大量蓝烟，且机油消耗量很大，通常是由于发动机气缸垫烧蚀，机油进入燃烧室造成的。此类故障需要拆缸盖，更换气缸垫。

2. "漏机油"的诊断方法

（1）首先检查发动机外部是否有漏油处。要特别注意曲轴前端和后端的油封处是否漏油。曲轴的前端油封破裂损坏、老化或曲轴带轮与油封接触面磨损，会引起曲轴前端漏油。曲轴后端的油封破裂损坏，或后主轴承盖的回油孔过小，回油受阻，会引起曲轴后端漏油。另外还应注意凸轮轴后端油封是否漏油。油封老化、破裂漏油应及时更换。除此之外，还要检查发动机润滑系统各零部件是否存在外漏现象。

（2）如果发动机的前后油封处漏油，甚至前后气缸盖罩、前后气门挺杆室、机油滤清器、油底壳衬垫等多处有机油渗出，但又找不到明显的漏油处，应检查曲轴箱通风装置，清理曲轴箱通风管道，尤其是检查PCV阀是否由于积炭和结胶卡滞造成工作不良。如果曲轴箱通风不良很可能会导致曲轴箱内压力升高，从而出现多处机油渗漏现象。

（3）如果机油滤清器及一些机油管路的接头处经过紧固后还是漏油，应注意检查机油压力是否过高，机油限压阀是否工作不良。

三、任务实施

1. 询问车主

向车主了解出现故障的时间；出现故障前是否有其他异常情况；发现故障后症状是否有

变化；车辆行驶的具体情况；车辆是否按时保养；故障发生后是否进行过其他维修。通过以上的问诊了解故障发生前后的情况及故障的具体信息，完成机油消耗过大的初步诊断。

  2. **试车与基本检查**

  首先检查发动机机油量是否正常，然后启动发动机，观察排气管是否冒蓝烟，以及冒蓝烟的程度；观察发动机工况变化，症状有无改变；观察发动机外部机件是否有明显漏油现象。

  3. **检测与诊断**

  对该车发动机外部进行检查，没有发现任何渗漏处。该车在大修时已同时更换过涡轮增压器，因此初步排除该处漏油。使用内窥镜深入到气缸内检视时发现，在气门背面存在较多积炭和胶质，还能看到气门杆上存在明显机油痕迹。通过现状分析认定机油应该是从气门导管及气门油封处渗入到燃烧室燃烧了，但是也不排除活塞环对口等原因，于是解体发动机。发动机解体后检查发现各缸活塞环未对口，并且密封性能良好，气缸直径也未超标，气缸的圆度和圆柱度以及与活塞的配合间隙等各项参数均正常，分解气缸盖后发现气门油封装配位置正常，气门和气门导管的配合间隙也正常。通过以上检查可以确定发动机上次大修时装配应该不存在问题。根据上述检查结果，综合引起机油消耗量大的主要原因，分析可能是曲轴箱压力过大。引起曲轴箱压力增大的主要原因有：活塞环与气缸之间密封性能下降，导致下窜气；曲轴箱强制通风管路堵塞。根据上述检查结果分析，引起曲轴箱压力增大的第一种原因可以排除，重点应该检查曲轴箱强制通风管路。该车型发动机有两条强制通风管路，分别是急速时通风管路（节气门关闭时）和负荷时通风管路（节气门开启时）。对通风管路所有止回阀检查未发现问题，但是在检查负荷时通风管路时发现射流泵附近有一截管路堵塞。此处由于存在积炭导致了堵塞，使发动机在负荷状态下工作时曲轴箱压力升高，在压力升高到一定程度时导致机油从气门导管及气门油封处渗进燃烧室中燃烧，最终使机油消耗量增大，汽车在大负荷时排气管冒蓝烟。

  4. **故障排除**

  对堵塞部位进行疏通处理并装复发动机后进行试车，故障排除。

  5. **检验交车**

  故障检修完毕，同时没有其他症状，向车主交车。

四、任务小结

  维修车辆时一定要注重细节，很小的疏忽就会引起严重的后果，该案例中的故障就是由于在大修作业时对强制通风管路未彻底清洁引起的。分析故障一定要讲究逻辑性，并且对相关的结构要熟悉，才能快速准确地找到故障部位。

五、任务报告单

专业		班级		姓名	
任务名称				学时	2
车型			发动机型号		
	考核项目	考核内容		分值	得分
任务完成过程	1. 故障症状描述			5	
	2. 故障可能的原因及分析			25	
	3. 检测与诊断过程			35	
	4. 故障排除			10	
	5. 故障诊断小结			10	
教师评价	作业质量、作业效率、作业安全等			15	
	总评分数			100	

六、知识拓展

【典型案例一】 一辆丰田皇冠汽车机油消耗量异常。

故障描述：在丰田维修技师按规程检查发动机油量时，发现该车机油尺测到的油平面离最低点只有2mm。通过与车主沟通得知，该车在此前曾做过3次检查，每次都发现机油量异常减少，这3次都进行了补加。

故障诊断与修复：通过与车主沟通，首先把发动机机油添加到油尺满位线处，交车让车主正常使用。车辆行驶500km后请车主回厂检查机油量发现已经减少了。用量杯渐渐添加机油到油尺满位线处，一共添加约300mL，按此计算出该车每行驶5000km的机油消耗量约3L，完全超出了正常的范围。

检查发动机各部位没有任何漏油迹象，检查各真空、进气管路、PCV阀没有异常机油泄漏迹象。除6缸火花塞比其他缸偏黑、缸压偏低一点外，也没有发现异常情况。由此分析，机油消耗异常的原因在发动机内部。于是拆卸分解发动机总成，逐缸检查发现活塞顶部积炭油泥较多，1缸、4缸和5缸的2号活塞环与油环的开口重合，1缸和6缸的活塞间隙超出规定值，其他缸的活塞间隙也达到或者接近规定值。由以上判定该发动机本体存在问题。由于车辆在保修期内，因此更换新的发动机裸机。发动机装复后经检验、运转、路试无误后交付车主使用。经过半个月后车辆回厂检查机油量正常，没有减少。

故障诊断小结：该车由于活塞环开口重合及一些缸的活塞间隙较大导致发动机将机油烧掉，使机油消耗量异常。机油消耗量可以通过一定的检测方法计算得出。

【典型案例二】 一辆2011款长安铃木天语SX41.8L汽车发动机机油消耗量大。

故障描述：车辆在行驶时发动机机油故障报警灯点亮，经检查机油油面过低，补加到正常液面，行驶一段时间后机油故障报警灯又点亮，经检查还是机油油面过低。

故障诊断与修复：

（1）检查发动机外部没有发现泄漏，急加油门，排气管有轻微的机油烧蚀味。

（2）用故障诊断仪读取故障码，结果无故障码。

（3）检查各缸缸压，正常，初步判断故障不是气缸磨损以及活塞环等故障。故障区域重点放在：VVT系统、凸轮轴油封、气门油封、气门、气门导管。

（4）检查VVT系统及相关管路没有发现泄漏。

（5）检查凸轮轴油封没有发现异常。

（6）拆检缸盖检查气门及气门油封没有发现异常。

（7）检查气门导管时发现气缸盖3缸进气门镶嵌气门导管处，气缸盖出现裂纹，如图2-2所示。裂纹导致发动机机油渗入燃烧室，因此急加速时，排气管有轻微的机油烧蚀味，并使机油消耗量大。于是更换气缸盖，试车，车辆正常。经3天后回访，车辆一切正常，故障完全排除。

图2-2 气缸盖3缸裂纹

故障诊断小结：该故障属于发生概率相对较小的典型故障，此故障的故障点比较隐蔽，因此需要按照机油消耗异常的可能原因，按照故障发生的特点和规律，逐一进行查找，逐步缩小故障范围，最终找到故障点。

任务四 机油变质故障诊断与修复

学习目标

1. 能根据报修车辆的故障现象确定问诊的方向及项目。
2. 能根据故障现象制定正确的故障诊断计划。
3. 能熟练查阅维修资料，能根据故障现象选用合适的检测与诊断设备并熟练使用。
4. 能根据诊断计划，运用合适的检修设备对机油变质故障进行检测。
5. 能对检测结果进行正确分析并确定机油变质的故障部位及原因。
6. 能对故障部位进行快速准确修复，并且消除故障隐患。

任务导入

任务资料：一辆长城哈弗CUV手自一体越野车，装备发动机型号为4G6454M，2.4L。车主反映的故障是机油变质、冷却液消耗异常，要求查找故障原因。

任务要求：根据该车辆的故障现象，查阅相关资料，并选用合适的检测与诊断设备进行故障诊断与修复，同时填写任务报告单。

一、故障分析

所谓机油变质指的是机油中混入了水分、灰尘、燃料，或其他机械物质而使机油的化学成分发生改变，导致机油润滑性能下降或者消失。

机油变质原因主要有以下几点：

（1）机件磨损杂质混入机油，使机油杂质含量增加。
（2）活塞环漏气造成未完全燃烧物进入曲轴箱，混入机油。
（3）曲轴箱通风不良，使有害气体不能及时排出。
（4）汽油、冷却水因泄漏进入油底壳。
（5）尘埃过多混入机油。
（6）发动机长时间在过热条件下工作导致机油氧化。

二、故障诊断

诊断机油变质故障时，首先要确认车辆是否按时保养，在保养正常的情况下再根据变质机油的特征确定故障的原因。

机油变质的诊断方法如下：

（1）检查机油是否由于使用时间过长，未定期更换导致机油变质。
（2）若机油呈浑浊乳化状且油面增高，说明冷却液进入机油。
（3）检查曲轴箱通风阀是否失效。
（4）机油呈灰色且有燃油气味，表明机油已被燃油稀释，这通常是由于气缸活塞组存在漏气，导致不完全燃烧的燃料窜到油底壳而造成的。

三、任务实施

1. 询问车主

向车主了解出现故障的时间；出现故障前是否有其他异常情况；发现故障后症状是否有

变化；车辆行驶的具体情况；车辆是否按时保养；故障发生后是否进行过其他维修。通过以上的问诊了解故障发生前后的情况及故障的具体信息，完成机油变质的初步诊断。

2. 试车与基本检查

首先检查发动机机油量和油质是否正常，然后启动发动机，观察发动机工作有无异常。

3. 检测与诊断

检查机油品质，发现机油呈浑浊乳化状，说明冷却液进入机油，消耗的冷却液进入了油底壳。

在冷车时，打开水箱盖，启动发动机，刚一启动，水箱中的冷却液猛烈喷出，于是迅速关掉钥匙门开关。分析上述状况，应该是气缸垫损坏，燃烧室的气体进入冷却系统。于是拆下气缸垫，检查后发现气缸垫完好，无任何损伤，检查气缸体，气缸体也完好。但是在活塞上却有防冻液，显然防冻液进入了燃烧室。于是检查了气缸盖，这次发现气缸盖在靠近燃烧室侧多处严重腐蚀，且每处都能导致燃烧室与水道相通，从而可以确定之前车主水箱漏水的原因就在此。

4. 故障排除

在确定气缸盖无法修复的情况下更换气缸盖。更换气缸盖后，再次启动发动机，防冻液不再从水箱盖喷出，冷却液中也没有气泡存在，至此故障排除。

5. 检验交车

故障检修完毕，同时没有其他症状，向车主交车。

四、任务小结

该故障的原因是冷却液从缸盖与缸垫之间的缝隙进入燃烧室，进而有一部分流到油底壳，最终导致机油变质。

气缸盖之所以腐蚀得如此严重，应该是由于车主加的是水，或者是不达标的防冻液，总之是没有注意对车辆的正确保养导致的。由此可见，在对车辆加注冷却液时，一定要首选防冻液，即使在没有条件的情况下加了水，也要及时在有条件的情况下更换成有品质保证的防冻液。

五、任务报告单

	专业		班级		姓名	
	任务名称				学时	2
	车型			发动机型号		
	考核项目		考核内容		分值	得分
任务完成过程	1. 故障症状描述				5	
	2. 故障可能的原因及分析				25	
	3. 检测与诊断过程				35	
	4. 故障排除				10	
	5. 故障诊断小结				10	
教师评价	作业质量、作业效率、作业安全等				15	
	总评分数				100	

六、知识拓展

【典型案例】 北京吉普汽车发动机机油变质。

故障描述： 一辆北京吉普汽车，在行驶中发动机突然熄火，再启动后，发动机运转不平

稳，且有异响，观察仪表，无机油压力指示，检查发动机机油发现机油变质。

故障诊断与修复：首先向车主询问，获知该车发动机机油没有按保养时间更换，因此怀疑机油变质是由于机油长时间不更换致使机油中杂质过多而造成的。于是从油底壳放出机油，检查发现机油集滤器已完全被杂质堵住。

然后清洗发动机机油集滤器及各润滑油道，更换新的机油和机滤，检查发现发动机启动正常，但发动机有异响。经过进一步检查发现发动机曲轴第5道主轴瓦烧蚀导致发动机异响，进行更换后，再试车，发动机工作正常。

故障诊断小结：该车因为没有按时进行保养，机油、机滤没有按规定更换，导致发动机机油变质且大量杂质久存于机油中，使机油变脏，以至于堵住了集滤器，使发动机内各运动机件得不到充分润滑，造成发动机烧瓦，所以在行驶途中突然熄火。

项目三

冷却系统故障诊断与修复

冷却系统故障主要分为两方面,一方面是冷却液循环系统故障;另一方面是冷却风扇及其控制电路部分故障。冷却系统常见故障特征主要有:发动机过热、冷却液异常消耗等。

学习目标

1. 能根据报修车辆的故障现象确定问诊的方向及项目。
2. 能根据故障现象制定正确的故障诊断计划。
3. 能熟练查阅维修资料,能根据故障现象选用合适的检测与诊断设备并熟练使用。
4. 能根据诊断计划,运用合适的检修设备对发动机过热故障进行检测。
5. 能对检测结果进行正确分析并确定发动机过热的故障部位及原因。
6. 能对故障部位进行快速准确修复,并且消除故障隐患。
7. 能具有良好的服务心态,认真的工作作风,提高安全意识。

任务导入

任务资料:一辆毕加索汽车,行驶里程12万千米,用户反映该车组合仪表上的发动机水温表指示过高,且发动机水温警报灯点亮,STOP灯也点亮。

任务要求:根据该车辆的故障现象,查阅相关资料,并选用合适的检测与诊断设备进行故障诊断与修复,同时填写任务报告单。

一、故障分析

发动机过热即通常所说的水温过高,其故障现象是发动机在工作过程中,水温表显示水温超过正常范围,水温报警灯点亮,甚至散热器伴随有"开锅"现象,发动机易出现爆震。

发动机过热故障原因主要有以下几点。

(1) 冷却液不足或者变质。
(2) 风扇皮带打滑、风扇不转或者无高速转。
(3) 节温器打不开或打开过迟。
(4) 冷却水管被挤压出现凹瘪。

(5) 散热器内部堵塞或外部脏堵；散热器和水套内沉积水垢过多。
(6) 水泵不工作或工作不良。
(7) 水温传感器、温控开关工作不良，或者其线路故障。
(8) 风扇控制模块或者控制电路故障。
(9) 点火时刻不正确使发动机不能正常燃烧，产生过多的热量。

二、故障诊断

(1) 检查冷却液液面高度，确定其规格、牌号是否符合要求。检查冷却液是否变质。
(2) 检查风扇转速是否正常；检查风扇皮带是否过松、叶片有无变形、风扇离合器是否失效等。
(3) 检查散热器有无变形、漏水，水垢是否过多；检查其各部分温度是否均匀。
(4) 检查水管是否有异常情况，触摸散热器及上下水管，若下水管温度较低，表明节温器有故障，应拆检节温器。
(5) 检查水泵皮带是否过松。检查时用手握住发动机顶部至散热器的通水管，然后由怠速加速到某一高速，如感到水管内的流速随发动机转速的增加而加快，说明水泵工作正常；否则说明水泵工作不良，应拆检水泵。
(6) 检查水温传感器、温控开关的技术状况，确认其技术状况是否良好。
(7) 检查风扇控制模块或者控制电路是否正常工作。
(8) 检查发动机点火系统是否有故障。

三、任务实施

1. 询问车主

向车主了解出现故障的时间；发现故障后症状是否有变化，出现故障前是否有其他异常情况；车辆行驶的具体情况；车辆是否按时保养；故障发生后是否进行过其他维修。通过以上的问诊了解故障发生前后的情况及故障的具体信息，完成水温高的初步诊断。

2. 试车与基本检查

首先检查发动机冷却液量，完全正常，然后启动发动机，观察发动机症状；观察冷却风扇工作情况。

3. 检测与诊断

启动发动机观察冷却系统工作情况，当发动机启动运转约 5min 时，发现发动机水温表指示到最高点，发动机水温警报灯点亮。同时，电动冷却风扇开始高速运转，经过几分钟的散热后，水温指示降低到正常值（90℃左右），电动风扇停止运转。

利用故障诊断仪 PROXIA3 读取故障信息：水温表指示灯故障，临时性故障；电动风扇高速运转故障，永久性故障。清除故障码，故障依旧。

由该车冷却系统工作原理可知：发动机温度到 97℃时，发动机控制单元控制冷却风扇开始低速运转进行散热；当发动机温度达到 101℃时，发动机控制单元控制冷却风扇开始中速运转进行散热；当发动机温度达到 105℃时，发动机控制单元控制冷却风扇开始高速运转进行散热；节温器在发动机温度 89℃时开启，发动机温度达到 101℃时完全打开。

分析认为，水温高很可能是由于节温器故障或水道中水垢过多造成的，于是将车辆发动机冷却液全部放掉，检查节温器及散热器总成，没有发现异常情况。更换新的冷却液，发现故障现象依然存在。

检查发动机冷却风扇控制电路、继电器都是正常的。

将发动机水温传感器拆下，测量其阻值并与标准值进行对比，发现存在较大差异，怀疑

此传感器存在故障。

4. 故障排除

更换一个新的发动机水温传感器,进行试车,故障消失。

5. 检验交车

故障检修完毕,同时没有其他症状,向车主交车。

四、任务小结

此故障是发动机温度传感器故障,导致发动机控制单元获得错误的水温信息,而出现水温报警的情况。在进行此类故障诊断时,可以通过数据流了解水温传感器的信号是否准确,避免盲目拆装和更换。

五、任务报告单

	专　　业		班　级		姓　名	
	任务名称				学　时	2
	车　　型		发动机型号			
	考核项目	考核内容			分　值	得　分
任务完成过程	1. 故障症状描述				5	
	2. 故障可能的原因及分析				25	
	3. 检测与诊断过程				35	
	4. 故障排除				10	
	5. 故障诊断小结				10	
教师评价	作业质量、作业效率、作业安全等				15	
	总评分数				100	

六、知识拓展

【典型案例一】 桑塔纳 2000GSI 型轿车发动机水温过高。

故障描述: 一辆桑塔纳 2000GSI 型轿车,行驶中出现水温报警、发动机温度过高现象。

故障诊断与修复: 首先用手分别触摸发动机上、下水管,发现二者温度基本一致,说明节温器是打开的。进一步检查后,发现发动机散热风扇没有正常转动。然后检查散热风扇的保险和温控开关,发现散热风扇的保险已经烧坏。更换同型号的保险片后试机,发动机的散热风扇可以正常运转,但 1 周后,同样的故障现象再次出现。这次更换同型号的保险片后,发动机散热风扇却不能正常运转。进一步检查,分别转动散热风扇的主动风扇和被动风扇叶片,手感阻力都很大,而且有发卡的现象,证明散热风扇的主、被动风扇都已经损坏。

更换相同规格、型号的散热风扇后,发动机水温高的现象再没有出现。

故障诊断小结: 因为散热风扇有卡滞问题,造成转动阻力较大,风扇工作的电流负荷加大,从而导致发动机散热风扇的保险烧坏,出现发动机温度过高现象。更换保险后又能正常运转,是因为散热风扇还能够克服风扇的卡滞阻力。但经过 1 周的运转,发动机散热风扇的卡滞现象更加严重,致使风扇电机不能转动,所以再次更换保险后散热风扇不能正常运转,使发动机的温度过高。

【典型案例二】 捷达 CIX 型发动机水温高。

故障描述: 一辆捷达汽车,行驶中发现发动机水温高,电子扇没有高速挡运转。

故障诊断与修复: 检查以后,先后更换了双温开关、电子扇、风扇控制器、节温器,故障依旧。

捷达风扇的控制电路如图 3-1 所示,双温开关根据发动机水温 95℃接通低速挡,直接将从保险丝提供的 30V 正电给风扇低速线圈,风扇低速运转。

发动机水温 105℃后高速挡接通,传递信号给风扇控制器,风扇控制器给风扇高速线圈供电,风扇以高速挡运转。

短接双温开关的线路后,低速挡正常运转,而高速挡还是不转,可以断定问题出在高速挡的电路上面。

检查双温开关插头 3 号线至风扇控制器 T10/7 号脚,检测电压为 12V,线路正常。

检查 S36 风扇控制器保险丝,电压 12V,检查风扇控制器 T10/9 线路,电压正常。

检查风扇控制器 T10/6 号脚与接地,接地正常。

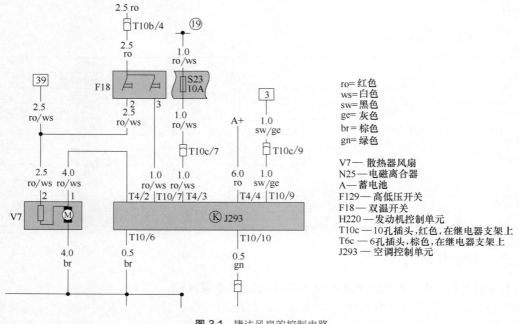

图 3-1 捷达风扇的控制电路

此时可以判定风扇控制器不工作。

又换了一个风扇控制器,故障依旧存在。单独从蓄电池正极引 30V 正电接入风扇控制器,风扇高速挡可以工作。

最后将保险丝盒拆下发现,36 号保险丝后面的线束已经磨断了,只有一点接触,测量时有电压,但是提供的电流不够,风扇控制器无法工作。将该电线连接后风扇工作正常,故障排除。

故障诊断小结:此故障是一个典型的线路电阻过大的故障,进行这类故障的诊断时,通过测量线路电阻的方式通常很难发现线路的异常,如果采用换件法也不能确定故障部位。这种故障可以采用测量风扇电路工作电流的方式来确定故障部位。此外,诊断时一定要结合系统的工作原理及线路进行分析。

项目四

汽车异响故障诊断与修复

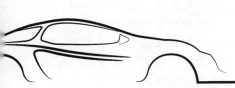

汽车异响是指由于运转或运动机件的非正常运动、磨损及老化等原因产生的非正常响声。汽车异响是汽车在使用中的常见故障,包括发动机异响和底盘异响。

汽车异响通常与正常的响声混杂在一起,维修人员在进行诊断时必须了解异响的特征和规律,才能迅速准确地确认故障来源并找到故障部位。

任务一 发动机异响故障诊断与修复

 学习目标

1. 能根据报修车辆的故障现象确定问诊的方向及项目。
2. 能根据故障现象制定正确的故障诊断计划。
3. 能熟练查阅维修资料,能根据故障现象选用合适的检测与诊断设备并熟练使用。
4. 能根据诊断计划,运用合适的检修设备对发动机异响故障进行检测。
5. 能对检测结果进行正确分析并确定发动机异响的故障部位及原因。
6. 能对故障部位进行快速准确修复,并且消除故障隐患。
7. 能具有严谨细致的工作态度,精益求精的工匠精神。

任务导入

任务资料: 一辆2011款捷达汽车,发动机在加速时发出"咯咯"的异响,凉车时声音小,热车时声音大。

任务要求: 根据该车辆的故障现象,查阅相关资料,并选用合适的检测与诊断设备进行故障诊断与修复,同时填写任务报告单。

一、故障分析

发动机异响是指发动机在工作时发出的各种不正常响声。发动机异响可以分为外部异响和内部异响。外部异响指的是皮带盘组件、发电机、水泵轴承、张紧轮等异响;内部异响指的是主轴承响、连杆轴承响、活塞敲缸响、活塞销响等。

异响与发动机转速、负荷、温度、润滑条件等多种因素有关，异响部位不同，其声响特征、伴随现象、发生时间各不相同，许多异响具有明显的声调特征，可以帮助确定故障部位。主要的异响特征包括以下几种：

（1）音频特征：发动机异响有不同的声调，如主轴承响为沉闷的"当当"声，而气门脚响为清脆的"嗒嗒"声。通过记录声响波形，可以对各自声响的频率、振幅、连续性进行观察。

（2）转速特征：一般情况下，异响会随发动机转速变化而改变，异响不同，异响最明显的转速范围也不同。如活塞敲缸响、活塞销响、气门脚响在怠速时较明显。连杆轴承响、气门座响在中速时较明显。主轴承响、连杆轴承响、活塞环响在急加速时较明显。

（3）负荷特征：有些异响与发动机负荷有关，负荷变化时异响加重或减弱。如曲轴主轴承响、连杆轴承响、活塞敲缸响和点火敲击响等均随负荷增大（爬坡、加速、满载等）而增强，随负荷减小而减弱。而有些异响与负荷无关，如气门响，负荷变化时异响不变。

（4）温度特征：有些异响与发动机温度有关，有些异响与发动机温度无关或关系不大。如活塞敲缸响在低温时响声明显，温度升高后异响减弱或消失；发动机过热引起的早燃突爆声、活塞因变形、配合间隙过小引起的敲缸异响等在低温时响声不明显，温度升高后异响明显或加重；主轴承响、连杆轴承响和气门脚响等受温度影响较小。

（5）缸位特征：单缸断火或复火时有明显变化的异响称为发动机上缸或响声上缸。如连杆轴承响、活塞环响以及因气缸配合间隙过大造成的活塞敲缸异响等，在单缸断火时响声减轻或消失；曲轴主轴承响在单缸断火时响声变化不明显，在相邻两缸断火时响声减轻或消失；气门脚响在单缸断火时响声不变或变化不明显。

（6）工作循环特征：发动机异响与工作循环有很大关系。如一般曲柄连杆机构异响每工作循环响2次，配气机构异响每工作循环响1次。

（7）异响听诊部位和振动区域：常见的异响在发动机上引起振动的区域为气缸盖部位、气缸体中上侧部位、气缸体下侧部位、油底壳与曲轴箱分界面部位及正时齿轮室部位和加机油口部位（或曲轴箱通风管口部位）。

（8）伴随现象：发动机出现异响时，常常伴随有其他故障现象出现。如机油压力降低、排气管排烟颜色异常、功率下降、运转无力、燃油消耗过大、个别缸不工作或工作不良、振抖、运转不稳定、回火、放炮、机油变质、排气管有"突突"声以及加机油口脉动冒烟等。

二、故障诊断

技术状况良好的发动机在运转过程中仅能听到均匀的排气声和轻微的噪声，当发动机运转过程中出现异常响声时，就表明相关部位出现故障。对于有异响的发动机，重要的是找出异响的特征和规律，分析产生原因，找出异响部位。

1. 曲轴主轴承响故障诊断

（1）故障现象

曲轴主轴承响的主要特征是发动机突然加速时发出沉重而有力的"当、当"或"刚、刚"的金属敲击声，严重时机体发生很大振动，响声随发动机转速的提高而增大，随负荷的增加而增强。产生响声的部位是在缸体下部的曲轴箱内，单缸断火时响声无明显变化，相邻两缸同时断火时，响声会明显减弱或消失，温度变化时响声无明显变化，响声严重时机油压力甚至会降低。

（2）故障原因

① 主轴承盖固定螺钉松动。

② 主轴承减摩合金烧毁或脱落。
③ 主轴承和轴颈磨损过大，轴向止推装置磨损过大，造成径向和轴向间隙过大。
④ 曲轴弯曲。
⑤ 机油压力过低或机油黏度过低。
（3）故障诊断
① 拔出机油尺，从机油尺管口处听诊，同时反复变换发动机转速进行试验，如果是主轴承响，可明显听到沉重有力的金属敲击声。
② 发动机在低速下运转，用手微微抖动并反复加大节气门进行试验，同时仔细倾听。如响声随着发动机转速的升高而增大，抖动节气门的瞬间响声明显，这一般是主轴承松旷；如发动机在怠速或低速运转时响声较明显，高速时显得杂乱，则可能是曲轴弯曲；如在高速时机体有较大振动，机油压力明显降低，则一般是主轴承松旷严重、烧毁或减摩合金脱落。
③ 用听诊器具听诊。在节气门开度不断变换的同时，将听诊器或大一字旋具，触在机体曲轴箱两侧与曲轴轴线齐平的位置上进行听诊，响声最强的部位即为发响的主轴承。
④ 断火试验。如 1 缸断火后响声明显减弱，则为第一道主轴承响；如最末缸断火后响声明显减弱，则为最后一道主轴承响；如任意相邻两缸同时断火响声明显减弱，则为两缸之间的主轴承响。
⑤ 踩离合器踏板试验。若怀疑曲轴轴向窜动发响时，可踩下离合器踏板保持不动，如果响声减弱或消失，则为曲轴轴向窜动产生的响声。

2. 连杆轴承响故障诊断
（1）故障现象
当发动机突然加速时，有"当、当、当"连续明显、轻而短促的敲击声，这是连杆轴承响的主要特征；轴承严重松旷时，怠速运转也能听到明显的响声，且机油压力降低；发动机温度变化时，响声不变化；发动机负荷变化时，响声随负荷增加而加剧；单缸断火，响声明显减弱或消失，但复火时又立即出现。
（2）故障原因
① 连杆轴承盖的固定螺栓松动或折断。
② 连杆轴承减摩合金烧毁或脱落。
③ 连杆轴承或轴颈磨损过甚，造成径向间隙过大。
④ 机油压力过低或机油黏度太低。
（3）故障诊断
① 听诊。如用听诊器触在机体上听诊，往往不易听清楚，但在机油尺管口直接倾听，可清楚地听到连杆轴承响。
② 改变发动机转速，怠速时声响较小，中速时较为明显，稍微加大节气门就有连续的敲击声，急加速时敲击声随之增加，高速时因其他杂音干扰而不明显。诊断时使发动机怠速运转，然后由怠速向低速、由低速向中速、再由中速向高速加大节气门进行试验，同时结合单缸断火法，并在机油尺管口处听诊。响声随转速的升高而增大，抖动节气门时，在加油的瞬间异响突出。响声严重时，在任何转速下均可听到清晰、明显的敲击声。
③ 单缸断火，响声明显减弱或消失，但复火时又立即出现，则可断定为该缸连杆轴承响。但当连杆轴承过于松旷时，单缸断火声响无明显变化。
④ 连杆轴承响伴随有油压明显降低现象，严重时机体振抖，这有别于活塞销响和活塞敲缸。可用手将旋具或听诊器抵住缸体下部或油底壳处，当触试相应的故障缸位时有明显振动感。

3. 活塞销响故障诊断

（1）故障现象

发动机在急速、低速和从急速向低速时抖动节气门，可听到清脆而又连贯的"嗒、嗒、嗒"的金属敲击声；响声严重时，随转速的升高而增大，随负荷的增大而加重，发动机温度变化时，对响声稍有影响但影响不大；机油压力不降低；单缸断火时响声明显减弱或消失，复火瞬间响声又出现或连续出现两个响声。

（2）故障原因

①活塞销与连杆小头衬套配合松旷。

②衬套与连杆小头孔配合松旷。

③活塞销与活塞上的销座孔配合松旷。

（3）故障诊断

① 听诊。在微抖节气门使发动机转速不断变化的情况下，用听诊器触在发响气缸上部，可听到清脆连贯的响声。打开加机油口盖听诊，也能清楚地听到这一响声。

② 抖动节气门试验。发动机急速运转，然后由急速向低速急抖节气门，响声随转速的变化而变化。每抖一次节气门，如能听到清脆而连贯的"嗒、嗒、嗒"响声，则有可能是活塞销响。

③ 若转速越高，响声越大，单缸断火时响声反而杂乱，则故障为活塞销与衬套间隙过大。

④ 急速运转时，响声为有节奏而较沉重的响声，提高转速声响不减，同时伴有机体轻微抖动，断火试验响声加重，则说明活塞销自由窜动。

⑤ 断火试验。将发动机稳定在响声明显的转速上，逐缸进行断火试验，如某缸断火后响声明显减弱或消失，在复火的瞬间又立即出现或连续出现两个响声，则可断定为此缸活塞销响。

4. 活塞敲缸响故障诊断

（1）故障现象

发动机在急速或低速运转时，气缸的上部发出清晰而明显的"嗒、嗒、嗒"的金属敲击声，在中速及中速以上运转时响声减弱或消失；发动机温度变化时响声也变化；多数情况下响声在冷车时明显，热车时减弱或消失，也有个别情况活塞敲缸响在温度升高后加重；负荷越大响声也越大，但机油压力不降低；单缸断火，响声减弱或消失。

（2）故障原因

① 活塞与气缸壁配合间隙过大。

② 活塞与气缸壁间润滑条件过差。

③ 活塞在常温时反椭圆或椭圆度过小。

④ 活塞销与活塞销座孔装配过紧。

⑤ 活塞销与连杆小头衬套装配过紧。

⑥ 连杆轴承装配过紧。

⑦ 活塞圆柱度过大。

（3）故障诊断

① 在不同水温下诊断。先在冷车时诊断，若冷车时有敲击声，热车响声消失，说明是活塞敲击响，且故障尚轻，车辆可继续运行；若发动机热起后响声虽有减弱，但仍明显，特别是大负荷低转速时听得非常清楚，说明响声严重，应停驶检修。

② 断火试验。将发动机置于敲击声最明显的转速下运转，逐缸进行断火试验，如某缸

断火后响声减弱或消失，则为该缸敲缸响。

③ 加机油确诊。为了进一步确诊是否是活塞敲缸响，可将发动机熄火，卸下有响声气缸的火花塞（或喷油器），向气缸内注入一定量的机油，转动曲轴数圈，使机油布满气缸壁与活塞之间。然后装上火花塞（或喷油器）启动发动机，若响声短时间内减弱或消失，过一会儿又重新出现，则可确诊为活塞敲缸响。

④ 听诊。将听诊器触在气缸上部的两侧进行听诊，一般发响气缸的上部响声较强并稍有振动，如听到"嗒、嗒、嗒"的声音，一般是气缸与活塞间隙太大造成的；如听到"刚、刚、刚"的声音，则可能是气缸壁润滑不良造成的。

5. 气门响故障诊断

（1）故障现象

气门脚响和气门落座响统称为气门响。其故障表现为：发动机怠速运转时发出连续不断而且有节奏的"嗒、嗒、嗒"（在气门脚处）或"啪、啪、啪"（在气门座处）的敲击声；转速增高时响声亦随之增高，温度变化和单缸断火时响声不减弱，若有数只气门响，则声音显得杂乱。

（2）故障原因

① 气门脚响有以下几种。

a. 气门间隙过大。

b. 气门间隙调整螺钉松动或该间隙处两接触面不平。

c. 配气凸轮过度磨损，造成缓冲段效能下降，加重了挺杆对气门的冲击。

d. 气门润滑不良。

② 气门落座响的故障原因有以下几种。

a. 气门杆与其导管配合间隙过大。

b. 气门头部与其座圈接触不良。

c. 气门座圈松动。

d. 气门脚间隙过大。

（3）故障诊断

① 听诊。发动机怠速运转时，听到有节奏的响声，转速增高响声增大，温度变化和逐缸断火时响声不减弱，响声来自气门室内，可诊断为气门响。

② 怠速时在气门室或气门罩处听诊异响非常明显，气门脚响清脆而有节奏，在发动机周围就能听到较为清晰的响声。

③ 检查气门间隙。打开气门室盖，用厚薄规检查气门脚间隙，间隙最大的往往是最响的气门。运转中的发动机，当用厚薄规插入气门脚间隙处可使响声减弱或消失时，即可确定是该气门响，且由间隙太大造成，如响声无变化，说明是气门落座响。气门落座响如是座圈松动造成，其响声不如气门脚响坚实，且带有破碎声。

6. 气缸漏气响故障诊断

（1）故障现象

发动机运转时，从机油尺管口处可听到曲轴箱内发出的漏气声，负荷越大时响声越强，转速越高时响声越小，当抬加速踏板或单缸断火时，响声减弱或消失。随着响声的出现，加机油口处脉动地向外冒烟，冒烟次数与发响次数相同。

（2）故障原因

① 活塞环与气缸壁的漏光度过大。

② 活塞环和气缸壁严重磨损。

③ 活塞环开口间隙过大或活塞环开口重合。
④ 活塞环弹力过弱或侧隙、背隙过小。
⑤ 活塞环卡死在环槽内。
⑥ 气缸壁拉伤，出现沟槽。

（3）故障诊断

① 断火试验。提高发动机转速至响声最明显处稳住，打开机油尺管口，若从口处向外冒烟，可初步诊断为气缸漏气响。若某缸断火后响声减弱或消失，且加机油口处的冒烟量明显减少，说明漏气异响是该缸发出的。

② 加机油法。拆下可能漏气气缸的火花塞，向气缸内注入少量机油，转动发动机数圈后，装好火花塞，重新启动发动机，若响声明显减小，则可确定是该缸漏气响。

7. 皮带、轴承磨损异响故障诊断

（1）故障现象

发动机上的附属部件包括发电机、空调压缩机、转向助力泵、水泵等。随着使用时间的增加，皮带会磨损引起打滑，或者因为皮带张紧器工作不良而引起皮带打滑，发出"吱、吱"的响声。同样，压缩机轴承、水泵轴承、发电机轴承等轴承件用久以后也会有"咝咝"或"沙沙"的异响。

（2）故障原因

皮带打滑异响主要是因为皮带用久以后磨损加剧，皮带的弹性下降，或者由于皮带张紧器工作不良导致皮带过松。轴承异响通常是由于轴承磨损松旷或润滑不良。

（3）故障诊断

皮带打滑会发出"吱、吱"的声音。诊断时可以将发动机熄火，用手按压皮带或用专用的检测设备检测皮带的松紧度，过松的皮带即是打滑的皮带。

轴承故障通常会发出"咝咝""沙沙"声。这种异响往往声音刺耳、音量较高且凉车明显。诊断时可以用听诊器或者一根金属棒抵在可能有异响的部件上，若异响比其他地方大，则该部件有异响。

三、任务实施

1. 询问车主

向车主了解出现故障的时间；出现故障前是否有其他异常情况；发现故障后症状是否有变化；车辆行驶的具体情况；车辆是否按时保养；故障发生后是否进行过其他维修。通过以上的问诊了解故障发生前后的情况及故障的具体信息，完成发动机异响故障的初步诊断。

2. 试车与基本检查

进行试车，对故障进行确认。听异响发出的部位，异响的特点和规律。

3. 检测与诊断

首先利用故障诊断仪进行诊断，发动机电控单元中没有故障码，检查爆震传感器数据正常，说明没有敲缸现象。然后做断缸试验，来判断异响的来源和部位。

拔下一缸、二缸、三缸的高压线，响声没有变化。

拔下四缸高压线时，异响消失，说明异响来自四缸缸体。

检查发动机气缸压力，一缸 1.1MPa，二缸 1.15MPa，三缸 1.13MPa，四缸 1.1MPa，4 个缸的压力都正常，说明发动机应该没有因气缸磨损而导致的敲缸异响。

检查机油压力，在发动机怠速时，压力比正常值偏低。

综合以上的检测与分析，异响应来自曲轴、活塞、连杆等部位，于是分解缸体，如

图 4-1 所示。检查活塞销、连杆轴承都正常，检查缸径都在标准范围内。

检查主轴瓦间隙，结果发现第 5 道主轴瓦间隙大于 0.76mm，故断定问题可能出在第 5 道曲柄或第 5 道主轴瓦。经检测，主轴径在规定范围内，则故障应在主轴瓦。由于第 5 道主轴瓦磨损导致间隙变大，从而发生异响。

4. 故障排除

更换第 5 道主轴瓦，异响排除。

5. 检验交车

故障检修完毕，发动机进行装复，试车没有其他异常，向车主交车。

四、任务小结

在进行异响诊断时，不能盲目进行拆卸，而应该详细了解异响来源，分析可能的原因，然后按步骤逐项进行诊断与排除。注意检测标准一定要依据维修手册。

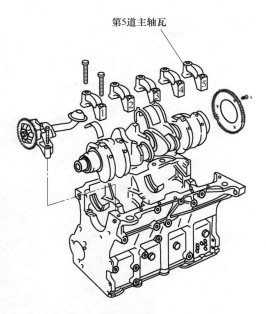

图 4-1 缸体分解图

五、任务报告单

	专 业		班 级		姓 名	
	任务名称				学 时	2
	车 型		发动机型号			
	考核项目	考核内容			分 值	得 分
任务完成过程	1. 故障症状描述				5	
	2. 故障可能的原因及分析				25	
	3. 检测与诊断过程				35	
	4. 故障排除				10	
	5. 故障诊断小结				10	
教师评价	作业质量、作业效率、作业安全等				15	
	总评分数				100	

六、知识拓展

【典型案例一】 2010 款速腾 1.6L 汽车发动机热车时有异响。

故障描述：一辆 2010 款速腾 1.6L 汽车在凉车时发动机声音正常，但热车时发动机前部有"吱吱"的异响。

故障诊断与修复：

(1) 询问车主此前是否进行过其他维修。车主说异响发生后更换过正时皮带、张紧轮、水泵。

(2) 检查该车是否有撞击痕迹。检查底盘、发动机和车身后，没有发现撞击痕迹。

(3) 查看声音来源，发现此声音不是来源于前部轮系。因为皮带异响一般是冷车时响，而热车时正常，此车故障现象恰恰相反，所以分析可能原因有两点。一个是凸轮轴油封异响，另一个是凸轮轴在 1 缸处与缸盖或端盖相连接部分相刮擦造成异响。于是将齿形皮带保

护罩拆下，进行详细检查。由于凸轮轴油封此时在外侧能看到，因此应先确定是不是凸轮轴油封异响。

凸轮轴油封由塑料、尼龙等制成，故也可能因热而出现问题，如果是它异响，使其位置发生变化，声音应该会有变化。于是用专用油封安装工具对油封重新安装，并使其位置发生变化。调整并重新安装后，异响明显变小，因此可基本判定该故障为凸轮轴油封导致的异响。

（4）拆下凸轮轴油封，检查凸轮轴安装油封处的轴颈没有问题，如图4-2所示，于是安装新油封。安装时要注意油封密封唇不能浸油，安装活塞不能位于上止点，凸轮轴轴颈必须无油。重新装回轮系，故障排除。

图4-2 凸轮轴轴颈

故障诊断小结：该故障在更换凸轮轴油封后消失，分析原因应为油封质量问题导致异响。

【典型案例二】 宝来汽车热车发动机异响。

故障描述：一辆宝来1.6L汽车，手动挡变速器，该车在热车时"唧咕、唧咕"响，急加油门之后响声尤为明显。

故障诊断与修复：发动机热车后正时皮带部位发出"唧咕""唧咕"声，分析认为可能如下部位会发出这种声音：发电机；正时皮带；张紧轮；水泵；发动机机械部分。

拆下发电机皮带后启动发动机检查，异响依旧，因此排除发电机异响。

按照一汽大众维修手册对正时皮带机构进行了组装，再次启动发动机，异响仍然存在；用水浇到皮带上声音没有改变，用胶带缠到张紧轮上装上试车，异响依旧存在；更换张紧轮和正时皮带做试验，响声依然没有排除。

用听诊器仔细听水泵部位声音，响声不明显。

检查机油油位、压力均正常，机油压力怠速时为340kPa（标准为在怠速时不低于200kPa），2000r/min时为390kPa（标准为2000r/min时不能高于700kPa），经比较机油压力也正常。

拆检发动机缸盖，发现凸轮轴有异常磨损，第2道、第3道、第4道轴瓦磨损都较严重。经仔细检查发现，轴瓦表面比较粗糙，从而导致凸轮轴异常磨损，进而导致发动机异响。更换新的气缸盖，故障排除。

故障诊断小结：对于异响特征不是非常明显的故障，首先应该从发动机外围容易发生异响的部件开始逐个检查，发动机异响部位的确定，可以依靠听诊器进行诊断。对于怀疑产生异响的零件可以采用隔离、浇水改变摩擦系数等方法进行相关试验后进行诊断。应根据先易后难、由表及里的原则逐步进行排除。

任务二　底盘异响故障诊断与修复

学习目标

1. 能根据报修车辆的故障现象确定问诊的方向及项目。
2. 能根据故障现象制定正确的故障诊断计划。
3. 能熟练查阅维修资料,能根据故障现象选用合适的检测与诊断设备并熟练使用。
4. 能根据诊断计划,运用合适的检修设备对底盘异响故障进行检测。
5. 能对检测结果进行正确分析并确定底盘异响的故障部位及原因。
6. 能对故障部位进行快速准确修复,并且消除故障隐患。

任务导入

任务资料:一辆2007款速腾1.8T汽车,行驶里程6.7万千米,用户反映低速大角度转向时车辆底盘发出"咕咕"的异响。

任务要求:根据该车辆的故障现象,查阅相关资料,并选用合适的检测与诊断设备进行故障诊断与修复,同时填写任务报告单。

一、故障分析

底盘异响是指汽车在行驶中从传动系统、行驶系统、转向系统和制动系统各总成部件或机构中发出的不正常噪声、响声及振动声。通常是由于汽车部件磨损或损坏、连接松动及配件质量差或装配不当等引起的。

变速器的异响特征主要包括:发动机怠速运转、变速器处于空挡位置时有异响,踏下离合器踏板时响声消失;换挡时异响或换入某挡后异响。

离合器分离和结合时产生的异响通常是离合器异响。

当传动轴或驱动桥转动时出现"咔啦咔啦"或"刚蹬刚蹬"的撞击声,且车辆发抖,通常是传动轴或驱动桥异响。

二、故障诊断

1. 离合器异响故障诊断

(1) 故障原因

① 分离轴承缺油或磨损,回位弹簧过软、折断或脱落。
② 分离杠杆螺钉折断或支承销及销孔磨损松旷。
③ 离合器摩擦片铆钉松动或铆钉头外露。
④ 离合器片的内孔花键槽与变速器主动轴花键齿磨损过甚。
⑤ 离合器片钢片碎裂或减振弹簧折断。
⑥ 踏板回位弹簧过软或折断、脱落。

(2) 故障诊断

① 无论离合器在分离和结合时,都会产生异响,同时在行驶中车辆有发抖现象,则很有可能是摩擦片裂缺破损或铆钉外露,或是从动盘与花键套铆钉出现松动等。

② 如果离合器踏板踩下时无明显异响,而当抬起踏板时异响十分明显,那么很有可能

是分离轴承存在着重大缺陷。此时分离轴承产生异响有两种情况。一种是分离轴承被卡死，在与分离杠杆头滑动摩擦时不断发出"唰、唰"声。另一种则是分离轴承因缺油或损坏发出的无节奏"哗、哗"声。

③ 如果踩下踏板少许，发出"沙、沙"声，抬起踏板时响声消失，则是因为离合器轴承缺少润滑油造成的。

④ 如果遇见离合器发出"咔吱、咔吱"的响声，那么应该马上将发动机熄火，这可能是离合器盖的固定螺杆松脱后与飞轮壳摩擦之后发出的响声。

2. 变速器异响故障诊断

（1）故障原因

① 主、被动齿轮之间齿隙过大；齿轮磨损过大；轮齿折断。

② 轴承磨损、破裂及润滑不良。

③ 同步器滑动齿轮拨叉内侧与变速杆下端头工作面出现严重磨损。

（2）故障诊断

变速杆处于空挡位置，变速器有"咯、咯"的响声，但踩下离合器踏板后响声消失，此时应检查第1轴后轴承是否磨损过甚或损伤。若响声均匀，踩下离合器踏板后声音减小或消失，说明常啮齿轮啮合不正常。

变速杆置入任何挡位行驶都有异响，但进入直接挡位时，响声减弱甚至消失，或在空挡时也无响声，此种故障的原因为中间轴与第2轴不平行，或第2轴轴承响。

变速杆置入低速挡位置时有异响，但在高速挡时声响减弱，空挡滑行时有"哗哗"声，可将驱动桥支起，使变速器在低速挡或倒挡运转。若在倒挡齿轮处听到响声明显，为第2轴后轴承松旷或损坏。若车速突然变化时响声增大，车速比较稳定时，响声是一种连续的"呜呜"声，且随车速提高而增大，则说明齿轮间隙过大或过小，应调整齿轮间隙。

汽车在不平的路面上行驶时，变速杆摆振，并发出摩擦声响，用手将变速杆稳住，响声消失，则说明换挡叉变形，固定装置松动，或换挡叉与叉槽磨损严重，可结合变速杆抖动情况分析处理。

发动机运转时，若听到变速器内有金属的摩擦声，则可能是润滑油不足，或润滑油变质过稀所致，此时应补添或更换符合要求的润滑油。

在行驶中挂入某挡时异响显著，则为该挡齿轮磨损过甚，或齿轮齿形有异常现象。新、旧齿轮啮合不良及边盖固定螺栓过长而碰击齿轮等都会引起异响。

3. 传动轴异响故障诊断

（1）故障原因

① 万向节长期缺油、万向节十字轴及滚针磨损松旷或滚针碎裂。

② 传动轴花键齿与叉管花键槽磨损松旷。

③ 变速器输出轴花键齿与突缘花键槽磨损过大。

④ 各连接部位螺栓松动。

⑤ 中间轴承磨损过甚或缺少润滑油。

⑥ 滚珠轴承损坏。

⑦ 中间轴承支架橡胶套损坏或支架位置不正。

⑧ 支架螺栓松动或松紧不一致。

⑨ 传动轴弯曲或传动轴两端的万向节叉安装不正确。

（2）故障诊断

① 汽车起步时发出撞击声，行驶过程中始终有异响，则是伸缩花键松旷、变速器输出

轴磨损、万向节松旷或缺油引起的。

② 汽车行驶中发出"呜呜"的响声，则是中间轴承发响。

③ 起步时无异响，加速时发出异响，脱挡滑行中更明显，则是万向节叉装错，传动轴弯曲。

④ 拉手制动时异常响声消失或减轻，则是手制动蹄或销套（盘式）发响。

4. 驱动桥异响故障诊断

（1）故障原因

① 驱动桥内各齿轮的齿隙过小或过大。

② 主动锥齿轮和从动锥齿轮的齿隙不均或装配不当。

③ 轴承预紧度调整不当。

④ 半轴管弯曲变形。

⑤ 齿轮损坏或齿面损伤。

⑥ 轴承损坏。

（2）故障诊断

① 驱动桥发出"哽哽"响声，滑行时不响，则是主减速器齿轮咬合不良。

② 挂1挡、2挡、3挡时发响，低速挡时更严重，则为主减速器被动齿轮或轴承松旷，主动锥齿轮轴承或螺母松旷；挂3挡、4挡、5挡时发响，高速挡时更严重，则为主动齿轮缺损。

③ 松开油门时发响，则是主减速器齿轮或轴承松旷，主动锥齿轮轴承或螺母松旷。加大油门时发响，则是减速器齿轮或轴承过紧。

三、任务实施

1. 询问车主

向车主了解出现故障的时间；出现故障前是否有异常情况；发现故障后症状是否有变化；车辆行驶的具体情况；车辆是否按时保养；故障发生后是否进行过维修。通过以上的问诊了解故障发生前后的情况及故障的具体信息，完成底盘异响故障的初步诊断。

2. 试车与基本检查

进行试车，对故障进行确认，发现故障车辆以20km/h的速度转弯时，其前部有异响。听异响发出的大致部位，异响的特点和规律。

3. 检测与诊断

把车辆举升后，任意一侧的驱动轮制动，异响仍然存在，排除车轮轴承和制动系统异响。

更换驱动半轴，异响仍然存在，排除半轴故障可能。因车辆只有在转弯时存在异响，故判断其为差速器响声。

分解变速器，测量差速器行星齿轮的齿轮间隙和啮合印痕，发现啮合印痕在齿根部位，如图4-3。因此判断是差速器不正常啮合，产生异响。

分析认为，差速器球形衬套的不正常磨损，造成差速器的行星齿轮啮合部位达到齿轮根部（正常应为齿轮中部啮合）。因为差速器行星齿轮只是在转弯时才发生转动，所以这种异响只在转弯时出现，异响比较明显。在判断是否为差速器异响的过程中，要求大角度（转向盘转角大于180°）转弯，并且伴随不同的加减速，如果异响能够随启动速度改变，则是差速器故障的概率较高。

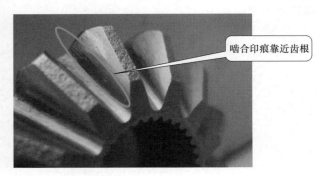

图 4-3　差速器齿轮啮合印痕

4. 故障排除

更换球形衬套，重新装配，测量新装配的差速器行星齿轮的齿隙在 0.4mm 左右，而发生异响的差速器的实际测量数据为 0.6mm 左右，试车发现异响排除。

5. 检验交车

故障检修完毕，没有其他异常，向车主交车。

四、任务小结

在进行异响诊断时，要在异响发生的条件下反复听，同时还要听在其他行驶状态下是否也会有异常情况。在基本确定故障来源后再进行相应的拆卸。

五、任务报告单

专　业			班　级	姓　名	
任务名称				学　时	2
车　型			发动机型号		
	考核项目	考核内容		分　值	得　分
任务完成过程	1. 故障症状描述			5	
	2. 故障可能的原因及分析			25	
	3. 检测与诊断过程			35	
	4. 故障排除			10	
	5. 故障诊断小结			10	
教师评价	作业质量、作业效率、作业安全等			15	
总评分数				100	

六、知识拓展

【典型案例一】 一辆 POLO 汽车底盘异响。

故障描述：一辆 POLO 1.6L 手动挡汽车，行驶里程 8.6 万千米。该车行驶在颠簸路上或过急弯时，底盘有时会发出"哒哒"的异响。

故障诊断与修复：进行试车，无论维修人员如何过弯，原地转动转向盘急加速或倒车，均未出现此故障现象。根据经验，造成 POLO 汽车发生此类异响的部位有：内外球笼或半轴磨损；前轮轴承松旷；外球笼大螺母松动或脱落；横向稳定杆变形或橡胶衬套磨损；横向稳定杆连接杆球头磨损。

于是举升起车辆对上述部位进行全面检查。检查发现左右两侧的内外球笼防尘套完好无裂纹，所有球头紧固良好无松旷；用双手晃动轮胎，没有发现前轮轴承松旷，也没有发现转

向横拉杆球头有间隙；紧固外球笼大螺母和轮胎螺栓，没有发现松动且紧固力矩均符合标准值；用手晃动横向稳定杆，没有发现橡胶衬套松旷。通过检查，没有发现异响部位。转弯异响一般由球笼磨损造成的可能性非常大，因为这个部位磨损无法通过外表检查而直接判断。为了证实这个判断，与车主一道又进行了多次路试，然而异响始终未曾出现。因此推断可能在球笼内部某一位置存在磨损。为慎重起见，对左右外球笼进行解体检查，出乎意料的是，并没有发现磨损迹象。

通过与车主交流获知，该车经常在比较颠簸的道路上行驶时出现异响，于是寻找类似的路况进行故障模拟试验。车辆在颠簸过弯时，终于听到从右前方悬挂下部传来几声"哒哒"的异响，声音是在右转急弯时才产生的。听声音比较沉闷，可以排除是球笼发出的异响；可以排除发动机或变速器所造成的异响。

举升起车辆，对右前悬挂处进行详细检查。发现右前半轴处有一道不易觉察的刮痕，但是在周围并没有发现异物；右前悬挂上的相关部件未发现碰撞过的痕迹，并且都保持着正常的间距，理论上不存在相互刮擦的可能。再进一步检查时，又发现该车的横向稳定杆虽然能保持紧固，但在撬棒的撬动下，却能左右移动少许，同时在横向稳定杆的末端也有一道不易觉察的刮痕。更换横向稳定杆的橡胶衬套后，故障排除。

故障诊断小结：此故障是车辆行驶在颠簸路面转弯时发出响声，该响声是由横向稳定杆与右前半轴撞击引起的。在诊断时一定要向车主了解清楚故障发生的条件和路况，以便在试车时可以快速了解异响的部位，并予以排除。

【**典型案例二**】 一辆 2011 款速腾汽车底盘异响。

故障描述：一辆 2011 款速腾汽车，行驶里程 5 万千米。该车行驶在颠簸路时右后部发出"咕嘟，咕嘟"的声音，类似减振器漏油失效的声音。

故障诊断与修复：与车主进行路试确认故障现象，故障现象比较明显。

车辆升起后，对后桥螺丝进行检查并按标准力矩紧固。目测底盘，减振器没有漏油的现象。未发现其他问题。因声音类似减振器损坏时的声音，于是更换了右后减振器，进行试车故障依旧。

再次将车辆举升后，对下控制臂及其他悬架连接件进行检查，同时对手刹拉线、油箱等进行检查，都未发现问题。

用手晃动两后刹车分泵时，发现左右分泵的旷量不一样，右侧的旷量比较大。于是与一辆其他车进行了比较，确认该车辆右后分泵旷量不正常。

拆下右后分泵及分泵支架进行检查，发现分泵支架导向螺栓磨损，旷量比较大。更换右后刹车分泵支架后进行试车，故障排除。

故障诊断小结：该车发生异响的部位集中在右后部，在此部位有相对运动的部件并不多。按照故障诊断的原则，从简单到复杂，应该先检查分泵支架及此处的其他部件，而不应该先更换减振器，大大增加了诊断时间。

项目五

发动机工作异常故障诊断与修复

发动机工作异常包括发动机启动异常、怠速运转异常、动力不足等故障现象。在进行故障分析时需要综合考虑与故障有关的多个系统，应在掌握发动机油路系统、点火系统等各系统故障诊断的基础上，掌握综合故障的分析与诊断。只有这样才能为所发生的故障制定全面合理的诊断方案，并选用合适的诊断工具进行科学诊断。

任务一 发动机无法启动故障诊断与修复

发动机无法启动是发动机常见故障之一。发动机无法启动故障涉及汽车上发动机系统、防盗系统等多个系统，发动机系统故障又涉及油路系统、点火系统、机械系统等。在进行发动机无法启动故障诊断时，首先要分析故障发生在哪个系统，然后再进一步检测故障发生在哪个部位，最终找到故障原因并予以修复。

学习目标

1. 能根据报修车辆的故障现象确定问诊的方向及项目。
2. 能根据故障现象制定正确的故障诊断计划。
3. 能熟练查阅维修资料，能根据故障现象选用合适的检测与诊断设备并熟练使用。
4. 能根据诊断计划，运用合适的检修设备对发动机无法启动故障进行检测。
5. 能对检测结果进行正确分析并确定发动机无法启动的故障部位及原因。
6. 能对故障部位进行快速准确修复，并且消除故障隐患。
7. 能具有精益求精的工匠精神和严谨细致的工作态度，增强环保意识。

任务导入

任务资料：一辆2010款速腾汽车，车主反映车辆停放一个晚上后，早晨不能启动。

任务要求：根据该车辆的故障现象，查阅相关资料，并选用合适的检测与诊断设备进行故障诊断与修复，同时填写任务报告单。

一、故障分析

1. 燃油量不足
发动机燃油量不足,导致油路无法建立正常的油压。

2. 发动机启动系统故障
(1) 蓄电池电量不足导致启动机运转无力。
(2) 蓄电池接线柱接触不良、启动机接线柱接触不良或断路。
(3) 启动继电器、启动保险、点火开关启动机故障,或者它们之间的线路断路或接触不良。

特别注意:如果是自动挡车辆出现启动时启动机不转动,需要查看变速杆是否在 P 挡或者 N 挡(可观察仪表台的挡位指示灯)。

3. 防盗系统故障
(1) 点火钥匙失效。
(2) 防盗电控单元或防盗模块故障。
(3) 识读线圈故障(不同车名称可能不同)。
(4) 防盗系统线路故障。

4. 点火系统故障
(1) 火花塞故障,导致火花塞不能点火或火弱,使发动机混合气无法正常燃烧。
(2) 高压线故障,导致火花塞跳火电压过低或无电压。
(3) 点火线圈故障,导致不能产生高压电。
(4) 分电器故障,导致高压电不能分配到各缸火花塞。
(5) 电控单元或点火模块及其线路故障,导致点火系统不能工作。

5. 油路系统故障
(1) 喷油器故障。喷油器堵塞、喷油器线路故障、喷油器损坏,导致喷油量过小或不能喷油。
(2) 油泵故障。油泵工作不良或损坏、油泵线路故障,导致油路油压低或无油压。
(3) 油路油压过低。油泵进油滤网堵塞、油泵工作不良、油泵线路接触不良、汽油滤清器堵塞,导致油路油压过低。
(4) 油路油压过高。油压调节器故障,导致油压过高、混合气过浓,发动机无法正常燃烧。

6. 点火正时错误
由于正时皮带过松、正时标记未对正等导致发动机正时偏差过大。

7. 曲轴位置传感器故障
曲轴位置传感器故障、线路故障,信号齿损坏或信号齿与传感器的距离变大,导致信号过弱。

8. 怠速控制系统故障
怠速控制阀卡滞不能打开、节气门体处过脏,导致进气量严重不足。

9. 发动机机械系统故障
气缸磨损过大、进排气门关闭不严,导致气缸压力严重不足。

10. 电控单元或线路故障
电控单元内部故障、电控单元供电线路或搭铁线路存在故障。

11. 燃油品质变差

燃油品质变差导致发动机不能正常燃烧。

12. 传感器故障

发动机除曲轴位置传感器以外，出现多个传感器不能工作或工作不良，导致发动机无法正常工作。

二、故障诊断

1. 首先通过观察仪表排除相关故障

（1）若显示油量不足，则应先添加油量。

（2）若防盗报警灯几秒钟不熄灭，而是闪烁或常亮，则初步判断防盗系统可能存在故障。

特别提示：有些车型，如桑塔纳2000，在防盗系统发生故障时，发动机能正常启动，只是启动后几秒钟会自动熄火。

（3）若发动机故障报警灯几秒钟后不熄灭，而是常亮，说明发动机电脑中已存有故障信息。

（4）若发动机故障报警灯不亮，则很可能发动机电控单元的供电、搭铁线路存在故障，也有可能是电控单元故障。

2. 打启动机，观察启动机运转情况

（1）若启动机运转无力，则检测启动系统，蓄电池可能亏电、启动线路可能存在故障、启动机可能存在故障。

（2）若启动机运转正常，则进行下面的检测。

特别注意：在打启动机时，要注意观察发动机转速表是否摆动。若发动机转速表表针不动，则很可能是发动机转速传感器发生故障。遇此情况，应重点检测发动机转速传感器（曲轴位置传感器）。

3. 利用故障诊断仪读取故障码，查看数据流

注意：若故障诊断仪无法与发动机电控单元进行通信，而能够进入其他电控系统，比如ABS系统、安全气囊系统，则应该检查发动机电控单元的供电线路和搭铁线路，这些地方很可能存在故障。

（1）若发动机电控单元中存在故障码，则应该对故障码进行分析，按照故障码进行故障查找。然后要看一下与启动有关的数据流，比如水温传感器、节气门位置传感器等的信息。

（2）若发动机电控单元中不存在故障码，则应进行下面的检测。

4. 检测点火是否正常，喷油器是否正常工作，油泵是否工作

首先打启动机（有些车打开点火开关，油泵会工作几秒钟），查看油泵是否在工作。

（1）若发动机能点火、喷油器也工作，但油泵不工作，则应检查油泵及其相应的线路是否存在故障。

（2）若火弱，则应查找点火系统相关部件，如检查火花塞是否存在故障、高压线是否电阻过大等。

（3）若无火，喷油器工作，则应查找点火模块及线路。

（4）若无火，喷油器也不工作，则应查找曲轴位置传感器，必要时还要查看正时是否严重错误，电控单元及线路是否有故障。

（5）若火正常，喷油器不工作，则喷油器线路可能存在故障。

（6）若火正常，喷油器工作正常，则应检查油路油压是否存在异常。若油压正常，则应检查怠速控制阀是否存在故障，另外查看发动机正时是否存在问题，发动机气缸压力是否存在不足。

特别提示：发动机无法启动时，别忘了检查是否存在燃油变质的问题。

三、任务实施

1. 询问车主

询问车主发生无法启动故障前有何症状；在何种情况下发生的该故障；发生故障后是否进行过维修；车辆发生故障前是否进行过其他的修理或加装设备；车辆行驶里程是多少；车辆是否按时保养等。

根据从车主处了解的车辆故障信息，初步排除某些故障的可能性，缩小故障诊断的范围。

2. 试车与基本检查

启动发动机，进行故障确认。同时观察仪表油量显示，观察发动机启动转速是否正常。观察发动机转速表指针的摆动幅度，是否偏离怠速期望值。观察进气道是否漏气、真空管有无脱落、破损，电线插接器有无松脱。观察是否存在漏油、漏水、漏气、漏电的四漏现象。观察节气门拉线是否调整合适。

3. 检测与诊断

用故障诊断仪 VAS5052A 对车辆系统进行诊断，各系统均没有故障码存储。点火钥匙打开，发动机不运转时的数据流也正常。

由于发动机控制单元能够用 VAS5052A 进行诊断，证明发动机控制单元通信、电源和接地没有问题。

检查发动机点火系统：拆下高压线，安装火花塞试火，发现点火正常，证明发动机点火系统和转速传感器没有问题。

检查供油系统：检查汽油泵压力。接上油压表后，启动车辆，发现油压能达到 280kPa，证明汽油泵及其控制电路都没有问题。

检查发动机机械部分：检查气缸压力，接上气缸压力表，测量气缸压力为 1.1MPa，气缸压力正常。在检查缸压时，发现火花塞全部都是干的，证明进入发动机气缸的汽油太少。

检查喷油器线路：在插头上面连接一个二极管试灯，启动发动机时试灯闪烁，说明喷油器控制线路正常。在启动车辆的同时喷入化油器清洗剂，发动机可以启动。

由此得出结论：发动机混合气过稀，导致发动机不能启动。

用 VAS5051 示波器检测喷油器启动时的喷油时间，如图 5-1 所示，正常的喷油器工作波形如图 5-2 所示。

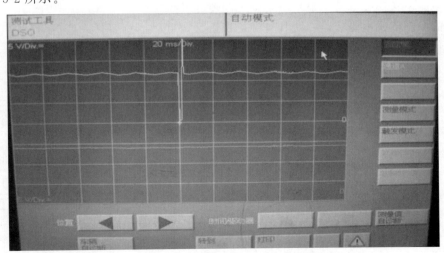

图 5-1 故障车辆启动时喷油器波形

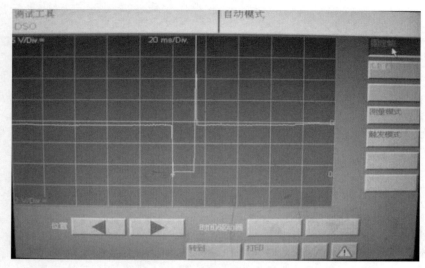

图 5-2 无故障车辆启动时喷油器波形

通过对比的两个波形,明显看出该故障车的喷油器喷油时间太短,使混合气太稀,从而导致发动机无法启动。

发动机的基本喷油时间取决于发动机负荷和转速。

进一步检测发动机转速传感器和进气压力传感器,均正常。

综合以上的检测和分析,故障很可能在发动机控制单元。

4. 故障排除

更换发动机控制单元,再利用故障诊断仪进行诊断,将电控单元中的故障码清除,同时查看所有数据流均在规定范围内,故障检修完毕,故障排除。

5. 检验交车

故障排除后,确认发动机没有其他症状,向车主交车。

四、任务小结

发动机控制单元接收发动机转速和负荷信号来控制喷油时间。当发动机控制单元发生故障时,即使能正常接收信号,也不能正确控制喷油时间。

发动机控制单元本身较难判断其自身是否正常,可以借助容易判断的传感器和执行器,用排除法来判断其是否正常。

五、任务报告单

	专 业		班 级		姓 名	
	任务名称				学 时	2
	车型		发动机型号			
	考核项目	考核内容			分 值	得 分
任务完成过程	1. 故障症状描述				5	
	2. 故障可能的原因及分析				25	
	3. 检测与诊断过程				35	
	4. 故障排除				10	
	5. 故障诊断小结				10	
教师评价	作业质量、作业效率、作业安全等				15	
	总评分数				100	

六、知识拓展

【典型案例一】 一辆三厢飞度轿车不能启动。

故障描述：一辆三厢飞度轿车，行驶3万千米，车主反映该车在行驶途中发动机突然熄火，再也无法启动。

故障诊断与修复：打开点火开关，仪表盘指示灯一切正常，启动发动机时，启动机转动有力，达到发动机启动转速要求，但是发动机不能启动。

发动机不能启动的故障原因很多，如油路系统故障、点火系统故障、机械系统故障、传感器故障等。

由于该车发动机有油压预制功能，因此先进行油路检测。将点火开关反复接通，同时打开燃油箱盖，听燃油泵工作情况，能听到燃油泵在接通电源时发出"嘶嘶"的声音。打开发动机罩，松开燃油轨道燃油进油管夹箍，有燃油喷出，初步判断供油系统正常。

于是检查电路故障。该车点火系统采用本田的 I-DSI（智能型独立双点火）系统，每个缸有前后2个点火线圈和火花塞。取下1缸、2缸的前点火线圈和火花塞，发现火花塞上有很湿的燃油液体，说明燃油已经进入气缸。将火花塞插入点火线圈，放在气缸盖上搭铁，启动发动机，火花塞无跳火火花，说明点火系统有故障。拔下该车点火线圈的三芯插头，3根线的颜色分别为黑/黄色、白色、黑色。查找手册，3根线分别为电源线、电脑控制回路线、搭铁线。打开点火开关，用万用表测量黑/黄色线（电源线）的电压，应为蓄电池电压，结果却无电压。按照电路图查找，发现驾驶员侧熔丝盒内的14号、15号熔丝熔断。14号熔丝为前点火线圈熔丝，15号熔丝为后点火线圈熔丝。更换新熔丝，打开点火开关后熔丝马上熔断，这说明存在点火系统短路故障。用万用表测量熔丝盒内14号、15号熔丝插座与搭铁之间的电阻，测量值为0Ω，说明电源对地短路。将点火线圈插接器全部拔下来，测量熔丝盒内14号、15号熔丝插座与搭铁之间电阻，测量值为∞，说明线路一切正常，故障点应该在点火线圈。于是，将8个（前4个，后4个）点火线圈逐一拆下测量，结果发现有2缸的前后点火线圈均有内部短路故障。于是更换这些点火线圈，装回所有的线路和熔丝，启动发动机，火花塞跳火火花强烈，说明点火系统故障已经排除。但是发动机还是不能启动。由于多次启动，这时发动机转速明显不够，说明蓄电池电量已明显下降。给蓄电池充足电后继续启动发动机。发动机有"突突"的声音，好像有启动的意思，但还是不能启动。在有油有火的情况下不能启动发动机，只能考虑机械和控制系统有问题。该车发动机配气正时传动采用静音式链条，又只跑了3万千米，分析认为点火正时应该不会出问题。用故障诊断仪读取发动机故障信息，电控单元中没有存储故障码。

打启动机读取数据流，发现发动机转速只有60r/min，明显比实际值低。因为发动机转速信号是由曲轴位置传感器获取的，所以怀疑曲轴位置传感器发生故障。检测曲轴位置传感器的电阻，完全正常。于是又拆下该传感器，这时发现传感器端部有非常明显的磨损现象。该车采用电磁感应式曲轴位置传感器，通过曲轴触发轮的转动来获取发动机转速，正常情况下，其与曲轴触发轮有一定的间隙，不应磨损。

因此怀疑触发轮存在故障，准备拆除油底壳检查。升起车辆时发现油底壳曾碰撞过，碰撞后将油底壳拆下进行重新焊接。

于是将油底壳拆下，发现油底壳内有一块齿轮，再查看传感器触发轮，只剩下一部分固定在曲轴上。曲轴触发轮已经裂为2块，其中有一块已掉在油底壳中。触发轮上的齿轮只能给传感器很低的发动机转速信号，并且还不连续，致使发动机有启动征兆但是不能启动。

更换触发齿轮后，发动机顺利启动，用故障诊断仪查看数据流，一切正常，故障排除。

事后得知，此车曾经进行过维修。可以断定是不规范的操作造成点火线圈无故损坏，而触发轮则是由于油底壳和曲轴带轮的间隙较小，拆卸油底壳时操作不当造成的。

故障诊断小结：发动机无法启动，但发动机还供油、火花塞还跳火的故障很容易让诊断人员走弯路，会误认为故障应该在机械部分。对于此类故障如果诊断人员能够用示波器连续监测喷油器或火花塞的跳火，会比较容易找到故障原因。

【典型案例二】 一辆北京现代2.0途胜汽车无法启动。

故障描述：一辆北京现代2.0途胜汽车，行驶5.8万千米，车主反映车辆正常行驶后停放了约1h发动机不能启动，仪表显示正常。

故障诊断与修复：了解该车属在保车辆，4S店保养记录正常，到现场后检查各种油液都正常后试车，证实了与车主所描述的故障。

拆卸火花塞打启动机检查无高压电。

利用故障诊断仪检查发动机电控系统发现有故障码存在：P0335曲轴转角传感器电路异常。

检查曲轴转角传感器的导线，连接良好。

电源电路检查：拔掉传感器插头，点火开关处于ON，测量传感器线束连接器电源端子与搭铁之间的电压为12.21V，如图5-3所示，与规定值一致。说明该线路及电控单元内部电路正常。

搭铁电路检查：点火开关处于OFF，测量传感器线束连接器的搭铁端子与搭铁之间的电阻，阻值小于0.5Ω，说明该线路及电控单元内部电路正常。

信号电路检查：点火开关处于ON，测量传感器线束连接器的信号端子与搭铁之间的电压为4.95V（标准值约5V），如图5-4所示，说明该线路及电控单元内部电路正常。

图5-3 传感器线束连接器电源端子与搭铁之间的电压

通过以上检查说明传感器线路以及控制单元正常。那么，故障应在曲轴位置传感器自身。更换曲轴位置传感器，试车发动机启动正常，利用故障诊断仪检测正常，如图5-5所示。

图5-4 传感器线束连接器信号端子与搭铁之间的电压

图5-5 故障诊断仪诊断结果

故障诊断小结：ECU根据曲轴位置传感器信号计算发动机的转速，以此控制喷油和点火。因曲轴位置传感器损坏、ECU接收不到该信号，所以车辆无法启动。

在日常的维修操作过程中，要严格按照标准操作流程作业，这样会减少诊断时间，提高故障诊断效率。

任务二　发动机有启动征兆，但不能启动故障诊断与修复

学习目标

1. 能根据报修车辆的故障现象确定问诊的方向及项目。
2. 能根据故障现象制定正确的故障诊断计划。
3. 能熟练查阅维修资料，能根据故障现象选用合适的检测与诊断设备并熟练使用。
4. 能根据诊断计划，运用合适的检修设备对发动机不能启动故障进行检测。
5. 能对检测结果进行正确分析并确定发动机不能启动的故障部位及原因。
6. 能对故障部位进行快速准确修复，并且消除故障隐患。

任务导入

任务资料：一辆2011款宝来1.6L汽车，手动挡轿车，行驶里程7.8万千米，发动机有启动迹象，但无法启动。

任务要求：根据该车辆的故障现象，查阅相关资料，并选用合适的检测与诊断设备进行故障诊断与修复，同时填写任务报告单。

一、故障分析

该故障症状是在启动发动机时，启动机能带动发动机正常转动，有启动征兆，但不能启动。可能原因有以下几种：

(1) 进气管有漏气，导致混合气过稀。
(2) 点火正时不正确，导致发动机不能正常燃烧。
(3) 高压火花过弱，导致混合气不能正常燃烧。
(4) 燃油压力过低，导致混合气过稀。
(5) 冷却液温度传感器有故障，导致空燃比失调。
(6) 空气滤清器堵塞，导致进气不足。
(7) 空气流量计有故障，导致空燃比失调。
(8) 喷油器堵塞或漏油，导致混合气过浓或过稀。
(9) 喷油控制系统有故障，导致混合气过浓或过稀。
(10) 气缸压力过低，导致混合气不能正常燃烧。

二、故障诊断

有启动征兆但不能启动，说明点火系统、燃油喷射系统和控制系统虽有故障，但没有完全丧失功能。此类故障通常先利用故障诊断仪进行检查，然后可以依次检查点火系统、进气系统、燃油系统等，最后检查发动机气缸压力。诊断步骤如下：

(1) 利用故障诊断仪检查有无故障码：如有故障码，则可按显示的故障码查找相应的故障原因。要注意所显示出的故障码不一定都与发动机不能启动有关系，间歇性故障一般不会影响发动机的启动性能。影响启动性能的部件主要有：曲轴位置传感器、冷却液温度传感

器、空气流量计等。

（2）检查高压火花：除了检查分电器高压总线上的高压火花是否正常外，还要进一步检查各缸高压分线上的高压火花是否正常。若总线火花太弱，应更换高压线圈；若总线火花正常而分线火花较弱或断火，说明分电器盖或分火头漏电，应更换。

（3）检查空气滤清器：如果滤芯过脏堵塞，可拆掉滤芯后再启动发动机。如能正常启动，则应更换滤芯。

（4）检查进气系统有无漏气：在空气流量计之后的进气管道有漏气会影响进气量测量的准确性，使混合气变稀。严重的漏气会导致发动机不能启动。检查中应仔细查看空气流量计之后的进气软管有无破裂，各处接头卡箍有无松脱，谐振腔有无破裂，曲轴箱通风软管是否接好。燃油蒸发回收系统和废气再循环系统在启动及怠速运转中是不工作的。如果它们在启动时就进入工作状态，则会影响启动性能。将燃油蒸发回收软管或废气再循环管道堵住，再启动发动机，若能正常启动，说明该系统有故障，应认真检查。

（5）检查火花塞：火花塞间隙过大、过小、有裂纹或积炭严重也会影响启动性能。火花塞正常间隙一般为0.8mm，有些高能电子点火系统火花塞间隙较大，可达1.2mm。如火花塞间隙过大、过小，应按车型维修手册所示标准值进行调整，同时注意检查火花塞有无积炭、裂纹等。

（6）检查燃油压力：如果燃油压力过低，应检查燃油滤清器、油压调节器及燃油泵有无故障。

（7）如果火花塞表面有大量潮湿汽油，说明喷油量过大，可拆下所有火花塞，将其表面汽油清洁，装上火花塞重新启动。如果存在仍喷油量过大现象，应拆卸喷油器，检查喷油器有无漏油。

（8）空气流量计或冷却液温度传感器故障也会引起喷油量过大或过小。如果出现这种情况，应对照车型维修手册中的有关数据测量这两个传感器。

（9）检查点火正时：如果点火提前角不准，应校准点火正时后再启动发动机检查故障是否排除。

（10）检查气缸压缩压力是否符合标准。

三、任务实施

1. 询问车主

询问车主发生无法启动故障前有何症状；在何种情况下发生的该故障；发生故障后是否进行过维修；车辆发生故障前是否进行过其他的修理或加装设备；车辆是否按时保养等。

根据从车主处了解的车辆故障信息，初步排除某些故障的可能性，缩小故障诊断的范围。

2. 试车与基本检查

启动发动机，进行故障确认。同时观察进气道是否漏气，真空管有无脱落、破损，电线插接器有无松脱，观察是否存在漏油、漏水、漏气、漏电等现象。

根据车辆的故障症状、基本检查及经验分析导致故障症状的可能原因。

3. 检测与诊断

（1）此车辆无法启动，将车辆拖回维修站内检查

① 使用VAS5052检测发动机和其他系统——无故障码。

② 检查发动机配气正时——正常。

③ 检查点火系统及火花塞——4个火花塞电极处比较湿，其他正常。

④ 进一步测量汽油压力时，测量汽油压力正常。拔掉汽油泵保险丝，多次启动后可以启动发动机，但发动机怠速发抖。

⑤ 打开加机油盖，此时发动机可以正常启动，但发现机油盖口有大量的白烟冒出，并且发动机怠速抖动厉害。

（2）根据上述试验分析，确定发动机本身存在机械方面问题　测量缸压后发现 2 缸只有 6kPa，压力明显偏低，如图 5-6 所示。而其他缸的缸压正常。往 2 缸内部加机油后，缸内压力没有变化，可以确定 2 缸活塞环存在问题。

（3）拆检第 2 缸活塞　发现活塞的第 2 道气环断裂成 3 段。如图 5-7 所示。

图 5-6　检测 2 缸气缸压力

图 5-7　损坏的气环

故障原因分析：发动机第 2 缸活塞气环断裂，大量的可燃混合气从活塞气环断裂处窜气到曲轴箱里，通过曲轴箱通风系统使"窜气"气体进入节气门后方，MAP 传感器判断进气量大（真空度低），进而造成喷油量过多，火花塞淹死，发动机有启动征兆但不能启动。

在打开机油加油盖后曲轴箱里的"窜气"气体从机油盖口排出，曲轴箱内的气体压力变小，无法把油气分离器的膜顶开，"窜气"气体无法通过曲轴箱通风系统进入到节气门后方，使启动时的可燃混合气正常，发动机可以正常启动，曲轴箱通风系统结构图如图 5-8 所示。

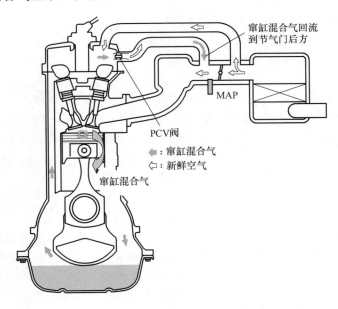

图 5-8　曲轴箱通风系统结构图

项目五　发动机工作异常故障诊断与修复　57

将汽油泵保险丝拔掉，多次启动发动机后，进油管内部汽油压力逐渐下降，使喷油器的喷油量下降，同时燃烧室内的部分可燃混合物被排出，此时发动机可以正常启动。

4. 故障排除

更换2缸活塞气环后进行装复试车，故障排除。

5. 检验交车

故障排除后进行试车，确认发动机启动正常，同时没有其他症状，再利用故障诊断仪进行诊断，将电控单元中的故障码清除，同时查看所有数据流在规定范围内，故障检修完毕。

四、任务小结

遇到发动机启动困难故障时，应用最基本的方法来制定维修技术方案，从可能引起该故障的原因进行逐步分析，不要盲目拆装使问题复杂化。

五、任务报告单

	专业		班级		姓名	
	任务名称				学时	2
	车型		发动机型号			
	考核项目	考核内容			分值	得分
任务完成过程	1. 故障症状描述				5	
	2. 故障可能的原因及分析				25	
	3. 检测与诊断过程				35	
	4. 故障排除				10	
	5. 故障诊断小结				10	
教师评价	作业质量、作业效率、作业安全等				15	
	总评分数				100	

六、知识拓展

【典型案例一】 一辆本田雅阁汽车不能启动。

故障描述：一辆本田雅阁汽车，行驶9万千米，在高速行驶中突然发现不能加速，进而只有怠速，空踩油门后发动机反而熄火，再也不能启动，但有启动征兆。

故障诊断与修复：首先检查高压火，经检查发现高压火正常。然后接上燃油压力表，压力表显示295kPa，说明燃油压力足够。在喷油器插头处连接LED灯，启动时LED灯闪烁，说明ECU将喷油信号传给执行器——喷油器。用点火正时枪检查启动时的点火提前角，在上止点附近变化，稍偏迟，说明无明显异常，至少还未达到不能启动的程度。怀疑启动时空燃比过浓，可能导致火花塞淹死。于是先将加速踏板踩到底进行启动，使之进入断油程序，但仍不能启动，且不管如何操纵节气门，均不能启动，但仍有启动征兆。于是拆下各缸火花塞，发现发动机火花塞是黑的，说明混合气偏浓。清洁火花塞，拔下喷油器插头，使其暂时不喷油，再次点火仍不能启动；插上插头启动，启动征兆似乎更明显了，但始终没能启动。鉴于该车在行驶途中突然出现无法启动故障，曲轴偶有反转现象，因此虽然点火正时枪未发现明显异常，但为保险起见，拆下了气门室盖，观察配气正时记号，并顺便检查了气门间隙，未见异常。在气门间隙正常的情况下，不可能出现4个气缸同时压缩压力不足而无法启动的现象，故气缸压力原因可以不考虑。分析故障应是由于混合气严重失调或排气管堵塞造成的。

用金德 KT600 检查，系统正常，无故障码。读取启动时的动态数据流，发现喷油脉宽达 17～18ms，进气歧管绝对压力传感器输出电压在 2.4～2.8V 之间变动，而排气管堵塞就会导致进气歧管真空度下降，MAP 电压升高。在启动时用手在排气管口处感觉排气压力，压力很小，排气系统有阻塞。拆下一个缸的火花塞启动时有明显的征兆，再配合踩加速踏板，发动机终于启动了，但可见大量的黑色废气从火花塞空隙中喷出。观察数据流，绝对压力传感器 2.1V。由此可见，排气系统阻塞无疑。拆下排气管，启动机加速极为顺畅，说明无其他故障。MAP 怠速电压 1.0V，喷油脉宽 4ms 左右。装上排气管，发动机可以启动，怠速平稳，MAP 怠速电压 1.2V。拆下三元催化器，发现其内部载体的三分之一没有了，烧结并附在载体上，且有石棉物质脱落。更换三元催化器，发动机顺利启动，进行路试，并且读取发动机数据流，均在正常范围。故障完全排除。一周后回访用户，再没有发现该故障。

分析故障原因，此车因三元催化器堵塞，排气不畅，导致进气歧管真空度下降。由于进气量由绝对压力传感器进行检测，导致混合气偏浓，燃烧不完全，使三元催化器温度升高，加剧其熔化，愈发堵塞。如此恶性循环，使混合气变得更浓，温度更高，载体熔掉，与其机壳之间的石棉物质在某次急加速之后掉落，进一步堵塞排气管，最终导致启动困难。拆下各缸火花塞，积压在排气管中的废气随着此缸排气门的打开而从该缸火花塞空隙中喷出。此时，该缸火花塞空隙充当了一个间歇排气的排气管，故发动机反而容易启动。

故障诊断小结：实际上，最终导致三元催化器堵塞的根源是燃油质量不合格。遇到有油有火的故障时，通常首先要考虑进排气系统是否有故障，比如混合气过稀、过浓、排气阻力过大等都会导致发动机不能启动。

【典型案例二】 一辆宝来汽车发动机无法启动。

故障描述：一辆宝来 1.8L 自动挡汽车，行驶 6 万千米，发动机有启动征兆，但无法启动。

故障诊断与修复：进行基本检查。用电脑 V.A.G5052 检测发动机系统正常无故障码。检查发动机的燃油压力和气缸压力都在正常范围内。检查配气相位、点火正时均正常。

检查火花塞时发现，虽然已经多次启动过发动机，可火花塞却没有被淹的迹象。从这一点推断，该故障会不会是由于喷油器供油过少，混合气过稀造成的呢？可又是什么原因导致混合气过稀呢？

通过读取该车静态发动机数据发现，发动机 ECU 输出的冷却液温度为 105℃，而此时发动机的实际温度只有 5℃左右，很明显，发动机 ECU 所收到的水温信号是错误的，说明水温传感器出现了问题，水温传感器电路图如图 5-9 所示。

仔细询问车主才知道，车主曾在发动机温度很高的情况下冲洗过发动机，这恰恰是引起此故障的关键。为了进一步确认该推断，更换了新的传感器进行试车，一切正常。分析认为由于车主的错误操作，使水温传感器输出的信号失真了。

故障诊断小结：该故障案例实际并不复杂，对于有经验的维修人员，可能会直接从水温传感器着手，找到问题原因。但该案例说明一个问题，那就是电控发动机系统的 ECU 对于某些故障是不进行记忆存储的，如该车的水温传感器，既没有断路，也没有短路，只是信号失真，ECU 的自诊断功能就不会认为是故障。在这种情况下，阅读数据块成为解决问题的关键。通过阅读控制单元数据，能够了解各传感器输送到 ECU 的信号值。通过与真实值比较，才能找出确切的故障部位。对于有故障码输出的 ECU 来说，阅读控制单元的数据也是至关重要的。

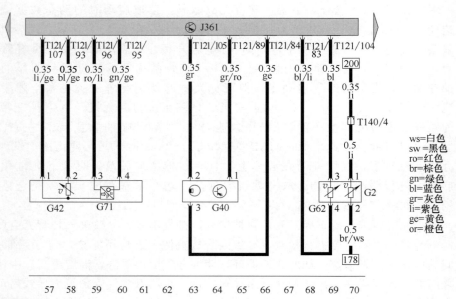

G2——冷却液温度传感器
G40——霍尔传感器
G42——进气温度传感器
G62——冷却液温度传感器
G71——进气压力传感器
J361——Simos多点喷射控制单元，在流水槽中部
T121——插头，121孔

图 5-9　水温传感器电路图

任务三　发动机启动困难故障诊断与修复

学习目标

1. 能根据报修车辆的故障现象确定问诊的方向及项目。
2. 能根据故障现象制定正确的故障诊断计划。
3. 能熟练查阅维修资料，能根据故障现象选用合适的检测与诊断设备并熟练使用。
4. 能根据诊断计划，运用合适的检修设备对启动困难故障进行检测。
5. 能对检测结果进行正确分析并确定启动困难的故障部位及原因。
6. 能对故障部位进行快速准确修复，并且消除故障隐患。

任务导入

任务资料：一辆2009款迈腾1.8T汽车，行驶里程9万千米，发动机冷车启动困难，多次启动才能启动，启动后怠速不稳、抖动大。

任务要求：根据该车辆的故障现象，查阅相关资料，并选用合适的检测与诊断设备进行故障诊断与修复，同时填写任务报告单。

一、故障分析

发动机启动困难是指启动机能带动发动机按正常速度转动,但是需要较长时间才能启动,或者需要连续多次启动才能启动。

可能的故障原因有以下几种:
(1) 进气系统漏气。
(2) 燃油压力过低。
(3) 空气滤清器滤芯堵塞。
(4) 冷却液温度传感器故障。
(5) 空气流量计故障。
(6) 怠速控制阀或附加空气阀故障。
(7) 喷油器故障(不工作、漏油、堵塞)。
(8) 点火正时不正确。
(9) 气缸压缩压力过低。
(10) 电控单元故障。

二、故障诊断

故障自诊断:如有故障码,则按故障码查找相应的故障原因。

检查怠速时进气管的真空度:若真空度小于66.7kPa,说明进气系统中有空气泄漏,应检查进气管各个管接头、衬垫、真空软管等处,以及废气再循环系统、燃油蒸气回收系统。

检查空气滤清器:如果滤芯堵塞,应清洗或更换。

如果节气门在1/4左右开度时发动机能正常启动,而节气门全关时启动困难,应检查怠速控制阀及附加空气阀是否工作正常。在冷车怠速运转中,拔下怠速控制阀线束插头,或者在冷车怠速运转时将附加空气阀进气软管用钳子夹住,如果发动机转速没有下降,说明怠速控制阀工作不正常,应检查怠速控制阀及其控制电路。

检查燃油压力:用一根导线将电动燃油泵的两个检测插孔短接,然后打开点火开关,让电动燃油泵运转。在这种状态下,燃油压力应达300kPa左右。如果压力太低,应检查油压调节器、喷油器有无漏油,燃油滤清器有无堵塞,燃油泵最大油压是否正常。

检查温度传感器和空气流量计:拔下温度传感器和空气流量计线束插头,用万用表欧姆挡测量温度传感器和空气流量计各接线端子之间的电阻。如果阻值不符合标准,应更换。

如果是在冷车时不易启动,而热车时启动正常,应检查冷启动喷油器工作是否正常。先检查在启动时冷启动喷油器线束插头处有无12V左右的电压。如果没有电压,则说明控制电路有故障,应检查冷启动温度时间开关及其控制电路。如果启动时线束插头处有电压,应检查冷启动喷油器电磁线圈电阻是否正常,喷孔有无堵塞等。

如果是在热车状态下不易启动(在热车状态下启动,如果打开启动开关转动曲轴超过3~4圈后才能启动,即可视为不易启动),应检查在点火开关关闭后,燃油系统的保持压力是否正常。接上油压表,在关闭点火开关(发动机熄火)后,5 min内燃油压力应保持不低于150kPa左右。如果保持压力过低,应检查油压调节器、电动燃油泵、喷油器等处是否漏油。

在发动机怠速运转时检查点火正时:如不符合标准,应予以调整。

检查启动开关至电控单元的启动信号是否正常:如果电控单元接收不到启动开关的启动信号,就不能进行启动加浓控制,也会导致启动困难。对此,应从电控单元线束插头处检查

启动时有无启动开关的信号传至电控单元。如无信号，应检查启动开关和线路。

检查气缸压缩压力：如压力过低，应拆检发动机。

如果上述检查均正常，可换一个新的 ECU。如有好转，则说明电控单元有故障，应更换电控单元。

三、任务实施

1. 询问车主

维修人员在接车后首先应向车主了解：故障出现的时间；车辆的行驶路况；车辆行驶里程；车辆是否按时保养；故障发生后是否进行过维修；车辆是否加装音响、防盗等设备。通过以上的问诊可对启动困难的原因做出初步判断，可以缩短检查时间，提高诊断效率。

2. 试车与基本检查

进行试车，对故障进行确认，测试车辆在各种工况下工作是否正常，从而对发动机的故障进行综合分析。观察发动机故障的特点和规律；观察各缸点火线圈、喷油器插头有无明显松脱，进气道有无明显漏气。

3. 检测与诊断

（1）用 VAS5052A 查询故障，得到图 5-10、图 5-11、图 5-12 所示的故障记忆。

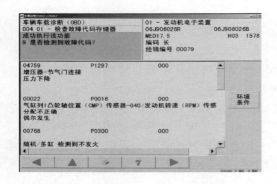

图 5-10　读取故障码（1）

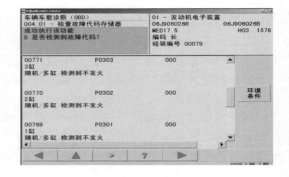

图 5-11　读取故障码（2）

（2）分析 04759——增压器-节气门压力下降故障可能的原因。空气流量计损坏；空气流量计后的增压管路有破损漏气；增压压力传感器损坏。

（3）分析 00022——凸轮轴位置传感器 G40/发动机转速分配不正确的可能原因。凸轮轴位置传感器 G40 和发动机转速传感器 G28 损坏；进气凸轮轴调节实际值有偏差。

（4）分析 00017——凸轮轴位置正时过多的可能原因。凸轮轴调解阀 N205 损坏或 N205 控制线路及控制单元损坏；进气凸轮轴上的液压控制阀损坏；发动机控制单元损坏。

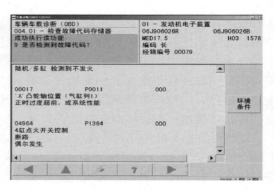

图 5-12　读取故障码（3）

（5）经检查进气系统无管路破损和漏气现象，加速时第 3 组数据块空气流量计数据及第 115 组增压压力数据能正常变化，基本排除空气流量计及增压系统的故障可能。

（6）读取第91组数据块并对比正常车辆数据发现凸轮轴调节实际值与额定值相差太大且该差值从启动时便一直存在。

（7）将N205拆卸后用VAS5052A做执行元件诊断，N205电磁阀能自如活动，N205及其控制电路正常。

（8）用螺丝刀拨动凸轮轴调节控制阀阀芯发现无法拨动，而正常车辆的应该能轻松拨动。经查看，控制阀有拆装过的迹象，拆卸时感觉很紧，与用户沟通得知该车由于事故维修过发动机正时系统。因此推断调节阀有故障。

分析认为，由于凸轮轴调节控制阀拧紧力矩过大造成变形，引起阀芯卡滞在提前调节位置，导致机油压力建立后进气凸轮一直处于过大的提前状态，造成进、排气门叠开角过大造成混合气过稀，并且增压压力在进、排气门叠开时被排出到排气管而产生故障记忆。

4. 故障排除

更换调节阀并按拧紧力矩35N·m拧紧后故障排除。

5. 检验交车

故障排除后，确认发动机没有其他症状，向车主交车。

四、任务小结

本故障的诊断充分利用了故障诊断仪读取故障码，并分析故障码的含义和产生条件，从而为诊断提供了很好的方向。同时结合数据流分析，更加准确地锁定了故障范围，然后再进行具体部位的拆装和检查即可找到故障部位。

五、任务报告单

专业			班级		姓名	
任务名称					学时	2
车型				发动机型号		
	考核项目		考核内容		分值	得分
任务完成过程	1. 故障症状描述				5	
	2. 故障可能的原因及分析				25	
	3. 检测与诊断过程				35	
	4. 故障排除				10	
	5. 故障诊断小结				10	
教师评价	作业质量、作业效率、作业安全等				15	
		总评分数			100	

六、知识拓展

【典型案例一】 一辆2008款迈腾1.8TSI汽车热车不易启动。

故障描述： 一辆2008款迈腾1.8TSI汽车，行驶19.2万千米，车辆冷车启动正常，热车停车短时间不易启动，踩油门踏板才能启动。

故障诊断与修复：

（1）读取故障码：使用VAS6150检查发动机控制单元存储故障码，如图5-13所示。

（2）分析故障码含义：08213进气歧管传感器虽然会影响发动机扭矩调节，但对启动和怠速时的混合气调节影响关系不大。

00370气缸列1燃油调整系统过浓，说明混合气处于较浓状态。

00769 1缸检测到不发火是偶发故障。

以上故障码无法判断故障的实际状态，需继续采集怠速混合气状态关键数据进行分析。

（3）读取数据流分析：发现发动机喷射脉宽 0.51ms 远低于正常值；进气量 2.1g/s、发动机负荷 15％也比正常值稍低。说明混合气过浓。

（4）通过以上数据分析判断发动机混合气过浓。

引起系统混合气过浓的原因有：喷油器磨损较大，引起漏油或滴油，雾化不良；燃油供油系统压力较高；发动机混合气有额外的油蒸气掺入燃烧，如燃油蒸气管路关闭不严等。

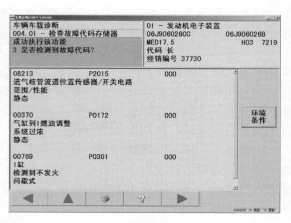

图 5-13　读取故障码（4）

（5）观察发动机怠速运行状态，发现其怠速运行较平稳，没有抖动现象，因此决定先检查燃油压力及燃油蒸气炭罐电磁阀部分。检测燃油系统压力正常，将与炭罐电磁阀相连燃油蒸气连接管堵塞喷油脉宽数据未见增加。

检查进气系统管路，没有发现漏气现象；对喷嘴拆检清洗，未发现喷嘴滴油或雾化不良现象。此时诊断陷入僵局。

经求教整理后，重新制定诊断方案，重点检查喷油器和高压泵。按照方案进行检查分析，热车熄火后拧开机油加注盖闻到较浓的燃油蒸气味，说明曲轴箱混入燃油，故障点与高压油泵有直接关系。于是更换高压油泵及机油、机滤，故障排除。

分析认为，因为高压油泵柱塞渗漏燃油进入曲轴箱机油中，导致热车后曲轴箱燃油蒸气过浓，使发动机空燃比始终处于较浓状态，发动机控制单元减少喷油脉宽也未能达到正常值。

故障诊断小结：目前，中高端车辆控制系统及结构较复杂，如果通过换件来查找故障既费时又增加劳动强度。车辆运行数据能准确反映其工况状态，通过数据来判断分析车辆故障范围，可以起到事半功倍的效果。

【典型案例二】　一辆 2011 款宝来汽车热车不易启动。

故障描述：一辆 2011 款宝来汽车，行驶 3 万千米，车主描述热车不好启动，只有踩油门才能启动。

故障诊断过程：经试车证实该车确实不好启动，即使能启动，刚开始怠速也很低，踩油门启动则一切正常。

（1）根据经验可知，热车不好启动一般是水温传感器有问题，但用电脑检测该部件没有故障，读数据块都正常。晃动水温传感器时水温也显示正常，发动机转速传感器也没有故障。

（2）检查燃油压力，结果为怠速时 250kPa，急加油时 300kPa，油压正常。这时怀疑喷油器有可能漏油，导致混合气过浓造成不好启动，把来油管和回油管用水管卡子卡住，经保压 30min，油压始终保持 200kPa，说明喷油器没有明显漏油。

（3）检查各真空管路没有漏气处，火花塞、缸线正常。

根据经验可知，宝来汽车的节流阀比较脏时，会有此现象，但此车节流阀经检测不太脏，开度 1.9。用试试看的心态把此车的节流阀清洗了，经试车启动正常。

故障诊断小结：在进行汽车诊断时，不但要有好的诊断设备和正确的维修方法，平时经验积累也是很重要的。在没有故障码，从数据流也不能明显看出故障部位的情况下，可以参照同类车的类似故障寻求解决方法。

任务四 发动机怠速不稳故障诊断与修复

怠速不稳是发动机最常见的故障之一。引起怠速不稳的原因很多，有可能是油路系统、点火系统、机械系统等发生故障。在进行怠速不稳诊断时，要分析怠速不稳的特点和规律，根据故障的具体特征确定诊断方案。特别是要了解故障车辆的使用、保养及维修情况。

学习目标

1. 能根据报修车辆的故障现象确定问诊的方向及项目。
2. 能根据故障现象制定正确的故障诊断计划。
3. 能熟练查阅维修资料，能根据故障现象选用合适的检测与诊断设备并熟练使用。
4. 能根据诊断计划，运用合适的检修设备对冷态怠速不稳故障进行检测。
5. 能对检测结果进行正确分析并确定冷态怠速不稳的故障部位及原因。
6. 能对故障部位进行快速准确修复，并且消除故障隐患。

任务导入

任务资料：一辆 2008 款迈腾 1.8T 汽车，行驶里程 16 万千米，用户反映发动机启动后怠速抖动，且动力下降。

任务要求：根据该车辆的故障现象，查阅相关资料，并选用合适的检测与诊断设备进行故障诊断与修复，同时填写任务报告单。

一、故障分析

1. 进气系统故障

（1）进气道或与其相连的气体管路及阀体泄漏 多余的空气进入进气道或进气歧管会使发动机混合气偏稀，导致发动机怠速不稳。同样，发动机怠速时，若废气再循环系统故障，使废气进入发动机，也会导致发动机怠速不稳。常见故障原因有：进气总管卡子松动或胶管破裂；进气歧管衬垫漏气；喷油器密封圈漏气；真空管插头脱落、破裂；曲轴箱强制通风（PCV）阀开度大；活性炭罐电磁阀关闭不严或者常开；废气再循环（EGR）阀关闭不严等。

（2）节气门或进气道积垢过多 节气门或周围进气道的积炭、污垢过多，空气通道截面积发生变化，使得电控单元无法精确控制怠速进气量，造成怠速不稳。

（3）怠速空气控制元件故障 怠速空气控制元件指的是控制发动机怠速的怠速电磁阀或怠速电机。若这些怠速空气控制元件发生故障不工作、工作不良，或者阀体上有油污和积炭都会导致怠速空气控制不准确，使发动机怠速不稳。

（4）进气量控制失准 若发动机水温传感器、进气压力传感器、空气流量计等传感器或其线路发生故障，电控单元就会接收到错误信号而进行错误的怠速控制，引起发动机怠速进气量控制失准。

2. 燃油系统故障

（1）喷油器故障　发动机个别缸的喷油器不工作或工作不良，以及各缸的喷油器喷油量不均、雾化不好，会使各缸发出的功率不一致从而导致发动机怠速不稳。

（2）燃油压力故障　油压过低会使喷油器喷出的燃油雾化不良，且使喷油量减少导致混合气过稀；油压过高，实际喷油量增加，使混合气过浓，这两种情况都能导致发动机怠速不稳。常见的燃油压力故障原因有：燃油滤清器堵塞、燃油泵滤网堵塞、燃油泵工作不良、油管变形、燃油压力调节器故障等。

（3）喷油量失准　若发动机水温传感器、进气压力传感器、空气流量计等传感器或其线路发生故障时，电控单元就会接收错误信号而进行错误的怠速控制，引起发动机怠速喷油量控制失准。

3. 点火系统故障

（1）点火模块与点火线圈故障　独立点火的发动机，个别缸点火模块或点火线圈不工作或工作不良，导致个别缸不工作或工作不良，造成发动机怠速不稳。如点火模块损坏，点火模块的电源电路、信号电路故障；点火线圈损坏或工作不稳定等。非独立点火的发动机，若点火模块或点火线圈工作性能不稳定同样会造成发动机怠速不稳。

近些年来，各车型多将点火模块与点火线圈制成一体，点火模块或点火线圈有故障主要表现为高压火花弱或火花塞不点火。常见原因有：点火触发信号缺失；点火模块有故障；点火模块供电或接地线的连接松动、接触不良；初级线圈或次级线圈有故障等。

（2）火花塞与高压线故障　火花塞、高压线故障导致火花能量下降或失火。常见原因有：火花塞间隙不正确；火花塞电极烧蚀或损坏；火花塞电极有积炭；火花塞瓷绝缘体有裂纹；高压线电阻过大；高压线绝缘外皮或插头漏电；分火头电极烧蚀或绝缘不良。

（3）点火提前角失准　由于发动机曲轴位置传感器、凸轮轴位置传感器及其线路故障，导致电控单元收到错误信号使点火提前角不正确。

4. 机械部分故障

（1）配气机构故障　配气机构故障导致个别气缸的功率下降过多，从而使各气缸功率不平衡。常见原因有：正时皮带安装位置错误，使各缸气门的开闭时间发生变化，导致配气相位失准，各气缸燃烧不正常；气门工作面与气门座圈积炭过多，气门密封不严，使各气缸压缩压力不一致；凸轮轴的凸轮磨损，各缸凸轮的磨损不一致导致各气缸进入空气量不一致；气门相关件有故障，如气门推杆磨损或弯曲，摇臂磨损，气门卡住或漏气，气门弹簧折断等。

若进气门背部存在大量积炭，则冷启动后积炭会吸附刚喷入的燃油，使进入气缸的燃油量减小、混合气过稀，从而导致冷车刚启动时怠速不稳。

此外，装有液压挺杆的发动机，在通往气缸盖的机油道上安装有一个泄压阀。当压力高于 300kPa 时，该阀打开。如果该阀堵塞，会使机油压力过高从而使液压挺杆伸长过多，导致气门关闭不严。

（2）发动机体、活塞连杆机构故障　发动机体的常见故障有：气缸衬垫烧蚀或损坏，造成单缸漏气或两缸之间漏气；活塞与气缸磨损，气缸圆度、圆柱度超差；气缸进水后导致连杆弯曲，改变压缩比。

活塞连杆机构的常见故障有：活塞环端隙过大、对口或断裂，活塞环失去弹性；活塞环槽内积炭过多。

发动机体、活塞连杆机构的这些故障都会使个别气缸功率下降过多，从而使各气缸功率不平衡。

(3) 其他原因　对于装备废气再循环系统的发动机，若 EGR 阀由于积炭等原因发生卡滞并在发动机怠速时开启，会使一部分废气进入燃烧室，导致发动机燃烧变得不稳定，从而怠速不稳。

发动机曲轴、飞轮等转动部件动平衡不合格，以及发动机支撑胶垫损坏、松动同样会引起发动机怠速不稳。

二、故障诊断

怠速不稳涉及的故障点很多，故障诊断时应该充分运用故障诊断仪，并结合其他检测和诊断设备，根据故障的特点和规律，制定合理的诊断方案，科学地检测与分析，才能快速准确地排除故障。

1. 利用故障诊断仪进行诊断

发动机电控单元都具有自诊断功能，因此应该先利用电控单元的自诊断功能，查看是否有故障信息记录，从而为维修人员提供诊断方向。

首先读取故障码，查看是否存在永久性或偶发性故障码，如果有故障码，则应该分析哪些故障码与怠速不稳故障有关。若有多个故障码，则应该对故障码进行分析，分析各故障码之间是否具有关联性，同时了解故障码发生的原因、影响因素。分析完成后，即可根据故障码进行下一步检修。若没有故障码，则应该按照常规诊断方法进行诊断，重点检查发生故障但电控单元不能进行监测和记录故障码的部件。

其次，查看分析数据流。数据流可以提供发动机运转中的实时数据。发生怠速不稳故障时要查看发动机转速、节气门开度、怠速空气流量学习值、怠速空气调节值、吸入空气量、点火提前角、冷却液温度等数据。数据实时值、学习值和调整值以实际值或百分率表示，工况以文字表示。如果发现哪项数据流的实际值超出规定范围，则应该分析引起数值偏差的原因，并对相应的部件及线路等进行检修。

此外，还可以利用故障诊断仪的主动测试功能对可能有故障的部件进行动态测试，比如对喷油器、燃油泵等进行主动测试，即可观察它们是否能工作，以此来判断其自身及其线路是否有故障。

2. 其他检测与诊断

根据故障现象、故障码内容、数据流数值确定检测内容。根据检测项目选择万用表、尾气检测仪、燃油压力表、真空表、气缸压力表、示波器等检测设备。尾气检测和波形分析很重要，非独立点火的发动机也可以用断缸法迅速找到输出功率小的气缸，使用真空表可以分析影响真空度的具体原因。检测的原则通常是从电到机、从简到繁，尽量在不拆卸或少拆卸的情况下确定故障部位。

诊断提示：在进行发动机怠速不稳的故障诊断时，要注意检查发动机在其他工况是否还存在工作异常情况，如发动机是否有启动不良、加速不良、动力不足、减速熄火等故障。若发动机只是怠速不稳，则在诊断时应该重点考虑影响发动机怠速不稳的故障原因；若还有其他症状，则在诊断时要综合考虑会同时引起多个工况工作异常的故障部位。

三、任务实施

1. 询问车主

维修人员在接车后应向车主了解：怠速不稳出现的时间；怠速不稳时车辆的行驶路况；车辆是否按时保养；故障发生后是否进行过维修；车辆是否加装音响、防盗等设备。通过以

上的问诊即完成了怠速不稳的初步判断，可以缩短检查时间，提高诊断效率。

2. 试车与基本检查

进行试车，对故障进行确认，测试车辆在怠速以外的工况工作是否正常，从而对发动机的故障进行综合分析。观察发动机抖动的特点和规律；观察各缸点火线圈、喷油器插头无明显松脱，进气道无明显漏气。

3. 检测与诊断

用故障诊断仪5052进行诊断，查询故障信息显示：2缸失火。

根据故障现象及诊断结果应先考虑是不是2缸不发火。检查火花塞发现2缸火花塞烧蚀，侧电极被烧蚀后缺失一部分。

分析认为，火花塞被烧蚀损坏严重，可能是火花塞工作不良导致2缸失火，发动机抖动应该就是它的问题。另外，该车火花塞还没有更换过，其他3个火花塞现状也明显不太好，表明都有积炭，也有不同程度的烧蚀情况。于是更换一组新的火花塞后试车，发动机还和原来一样运转不稳。由此可以暂时排除点火系统故障。

油路出现问题，如喷油器堵塞、喷油器电磁阀不工作，也会造成怠速不稳。于是拆掉喷油导轨和喷油器进行检查，拆下喷油器观察无异常情况，喷油器喷孔周围有轻微积炭属于正常现象，把喷油器装到导轨上启动电机直观测试喷油情况，4个喷油器喷油没有什么差别，都很正常。这说明油路方面没有故障。

诊断到此又怀疑可能是点火线圈故障导致点火不良，更换新的点火线圈再试车，发动机情况仍然没有好转，又找了一只新火花塞装到点火线圈上测试火花塞跳火情况，结果也很正常，这说明点火线圈没有问题。

油路没有问题，电路也没有问题，因此分析故障应该是气缸压力有问题。拆掉火花塞后，用气缸压力表测试气缸压力，结果发现2缸气缸压力接近"0"，气缸压力低的原因可能是气门问题或气缸密封不良，该车曲轴与凸轮轴的装配应该没问题，因为其他几个缸工作正常，只有2缸失火。要想找到真正的故障所在，就必须拆检气缸盖。

拆开气缸盖后发现，气缸表面磨损正常，活塞顶部完好无损，但是2缸的一个排气门烧掉一块，如图5-14所示。

分析认为，由于用户没有更换过火花塞，致使因烧蚀掉下的2缸火花塞侧电极熔块夹在了排气门与气门座圈之间，造成排气门关闭不严而漏气。在这种条件下，燃烧的高温火焰在气门与座圈形成的缝隙流过，造成排气门局部高温烧蚀并严重损害，导致发动机怠速不稳。

4. 故障排除

更换全部火花塞、2缸排气门后，重新装复发动机，发动机运转平稳。再利用故障诊断仪进行诊断，将电控单元中的故障码清除，故障检修完毕。

5. 检验交车

故障排除后，确认发动机没有其他症状，向车主交车。

图 5-14 损坏的排气门

四、任务小结

在诊断发动机怠速不稳，电控单元报出某缸失火的故障时，不仅要考虑点火系统、油路系统，还要考虑机械系统的故障。可以通过检测气缸压力来判断活塞缸筒密封性、气门密封性，此外还可以使用内窥镜来检查燃烧室内的情况。

五、任务报告单

专　业			班　级		姓　名	
任务名称					学　时	2
车　型			发动机型号			
	考核项目	考核内容			分　值	得　分
任务完成过程	1. 故障症状描述				5	
	2. 故障可能的原因及分析				25	
	3. 检测与诊断过程				35	
	4. 故障排除				10	
	5. 故障诊断小结				10	
教师评价	作业质量、作业效率、作业安全等				15	
	总评分数				100	

六、知识拓展

【典型案例一】 一辆2010款捷达汽车发动机怠速不稳。

故障描述：一辆2010款捷达汽车，行驶18万千米，汽车在行驶中发现发动机怠速不稳。

故障诊断与修复：用大众专用诊断仪VAS5052检测，显示节气门故障。检测燃油压力，启动、怠速压力都正常。

拆检火花塞，检查高压火，跳火正常。

检测气缸压力为1缸1.13MPa，2缸1.16MPa，3缸1.09MPa，4缸1.12MPa，缸压都在正常范围。

拆检喷油器，检查喷油量、雾化性良好，无滴油现象。

检查点火正时，完全正常。

拆检缸盖，检查配气机构，发现1缸进气气门弹簧折断。

分析认为启动时电机转速低，活塞压缩时，压缩气体力能将进气门关闭，因此低转速检测缸压正常。启动后转速升高，进气门不受凸轮的控制，不能及时关闭，所以在发动机正常工作时缸压不足，导致1缸工作不良，怠速不稳。

更换气门弹簧，故障排除。

故障诊断小结：怠速不稳的故障部位及原因很多，诊断难度很大，在诊断时一定要依据各系统的工作原理进行科学合理分析，才能快速准确地排除故障。

【典型案例二】 一辆北京现代御翔2.4L汽车发动机怠速抖动。

故障描述：一辆北京现代御翔2.4L汽车，车主反映发动机故障灯亮，怠速时车抖，等红灯时偶尔出现熄火。

故障诊断与修复：维修人员进行试车，发现故障如车主所说，发动机怠速时车辆抖动严重，但加速正常。用故障诊断仪读取了故障代码：P0170—燃油修正故障；P2187—怠速时系统过稀（现有故障）。

分析故障码的含义如下。

① 出现故障代码P0170的原因：空燃比控制达到最大或最小限度时，系统将不能进行空燃比控制并记录DTC P0170。

② 出现故障代码P2187的原因：空燃比控制在怠速时达到最大界限后记录DTCP2187。

综合上述两个故障码的故障可能原因有以下几种。

① 前氧传感器、进气流量传感器故障。

② 炭罐电磁阀及进气系统故障。
③ 相应线路故障。

故障诊断过程如下。

① 用检测仪查看数据流，前氧传感器数据波形低位 0.01V 没有明显变化。分离前氧传感器插头后发动机抖动依然没有好转。通常情况下，如果是前氧传感器故障，当分离插头后发动机会趋于平稳。

② 检查进气流量传感器，未见异常。清洗节气门故障没有排除。因为没有相应传感器的故障码出现，各传感器本身故障的可能性较小，所以直接对进气系统做检查。

③ 检查炭罐电磁阀。启动发动机用尖嘴钳捏住炭罐电磁阀侧软管，发动机没有变化，未发现有漏气现象。在检查进气系统过程中发现喷油器有拆过的痕迹。用清洗剂喷进气歧管与喷油器连接处发现，喷每个喷油器时，怠速都会有明显上升。拆下喷油器后发现 4 个喷油器密封圈都比原有的小一号，无法起到密封作用。至此判定为喷油器密封圈安装错误造成上述故障。

更换喷油器密封圈后发动机抖动现象消失。查看前氧传感器数据波形 0.1～0.9V 变化恢复正常，故障码没有再次出现，故障排除。

故障诊断小结：喷油器密封不良，进气增多，造成空燃比过稀并已超过最大调节限度，ECM 根据氧传感器反馈的信号确认已无法进行修复，停止空燃比控制，并记录故障码 DTC P0170、P2187。怠速时在喷油量不变的情况下，进气额外增多使发动机出现抖动现象。

任务五　发动机动力不足故障诊断与修复

学习目标

1. 能根据报修车辆的故障现象确定问诊的方向及项目。
2. 能根据故障现象制定正确的故障诊断计划。
3. 能熟练查阅维修资料，能根据故障现象选用合适的检测与诊断设备并熟练使用。
4. 能根据诊断计划，运用合适的检修设备对发动机动力不足故障进行检测。
5. 能对检测结果进行正确分析并确定发动机动力不足的故障部位及原因。
6. 能对故障部位进行快速准确修复，并且消除故障隐患。

任务导入

任务资料：一辆迈腾 1.8TSI 汽车，发动机启动正常，车速最高仅能达到 80km/h。

任务要求：根据该车辆的故障现象，查阅相关资料，并选用合适的检测与诊断设备进行故障诊断与修复，同时填写任务报告单。

一、故障分析

发动机动力不足是指发动机无负荷运转时基本正常，但带负荷运转时加速缓慢，上坡无力，加速踏板踩到底时仍感到动力不足，车速提升很慢，达不到最高车速。

发动机动力不足的常见故障原因主要包括以下几种。

(1) 发动机进、排气系统堵塞。
(2) 节气门调整不当，不能全开。
(3) 燃油压力过低。

(4) 喷油器堵塞或雾化不良。
(5) 冷却液温度传感器故障。
(6) 空气流量计故障。
(7) 点火正时不当或高压火太弱。
(8) 发动机气缸压缩压力不足。
(9) 涡轮增压器不工作或工作不良。
(10) 进、排气系统不工作或工作不良。

二、故障诊断

(1) 将加速踏板踩到底，检查节气门是否存在卡滞、能否全开。

(2) 检查空气滤清器有无堵塞：如有堵塞应更换。

(3) 进行故障自诊断，检查有无故障码出现：影响发动机动力性的传感器和执行器有冷却液温度传感器、空气流量计或进气歧管绝对压力传感器、点火器、喷油器等。按所显示的故障码查找故障原因。

(4) 检查节气门位置传感器的怠速开关和全负荷开关是否调整正确：如不正确，应按标准重新调整。

(5) 检查点火正时：当发动机温度正常后，怠速时点火提前角及加速时点火提前角都应符合规定。如怠速时的点火提前角不正确，应调整初始点火提前角；如果加速时点火提前角不正常，应检查点火提前控制线路及曲轴位置传感器、点火器等。

(6) 检查冷却液温度传感器：在不同温度下，冷却液温度传感器的电阻应能按规定标准值变化。如不符合标准值，应更换冷却液温度传感器。

(7) 检查空气流量计或进气歧管压力传感器：如有异常应更换。

(8) 检查各缸火花塞、高压线、点火线圈、点火器等：如有异常应更换。

(9) 检查燃油压力：如压力过低，应进一步检查电动燃油泵、油压调节器、燃油滤清器等。

(10) 拆卸喷油器，检查喷油量是否正常：如喷油量不正常或喷油雾化不良，应清洗或更换喷油器。

(11) 测量气缸压缩压力：如压力过低，应拆检发动机。

三、任务实施

1. 询问车主

向车主了解出现故障的时间；出现故障前是否有异常情况；车辆行驶的路况；车辆是否按时保养；故障发生后是否进行过维修。通过以上的问诊了解故障发生前后的情况及故障的具体信息，完成发动机动力不足的初步诊断。

2. 试车与基本检查

进行试车，对故障进行确认。检查进气管路是否有漏气，检查喷油器插头、点火模块插头等是否连接良好。

3. 检测与诊断

利用故障诊断仪 VAS5051 读取故障码，发现存有故障码"17957 P1549 增压压力限制电磁阀-N75 断路/对地短路"。故障可能原因有：增压压力限制电磁阀线束或线束连接器故障；增压压力限制电磁阀故障。

查看数据流，进入发动机地址 01-08-115 组数据组第 3、4 区。怠速时进气压力规定值和实际值都是 80kPa，急加速时规定值为 160kPa，实际值为 78kPa。实际值比规定值小很

多，说明增压器没有增压效果。

无增压的可能原因有：进气系统堵塞；排气系统堵塞；涡轮增压器失效。

将涡轮增压器压力单元的压力软管断开，故障依旧。

断开增压压力限制电磁阀插头，用万用表测量1号线为12.2V，电压值正常。检查插头和线束无异常。互换涡轮增压压力限制阀，故障依旧。说明该电磁阀及线路无故障。

将空气滤清器、进气歧管、中冷器的连接拆开检查，未见发现异物堵塞进气道。

拆下涡轮增压器空气循环阀，从插头端检测电压12.2V，电压正常，对空气循环阀进行通电测试，电磁阀能正常吸合。说明电磁阀及线路无故障。

拆除氧传感器，增加排气量，故障依旧，说明三元催化器未堵塞。

拆下涡轮增压器，经拆检发现废气侧涡轮轴的调节垫片断裂将废气侧涡轮轴卡死，废气涡轮不能转动，故无涡轮增压。

4. 故障排除

更换涡轮增压器总成，车辆装复后再进行试车，故障排除。

5. 检验交车

故障检修完毕试车换挡正常，同时没有其他症状，向车主交车。

四、任务小结

发动机动力不足是维修中常遇到的问题，维修过程中要依据实际的故障表现进行分析，更要注意结合发动机相关数据流进行诊断。

对于大众废气涡轮增压系列发动机，在发生发动机动力不足的故障时要注意涡轮增压器的故障影响。

五、任务报告单

	专 业		班 级		姓 名	
	任务名称				学 时	2
	车 型		发动机型号			
	考核项目	考核内容			分 值	得 分
任务完成过程	1. 故障症状描述				5	
	2. 故障可能的原因及分析				25	
	3. 检测与诊断过程				35	
	4. 故障排除				10	
	5. 故障诊断小结				10	
教师评价	作业质量、作业效率、作业安全等				15	
	总评分数				100	

六、知识拓展

【典型案例一】 一辆2011款捷达汽车加速无力。

故障描述： 发动机怠速运转正常，但是加速无力，同时在加速时发动机抖动严重。

故障诊断与修复：

（1）用大众专用诊断仪进行检测，发动机无任何故障码。

（2）检查发动机数据流，怠速稳定在750r/min，节气门开度2.2，正常。

（3）检查发动机进气系统压力，怠速无负荷时30kPa，正常。

（4）用油压检测仪检查燃油压力：0.28MPa，油压正常；对喷油器进行清洗后再进行喷

油测试，喷油雾化正常，且无滴漏现象，说明喷油器工作正常。

（5）检测高压线点火波形，波形正常；拆卸火花塞，火花塞电极间隙正常，将高压线插入火花塞，火花塞跳火正常，说明点火系统工作基本正常。

（6）判断有可能是点火线圈热稳定故障，造成高温断火，于是更换点火线圈路试；故障依旧。

（7）怀疑发动机电控单元内部存在故障，于是更换发动机控制单元，故障依旧。

（8）在加速时发现尾气排放量比正常车少，分析可能是发动机排气不畅。

（9）更换三元催化器，试车，故障排除。

故障诊断小结：排气管中三元催化转换器堵塞导致发动机动力不足在故障诊断中容易被忽视，特别是经验不足的维修人员。在检测故障率比较高的点火系统、油路系统没有故障时，要考虑到三元催化转换器堵塞的故障。检测三元催化转换器堵塞最简单有效的方法是用红外测温仪检测，当三元催化转换器堵塞后，其入口比出口温度要高，而正常情况下应该是出口比入口高20℃以上。

【典型案例二】 一辆北京现代索纳塔2.0GLSAT汽车提速无力。

故障描述：一辆北京现代索纳塔2.0GLSAT汽车，行驶13万千米，车主反映汽车提速无力，达不到最高车速。

故障诊断与修复：通过与车主沟通获知该车在汽修厂做过全面检查，更换了火花塞及缸线不起作用，有故障码P0340—凸轮轴位置传感器电路故障。汽修厂维修人员建议更换发动机模块。

进行试车，行驶中发现车辆加速时车速提升缓慢，最高车速仅为120km/h。

使用解码仪进入发动机及变速器查看，除有故障码P0340外，发动机和变速器各数据流均正常。清码后启动发动机，故障码会再次出现。

根据故障码P0340进行诊断。

关闭点火开关，拔下凸轮轴位置传感器插头。打开点火开关，测量传感器1号端子有12.5V电源电压，2号端子有4.8V的信号电压，3号端子的接地正常。检查至此可以确定CMP线路没有问题，很可能是凸轮轴位置传感器内部电路短路或断路，更换传感器试车，故障症状依旧，且故障码还是消不掉。故障诊断到此陷入困境。于是重新整理思路，从发动机无力的现象入手进行检查。

检查火花塞、高压线，完全正常。检查燃油压力350kPa，正常。检查气缸压力，也正常。检查三元催化转换器，无堵塞现象。

由于该车在外面的汽修厂检查时已更换过油箱内燃油，因此燃油品质方面的问题也可以排除。那还有什么故障能引起发动机无力呢？能引起发动机加速无力的故障就只有发动机正时系统和配气相位了。接下来检查发动机正时。

打开凸轮轴皮带盘上罩壳，转动曲轴皮带盘，使1缸停留在压缩冲程上止点位置，查看气门正时，发现凸轮轴皮带盘与正时标记错过了一个齿。

拆卸正时皮带，重新对准正时。故障诊断仪清除故障码后进行试车，发动机动力恢复正常，经查看P0340故障码不再出现。

故障诊断小结：在与客户交流车辆故障的过程中要细致、全面，应尽量准确地了解故障发生时间，发生现象，发生地点，以及曾经维修过哪些项目等。这样，在维修过程中就能少走或不走弯路，就能减少维修时间，提高维修效率。

此外，对发动机发生的故障要具有综合分析能力，了解故障的特点和规律。实际上，能使电控单元产生关于CMP的故障码，又会导致发动机行驶无力的故障，通常是发动机正时存在错误。

项目六

传动系统故障诊断与修复

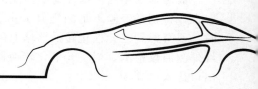

任务一 离合器打滑故障诊断与修复

学习目标

1. 能根据报修车辆的故障现象确定问诊的方向及项目。
2. 能根据故障现象制定正确的故障诊断计划。
3. 能熟练查阅维修资料,能根据故障现象选用合适的检测与诊断设备并熟练使用。
4. 能根据诊断计划,运用合适的检修设备对离合器打滑故障进行检测。
5. 能对检测结果进行正确分析并确定离合器打滑的故障部位及原因。
6. 能对故障部位进行快速准确修复,并且消除故障隐患。
7. 能增强规范意识,具有精益求精的工匠精神。

任务导入

任务资料:一辆速腾2.0汽车,行驶里程为9万千米,当转速到达3000r/min时5挡车速仅能达到45km/h。

任务要求:根据该车辆的故障现象,查阅相关资料,并选用合适的检测与诊断设备进行故障诊断与修复,同时填写任务报告单。

一、故障分析

离合器打滑的故障分析:在起步时离合器踏板接近完全放松汽车方能起步,离合器接合后,发动机动力不能完全传给驱动轮,会出现汽车起步困难、油耗上升、行驶中或加速时发动机转速过高但车速提高缓慢等现象。

(1)汽车在起步时离合器踏板接近完全放松汽车才能起步,即起步困难。
(2)汽车在行驶中加速时,发动机转速升高,但车速不能同步增加,即出现加速不良,行驶无力。

此外,离合器打滑还会出现汽车油耗升高,达不到最高车速,甚至在上坡、重载时还可

能嗅到一股焦煳味。

离合器打滑的主要原因如下：

（1）离合器无自由行程或自由行程过小。

（2）从动盘摩擦片磨损过度或铆钉外露，摩擦片黏油、碳化、烧损、破损。

（3）离合器压盘弹簧过软或折断，膜片弹簧破损，压盘工作端面磨损超过0.3mm、变形，安装螺钉松动，分离指端跳超过1mm。

（4）飞轮工作面磨损大，超过0.5mm。

（5）分离拨叉或分离轴承无游动余量。

（6）离合器总泵回油孔堵塞。

（7）离合器分泵不回位。

二、故障诊断

拉紧驻车制动，启动发动机，踩下离合器踏板，挂上1挡，松离合器踏板并踩下加速踏板，如果发动机迅速熄火，证明离合器不打滑；如果发动机熄火缓慢或不熄火，就确认是离合器打滑故障。

三、任务实施

1. 询问车主

维修人员在接车后首先应向车主了解：离合器打滑出现的时间；离合器打滑时车辆的行驶路况；车辆是否按时保养；故障发生后是否进行过维修；车辆是否加装音响、防盗等设备。通过以上的问诊完成离合器打滑故障的初步判断，可以缩短检查时间，提高诊断效率。

2. 试车与基本检查

进行试车，对故障进行确认，确认停车后在离合器附近能否嗅到焦煳味。

3. 检测与诊断

检查离合器踏板自由行程太小，同时离合器踏到底再松到很高程度，才能起步。拆下离合器分泵，轻轻按压离合器分泵的推杆，能按压到底，并能回位。轻踏离合器踏板，分泵推杆能伸出，放松离合器踏板，分泵推杆能回位。这与新车相同，大致判定离合液压系统正常。这时用手晃动分离拨叉，发现拨叉没有游动余量，同时拨叉烫手，不能回位。

在大多数情况下，离合器片、压盘与飞轮都处于结合的状态，以保证动力的最大传递。此时，分离拨叉与分离轴承处于自由状态，不参与工作。只有当离合器打滑时，离合器片才摩擦生热，产生的热量通过压盘、分离轴承，才能传到分离拨叉，造成分离拨叉温度异常。分离拨叉为什么没有一定的间隙？带着这个疑问，通过仔细检查，发现固定换挡支架的固定螺栓拧入变速器壳体过多，正好挡住分离拨叉，致使分离拨叉不能回位。这是造成离合器打滑的根本原因。通过与新车对比，发现固定支架橡胶内应有一个铁套，所修的车上没有铁套，造成螺栓拧入过多，挡住分离拨叉，使其不能回位，导致离合器打滑。

4. 故障排除

装上相同规格的铁套，重新装复试车，故障排除。

5. 检验交车

故障检修完毕试车车速正常，同时没有其他症状，向车主交车。

四、任务小结

根据故障现象，做好每一项检查和分析工作，才能提高故障诊断的效率。在故障诊断中

要依据机构的工作原理进行分析，不要过度依赖维修经验。

五、任务报告单

专 业			班 级		姓 名	
任务名称					学 时	2
车 型			发动机型号			
	考核项目	考核内容			分 值	得 分
任务完成过程	1. 故障症状描述				5	
	2. 故障可能的原因及分析				25	
	3. 检测与诊断过程				35	
	4. 故障排除				10	
	5. 故障诊断小结				10	
教师评价	作业质量、作业效率、作业安全等				15	
	总评分数				100	

六、知识拓展

【典型案例】 一辆东风标致 307 汽车加速不良。

故障描述： 一辆东风标致 307 汽车，手动挡，行驶 12 万千米，汽车在急加速时发动机转速瞬间可达 5000r/min，但车速提升缓慢。

故障诊断与修复： 进行试车，故障完全如车主描述。分析认为很可能是离合器片过薄造成的。于是更换离合器片，装复后试车，故障消失，于是交车。

几天后车主又来反映出现离合器打滑现象，故障和上次一样。于是再次试车，发现该车在 3 挡急加速时，发动机转速瞬间从 2000r/min 上升到 5000r/min。引起离合器打滑，除了离合器片过薄，还可能因为离合器分泵或总泵发卡导致在松开离合器踏板后，离合器压盘不能完全压住离合器片。到底会有哪些原因导致离合器分泵或总泵发卡呢？具体有两方面原因，一方面是离合器工作液太脏，另一方面是离合器分泵或总泵损坏。经检查发现，该车离合器液非常脏，更换后进行试车，故障依旧。

拆下离合器分泵进行检查，一个人在车上踩离合器踏板，另一个人用手顶住分泵。当踩下离合器踏板时，离合器分泵能正常顶出，释放离合器踏板时下面的人能把离合器分泵压回位，这说明离合器分泵或总泵没有发卡现象。

为了诊断到底是离合器操纵机构问题还是离合器压盘及离合器片的问题，把离合器分泵拆掉，使离合器操纵机构和离合器片、离合器压盘完全分离，拆掉后试车 5km，急加速后发动机不再空转，离合器工作恢复正常，至此可以确定故障在离合器分泵或总泵，更换离合器分泵后试车，故障依旧，更换离合器总泵后试车，故障完全消失，于是交车。

故障诊断小结： 离合器打滑是汽车加速不良较常见的故障，多数故障是因为离合器片磨损过大，更换后故障即排除。本故障车辆是液压控制的离合器，故障发生在离合器总泵，分析认为是由于离合器油过脏致使离合器总泵故障，最终导致离合器片压紧力不足而打滑。判定离合器操纵机构是否有故障时，最好采用隔离法，即切断离合器操纵机构试车，如果故障消失即为该部分故障。

任务二　手动变速器换挡困难故障诊断与修复

学习目标

1. 能根据报修车辆的故障现象确定问诊的方向及项目。
2. 能根据故障现象制定正确的故障诊断计划。
3. 能熟练查阅维修资料，能根据故障现象选用合适的检测与诊断设备并熟练使用。
4. 能根据诊断计划，运用合适的检修设备对手动变速器换挡困难故障进行检测。
5. 能对检测结果进行正确分析并确定手动变速器换挡困难的故障部位及原因。
6. 能对故障部位进行快速准确修复，并且消除故障隐患。

任务导入

任务资料：一辆 2011 款大众宝来 1.6L 汽车，行驶里程为 12 万千米，车主反映该车在停车时挂 1、2 挡很好挂，可是在汽车行驶过程中由 1 挡换 2 挡或者由 2 挡换 1 挡就会出现换挡困难。

任务要求：根据该车辆的故障现象，查阅相关资料，并选用合适的检测与诊断设备进行故障诊断与修复，同时填写任务报告单。

一、故障分析

换挡困难是指变速器换挡时不能顺利地进入所需要的挡位，通常还会发出齿轮撞击声。变速器换挡困难的原因主要来自变速操纵机构和齿轮变速传动机构两部分。

1. 变速操纵机构的原因
(1) 远距离操纵机构传动杆件工作不可靠。
(2) 拨叉轴弯曲变形。
(3) 拨叉弯曲变形、固定销钉松动、拨叉下端面磨损严重。
(4) 变速杆球形支承铰磨损过度。
(5) 拨块磨损过度。

2. 齿轮变速传动机构的原因
(1) 变速器自锁互锁装置失效。
(2) 同步器磨损过度、配合松旷、失效。

3. 其他原因
(1) 变速器壳体连接螺栓松动。
(2) 严寒地区，使用齿轮油牌号不对，产生凝固。
(3) 异物阻挡齿轮的正常啮合。

二、故障诊断

出现换挡困难的故障后，千万不要盲目地拆卸，应当结合工作原理，按照合理的顺序查找原因，然后采取相应的处置措施。

(1) 如果换挡时各挡位都有齿轮撞击声，可能是发动机的动力无法暂时切断，应当检查离合器是否分离不清。检测离合器的自由行程、分离杠杆的高度等是否正常。

（2）如果离合器正常，再检查变速器齿轮油的品质和油量是否符合要求。应当按照季节、转速和负荷的不同选用合格的齿轮油。

（3）有的车辆采用远距离操纵的变速器操纵机构，应当检查远距离操纵机构的调整是否合适，杆件是否变形或者卡滞。如果有异常，应当拆下来矫正、紧固或者修理。

（4）如果上述检查都正常，再检查变速器第 1 轴是否变形，花键是否磨损。如果不正常，应当拆下来矫正、焊修或者更换新件。

变速器换挡困难的排除过程如图 6-1 所示。

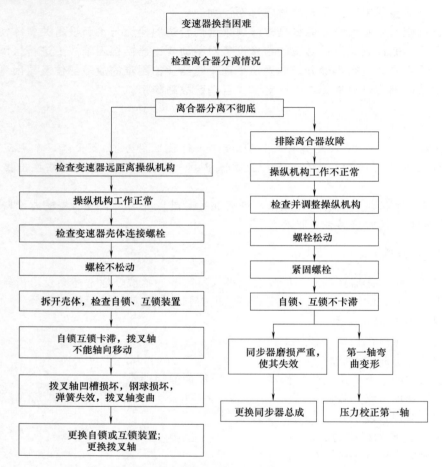

图 6-1　变速器换挡困难的故障排除流程图

三、任务实施

1. 询问车主

维修人员在接车后首先应向车主了解换挡困难出现的时间；车辆是否按时保养；故障发生后是否进行过维修。问诊可以对离合器换挡困难进行初步判断，可以缩短检查时间，提高诊断效率。

2. 试车与基本检查

试车对故障进行确认。通过试车发现，确实存在 1 挡 2 挡换挡困难的现象，但是其他挡位换挡平顺。

3. 检测与诊断

分析认为，该车属于个别挡位行车存在换挡困难，基本可以排除是离合器、连接螺栓以及润滑油等原因导致的故障。

按照故障排除的过程，首先检查变速器操纵机构，杆件无变形和卡滞。

然后，拆下变速器盖，检查变速器拨叉、自锁和互锁机构等，发现这些部件技术状况良好。检查变速传动机构，在检测的过程中发现1挡2挡同步器同步锥环磨损严重。

4. 故障排除

将该同步器更换，重新装复试车，故障排除。

5. 检验交车

故障检修完毕试车车速正常，同时没有其他症状，向车主交车。

四、任务小结

变速器出现换挡困难故障时一定要进行充分试车，了解故障的范围和特点。当变速器出现个别挡位换挡困难时，应该有的放矢，针对这些挡位的有关部件进行技术检测，而不要进行盲目拆装，以免走弯路。

五、任务报告单

	专业		班级		姓名	
	任务名称				学时	2
	车型		发动机型号			
	考核项目	考核内容			分值	得分
任务完成过程	1. 故障症状描述				5	
	2. 故障可能的原因及分析				25	
	3. 检测与诊断过程				35	
	4. 故障排除				10	
	5. 故障诊断小结				10	
教师评价	作业质量、作业效率、作业安全等				15	
	总评分数				100	

六、知识拓展

【典型案例一】 一辆大众POLO汽车换挡困难。

故障描述：一辆大众POLO1.4L汽车，行驶2000km，车主反映该车变速器一直换挡很平顺，手感良好。但是最近在汽车行驶的过程中换挡明显感觉困难，即使强行挂上挡位，也会伴随"咔咔"的金属摩擦异响。

故障诊断与修复：进行试车，试车发现该车每个挡位均存在换挡困难的现象。

考虑到该车属于新车，变速器技术状况下降导致故障的可能性较小，因此先对离合器的工作状态进行了检测。在准备进行离合器踏板自由行程检测之前，发现在车主进行汽车内部装饰时，铺了厚厚的一层地毯，导致离合器踏板行程减小。于是将驾驶员这一侧的地毯取出，进行试车，故障排除。

故障诊断小结：在进行变速器相关故障诊断时，先要对其外部结构以及离合器的技术状况进行检测，不能盲目地进行变速器分解。在确定不是外部原因所导致故障的情况下，再进行变速器分解。同时需要提示车主，在进行汽车内部装饰时，不要在离合器、制动器踏板部位铺设较厚的地毯或地胶，这样很容易导致离合器踏板不能踩到底，造成离合器分离不彻

底，从而导致换挡困难等故障。

【典型案例二】 一辆奇瑞旗云汽车换挡困难。

故障描述： 一辆奇瑞旗云轿车，行驶 12 万千米，车主反映无论在行驶中还是原地换 3 挡都较困难。

故障诊断与修复： 通过与车主交流获知，该车曾碰破了变速器壳体，在其他奇瑞维修站更换过变速器壳体，但是维修后返回途中出现 3 挡换挡困难的故障。

检查发现发动机无论启动还是不启动，3 挡的换挡都很困难，而其他挡位，尤其是 4 挡，与 3 挡共用一套同步器和一个拨叉，却能实现换 4 挡轻松自如。3 挡可以顺利换挡的情况是：在发动机不启动的条件下，偶然换入一次，且不再换其他挡位，此时反复换 3 挡都轻松自如。发动机运转时换 3 挡，偶尔也很顺利。分析认为，故障部位应集中在 3、4 挡同步器滑套（外套）及同步环等部件。

分解变速器，检查发现 3、4 挡同步器滑套内齿的齿端，一边倒角，端头成尖角；一边未倒角，端头成平面。未倒角一边正是与 3 挡齿轮接合端，此时，产生故障的原因终于真相大白。有倒角的一边（4 挡），在换挡的过程中，滑套与齿轮圆周速度同步的瞬间，同步滑套受换挡的轴向作用力与同步环和相应齿轮的反向作用力，两尖角的接触可使换挡的轴向作用力的一部分，分解成两个方向相反的旋转力，使同步滑套与欲挂入的齿轮发生相对转动，实现滑套与齿轮顺利啮合，轻松换挡。而无倒角一边（3 挡）的滑套在换挡的过程中是滑套内齿的平面与 3 挡齿轮的尖角接触，当 3 挡齿轮的尖角顶在滑套的平面上时，换挡的轴向作用力不能分解成两个方向相反的作用力，滑套与齿轮没有相对转动，因此很难实现换挡。只有滑套的内齿与齿轮的齿隙正好对正时，3 挡才能顺利挂入。

据用户反映，在未换变速器壳前，并没有此种现象，但毫无疑问，同步器滑套的内齿端部应该是倒角。带着这个问题进一步观察，发现 5 挡的同步滑套与 3、4 挡同步器的滑套外形几何形状大体一致，是不是装错了位置？承修人员并不认同这个设想：换变速器壳不需要分解上述部件，不可能装错。可不合格的 3、4 挡滑套又是从何而来？根据 3、4 挡同步器滑套与 5 挡同步器滑套几何形状大体一致的情况来看，还是决定对 5 挡同步器进行分解，并对两个同步器滑套进行了比较，发现它们不仅几何形状一致，几何尺寸也一致，且两端都有倒角。根据这一特征，将两个滑套互换位置，装复试验，故障排除。

故障诊断小结： 奇瑞旗云轿车变速器的 3、4 挡同步器滑套与 5 挡的同步器滑套不能互换。维修人员要了解各种机械结构的特点、性能与工作原理，这样在修理作业中才能对出现的各种异常故障做出准确的判断。

项目七 自动变速器故障诊断与修复

任务一 不能行驶故障诊断与修复

学习目标

1. 能根据报修车辆的故障现象确定问诊的方向及项目。
2. 能根据故障现象制定正确的故障诊断计划。
3. 能熟练查阅维修资料,能根据故障现象选用合适的检测与诊断设备并熟练使用。
4. 能根据诊断计划,运用合适的检修设备对不能行驶故障进行检测。
5. 能对检测结果进行正确分析并确定不能行驶故障部位及原因。
6. 能对故障部位进行快速准确修复,并且消除故障隐患。
7. 能具有精益求精勇于创新的精神,提高团队合作能力。

任务导入

任务资料:一辆别克 GL8 商务车,行驶里程为 13 万千米,自动变速器型号为 4T-65E,该车在上坡行驶时突然失去动力,再次挂挡失败,同时变速杆处于任何挡位上都无法行驶。

任务要求:根据该车辆的故障现象,查阅相关资料,并选用合适的检测与诊断设备进行故障诊断与修复,同时填写任务报告单。

一、故障分析

变速杆无论在前进挡或者倒挡,汽车都不能行驶,或者汽车在行驶一段路程后又不能行驶。其故障原因主要包括以下几种。

(1) 自动变速器油发生泄漏,使油液严重不足。
(2) 变速杆与手动阀摇臂之间的连杆或拉索松脱,使手动阀保持在空挡或停车挡位置。
(3) 油泵故障或者滤清器严重堵塞导致主油路不能建立正常油压。
(4) 自动变速器发生机械故障,如涡轮花键毂严重磨损、行星齿轮系统损坏等。

二、故障诊断

（1）检查自动变速器的液面高度。如果液面过低或者无油，则应检查自动变速器油底壳、变速器油散热器、油管等处有无破损而导致漏油。如有漏油处，应修复后重新加油。

（2）检查变速杆与手动阀摇臂之间的连杆或拉索是否有松脱。如果有松脱，应予以装复并调整好变速杆的位置。

（3）检测主油路油压。如果油压过低，应打开油底壳，检查滤清器是否堵塞。如果滤网无堵塞，说明油泵故障或主油路严重泄漏。对此，应拆解自动变速器进行进一步检查。如果主油路油压正常，则故障应为涡轮花键毂严重磨损、行星齿轮系统损坏等机械故障。若冷车启动时主油路有一定的油压，但热车后油压明显下降，说明油泵磨损过大或者滤清器堵塞。

特别提示：当发生冷车启动后汽车能行驶一小段路程，而热车状态下汽车不能行驶的故障时，通常故障应为滤清器堵塞。原因是冷车时滤清器堵塞不严重，车辆可以行驶，热车后滤清器上吸附的杂质逐渐增多，油泵的吸力还会使滤网夹层紧紧地吸合在一起，最终使变速器油不能通过滤网，从而造成热车后不能行驶的故障。

三、任务实施

1. 询问车主

首先向车主了解出现故障的时间；出现故障前是否有异常情况；车辆行驶的路况；车辆行驶里程；车辆是否按时保养；故障发生后是否进行过维修。通过以上的问诊了解故障发生前后的情况及故障的具体信息，完成不能行驶故障的初步诊断。

2. 试车与基本检查

进行试车，对故障进行确认，检查ATF液面正常，油色已发黑，ATF油有烧焦味。

3. 检测与诊断

启动发动机，挂入各挡位运转未发现有异响。于是打开油底壳，发现油底壳上有较多的金属颗粒。于是拆下变速器，进行分解并检查阀体、前进制动带处的单向滚子离合器，未发现异常。发现变速器的滤清器滤网已被杂质污垢严重堵塞结成胶状。分析认为，造成驱动轮总成动力无法输出的原因就是自动变速器滤网严重堵塞，导致ATF油无法吸入油泵内，使油路的液压油从不足到最终几乎没有。这个过程实际上是一个渐进、缓慢的过程，但车主没有注意到车子的行驶变化。继续拆解时，发现驱动太阳轮轴处的铜套脱落，并且磨损开裂。另外，驱动总成太阳轮轴已经沿轴向开裂，并且两端已断裂，这是金属颗粒的来源。

4. 故障排除

将损坏的驱动轮总成、已经磨损的离合器片和滤清器更换，装配前彻底将变矩器、散热器和阀体等清洗干净，重新装复试车，故障排除。

5. 检验交车

故障检修完毕试车换挡正常，同时没有其他症状，向车主交车。

四、任务小结

经询问车主得知，此车变速器油一直没有更换过，且经常在高速、大负荷条件下运行，因此变速器损坏的原因是变速器油使用周期过长，长期不换而变质。油的性能变差后，使一些摩擦元件因润滑不良，出现打滑和发热现象，加速了相应摩擦元件的磨损。而离合器、制动器打滑和磨损使大量磨屑进入油中，又加速了变速器油的变质与污染，变质和污染的ATF油垢最终将滤清器滤网严重堵塞，造成行驶中突然失去动力的故障。

五、任务报告单

专　业		班　级		姓　名	
任务名称				学　时	2
车　型		发动机型号			
	考核项目	考核内容		分　值	得　分
任务完成过程	1. 故障症状描述			5	
	2. 故障可能的原因及分析			25	
	3. 检测与诊断过程			35	
	4. 故障排除			10	
	5. 故障诊断小结			10	
教师评价	作业质量、作业效率、作业安全等			15	
	总评分数			100	

六、知识拓展

【典型案例】 一辆新帕萨特轿车无法行驶。

故障描述： 一辆新帕萨特轿车在行驶时，遇到路面的石块。由于避让不当，造成石块拖底，随即车速下降，停车后汽车无论挂何挡位均无法继续行驶。

故障诊断与修复： 将车辆拖到修理厂后进行检查，发现故障灯亮，用 VAG1552 故障检测仪进行检测，显示变速器转速传感器和 N89 换挡电磁阀断路或短路。将车辆举升起来，发现变速器油底壳碰瘪严重。打开油底壳，发现 N89 换挡电磁阀端子已经脱开，变速器转速传感器外观未见异常，变速器机油滤芯变形。用数字万用表分别检查电控单元、变速器转速传感器和 N89 换挡电磁阀的线束，电阻值都小于 1Ω，线间及对地电阻无穷大，说明线束正常。用万用表检测变速器转速传感器和 N89 换挡电磁阀的电阻值为∞，说明变速器转速传感器和 N89 换挡电磁阀损坏。大众自动变速器电控单元自诊断系统发现传感器或电磁阀断路或短路后，会进入失效保护程序，在"D"位会有一个 3 挡，最高车速能达到 150km/h，该车却不能行驶。所以进一步检查滤清器，发现滤清器不能过油，于是更换了新的电磁阀、变速器转速传感器以及变速器油底壳和滤清器，试车一切正常，故障排除。

故障诊断小结： 本故障原因是自动变速器油底壳发生拖底，油底壳变形堵住自动变速器的油液滤清器进油口，同时造成电磁阀损坏，最终使汽车无法行驶。在对此类事故车辆进行诊断时要分析事故的部位及对变速器相应可能的影响，从而更准确地确定故障诊断方向。

任务二　换挡冲击故障诊断与修复

学习目标

1. 能根据报修车辆的故障现象确定问诊的方向及项目。
2. 能根据故障现象制定正确的故障诊断计划。
3. 能熟练查阅维修资料，能根据故障现象选用合适的检测与诊断设备并熟练使用。
4. 能根据诊断计划，运用合适的检修设备对换挡冲击故障进行检测。
5. 能对检测结果进行正确分析并确定换挡冲击故障部位及原因。

项目七　自动变速器故障诊断与修复

6. 能对故障部位进行快速准确修复，并且消除故障隐患。

任务导入

任务资料：一辆 2011 款速腾汽车，行驶里程 8 万千米。车主反映该车挂 D 挡，起步加速时 1 挡升 2 挡过程中车身耸动、换挡冲击大，且每次从 D 挡起步时均有此现象发生，3、4、5 挡之间换挡过程均正常。

任务要求：根据该车辆的故障现象，查阅相关资料，并选用合适的检测与诊断设备进行故障诊断与修复，同时填写任务报告单。

一、故障分析

换挡冲击指的是汽车在起步时，由停车挡或空挡换入前进挡或倒挡时，发生入挡冲击；汽车在行驶中自动变速器在升降挡瞬间有明显的冲击或者个别挡位有严重的换挡冲击。

1. 所有挡位均有入挡冲击

所有挡位均有入挡冲击时，通常是由发动机怠速过高、变速器油位过高、节气门拉线过紧或节气门位置传感器信号异常，以及电控单元进入失效保护程序等原因造成的。

2. 所有挡位均有换挡冲击

所有挡位均有换挡冲击，通常是由主油压过高造成的。

3. 个别挡位有严重的换挡冲击

个别挡位有严重的换挡冲击，通常是由对应挡位的油压缓冲系统相关部件工作不良或者离合器、制动器活塞的密封性不良等原因造成的。

二、故障诊断

引起自动变速器换挡冲击的原因较多，在诊断故障的过程中，应遵循由表及里、从简到繁的原则，对自动变速器的各个部分做认真的检查。在基本检测的基础上，有针对性地进行分解修理，不要盲目地拆修。如果是由于调整不当所造成的故障，只要稍作调整即可排除；如果是自动变速器内部控制阀、蓄压器或换挡执行元件有故障，应先分解阀体再分解自动变速器，予以修理；如果是电子控制系统有故障，应对电子控制系统进行检测，找出具体原因，加以排除。具体检修过程如下。

1. 检修所有挡位均有入挡冲击

发生该故障时，首先应检查发动机怠速是否过高，如果怠速高，应检查发动机，查找引起怠速高的原因；检查节气门拉线是否过紧或节气门位置传感器信号是否异常，如果存在问题进行修复；检查变速器油位是否过高，如果油位过高，需将多余的油放掉，使油面达到规定范围；利用故障诊断仪检查变速器是否进入失效保护状态，如果确实进入失效保护状态，则应进一步检查引起失效保护的原因。

2. 检修所有挡位均有换挡冲击

发生该故障时，首先应检查主油路油压，如果油压过高，则可以确定故障发生在主油路调压电磁阀或主油路调压阀。此时应先检查油压调节电磁阀的线路以及油压电磁阀工作是否正常，电脑是否在换挡的瞬间向油压电磁阀发出控制信号。如果电磁阀线路有故障，应予以修复；如果电磁阀损坏，应更换电磁阀；如果电脑在换挡的瞬间没有向油压电磁阀发出控制信号，说明电脑有故障，应更换电脑。如果电磁阀工作正常，通常需要拆解自动变速器阀体，检查主油路调压阀是否发生卡滞。如果发生卡滞应用 1200 号细砂纸沿圆弧方向进行打磨，如果阀体发生严重损坏不能修复，则应进行更换。

3. **检修个别挡位有严重的换挡冲击**

发生个别挡位有严重的换挡冲击故障时，首先应进行道路试验，如果发现有个别挡位升挡过迟，则说明换挡冲击大的故障是升挡过迟所致。如果在升挡之前发动机转速异常升高，导致在升挡的瞬间有较大的换挡冲击，则说明离合器或制动器打滑，应检测该挡油路油压是否正常，必要时需分解自动变速器，予以修理。

其次，应检测发生换挡冲击的挡位的换挡油压，若发现某个挡位在换挡时油压保持稳定，则说明负责该挡的油压缓冲系统相关部件发生故障。在各挡装备蓄压器的变速器上，若蓄压器活塞密封圈泄漏，通常会造成热车时换挡冲击严重；若蓄压器活塞卡滞，同样不能起到油压缓冲作用，从而导致换挡冲击。在装备滑行调节阀的变速器上，换挡瞬间该阀减小液压油的通道，使离合器或制动器缓慢结合，若该阀卡滞也会使相应挡位产生换挡冲击。此外，在装备单向球阀的变速器上，如果球阀磨损、装错或漏装，会使离合器和或制动器结合过快，也会造成严重的换挡冲击。

另外，离合器或制动器活塞的密封圈密封不良，会使其结合时间滞后，则其负责的挡位会出现换挡冲击。离合器或制动器活塞的密封性可以通过加压进行测试。

三、任务实施

1. **询问车主**

向车主了解出现故障的时间；出现故障前是否有异常情况；车辆行驶的路况；车辆行驶里程；车辆是否按时保养；故障发生后是否进行过维修。通过以上的问诊了解故障发生前后的情况及故障的具体信息，完成换挡冲击的初步诊断。

2. **试车与基本检查**

首先进行试车，对故障进行确认，然后检查变速器外表面无油液渗漏或损伤。检查自动变速器油位和油质正常，无明显的色泽变化（正常是暗红色）及烧焦气味。

3. **检测与诊断**

用 VAS5051 进入网关安装列表查询，无故障存储，进入 02（自动变速器系统）读取自动变速器测量数据块显示正常。自动变速器控制单元编码正确。

对自动变速器进行失速试验，发动机转速在 2000r/min 左右，在正常范围，证明自动变速器内部离合器与制动器等摩擦元件正常。

根据 09G 自动变速器升挡工作原理：1 挡升 2 挡过程中，自动变速器 1、2 挡切换时参加的执行元件有 K1 和 B1，相应的电磁阀是 N92 与 N283。检查电磁阀 N92 与 N283 线路，无短路和开路现象。

拆下自动变速器的滑阀箱：检查 N283 电磁阀工作性能，包括是否有堵塞、卡滞，经检查完全正常。拆检与 N283 电磁阀相连的机械阀，发现机械阀的弹簧断成两段，如图 7-1 所示。

自动变速器阀板中，与 N283 电磁阀相连的机械阀弹簧本身存在瑕疵，在正常使用一段时间后断成两段，机械阀弹簧断成两段后总弹簧力小于原来值。在 N283 电磁阀通入占空比信号后，机械阀弹簧不能迅速推动机械阀移动进行油道切换，导致 B1（制动器）的活塞不能迅速移动，结合迟缓，造成 1 挡升 2 挡时车身耸动，换挡冲击大。

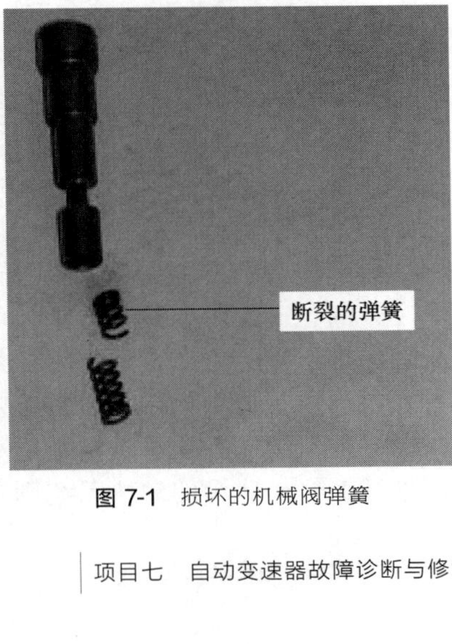

图 7-1 损坏的机械阀弹簧

4. 故障排除

更换新的 09G 自动变速器阀板，车辆装复后再进行试车，故障排除。

5. 检验交车

故障检修完毕试车换挡正常，同时没有其他症状，向车主交车。

四、任务小结

在诊断此类故障时要先了解发生冲击时的特点和规律，再依据变速器换挡控制的工作原理加以分析，然后逐一排除，查找故障原因。

五、任务报告单

	专业		班级		姓名	
	任务名称				学时	2
	车型		发动机型号			
	考核项目	考核内容			分值	得分
任务完成过程	1. 故障症状描述				5	
	2. 故障可能的原因及分析				25	
	3. 检测与诊断过程				35	
	4. 故障排除				10	
	5. 故障诊断小结				10	
教师评价	作业质量、作业效率、作业安全等				15	
	总评分数				100	

六、知识拓展

【典型案例一】 一辆帕萨特汽车换挡冲击。

故障描述： 一辆帕萨特汽车（01N 自动变速器）车主反映，此车曾经在去年下雨的时候涉水。从那以后，过了大概两个月，车辆渐渐出现工作不平稳，换挡时有明显的冲击现象。

故障诊断与修复： 试车发现每次挂挡起步时，车辆在前进挡、倒挡都有冲击，将油门踏板加速至 2000～3000r/min 时车辆有明显冲击后才能缓慢行驶。在冷车时车辆可以自由换挡，待油温达到正常温度后，车辆 2—3 挡出现空转现象，车辆行驶无力，车速提升困难，车速最高仅能达到 80km/h 左右，但此时发动机转速已达 4000r/min。

（1）连接上海大众专用检测仪器 5051B，进入自动变速器系统 02 检测故障码为：P0735——检测到挡位不可靠信号；P0712——变速器油温传感器故障；P0741——锁止离合器机械故障。

（2）试车现象为 2 挡升 3 挡打滑，结合该车的涉水经历，分析可能是变速器内部进水，变速器 ATF 油与水混合，导致变速器油失去了缓冲、润滑、散热、驱动等功能。变速器工作换挡需要变速器油驱动，离合器摩擦片也需要变速器油润滑、散热，可此时变速器油失去了上述功能，同时阀体压力调节也因此失常。故障初期只是造成变速器冲击，但由于没能及时维修导致主油路压力调节阀部分卡滞，使得离合器长期处于半离合工作状态，造成变速器油温度升高。高温将内部最常使用的 3 挡离合器摩擦片烧蚀，导致变速器输入与车速传感器检测到的输出比有误差。此错误信号传输到变速器 ECU 内，电控单元将此信号与变速器电控单元内部的正确数据相比后，确定与正确信号不符，因此就出现变速器挡位信号不可靠。

（3）此车锁止系统设置与其他车型不同。多数情况下，锁止工作后再将变扭器内部的液压油进行散热，此车的锁止系统则是油泵建立压力后，将油压发布到各个调压阀以及变扭器

压力调节阀后,经散热器散热,到达 TCC 阀,最终才到锁止离合器。此时变速器内部的磨损已经产生许多铁屑,它们与变速器油一起流进散热器,最终到达阀体内部锁止阀导致锁止阀芯卡滞,造成锁止离合器不能正常建立工作压力,使锁止离合器打滑。变速器电控单元检测到锁止离合器有空转现象,将此现象存储到电控单元故障存储器内。

(4) 液压测试:将压力表连接到变速器油路压力测试口,检测变速器油路压力,观察压力表显示结果,系统压力偏低(怠速:D—2.5kPa、R—3kPa,失速:D—6kPa、R—6kPa,正常的压力为 D 位怠速 3.8kPa、失速 11.5kPa,R 位怠速 5.8kPa、失速 24.5kPa)。由此可以得出,此时变速器内液压系统已有卡滞,主油路压力调节已经失常,不能调节离合器、制动器所需的压力,使得变速器无法正常工作。

(5) 经过以上的测试和分析,最后确定将变速器进行大修。经车主同意后,将变速器从车上拆下进行分解,发现其内部已经严重受损,所有的离合器制动器摩擦片均已损坏。拆解阀体发现,阀体内主油压调节阀、锁止阀均已卡滞。现已确定导致变速器故障的原因,接下来将变速器进行大修,更换内部受损元件,将离合器活塞进行打压试验,离合器间隙重新调整,然后将变速器重新组装。连接上海大众专用检测仪器清除变速器电控单元内存储的故障信息,再试车,故障排除。

故障诊断小结:自动变速器由 ATF 油驱动、散热、润滑,所以必须定期检测更换 ATF 油,以保证自动变速器正常工作。

自动变速器故障的诊断一定要做到先检测确定故障部位后再进行拆卸,以免走弯路,或者找不到真正的故障原因。

【**典型案例二**】 一辆大众 2010 款宝来汽车换挡冲击。

故障描述:一辆大众 2010 款宝来汽车,装备 01M 自动变速器,该车在 D 位、3 位、2 位运行时各换挡点均有明显冲击。

故障诊断与修复:首先用故障诊断仪读取故障码,没有故障码,然后读取数据流,显示油压调节电磁阀的实际电流值与额定电流值一致。

换挡冲击的故障原因很多,主要有油压高、换挡电磁阀故障、离合器和制动器故障等。该自动变速器各换挡点均有冲击,主油压过高的可能性较大。连接油压表检测变速器的主油压测得 N 位怠速主油压值为 550kPa(规定值为 450kPa),明显高于规定值。由于油压调节电磁阀已经在之前的维修中更换过,而且看其数据流也正常,因此故障发生在主调压阀的可能性较大。拆卸阀板,检查主调压阀,发现主调压阀弹簧侧的阀孔已严重磨损,此处磨损泄漏会使主调压阀阀芯右端油压增大,从而导致主油压过高,最终导致各个挡位的换挡冲击。

故障诊断小结:自动变速器升挡冲击通常是由换挡电磁阀故障、油压过大等原因造成的,首先应利用故障诊断仪进行故障查找,然后再从影响油压过大的原因进行分析。

任务三 自动变速器异响故障诊断与修复

学习目标

1. 能根据报修车辆的故障现象确定问诊的方向及项目。
2. 能根据故障现象制定正确的故障诊断计划。
3. 能熟练查阅维修资料,能根据故障现象选用合适的检测与诊断设备并熟练使用。

4. 能根据诊断计划，运用合适的检修设备对变速器异响故障进行检测。
5. 能对检测结果进行正确分析并确定变速器异响的部位及原因。
6. 能对故障部位进行快速准确修复，并且消除故障隐患。

任务导入

任务资料：一辆宝来1.6L轿车，在行驶中自动变速器伴有"嗡嗡"响声，而且随车速的升高声音增强。

任务要求：根据该车辆的故障现象，查阅相关资料，并选用合适的检测与诊断设备进行故障诊断与修复，同时填写任务报告单。

一、故障分析

1. 发动机在运转过程中，自动变速器内始终有异响

发动机在运转过程中，自动变速器内始终有异响，而将变速杆从P挡或N挡换入其他挡位时，异响消失，通常为油泵或变矩器故障。

2. 汽车在行驶过程中自动变速器有异响，而在停车挡或空挡异响消失

汽车在行驶过程中自动变速器有异响，而在停车挡或空挡异响消失，通常是由于行星齿轮机构磨损、断裂或者行星齿轮与行星架之间轴向间隙过大等造成的。

二、故障诊断

1. 发动机在运转过程中，自动变速器内始终有异响

如果在任何挡位下自动变速器中始终有连续的异响，通常需拆下油泵和变矩器，检查油泵有无磨损，变矩器内有无大量摩擦粉末。如有异常，应更换油泵或变矩器。

2. 汽车在行驶过程中自动变速器有异响，而在停车挡或空挡异响消失

如果自动变速器只在行驶中才有异响，停车挡或空挡时无异响，则为行星齿轮机构异响。对此，应分解自动变速器，检查行星排各个零件有无磨损痕迹，齿轮有无断裂，单向超越离合器有无磨损、卡滞，轴承或止推垫片有无损坏，行星齿轮与行星架之间轴向间隙是否过大。如有异常，应予以更换。

特别提示：若自动变速器在直接挡没有异响，而在其他挡均有异响，通常故障在行星齿轮机构。相反若在其他挡没有异响，而在直接挡有异响，则故障不会在行星齿轮机构。若改变车速或换挡时异响有变化但始终存在，则故障很可能在液压系统。

三、任务实施

1. 询问车主

向车主了解出现故障的时间；出现故障前是否有其他异常情况；发现故障后症状是否有变化；车辆行驶的具体情况；车辆是否按时保养；故障发生后是否进行过其他维修。通过以上的问诊了解故障发生前后的情况及故障的具体信息，完成变速器异响的初步诊断。

2. 试车与基本检查

进行路试，确认"嗡嗡"声确实来自变速器内部，且随车速的升高而增大。检查变速器油量和油质，没有发现明显异常。

3. 检测与诊断

将变速杆置于"1"位，加速时"嗡嗡"声不明显；置于"2"位，汽车以2挡速度行驶时异响有所增强。变速杆置于"3"位，车速约50km/h行驶时响声较明显，这时略微松开

加速踏板和压紧加速踏板，声音无明显变化。若汽车以 4 挡行驶，则响声显著增强。

通过整个试车的过程中可以判定，不是某个挡位齿轮发出的响声。因为在 3 挡（直接挡）的时候变速器内部拉维那行星齿轮之间不存在相对转动，所以可以判定故障部位一定是在 1、2、3、4 挡行驶时均参加工作的元件。

故障原因仅有两种可能：齿轮响或轴承响。

将车辆举起挂入"D"挡并保持行驶状态，用听诊器在车下方可以听见声音是从变速器后盖处发出。从响声的特点可以判定是轴承发出的"嗡嗡"声，而不是齿轮发出的"咔啦、咔啦"声。拆下后盖检查主动齿轮和被动齿轮，发现被动齿轮轴承已被磨出麻点。

4. 故障排除

更换被动齿轮轴承，故障排除。

5. 检验交车

故障检修完毕，同时没有其他症状，向车主交车。

四、任务小结

异响故障是比较难诊断的故障。在诊断时需要在不同挡位、不同负荷和车速下试车，了解异响的特点和规律；通过仔细听，缩小异响的故障范围；最后通过对发出异响部位进行拆解、检查找到故障部位。

五、任务报告单

	专 业		班 级		姓 名	
	任务名称				学 时	2
	车 型		发动机型号			
	考核项目	考核内容			分 值	得 分
任务完成过程	1. 故障症状描述				5	
	2. 故障可能的原因及分析				25	
	3. 检测与诊断过程				35	
	4. 故障排除				10	
	5. 故障诊断小结				10	
教师评价	作业质量、作业效率、作业安全等				15	
	总评分数				100	

六、知识拓展

【典型案例一】 一辆别克君威汽车行驶到一定车速时变速器侧面异响。

故障描述：一辆别克君威汽车，装有 4T65E 自动变速器，当车辆行驶到一定车速时，从变速器侧面发出异响。在发动机运转状态下，踩住制动踏板变速器异响消失。

故障诊断与修复：进行路试，现象和车主所反映的基本一样。分析异响可能来自液力变矩器涡轮、驱动链轮、传动链、从动链轮、输入离合器、输入支柱单向离合器和行星齿轮组。因为在"P"或"N"挡时上述元件都是运转的。在挂入"R"挡或前进挡时踩住制动踏板不发出响，当车辆运行至一定时速时，即发动机以一定转速运转时发生异响，又因为异响从侧面位置发出，因此判断异响来自驱动链轮、传动链和从动链轮的可能性大。于是分解变速器。仔细查看驱动链轮、传动链和从动链轮，发现链条磨损较多，测量变速器与驱动链之间的距离，已经小于厂家给定的 3.2mm 标准。更换驱动链轮、传动链和从动链轮，故障排除。

故障诊断小结：在进行异响诊断时，首先应从不同工作条件下各元件的状态（静止或运转）着手，一般运动的元件产生异响的可能性大。然后从异响的位置着手，这要求对自动变速器内部各元件的空间位置清楚了解，如果不熟悉其内部结构，则很难做出准确判断。在确认故障时，如能够找到技术资料，应以厂家提供的技术参数为依据，避免主观臆断，错误换件。像这样由于磨损引起的异响，如果没有厂家提供的技术参数为依据，较难确认。

【典型案例二】 一辆本田雅阁汽车倒挡异响。

故障描述：一辆维修过的本田雅阁汽车，装备 MPOA 型变速器，修复后试车，前进挡正常，倒挡有异响。

故障诊断与修复：首先检查自动变速器的油面高度和油质，未见异常。然后调取故障码无码，试车听声音，应该是齿轮摩擦的声音，怀疑是不能将挡位挂到位。于是将车辆升起，拆掉变速杆拉线，启动发动机，用手拨动手动阀挂挡。此时从 P 挡换到 R 挡，从 N 挡换到 R 挡，并不断地改变发动机转速，均有倒挡，且没有听到有任何不正常的响声。又将变速杆的拉线装上，挂入 R 挡时，变速器异响再次出现。可基本确定，异响并非出在自动变速器内部。进一步检查变速杆及拉线，发现调整螺母已经松动，调整拉线并紧固调整螺母，试车，变速器异响消失。此车故障是拉线长度发生变化，使倒挡不能挂到位造成的。

故障诊断小结：本田雅阁 MPOA 自动变速器为平行轴式，倒挡是利用拨叉滑套和从动齿轮啮合来实现的。因变速杆调整螺母松动，使倒挡滑套不能和从动齿轮完全啮合，从而导致倒挡异响（工作原理基本同手动变速器）。在检修自动变速器时，应首先了解变速器的基本结构特点，再进行外部检查和调整，按先外后内、由简到繁的顺序进行检修，达到快速检修的目的。

任务四　升挡迟滞故障诊断与修复

学习目标

1. 能根据报修车辆的故障现象确定问诊的方向及项目。
2. 能根据故障现象制定正确的故障诊断计划。
3. 能熟练查阅维修资料，能根据故障现象选用合适的检测与诊断设备并熟练使用。
4. 能根据诊断计划，运用合适的检修设备对升挡迟滞故障进行检测。
5. 能对检测结果进行正确分析并确定升挡迟滞的故障部位及原因。
6. 能对故障部位进行快速准确修复，并且消除故障隐患。

任务导入

任务资料：一辆一汽大众宝来 1.6L 汽车，自动变速器型号为 01M，行驶里程为 6 万千米，该车在平稳加速时，从 1 挡升挡到 4 挡，每次升挡都迟滞，升挡时发动机转速明显超过正常转速范围。

任务要求：根据该车辆的故障现象，查阅相关资料，并选用合适的检测与诊断设备进行故障诊断与修复，同时填写任务报告单。

一、故障分析

升挡迟滞通常表现为达到升挡车速范围不能升挡，要有较高的车速和发动机转速才能升挡，也叫升挡过迟。升挡迟滞的故障原因有以下几种：

(1) 节气门位置传感器或车速传感器信号不良或其线路故障。
(2) 自动变速器油量不足、变质等。
(3) 离合器或制动器等液压执行元件打滑。
(4) 主调压阀或手控阀故障。
(5) 油路泄漏或者集滤器堵塞等造成主油路油压过低。
(6) 电控单元或其线路故障。
(7) 液力变矩器工作不良。
(8) 涡轮轴或者行星齿轮组发生机械损坏。

二、故障诊断

首先应检查自动变速器油量是否充足，是否存在油变质。

然后利用故障诊断仪读取有无故障码存储，同时查看影响升挡迟滞的数据流，比如发动机水温、变速器油温、节气门开度等。

检测油路油压，通过检测油压来判断故障在液压系统还是机械系统。

若油压偏低，则故障在液压系统，需进一步检查油泵、油压调节阀等是否有故障。

若油压正常，则故障在机械系统，需解体进一步检查可能出现故障的机械部件。

三、任务实施

1. 询问车主

向车主了解出现故障的时间；发现故障后症状是否有变化；出现故障前是否有其他异常情况；车辆行驶的具体情况；车辆是否按时保养；故障发生后是否进行过其他维修。通过以上的问诊了解故障发生前后的情况及故障的具体信息，完成升挡过迟的初步诊断。

2. 试车与基本检查

试车发现平稳加油时，1挡升2挡迟滞，2挡升3挡时发动机转速超过3000r/min，3挡升4挡时，发动机转速超过3500r/min，转速值都远远超过正常的范围。

通过检查自动变速器油面与油质，没有发现异常。

3. 检测与诊断

首先利用VAS5051检查，无故障码存储。检查影响升挡迟滞的数据流：油温通常低于105℃，偶尔达到120℃；发动机负荷在全速试车时处于10%～150%和0～260N·m范围内；节气门位置在全速试车时，在0～100%时，节气门角度G188处于97%～3%，G187处于3%～93%；水温在80～105℃范围内。

检测结果发现以上数据基本正常，只是油温偶尔略高，说明可能因散热不良导致离合器与制动器打滑故障。因此清洁散热器，故障依旧。

通过以上检查来判断，故障很可能在液压系统或机械系统。于是对油压进行检测：当油温升到60℃时，检测急速时D挡油压为370kPa，正常值在340～380kPa之间，油压正常。在油压正常情况下离合器出现打滑，可以推断故障点为离合器。

通过分析换挡执行元件工作表（图7-2）可知由于1挡和倒挡无故障，说明K1、B1和K2没问题，问题可能在B2和K3。

通过模拟 3 挡（拔下电磁阀插头）失速测试，与相同车型相比，发现该车发动机转速偏高，故障原因可能为 K3 打滑。

解体自动变速器，检查 K3 离合器和 B2 制动器，发现间隙偏大。

4. 故障排除

更换离合器 K3 和制动器 B2 的摩擦片，故障排除。

5. 检验交车

故障检修完毕，装复试车，没有其他症状，向车主交车。

		B1	B2	K1	K2	K3	F	LC
R		×			×			
1	H			×			×	
	M			×			×	×
2	H		×	×				
	M		×	×				×
3	H		×	×		×		
	M		×	×		×		×
4	H		×		×	×		
	M		×		×	×		×

图 7-2　换挡执行元件工作表

四、任务小结

由于离合器 K3 和制动器 B2 间隙偏大导致打滑，使变速器升挡迟滞。因为这两个元件在从 1 挡升 4 挡的过程中都参与工作，所以每次升挡都有打滑。

在诊断时一定要充分运用好故障诊断仪，读取故障信息，同时查看相关数据流。再结合相应的检测，综合各方面的信息，按照故障诊断流程就可以提高诊断的效率，并顺利找到故障部位。

五、任务报告单

专　　业		班　　级		姓　　名	
任务名称				学　　时	2
车　　型			发动机型号		
	考核项目	考核内容		分　值	得　分
任务完成过程	1. 故障症状描述			5	
	2. 故障可能的原因及分析			25	
	3. 检测与诊断过程			35	
	4. 故障排除			10	
	5. 故障诊断小结			10	
教师评价	作业质量、作业效率、作业安全等			15	
	总评分数			100	

六、知识拓展

【典型案例一】 一辆丰田凯美瑞 2.0L 汽车，2 挡升 3 挡发动机转速过高。

故障描述： 一辆丰田凯美瑞 2.0L 汽车，装备 A140E 自动变速器。变速器 1、2 挡升挡正常，但升 3 挡时，发动机转速很高才能升挡，且没有超速挡，同时"OD OFF"指示灯一直闪亮。

故障诊断与修复： 试车，故障现象和车主反映的基本一样。自动变速器 1 挡、2 挡基本正常，2 挡升 3 挡则非常迟缓，不能升入超速挡，且在高速挡时，发动机转速较高。"OD OFF"指示灯一直闪亮。基本检查未见异常，说明自动变速器的电子控制系统有故障的可能性大。连接解码器，读取故障码"62"，即 1 号电磁阀或线路故障。检查电控单元到电磁阀的线路，没有发现导线破损、搭铁、短路现象，线路正常。测量两个换挡电磁阀的电阻，1 号电磁阀的阻值是 4.5Ω，2 号电磁阀的阻值是 15.2Ω，A140E 自动变速器换挡电磁阀的正常阻值为 14～16Ω，显然 1 号电磁阀的电阻太小，说明电磁线圈匝间短路。更换新的 1 号电磁阀，装复试车，故障排除。

故障诊断小结： 利用解码器检查到 1 号换挡电磁阀故障，又因为 A140E 自动变速器在 1

挡工作时，1号电磁阀通电，2号电磁阀断电；在2挡工作时，两个电磁阀都通电；3挡工作时，1号电磁阀断电，2号电磁阀通电；在4挡工作时，两个电磁阀都断电。根据控制原理和此车的故障现象判断是1号电磁阀出现故障。检测与维修手册两者结合起来进行分析，有利于故障的诊断与排除。

【典型案例二】 一辆本田雅阁汽车升挡过迟。

故障描述： 一辆本田雅阁2.0L汽车，车主反映自动变速器出现升挡过迟，升挡时发动机存在空转现象，冷车时该故障不明显，但行驶几千米后，上述故障现象就变得十分明显。

故障诊断与修复： 试车，发现自动变速器升挡明显过迟，轻踩加速踏板，发动机转速到2300r/min以上时才升挡，稍快点踩加速踏板，发动机转速达到3000r/min时才开始升挡，在3挡升4挡的瞬间发动机空转，转速会突然上升至3500r/min以上，然后再降到2800r/min左右，即有明显的瞬间打滑现象。

检查自动变速器油量符合要求，但油中有一股焦烟味，其中未发现杂质；节气门拉索松紧度适中；仪表盘上的"S"指示灯没有闪亮，说明PCM没有检测到自动变速器系统电器有故障；汽车行驶时车速表显示正常，说明车速传感器也没问题。

做失速试验，将变速杆置于D4、D3、1、R位时的失速转速均为2400r/min左右，完全正常；置于2位时的失速转速也在正常范围内。脱开换挡电磁阀导线侧连接器，在D4、D3位做失速试验，结果失速转速也正常。上述试验说明各离合器不打滑。

检查节气门位置传感器信号电压。在节气门位置传感器处测量，发动机怠速时，其信号电压为0.45V，节气门全开时，其信号电压为4.4V左右，而且随着节气门开大，其信号电压平稳变化。

检查主轴转速传感器和副轴转速传感器的电阻，都在正常范围内。检查"S"换挡程序开关，也正常。拆下PCM盖板检查，没有发现明显问题。顶起两前轮，启动发动机，将变速杆置于D4位试车，发现同路试时一样存在换挡过迟，3挡升4挡瞬间打滑的现象。将变速杆置于D3位，加速到70km/h再将变速杆推至D4位，在换入4挡的瞬间仍会打滑。将变速杆置于D4位，保持变速器在3挡行驶，并迅速断开换挡电磁阀导线侧连接器，自动变速器能迅速换入4挡，而不瞬间打滑。由此可以断定，故障部位还是在自动变速器电控部分。由于冷却液温度信号、节气门位置信号、车速信号、转速信号，以及各电磁阀线路，PCM的供电及搭铁情况等均正常，因此怀疑是PCM有故障导致自动变速换挡过迟，换挡瞬间自动变速器打滑。

于是更换PCM后试车，自动变速器在2000r/min左右就可以升挡了，而且换挡时瞬间打滑现象也消失了。

故障诊断小结： 此故障是由于自动变速器电控单元故障使换挡控制不正常，出现换挡迟滞故障。因为该故障没有故障码且自动变速器油液有焦烟味，所以诊断时在确定变速器打滑的情况下，只能按照引起自动变速器打滑的故障原因逐个去分析，当电控单元以外的故障被排除后即可判断是电控单元故障，通过更换电控单元进行测试即可确定故障原因。

任务五　打滑故障诊断与修复

学习目标

1. 能根据报修车辆的故障现象确定问诊的方向及项目。

项目七　自动变速器故障诊断与修复　93

2. 能根据故障现象制定正确的故障诊断计划。
3. 能熟练查阅维修资料，能根据故障现象选用合适的检测与诊断设备并熟练使用。
4. 能根据诊断计划，运用合适的检修设备对打滑故障进行检测。
5. 能对检测结果进行正确分析并确定打滑的故障部位及原因。
6. 能对故障部位进行快速准确修复，并且消除故障隐患。

任务导入

任务资料：一辆上海别克新世纪轿车装备 4T65-E 型自动变速器，因多次烧损制动带而导致自动变速器打滑故障。多次进行维修，并更换阀体等一些重要部件，每次维修后，都会出现起步困难，无倒挡。起步后，车速能正常上升，但当车速超过 120km/h 以上加速时，便会出现发动机转速升高而车速却不能相应提高的打滑现象。

任务要求：根据该车辆的故障现象，查阅相关资料，并选用合适的检测与诊断设备进行故障诊断与修复，同时填写任务报告单。

一、故障分析

自动变速器打滑故障具有以下一个或多个特征：
（1）汽车起步时，踩下加速踏板，发动机转速升高很快，但车速升高缓慢。
（2）汽车在行驶过程中升挡车速较高，升挡时发动机转速升高但车速没有很快提高。
（3）在车辆行驶过程中，换入某个挡位时，发动机转速突然升高，但车速提高缓慢。
（4）车辆在上坡或急加速时，发动机转速升高很快，但车辆行驶缓慢。
（5）自动变速器油温易升高，甚至可能闻到自动变速器有焦煳味。

自动变速器打滑故障主要原因有以下几种：
（1）自动变速器油液面高度过低或过高。
（2）变速器油品种变差。
（3）阀体泄漏（包括电磁阀）。
（4）离合器、制动器或单向离合器本身严重磨损，产生打滑。如果是新大修的自动变速器，要考虑离合器片组间隙是否正确，或制动带间隙调整是否正确。
（5）离合器或制动器活塞密封圈损坏，导致漏油。
（6）主油压过低造成打滑。自动变速器油液面过低、滤清器堵塞、油泵严重磨损、主油路泄漏、主调压阀或压力控制电磁阀失效等，均会导致主油压过低，从而造成多个执行元件打滑、烧损。
（7）单个执行元件的工作油压过低。执行元件的活塞密封圈损坏、油路密封圈损坏、蓄压器泄漏、节流装置堵塞等，都会造成该执行元件打滑和烧损，表现为在相应挡位出现打滑，这种打滑往往还伴有冲击，即先打滑后冲击。

二、故障诊断

自动变速器打滑是最常见的故障之一。自动变速器打滑往往都伴有离合器或制动器摩擦片严重磨损甚至烧焦等现象，但如果只是简单地更换磨损的摩擦片而没有找出打滑的真正原因，则会使修后的自动变速器使用一段时间后又出现打滑现象。因此，对于出现打滑的自动变速器，不要急于拆卸分解，应先做各种检查测试，以便找出造成打滑的真正原因。

1. 检查液压油高度

如果液压轴过低或过高，应找出原因，修复后调整到正常位置。

2. 检查自动变速器油（ATF）品质

如果 ATF 油已变色且有烧焦气味，说明自动变速器内部有离合器或制动器摩擦片烧坏，此时要慎重试车，避免做失速试验，以免进一步损坏元件。可先放出 ATF 油，拆下自动变速器油底壳，检查是否有较多的磨屑。磨屑中的黑色、棕色颗粒是脱落的摩擦材料；银色粉末是被磨下来的钢片或金属壳体材料；红色、棕色粉末是磨下来的铜套材料。有上述情况时，需解体自动变速器进行大修。

3. 测量油压

大多数自动变速器都设有主油压测试口，有些自动变速器还有各离合器或制动器的油压测试口。油压测试是判断自动变速器打滑故障最直接、最有效的手段。

油压测试口的位置及油压标准值可参见相应资料。如果主油路压力正常，则只要更换磨损或烧焦的摩擦元件即可。如果测量出油压偏低，可先拆下自动变速器油底壳，检查 ATF 滤清器是否堵塞。有些型号的自动变速器滤清器没有螺栓固定，如果装用劣质配件，常常造成滤清器脱落。如果滤清器正常，应拆检阀体，清洗油路，检查或试换油压调节阀。如果经以上处理无效，则需解体自动变速器，检查油泵及各密封件是否良好，按需要更换密封圈和密封环。

4. 进行道路试验

道路试验可以确定自动变速器是否打滑，并确定打滑的挡位和打滑的程度。对于打滑的自动变速器进行路试时一定要慎重，不宜急加速或做失速试验，以免自动变速器进一步损坏。

在汽车行驶过程中，将操纵手柄拨入不同的位置，若自动变速器升至某一挡位时发动机转速突然升高，但车速没有相应地提高，即说明该挡位打滑。打滑时发动机转速升高越快，说明打滑越严重。根据打滑的规律，可以判断出打滑的执行元件。

三、任务实施

1. 询问车主

向车主了解出现故障的时间；出现故障前是否有其他异常情况；发现故障后症状是否有变化；车辆行驶的具体情况；车辆是否按时保养；故障发生后是否进行过其他维修。通过以上的问诊了解故障发生前后的情况及故障的具体信息，完成自动变速器打滑的初步诊断。

2. 试车与基本检查

试车进行故障确认，检查自动变速器的油面高度和油质，没有发现异常。

3. 检测与诊断

用别克检测仪 TECH2 读取自动变速器的故障码，无故障码显示。将换挡操纵手柄挂到 N（空）挡，加大油门，发动机转速能达到 5000～6000r/min，且发动机运行声音正常，说明发动机无故障。连接油压表，检测自动变速器的管路压力，经检测，变速杆在前进挡（D）位时，D1 挡和 D4 挡油路压力偏低。变速杆在倒挡（R）位时，油路压力仅为 830kPa，远远低于标准值 1540～1869kPa。这说明 D1 挡、D4 挡和倒挡油路存在泄漏。由于此车的变速器已经多次维修，并都是因同一故障而维修的，在没有找到故障的真正原因之前，没有对变速器进行解体检修，而是先分析 4T65-E 型自动变速器的结构。

4T65-E 型自动变速器的行星齿轮采用辛普森 Ⅱ 型行星轮系，行星齿轮机构只有前后两个行星排，由 10 个换挡执行元件操纵 3 个离合器、4 个制动器（3 个带式制动器、1 个片式制动器）和 3 个单向离合器，构成具有 4 个前进挡和 1 个倒挡的行星齿轮变速器。

4T65-E 型自动变速器的传动路线如图 7-3 所示。各挡位时离合器与制动器的工作情况

如表 7-1 所示。

根据图 7-3 和表 7-1 可分析出 4T65-E 型自动变速器的各挡传动路线。

在 D1 挡时，参与工作的执行元件有输入离合器 C3、前进挡制动器 B4，且由于该车倒挡工作也不正常，而在倒挡工作时，输入离合器 C3 也参与工作，所以推测输入离合器 C3 有故障。又根据图 7-3 和表 7-1 可以看出，D1 挡正常工作时，若前进挡制动器 B4 不能实现制动，此时后排太阳轮便可以自由转动，使动力不能输出。自动变速器必然没有 D1 挡。因此，认为前进挡制动器 B4 的活塞密封不好，其控制油路可能也存在问题。由于检查输入离合器 C3 和前进挡制动器 B4 的工作状况必然要拆解自动变速器，因此在拆解自动变速器之前，分析控制油路引发故障的可能性，这样可以避免不必要的自动变速器拆解。

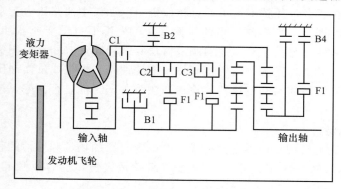

图 7-3　4T65-E 型自动变速器传动线路图

表 7-1　离合器与制动器的工作情况

挡位		S1	S2	C1	C2	C3	B1	B2	B3	B4	F1	F2	F3
P	驻车	ON	ON			A*						H*	
R	倒挡	ON	ON			A		A				H	
N	空挡	ON	ON			A*						H	
D	1 挡	ON	ON			A				A		H	H
	2 挡	OFF	ON	A		A*				A		H	O
	3 挡	OFF	OFF	A	A				A	A*	H		O
	4 挡	ON	OFF	A	A*					A*	O		O
3	1 挡	ON	ON			A				A		H	H
	2 挡	OFF	ON	A		A*				A		H	O
	3 挡	OFF	OFF	A	A				A	A*	H		O
2	1 挡	ON	ON			A				A		H	H
	2 挡	OFF	ON	A		A*				A		H	O
1	1 挡	ON	ON			A	A			A		H	H

注：ON，电磁阀通电；OFF，电磁阀不通电；A，结合（Appled）；H，同步（Holding）；*，无负荷时结合或同步；O，超越（Overrun）；S1，1-2/3-4 挡换挡电磁阀；S2，2-3 挡换挡电磁阀。

4T65-E 型自动变速器共采用两个换挡电磁阀，1-2/3-4 挡换挡电磁阀（换挡电磁阀 S1）控制 1-2/3-4 挡换挡，2-3 挡换挡电磁阀（换挡电磁阀 S2）控制 2-3 挡换挡。换挡电磁阀是由 PCM 根据车速和传动比进行控制的，在断电时，换挡电磁阀将从油泵来的油路压力释放掉，在通电时，换挡电磁阀关闭泄压口，使得从油泵来的油路压力全部传到换挡阀上，从而实现换挡动作。换挡电磁阀发生故障，有两种可能性：电子故障和机械故障。当任何一个换挡电磁阀发生电子故障时，自动变速器故障指示灯（MIL）应该闪烁，并且，自动变速器进入强制 D3 挡应急模式，但从该车的故障现象来看，该车发生故障时并没有进入强制 D3 挡应急模式，且用 TECH2 诊断仪也没有读到故障码，从而可初步断定换挡电磁阀发生电子故

障的可能性不大，应重点检查换挡电磁阀"机械"方面的问题。当换挡电磁阀发生机械故障时，换挡电磁阀在 PCM 的控制下虽然动作了，但却没有起到控制油液的作用，因此判定换挡电磁阀如果发生机械故障则应在其密封性能方面。

根据上述结构分析可以看出，故障应该集中在前进挡制动器 B4、输入离合器 C3 的活塞密封状况和换挡电磁阀的密封状况上。由于换挡电磁阀位于油路板上，拆检比较方便，因此决定首先检查换挡电磁阀的密封状况。将换挡电磁阀拆下，仔细检查换挡电磁阀各个部位，结果发现 1-2/3-4 挡换挡电磁阀（换挡电磁阀 S1）的滑阀工作表面已经严重磨损。

4. 故障排除

更换 1-2/3-4 挡换挡电磁阀，试车，故障完全排除。

5. 检验交车

故障检修完毕，同时没有其他症状，向车主交车。

四、任务小结

在 D1 挡时，1-2/3-4 挡换挡电磁阀（换挡电磁阀 S2）接收到 PCM 发来的开启（ON）指令后，泄压口应该关闭，保持油压。但由于该换挡电磁阀的滑阀工作表面已经严重磨损，故在滑阀处自动变速器油泄漏，从而导致油路油压太低。在低油压作用下 1-2/3-4 挡换挡电磁阀不能动作，导致前进挡制动器 B4 活塞无油压驱动，后排行星齿轮机构的太阳轮无法实现制动，造成没有 D1 挡，所以起步困难。在 D4 挡时，该阀不工作导致 4 挡制动器 B1 活塞无油压驱动，前排行星齿轮机构的太阳轮无法实现制动，从而造成没有超速挡。在倒挡时，该阀不工作导致倒挡制动器（带式）B2 活塞无油压驱动，前行星架及后齿圈无法实现固定，从而造成没有倒挡。而在 D2 和 D3 挡时，1-2/3-4 挡换挡电磁阀不参与工作，所以 2-3 挡换挡阀能正常工作。

通过此故障的排除可以看出，在进行自动变速器故障诊断时，结合自动变速器的传动路线和自动变速器执行工作表进行故障诊断非常重要，可以提高诊断效率，避免盲目拆装。

五、任务报告单

	专业		班级		姓名	
	任务名称				学时	2
	车型		发动机型号			
	考核项目	考核内容			分值	得分
任务完成过程	1. 故障症状描述				5	
	2. 故障可能的原因及分析				25	
	3. 检测与诊断过程				35	
	4. 故障排除				10	
	5. 故障诊断小结				10	
教师评价	作业质量、作业效率、作业安全等				15	
	总评分数				100	

六、知识拓展

【典型案例一】 一辆标致轿车自动变速器打滑。

故障描述： 一辆标致轿车，配备 4HP14 型自动变速器。该车在行驶中先是自动变速器打滑，然后车下冒烟，接着就不能行驶了。

故障诊断与修复： 检查自动变速器油位，发现冷机时的油位比上限（MAX）高出

1.5cm 左右，且油液很脏，有烧焦的气味。进行运转试验，使自动变速器油升温。进入 4 挡后，发动机加速自动变速器就开始打滑。将变速杆置于"3"位，在 3 挡自动变速器恢复正常状态。做失速试验，不管是前进还是后退，发动机的失速转速都为 2100r/min，这是正常的。举起车辆检查，发现在自动变速器与发动机之间的区域、副车架与动力转向泵之间的区域有许多漏出的自动变速器油。拆下自动变速器油底壳，发现油底壳内有大量离合器磨屑。鉴于这种情况，只好分解自动变速器进行检查。

首先取出 E 离合器，发现其制动鼓部分已因受热而变色，摩擦片严重磨损，钢片都露出来了。由于受热，活塞密封件硬化。然后检查其余的 A、B、C、D 各离合器，内部都没有异常。沿着 E 离合器的压力油供给通道进行检查，发现压力油是从泵罩内部的孔通过涡轮轴的孔进入 E 离合器活塞里侧的，用手触摸感觉有明显的磨损台阶，已形成沟状，这可能就是 E 离合器磨损的原因。更换钢环、摩擦盘、密封套件，调整轴向间隙，清洗自动变速器本体和扭矩变换器。装复自动变速器，在连接油压表的情况下进行行驶试验，结果升挡点良好，自动限位跳合和降挡时没有振动，发动机制动良好。

该车的故障一是自动变速器漏油，二是冷机时油位偏高。如果是在油温较低时补充油液，则油位应控制在比下限（MIN）低 1.5cm 的水平上。在有的进口车型中，刻有冷、热两种状态的加油水平线，有的则只刻有 MIN（最少）和 MAX（最多）两条线，本车就属于后者的类型，因此在油温未达到 60℃ 以上时，很难判断加多少油合适。该车自动变速器油添加过量，在高速行驶中，油液因温度升高而膨胀，最后从冷却器溢出，掉在排气管上，所以冒烟。同时，油温升高后起泡，加上套筒磨损，导致油压过低，高速行驶时离合器因负荷过大而烧损，车辆不能行驶。

故障诊断小结：自动变速器打滑故障原因很多，诊断难度大，但只要掌握自动变速器的基本结构和原理，再围绕制动器、离合器和油路几方面去检查、分析，就能比较顺利地找到故障的部位并分析出原因。

【典型案例二】 一辆本田雅阁 2.0L 汽车 3 挡升 4 挡时瞬间打滑。

故障描述：一辆本田雅阁 2.0L 汽车，车主反映自动变速器升挡太迟，升挡时发动机有空转现象，行驶几千米就会出现升挡迟缓的现象。

故障诊断与修复：试车，在较小油门下进行加速时发现发动机在 2300r/min 以上才升挡，在较大油门下则要到 3000r/min 以上才升挡；在 3 挡升 4 挡的瞬间发动机空转，转速突然上升到 3500r/min 甚至更高，再降到 2800r/min 左右，即有明显的瞬间打滑现象。其余工作时间发动机转速与车速基本保持一致，说明没有打滑现象。

检查自动变速器油量正常，油质有点焦糊味，但无明显杂质，由于经过较长时间未更换也属基本正常。检查节气门拉线没有问题，进行时滞试验也正常。故障灯没有闪亮说明电脑未检测到故障，行驶时车速表指示正常，说明车速传感器正常。做失速试验 D4 挡、D1 挡、1 挡、R 挡失速转速均为 2400r/min 左右，均正常，2 挡失速转速也正常。脱开换挡电磁阀插头在 D4 或 D3 挡做失速试验，结果失速转速也正常。这说明各挡离合器未打滑。

由于换挡过迟发生在车速表指示正常的情况下，于是检查节气门位置传感器信号，在节气门位置传感器处测量，怠速时信号电压为 0.45V，全开为 4.4V 左右，且随着节气门开大平稳变化，正常。检查电磁阀阻值、主轴转速传感器、副轴转速传感器均正常。检查"S"换挡程序开关也正常。拆开变速器控制电脑盖板目视也未发现什么故障迹象。

顶起两前轮启动发动机，置于"D1"挡运行结果同路试一样换挡过迟，3 挡升 4 挡瞬间打滑故障依旧。置于"D3"挡运行，加速到 70km/h 左右将变速手柄迅速推到"D4"挡结果在换入 4 挡瞬间仍有打滑现象。在"D1"挡运行并使之保持在 3 挡迅速断开两换挡电磁

阀插头，结果自动变速器能迅速换入 4 挡而无瞬间打滑现象。由此可基本断定故障仍在电控部分，而不是换挡电磁阀及其油路控制阀体、执行元件动作缓慢的原因造成的。

由于自动变速器电控线路部分，包括水温信号、节气门位置信号、车速信号、转速信号、电磁阀线路、电脑电源、搭铁线路等均良好，于是断定电脑有故障。更换自动变速器电脑试车，在 2000r/min 左右就升挡了，也无瞬间打滑现象了，换挡品质良好，证实换挡过迟及瞬间打滑确实为电脑故障造成。

故障诊断小结： 自动变速器电控单元故障导致升挡瞬间打滑故障比较少见，诊断难度较大。升挡瞬间打滑通常会认为是由变速器内部换挡阀或换挡执行元件工作不良造成的。诊断此类故障时一定要进行模拟换挡试验、手动换挡试验等试验，以区分是电路故障还是机械故障，而不要轻易地分解自动变速器去查找故障部位。

项目八

转向系统故障诊断与修复

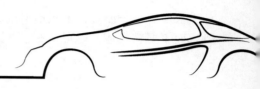

任务一 液压助力转向系统转向沉重故障诊断与修复

学习目标

1. 能根据报修车辆的故障现象确定问诊的方向及项目。
2. 能根据故障现象制定正确的故障诊断计划。
3. 能熟练查阅维修资料，能根据故障现象选用合适的检测与诊断设备并熟练使用。
4. 能根据诊断计划，运用合适的检修设备对液压助力转向系统转向沉重故障进行检测。
5. 能对检测结果进行正确分析并确定液压助力转向系统转向沉重的故障部位及原因。
6. 能对故障部位进行快速准确修复，并且消除故障隐患。
7. 能具有较强的责任心，严谨细致的工作态度，提高团队合作能力。

任务导入

任务资料：一辆大众捷达王轿车，车主反映该车转向一直较沉，经检查发现储液罐内缺少助力油。按规定加油后，试车，转向反而更沉了，似乎没有助力。

任务要求：根据该车辆的故障现象，查阅相关资料，并选用合适的检测与诊断设备进行故障诊断与修复，同时填写任务报告单。

一、故障分析

转向沉重指的是汽车在行驶中左右转动转向盘感到沉重费力，转弯后不能及时回正。
转向沉重的原因主要有以下几种。
（1）轮胎气压过低：轮胎的气压过低导致转向力矩增大。
（2）四轮定位不准：四轮定位不准确，如主销后倾角过大、主销内倾角不当等。
（3）机械部分故障

① 各连接配合过紧，如：横直拉杆球头锈蚀、缺油使配合间隙过紧，使加在转向盘上克服转向节转动的阻力增加，从而使转向不轻便。

② 车架变形、横直拉杆弯曲使前轮定位参数不准。如车架变形使主销内倾角、主销后倾角改变，从而使转向沉重；横直拉杆弯曲使前轮前束、前轮外倾角变大或变小，从而加大了轮胎与地面的摩擦阻力使转向沉重。

③ 转向器缺油、发卡使其内部的摩擦增加，从而使克服转向器的阻力增加，使转向沉重。

（4）动力转向系统故障：转向助力油不足；油液过脏、油路中有空气；油泵驱动皮带打滑，油泵磨损严重；安全阀泄漏严重；流量控制阀不密封，泄漏严重，造成泵油压力不足；转向控制阀密封圈不密封，造成各油道间泄漏；转向动力缸不密封造成泄漏，使压力不足。

二、故障诊断

1. 检查轮胎及配合

首先考虑轮胎气压是否过低，轮胎规格是否符合要求。如果是新修的汽车，应考虑主销与衬套装配是否过紧，横直拉杆球头装配是否过紧。

2. 检查油泵驱动皮带是否过松

皮带过松会出现打滑现象，导致油泵泵油压力不足。

3. 检查转向助力油的油量和油质

在发动机怠速运转状态下，原地转动转向盘数次，使液压油升温至 80℃ 左右，油面应在油尺正常标记处（油温在 80℃ 时，应在油尺的热刻线，常温时应在冷刻线），并查看储液罐内的油液有无气泡、油液是否混浊。

若油量不足应检查各管接头和各接合面螺栓是否松动，密封件是否损坏，油管是否破裂，发现泄漏的部位应进行修整或更换。

若油液中有泡沫，说明液压系统内混有空气。液压系统内混有空气要先进行排气。

4. 测试油泵油压

把压力表连接到动力转向装置的回路中，使油液升温至 80℃，保持发动机怠速运转。此时若油压达不到规定值，且在逐渐关闭手动阀时油压也不升高，可判定为油泵有故障，或安全阀未调整好。应拆检修复并重新调整油压，必要时应更换新件。

5. 检查机械部分故障

架起车辆的前桥打转向盘，若此时转向不沉重，则可以判断是由于前轮定位的不准造成故障（如：主销后倾角过大、主销内倾角过小或过大、前轮前束、前轮外倾角），应先进行四轮定位。若此时转向沉重，则可以说明连接配合过紧（如：横直拉杆球头配合，主销平面轴承的配合间隙过紧）或是转向器缺油、发卡及转向轴弯曲、管柱凹曲。

检查横直拉杆是否弯曲、变形（影响主销后倾角和主销内倾角）。

检查车架是否弯曲、变形（影响主销后倾角的主销内倾角）。若弯曲、变形，则应校正或换新件；若不弯曲、变形，则应检查转向节是否弯曲（影响主销后倾角和主销内倾角）；若弯曲，则应校正或换新件。检查时应按照先易后难的原则。

若是由于连接过紧引起的转向沉重，则应先检查转向球头是否配合过紧、锈蚀、缺油，若过紧、锈蚀、缺油，则应更换主销平面轴承；若正常，则应检查主销平面轴承是否锈蚀；若锈蚀，则应更换主销平面轴承；若正常，则应检查转向轴是否有故障。

若不是连接过紧引起的转向沉重，则应检查转向轴是否弯曲，若弯曲则应校正或更换转向轴；若不弯曲则应检查管柱是否凹曲，若凹曲则应校正或更换新件；若不凹曲，则应检查转向器是否缺油、发卡等。

三、任务实施

1. 询问车主

向车主了解出现故障的时间；出现故障前是否有其他异常情况；发现故障后症状是否有变化；车辆行驶的具体情况；车辆是否按时保养；故障发生后是否进行过其他维修。通过以上的问诊了解故障发生前后的情况及故障的具体信息，完成转向沉重的初步诊断。

2. 试车与基本检查

首先进行试车，对故障进行确认。然后检查轮胎气压是否符合规定值，检查转向助力液是否充足，制动管路有无明显漏油现象。以上检查均未发现问题。

3. 检测与诊断

首先检查助力泵的皮带松紧度，完全正常。于是怀疑是转向助力泵损坏，更换一个助力泵后试车，没有解决问题。在原地打转向，经观察发现动力转向管路回油不好。于是将油管及储液罐拆下，发现在储液罐中有一个塑料片，就是它将出油孔给堵住了。油面较低时，压力较小，动力油还能通过一些，因此还有一些助力作用；加满油后，压力大了，将塑料片压在出油孔上，动力油不能通过，从而不能到达动力泵及转向机，造成没有动力转向的现象。储油罐里面为什么会有塑料片呢？带着疑问，仔细检查锁紧盖，发现是锁紧盖里面的一层起挡油作用的塑料片脱落，造成了此车故障。

4. 故障排除

清除塑料片，重新换回原车助力泵，更换新的储液罐，按规定加注动力油后试车，故障排除。

5. 检验交车

故障检修完毕，同时没有其他症状，向车主交车。

四、任务小结

通常，动力转向系统出现故障，总是容易先怀疑助力泵及转向机等零部件有问题，而很少仔细检查管路及储液罐等小部件。但有时小部件也能引起大故障，这是需要我们在今后的维修工作中引起注意的。

五、任务报告单

	专 业		班 级		姓 名	
	任务名称				学 时	2
	车 型		发动机型号			
	考核项目	考核内容			分值	得分
任务完成过程	1. 故障症状描述				5	
	2. 故障可能的原因及分析				25	
	3. 检测与诊断过程				35	
	4. 故障排除				10	
	5. 故障诊断小结				10	
教师评价	作业质量、作业效率、作业安全等				15	
	总评分数				100	

六、知识拓展

【典型案例一】 一辆丰田皇冠 2.8L 汽车转向沉重。

故障描述： 一辆丰田皇冠 2.8L 汽车转向沉重，需用较大的力才能使车轮偏转。

故障诊断与修复： 经询问，车主反映行驶中转向时越来越费力，直至感觉转向沉重。因此怀疑其动力转向系统有问题。首先进行外观检查，没有发现漏油之处；检查油面，高度正常。然后检查油泵，在油泵的输出端和转向助力器的输入端接入油压表，测得油压为 3.5MPa（标准值为大于 7.0MPa），说明油压过低。将转向盘转到左或右极限位置，分别测量油压，仍为 3.5MPa，这说明转向助力器、安全阀、溢流阀均正常，故障可能在油泵。拆检叶片泵，发现叶片泵各滑片表面磨损严重，厚度仅为 1.35mm（标准值为 1.55mm）。叶片磨损，导致油泵泵油压力不足，助力效果明显减弱，造成转向沉重。更换一套（6组）滑片、弹簧、弹簧座后，泵油压力恢复正常，故障排除。

故障诊断小结： 本车故障诊断在确认油泵是否有故障时，选用了通过检测转向时的油路油压的方法进行判定，没有采用随意换件的方法，符合诊断的思路。需注意，在采用检测法时一定要参照维修手册的规定值。

【典型案例二】 一辆桑塔纳轿车转向沉重。

故障描述： 一辆桑塔纳轿车，行驶中转动转向盘时，突然出现转向沉重。

故障诊断与修复： 顶起前桥，转动转向盘，感到转向盘转动沉重，表明故障不在前轮定位。在发动机熄火状态下，原地转动转向盘与发动机启动后原地转动转向盘进行比较，两者转向均较为沉重，说明该车的故障部位在液压助力机构。检查助力泵驱动皮带的松紧度，松紧适度。启动发动机，检查传动液液面，发现液面偏低，于是添加传动液到正常液面高度，经过试车发现，故障稍微好转，但仍然转向沉重。说明转向沉重不仅是传动液不足，还有其他原因。

分析认为传动液中很可能有空气存在，经原地转动转向盘测试，液面确实有气泡冒出。同时结合液面过低现象，说明液压系统中有泄漏部位。于是启动发动机，左、右转动转向盘至极限位置固定，使管内油压达到最大值，仔细检查分配阀、齿条密封及进、回油管接头，结果发现进油管接头处漏油。更换进油管接头密封环、紧固密封环螺栓后，不停地转动转向盘至左、右极限位置，直至液面稳定并且无气泡冒出为止。路试，转向盘转向轻便、自如。

故障诊断小结： 转向助力机构的管路中出现漏油渗气部位后，管路中的传动液中就会有空气存在，影响动力的传递。同时因转动转向盘时管路漏油，也造成了管路中压力不足，所以转动转向盘时出现沉重的感觉。

任务二　电子助力转向系统转向沉重故障诊断与修复

学习目标

1. 能根据报修车辆的故障现象确定问诊的方向及项目。
2. 能根据故障现象制定正确的故障诊断计划。
3. 能熟练查阅维修资料，能根据故障现象选用合适的检测与诊断设备并熟练使用。
4. 能根据诊断计划，运用合适的检修设备对电子助力转向系统转向沉重故障进行检测。
5. 能对检测结果进行正确分析并确定电子助力转向系统转向沉重的故障部位及原因。
6. 能对故障部位进行快速准确修复，并且消除故障隐患。

> **任务导入**

任务资料：一辆 2011 款迈腾汽车，车辆行驶中，电子助力转向盘灯红色报警，转向瞬间沉重，无法正常行驶。故障发生后，车主为应急恢复车辆，关闭钥匙后，把蓄电池负极拆掉，试验用断电的方式清除故障，重新装上蓄电池负极后故障依旧。

任务要求：根据该车辆的故障现象，查阅相关资料，并选用合适的检测与诊断设备进行故障诊断与修复，同时填写任务报告单。

一、故障分析

电子助力转向系统转向沉重的故障原因有以下几种：
（1）CAN 线路故障导致不能进行信号通信。
（2）转向机线路故障，如保险丝断路或虚接、搭铁不良等。
（3）转向机控制单元电源、搭铁线断路或虚接。
（4）方向转角传感器信号不良。
（5）转向机控制单元内部故障。

二、故障诊断

首先使用故障诊断仪读取故障码，通过对故障码的分析确定故障的检测方向，如果出现 CAN 线路故障导致不能进行信号通信，则电控单元中会存储故障码。然后使用万用表进行线路检测，检测方向转角传感器信号是否正常，检测转向机是否发生机械故障。如果检查该系统所有部位均正常，则故障在电控单元。

三、任务实施

1. 询问车主

向车主了解出现故障的时间；出现故障前是否有其他异常情况；发现故障后症状是否有变化；车辆行驶的具体情况；车辆是否按时保养；故障发生后是否进行过其他维修。通过以上的问诊了解故障发生前后的情况及故障的具体信息，完成机油压力过高的初步诊断。

2. 试车与基本检查

首先检查发动机机油量是否正常，然后启动发动机，观察排气管是否冒蓝烟，以及冒蓝烟的程度；观察发动机工况变化，症状有无改变；观察发动机外部机件是否有明显漏油现象。

3. 检测与诊断

正常车辆在拆装蓄电池线后，打开点火开关，电子助力转向盘灯应显示黄色，而该车拆装蓄电池线后显示为红色。如图 8-1 所示。

图 8-1　电子助力方向盘灯显示红色

（1）运用 VAS5051，进入网关列表检测，显示地址码 44 动力转向系统有故障。

（2）进入 44-02 地址码，检测故障码为 00569，含义为电流，动力转向马达超过上极限。

进入 44-05 故障清除功能，故障码可清除，转向盘红色报警灯亦可熄灭，但转向盘依然沉重。再次点火后红色报警灯重新点亮，查询故障码依然为 00569。

（3）进入 44-08，查看数据流。从数据流 08-02 中可以看出电源正常；从 08-03 中看到控制单元中可以识别发动机运转状态，发动机转速正常。

转向助力工作的前提是有 15 号正电和正常的发动机转速，通过上述数据说明前提条件正常。

读数据 08-04。从该车 08-04 数据中可以看出，数据一区显示 6 属于故障状态（正常的动力转向系统数据应为 3，即表示系统正常）。数据二区显示点火开关处于接通状态。

读数据流 08-05。对于工作正常的转向机而言，在转动转向盘时 08-05 数据流应是不断变化的。其数据应为一区：±5N·m，助力力矩理论值；二区：±5N·m；三区：助力电机输出力矩 MAX=4.375N·m；四区：扭力杆力矩 MAX=11N·m。而该车 4 个区均显示 0.000N·m，依此可以看出扭矩传感器 G269 没有扭矩输出。

读数据 08-06。正常工作的动力转向系统，二区显示为：接通。但该车二区显示为：关闭，说明转向机根本不工作。

读数据 08-07。从数据可以看出方向转角传感器 G85 是工作正常的，这说明该车故障原因与 G85 无关。

读数据 08-125 和 08-126 显示各控制单元之间通信正常。

根据以上数据综合分析，该车转向辅助控制单元 J500 没有控制转向机助力马达工作。

（4）为了进一步分析助力马达没有工作的原因，对电路图进行分析，并对线路进行检查。

检查 SA2 和 SC3 保险丝，正常。检查空滤壳下的搭铁线（即接地点 2）及插头接触均正常。

（5）综合判断转向辅助控制单元 J500 没有控制转向机助力马达工作，由于转向辅助控制单元 J500 与转向机机械装置为一个总成，所以应更换转向机总成。

4. 故障排除

更换转向机总成后，打开点火开关，转向盘红灯立刻变为黄灯。将转向盘左右打到底，再回到中间位置，起步运行 20m 后，ESP 灯和转向盘灯同时熄灭，检测 44-02 中的故障码自动消除，转向盘动力转向恢复正常。

至此该车转向盘转向沉重故障排除，该车恢复正常运行。

5. 检验交车

故障检修完毕，同时没有其他症状，向车主交车。

四、任务小结

（1）对于新款大众车型（PQ35、PQ46）来说，用断电瓶线的方法消除故障记忆是基本无效的。

（2）该车故障诊断，因有故障码提示，较为容易。关键是要注意，更换转向机总成后，感觉转向机有助力和电子助力转向盘灯熄灭了，此时故障并没有完全排除，需要进入转向辅助装置 44 地址码进行新转向盘总成激活设置，进入 44-10-03 中将 1 改为 0，进行储存，并将 03 ABS 的故障码清除。在网关列表检查，各个系统完全正常后，故障才完全排除，车辆恢复正常。

五、任务报告单

专业		班级		姓名	
任务名称				学时	2
车型		发动机型号			
	考核项目	考核内容		分值	得分
任务完成过程	1. 故障症状描述			5	
	2. 故障可能的原因及分析			25	
	3. 检测与诊断过程			35	
	4. 故障排除			10	
	5. 故障诊断小结			10	
教师评价	作业质量、作业效率、作业安全等			15	
	总评分数			100	

六、知识拓展

【典型案例一】 一辆大众CC汽车转向沉重。

故障描述：一辆2010款大众CC汽车，行驶12万千米，车主反映该车在行驶中发现转向沉重，指示灯红灯报警。

故障诊断与修复：分析转向沉重的故障原因，该故障可能出现的原因主要有以下几种。

（1）CAN线系统故障。

（2）保险丝SC3、SA2断路或虚接。

（3）转向机控制单元搭铁线断路或虚接。

（4）转向机电源插头松动。

（5）转向机控制单元内部故障。

大众CC汽车配备的电子助力转向，转向助力由转向助力控制单元进行控制，因此先利用系统自诊断进行分析。

利用大众专用诊断仪VAS5052检测网关列表，除地址44其余单元系统正常。地址44故障码如图8-2所示。

根据读取网关列表除地址44外其余系统正常，并且能读取到地址44的故障码，首先排除了CAN总线系统故障。

根据电路图分析得到以下结果：

（1）检查SA2和SC3保险丝无断路或虚接现象。

（2）检查转向机控制单元搭铁点和线路无虚接现象。

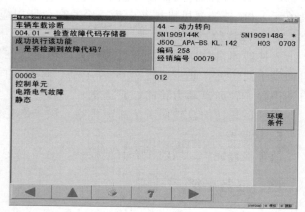

图8-2 地址44故障码

（3）拔下转向机控制单元插头检查没松动现象，用万用表测量其电压为12.65V（电源正常）。

（4）排除上述可能因素后分析，可能是转向机控制单元内部故障。

于是更换转向机，并对转向机进行匹配，然后以低于20km/h的车速匀速行驶，转向盘往左打到底踩住刹车，等听到3声报警声后，再往右打到底踩住刹车，等听到3声报警声

后，把转向盘回正。这时指示灯黄灯熄灭，清除系统故障码，试车故障排除。

故障诊断小结：该故障诊断过程充分结合了故障诊断仪的诊断与电路图的使用，同时根据转向助力系统的工作原理进行分析，诊断过程有比较强的逻辑性。注重诊断和分析，避免依靠经验盲目拆装换件，这是对电控系统诊断需要具备的基本能力。

【典型案例二】 一辆大众POLO汽车转向沉重。

故障描述：一辆大众POLO手动挡汽车，行驶里程15万千米，该车在行驶过程中转向沉重，仪表板上的故障警告灯偶尔出现全部闪烁报警的现象。

故障诊断与修复：试车，打开点火开关，仪表指示灯显示正常。起步后，发现转向确实沉重。行驶一段路程后发现仪表板上的动力转向故障指示灯点亮。利用故障诊断仪进入"辅助转向"系统读取故障码，显示01309辅助转向（J500）控制单元。清除故障码后启动发动机发现仪表板上的故障警告灯全部闪烁报警，再次连接故障诊断仪却不能进入"辅助转向"系统。利用故障诊断仪进入发动机系统进行检测，结果显示"系统正常"。进入车载网络控制单元后，发现2个故障码：01312动力系统数据总线；01760辅助转向控制单元（J500）无通信。进入网关（J533）数据总线，也检测到了2个相同的故障码。结合电路图检查辅助转向控制单元电路及线路，均正常。接下来检查网关J533。因网关J533与车载网络控制单元J519是一体的，只能更换车载网络控制单元J519，替换后，故障依旧存在。根据前面所检测到的故障码的提示，该故障也可能与转向助力控制单元有关。于是将转向助力控制单元J500上的插头拔下，并观察仪表板，结果发现除了转向助力报警灯点亮外，其余的报警灯都熄灭了。至此，发现故障，将转向助力控制单元更换后，用故障诊断仪对辅助转向控制单元编码后，故障排除。

故障诊断小结：该车采用新一代的CAN-BUS系统，为汽车的控制器之间进行数据交换，在系统内的控制单元之间采用了铜缆（双绞线）串行连接方式，即各控制单元都串行连接在一起。由于转向助力控制单元损坏，使得其他控制单元均无法通信，这种故障属于CAN-BUS系统在控制单元内线路的短路。

项目九

制动系统故障诊断与修复

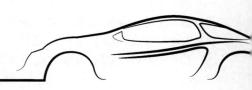

制动系统故障可分为制动不灵、制动失效、制动跑偏、制动拖滞及驻车制动失效等。

因各种类型制动系统的结构和工作原理的不同,尽管制动系统故障现象都基本相同,但故障产生的原因是不相同的,所以在诊断故障时,应有所区别。同时应注意到制动系统故障产生的原因不应局限于制动装置。车架、悬架、行驶机构等系统故障,以及道路状态、装载状况等外界使用条件,环境因素也可以影响到制动系统的效能。使用制动试验台检测汽车制动,对诊断和排除故障帮助较大。

任务一 制动力不足故障诊断与修复

学习目标

1. 能根据报修车辆的故障现象确定问诊的方向及项目。
2. 能根据故障现象制定正确的故障诊断计划。
3. 能熟练查阅维修资料,能根据故障现象选用合适的检测与诊断设备并熟练使用。
4. 能根据诊断计划,运用合适的检修设备对制动力不足故障进行检测。
5. 能对检测结果进行正确分析并确定制动力不足的故障部位及原因。
6. 能对故障部位进行快速准确修复,并且消除故障隐患。
7. 能具有严谨细致的工作态度,提高安全与服务意识。

任务导入

任务资料:一辆丰田威驰1.5L,行驶16万千米,车主反映车辆制动力不足,而且症状越来越严重。

任务要求:根据该车辆的故障现象,查阅相关资料,并选用合适的检测与诊断设备进行故障诊断与修复,同时填写任务报告单。

一、故障分析

制动力不足是指车辆在进行制动时制动器效能明显下降,制动减速度不够,制动距离变

长。地面没有轮胎拖痕或拖痕很短（有 ABS 的汽车除外）。

制动力不足的主要原因有以下几种：

（1）制动系统中制动液不足或变质。

（2）制动管路中有气体。

（3）制动摩擦片磨损过大。

（4）制动踏板自由行程过大，踏板传动机构松旷。

（5）刹车总泵故障：液压总泵活塞与缸壁磨损过大，导致配合松旷，漏油；液压总泵出油阀弹簧过软、折断，或出油阀密封不严；液压总阀回油阀密封不严；液压总阀回油孔堵塞。

（6）制动分泵故障：液压分泵皮碗、皮圈老化、发胀、磨损或变形；液压分泵活塞与缸壁磨损过大，导致配合松旷、漏油；液压分泵活塞回位弹簧过软或折断。

（7）制动管路故障：制动管路凹瘪，破损漏油，制动软管老化、发胀；制动管路接头破损、松动、密封不严导致漏油。

（8）真空伺服制动装置故障：各真空管接头破损、松动引起漏气；各真空管破裂、凹瘪、扭曲导致漏气，不畅通；真空储气筒单向阀密封不严；控制阀中的空气阀或真空阀密封不良；控制阀膜片破损；控制阀活塞和皮圈磨损，密封不良；加力气室膜片破裂；增压缸活塞磨损过多，皮圈磨损导致漏油；增压缸活塞回位弹簧过软；增压缸活塞球阀密封不良。

二、故障诊断

（1）检查制动系统有无泄漏，制动液液位、油质是否正常。

（2）检查制动磨损片是否过薄。

（3）检查踏板自由行程、制动行程是否正常。

（4）检查制动真空助力器工作是否正常。

（5）检查制动管路是否存在异常。

（6）更换制动液并进行排气。

（7）在制动时检测制动油压，判断制动总泵是否正常。

三、任务实施

1. 询问车主

向车主了解出现故障的时间；出现故障前是否有异常情况；车辆行驶的路况；车辆行驶里程；车辆是否按时保养；故障发生后是否进行过维修。通过以上的问诊了解故障发生前后的情况及故障的具体信息，完成制动力不足故障的初步诊断。

2. 试车与基本检查

进行试车，对故障进行确认，检查制动液油位和油质都正常。

3. 检测与诊断

通过与车主沟通获知，该车制动磨损片刚刚更换不久，因此暂时排除摩擦片磨损过大的故障。检查踏板自由行程、制动行程都正常。检查真空助力器工作正常。检查制动管路没有凹瘪等异常。更换制动液并进行排气试车，故障依旧。在制动时检测制动油压，发现制动油压明显比正常值低，由此判断制动总泵故障。

4. 故障排除

更换制动总泵后，故障排除。

5. 检验交车

故障检修完毕，车辆制动完全正常，向车主交车。

四、任务小结

在进行制动力不足这种常规故障诊断时，按照导致制动力不足的概率，由大到小进行诊断即可，不要完全按照经验进行诊断。特别是对总泵的故障判断，一定要通过制动油压的检测进行判断，不能盲目进行换件测试。

五、任务报告单

	专 业		班 级		姓 名	
	任务名称				学 时	2
	车 型		发动机型号			
	考核项目	考核内容			分 值	得 分
任务完成过程	1. 故障症状描述				5	
	2. 故障可能的原因及分析				25	
	3. 检测与诊断过程				35	
	4. 故障排除				10	
	5. 故障诊断小结				10	
教师评价	作业质量、作业效率、作业安全等				15	
	总评分数				100	

六、知识拓展

【典型案例一】 一辆北京现代伊兰特轿车制动力不足。

故障描述： 一辆北京现代伊兰特轿车，行驶16万千米，车主反映该车制动力不足。

故障诊断与修复： 首先检查制动液，发现制动液不足，而且制动液有些变质。通过与车主沟通获知，该车从未更换过制动液。

更换制动液并进行排气，检查制动摩擦片磨损不大，没有进行更换，试车后发现故障依旧。

检查制动管路，没有凹瘪、变形的地方。

在制动时检测制动油压，发现制动油压明显比正常值低，由此判断制动总泵故障。于是更换制动总泵，试车后发现故障依旧。

分析认为，故障只可能发生在ABS泵。因此更换ABS泵，试车故障排除。

故障诊断小结： 当遇到此类故障时，在进行常规检查没有发现故障的情况下，应该进行制动油压的检测，这样可以避免反复拆装，节省诊断的时间，需要注意的是在进行油压检测时应将油压表接在制动总管上。

【典型案例二】 一辆PASSAT 1.8T汽车制动力不足。

故障描述： 一辆PASSAT 1.8T手动挡轿车，行驶里程8万千米，车主反映该车在制动时，感觉制动偏软，有停不住车的感觉。

故障诊断与修复： 首先进行试车，发现故障现象确如车主所述。造成制动不良、制动距离长的原因有：制动液不足；制动总泵有故障；制动分泵有故障；制动片与制动盘磨损过度；制动管路中有空气；制动液性能变差。

根据以上分析进行逐项检查。首先检查了制动液在规定范围，制动管路及各个油管接头紧固良好，无松动泄漏，油管无老化、变形；制动分泵皮碗良好，没有制动液渗

漏；制动盘与制动片磨损正常；制动液颜色清澈透明。

对制动系统进行排气，管路中没有空气。根据以往的经验制动总泵引起该故障最多，于是更换制动总泵。试车，没有上述故障现象出现，于是交车。过了一周后，车主又来反映故障和以前一样。于是，对制动液、管路等部件又一次全面检查，没发现什么异常。仔细询问车主得知，只有长时间行驶后以及在市区行驶时频繁踩制动踏板后才会出现该故障，而且早上出现的概率小，下午出现的概率大。根据车主反映的情况又作进一步仔细分析，怀疑是热衰退使制动性能下降。但是，通常来说频繁使用制动器也不会使制动器过热而影响制动，且其他车没出现过这种现象。分析认为，很可能是制动盘通风散热性能变差导致该故障。于是拆下前制动盘检查，发现制动盘中间的通风槽内有许多泥土，由此可以判定造成该故障的原因就在前制动盘上。因前制动盘通风槽内有泥土堵塞，造成制动器散热不良从而影响了制动性能。于是，清洁了两前制动盘，装复试车，一切正常。此故障再没有出现。

故障诊断小结：该故障的原因是制动盘通风散热性能变差导致热衰退使制动性能下降，这种故障在维修中较少遇到。影响制动力不足的因素只有制动系统中的相关元件，维修人员一方面要了解制动系统的工作原理，另外需要做好问诊工作，了解故障发生的条件、环境和规律等，这些信息可以帮助维修人员确定故障诊断的方向。

任务二 制动跑偏故障诊断与修复

学习目标

1. 能根据报修车辆的故障现象确定问诊的方向及项目。
2. 能根据故障现象制定正确的故障诊断计划。
3. 能熟练查阅维修资料，能根据故障现象选用合适的检测与诊断设备并熟练使用。
4. 能根据诊断计划，运用合适的检修设备对制动跑偏故障进行检测。
5. 能对检测结果进行正确分析并确定制动跑偏的故障部位及原因。
6. 能对故障部位进行快速准确修复，并且消除故障隐患。

任务导入

任务资料：一辆 2011 款捷达，行驶 9 万千米，车主反映该车踩刹车时轻微甩尾。

任务要求：根据该车辆的故障现象，查阅相关资料，并选用合适的检测与诊断设备进行故障诊断与修复，同时填写任务报告单。

一、故障分析

制动跑偏是指在制动时，汽车维持直线行驶的方向性能力变差，不能沿直线方向停下，而是偏向道路一侧。

影响车辆制动跑偏的主要因素有制动器、悬架系统、前轮定位和轮胎等。

1. 制动器的影响

（1）同轴左右制动力不等。这种现象在路试过程中主要表现为紧急制动时，一侧车轮已经抱死，另一侧车轮只是减速而没有抱死。汽车偏驶向车轮抱死的一侧，从制动轮与地面的

拖痕来看，一边拖痕很深，而另一边拖痕很浅，甚至没有拖痕。造成该故障的主要原因是：某一制动气室膜片破裂或制动分泵密封圈损坏，制动气管或油管漏气、漏油；某一制动气室推杆变形或卡死，制动分泵活塞发咬；某一制动凸轮轴锈蚀，动作不灵活，调节器损坏；制动蹄片支承销锈蚀发咬；左右制动器与蹄片间隙大小不等；左右制动器摩擦片材料不同、厚薄不均、摩擦系数不同；某一制动摩擦片有油污等。

(2) 同轴左右制动力增长快慢不一致。这种现象在路试过程中表现为汽车制动时一侧车轮减速快，而另一侧车轮减速慢，汽车在减速过程中明显偏向车轮减速快的一侧。造成该故障的主要原因是：左右制动器的回位弹簧张力大小不等；左右制动气室推杆长度不一致；个别制动鼓磨损严重或失圆；个别车轮的凸轮轴衬套和蹄片支承销松旷等。

2. 悬架系统的影响

汽车车架变形与悬架系统出现故障将造成车轮载荷分布不均、前轮定位不正确、前后轴移位等现象，这些都将导致制动跑偏。制动时，在左右轮制动力大小相等、制动力增长快慢一致的情况下，承受载荷小的车轮必然先抱死，而承受载荷大的车轮由于惯性的作用必然后抱死，故而出现制动跑偏的现象。这种现象在汽车有装载的情况下才会较明显，空载的情况下一般不会发生。在制动台上检验也没有明显的反应。造成该故障的主要原因是：车架变形；减振器损坏；钢板弹簧变形、折断、疲劳；悬架系统的导向杆或平衡杆变形等。汽车在装载过程中，人为地将货物堆放不均匀，也将造成车辆左右轮载荷分布不均而导致制动跑偏。

3. 前轮定位

前轮定位不正确将造成转向轮"发摆"、转向自动"跑偏"、轮胎异常磨损等现象，破坏了汽车行驶的稳定性，在制动时也将造成制动跑偏，主要是前制动时跑偏。在路试过程中，可以发现制动跑偏的方向不是固定不变，而是时左时右。在制动检验台上试验时没有明显反应。造成该故障的主要原因是：车架变形；悬架系统损坏变形；前轴变形；转向节松旷及前束调整不当等。

此外，车辆在严重超载的情况下，使车架变形、弹簧钢板的弧度发生较大变化，也将造成前轮定位不正确，引起制动跑偏。这种现象应当引起驾驶员的高度重视，以免造成安全事故。前后轴移位（左右轴距差过大）、车架变形、前后轴弹簧钢板的U形螺栓松动、弹簧钢板中心螺栓折断等都可能造成前后轴移位（左右轴距差过大），导致汽车在直线行驶和制动时均出现跑偏现象。

4. 轮胎的影响

汽车要实现制动，不仅需要有足够的制动力，而且需要轮胎与地面之间有足够的附着系数。如果同轴上的轮胎气压、花纹、磨损程度不一致，轮胎的附着系数就不同，可造成制动跑偏。同一轴上的轮胎规格不一致（直径大小不相等），会导致左右轮产生的制动力不相等，也将造成制动跑偏。在路试过程中可以发现，由轮胎引起的制动跑偏也是无规则的，时左时右。因此，在对车辆进行维修时，应按照规定及时对轮胎进行合理调配和换位，避免轮胎的异常磨损。由于路面泥泞、凹凸不平、偏斜等原因，汽车制动时也将出现制动跑偏，这就要求在进行道路试验时必须在平直、干燥、清洁、附着系数较高的水泥或沥青路面上进行，以排除道路因素对汽车制动跑偏的影响。

二、故障诊断

(1) 检查左右轮胎气压和轮胎规格是否一致。
(2) 检查车架、悬架系统是否有变形。

（3）车辆进行路试（ABS系统功能取消），进行紧急制动，观察路面轮胎拖痕，无拖痕或拖痕短的一侧制动器存在问题，应重点检查，如摩擦片的厚度、制动鼓磨损程度、制动分泵的工作情况等。

（4）进行四轮定位检测，查看前轮定位角是否存在异常。

三、任务实施

1. 询问车主

向车主了解出现故障的时间；出现故障前是否有异常情况；车辆行驶的路况；车辆行驶里程；车辆是否按时保养；故障发生后是否进行过维修。通过以上的问诊了解故障发生前后的情况及故障的具体信息，完成制动跑偏的初步诊断。

2. 试车与基本检查

进行试车，对故障进行确认，检查轮胎气压、规格是否一致，车身有无倾斜等。

3. 检测与诊断

（1）拔下ABS电脑插头试车。车速达到45km/h时拉手制动，发现右后轮制动正常拉带，左后轮无拉带，不正常。

（2）试车说明左后轮制动力不足。可能是制动鼓和制动片配合不良，制动力低。

（3）拆下左后轮制动鼓检查，没有发现有油迹和安装问题，检查制动片正常。判断原因是制动鼓与制动片配合间隙过大。

4. 故障排除

拆下左后制动片进行更换，试车能正常拉带，没有甩尾现象，故障排除。

5. 检验交车

故障检修完毕，制动正常，同时没有其他症状，向车主交车。

四、任务小结

此故障是左后轮制动鼓片磨损过大，制动力明显低于右后轮。更换左右制动片，左右制动动力相等，制动甩尾故障消失。此故障相对简单，运用常规的制动跑偏故障诊断流程即可顺利排除。

五、任务报告单

专 业			班 级		姓 名	
任务名称					学 时	2
车 型			发动机型号			
	考核项目	考核内容			分 值	得 分
任务完成过程	1. 故障症状描述				5	
	2. 故障可能的原因及分析				25	
	3. 检测与诊断过程				35	
	4. 故障排除				10	
	5. 故障诊断小结				10	
教师评价	作业质量、作业效率、作业安全等				15	
	总评分数				100	

六、知识拓展

【典型案例一】 一辆北京 BJ2022 型"勇士"汽车制动跑偏。

故障描述：一辆北京 BJ2022 型"勇士"汽车，制动时，右前轮无拖印，方向严重向左跑偏。

故障诊断与修复：进行试车，发现右前轮制动力不足，拆下右前轮胎，检查发现右前轮制动蹄片与制动鼓的间隙过大，但按标准调整后，故障未能排除。对该车前制动的驱动机构进行检查，踏下制动踏板时，发现右前轮制动气室支架变形量比左前轮的大，而且制动气室回位弹簧歪斜，推杆连接叉也到达不到相应位置。更换右前制动气室和制动臂调整总成后，故障排除。

故障诊断小结：由于右前轮制动气室支架变形过大，制动气室回位弹簧歪斜，推杆连接叉不能到位，导致该制动气室推杆的有效工作行程减小，从而使右前轮制动力下降，引起制动跑偏。

【典型案例二】 一辆大众速腾 1.8TSI 汽车紧急制动甩尾。

故障描述：一辆大众速腾 1.8TSI 汽车，行驶 7.9 万千米，紧急制动时车辆有甩尾现象，此时 ABS 正常工作。

故障诊断与修复：检查发现紧急制动时甩尾严重，左前轮没有制动力。

拆检左前轮检查制动片及制动钳，没有发现渗漏及其他问题，按"Sagitar2006 制动装置"对制动系统排气之后，经试车左前轮没有制动力及制动时甩尾的现象依旧。

检查制动系统没有发现制动管路有不正常的变形或挤压痕迹，接下来连接制动系统检测设备 V.A.G1310A、适配接头 V.A.G1310/6 在压力下进行密封性检测，检测结果符合维修手册的要求：预压制动踏板，在 45s 的检测期间内压力下降没有超过 400kPa。压降符合标准。

左前轮连接 V.A.G1310A 时快速踏下制动踏板，左前轮压力表上升缓慢（右前轮能快速达到 10MPa）。原来是因为左前轮制动力来得过晚导致制动力不平衡，制动时甩尾。更换 ABS 泵后故障排除。

故障诊断小结：制动时制动系统处于建压阶段，如果车辆两侧车轮制动力增长的幅度不一样会造成车辆跑偏或者甩尾，在制动时测量制动压力是判断制动系统是否有故障的较好方式。

任务三　ABS 系统故障诊断与修复

学习目标

1. 能根据报修车辆的故障现象确定问诊的方向及项目。
2. 能根据故障现象制定正确的故障诊断计划。
3. 能熟练查阅维修资料，能根据故障现象选用合适的检测与诊断设备并熟练使用。
4. 能根据诊断计划，运用合适的检修设备对 ABS 系统故障进行检测。
5. 能对检测结果进行正确分析并确定 ABS 系统的故障部位及原因。
6. 能对故障部位进行快速准确修复，并且消除故障隐患。

任务导入

任务资料：一辆 2010 款速腾 1.6L 手动挡轿车，ABS 警报灯亮起，不能熄灭。

任务要求：根据该车辆的故障现象，查阅相关资料，并选用合适的检测与诊断设备进行故障诊断与修复，同时填写任务报告单。

一、故障分析

ABS 系统电控单元具有自诊断功能，当电控单元检测到系统发生故障时，电控单元会点亮故障指示灯，同时在电控单元中存储故障码。

常见的 ABS 系统故障原因有以下几种：
（1）轮速传感器故障导致无信号或信号不良。
（2）ABS 系统线路故障。
（3）电控单元故障。
（4）液压控制单元故障。

二、故障诊断

首先要使用故障诊断仪读取故障码，通过对故障码分析确定故障的检测方向。然后使用万用表进行检测，包括轮速传感器插头、信号及其线路；电控单元电源、搭铁、信号线路等。另外，可以通过检测制动油压来判断 ABS 液压控制单元是否工作正常。

如果检查该系统所有部位均正常，则故障在电控单元。

三、任务实施

1. 询问车主

向车主了解出现故障的时间；出现故障前是否有异常情况；车辆行驶的路况；车辆行驶里程；车辆是否按时保养；故障发生后是否进行过维修。通过以上的问诊了解故障发生前后的情况及故障的具体信息，完成 ABS 系统故障的初步诊断。

2. 试车与基本检查

进行试车，对故障进行确认，检查制动液油位和油质正常。

3. 检测与诊断

利用大众专用诊断仪 VAS5051 检测，发现有右后轮轮速传感器信号错误的故障，并且故障不能清除。进入 ABS 控制单元读取数据块，查看 001 组发现第 1、2、4 组在接通与关闭之间来回变化，只有第三组始终是接通状态不变化。因此判断故障可能由以下几方面导致：
（1）右后轮速传感器故障。
（2）右后轮速传感器线存在短路或断路。
（3）右后靶轮损坏或与传感器之间存在异物。
（4）ABS 控制单元内部故障。

首先检查右后轮速传感器，从外表看无损坏，测量内部两插头电阻，因无准确数值，与左侧的轮速传感器进行比较发现二者一致，基本判断轮速传感器没问题。

为了进一步确定刚才的判断，更换新的轮速传感器，结果更换后故障码可清除，但 ABS 警报灯仍亮，路试了一会，再用 5051 检测，还是和原来一样，判定轮速传感器没问题。

再检查由 ABS 泵到轮速传感器的连接线，用万用表测量没有短路或断路的现象。

接下来检查轮速传感器的靶轮。拆下外部的制动分泵支架等部件，发现靶轮与轴承集成在一起，带磁性的表面上吸上了些铁屑，怀疑这是导致故障的原因。

4. 故障排除

对靶轮与轴承表面进行清洁，车辆装复后，再进行试车，故障排除。

5. 检验交车

故障检修完毕试车，ABS 警报灯熄灭，制动正常，同时没有其他症状，向车主交车。

四、任务小结

此车的轮速传感器与靶轮采用了与捷达 SDI 发动机转速传感器类似的结构，靶轮与后轮轴承集成在一起，上面具有间隔的磁极，吸附铁屑后导致传感器信号异常，使故障灯亮起。

通过 5051 的读取故障记忆与数据块基本确定了导致故障的可能因素，按照由简到难的原则，一步步把故障排除。

五、任务报告单

专业			班级		姓名	
任务名称					学时	2
车型			发动机型号			
	考核项目		考核内容		分值	得分
任务完成过程	1. 故障症状描述				5	
	2. 故障可能的原因及分析				25	
	3. 检测与诊断过程				35	
	4. 故障排除				10	
	5. 故障诊断小结				10	
教师评价	作业质量、作业效率、作业安全等				15	
	总评分数				100	

六、知识拓展

【典型案例一】 一辆捷达汽车踩刹车 ABS 灯常亮。

故障描述：一辆捷达汽车，行驶 12 万千米，踩刹车 ABS 灯长亮。

故障诊断与修复：用 VAS5051 检测 ABS 系统，发现故障为 00290 左后轮不可靠信号。用电脑 VAG1552 读取数据，不踩刹车时 ABS 数据正常，轻踩刹车踏板左后轮数据与其他车轮数据有误差。

经检查左后轮 ABS 传感器阻值在正常范围，测量工作电压发现左后轮电压过高为电瓶电压。

检查线路发现 ABS 与车身线束插头腐蚀，由于插头内的刹车开关线和 ABS 左后轮传感器线短路，导致踩刹车 ABS 灯亮。

清洗线束插头，经路试故障排除。

故障诊断小结：该故障诊断从电控单元所报故障码开始，在工作状态下读取动态数据流，然后再结合万用表检测，最终找到故障点。对于这种在静态下不显示故障，而在工作状态报故障的系统，应该在系统工作时进行检测才可以更快更准地找到故障部位。

【典型案例二】 一辆新宝来轿车低速轻踩刹车 ABS 工作。

故障描述：一辆新宝来轿车，行驶10万千米，低速轻踩刹车ABS工作。

故障诊断与修复：试车确认故障现象，踩刹车，每当车速降到10km/h时ABS开始工作。读取数据流，发现左前/左后/右后车轮速度为10km/h左右时，右前轮为0。拆解右前轮，发现ABS传感器与齿圈间隙大。

更换法兰，调整传感器与齿圈间隙，试车，读取数据，四轮一样，轻踩刹车时ABS不再误工作，故障排除。

故障诊断小结：此车为事故车，更换过非原装法兰，导致传感器与齿圈间隙过大，从而造成车辆低速时ABS传感器的磁通量变化不大，因而控制单元误认为车轮抱死，驱动ABS误工作。此故障不难维修，但找准故障的切入点很重要。ABS工作的目的是控制车轮抱死而抑制侧向滑移，所以ABS工作时一定是控制单元认为某个车轮抱死，这就有必要先读取车轮的转速差。确认好故障着手点可以提高诊断速度。

项目十

行驶系统故障诊断与修复

任务一 汽车行驶跑偏故障诊断与修复

学习目标

1. 能根据报修车辆的故障现象确定问诊的方向及项目。
2. 能根据故障现象制定正确的故障诊断计划。
3. 能熟练查阅维修资料,能根据故障现象选用合适的检测与诊断设备并熟练使用。
4. 能根据诊断计划,运用合适的检修设备对行驶跑偏故障进行检测。
5. 能对检测结果进行正确分析并确定行驶跑偏的故障部位及原因。
6. 能对故障部位进行快速准确修复,并且消除故障隐患。
7. 能具有吃苦耐劳的精神,较强的责任心,严谨细致的工作态度。

任务导入

任务资料:一辆 2011 款迈腾 2.0,发动机号为 BYJ。车主反映车辆行驶中跑偏,而且一会儿向左跑,一会儿向右跑,已经维修过两次,更换过前轮的左右悬挂和转向机,但故障没有任何好转。

任务要求:根据该车辆的故障现象,查阅相关资料,并选用合适的检测与诊断设备进行故障诊断与修复,同时填写任务报告单。

一、故障分析

汽车直线行驶一段后,在转向盘不动的情况下,汽车行驶方向向一侧偏行,即为行驶跑偏。汽车行驶跑偏导致汽车维持直线行驶的能力下降,驾驶员需不断地修正行驶方向,才能保持汽车的正常行驶。

(1) 行驶系统故障 两前轮轮胎气压不相等或轮胎规格不一致;两前轮主销后倾角或车轮外倾角不相等;前轮前束值过大或过小;前悬架弹簧折断,钢板弹簧错位或左右两侧弹簧力不一致;车架变形或前桥变形;车桥发生位移或驱动桥变形;前后桥左右轮距相差过大(出现推力角);前后桥左右轮毂轴承预紧度调整不一致,相差太大。

（2）转向系统故障　转向器调整不当，蜗杆轴承过紧，啮合过紧、发卡；转向节主销、独立悬挂的球销间隙过大或过小，引起松旷或运转不灵活；左、右转向节梯形臂不一致，有一侧转向梯形臂变形；独立悬架的左、右横拉杆不等长，调整不当；转向器垂臂不在中间位置、安装记号未对正。

另外，有液压转向助力装置的汽车在行驶中跑偏，通常是控制阀有故障，造成动力缸活塞两侧有压力差而自动产生助力作用所致。

（3）制动系统故障　有一侧车轮制动器的制动间隙调整过小；有一侧车轮制动器不回位；有一侧车轮的轮毂轴承间隙过大，引起制动鼓偏斜、拖滞。

（4）其他故障　车辆偏载严重；因路面、轮胎花纹磨损不一致等原因，使左右驱动车轮附着力有差异；差速器装配、调整不当，使左右驱动轮转速有差异；路面向一侧倾斜。

二、故障诊断

首先检查左、右轮胎（重点在前轮）的气压是否一致，轮胎规格是否一致。

如果轮胎符合要求，则用手摸跑偏一侧的制动鼓（盘）或轮毂有无发热现象，并与另一侧的制动鼓（盘）和轮毂相比较。

如跑偏侧的制动鼓温度高于另一侧的制动鼓温度，说明该侧有制动拖滞现象，需拆检该侧车轮制动器处理。

如跑偏侧的轮毂温度高于另一侧的轮毂温度，说明该侧轮毂轴承调整过紧、缺油，需检修、调整。

如制动鼓、轮毂温度正常，则应检查悬架弹簧有无错位、折断，检查左右弹簧的弹力是否一致。不符合要求则应修理或更换。

检查时可在汽车前方观察车身是否歪斜。注意检查时应使汽车空载或均载，将车辆停放在平坦、干燥、坚硬的地面上进行。

如以上项目经检查均符合要求，则应检查以下各项内容：

（1）检查前轮定位参数是否正确，如不符合要求则需重新调整。
（2）检查前桥、后桥有无变形、移位，如有则需修理或更换。
（3）检查转向系统各机构安装、调整情况。
（4）检查前、后桥左、右轮轴距是否一致。

三、任务实施

1. 询问车主

向车主了解出现故障的时间；出现故障前是否有异常情况；车辆行驶的路况；车辆行驶里程；故障发生后是否进行过维修。通过以上的问诊了解故障发生前后的情况及故障的具体信息，完成行驶跑偏的初步诊断。

2. 试车与基本检查

首先进行试车，对故障进行确认。试车后发现车辆在行驶时不但跑偏，而且在驾驶过程中转向盘手感不好，向左打方向轻，向右打方向重。

然后检查汽车底盘有无碰撞，经查底盘无磕碰现象。检查轮胎型号，四轮轮胎均为同一型号。

3. 检测与诊断

检测胎压，同轴胎压基本一致。

检查轮胎磨损，发现左后轮存在异常磨损，轮胎的左右磨损面位置不一致，整个轮胎的磨损面严重向右偏移，且磨损程度严重，如图10-1所示，这说明车辆的定位有问题。从车

主处获知，该车辆已经做过两次四轮定位，但是都没解决问题。查看四轮定位的打印报告，两次定位数据差别很大，甚至有一份的标准数据都是错的，所以这两次定位并不完全可信。

拆下四条轮胎，换上新轮胎试车，症状稍有好转。

车辆举升，转向横拉杆球头不存在松旷，转向机间隙也正常。

检查副车架和转向节胶套无明显磨损、旷动。

4. 故障排除

最终决定重新给车辆做四轮定位，在给四轮定位及举升机标定后，按照标准操作给车辆定位，定位过程中发现后轮前束值和外倾角均有较大偏差，将车轮定位角调整到规定范围。在定位结束后检查"附加检测值"查看车身是否有变形，结果附加检测值反映车身良好，无变形。定位完成后试车，汽车行驶完全正常，故障消除。

5. 检验交车

故障检修完毕，车辆行驶平稳无跑偏，向车主交车。

图 10-1 异常磨损的轮胎

（请注意观察轮胎磨损面的左右位置，整个轮胎的磨损面严重向右偏移）

四、任务小结

诊断车辆跑偏故障不能简单换件，而是应按照车辆跑偏的特征确定故障的可能原因，再逐项进行诊断。在做四轮定位时一定要保证定位设备准确，同时操作要规范。实际上，很多跑偏的故障可能仅仅是定位数据不准造成的。

五、任务报告单

	专 业		班 级		姓 名	
	任务名称				学 时	2
	车型		发动机型号			
	考核项目	考核内容			分值	得 分
任务完成过程	1. 故障症状描述				5	
	2. 故障可能的原因及分析				25	
	3. 检测与诊断过程				35	
	4. 故障排除				10	
	5. 故障诊断小结				10	
教师评价	作业质量、作业效率、作业安全等				15	
	总评分数				100	

六、知识拓展

【典型案例一】 一辆速腾 1.8T 轿车行驶中向左跑偏。

故障描述： 一辆大众速腾 1.8T 轿车，装备手动变速器，在直线行驶时松开转向盘后车辆会向左跑偏。

故障诊断与修复： 接车后试车，确认故障现象属实，但当轿车直线行驶时转向盘位置正确。车主反映，该车为在一综合汽车修理厂刚修过的事故车，事故位置在左前悬架上，已更

换了左前悬架的大部分零件、主气囊、副气囊和仪表台总成，并做过四轮定位。一般轿车跑偏的原因有：四轮定位不准，轿车左、右轴距不一致，左、右轮胎气压不一致或左、右轮胎品牌或花纹不一致等。该车已经做过四轮定位，并且车主提供的四轮定位打印数据都在标准范围之内；测量轿车的左、右轴距，相同；测量左、右轮轮胎的气压，也正常。为排除轮胎方面的原因，把车的左、右前轮胎对调后试车，故障现象依旧。

接着从助力转向系统方面分析故障原因。速腾轿车的助力转向系统与普通车辆的不同，其助力方式为双齿轮式机械电动助力式，它的功能有随速转向功能和主动回正功能。助力转向系统中有转向角传感器（G85），它可识别转向盘的转动角速度和转角位置，轿车转向盘不受力时，如果它识别到转向盘不在中心位置（转向盘转角为0°），则助力转向控制单元（J500）会根据 G85 的信号控制转向电动机（V187）工作。通过转向机器向转向盘提供一个回正力矩，从而使转向盘回到中心位置。G85 识别的转向盘转角可用 VAS5052（44-08-007 区第 1 组数据）读得。

把转向盘转到轿车直线行驶方向（转向盘的中心位置），用 VAS5052 读取 G85 的数据（转向盘转角），为 -7.52°，只有把转向盘再向左转一定角度后 G85 的数据才会为 0°。至此故障原因找到了，在轿车直线行驶时，虽然转向盘位置是正确的，但 G85 所识别到的转向盘转角不为 0°，所以 J500 通过转向器给予转向盘一个向左的回正力矩，结果轿车向左跑偏。

用 VAS5052 功能引导程序做 G85 的零点基本设置，然后试车，故障排除。再次用 VAS5052 读取转向盘中心位置 G85 的数据为 0°。

故障诊断小结：本故障是助力转向控制单元基本零点设置错误导致的，电控单元会收到错误的信号，从而进行错误控制。

【典型案例二】 一辆丰田大霸王行驶中向右跑偏。

故障描述：一辆丰田大霸王以 60km/h 的速度在城市环路上行驶时向右跑偏，需用手轻微用力逆时针方向拽转向盘，才能使车辆直线行驶。

故障诊断与修复：检查车辆轮胎，四轮轮胎型号均为 215/55R17 94V，轮胎外观良好，无异常磨损。将轮胎气压调整至 280kPa。检查车辆左右高度，左边比右边略高 3mm，应不是主要问题。检查左右轴距完全相同。

检查前轮定位情况如下。

① 前束。前短后长相差 1mm，标准值：1.0mm±2.0mm。

② 外倾角。左侧：-0°15″；右侧：0°20″；标准值：-0°10″±45″。

③ 后倾角。左侧：5°15″；右侧：5°55″；标准值：5°45″±45″。

④ 转向轴线内倾角。左侧：12°45″；右侧：12°36″；标准值：11°22″±45″。

经检查前轮定位基本符合维修手册所提供的维修数据。

根据以往修理经验将两前轮轮胎左右互换位置后试车，故障依然存在。

考虑在检查前轮定位时，外倾角（左侧：-0°15″；右侧：+0°20″）虽符合标准，但外倾角均向右侧倾斜，怀疑与车辆故障有关。所以将左侧外倾角调整为 +0°10″，将右侧外倾角调整为 -0°15″，经试车故障排除，车辆恢复正常状态。三天后回访车辆状况，车主反映车辆状态良好。

故障诊断小结：该车行驶跑偏的故障最终是通过调整前轮定位排除的。虽然此车前轮定位的数据符合维修手册数据，但其数据在规定的偏差范围内有一定的调整空间，左右两轮的定位值一个正值一个负值，而且两轮之间偏差较大，因此导致该车向右跑偏，也就是说定位值在规定范围内也可能导致车辆跑偏。

任务二　轮胎异常磨损故障诊断与修复

学习目标

1. 能根据报修车辆的故障现象确定问诊的方向及项目。
2. 能根据故障现象制定正确的故障诊断计划。
3. 能熟练查阅维修资料，能根据故障现象选用合适的检测与诊断设备并熟练使用。
4. 能根据诊断计划，运用合适的检修设备对轮胎异常磨损故障进行检测。
5. 能对检测结果进行正确分析并确定轮胎异常磨损的故障部位及原因。
6. 能对故障部位进行快速准确修复，并且消除故障隐患。

任务导入

任务资料：一辆日产蓝鸟轿车，两个前轮轮胎外侧磨损严重，内侧边缘花纹沟边部呈羽毛状磨损，磨损痕迹从内到外，逐步加重，横过胎面，而且右前轮外侧的磨损尤其严重。

任务要求：根据该车辆的故障现象，查阅相关资料，并选用合适的检测与诊断设备进行故障诊断与修复，同时填写任务报告单。

一、故障分析

（1）前轮定位失准。前束值过大时，转向盘发飘。前轮外侧磨损，内侧花纹沟边呈羽毛状。前束值过小时转向沉重，车轮内侧磨损严重，外侧花纹沟边呈羽毛状磨损。主销后倾过大时，车轮转向后自动回正阻力过大，低速时使轮胎过度摇晃，而高速时则引起飘荡，增加对路面的冲击，使胎面严重磨损。主销后倾角失准时，制动中将使两前轮拖拽不均，制动性能变坏，轮胎偏磨。主销后倾角、主销内倾角一般由车身本身决定，不直接引起轮胎的异常磨损，而是轮胎异常磨损的主要诱导原因。

（2）驾驶操作技术不良。起步快、频繁紧急制动、转弯过急、高速通过障碍等，均可使轮胎受到剧烈冲击而损坏。

（3）后桥、车架变形。交通事故或长期超载、偏载均会引起前后桥、车架变形，导致车轮不正常摇摆，转向轮滑动磨损增大，轮胎胎面形成有规则的间隔斜磨。

（4）悬挂技术状况不良、钢板总成装备不妥、左右钢板弹簧刚度不一，导致动载荷交替变化，车轴产生不良的摇摆现象，可引起轮胎磨损不均。

（5）制动器工作不良。制动鼓磨损过限引起制动不均匀，制动发滞咬死，轮胎拖拽，加剧轮胎的磨损。

（6）轮距不等。车辆前后桥扭曲或位移，大梁变形，钢板弹簧吊耳铆钉松动或脱落，钢板弹簧中心螺栓弯曲或折断错位等，都会使轴距变化，车轮运转不在一条直线上，引起轮胎的偏磨产生机件伤胎。

二、故障诊断

（1）胎冠两肩花纹磨损。由于轮胎气压过低，长期缺气或由于经常超载行驶而压缩变形，致使胎冠中部向里弯曲，胎面边缘负荷剧增，使胎面磨损不匀。

（2）胎冠中间磨损。由于轮胎长期气压过高，帘布过度伸张，胎体疲劳过程过快，使轮

胎接触面积减小，增加了单位压力负荷致使胎冠中部磨损。

（3）边磨耗，即胎外侧偏磨，多属轮胎规格尺寸不一，负荷不一；或长期行驶在拱形路面上；或未定期进行轮胎换位。

（4）胎侧呈锯齿形磨损。由于长期超载使用或缺气行驶而未及时进行轮胎换位，制动过于频繁，以致轮胎在制动力作用下经常单向与路面摩擦，引起不规则磨损。

（5）胎内侧磨损严重，外侧花纹沟边起毛。多是由转向横拉杆变形、转向臂弯曲、前桥扭曲及车架前端变形等引起前轮定位失准，造成的偏磨及拖拽磨损。

（6）胎冠呈波浪形磨损。这是由于胎面接触坚硬路面时，瞬间花纹块前端受压挤变形、后端在离地时产生滑磨、轮胎平衡不良、轮毂松旷、轮辋拱曲或经常使用紧急制动等造成的。

三、任务实施

1. 询问车主

向车主了解出现故障的时间；发现故障后症状是否有变化，出现故障前是否有其他异常情况；车辆行驶的具体情况；车辆是否按时保养；故障发生后是否进行过其他维修。通过以上的问诊了解故障发生前后的情况及故障的具体信息，完成轮胎异常磨损的初步诊断。

2. 试车与基本检查

观察左右轮胎气压、轮胎规格，完全符合要求，目视观察车身无明显倾斜。试车，测试车辆是否存在行驶跑偏、转向盘摆振等情况。

3. 检测与诊断

根据对该车轮胎异常磨损的实际状况观察和以上造成异常磨损原因的综合分析，可以初步判断该故障是由于该车的前轮定位参数不当所致。

从前轮定位的4个参数对轮胎的异常磨损造成的不同影响来看，前轮前束和前轮外倾角不当会引起轮胎的单肩侧磨，而前束和外倾角过大都会引起外侧磨损过度，这与该车的实际情况相吻合。通过对该车仔细观察，发现该车在行驶时有转向盘发飘、操纵不稳的现象。因此，基本上可以确定该车前轮前束和外倾角可能会过大。而其他的原因，包括主销后倾和主销内倾不当，转向器和转向传动机构磨损松旷，悬架支承和避振器松旷以及轮胎不平衡和气压不当，轮辋变形，驾驶技术不当等，主要会引起汽车行驶时出现摆振，造成轮胎径向异常波浪形磨损。这与该车损坏的实际情况不符，其影响基本上可以排除。故障的原因很可能是前轮前束和外倾角不正确。

利用四轮定位仪检测前轮定位与前轮前束。测量的结果为前轮前束：＋8mm；前轮外倾角：1°08′；主销后倾角：3°30′；主销内倾角：10°30′。从以上测量数据看，该车的前轮外倾角、主销内倾角和主销后倾角均正常，不必调整。测量的结果还表明，该车前束过大。

检查影响前轮前束的部位，即检查前桥总成及转向机构部件是否有损坏和变形等，经检查转向拉杆、球头销及销座、转向节无异常，前轮轴承不松旷，车架和悬架无变形。

前轮前束调整前检查：按标准为轮胎充气；检查减振器有无漏油和损伤；车架已正确校正，悬架活动自如；转向器调整正确，前悬架无大的间隙和损坏。

4. 故障排除

调整前束后试车，经过一段时间反馈无轮胎异常磨损状况出现，故障排除。

5. 检验交车

故障检修完毕，没有其他症状，向车主交车。

四、任务小结

该车轮胎异常磨损是由前轮前束异常导致的,经四轮定位检测和调整后故障排除。在检测中仍然不要忽视对基本项目的检查,比如轮胎的规格、气压,车身、悬架等有无异常等。只有这样才能准确地分析出故障原因并予以排除。

五、任务报告单

专　业			班　级		姓　名	
任务名称					学　时	2
车型			发动机型号			
任务完成过程	考核项目	考核内容			分　值	得　分
	1. 故障症状描述				5	
	2. 故障可能的原因及分析				25	
	3. 检测与诊断过程				35	
	4. 故障排除				10	
	5. 故障诊断小结				10	
教师评价	作业质量、作业效率、作业安全等				15	
	总评分数				100	

项目十一

安全气囊系统故障诊断与修复

学习目标

1. 能根据报修车辆的故障现象确定问诊的方向及项目。
2. 能根据故障现象制定正确的故障诊断计划。
3. 能熟练查阅维修资料,能根据故障现象选用合适的检测与诊断设备并熟练使用。
4. 能根据诊断计划,运用合适的检修设备对安全气囊系统故障进行检测。
5. 能对检测结果进行正确分析并确定安全气囊系统的故障部位及原因。
6. 能对故障部位进行快速准确修复,并且消除故障隐患。
7. 能具有严谨细致的工作态度,提高安全意识与团队合作能力。

任务导入

任务资料: 一辆 2010 款大众 CC 汽车,车主反映车辆在行驶中仪表气囊故障灯常亮。

任务要求: 根据该车辆的故障现象,查阅相关资料,并选用合适的检测与诊断设备进行故障诊断与修复,同时填写任务报告单。

一、故障分析

安全气囊系统电控单元具有自诊断功能,当电控单元检测到系统发生故障时,电控单元会点亮故障指示灯,同时在电控单元中存储故障码。

常见的安全气囊故障原因有以下几种:

(1) 碰撞传感器故障。
(2) 安全气囊系统线路故障,包括螺旋线束及其他线路。
(3) 电控单元故障。

二、故障诊断

首先要使用故障诊断仪读取故障码,通过对故障码分析确定故障的检测方向。然后使用万用表进行线路检测。碰撞传感器不能进行检测,可以通过替换法进行故障确认。

如果检查该系统所有部位均正常,则故障在电控单元。

三、任务实施

1. 询问车主

向车主了解出现故障的时间；出现故障前是否有异常情况；车辆行驶的路况；车辆行驶里程；故障发生后是否进行过维修。通过以上的问诊了解故障发生前后的情况及故障的具体信息，完成故障的初步诊断。

2. 试车与基本检查

进行试车，对故障进行确认。

3. 检测与诊断

用大众专用诊断仪 5051 读取故障码，如图 11-1 所示。故障码显示"01639 后排侧面安全气囊碰撞传感器（乘客侧）—G257 断路/对正极短路 间歇式"，清除故障码后故障灯熄灭，试车一段路程故障再现。

根据故障码内容判断可能的故障原因有以下几种：

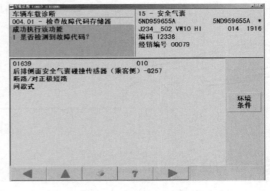

图 11-1 5051 读取的故障码

(1) J234 安全气囊控制单元损坏。

(2) G257 后排侧面安全气囊碰撞传感器（乘客侧）故障。

(3) J234 和 G257 之间的线路故障。

分析认为碰撞传感器有可能损坏，于是先更换 G257 后排侧面安全气囊碰撞传感器（乘客侧），试车后故障再现。

用万用表检查传感器到气囊控制单元的线路，线路如图 11-2 所示。传感器插脚 1（绿色线）到气囊控制单元的阻值为 0.3Ω，线路完全正常；插脚 2（棕色线）到气囊控制单元阻

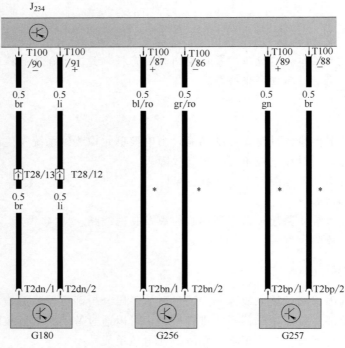

图 11-2 大众 CC 安全气囊系统电路图

值 0.2Ω，没有短路、断路现象。

安装好气囊控制单元与线束接口，读取故障码，发现故障码由"间歇式"变为"静态式"，不能清除，由此判断气囊控制单元与线束接口很可能存在接触不良。

将气囊控制单元 T100/8 和 T100/88 针脚退出，用钳子将接口夹紧，重新装后故障码定义为偶发，清除故障后试车未再出现气囊灯亮，经过几天的后续跟踪，故障未再现。

由于气囊控制单元插头上 T100/8 或 T100/88 针脚与导线间接触不良造成 G257 间歇故障。

4. 故障排除

用钳子将针脚再次紧固，故障排除。

5. 检验交车

故障检修完毕，没有其他症状，向车主交车。

四、任务小结

（1）根据故障码定义分析，结合电路图对线路进行测量诊断，是排除故障的常规思路。

（2）检查线路的通断，要有耐性和清晰的思路。

（3）通过案例理解故障码类型定义"间歇式"和"静态式"，此两种故障码类型定义提示可以帮助我们诊断故障。

五、任务报告单

	专业		班级		姓名	
	任务名称				学时	2
	车型		发动机型号			
	考核项目	考核内容			分值	得分
任务完成过程	1. 故障症状描述				5	
	2. 故障可能的原因及分析				25	
	3. 检测与诊断过程				35	
	4. 故障排除				10	
	5. 故障诊断小结				10	
教师评价	作业质量、作业效率、作业安全等				15	
	总评分数				100	

六、知识拓展

【典型案例一】 一辆 2011 款宝来汽车，气囊报警灯亮。

故障描述： 一辆 2011 款大众宝来汽车，行驶中安全气囊报警灯点亮。

故障诊断与修复： 首先，用大众专用诊断仪 5052 读取故障码，驾驶员侧安全气囊引爆装置电阻值过大（偶发），清除故障代码，再检测一切正常。车主同意先将车开走，行驶数天后再次报警。

再次读取安全气囊故障码为：驾驶员侧安全气囊引爆装置电阻值过大（偶发）。

考虑到气囊线路特殊性，先更换相关元件，进行测试。先后更换气囊滑环、主气囊、气囊控制单元，故障未解决。

只能根据线路图重新检查相关线路，电路如图 11-3 所示。检查控制单元与主气囊间的连线及插头时发现气囊复位环与线束 T5 插头 4 号脚折断虚接，如图 11-4 所示。

用专用工具更换相同型号线束插脚后，用热缩管连接连接点确保连接牢固，故障解决。

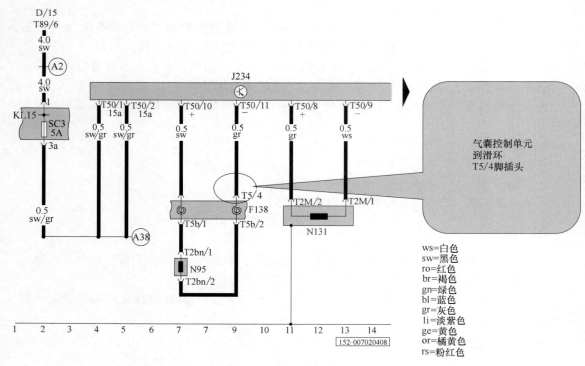

图 11-3 安全气囊系统电路图

故障诊断小结：此故障为线路断裂后虚接造成气囊灯报警。建议处理类似偶发故障时，尽量使用模拟故障发生状态（振动/摇晃线束），并且遵守气囊线路维修操作要求，维修时耐心细致，避免盲目换件试车。

【典型案例二】 一辆 2011 款宝来汽车，安全气囊报警灯亮。

故障描述：一辆 2011 款大众宝来汽车，车主反映安全气囊报警灯点亮。

故障诊断与修复：首先用 VAS5051 故障查询，故障码 01217-029，即驾驶员侧侧

图 11-4 损坏的接线端子

面气囊引爆器 N199 对地短路偶发。清除故障码后故障消失，同时检查座椅下的侧面安全气囊线束及插头未见松动或固定不实的现象（因为好多车辆装地胶或者后座脚垫等会造成插头脱落以及线束未固定导致气囊灯亮的故障，所以交车）。

但用户车辆行驶几天后气囊灯再次亮起。再次查询故障，故障码还是 01217-029，清除故障后又恢复正常。但考虑故障频繁出现，因此拆装座椅并按照气囊系统电路图（如图 11-5）进一步检查气囊系统线路，经检查未见线束或插头安装不实等现象，用万用表检测气囊电脑一侧线束未见异常。

当翻过座椅顺着气囊线束往座椅内看时发现线束是从手动调节压杆处出来的，因此怀疑气囊线束在此处被挤压了，故继续拆装座椅侧面饰板检查。当拆开座椅调节压杆后发现在压杆末端齿轮处的气囊线束破损，故障点在此已毫无疑问，如图 11-6 所示。更换驾驶员侧侧

面安全气囊总成故障排除。

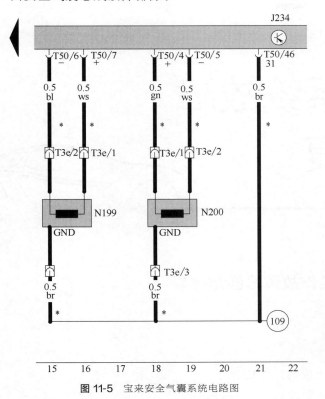

图 11-5 宝来安全气囊系统电路图

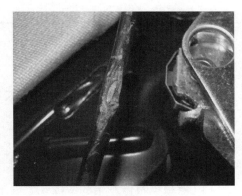

图 11-6 损坏的气囊线束

故障诊断小结：首先对故障码含义进行分析，这种故障多数为插头未插或插得不实，少数为气囊本体的故障；另一种故障为 N199 引爆装置电阻太小，这种故障少数为控制单元到气囊间的线路短路（这种情况极少发生），出现电阻太小故障多为气囊本体故障。此故障显示 N199 对地短路应该是气囊控制单元到 N199 间的正极线对地短路，所以应该着重于检查控制单元到 N199 间的线路。

对于维修安全气囊的故障一定要有细心负责的态度，不要简单清除故障或盲目换件，以免发生事故时气囊不能正常引爆带来损失。

项目十二

汽车空调系统故障诊断与修复

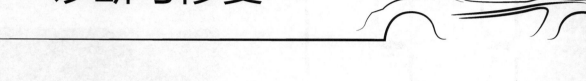

任务一 空调系统不工作故障诊断与修复

学习目标

1. 能根据报修车辆的故障现象确定问诊的方向及项目。
2. 能根据故障现象制定正确的故障诊断计划。
3. 能熟练查阅维修资料,能根据故障现象选用合适的检测与诊断设备并熟练使用。
4. 能根据诊断计划,运用合适的检修设备对空调系统不工作故障进行检测。
5. 能对检测结果进行正确分析并确定空调系统不工作的故障部位及原因。
6. 能对故障部位进行快速准确修复,并且消除故障隐患。
7. 能具有严谨细致的工作态度,提高服务意识。

任务导入

任务资料:一辆桑塔纳 3000 汽车,配备自动空调。该车打开空调后,压缩机不工作,不能制冷,其他功能正常。

任务要求:根据该车辆的故障现象,查阅相关资料,并选用合适的检测与诊断设备进行故障诊断与修复,同时填写任务报告单。

一、故障分析

空调系统不工作指的是在开启空调开关后,空调压缩机不工作。
空调系统不工作的主要原因包括以下几种:
(1) 空调压缩机或者其线路故障。
(2) 空调系统中制冷剂不足。
(3) 空调 A/C 开关损坏。
(4) 空调放大器或者其线路故障。
(5) 蒸发器表面温度传感器或温控开关故障。

（6）发动机水温太高。
（7）外界温度太低而调定温度太高。
（8）空调电控单元或其线路故障。

二、故障诊断

（1）若是自动空调，首先应利用故障诊断仪读取故障码，如果有故障码，按照故障码进行检查，如果无故障码，读取数据流，查看与压缩机启动有关的传感器及开关是否正常。

若是手动空调，首先应利用空调压力表检查制冷剂是否充足，进而检查空调压力开关是否工作正常。

（2）检查电磁离合器及其线路是否正常。
（3）检查蒸发器表面温度传感器或热敏开关是否正常。
（4）如各开关和电磁离合器能正常工作，而压缩机不转，则检查压缩机。
（5）若故障诊断仪无法与空调电控单元正常通信或者空调控制单元无法控制执行器工作，则空调控制单元故障。

三、任务实施

1. 询问车主

向车主了解出现故障的时间；出现故障前是否有其他异常情况；发现故障后症状是否有变化；车辆行驶的具体情况；车辆是否按时保养；故障发生后是否进行过其他维修。通过以上的问诊了解故障发生前后的情况及故障的具体信息，完成空调不工作的初步诊断。

2. 试车与基本检查

进行试车，对故障进行确认。停车后检查空调管路是否有油迹，电磁离合器、压力传感器或压力开关插头是否连接牢固。此外要确定该车空调系统的结构特征和线路连接方式。

3. 检测与诊断

检测空调系统内制冷剂的压力，发现压力正常、制冷剂充足。对发动机舱内的一些与空调有关的插接件进行初步检查，未发现松动、脱落。随即将车发动，打开空调，进行进一步检查。打开位于发动机舱左侧的"继电器-保险丝盒"，拔下位于RL2位的电磁离合器继电器J44，用试笔测量继电器座上的2/30号插脚无电。用一根导线由蓄电池向插座的5/87a号脚直接供电，压缩机正常工作制冷，说明147B继电器至压缩机线路正常，空调系统本身也没有问题，故障出在控制线路上。继续对线路进行检查，147B继电器的2/30号插脚通过位于干燥罐上的空调压力开关F129供电。拔下插头T4at，测量2号脚无电，因该线通向空调控制单元J127的T32e/23脚，故先对J127进行检查。检查过程中发现控制面板显示的各项状态都很正常，于是激活自动空调的读数据块功能进行查看。检查车内外温度、蒸发器温度、水温、太阳光辐射（采样值1/20）、进气口温度、车速（采样值1/5）数据都正常。

于是又激活空调的自诊断功能。经检查也未有任何故障提示。拆下空调控制单元，无意晃动空调控制单元时，内部发出异物响声，如同有东西在里面脱落了。于是分解控制单元J127，发现脱落的异物竟然是一枚电路板上的贴片电阻。安装好新的空调控制单元后，空调仍不工作。又将空调控制单元拆下，用12V电直接向T32e/23脚供电（T32e/23脚内插入一枚大头针），压缩机开始工作，正常制冷。怀疑还是线路有问题，再次直接向T32e/23脚供电，在连接的一瞬间冒出了巨大的火花，插入T32e/23脚内的大头针也被熔化了，说明线路中存在严重的搭铁短路现象。于是将仪表盘的下饰板拆掉，对空调线束进行仔细检查，

最后在拆下中央保险盒后发现空调的线束被缠进了离合器踏板支架上的轴内，线束已经被挤压得严重破损了。

4. 故障排除
把线束取出包扎完毕后，启动空调，空调系统工作正常，故障排除。

5. 检验交车
故障检修完毕，装复试车，没有其他症状，向车主交车。

四、任务小结

在汽车维修工作中，维修方案的制订至关重要，合理的方案可以提高工作效率，而合理方案的制订是基于对故障原因全面分析基础之上的。这既要考虑故障原因的主次关系，同时也要考虑故障排查难易程度，即遵循"由主至次，由简至繁"的检修原则。

五、任务报告单

专　业		班　级		姓　名	
任务名称				学　时	2
车　型		发动机型号			
	考核项目	考核内容		分　值	得　分
任务完成过程	1. 故障症状描述			5	
	2. 故障可能的原因及分析			25	
	3. 检测与诊断过程			35	
	4. 故障排除			10	
	5. 故障诊断小结			10	
教师评价	作业质量、作业效率、作业安全等			15	
	总评分数			100	

六、知识拓展

【典型案例一】 一辆大众速腾 1.8T 汽车空调不制冷。

故障描述：一辆 2010 款大众速腾 1.8T 汽车，行驶里程 5 万千米，车主反映高速行驶时，空调突然不制冷。

故障诊断与修复：首先对车辆空调系统用电脑（5052A）进行了相关的检测，无故障记录。检查空调保险及制冷剂加注量正常。

读取其他系统发现 09 系统中有 2 个故障：01333 车门控制单元-左后-J388 无信号/通信（偶发）；交流发电机端子 DF 负荷信号，不可靠信号（偶发）。

由此说明故障应该发生在控制部分。于是用万用表测得发电量在 11.8～12.0V 之间变化。测量发电机的磁场电压为 0V。从而可以确定故障点为汽车电源。检查全车正极和负极连接点，一切正常。

按照相关电路图（如图 12-1、图 12-2）进行检查发现：从发电机 T2/1 到 J519F/4 之间的导线不通。于是检查 T4t/2 的 4 脚连接插头，发现插头脱落。重新安装插好后，发电量正常，空调工作正常，故障排除。

故障诊断小结：此故障是由插头断开导致发电机、车门、空调等多个系统出现故障，这些系统线路都涉及了该插头。解决这类故障时可以先读取故障码，通过对多个故障码的综合分析，即可判断是涉及这多个系统的插头存在故障。

【典型案例二】 一辆大众宝来 1.6 汽车空调不工作。

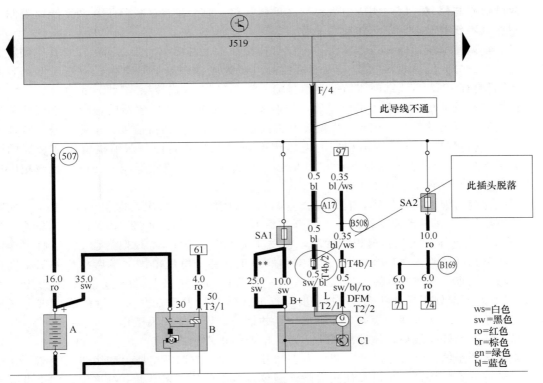

图 12-1 空调系统电路图（1）

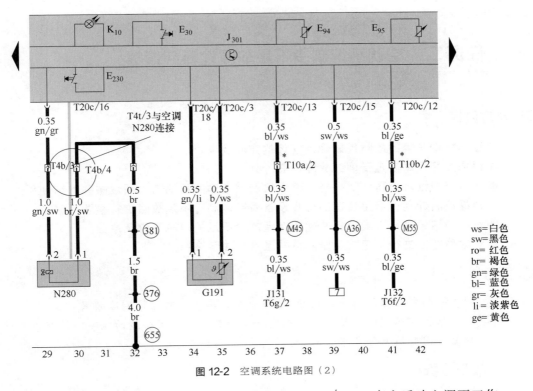

图 12-2 空调系统电路图（2）

故障描述：一辆大众宝来 1.6 汽车，行驶里程 9×10^4 km，车主反映空调不工作。

项目十二　汽车空调系统故障诊断与修复 | **133**

故障诊断与修复：用空调压力表检测高低压管路，完全正常。排除了空调系统内无制冷剂或制冷剂不足导致空调不工作的可能性。

拔下空调压缩机电磁离合器插头，用试灯连接插头上的两个插脚，测量在打开空调状态下的电压，无灯光闪烁现象（宝来压缩机控制电压为脉宽调制信号电压，不能用万用表测量），继而检查 J293 空调继电器压缩机信号输出端 T14/10（连接绿/黑线）无电。

根据宝来发动机空调系统工作原理，控制单元 J220 接收各传感器的信号（空调开关的信号、高低压开关的信号、F38 外部温度开关的信号、水温传感器信号、车速信号、特殊工况信号），进行分析处理后输出相应的电压传递到 J293，从而控制压缩机电磁离合器的吸合。测量 J293 空调继电器控制单元 J220 信号输入端 T14/3（连接绿线）无电。说明相应传感器信号不正常导致了空调不工作。

根据先简后繁的检修原则，首先检查空调开关的信号识别状况，即 J293 的 T14/8 插脚（连接蓝/红线），在发动机工作状态下打开空调开关，此时电压为 12V，关闭 AC 开关变为 0V。再检查高低压开关的信号识别状况，在发动机工作状态下，J293 的 T14/2 插脚（连接白线）所感知高压管内电压为 2.9V，属空调静态正常感知电压范围。最后检查外部温度开关的线路，检查 T14/14 插脚（连接绿/蓝线）和 T14/5（连接蓝/红线）间电阻为无穷大（正常在常温下应处于导通状态）。进一步检查 F38 线束，发现在开关附近的线束被老鼠咬断，造成断路，从而传递给控制单元空调切断的信号，导致空调不工作。

修复好外部开关线束，压缩机正常运转，空调能正常制冷。

故障诊断小结：此故障借助空调压力表和万用表进行空调系统压力和线路的检测，并通过原理进行故障分析，但是没有使用故障诊断仪。对于此款宝来空调系统来说，完全可以通过故障诊断仪读取故障码和数据流，然后再根据故障码的信息去检查相应故障，这样可以大大提高诊断效率。

任务二　空调系统制冷不足故障诊断与修复

学习目标

1. 能根据报修车辆的故障现象确定问诊的方向及项目。
2. 能根据故障现象制定正确的故障诊断计划。
3. 能熟练查阅维修资料，能根据故障现象选用合适的检测与诊断设备并熟练使用。
4. 能根据诊断计划，运用合适的检修设备对空调制冷不足故障进行检测。
5. 能对检测结果进行正确分析并确定空调制冷不足的故障部位及原因。
6. 能对故障部位进行快速准确修复，并且消除故障隐患。

任务导入

任务资料：一辆本田雅阁轿车，行驶 16 万千米，车主反映空调制冷效果差。

任务要求：根据该车辆的故障现象，查阅相关资料，并选用合适的检测与诊断设备进行故障诊断与修复，同时填写任务报告单。

一、故障分析

所谓制冷不足是指压缩机运转正常，但出风口冷气不足，制冷效果差。

制冷不足的故障原因有以下几种：
（1）电源、电压过低使压缩机电离合器吸力下降或电离合器压板与皮带盘间有油污。
（2）压缩机驱动带过松。
（3）制冷剂过多，这一般都是在维修时过量加注制冷剂而造成的。
（4）制冷剂过少，其原因大多是系统中的制冷剂微量泄漏。
（5）制冷剂与冷冻机油内含杂质过多、微堵。
（6）空调制冷系统中有水分渗入。
（7）系统中有空气。
（8）冷凝器散热能力下降。
（9）膨胀阀损坏。

二、故障诊断

1. 检查压缩机皮带是否过松

在发动机处于停机时，在皮带中间位置用手拨动皮带，如果能翻转大约90°，说明松紧适当；若转动过多，则说明皮带过松，应张紧。若收紧无效或皮带已有裂纹老化等损伤，应更换新皮带。

2. 检查制冷剂是否过多或过少

可以从储液干燥罐上方视液镜中观察。如果汽车空调在运转过程中从视液镜中看不到气泡，压缩机停转后也无气泡，说明制冷剂过多。

如制冷剂过多，可以在空调系统低压侧的维修口处缓慢地放出一些。在空调正常运转时，如视液镜中有连续不断的缓慢的气泡产生，则说明制冷剂不足。如出现明显的气泡翻转的情况，则表示制冷剂严重不足。制冷剂若不足，应添加制冷剂。如果加的冷却机油量过多，则在空调系统正常运转时，能从视液镜中看到较为混浊的气泡。

3. 检查制冷剂与冷冻机油内的杂质情况

可以从干燥罐上方视液镜中观察，空调系统正常运转时，能从视液镜中看到较为混浊的气泡，则说明系统内杂质过多，应更换制冷剂。

4. 检查制冷系统中是否有水渗入

当空调制冷效果变差，停机一会儿，制冷系统又会出现正常的状态，这说明系统中有水。同时为了更好地检测系统中水的多少，有些汽车上所使用的干燥剂，不含水时的颜色为蓝色，一旦水过多，干燥剂便成为红色。如制冷剂含水过多，应更换干燥剂或干燥罐，重新对系统抽真空，重新注入新的适量的制冷剂。

5. 检查冷凝器散热能力

首先检查装在汽车发动机前方的冷凝器表面是否有油污泥土或杂物，如有，应用软毛刷刷除冷凝器表面的脏物。然后检查冷却风扇是否正常工作，如驱动带过松、风扇转速下降等问题，这也会导致冷凝器散热能力下降。如风扇存在问题，应维修或更换电风扇故障。

6. 检查制冷系统的其他情况

检查制冷系统的堵塞、泄漏以及系统内有无空气。

三、任务实施

1. 询问车主

向车主了解出现故障的时间；出现故障前是否有其他异常情况；发现故障后症状是否有变化；车辆行驶的具体情况；车辆是否按时保养；故障发生后是否进行过其他维修。通过以

上的问诊了解故障发生前后的情况及故障的具体信息，完成制冷不足的初步诊断。

2. 试车与基本检查

进行试车，对故障进行确认。停车后检查空调管路是否有油迹，冷凝器表面是否过脏，散热风扇是否工作正常。

3. 检测与诊断

检查压缩机及离合器，工作正常。

发动机运转一段时间后保持怠速运转，接通空调开关，从储液罐观察窗可以见到有连续的气泡，摸低压管路不够冷且表面无水珠，空调出风口空气不冷，初步诊断是缺少制冷剂。

利用歧管压力表检测高、低压端显示的压力值均偏低，验证了缺少制冷剂的判断。缺少制冷剂，多数为制冷系统有泄漏。经检查，发现储液罐的接头部位有泄漏处。

4. 故障排除

更换垫圈，按规定力矩拧紧螺母。加注制冷剂直至高压表上的压力达到正常值，然后再进行气体泄漏检测，确认没有泄漏。发动机运转过程中，从视窗观察制冷剂无气泡，而且出风口空气是冷的，表明制冷剂量适当，制冷效果良好，故障排除。

5. 检验交车

故障检修完毕，装复试车，没有其他症状，向车主交车。

四、任务小结

该故障属于制冷系统泄漏导致制冷剂不足的常规故障，因此进行空调系统压力检测即可判断出故障原因为制冷剂泄漏。关键是要找到制冷剂泄漏的根本原因并予以解决，消除故障隐患。

五、任务报告单

专　业			班　级		姓　名	
任务名称					学　时	2
车　型				发动机型号		
任务完成过程	考核项目		考核内容		分　值	得　分
	1. 故障症状描述				5	
	2. 故障可能的原因及分析				25	
	3. 检测与诊断过程				35	
	4. 故障排除				10	
	5. 故障诊断小结				10	
教师评价	作业质量、作业效率、作业安全等				15	
	总评分数				100	

六、知识拓展

【典型案例一】 一辆大众捷达轿车空调制冷不良。

故障描述：一辆大众捷达 1.6L 轿车，空调制冷效果不良。

故障诊断与修复：首先观察空调管路接头，无明显油迹，说明无明显泄漏。压缩机运转时无异响。

然后用压力表测量空调系统压力，具体值如下。

测量工况。发动机转速：1500～2000r/min；环境温度：25～30℃。

测量实际压力。低压压力：0.33MPa；高压压力：1.1MPa。

正常系统低压压力：0.15～0.25MPa；正常系统高压压力：1.2～1.5MPa。

通过低压压力、高压压力和相应的正常系统压力对比可知，低压压力明显高于正常值。若出现低压压力高、高压压力低的情况，则故障部位通常在压缩机。

更换膨胀阀后，试车故障依旧。更换压缩机后试车故障排除。

故障诊断小结：通过检测空调系统压力确定了该故障的诊断方向，故障部位通常应在压缩机，膨胀阀故障概率相对较小。该故障排除时本应先更换压缩机而不是膨胀阀，检修走了弯路。

【典型案例二】 一辆上海大众朗逸汽车空调制冷量不足。

故障描述：一辆2011款上海大众朗逸汽车，装配1.6L CDE发动机，手动空调，行驶里程2.5万千米。车主反映开启空调制冷系统后，感觉制冷量不足。

故障诊断与修复：维修人员接修此车后，首先确认空调系统制冷量不足的现象是否存在。启动发动机，开启空调制冷功能，风速开至2挡，风向选择为中部出风，用温度计测量出风口温度，5min后温度计显示16.7℃，大大高于"出风口温度＜11℃"的标准值，明显存在故障。

该款车的空调系统由制冷系统、供暖系统、送风系统、电子控制系统组成。因为报修的是制冷问题，所以这里可以不考虑供暖系统。首先使用冷媒分析仪16900对管路中的冷媒进行纯度分析，分析结果合格；然后连接压力表，高低压的指数也都在正常的范围内；检查冷凝器，干净无脏污；目测低压管上有露水，用手触摸管路，感觉很凉。通过这些初步检查感觉制冷量方面没有问题，基本可以排除是制冷系统的问题。既然制冷系统压缩机能正常工作，证明空调的控制系统也没有问题，剩下的可疑部位只有送风系统了。于是拆下仪表台，对鼓风箱壳体进行检查。检查发现，箱体内冷热风门上的塑胶蒙皮已经严重脱落和褶皱，如图12-3所示。这使得冷热风门无法完全关闭，使一部分热空气同制冷后的空气混合，送出出风口，导致出风口温度不能达到正常范围。

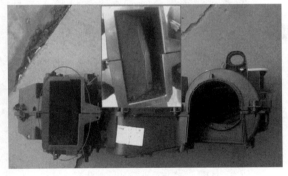

图12-3　褶皱的冷热调节风门

虽然发现冷热风门存在明显的问题，但因没有单独的风门配件，故更换了整个鼓风箱总成。更换完毕后，运转发动机，开启空调，风速开至2挡，风向选择为中间出风口，测量出风口温度，5min后温度计显示12.2℃，温度对比之前有所下降，但仍高于正常范围。通过手感空调低压管的温度也很低，说明制冷是没问题的，那造成出风口温度低不下来的原因还会是什么呢？除了冷热风门关闭不严外，还有其他因素在影响出风口的温度。

如果蒸发器对空气降温不足，也会造成通过蒸发器的空气不能被充分制冷，这样从出风口送出的空气温度也会变高，蒸发器的工作方式如图12-4所示，热空气通过蒸发器后即被降温成冷空气。于是拆下鼓风机，用手触摸鼓风箱内的蒸发器外壳，发现其外壳温度明显高于空调低压管的温度，只是微微凉，不像低压管那样冰手，明显不正常。由此判断蒸发器内部堵塞，造成热交换不良。再次拆下鼓风箱，更换蒸发器

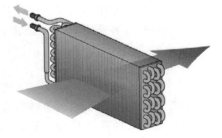

图12-4　蒸发器工作示意图

后装复试车。经过测试，出风口温度降低到4℃，符合出风口温度的标准，空调制冷量不足故障排除。

故障诊断小结：该故障为综合性故障，根本原因是蒸发器内部堵塞，造成通过蒸发器的空气不能被充分冷却，同时送风系统的冷热风门也存在关闭不严，造成本来就温度偏高的空气再与热空气混合后送出，最终导致出风口送风温度过高。对于空调系统的故障，在诊断时最好根据空调系统的组成，按照制冷系统、供暖系统、送风系统、电子控制系统的顺序，进行分系统诊断，这样可以大大地简化诊断流程和提高诊断效率。

任务三 空调易结冰故障诊断与修复

学习目标

1. 能根据报修车辆的故障现象确定问诊的方向及项目。
2. 能根据故障现象制定正确的故障诊断计划。
3. 能熟练查阅维修资料，能根据故障现象选用合适的检测与诊断设备并熟练使用。
4. 能根据诊断计划，运用合适的检修设备对空调易结冰故障进行检测。
5. 能对检测结果进行正确分析并确定空调易结冰的故障部位及原因。
6. 能对故障部位进行快速准确修复，并且消除故障隐患。

任务导入

任务资料：一辆迈腾1.8TSI汽车，行驶里程6.5万千米，该车空调处于制冷状态，并在高速行驶约30分钟后，空调出风口无风吹出，制冷功能失效。

任务要求：根据该车辆的故障现象，查阅相关资料，并选用合适的检测与诊断设备进行故障诊断与修复，同时填写任务报告单。

一、故障分析

该故障表现为在打开空调一段时间后，空调制冷效果明显下降，同时蒸发器的进、出管上结霜，将霜除去后制冷效果恢复。

造成此故障的原因有以下几种：

（1）蒸发器表面温度传感器或温度开关工作不良。
（2）制冷剂的加注量不正确。
（3）系统的管路堵塞。
（4）系统中有水分。
（5）膨胀阀工作不正常。
（6）压缩机本身调节功能失效。

二、故障诊断

（1）检查制冷剂加注量。从干燥罐上方视液镜中观察，如果汽车空调在运转过程中从视液镜中看不到气泡，压缩机停转后也无气泡，说明制冷剂过多。

（2）利用故障诊断仪读取故障码，若有故障码，按故障码去排除故障。读取蒸发器表面温度传感器的数据流是否正常，以及温度开关的开闭是否正常。

（3）利用空调压力表检测高低压管路的压力，将检测的压力值与正常值进行对比来判断故障的部位。

（4）可以将空调系统中的制冷剂回收，按规定数量重新加注制冷剂，以消除系统中的水分。

三、任务实施

1. 询问车主

向车主了解出现故障的时间；出现故障前是否有其他异常情况；发现故障后症状是否有变化；车辆行驶的具体情况；车辆是否按时保养；故障发生后是否进行过其他维修。通过以上的问诊了解故障发生前后的情况及故障的具体信息，完成空调易结霜的初步诊断。

2. 试车与基本检查

进行试车，对故障进行确认。停车后检查空调管路，发现空调低压管出现结冰现象。

3. 检测与诊断

利用故障诊断仪 VAS5052A 读取故障码，无故障码显示，进入 08-08 读取空调系统数据流，发现第 6 组数据流显示异常。

正常车辆第 6 组数据——第 1 区：蒸发器后的温度显示为 1～2℃。

故障车辆第 6 组数据——第 1 区：蒸发器后的温度显示为 5～10℃。

蒸发器后的温度是由蒸发器后出风温度传感器检测的。

由于该传感器数据会随空调工作状态的改变而动态变化，因此无故障码。结合数据流的异常显示，可基本判定应为蒸发器后出风温度传感器异常。

于是拆下位于副驾驶蒸发器处的传感器检查，发现该传感器装错，误将速腾手动空调的蒸发器后出风温度传感器，装在迈腾自动空调上。迈腾自动空调装备的蒸发器后出风温度传感器比速腾的传感器长度长。

由于速腾手动空调的蒸发器后出风温度传感器比迈腾自动空调的传感器长度短，因此感知不到蒸发器的实际温度，当蒸发器出口温度已接近 1～2℃时，反映的温度是 5～10℃，空调电控系统根据该信号控制压缩机以较大排量工作，导致蒸发器结冰。当蒸发器结冰后，空调无冷风吹出，蒸发器后出风温度传感器反映的温度继续上升，空调控制系统将据此信号以更大的排量工作，从而使空调蒸发器加速结冰，冷风无法吹出，进而使空调低压管结霜。

4. 故障排除

更换蒸发器后出风温度传感器，故障排除。

5. 检验交车

故障检修完毕，装复试车，没有其他症状，向车主交车。

四、任务小结

该案例故障分析主要是从数据流中寻找故障原因。第 6 组第 1 区的蒸发器出口温度传感器的数据比正常值高，该故障源于蒸发器出口温度传感器装配错误。此类故障诊断不但需要诊断知识，还需要对汽车配件比较熟悉。

五、任务报告单

专　业		班　级		姓　名	
任务名称				学　时	2
车　型			发动机型号		

续表

考核项目		考核内容	分 值	得 分
任务完成过程	1. 故障症状描述		5	
	2. 故障可能的原因及分析		25	
	3. 检测与诊断过程		35	
	4. 故障排除		10	
	5. 故障诊断小结		10	
教师评价	作业质量、作业效率、作业安全等		15	
总评分数			100	

六、知识拓展

【典型案例】 一辆2004款奥迪A6 2.4L汽车空调蒸发器结冰。

故障描述：一辆奥迪A6 2.4L汽车，车主反映，在长途行驶后，空调制冷不良，出风口风量减小，停车一会儿或将空调关一会儿后重开空调，空调又恢复正常，在驾驶员侧地板上面有大量的空调水。

故障诊断与修复：根据车主的描述，初步判断是由于空调系统蒸发器结冰造成的故障现象。首先检查空调系统的压力，开空调时检查高低压端的压力正常，高压1600kPa，低压280kPa。系统的压力正常。

用VAS5052检查空调控制单元，未检测到故障码，用数据块检查空调控制单元各个出风口传感器的值也正常。

奥迪A6车采用的是变排量式压缩机，初步判断有可能是车辆在长途行驶中压缩机的调节功能失效，一直处在大负荷的制冷状态造成空调系统的蒸发器结冰。造成蒸发器结冰的可能原因有：压缩机本身调节功能失效；制冷剂的加注量不正确；系统中有水分；系统的管路堵塞。系统的压力虽然在工作时正常，但是压力值正常并不能代表空调系统制冷剂的加注量正常，在回收该车空调系统的制冷剂时，发现该车空调系统的制冷剂量是510g，正常值应该是（650±50）g。抽真空并进行系统检漏后，重新加注650g制冷剂，试车，蒸发器结冰的故障排除。

故障诊断小结：维修人员在进行车辆故障判断时一定要确认车辆的故障现象和故障表征，应该通过实际的检测作出判断，而不能通过猜测去诊断。通过此故障我们知道空调系统制冷剂的加注量一定要按照车辆给出的原厂数据进行加注，不能过多或过少。另外，维修人员一定要详细地了解系统的工作原理，并根据工作情况分析故障产生的原因，才能快速准确地判断故障并找到引起故障的原因。

项目十三

车身电器故障诊断与修复

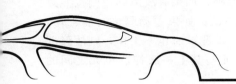

任务一 中控门锁故障诊断与修复

📚 学习目标

1. 能根据报修车辆的故障现象确定问诊的方向及项目。
2. 能根据故障现象制定正确的故障诊断计划。
3. 能熟练查阅维修资料,能根据故障现象选用合适的检测与诊断设备并熟练使用。
4. 能根据诊断计划,运用合适的检修设备对中控门锁故障进行检测。
5. 能对检测结果进行正确分析并确定中控门锁故障的部位及原因。
6. 能对故障部位进行快速准确修复,并且消除故障隐患。
7. 能具有严谨细致的工作态度,提高安全与服务意识。

任务导入

任务资料:一辆 2010 款捷达汽车,行驶里程 13 万千米,车主反映四门玻璃升降器不能升降,在外面多次维修,更换过升降器保险,当时好用但是过一段时间故障又出现了。

任务要求:根据该车辆的故障现象,查阅相关资料,并选用合适的检测与诊断设备进行故障诊断与修复,同时填写任务报告单。

一、故障分析

中控门锁的工作方式主要分为两大类,一类是开关或模块直接控制;另一类是由车载网路传输信号和电控单元控制。第一类故障诊断相对比较简单,不涉及车载网路,工作的电路只是普通导线。在此只分析车载网路传输信号并由电控单元控制的中控门锁。这种控制方式涉及多个电控单元,工作的电路既有普通导线,又有 CAN 或 Lin 总线,工作原理比较复杂。

中控门锁不工作的主要原因包括以下几种:
(1)锁控制开关故障。

(2) 控制单元及其线路故障。
(3) 锁电机及其线路故障。
(4) 锁 CAN 或 Lin 信号线路故障。
(5) 网控制单元故障。
(6) 锁机械故障。

二、故障诊断

(1) 车门中控门锁不工作，应该先用故障诊断仪读取故障码，如果有故障码，则按照故障码去查找故障部位。此外还可以使用故障诊断仪进行主动测试，如果主动测试时能工作，则故障部位在开关和开关到其控制单元的线路及插头。如果主动测试时也不工作，则故障部位很可能在：中控门锁控制单元及其电源搭铁电路；控制单元与其上一级控制单元之间的 CAN 或 Lin 信号线路；中控门锁；中控门锁机械部分。

(2) 中控门锁都不工作，应该先用故障诊断仪读取故障码，如果有故障码，则按照故障码去查找故障部位。此外，应检测所有中控门锁控制单元的上一级主控单元及其 CAN 或 Lin 信号线路。

三、任务实施

1. 询问车主

向车主了解出现故障的时间；出现故障前是否有其他异常情况；发现故障后症状是否有变化；车辆行驶的具体情况；车辆是否按时保养；故障发生后是否进行过其他维修。通过以上的问诊了解故障发生前后的情况及故障的具体信息，完成中控锁故障的初步诊断。

2. 试车与基本检查

进行门锁功能测试，了解故障特征，对故障进行确认。此外要确定该车中控门锁的结构特征和线路连接方式。

3. 检测与诊断

测量保险丝（S111）有没有电源，在测量时发现该保险丝非常热。部分捷达车玻璃升降器保险丝是热保护的，如果出现用电量过大或者正极对地短路等情况时，保险会自动断开。

由此可以判断保险丝之后的电器有异常。查看玻璃升降器的电路图可知，该保险为 4 个车门的电机供电，因此进一步检测保险后面的电路。

检测的方法有以下几种：

(1) 拆开四门里板断开电机插头看看保险还热不热。
(2) 找到四门正极连接点逐一断开。
(3) 使用电流感应钳感应四门放电量。

这里选择了第二种方法，逐一断开 4 个门的供电线。

观察发现当断开右前门时放电量消失保险不再过热，由此可以判断故障点就在右前门线束或者电机内部。拆开右前门里板检查电机及线束，发现右前门折合部位，线束被磨损，正极线外露接地，故障点如图 13-1 所示。

图 13-1 破损的线束

4. 故障排除

重新包扎线束，试车故障排除。

5. 检验交车

故障检修完毕，装复试车，没有其他症状，向车主交车。

四、任务小结

通过该故障案例我们认识到，在维修故障时可以列出几个可行的方案并找到一个比较简便的方法进行排查，这样能使我们更快更准地找到故障点。

五、任务报告单

专　业			班　级		姓　名	
任务名称					学　时	2
车　型				发动机型号		
	考核项目	考核内容		分　值	得　分	
任务完成过程	1. 故障症状描述			5		
	2. 故障可能的原因及分析			25		
	3. 检测与诊断过程			35		
	4. 故障排除			10		
	5. 故障诊断小结			10		
教师评价	作业质量、作业效率、作业安全等			15		
	总评分数			100		

六、知识拓展

【典型案例一】 一辆雪佛兰赛欧汽车仅能打开左前车门。

故障描述：一辆雪佛兰赛欧汽车，手动挡轿车，行驶6.2万千米，车主反映中控锁系统失效，无论从车内还是车外仅能打开左前车门。

故障诊断与修复：该车具有防盗锁死功能，即处于电子防盗锁定状态时，除非用钥匙在左前门打开车锁外，其他方法都打不开车锁。

根据故障现象，怀疑可能的原因有线路问题、中控模块故障和S41开关故障等。检测时遵循由简单到复杂，由外围到内部的原则，先对线路进行检测，然后检测中控模块，最后检测S41开关。

首先用钥匙对行李箱进行开锁和上锁的操作，结果行李箱锁工作状态正常。打开左前车门进入车厢内，拆卸中控模块。根据中央控制门锁系统的电路图，用试灯一端接12V电源，另一端测量中控模块的7端子。当钥匙转动左前门锁芯于开锁位置时试灯能够亮，转回时试灯又熄灭了，更换另一侧右前重复以上的测试，结果一样，说明有开锁信号向中控门锁模块传送。再用试灯测量中控模块的8端子，试灯一端接地，另一端接8端子，结果试灯不亮，说明中控模块并没有正确的开锁信号输入。可能原因有两种：一是中控模块内部失效，更换中控模块之后故障依然存在，故排除中控模块故障；二是中控系统进入了防盗模式，不对任何输入信号作反应。左前门锁的防盗仅依靠机械防盗并没有电子锁定防盗，所以该侧的车锁仍可以自由开锁和锁定。使中控门锁进入防盗设定并且保持这种状态的方法是开关S41中1和2端子接通，因此很有可能是S41开关故障。拆卸左前门外拉手连锁芯总成上的S41开关的连接插头，然后用钥匙开锁，车门都打开了，中控系统恢复正常。当重新插回插头

后，中控系统又重现了先前的故障。

将防盗死锁开关拆卸下来，测量后发现开关的 1 和 2 端子粘接在一起，导致了中控模块长期处于防盗死锁状态，即便接收到开锁的信号也由于执行了内部程序而将信号忽略，所以锁定了其余 3 个车门。更换防盗死锁开关，故障彻底解决。

故障诊断小结：本故障原因在主驾驶的防盗死锁开关上，这主要缘于赛欧轿车门锁具备死锁功能的特殊性。在汽车维修中，一定要仔细分析系统电路及内在的控制特点，这样才能够有的放矢地找出故障原因，准确排除故障。

【典型案例二】 一辆 2010 款高尔夫 6 汽车中控锁锁止指示灯不亮。

故障描述：一辆 2010 款高尔夫 6 汽车，该车是事故车辆，在维修后的检验交车时，发现中控锁锁止指示灯不亮，同时在锁止过程中，锁块部位发出 2~3 声动作的声音。

故障诊断与修复：利用大众专用故障诊断仪进行故障诊断，出现两个故障码，分别是中控锁锁止单元驾驶员侧—F220 不可靠信号和驾驶员侧中控锁保险/锁止信号不可靠信号，如图 13-2 所示。

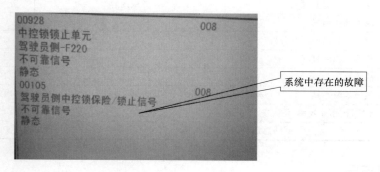

图 13-2　读取故障码

由于该车是事故维修车辆，而且还更换了左前门及所有附属部件，初步诊断事故中可能损伤到其他线路，造成该故障的存在（因为该中控门锁的部件都是新的）。按照如图 13-3 所示的电路图对相应的电路进行检查，没有发现线路有短路、断路的情况。因此将问题锁定在

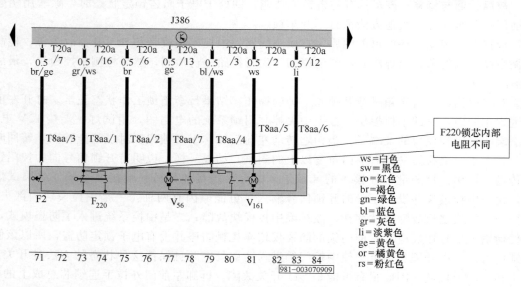

图 13-3　高尔夫 6 中控门锁系统电路图

所更换的备件上。无意中，拔掉锁块的插头，按压锁止按键，指示灯点亮。怀疑是锁块的线束出现问题，对锁块的线路进行了重新检查，发现将锁块的搭铁线断开后，按压锁车键，指示灯点亮。因为车上安装的锁块已经是新的，查询该车的备件，查到了两种锁块，其中一种零件号为 L5K1 837 015C，另一种为不带尾号 C，带尾号的是高尔夫、新速腾所用的，不带尾号的是高尔夫的车型使用。因为是事故车，原车安装的零件号已经无法确认了，该车的线路也检查完好，同时电脑故障指示锁块存在问题，更换了尾号为 C 的锁块，故障变成偶发，确定故障点应该是内部锁块型号不正确，于是更换锁块，故障彻底排除。

故障诊断小结：不同备件，内部结构不同，虽然可以安装使用，但可能带来一些功能的受限。更换备件，特别是通用备件，内部结构很可能存在差异，备件 L5K1 837 015 是高尔夫车型安装的锁块，但是该车安装的是带有尾号 C 的备件，两种锁块内部电阻不同，导致指示灯不亮，功能受限。

任务二　电动玻璃升降器故障诊断与修复

学习目标

1. 能根据报修车辆的故障现象确定问诊的方向及项目。
2. 能根据故障现象制定正确的故障诊断计划。
3. 能熟练查阅维修资料，能根据故障现象选用合适的检测与诊断设备并熟练使用。
4. 能根据诊断计划，运用合适的检修设备对电动玻璃升降器故障进行检测。
5. 能对检测结果进行正确分析并确定电动玻璃升降器故障的部位及原因。
6. 能对故障部位进行快速准确修复，并且消除故障隐患。

任务导入

任务资料：一辆 2010 款捷达汽车，行驶里程 7 万千米，车主反映锁车后四门升降器没有自动升窗功能。

任务要求：根据该车辆的故障现象，查阅相关资料，并选用合适的检测与诊断设备进行故障诊断与修复，同时填写任务报告单。

一、故障分析

电动玻璃升降器的工作方式主要分为两大类，一类是开关或模块直接控制；另一类是由车载网路传输信号和电控单元控制。第一类故障诊断相对比较简单，不涉及车载网络线路，工作的电路只是普通导线。在此只分析车载网路传输信号并由电控单元控制的电动玻璃升降器。这种控制方式涉及多个电控单元，工作的电路既有普通导线，又有 CAN 或 Lin 总线，工作原理比较复杂。

电动玻璃升降器不工作的主要原因包括以下几种：

(1) 电动玻璃升降器控制开关故障。
(2) 电动玻璃升降器控制单元及其线路故障。
(3) 电动玻璃升降器电机及其线路故障。
(4) 电动玻璃升降器 CAN 或 Lin 信号线路故障。

(5) 车载电网控制单元故障。
(6) 电动玻璃升降器机械故障。

二、故障诊断

（1）若个别车门电动玻璃升降器不工作，应该先用故障诊断仪读取故障码，如果有故障码，则按照故障码去查找故障部位。此外还可以使用故障诊断仪进行主动测试，如果主动测试时能工作，则故障部位在开关和开关到其控制单元的线路及插头；如果主动测试时也不工作，则故障部位很可能在：电动玻璃升降器控制单元及其电源搭铁电路；控制单元与其上一级控制单元之间的 CAN 或 Lin 信号线路；电动玻璃升降器电机；电动玻璃升降器机械部分。

（2）若所有车门电动玻璃升降器都不工作，应该先用故障诊断仪读取故障码，如果有故障码，则按照故障码去查找故障部位。此外应去检测所有电动玻璃升降器控制单元的上一级主控单元及其 CAN 或 Lin 信号线路。

三、任务实施

1. 询问车主

向车主了解出现故障的时间；出现故障前是否有其他异常情况；发现故障后症状是否有变化；车辆行驶的具体情况；车辆是否按时保养；故障发生后是否进行过其他维修。通过以上的问诊了解故障发生前后的情况及故障的具体信息，完成电动玻璃升降器故障的初步诊断。

2. 试车与基本检查

进行电动玻璃升降器功能测试，了解故障特征，对故障进行确认，此外确定该车电动玻璃升降器的控制方式和线路连接方式。

3. 检测与诊断

检查四门升降器，单独控制均正常，中控锁也正常工作，但左前主控开关不能控制右后门，右后门开关可以单独控制。由于此车为 2005 年 2 月 22 日以后生产的车型，具有锁车升窗功能。该车具有 Lin 总线通信功能和具备 K 线诊断功能，于是用 5051 进入地址 46-舒适系统，进行故障查询，故障为 V27 右后门玻璃升降电机故障。根据上述情况分析，故障点有可能是线束有短路现象或控制单元损坏。

根据电路图（如图 13-4）测量线束，发现 T23/3 脚到 T69-2Lin 线断路。经查找，发现在驾驶员座椅下的 Lin 线老化磨断。修复后右后升降器工作正常，但锁车时还是不升窗。

于是分析控制单元有故障。

4. 故障排除

更换控制单元后，试车，故障排除。

5. 检验交车

故障检修完毕，装复试车，没有其他症状，向车主交车。

四、任务小结

该故障共有两个故障点，由于线路故障最终导致电控单元也损坏。在故障排除时应了解系统的工作方式，同时要借助电路进行故障分析。需要注意 2005 年 2 月 22 日以后生产的捷达车都有锁车升窗功能，另外需要注意电脑外观零件号。

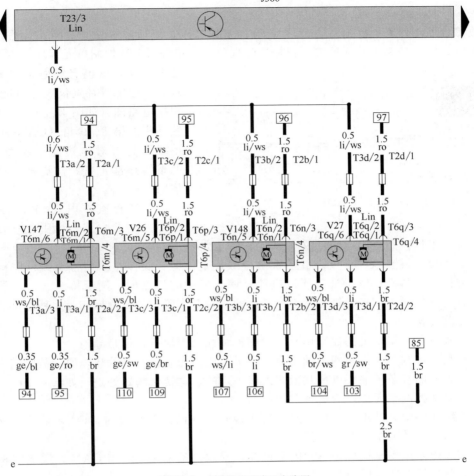

图 13-4 电动玻璃升降器电路图

五、任务报告单

专 业			班 级		姓 名	
任务名称					学 时	2
车 型			发动机型号			
	考核项目		考核内容		分 值	得 分
任务完成过程	1. 故障症状描述				5	
	2. 故障可能的原因及分析				25	
	3. 检测与诊断过程				35	
	4. 故障排除				10	
	5. 故障诊断小结				10	
教师评价	作业质量、作业效率、作业安全等				15	
	总评分数				100	

六、知识拓展

【典型案例一】 一辆大众宝来汽车四门玻璃升降器无法正常升降。

故障描述：一辆大众宝来汽车，行驶 6.2 万千米，车主反映四门玻璃升降器无法正常升

项目十三 车身电器故障诊断与修复 | 147

降，门灯时亮时不亮，按几次中控锁门灯就亮，而且不亮时防盗灯闪。行驶中中控锁自己跳来跳去。

故障诊断与修复：首先用5051检测有如下故障码：舒适系统总线故障；舒适系统单线模式运行；四门控制单元无反应。根据故障现象，怀疑舒适系统控制单元损坏，更换后故障依旧。仪表里也有舒适系统单线模式运行的故障，怀疑仪表也可能有问题。根据电路图（如图13-5），检测仪表右侧插头的第8、9角（CAN-H、CAN-L线）是否对地短路，检查后发现，两条线路都正常。试更换仪表，故障依旧。

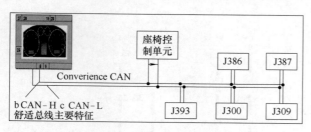

图13-5 舒适系统CAN总线电路图

继续检查，用5051示波器检测CAN-H、CAN-L两根线的波形，发现有一根不工作。用万用表测量仪表检测左前门线束，连接正常。

这时发现一根表笔放在仪表舒适系统橙绿线上，另一头接左前门橙绿线、橙棕线都导通，而橙棕线不与橙绿线导通。所以应该是两根线中有短路的。测量橙绿线、橙棕线两根线，两者之间导通，调换表笔却又不导通。此时可基本确定故障原因，是总线之间相当于用二极管短路连接了。

逐个拔下各个车门上的控制单元，检测橙绿线与橙棕线，还是导通。

此车是有控制单元控制的电动座椅，当拔下座椅控制单元删除故障码后故障消失。

控制单元的各条传输线以星状形式汇聚一点的，这样做的好处是，如果一个控制单元发生故障，其他控制单元仍可发送各自的数据。

该系统线路中某处出现对地短路、对正极短路或断路等情况时，CAN系统会立即转为应急模式运行或转为单针模式运行。

此车故障是由于座椅控制单元内部损坏，导致舒适CAN-H与CAN-L线之间相当于用二极管短路连接，造成橙绿与橙棕导通，反之不通。故障使得舒适系统CAN总线单线模式运行。

更换座椅控制单元后，进行四门玻璃升降器功能测试，恢复正常。

故障诊断小结：此案例中，由于车载网络系统中的座椅控制单元出现内部故障，导致网络传输线路故障，最终使四门玻璃升降器出现故障。这类故障是目前使用车载网络控制的车辆中常见的典型故障，也就是说某系统功能失常时，不仅要考虑所在系统部件及线路故障，还要考虑网络系统故障。

【典型案例二】 一辆2010款大众速腾汽车左前门玻璃升降器无法升降。

故障描述：一辆2010款大众速腾汽车，行驶5.8万千米，车主反映左前门玻璃升降器无法升降，其余玻璃升降器功能正常。

故障诊断与修复：

（1）用VAS5052A读取故障码，如图13-6所示。检查发现有两个故障记忆。

① 00932 驾驶员侧车窗升降机马达-V147电路电气故障（静态）。

② 00120 驾驶员侧车外警告灯/车门出口灯电路电气故障（静态）。

（2）查阅电路图，对线路进行如下检查。

① 检查执行元件电源-保险丝SC12，电压12V，正常。

② 测量左前门控制单元J386插接端子T20a/12无电压。

③ 断开左前门连接插头 T28，检查端子 T28/1 电压为 12V，判定车门内部线路出现断路。剥开线束检测发现线束断路，如图 13-7 所示。修复线束，故障排除。

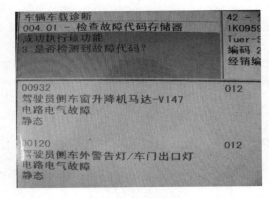

图 13-6　读取故障码

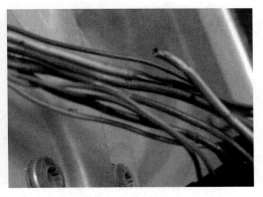

图 13-7　损坏的线束

故障诊断小结：故障码分析只是诊断汽车电子控制系统故障的第一步，重要的是能够判定故障码产生的原因。对于此类故障应该按照电路图检查执行元件的电路，即检查执行器的电源电路与接地电路，然后检查相关联的电气系统。

任务三　汽车照明系统故障诊断与修复

学习目标

1. 能根据报修车辆的故障现象确定问诊的方向及项目。
2. 能根据故障现象制定正确的故障诊断计划。
3. 能熟练查阅维修资料，能根据故障现象选用合适的检测与诊断设备并熟练使用。
4. 能根据诊断计划，运用合适的检修设备对汽车照明系统故障进行检测。
5. 能对检测结果进行正确分析并确定汽车照明系统的故障部位及原因。
6. 能对故障部位进行快速准确修复，并且消除故障隐患。

任务导入

任务资料：一辆 2012 款北京现代悦动汽车，行驶里程 7 万千米，客户反映两侧大灯灯光亮度不一致，右前亮度正常，左前亮度不够。

任务要求：根据该车辆的故障现象，查阅相关资料，并选用合适的检测与诊断设备进行故障诊断与修复，同时填写任务报告单。

一、故障分析

汽车照明系统的工作方式主要分为两大类：一类是开关直接控制；另一类是电控单元控制。

1. 开关直接控制的汽车照明系统故障分析

开关直接控制的汽车照明系统，在开关闭合后，所有灯的供电电路接通，所有灯应点亮。

(1) 照明系统开关接通后所控制的灯全部不亮
① 开关故障；
② 保险故障；
③ 继电器故障（多数车型前照灯、雾灯控制电路有继电器）；
④ 供电线路故障。
(2) 照明系统开关接通后所控制的灯部分不亮
① 灯泡故障；
② 灯插头端子或其供电线路故障；
③ 灯搭铁线路故障。

开关直接控制的照明系统故障诊断相对比较简单，不涉及车载网络及电子控制单元，工作的电路只是普通导线。

2. 电控单元控制的照明系统故障分析

电控单元控制的照明系统中电控单元接收灯光开关的闭合信号，然后电控单元分别向各个灯泡供电，灯的搭铁线路直接搭铁，所有灯点亮。

(1) 电控单元控制的照明系统开关接通后所控制的灯全部不亮
① 开关故障；
② 开关所在的信号线路故障；
③ 电控单元局部故障；
④ 汽车网络线路故障（有些灯开关信号需要通过网络传输）。
(2) 电控单元控制的照明系统开关接通后所控制的部分灯不亮
① 灯泡故障；
② 灯插头端子或其供电线路故障；
③ 灯搭铁线路故障；
④ 电控单元局部故障。

二、故障诊断

1. 开关直接控制的汽车照明系统故障诊断

(1) 照明系统开关接通后所控制的灯全部不亮
① 首先检测保险是否熔断，如果熔断则更换新件保险，如果保险正常则进行下一步检测。
② 检测灯光控制继电器（部分灯光控制没有继电器），继电器损坏则更换新继电器，如果继电器正常则进行下一步检测。
③ 检测灯光开关接通是否正常，如果开关不能正常接通则更换新开关，如果开关正常则进行下一步检测。
④ 检测供电线路是否存在断路或虚接，如果线路故障则修复线路或者更换线束。
(2) 照明系统开关接通后所控制的部分灯不亮
① 检查灯插头连接是否正常，如果接触不良则进行修复，如果正常则进行下一步检测。
② 检查灯泡是否损坏，如果损坏则更换新灯泡，如果灯泡正常则进行下一步检测。
③ 检测灯的供电线路是否存在断路、短路或虚接，如果线路故障则修复线路或者更换线束。
④ 检测灯的搭铁线路是否存在断路或虚接，如果线路故障则修复线路或者更换线束。

2. 电控单元控制的照明系统故障诊断

电控单元控制的照明系统开关接通后所控制的灯全部不亮：

① 首先用故障诊断仪读取故障码，如果有故障码（有些车的电控单元能对所有灯及其线路进行监测，有故障就会生成故障码），则按照故障码去查找故障部位。

② 用故障诊断仪读取开关状态的数据流，若开关接通和断开时诊断仪不能正常显示出相应的数据流，则进一步检查灯光开关及其信号线路，甚至检查车载网路线路等。若开关接通和断开时诊断仪能正常显示出相应的数据流，则说明开关及信号线路正常。

③ 用故障诊断仪进行执行元件测试，如果在测试时灯仍不亮，则检测灯及供电、搭铁线路是否有故障，有故障则进行排除，若这些都没有故障，则故障部位在控制单元内部；如果在测试时灯正常亮，则说明故障也在控制单元内部。

三、任务实施

1. 询问车主

向车主了解出现故障的时间；出现故障前是否有其他异常情况；发现故障后症状是否有变化；车辆行驶的具体情况；车辆是否按时保养；故障发生后是否进行过其他维修。通过以上的问诊了解故障发生前后的情况及故障的具体信息，完成汽车照明系统故障的初步诊断。

2. 试车与基本检查

进行汽车故障测试，了解故障特征，对故障进行确认，此外确定该车照明系统的结构特征及线路连接方式。

3. 检测与诊断

检查左前大灯远近光连接插头，插头连接正常，检查左侧近光灯保险片，保险片插接良好，没发现虚接现象。由于左右远光灯共用一个保险，而右侧大灯工作正常，因此大灯远光保险应正常。拔下左侧远近光灯插头，检测3号端子，电压为12V，电压正常，检查远近光灯泡，灯泡正常，将插头插好，再次测量3号、4号端子之间的电压为8V，正常应为12V，断开插头检测搭铁端子4与车身之间的电阻为2Ω，正常电阻应该接近零，由此判断左侧大灯线路的搭铁应该有问题。查找电路图（如图13-8），找到搭铁点GE11位置，查看搭铁点固定螺栓，发现此螺栓紧固正常，但是螺栓表面锈蚀严重，拆卸搭铁点，取下螺栓后发现螺栓四周锈蚀严重。

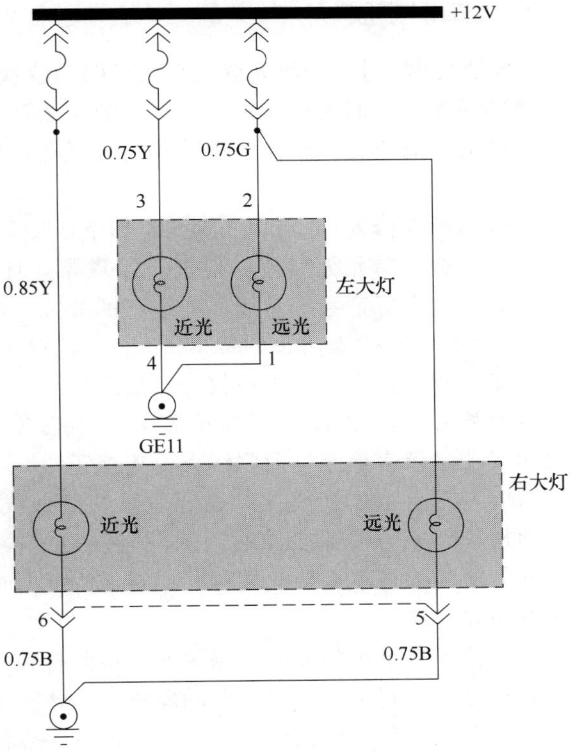

4. 故障排除

对搭铁点、搭铁螺栓和搭铁线接线端子进行除锈处理，重新固定搭铁线后故障排除。

5. 检验交车

故障检修完毕，装复试车，没有其他症状，向车主交车。

图 13-8　前大灯电路图

四、任务小结

搭铁螺栓螺纹处锈蚀严重造成搭铁不良，导致线路接地电阻过大，电路电流减小，从而出现灯泡亮度不够现象，检测灯泡两端电压比正常电压低。此类故障在确定故障现象后应首先查看电路图，了解左右两侧大灯的线路特点，然后进行综合分析，这样就可以有目的性地去重点部位进行检测，提高检修的效率。

五、任务报告单

专业		班级		姓名	
任务名称				学时	2
车型			发动机型号		
	考核项目	考核内容		分值	得分
任务完成过程	1. 故障症状描述			5	
	2. 故障可能的原因及分析			25	
	3. 检测与诊断过程			35	
	4. 故障排除			10	
	5. 故障诊断小结			10	
教师评价	作业质量、作业效率、作业安全等			15	
	总评分数			100	

六、知识拓展

【典型案例一】 一辆大众宝来汽车四门玻璃升降器无法正常升降。

故障描述：一辆大众宝来汽车，行驶 6.2 万千米，车主反映四门玻璃升降器无法正常升降，门灯时亮时不亮，按几次中控锁门灯就亮，而且不亮时防盗灯闪。行驶中中控锁自己跳来跳去。

故障诊断与修复：用 5051 检测有如下故障码：舒适系统总线故障；舒适系统单线模式运行；四门控制单元无反应。根据故障现象，怀疑舒适系统控制单元损坏，更换后故障依旧。仪表里也有舒适系统单线模式运行的故障，怀疑仪表也可能有问题。根据电路图（如图 13-9），检测仪表右侧插头的第 8、9 脚（CAN-H、CAN-L 线）是否对地短路，检查后发现，两条线路都正常。试更换仪表，故障依旧。

继续检查，用 5051 示波器检测 CAN-H、CAN-L 两根线的波形，发现有一根不工作。用万用表测量仪表检测左前门线束，连接正常。

这时发现一根表笔放在仪表舒适系统橙绿线上，另一头接左前门橙绿线、橙棕线都导通，而橙棕线不与橙绿线导通。所以应该是两根线中有短路的。测量橙绿线、橙棕线两根线，两者之间导通，调换表笔却又不导通。此时可基本确定故障原因，是总线之间相当于用二极管短路连接了。

逐个拔下各个车门上的控制单元，检测橙绿线与橙棕线，还是导通。

此车是有控制单元控制的电动座椅，当拔下座椅控制单元删除故障码后故障消失。

控制单元的各条传输线以星状形式汇聚一点的，这样做的好处是，如果一个控制单元发生故障，其他控制单元仍可发送各自的数据。

该系统线路中某处出现对地短路、对正极短路或断路等情况时，CAN 系统会立即转为应急模式运行或转为单针模式运行。

此车故障是由于座椅控制单元内部损坏，导致舒适 CAN-H 与 CAN-L 线之间相当于用

二极管短路连接,造成橙绿与橙棕导通,反之不通。故障使得舒适系统 CAN 总线单线模式运行。

更换座椅控制单元后,进行四门玻璃升降器功能测试,恢复正常。

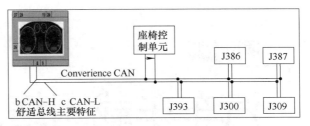

图 13-9 舒适系统 CAN 总线电路图

故障诊断小结:此案例中,由于车载网络系统中的座椅控制单元出现内部故障,导致网络传输线路故障,最终使四门玻璃升降器出现故障。这类故障是目前使用车载网络控制的车辆中常见的典型故障,也就是说某系统功能失常时,不仅要考虑所在系统部件及线路故障,还要考虑网络系统故障。

【典型案例二】 一辆 **2010 款大众速腾汽车左前门玻璃升降器无法升降**。

故障描述:一辆 2010 款大众速腾汽车,行驶 5.8 万千米,车主反映左前门玻璃升降器无法升降,其余玻璃升降器功能正常。

故障诊断与修复:

(1) 用 VAS5052A 读取故障码,如图 13-10 所示。检查发现有两个故障记忆。

① 00932 驾驶员侧车窗升降机马达-V147 电路电气故障(静态)。

② 00120 驾驶员侧车外警告灯/车门出口灯电路电气故障(静态)。

(2) 查阅电路图,对线路进行如下检查。

① 检查执行元件电源——保险丝 SC12,电压 12V,正常。

② 测量左前门控制单元 J386 插接端子 T20a/12 无电压。

③ 断开左前门连接插头 T28,检查端子 T28/1 电压为 12V,判定车门内部线路出现断路,剥开线束检测发现线束断路,如图 13-11 所示。修复线束,故障排除。

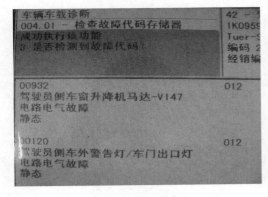

图 13-10 读取故障码

图 13-11 损坏的线束

故障诊断小结:故障码分析只是诊断汽车电子控制系统故障的第一步,重要的是能够判定故障码产生的原因。对于此类故障应该按照电路图检查执行元件的电路,即检查执行器的电源电路与接地电路,然后检查相关联的电气系统。

项目十四

汽车车载网络系统故障诊断与修复

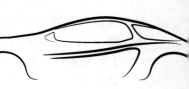

学习目标

1. 能根据报修车辆的故障现象确定问诊的方向及项目。
2. 能根据故障现象制定正确的故障诊断计划。
3. 能熟练查阅维修资料,能根据故障现象选用合适的检测与诊断设备并熟练使用。
4. 能根据诊断计划,运用合适的检修设备对汽车车载网络系统故障进行检测。
5. 能对检测结果进行正确分析并确定汽车车载网络系统的故障部位及原因。
6. 能对故障部位进行快速准确修复,并且消除故障隐患。
7. 能具有精益求精勇于创新的精神,严谨细致的工作态度。

任务导入

任务资料:一辆大众帕萨特轿车,偶尔出现安全气囊黄色灯报警,同时机油灯报警。

任务要求:根据该车辆的故障现象,查阅相关资料,并选用合适的检测与诊断设备进行故障诊断与修复,同时填写任务报告单。

一、故障分析

通过汽车网路拓扑图,了解汽车网络信息传输方式,比如目前大众奥迪等车系普遍采用 CAN 数据总线,包括一个独立的网关,以及与网关相连的动力网、舒适网、信息娱乐网等多路网络。

CAN 数据总线使各个电控系统之间数据、信息实现了实时的交换、传递和共享,这也使得某一个故障不但影响本电控系统,同时使相关电控系统也因此受到影响,从而出现更多的故障现象。

汽车 CAN 数据总线系统的故障包括两类:一是 CAN 数据总线系统信息传输的节点即电控单元本身故障;二是 CAN 数据总线信息传输线路故障。

CAN 数据总线系统出现故障,在相关控制单元存储器里必然存有相关的故障码信息。

二、故障诊断

(1) 读取故障码,并分析故障码的含义。

（2）若出现诊断仪与所有电控单元都无法通信，则应重点检查诊断接口到网关之间的 CAN 线路、网关的供电线路及网关自身是否存在故障。

（3）若出现诊断仪与个别电控单元无法通信，则应重点检查电控单元供电线路及其自身是否存在故障，也可能是该电控单元 CAN 线到网络节点之间出现断路。

（4）若出现诊断仪与某一路总线的所有电控单元无法通信，与其他总线的所有电控单元通信正常，则应重点检查该路总线是否存在线路故障，也有可能是该路总线上的某个电控单元内部出现短路等故障。

注意，通常 CAN 数据总线中的动力总线不能单线传输信息，但舒适总线能单线传输信息，且车辆无明显故障现象（有些高速传输的舒适总线出现故障后故障特征也比较明显）。

若个别电控单元内部出现故障导致某一路总线系统故障，可以通过逐个断开各控制单元的方法查找故障，当断开某个控制单元后其所在总线系统恢复正常，就说明控制单元内部存在故障。

若网路线路存在故障，可以通过双通道示波器对总线进行波形检测，通过分析波形特征即可确定故障的类型，再逐段查找总线，最终确定故障点。

三、任务实施

1. 询问车主

向车主了解出现故障的时间；出现故障前是否有异常情况；车辆行驶的路况；车辆行驶里程；故障发生后是否进行过维修。通过以上的问诊了解故障发生前后的情况及故障的具体信息，完成故障的初步诊断。据车主讲述该故障已经维修多次，始终未解决。

2. 试车与基本检查

进行汽车故障测试，了解故障特征，对故障进行确认，此外要确定该车车载网络的特征和线路连接方式。

3. 检测与诊断

运用大众专用诊断仪进入"引导性故障查寻"功能对所有电控系统故障信息进行全面检测。检测数据如下。

故障代码存储器内容：

数据总线驱动链缺少来自安全气囊控制模块的信息　偶发故障；数据总线驱动链没有来自仪表板的信息　偶发故障；数据总线的诊断接口没有通信　偶发故障；驱动链数据总线损坏；发动机控制单元无信息交换；安全气囊控制单元 J234 无信息交换。

对整个检测数据进行分析：

在安全气囊、仪表、发动机电控系统都有数据总线的故障信息提示，其中有关于安全气囊控制模块和数据通信接口，在各个系统中都存在故障信息。

这里共同的故障点是：所有的故障信息中都有安全气囊数据总线的通信信息不正常，同时还有仪表系统与发动机电控系统通信的故障信息。

考虑到安全气囊灯常亮，分析其故障原因，安全气囊系统中的故障码信息，需进一步检查安全气囊电控系统，尤其是安全气囊 CAN 数据总线。

安全气囊 CAN 数据总线和安全气囊电脑位于驾驶室胶质地板底下，检查该线束需要拆下仪表台及仪表台内部支架，拆装暖风水箱、蒸发箱及仪表盘下部主保险丝盒线束等，拆装全部座椅，将换挡杆中间护罩拆下，前左右门框下护板拆下，最后，将整个胶质地板掀起。地板移开后，就将底部的连接舒适电脑和安全气囊电脑的多路线束露了出来。

检查安全气囊电脑正常，检查线束也无明显破损或接触不良之处。

仔细分析，故障码：01299 049 数据总线的诊断接口没有通信，是指没有数据传递到诊断接口，这包含了因线路导致的无法传递；驱动链数据总线损坏，其含义是数据链总线本身的问题。这二者都在指向一个原因就是数据链路故障，因此判断问题还是出在 CAN 数据线束上。

基于这个分析反复仔细检查安全气囊电脑线束，特别注意 CAN 数据总线的双绞线。该线束位于换挡杆支架后部的地板，仔细检查发现安全气囊 CAN 双绞线绝缘胶皮上有一条非常细的缝隙，在不受外力挤压的情况下，该线胶皮是看不出缝隙的，只有将线弯曲时才会出现缝隙。该线是被手动挡把手支架后侧的锋利的 U 形支架的钢板切开的。

4. 故障排除

用绝缘胶带将裸露的双绞线处理好后，并将该线束整个线束包扎好，并固定在 U 形支架后部。

5. 检验交车

故障检修完毕，装复试车，故障现象消失，没有其他症状，向车主交车。

四、任务小结

该车故障原因是安全气囊的 CAN 数据总线双绞线绝缘层被割开后，车辆在颠簸时，有时数据总线被同时搭铁，有时又脱离搭铁，从而形成了该车故障的间歇性。总线搭铁，其电位被拉低，并造成 CAN 数据总线信息传递异常，安全气囊电脑首先检测并记录该故障，同时通过 CAN 数据总线将该信息传递到发动机电控单元和仪表电控单元。总之，对于 CAN 数据总线系统故障诊断，要通过分析故障码信息，找出多个系统中共有的信息，确定出源性故障信息系统；在此基础上，对源性故障信息系统进行具体故障点的分析。在判断思维上要依靠逻辑推理判断，对于故障信息和各系统进行全面的分析，由多个系统到单一系统，再对单一系统内的故障范围进行测试、推理、分析、判断，最终确定故障点。

五、任务报告单

	专　　业		班　　级		姓　　名	
	任务名称				学　　时	2
	车　　型		发动机型号			
	考核项目	考核内容			分值	得分
任务完成过程	1. 故障症状描述				5	
	2. 故障可能的原因及分析				25	
	3. 检测与诊断过程				35	
	4. 故障排除				10	
	5. 故障诊断小结				10	
教师评价	作业质量、作业效率、作业安全等				15	
	总评分数				100	

六、知识拓展

【典型案例一】　一辆迈腾 B7L 汽车不能自动落锁。

故障描述：一辆迈腾 B7L1.8T 汽车经常出现不能自动落锁故障。

故障诊断与修复：

（1）利用大众专用诊断仪的引导性功能启用车辆自动落锁功能，车辆不能自动落锁。

（2）利用大众专用诊断仪进入网关列表：舒适系统控制单元显示"故障"或"无法达

到"，如图 14-1 所示。

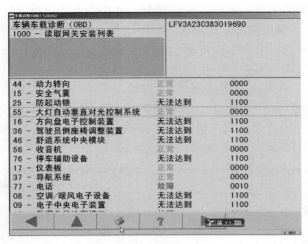

图 14-1　网关控制单元列表

（3）利用诊断仪单独进入每个控制单元，都能单独进入，但进入控制单元偶尔会出现控制单元无反应的提示；通过这个现象可以证明控制单元偶尔无法达到，因为在无法达到的情况下诊断仪会提示控制单元无反应，与在网关列表里面看到的现象相符合。

（4）利用诊断仪进入网关读取故障码，在网关里面出现：故障码 00470 组合舒适系统数据总线处于单线模式下　断路，如图 14-2 所示。

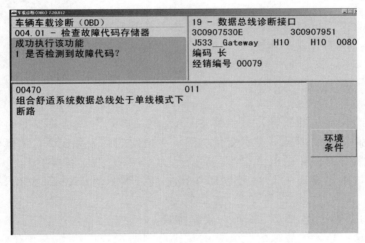

图 14-2　网关故障码

（5）通过上面的数据可以看出，驾驶员侧车门处于单线模式。拆下左前门线束插头，用万用表测量驾驶员侧车门 J386 与网关 J533 间的 CAN 总线，当测量 CAN-L 时，发现断路。修复 CAN-L 线，再用诊断仪进行诊断，发现故障依旧存在，网关里面还是显示单线模式。

（6）拆下网关插头，测量 J533 与 J386 间的 CAN 线，此时线路连接正常。网关插头装回，此时再次读取数据流，显示正常。摇动网关插头后再次出现单线模式，说明网关插头或网关存在接触不良的故障，检查网关插头无异常，则判断应为网关故障。

（7）更换网关后故障排除。

故障诊断小结：此车故障是由两个故障组合在一起，诊断故障时应先按控制单元所给的

提示进行维修。由于舒适总线具有单线模式，所以客户感觉不到车辆出现问题，只有当网关出现接触不良引起舒适系统接收不到车速信号时，才出现不能自动落锁故障。

【典型案例二】 一辆速腾汽车在车辆行驶中熄火，无法再启动。

故障描述： 一辆速腾汽车在车辆行驶中突然出现气囊灯、排放灯、防侧滑灯等故障警报灯报警，同时发动机熄火，熄火后无法启动。

故障诊断与修复： 利用大众专用诊断仪器检测各控制单元，发现 19-网关里存储有"01312 传动系数据总线无信号/通信　间歇式"等故障码，可以清除，清除后车辆可以启动，但行驶一段时间后故障会再现，依然无法启动车辆；01-发动机电脑里有"28836 空调控制单元-J301 无通信　间歇式"等故障码；如图 14-3、图 14-4 所示。

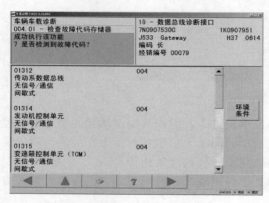

图 14-3　网关中的故障码

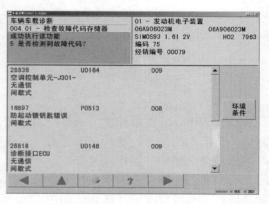

图 14-4　发动机电控单元中的故障码

根据故障码含义，可以看出都是动力总线相关的控制单元报故障，可以初步判断导致该故障现象的原因，可能有以下几种：

（1）驱动 CAN 总线上某一控制单元损坏；

（2）网关故障；

（3）驱动 CAN 总线故障。

结合故障诊断仪显示的故障，对照驱动 CAN 网络图，对驱动总线上的各控制单元逐一断开和检查，存储器的故障显示没有变化，然后更换新的网关和仪表，故障依旧，因该车为新车，分析控制器本身损坏的概率很小，后对动力 CAN 总线上各控制器的线路进行排查。

经过进一步排查，发现从 J533 控制器 T20/6 插针到驱动 CAN-L 总线节点 B390 之间的线路出现断路。

修复 CAN-L 总线断路部分，试车，故障排除。

故障诊断小结： 导致该故障的原因应该是线束制造过程中线束节点有一根线没有压住，直接用胶带和节点绑在一起，在车辆使用过程中接触不良，导致总线故障，由于连接点并没有完全脱开，所以出现了间歇式故障。

对于总线故障，采取逐个断开相关总线上的控制单元来判断哪个控制单元或控制单元相连线束故障是常采用的有效方法。

参考文献

[1] 朱军. 汽车故障诊断方法. 北京：人民交通出版社，2008.
[2] 《汽车维修与保养》杂志社. 汽车维修案例：专家点评典型故障. 北京：人民交通出版社，2011.
[3] 邹喜红. 汽车故障诊断技术. 北京：中国铁道出版社，2016.
[4] 罗富坤. 汽车故障诊断技术. 北京：化学工业出版社，2014.
[5] 李庆军. 汽车发动机构造与维修. 北京：中国铁道出版社，2016.
[6] 谢剑. 汽车底盘构造与维修. 北京：中国铁道出版社，2016.
[7] 文爱民. 汽车故障诊断技术. 北京：人民交通出版社，2021.
[8] 张俊峰. 汽车综合故障诊断. 北京：机械工业出版社年出版，2021.

Bilingual Textbooks of Vocational Education
职业教育双语教材

Automobile Integrated
Fault Diagnosis and Repair

汽车综合故障诊断与修复

Edited by Xianghong Cao

曹向红 主编

Chemical Industry Press
化学工业出版社

BeiJing
·北京·

Preface

The Integrated Fault Diagnosis and Repair of Automobile is a series of bilingual textbooks for automobile majors of higher vocational education. It is a school-enterprise cooperation achievement developed by the teacher team of Tianjin Transportation Technical College and technical backbones of FAW-Volkswagen Automobile Co., Ltd., the achievement of teaching material and teaching method reform of High-level Vocational Schools and Professional Construction Plan with Chinese Characteristics (Double High-levels Plan), and one of the high-quality teaching achievements of Luban Workshop, a famous brand of humanities exchange initiated and practiced firstly in Tianjin.

This book designs 14 learning items and several learning tasks, including querying the owner, test run and basic inspection, detection and diagnosis, troubleshooting, inspection and delivery, etc., based on the international advanced education concept, taking project orientation, task-driven and case teaching as the carrier, the standard, safety, environmental protection, service, cooperation and other elements and the spirit of artisans and craftsmen of excellence as guide, referring to the typical work flow of automobile maintenance enterprises, and according to the core work content, task and post specification of the solid automobile enterprises. Each learning task leads out fault problem analysis, diagnosis knowledge points and post literacy requirements through typical automobile fault phenomena, and systematically and comprehensively elaborates the diagnosis and repair process and technical specifications of typical cases. The typical fault cases attached to this book cover the Volkswagen, Toyota, Audi and other brands. This book can be used by international automobile professionals such as automobile inspection and maintenance technology, and can be used for on-the-job training of employees in automobile maintenance enterprises.

This book breaks the traditional textbook format in writing style. Each learning item consists of learning objective, task introduction, task implementation, task summary, task report sheet. Each task is equipped with a task report sheet like a workbook, which can be completed in the form of group collaboration, which is helpful for students to carry out process quantitative assessment and learning feedback in aspects of learning attitude, cooperation ability and practical ability.

This book is mainly edited by Cao Xianghong of Tianjin Transportation Technical College, with a deputy editor, Zeng Kaikai from Tianjin Branch of FAW-Volkswagen Automobile Co., Ltd., and two participants in editing Liu Xinyu and Liu Bingyue of Tianjin Transportation Technical College. Among them, Cao Xianghong compiles the introduction, Item I to Item VI, Item XIV, Zeng Kaikai compiles Item VIII to Item XI, Liu Xinyu compiles Item XII, Item XIII, and Liu Bingyue compiles Item VII. This book is mainly reviewed by Professor Guan Zhiwei of Tianjin Sino-German University of Applied Sciences. During the writing, we have obtained the selfless help of Tianjin Society of Automotive Engineering, some member units and many professional technicians. Thank you very much!

Because of the limited editorial level, there are inevitable omissions and inappropriateness in the book, so please criticize and correct.

Editor
May 2022

Content

Introduction　Basic Knowledge of Automobile Fault Diagnosis ⋯⋯ 1

Item Ⅰ　Fault Diagnosis and Repair of Charging System ⋯⋯⋯⋯ 21

Item Ⅱ　Fault Diagnosis and Repair of Lubrication System ⋯⋯⋯ 25

Task Ⅰ　Fault Diagnosis and Repair of Low Oil Pressure ⋯⋯⋯⋯⋯⋯⋯⋯⋯⋯⋯ 25
Task Ⅱ　Fault Diagnosis and Repair of High Oil Pressure ⋯⋯⋯⋯⋯⋯⋯⋯⋯⋯ 29
Task Ⅲ　Fault Diagnosis and Repair of Excessive Oil Consumption ⋯⋯⋯⋯⋯ 33
Task Ⅳ　Fault Diagnosis and Repair of Oil Deterioration ⋯⋯⋯⋯⋯⋯⋯⋯⋯ 39

Item Ⅲ　Fault Diagnosis and Repair of Cooling System ⋯⋯⋯⋯⋯ 43

Item Ⅳ　Fault Diagnosis and Repair of Abnormal Sound of
Automobile ⋯⋯⋯⋯⋯⋯⋯⋯⋯⋯⋯⋯⋯⋯⋯⋯⋯⋯⋯⋯ 49

Task Ⅰ　Fault Diagnosis and Repair of Abnormal Engine Sound ⋯⋯⋯⋯⋯⋯ 49
Task Ⅱ　Fault Diagnosis and Repair of Abnormal Chassis Sound ⋯⋯⋯⋯⋯⋯ 60

Item Ⅴ　Fault Diagnosis and Repair of Abnormal Engine
Operation ⋯⋯⋯⋯⋯⋯⋯⋯⋯⋯⋯⋯⋯⋯⋯⋯⋯⋯ 68

Task Ⅰ　Fault Diagnosis and Repair of Engine Failure to Start ⋯⋯⋯⋯⋯⋯ 68
Task Ⅱ　Fault Diagnosis and Repair of Engine with Signs of starting but
Failing to Start ⋯⋯⋯⋯⋯⋯⋯⋯⋯⋯⋯⋯⋯⋯⋯⋯⋯⋯⋯⋯ 77
Task Ⅲ　Fault Diagnosis and Repair of Engine Starting Difficulty ⋯⋯⋯⋯ 85
Task Ⅳ　Fault Diagnosis and Repair of Engine Idle Unsteady ⋯⋯⋯⋯⋯⋯ 91
Task Ⅴ　Fault Diagnosis and Repair of Engine Power Shortage ⋯⋯⋯⋯⋯⋯ 99

Item Ⅵ　Fault Diagnosis and Repair of Transmission
System ⋯⋯⋯⋯⋯⋯⋯⋯⋯⋯⋯⋯⋯⋯⋯⋯⋯⋯⋯⋯ 105

Task I   Fault Diagnosis and Repair of Clutch Slipping ················· 105

Task II   Fault Diagnosis and Repair of Shifting Difficulty of Manual
Transmission ················· 109

Item VII   Fault Diagnosis and Repair of Automatic Transmission ················· 114

Task I   Fault Diagnosis and Repair of Failure to Drive ················· 114

Task II   Fault Diagnosis and Repair of Shifting Shock ················· 117

Task III   Fault Diagnosis and Repair of Abnormal Sound of Automatic
Transmission ················· 123

Task IV   Fault Diagnosis and Repair of Upshifting Hysteresis ················· 127

Task V   Fault Diagnosis and Repair of Slipping ················· 132

Item VIII   Fault Diagnosis and Repair of Steering System ············ 141

Task I   Fault Diagnosis and Repair of Heavy Steering of Hydraulic Power
Steering System ················· 141

Task II   Fault Diagnosis and Repair of Heavy Steering of Electronic
Power Steering System ················· 146

Item IX   Fault Diagnosis and Repair of Brake System ··············· 152

Task I   Fault Diagnosis and Repair of Insufficient Braking Force ················· 152

Task II   Fault Diagnosis and Repair of Brake Deviation ················· 156

Task III   Fault Diagnosis and Repair of ABS System ················· 161

Item X   Fault Diagnosis and Repair of Driving System ············ 165

Task I   Fault Diagnosis and Repair of Vehicle Running Deviation ················· 165

Task II   Fault Diagnosis and Repair of Abnormal Tire Wear ················· 170

Item XI   Fault Diagnosis and Repair of Airbag System ··············· 175

Item XII   Fault Diagnosis and Repair of Automotive Air Conditioning System ················· 181

Task I   Fault Diagnosis and Repair of Inoperative Air Conditioning System ········· 181

Task II   Fault Diagnosis and Repair of Insufficient Cooling of Air
Conditioning System ················· 187

Task III   Fault Diagnosis and Repair of Air Conditioning Easy to Ice ················· 192

Item XIII Fault Diagnosis and Repair of Body Electrical Apparatus ················· 197

Task I   Fault Diagnosis and Repair of Central Control Door Lock ················· 197
Task II Fault Diagnosis and Repair of Electric Window Regulator ················ 202
Task III Fault Diagnosis and Repair of Automobile Lighting System ··············· 208

Item XIV Fault Diagnosis and Repair of Automobile Onboard Network System ················· 215

Introduction

Basic Knowledge of Automobile Fault Diagnosis

Ⅰ. Basic Concepts of Automobile Fault Diagnosis

1. Basic terms and definitions

(1) Technical condition of automobile: Sum of quantitatively measured parameters that characterize the appearance and performance of an automobile at a given time.

(2) Automobile inspection: Inspection to determine the technical condition and working capacity of an automobile.

(3) Automobile fault: A phenomenon of partial or total incapacity of an automobile.

(4) Automobile fault phenomenon: Specific manifestations of an automobile fault.

(5) Automobile diagnosis: Under the condition of not disassembling or only removing individual small parts, determination of the technical condition of an automobile to find out the fault position and cause.

(6) Diagnostic parameter: A parameter used for diagnosis to characterize the technical status of an automobile, its assemblies and mechanisms.

(7) Automobile maintenance and repair: A general term for automobile maintenance and repair.

(8) Automobile maintenance: Work carried out to maintain sound technical condition or working capacity of an automobile.

(9) Automobile repair: Work carried out to restore the sound technical condition or working capacity and service life of an automobile.

2. Relationship between Automobile Inspection and Fault Diagnosis

The purpose of automobile detection is to judge whether the technical indexes and performance indexes of an automobile under test conform to the regulations. Automobile detection is a qualitative analysis.

Automobile fault diagnosis includes two links: "inspection" and "judgement". The process of automobile fault diagnosis is that the diagnostic technician, starting from automobile fault phenomena, skillfully uses all kinds of detection devices to carry out the corresponding inspection on the automobile, that is, the first link "inspection" is done. At the same time, by using the deep understanding of the principle and structure of the automobile,

he makes an accurate judgment on the fault position and cause after comprehensively analyzing the test results, then, the second link "judgement" is done.

The purpose of automobile fault diagnosis is to judge the fault position and cause of the automobile. Automobile inspection is the basis of automobile fault diagnosis.

II. Classification of Automobile Faults

1. Classification by fault location

Automobile fault can be divided into overall fault and local fault.

(1) The overall fault refers to the overall performance fault caused by the overall aging after the automobile reaches the design life. It shows the overall decline of power, safety, economy, reliability, braking, maneuverability, environmental protection and smoothness.

(2) The local fault refers to the fault of a part of the automobile. The function of this part cannot be realized, but the functions of other parts are still intact.

2. Classification by fault development process

Automobile fault can be divided into sudden fault and gradual fault.

(1) The sudden fault refers to a fault that occurs suddenly without any detectable symptom, which is the result of the combined action of various unfavorable factors and incidental external influence, exceeding the limit that the product can bear.

(2) The gradual fault refers to a fault that occurs gradually, is gradually formed from weak to strong, which is usually related to service time. With the extension of service time, the fault is gradually obvious, which is characterized by gradual strength and inevitability, with obvious quantitative change characteristics. The gradual fault can be diagnosed and corrected as soon as they occur.

3. Classification by fault occurrence frequency

Automobile fault can be divided into incidental fault and frequently occurring fault.

(1) The incidental fault refers to a fault with a very low probability of occurrence, i. e. , a fault with very few occurrences. For example: A sudden engine stalling occurs only once or twice in a long time while driving.

(2) The frequently occurring fault refers to a fault with high probability of occurrence, i. e. a frequently occurring fault.

4. Classification by fault impact

Automobile fault can be divided into partial fault and complete fault.

(1) The partial fault refers to a fault of partial loss of working capacity of an automobile, i. e. the performance of the automobile is reduced. For example: Poor braking performance, poor acceleration performance, poor idle speed, etc.

(2) The complete fault refers to a fault of complete loss of working capacity of an automobile, i. e. complete loss of service performance. For example: There is no braking at all, no acceleration at all (flameout when accelerating), no idle speed, etc.

III. Automobile Fault Diagnosis Methods

1. Manual empirical diagnosis

The manual empirical diagnosis is a diagnostic method by which the diagnosis worker in-

spects, tests, analyzes and determines the cause and position of an automobile fault by simple inspection means such as seeing, listening, toughing, smelling, etc., based on rich practical experience and certain theoretical knowledge without disassembling or partially disassembling the automobile. The manual empirical diagnosis is not only a traditional method but also a basic method for automobile fault diagnosis. Even in today's rapid development of modern instruments and diagnostic technologies, the manual empirical diagnosis can not be replaced.

(1) "Seeing" "Seeing" refers to a method to observe all parts of an automobile mainly by naked eyes directly or by means of a magnifier and an endoscope, to check whether there is abnormal phenomenon and find out the trace of the fault. It is the most applied, basic and effective fault diagnosis method.

Items and parts that can be seen in automobile fault diagnosis mainly include the following aspects.

① Indication of automobile fault indicator lights; Display of automobile instruments and alarm lights and indicator lights.

② Whether there is air leakage, water leakage or oil leakage; Whether fluid flow is normal; Whether the color and liquid level of oil, transmission fluid, brake fluid, coolant, etc. are normal.

③ Whether the exhaust color of the engine is normal.

④ Whether the movement of each component is normal; Check whether the connecting parts are loose, cracked, deformed or fractured.

⑤ Whether the line is damaged, loosened or broken; Check whether there are abnormal conditions such as corrosion and deformation of wiring terminal.

⑥ Check whether the oil pipe and the gas pipe are compressed, bent, damaged, cracked, etc.

⑦ Check whether each lever, cable and pull rod are properly adjusted.

⑧ Check whether there is coking in intake pipe, intake and exhaust valve and cylinder.

⑨ Whether the tire pressure and tire wear are normal; Whether there is obvious deformation of frame, axle, automobile body and shell and guard board of each assembly, and whether there are scratch marks on relevant parts.

There are many items and parts listed above for seeing. However, in the actual fault diagnosis, the area where the specific fault occurs and the part or item associated with the fault are observed.

The fault diagnosis by "seeing" is similar to a doctor of traditional Chinese medicine to detect the visceral lesion of a patient by observing the spirit, color, shape, state, tongue image and so on. On the one hand, by seeing, we can find out the faults occurring on the surface of an automobile to avoid detour; On the other hand, the fault information inside the automobile can be obtained by observing. For example, by seeing the color of the automatic transmission fluid and the substance contained in the fluid, the cause of the transmission fault can be roughly understood.

(2) "Touching" "Touching" is to feel the temperature, pressure, vibration, etc. of the machine parts by human hand, so as to obtain the fault information of the automobile,

just like pulse-taking in traditional Chinese medicine. This is also an effective fault diagnosis method.

Faults and items that can be diagnosed by touching mainly include the following aspects.

① The engine water temperature is abnormal; Automatic transmission fluid temperature is abnormal.

② Partial fault of air conditioning system; Partial fault of automobile suspension system and shock absorber.

③ Touching by hand can judge whether the plug and wire connection of the line are loose, whether there is abnormal high temperature at the connection of the line, and judge whether there is bad contact at this place.

④ The vibration of fuel injectors, various solenoid valves and motors can be sensed by hand to determine whether they work.

⑤ Touch the surface temperature of electrical appliances and electronic components such as ignition module, ignition coil, relay and motor by hand to judge whether they work normally.

⑥ Check the tightness of the belt and judge whether the belt is slipping.

⑦ Touch the generator, air-conditioning compressor and other components by hand to determine whether the connection is loose.

⑧ Feel the viscosity of oil, ATF, gear oil and other impurities by hand to judge the quality and possible faults.

⑨ Feel the pressure fluctuation of cooling water pipe and fuel pipe by hand to understand the circulation of cooling water and oil supply.

⑩ Check the wear of the friction surface, check the fitting clearance of friction pairs and the running smoothness of rotating parts, and judge whether these parts are faulty.

⑪ Touch the clutch, brake drum or brake disc by hand and sense their temperature to determine whether there are clutch slipping and brake drag fault.

For example, in case of high engine water temperature fault, touch the upper and lower water pipes by hand to determine whether the thermostat can be opened normally, touch the radiator surface to feel whether there is temperature difference between parts and know whether there is pipe blockage inside the radiator.

(3) "Listening" "Listening" mainly monitors the sound emitted by an automobile directly through ears or by a stethoscope, so as to judge the fault location and type, and then find out the cause. This method is mainly used to find out the abnormal sound of the automobile mechanical part and judge whether some electrical components work.

In the automobile fault diagnosis, faults and items involved listening include the following aspects.

① Intake and exhaust system has abnormal sounds.

② Drive belt slips and rattles abnormally.

③ Abnormal sounds of generator, air conditioning compressor, etc.

④ Various abnormal sounds of engine: Abnormal valve sound, piston pin sound, piston knocking, crankshaft bearing sound, connecting rod bearing sound, etc. ; Abnormal sound

of mechanical transmission part: clutch, transmission, final drive, etc.

⑤ Leakage of high voltage line of ignition system.

⑥ Check whether relays, fuel injectors, solenoid valves, etc. are connected and whether there are running sounds of the motor, oil pump, etc. by listening, to see whether they can operate.

⑦ The steering system sounds abnormally.

⑧ The brake system sounds abnormally.

⑨ The automobile suspension sounds abnormally.

⑩ Body and wheel rattle abnormally while driving.

Pay attention to the methods and means when making diagnosis by "listening". For example, when checking abnormal sound fault of an engine, generally start the engine under shutdown state to make the engine run at different speeds. According to different sounds emitted from different fault parts, such as continuous sound and intermittent sound, brittle sound and dull sound, regular sound and irregular sound, etc., the sound position can be judged, sometimes by means of a stethoscope. For abnormal sound fault of the transmission system, it is often necessary to drive around the condition of abnormal sound by road test to determine the abnormal sound position.

(4) "Smelling" "Smelling" mainly senses the abnormal smell produced by every part of an automobile by nose. Faults or items can be diagnosed through "smelling" include the following aspects.

① The engine working condition is judged by the smell of engine exhaust, which provides important information for fault diagnosis.

② Judge the quality of oil and the operation condition of corresponding system according to the abnormal smell of oil such as engine oil and ATF.

③ Judge clutch slipping, brake drag and other faults according to the scorching smell of non-metallic materials.

④ The rubber plastic smell of rubber and plastic parts after overheating is used to find faults such as wire overheating and short circuit.

2. Instrument and device diagnosis

The instrument and device diagnosis refers to a diagnostic method that the diagnostic worker can detect, test and analyze various diagnostic parameters of the automobile by using various diagnostic and inspection devices without disassembling or less disassembling the parts of the automobile, so as to understand the technical conditions of each part of the automobile, and finally determine the fault cause and position of the automobile. There are many devices used for automobile diagnosis and detection, such as multimeter, fuel pressure gauge, cylinder pressure gauge, vacuum gauge, oscilloscope, fault scan tool, timing light, etc. These devices have their own inspection functions. In actual fault diagnosis, corresponding device can be selected according to the items to be inspected.

For example, when a fuel system may fail, use a fuel pressure gauge to inspect the fuel pressure to determine whether the fuel system is indeed faulty; When there is a possible leak in a engine intake manifold, the vacuum level of the intake manifold can be detected by a vacuum gauge to determine if there is a leak in the intake manifold.

3. Test Method

The test method uses certain methods and means to carry out the corresponding test a-round the fault, so as to determine the fault location.

Common test methods mainly include the following.

(1) Interchange and replacement comparison test

① Interchange comparison test: It refers to a test in which a part that may be faulty on the automobile is interchanged with other identical part, if the fault is transferred to another place, it indicates that the suspected part is indeed faulty. For example, the cylinder 2 of the single cylinder independent ignition engine does not operate and the fault is likely to occur in the ignition coil of the cylinder. The ignition coil of the cylinder can be interchanged with other cylinder. If the fault is transferred to other cylinder, the fault is indeed the ignition coil of cylinder 2.

② Replacement comparison test: It refers to a test in which a part that may be defective in an automobile is replaced with a good one, if the fault disappears, it is proved that the fault occurs in this part. This method is particularly suitable for use without maintenance data and information and with sufficient accessories. This method is simple, does not require inspection devices, and is highly efficient in the diagnosis of some faults.

For example, if it is judged that the fault may occur in the air flow meter when the engine fails to accelerate normally, it can be replaced with a good air flow meter. If the fault is removed after replacement, it can be determined that the fault occurs in the air flow meter.

(2) Vibration simulation test   When vibration may be the main cause of a fault, the vibration method can be used for inspection. The test methods mainly include: lightly swinging connectors, harnesses, wire connectors, etc. horizontally and vertically; Tapping the sensors, actuators, relays and switches with hand gently. If the fault reappears or disappears during the vibration simulation test, it indicates that there is a fault in the part applied with vibration.

(3) Heating simulation test   When the fault is caused by the heating of some sensors or other parts, heating tools such as an electric heating blower can be used to properly heat the parts that may cause the fault. If the fault reappears, it indicates that there is a fault in the heated part.

(4) Humidification simulation test   The spray humidification test may be performed when a fault occurs in a rainy day or under a high humidity condition. During the test, spray water on the front of the radiator or on the top of the automobile. If the fault is repeated, focus should be the parts that are susceptible to moisture.

(5) Separation (isolation) comparison test   This is a method of separating (isolating) certain systems or components, stopping them from working, and determining the location or extent of the fault by fault phenomenon change.

① If the fault disappears when the electrical component or wiring is isolated, the fault is in the isolated component or wiring. For example, if an automobile has a short circuit fault and the fault is locked at an area, the parts in that shall be isolated one by one, and when certain part is isolated and the fault disappears, then the fault is in the area where the part is located.

② If the fault disappears when the machine part is removed, the fault will be in the part. For example, if an automobile has a poor acceleration fault and the fault may be caused by air filter blockage, the air filter may be removed for test-drive. If the fault disappears, the fault is caused by the air filter. In addition, it also belongs to this method to check the abnormal sound or unstable idle speed of the engine by the single cylinder fire cut-off test.

③ Block the oil and gas lines to see if the fault phenomenon changes. For example: Pinch the vacuum line, and if the vacuum degree of the intake manifold rises, it indicates that the vacuum pipe is leaking; Pinch the fuel return line. If the oil pressure rises, the too low oil pressure will occur.

4. Fault self-diagnosis

The fault self-diagnosis is a method that uses the automobile computer scan tool to call the fault code, and then diagnoses the fault according to the fault code diagnosis flow chart provided in the maintenance manual. The fault self-diagnosis is a special form of the instrument and device diagnosis. It is a method of automobile fault diagnosis based on the fault code of automobile electronic control system called by the automobile computer scan tool. Fault code and data flow are the most important display modes of the automobile computer scan tool in self-diagnosis analysis. Fault code can give description of fault point qualitatively and data flow can give quantitative display of batch data parameters. These parameters can not only display input/output information of electronic control unit in multi-path instantly, but also display dynamic change of control process parameters of electronic control unit.

Ⅳ. Basic Process of Automobile Fault Diagnosis

The basic flow of automobile fault diagnosis is the most basic diagnosis process of automobile fault diagnosis, which is the most general summary of diagnosis content. The basic content of automobile fault diagnosis includes starting from fault symptoms, through inquiry and test-drive (verifying fault symptoms), analytical research (analyzing structural principle), reasoning and hypothesis (reasoning possible causes), flow design (proposing diagnostic steps), test and confirmation (testing and confirming fault point), repair and verification (verification after troubleshooting), finally achieving the purpose of finding the final cause of a fault.

The basic flow chart of automobile fault diagnosis is shown in Figure 0-1.

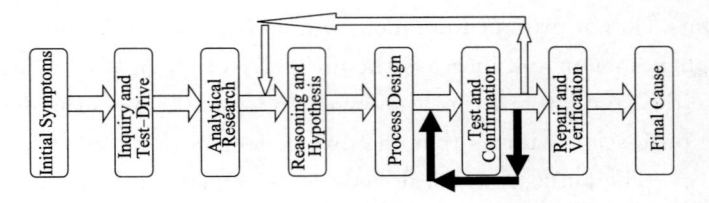

Figure 0-1   Basic Flow of Automobile Fault Diagnosis

1. Initial Symptoms

Initial symptoms refer to the fault characteristics of an automobile requiring repair. It is important for maintenance personnel to understand and describe the fault phenomena accurately, which is related to the direction and efficiency of diagnosis. Because an automobile

owner can only judge automobile faults from the abnormality in automobile use, maintenance personnel need to accurately describe the fault symptoms according to the owner's description and self-observation.

2. Inquiry and Test-Drive

Inquiry is a process of knowing the fault symptoms of an automobile by asking the owner, and test-drive is a process of further confirming the symptoms by verifying the actual fault symptoms.

(1) Inquiry   Inquiry is a process by which maintenance personnel ask the owner about the automobile fault, just as a doctor asks a patient about his condition. Inquiry should be the first step in an automobile fault diagnosis. Inquiry is very important in the automobile fault diagnosis, grasping this link can determine the direction of the next fault diagnosis, even lock the fault range.

General inquiry shall include the following.

① The condition in which the fault occurs.

• The time of the first fault, the state of the automobile.

• Whether the fault is accompanied by other performance changes and what symptoms are there before the fault.

• Frequency of fault occurrence: Frequent; Sometimes; Under certain conditions; Only once.

• Degree of change after the fault: No change; Increasingly serious; Deteriorated rapidly.

• Environment where the fault occurs: Temperature, climate, road conditions, etc. When the fault occurs.

② Repair and maintenance.

• Whether the fault has been repaired, what repairs have been carried out, and which parts have been replaced.

• Check whether a device has been installed before the fault occurs, whether certain circuit is changed or certain part is changed.

• Whether the automobile is maintained on time, and whether it is maintained in a regular maintenance enterprise.

In addition, it is necessary to know the owner's driving habits, frequent driving road conditions, driving speed, gear, fuel label, quality and additive usage.

Note that you must master the inquiry skills. Ask the owner to speak more when asking about the symptoms. Do not prompt too much, otherwise it will mislead the owner to say the ambiguous fault phenomenon and increase the difficulty of diagnosis. In addition, when asking questions, use the familiar words of the owner to make the owner understand easily, and try not to use the professional terms that the owner does not understand.

(2) Test-drive   The purpose of test-drive is to reproduce the fault symptoms described by the owner to verify the authenticity of the fault symptoms, and to test the objective states such as characteristics, time, location, environment, conditions and working conditions when the fault symptoms are reproduced, so as to prepare for further analysis of the fault cause.

After the fault symptoms are reproduced after the test-drive, the maintenance personnel shall repeatedly understand and observe the subtle processes such as various conditions, working conditions, environment and conditions when the fault symptoms appear, and carefully record them and

confirm the fault symptoms. The test-drive is a process that maintenance personnel feel the fault symptoms of the automobile, and it is of great significance for maintenance personnel to understand the fault symptom features. The complete test-drive shall include the test process of various performances of the automobile, i. e. , the running conditions of the whole process from engine cold start, high idle speed of cold engine, warm-up to hot engine idle speed, acceleration and rapid acceleration, as well as instrument indications. In addition, it shall also include driving condition test during automobile starting, shifting, acceleration, deceleration, braking and steering. According to the automobile fault, the automobile dynamic performance, braking performance, driving stability performance, handling reliability performance, vibration swing abnormal sound and other conditions shall be selected and checked, to feel various reactions during driving and handling, so as to check any automobile fault symptoms that are not felt by the owner.

3. Analytical Research

The analytical research is to research and analyze the structure and principle of an automobile according to the fault symptoms after the inquiry and test-drive. The purpose is to analyze the mechanism of fault generation, the conditions and characteristics of fault generation, so as to prepare for reasoning the fault cause in the next step. In the analytical research, first of all, the maintenance personnel should collect the structural principle data of automobile fault parts, understand the normal operating conditions and rules of the automobile, and make a comparative analysis with the fault conditions. The basic materials of the analytical research are knowledge of automobile structure and principle, as well as important information such as mechanical and hydraulic principle structure diagrams, oil circuit, electric circuit and gas line diagrams, electronic control system block diagram, control schematic diagram, technical parameter table and technical information bulletin provided by the repair manual of the automobile.

4. Reasoning and Hypothesis

After analyzing the structure and principle of the automobile fault parts, looking for and comparing the automobile technical data, the maintenance personnel should make the reasoning and hypothesis for the possible cause of the fault according to the logic analysis and experience judgment. The reasoning and hypothesis is a preliminary judgment of the fault cause, which is based on both theory and practice. Theoretically, it means that according to the knowledge of structure and principle and the manifestation of fault symptoms, the possible causes of fault symptoms are derived from logic analysis. This deduction is logical reasoning which can be established in principle, which is the logic reasoning based on theory. In practice, it refers to the empirical inference of the possible fault causes of similar faults with the same or similar structure according to the experience of previous fault diagnosis. This inference has the property of analogy judgment, which is the empirical inference based on practice.

Reasoning is a process of deducing fault principle according to the working principle and fault symptom. In this link, besides having a profound understanding of the working principle, the maintenance personnel should also pay attention to the fault essence corresponding to the fault symptom. That is to say, although we still don't know what the final cause leads to the fault symptoms or where the fault point is, the mechanism of fault occurrence at this

Introduction　Basic Knowledge of Automobile Fault Diagnosis | **9**

time should be basically clear. For example, although it is unknown which component is damaged and caused the black smoke emitted by the engine, it must be caused by thick mixture in principle. The hypothesis is a process of further inferring the cause of the next fault from the reasoning result. For example, a further analysis of the reasons for the thick mixture shows the two reasons, one is more fuel and the other is less air. Further reasoning shows that there are two reasons for more fuel: high oil pressure and long injection time, while longer injection time may be caused by abnormal control injection time and poor fuel injector closing. If less air may be two kinds of cases: true less air and false less air. The true less air is caused by blockage of intake system, and false less air is caused by high output signal of air flow meter. This is a process of making hypotheses step by step. Reasoning is to deduce the basic mechanism cause of fault symptoms. Hypothesis is the result of further analyzing its cause to the next level of fault by using the method of logic reasoning, based on the deduced fault mechanism. It is clear that the cause mechanism of the fault symptom emission of black smoke in the above example is caused by thick mixture, which is empirically confirmed, and therefore this reasoning is the result of empirical judgment. If that fault symptom occur on an automobile with new technology and new structure, such as hybrid automobile and diesel common rail injection system, the corresponding mechanism of the fault symptom cannot be obtained directly from the empirical judgment. At this time, the composition and working principle of the structure must be deeply analyzed, so that the direction of the possible fault mechanism cause can be introduced, and then the hypothesis of the deep cause can be made. Therefore, the logical reasoning should be used here.

The reasoning and hypothesis process is a process of finding the fault cause in a large direction, which explores the basic mechanism and direction of the fault.

5. Process Design

Process design is to design the fault diagnosis flow of practical application according to the possible fault cause of hypothesis after reasoning and hypothesis. During the design, the items to be tested should be determined first, then the inspection methods for distinguishing the faults of major components or assemblies of the automobile should be determined, and then the inspection methods for the working performance of various systems and devices of the automobile should be determined. Finally, the testing methods of components and circuits should be determined. The purpose of these test methods is to gradually narrow the range of fault suspicion and eventually lock out the fault point.

6. Test and Confirmation

Test and confirmation is to test each item one by one according to the procedures of the process design after the design of the fault diagnosis process. The test and confirmation is a test process of automobile overall performance, system or assembly performance, mechanical and electrical device performance, pipe line status and component performance without disassembly or disassembling only a few parts. It includes three parts: inspection, test and confirmation. The contents of the three parts are different. The inspection mainly refers to a technical inspection process completed through inspection and measurement by manual direct observation and device and instrument analysis, and the test mainly refers to a technical inspection process completed through simulation experiment and dynamic analysis of the system. Confirmation mainly refers to a process to finally confirm the loca-

tion of the fault point through the logical analysis of the diagnosis flow, the judgment of inspection and test results.

7. Repair and Verification

Repair and verification refers to the repair of the fault point and the verification of the result after repair after the minimum fault point location is found through the test and confirmation. It is divided into two parts: determination of repair method and verification after repair.

(1) Determination of repair method   The repair method shall be determined according to the fault performance mode of the fault point. The fault point is the low-end event leading to the fault and the smallest unit of the fault. The different performance modes of the fault points determine the different methods to be adopted in the repair.

① The component damage, component aging and component misuse and the like are usually repaired by replacement.

② The installation loosening, assembly error and improper adjustment are usually repaired by re-installation and adjustment.

③ The poor lubrication is repaired by means of maintaining lubrication.

④ For leaky sealing, the rubber parts are usually replaced, and the mechanical parts are repaired by surface repair process or replacement.

⑤ The oil deficiency is usually repaired by refilling, but for the defect caused by leakage and abnormal consumption, it is necessary to find out the root cause and then to repair.

⑥ The gas or liquid leakage or plugging is repaired by plugging or dredging.

⑦ The coking scale is generally repaired by cleaning and decoking.

⑧ The rust and oxidation is generally repaired by derusting and de-oxidation.

⑨ The motion interference is usually repaired by restoring shape, adjusting position and strengthening fastening.

⑩ Control disorder, entry into emergency/standby mode, and improper match are repaired by readjusting, restoring to zero, and re-matching.

⑪ Short circuit, open circuit, line damage, dummy welding and ablation shall be repaired by repairing damage, cleaning ablation, re-welding and local replacement of wiring.

⑫ The leakage breakdown and poor contact shall be repaired by replacement or cleaning.

(2) Verification after repair   The verification after repair refers to the function test of the repaired automobile. If the fault disappears completely and the function returns to normal, the automobile can be confirmed to have been completely repaired.

8. Final Cause

After repairing and verifying the minimum fault point found in the preceding link, the fault may be eliminated, but it cannot be considered that the fault diagnosis work can be finished here. Because the final cause at this minimum fault point has not been determined yet. If the determination is not continued, the maintenance is completed and the automobile continues to drive from the factory, the fault may occur again. To analyze the final fault cause of the fault point, find out the internal and external causes, completely eliminate the root cause and eliminate the recurrence is the important content of the last link of the basic process of automobile fault diagnosis.

V. Common Fault Detection and Diagnosis Equipment of Automobile

1. Test light

Test lights are generally divided into diode test lights and common bulb test lights, as shown in Figure 0-2 and Figure 0-3.

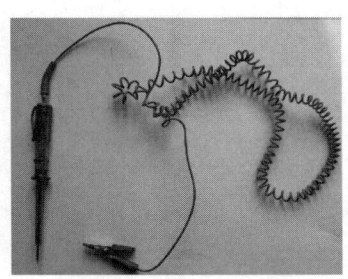

Figure 0-2　Diode Test Light

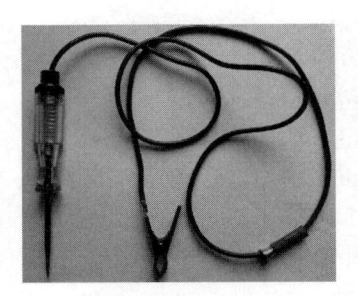

Figure 0-3　Common Bulb Test Light

Test light is easy to use, convenient and intuitive, so it is widely used in automobile inspection. However, it should be noted that when detecting the circuit connected with the electronic control unit of an automobile, the test light made of common bulb cannot be used, but only the test light made of light emitting diode can be used, otherwise the electronic components of the automobile may be damaged.

The test light can be used to detect whether the circuit is live. One end of the test light is connected to the negative electrode of battery or grounded, and the other end is connected to the tested part. If the test light is on, it indicates that the circuit is powered, otherwise, the circuit is not powered.

The test light can be used to detect a circuit for open circuit. If the test light is used and detected that a point in the power supply circuit of an appliance has power, but no power is detected at the next point of the circuit, it indicates that there is an open circuit in this section of circuit.

The test light can be used to detect the presence of a signal in the signal circuit. When signal circuits such as ignition signal and Hall camshaft position sensor are detected with the test light, the test light shall flash regularly, otherwise, the circuit or relevant components are faulty.

2. Multimeter

The automobile multimeter is shown in Figure 0-4. It is the most commonly used detection tool in the automobile fault diagnosis. Generally, it has the functions of measuring voltage, resistance and current, and some can test items such as duty cycle, temperature and frequency.

Note that the pointer multimeter shall not be used to test the computer and sensor except for special requirements during the test. The high impedance digital multimeter shall be used. The internal resistance of the multimeter shall not be

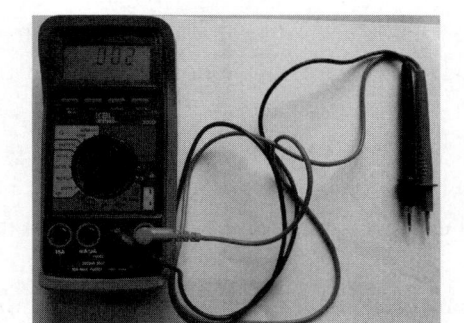

Figure 0-4　Multimeter

less than $10k\Omega$.

(1) Voltage detection   When measuring the voltage between two terminals or between two lines, the two probes of the multimeter (voltage gear) should be contacted with the measured two terminals or two wires.

When measuring the voltage of a terminal or circuit, the positive probe of the multimeter shall be contacted with the tested terminal or line, and the negative probe of the multimeter shall be contacted with the ground wire.

(2) Resistance detection   When checking open circuit fault, the connector between computer and corresponding sensor shall be disconnected first, and then the resistance between corresponding terminals of the connector can be measured to determine whether there is open circuit or poor contact.

When checking the ground short circuit fault of the circuit, the connectors at both ends of the line shall be disconnected, and then the resistance value between the terminal tested of the connector and the automobile body (ground) shall be measured. If the measured resistance value is small or has no resistance value, it can be determined that there is a short circuit ground fault between the wire and the body. There is no fault if the resistance value is greater than $1M\Omega$.

When checking the continuity of terminals, contacts or wires, the resistance value can be measured with a multimeter (resistance gear). If conducting, the resistance value shall be small or zero, and if it is not conducted, the resistance value shall be ∞.

Note that the electronic control system circuit of the engine shall be removed during resistance detection. Before this, the power supply shall be cut off first, i. e. the ignition switch shall be turned off.

(3) Current detection   First disconnect the circuit under test, then select the AC gear or DC gear of the multimeter according to the measured current (AC or DC), select the range and connect the multimeter in series into the circuit. The red probe shall be connected to the breakpoint connected to the positive electrode of the power supply, and the black probe shall be connected to the breakpoint point connected to the negative electrode of the power supply.

(4) Duty cycle detection   Duty cycle refers to the ratio of power-up time to cycle within one power-up cycle. Many signals on the automobile are duty cycle signals, such as camshaft position sensor, crankshaft position sensor, carbon canister solenoid valve, etc.

When connecting, the red probe is connected to the signal circuit, and the black probe is grounded or connected to the negative electrode of the battery.

3. Vacuum gauge

The vacuum gauge for automobile diagnosis is shown in Figure 0-5. It can judge the causes and locations of various faults by detecting the vacuum degree by the vacuum gauge. It plays a more and more important role in automobile diagnosis.

When the engine operates under different conditions, the

Figure 0-5   Vacuum Gauge

vacuum in the intake pipe is different. The vacuum gauge is connected to the intake manifold behind the throttle valve. Using the vacuum gauge to detect the vacuum degree in the intake manifold of the engine under different working conditions can help diagnose various faults of the engine.

(1) Start-up condition detection   To get a accurate test result, the start-up test needs to be performed when the engine is hot. If the engine fails to start due to a fault, it can also be measured when the engine is cold, but the accuracy will be reduced. When measuring, close the throttle valve, disconnect the fuel injector plug, start the engine and observe the value on the vacuum gauge. When each part of the engine is normal, the value is usually between 11 and 21 kPa. If less than 10 kPa, the possible causes include the following: too low engine speed, worm piston ring, stuck or ablated throttle valve, leaked intake manifold, too large idle bypass air passage opening, etc.

(2) Idle condition detection   Intake manifold vacuum is usually 50 to 70 kPa (depending on engine displacement and compression ratio) when the engine is idle. If the measured value is not within this range, or if it is too large or too small compared to the normal value, the engine is faulty.

① If the value of the vacuum gauge drops regularly by 6 to 9 kPa and the value is stable, check the initial ignition timing, valve timing, cylinder pressure, positive crankcase ventilation valve and exhaust gas recirculation system, throttle seal and idle bypass valve, and check for inoperative spark plugs.

② If the value of the vacuum gauge drops irregularly by $10 \sim 27$ kPa, the spark plug may not work properly, or the valve is stuck, the valve tappet or hydraulic tappet is stuck, or the camshaft may be severely worn.

③ If the value of the vacuum gauge is slowly displayed back and forth between 27 and 34 kPa, check whether the mixture is too thick (focus on the oil supply system) and the spark plug gap is too small.

④ If the value of the vacuum gauge changes quickly from 47 to 61 kPa, check whether the inlet valve tappet and guide are worn and the fitting is loose. If the value of the vacuum gauge is displayed slowly back and forth from 34 to 76 kPa and with the increased engine speed, its numerical variation is intensified, which is likely caused by insufficient elastic force of the valve spring.

⑤ If the value of the vacuum gauge varies greatly from 18 to 65 kPa, it is likely that the cylinder liner is leaking.

⑥ If the engine idle speed is too high and the vacuum degree of the intake manifold is less than 40 kPa, it indicates that the intake manifold or main pipe behind the throttle valve of the engine is leaking. The air leakage position is generally the intake manifold pad and many pipelines connected with the intake manifold, such as vacuum booster air pipe.

⑦ If the engine is difficult to start and cannot guarantee stable idle speed operation, but the vacuum degree of the intake manifold of the engine is above 50 kPa, it means that there is no problem with the intake pipe and cylinder seal of the engine. The fault mainly lies in the poor ignition or poor fuel injection of the electronic control system, such as abnormal ignition coil.

(3) Detection of rapid acceleration and rapid deceleration conditions   If each system of the en-

gine is normal, the value of the vacuum gauge shall drop suddenly during rapid acceleration, and the value of the vacuum gauge shall increase greatly at the original idle speed. When the throttle is opened and closed quickly, the value of the vacuum gauge shall fluctuate from 7 to 86 kPa. If the piston leaks seriously, the variation in the value of the vacuum gauge will not be significant. The wider the variation in the value of the vacuum gauge indicates the better the technical condition of the engine. If the value of the vacuum gauge at idle speed is lower than the normal value, the value during rapid acceleration drops to near 0, and the value of the vacuum gauge cannot rise to about 86 kPa when the throttle is suddenly closed, it indicates that the piston ring, intake pipe or throttle body gasket is leaking.

(4) Detection of exhaust system blockage   If the exhaust pipe is blocked while opening, the back pressure during exhaust will increase, which will reduce the vacuum degree of intake manifold. The vacuum at idle speed shall generally be 50 ∼ 70 kPa. Accelerate slowly so that the speed reaches 2, 000∼2, 500 r/min. At this time, the value of the vacuum gauge shall be equal to or near the vacuum value at idle speed. Return the throttle quickly to idle state, and the vacuum gauge reading shall be increased rapidly by an amplitude (e. g. 15-20 kPa) and then dropped back.

When the engine is at 2, 500 r/min, the value of the vacuum gauge is gradually lower than the idle speed value or does not increase when the engine drops suddenly from 2, 500 r/min to idle speed, it indicates that the back pressure in the exhaust system is too high and the exhaust resistance is too high, which is likely to be that the three-way catalytic converter is blocked or the exhaust pipe and the silencer are blocked. At this time, remove the exhaust pipe and try again. If the vacuum returns to normal, it can be confirmed that the exhaust pipe is blocked.

If the engine fails to start, the vacuum fluctuates around zero, and even positive pressure occurs, the exhaust pipe or three-way catalytic converter is blocked.

Particularly, since the vacuum value of an engine varies with the altitude and the air density, the standard value for each engine will vary.

4. Oil pressure gauge

The oil pressure gauge is shown in Figure 0-6. The oil system fault can be analyzed and judged by an oil pressure gauge.

(1) Oil pressure detection   Remove the oil pressure sensor or oil pressure switch, select the proper connector to connect the oil pressure gauge, start the engine and read the oil pressure values

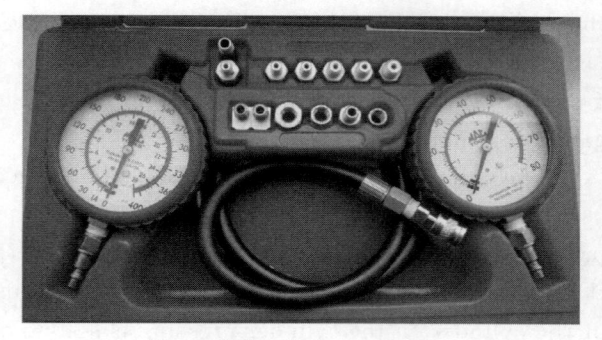

Figure 0-6   Oil Pressure Gauge

under idle speed, acceleration and heavy load. Compare them with the specified values, determine whether the oil pump, oil pressure sensor or oil pressure gauge is faulty.

(2) Fuel pressure detection   Firstly, disconnect the fuel line and connect the oil pressure gauge to the fuel line by a suitable connector. Start the engine and read the fuel pressure values under idle speed, acceleration and heavy load, and compare them with the specified values to determine whether the fuel pump or the oil pressure regulator is faulty. Shut down

the engine, wait for 10min and observe the pressure value of the pressure gauge. Generally, it shall not be lower than 0. 20 MPa, otherwise, the oil pump check valve is faulty.

(3) Brake pressure detection Firstly, disconnect the oil circuit connecting the master cylinder and connect the oil pressure gauge to the brake line by a suitable connector. Depress the brake pedal, observe the oil pressure value and compare it with the specified value. If the oil pressure value is normal and the pressure can be kept constant, the master cylinder shall be free of fault. If the oil pressure drops slowly, the brake cylinder and piston of the brake master cylinder wear too much.

(4) Oil pressure detection of automatic transmission Firstly, remove the nut from the automatic transmission pressure tap, then select a suitable connector to connect the oil pressure gauge to the pressure tap. Start the engine, observe the oil pressure under idle speed and various gear conditions, and compare it with the specified value. If the main oil pressure is not within the specified range, it indicates that the oil pump and the oil pressure regulator are faulty. If the oil pressure of each gear is not within the specified range, it indicates that the solenoid valve and shift valve of each gear are faulty.

5. Cylinder pressure gauge

The cylinder pressure gauge is shown in Figure 0-7 to detect the engine cylinder pressure so that the engine mechanical system can be fault-diagnosed.

Cylinder pressure gauges can be divided into push-in type and threaded interface type. The push-in cylinder pressure gauge is used for the detection of gasoline engine, and the threaded interface cylinder pressure gauge is used for the detection of diesel engine. When the compression force of the diesel engine is large, the pressure gauge head must be tightly fastened to the fuel injector hole before measurement. The compression force of gasoline engine is relatively small, and the pressure gauge can be held by hand and measured directly against the spark plug hole.

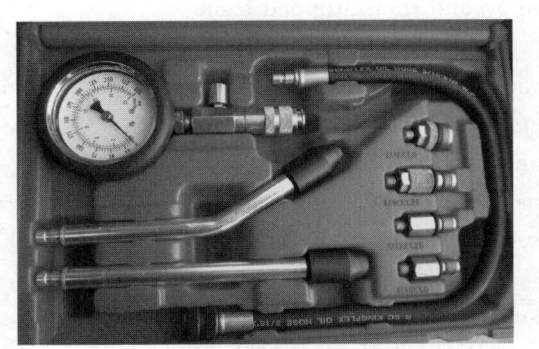

Figure 0-7 Cylinder Pressure Gauge

The cylinder pressure is detected and analyzed as follows.

(1) Test conditions Before testing, start the engine and let it run for a period of time, preheat it to make the water temperature rise to 75~90℃, and after the oil pressure reaches the normal value, then stall for test. This is because the influence of the lubrication condition of the cylinder on the cylinder pressure is second only to the speed of the crankshaft, and the lubrication condition of the cylinder is closely related to the oil temperature. During measuring, the more close to the actual working condition, the more accurate the measurement results are. The measured results must also be analyzed in combination with the use and maintenance conditions to draw the correct conclusion.

(2) Test method After the engine is shut down, blow the dust and dirt around the spark plugs or fuel injector with compressed air, then remove all spark plugs (for the diesel engine, remove the fuel injector) and place them in the cylinder sequence. Insert the rubber

joint of the cylinder pressure gauge into the spark plug hole of the cylinder under test to straighten and press it. Turn the crankshaft 3~5s with the starter when the throttle is at the fully open position, and stop rotating after the pressure gauge head pointer indicates and maintains the maximum pressure. Remove the cylinder pressure gauge, read and record the reading, press the check valve to return the pressure gauge pointer to zero. Measure each cylinder in sequence according to the above method, and each cylinder shall be measured at least twice. When detecting the cylinder pressure of the diesel engine on the automobile, except for the cylinder pressure gauge where the screw joint shall be used, other detection conditions and detection method are the same as those of gasoline engine.

(3) Analysis of cylinder pressure detection result   Standard value of cylinder compression pressure is generally provided by automobile manufacturer. According to regulations, the pressure of each cylinder of automobile engine in use shall not be less than 85% of original design value. The difference between the pressure of each cylinder and the average pressure of cylinders shall not exceed 8% for gasoline engine and 10% for diesel engine.

If the measured result is higher than that specified in the original design, it may be caused by excessive carbon deposition in the combustion chamber, too thin cylinder liner, or excessive repair and machining of the connecting plane between cylinder block and cylinder head, which generally occurs rarely. If the measured result is lower than that specified in the original design, a proper amount of engine oil can be injected into the spark plug or fuel injector hole of the cylinder, and the cylinder pressure shall be remeasured with the cylinder pressure gauge and analyzed.

① The pressure measured for the second time is higher than that of the first time and is close to the standard pressure, which indicates that the cylinder seal is not tight due to excessive wear of cylinders, piston rings and pistons, or due to piston ring matching, jamming, fracture and cylinder wall strain.

② The pressure measured for the second time is slightly the same as that of the first time, i. e. still lower than the standard pressure, indicating that the inlet and exhaust valves or cylinder gaskets are not sealed.

③ Both test results indicate that the pressures of two adjacent cylinders are quite low, indicating that the cylinder gaskets at the adjacent parts of two cylinders are burnt and blown-by.

6. Infrared thermometer

The infrared thermometer is shown in Figure 0-8. The surface temperature of automobile parts can be detected by this equipment to determine whether the parts and relevant systems are working normally.

The infrared thermometer does not need to touch the surface of the object under test. This instrument has large measuring range, is easy to use, simple, and can conduct accurate and safe measurements.

(1) Engine operating condition detection   Check the exhaust temperature of the engine to determine whether a certain cylinder is working or whether a certain cylinder is working normally. If the ex-

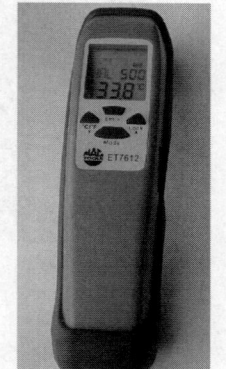

Figure 0-8   Infrared Thermometer

haust temperature of a certain cylinder is significantly lower than that of other cylinder, the cylinder is not working, and if the exhaust temperature of the cylinder is relatively lower than that of the other cylinder, it indicates that the cylinder is not working well.

(2) Cooling system detection If the engine water temperature is too high and the coolant quantity is normal and the fault position cannot be directly judged, it is likely that the internal pipeline of the cooling system is blocked, the thermostat or the water pump are faulty.

The temperature difference between the inlet pipe and the outlet pipe of the radiator shall be very obvious, and the temperature of each part of the radiator surface shall be consistent, otherwise, the radiator is faulty.

When the engine water temperature reaches the normal value, the temperature of the engine outlet pipe shall be significantly rose. If the temperature rise is not obvious or doesn't occur, it indicates that the thermostat works badly.

(3) Detection of engine exhaust pipe temperature The temperature at the outlet end of the three-way catalytic converter should be several tens of degrees Celsius higher than the inlet temperature, otherwise, the three-way catalytic converter is not working well.

7. Manual Vacuum Pump

The manual vacuum pump is shown in Figure 0-9. Apply vacuum to the tested part through this device, and judge whether the vacuum degree can be maintained to determine whether the part works normally.

A manual vacuum pump can be used to detect vacuum control valves and gas control solenoid valves, such as carbon canister solenoid valves, exhaust gas recirculation valves, etc. When testing, select an appropriate connector and a hose. One end is connected with the vacuum pump and the other end is connected with the tested component, as shown in Figure 0-10. Press the pump rod several times to observe the reading. When the valve is closed, the value shown on the gauge shall remain unchanged, otherwise it means that the valve body is not closed tightly and air leaks.

Figure 0-9 Manual Vacuum Pump

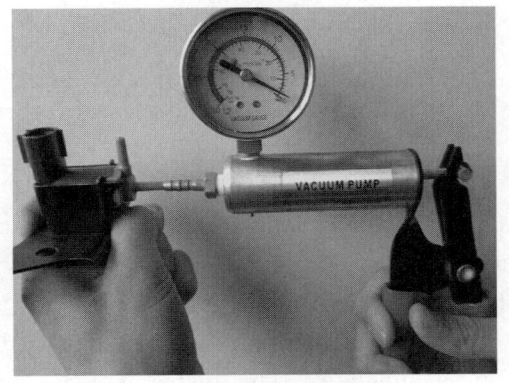

Figure 0-10 Detection of Carbon Canister Solenoid Valve by Manual Vacuum Pump

8. Automobile Scan Tool

The automobile scan tool is divided into general type and special type. As shown in Figure 0-11, a general-purpose automobile scan tool is used to detect the electronic control sys-

18 Automobile Integrated Fault Diagnosis and Repair

tems of common automobiles, while the special type is used to detect the electronic control system of a certain automobile.

The scan tool is a very important tool in maintenance and generally has several or all of the following functions:

① Read out the fault code.

② Clear the fault code.

③ Read the dynamic data flow of electronic control system.

④ Oscilloscopic function.

⑤ Component action test.

⑥ Matching, setting and coding, etc.

Typically, there are the following steps when using a scan tool.

① Find the diagnostic seat on the automobile.

② Select the corresponding diagnostic connector.

③ According to the automobile model, enter the corresponding diagnosis system to carry out corresponding detection and diagnosis.

With the scan tool, the fault code stored in each electronic control unit on the automobile can be read, as shown in Figure 0-12. The maintenance personnel can understand the location and type of the fault through the fault code, which provides the diagnosis direction for the fault diagnosis. The fault code stored in the electronic control unit can be cleared by the fault code clear command issued by the scan tool.

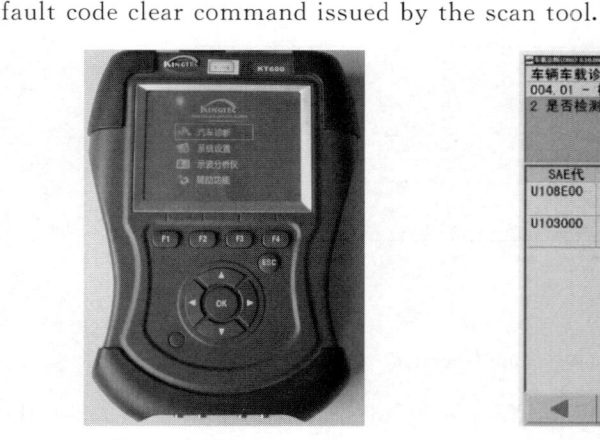

Figure 0-11 Scan Tool

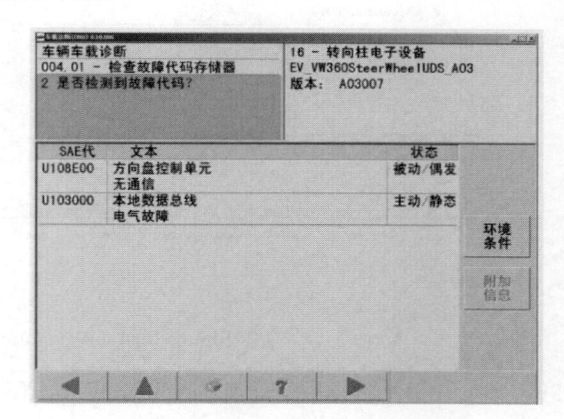

Figure 0-12 Reading Fault Code

Reading dynamic data flow refers to reading various signal information received by each electronic control unit on the automobile. The electronic control unit can process the DC, AC, serial data and other signals obtained from the sensor to display the actual value. If the voltage transmitted by the engine water temperature sensor to the engine electronic control unit is 1.6V and the corresponding engine water temperature is 70℃, the data flow read by the scan tool is 70℃ water temperature.

When troubleshooting, if there is no fault code display, you can view the data flow and compare it with the standard value to analyze whether the relevant system or component is faulty. Data flow is shown in Figure 0-13.

Oscilloscopic function is an important function of many scan tools. Oscilloscopic function

Introduction Basic Knowledge of Automobile Fault Diagnosis | **19**

usually has four display modes, single channel, dual channels, three channels and four channels. For example, dual-channel oscilloscopic function can display two different signal waveforms independently at the same time, and can select the same signal source or select different signal source. There is a test probe and a grounding clamp at the input end of the oscilloscope. Ground the clamp during measurement, and place the probe at the point to be tested. The measured signal waveform is shown in Figure 0-14.

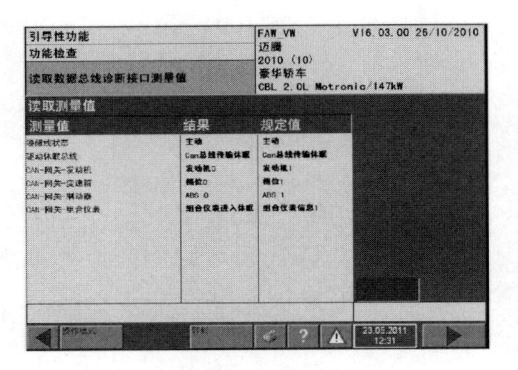

Figure 0-13　Reading Data Flow

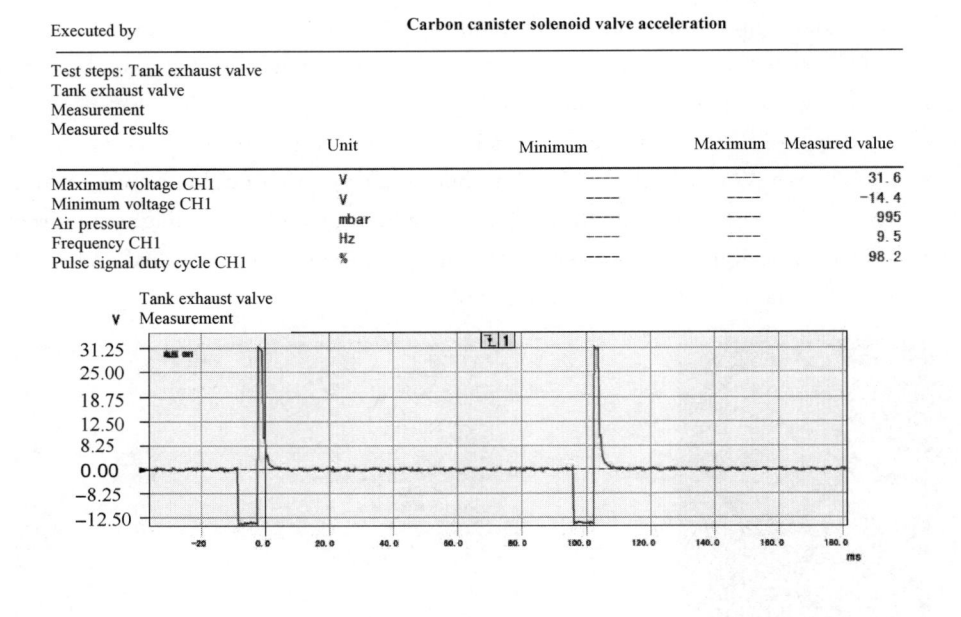

Figure 0-14　Waveform Detection

The scan tool can adjust the amplitude and frequency of signal waveform to make the displayed waveform clear and complete. The signal type and the process of signal change can be understood from the waveform. Comparing the detected waveform with the standard waveform, it can be analyzed whether the relevant components and circuits are faulty.

Note that when testing ignition high voltage line, special capacitance probe must be used, and the oscilloscope probe cannot be directly connected to ignition secondary circuit.

Component action test means that the scan tool sends a command to the electronic control unit of the automobile, then the electronic control unit controls the operation of an actuator (such as fuel injector, fuel pump and carbon canister solenoid valve) on the automobile to judge whether the actuator and the circuit are faulty by judging whether the component responds. Component action test can be performed for components in operation, such as idle motors, or components in non-operating conditions, such as fuel pumps.

20　Automobile Integrated Fault Diagnosis and Repair

Item I

Fault Diagnosis and Repair of Charging System

There are many faults of charging system, such as generator fault, regulator fault, faults in the circuit and instrument display of the charging system, as well as mechanical faults like slipping of the drive belt of the generator and unstable fixing of the generator. Common faults of charging system mainly include: The generator does not generate electricity, the generator voltage is too low, the generator voltage is too high, and the generator voltage is unstable, etc.

Learning Objectives

1. Be able to determine the direction and items of inquiry according to the fault phenomena of the automobile for repair.

2. Be able to prepare a correct fault diagnosis plan according to fault phenomena.

3. Be able to consult maintenance data skillfully, select appropriate detection and diagnosis devices according to fault phenomena and use them skillfully.

4. Be able to detect the fault of charging system with appropriate maintenance devices according to the diagnosis plan.

5. Be able to correctly analyze the test results and determine the fault location and causes of the charging system.

6. Be able to repair the fault parts quickly and accurately and eliminate the hidden troubles.

7. Be able to work rigorously and carefully and improve safety awareness.

Task Import

Task Material: A Jetta car has a driving mileage of 110,000 km. The user said that the engine could not be started and the battery was insufficient when the automobile was parked for a long time. The engine started normally after charging the battery. No abnormality was found on the display of the instrument charging indicator light.

Task Requirements: According to the fault phenomena of the car, consult relevant materials, select appropriate detection and diagnosis devices for fault diagnosis and repair, and fill in the task report.

Ⅰ. Fault Analysis

Insufficient battery capacity may be a battery problem or a charging system fault. The specific reasons are as follows:

(1) Battery fault or aging may result in insufficient battery storage.

(2) Poor contact between the power cord and the battery pole.

(3) The generator and its wiring fault causes the battery to be undercharged.

(4) The generator drive belt slips, causing low generator voltage.

Ⅱ. Fault Diagnosis

(1) Check whether the contact between the power cord and the battery pole is loose, and fasten it if it is loose.

(2) Check whether the connection plug of the generator is connected well. If there is any abnormality, repair it.

(3) Check whether the drive belt of the generator is too loose, and fasten it if too loose.

(4) After the engine is started, check whether the generator voltage is normal at the battery terminal, and the normal voltage shall be around 14V.

(5) After starting the engine, check whether the generator voltage is normal at the generator output terminal, and the normal voltage shall be around 14V.

(6) Check whether there is any problem in the generator circuit. If there is any abnormality, it shall be repaired.

Ⅲ. Task Implementation

1. Inquiry

Know the time of fault from the owner; Whether the symptoms change after the fault is found, and whether there are other abnormal conditions before the fault; Details during driving; Whether the car is maintained on time; Have other repairs been performed after the fault. The preliminary diagnosis of the charging system fault can be completed by knowing the situation before and after the fault and the specific information via inquiry.

2. Test-drive and Basic Inspection

Carry out the test-drive to confirm the fault. Observe whether the instrument charging indicator displays normally. Check whether the power cord and the battery pole are in good contact without looseness. Check whether the connection plug of the generator is in good condition. Check whether the tightness of the drive belt of the generator meets the requirements. In addition, it is necessary to determine the structure characteristics and wire connection mode of the charging system.

3. Detection and Diagnosis

After starting the engine, detect the generator voltage at generator output terminal to be 14.2V, and the voltage is normal.

After the engine is started, use a multimeter to detect the generator voltage at the battery terminal, the voltage is 14.2V and is normal.

After the power cord is re-tightened to the battery pole, the fault is not eliminated.

After replacing the battery, the fault remains.

The engine runs at idle speed after starting, start the all electric devices of the car, and test the generator voltage at the battery terminal with a multimeter again. The voltage is 13.5V, lower than the voltage at the output terminal of the generator.

Check the fuse in the charging circuit in the fuse block and the ablation phenomenon at the fuse terminal is found after pulling the fuse out.

4. Fault Elimination

After handling the fuse seat and replacing a new fuse, carry out the test-drive and the fault disappears.

5. Inspection and Delivery

After troubleshooting and without any other symptoms, hand over the car to the owner.

IV. Task Summary

This fault is caused by the increase of the resistance at the plug connection caused by the insecure fuse plug connection. After a long time of large current flow, the fuse terminal corner is ablated, resulting in the decrease of charging current, insufficient charging of the battery, and long shutdown time and difficulty to start. During such fault diagnosis, besides checking some conventional items, it should also be tested when the generator load is large, so as to obtain more accurate detection results and avoid blind disassembly and replacement.

V. Task Report

Major			Class		Name	
Task Name					Class Hours	2
Model				Engine Model		
Task Completion Process	Assessment Items		Assessment Contents		Maximum Score	Score
	1. Description of fault symptoms				5	
	2. Possible causes and analysis of fault				25	
	3. Detection and diagnosis process				35	
	4. Fault Elimination				10	
	5. Summary of fault diagnosis				10	
Teacher Evaluation	Operation quality, operation efficiency, operation safety, etc.				15	
Total Score					100	

VI. Knowledge Expansion

〔Typical Case Ⅰ〕 **The power generation of a Santana 2000GSi car was insufficient.**

Fault Description: The battery of a Santana 2000GSi car often lost electricity, causing the starter ran weakly, the headlights dim, and the battery recharged every few days.

Fault Diagnosis and Repair: Checked whether the battery pole was fixed properly and the tightness of the generator belt was normal. It was known from communication with the user that the battery had been used for more than 2 years, so it was recommended that the owner replace the battery, but the fault remained shortly after replacing a new battery.

Started the engine, used a multimeter to detect the generator output voltage of 14.5 V, and the charging voltage was normal. Checked the generator circuit and found no abnormality.

Item Ⅰ Fault Diagnosis and Repair of Charging System **23**

The battery fault can be eliminated by replacing the new battery, so the fault was likely to be inside the generator.

Started the engine to turn on all lights of the car, increased the engine speed to 2,000 r/min, detected the output current of the generator and the current value was 1A, which was significantly lower than the current required by the lights. Therefore, it was judged that the fault was inside the generator.

When the generator of the same model was replaced, the fault disappeared.

Summary: Because of local faults inside the generator, such as brush wear, partial fault of rectifier, fault of stator winding, etc., the generator generates normal voltage when the power load is small, but when the power load is large, the battery cannot be fully charged due to insufficient power generation.

[Typical Case Ⅱ] The combination cluster did not work because the generator voltage of the new Magotan car was too high.

Fault Description: In a brand new Magotan sedan driving 30,000 km, the combination cluster did not work when the engine speed reached more than 3,000 r/min.

Fault Diagnosis and Repair: A Volkswagen special scan tool VAS6150 was used to read out the fault codes of the engine control unit and the instrument control unit and no fault codes were found.

Through inspection, it was found that the power supply fuse of the combination cluster was OK and the grounding wire of the combination cluster had no problem. The fault remained after replacing a new combination cluster.

Considering that the fault phenomenon was related to the engine speed, the VAS6150 was connected, but the fault remained when the engine speed gradually rose to about 3000 r/min. Read the basic operating status of each electronic control system of the car. When reading the charging voltage of the generator of the electronic control system of the engine, the generator voltage gradually rose with the speed and even reached more than 16V. It was preliminarily judged that the generator voltage regulator was faulty.

When the generator voltage at the generator output terminal was above 16V, it was judged that the generator had an internal fault.

The fault disappeared after replacing a generator.

Summary: This fault is a combination cluster fault due to high generator voltage. The fault is characteristically related to the engine speed, so the engine speed should be raised to the fault occurrence state when inquiring about the fault. In this state, abnormal data flows should be found to find the direction of the fault.

Item II

Fault Diagnosis and Repair of Lubrication System

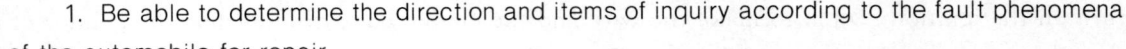

The lubrication system faults are mainly divided into two aspects, on the one hand, faults of main parts or oil circuit; On the other hand, low oil pressure and deterioration due to engine fault. Common lubrication system faults include too low oil pressure, too high oil pressure, excessive oil consumption, oil deterioration, etc.

Task I   Fault Diagnosis and Repair of Low Oil Pressure

Learning Objectives

1. Be able to determine the direction and items of inquiry according to the fault phenomena of the automobile for repair.

2. Be able to prepare a correct fault diagnosis plan according to fault phenomena.

3. Be able to consult maintenance data skillfully, select appropriate detection and diagnosis devices according to fault phenomena and use them skillfully.

4. Be able to detect low oil pressure fault with appropriate maintenance devices according to the diagnosis plan.

5. Be able to correctly analyze the test results and determine the fault location and cause of low oil pressure.

6. Be able to repair the fault parts quickly and accurately and eliminate the hidden troubles.

7. Be able to have strong sense of responsibility, good service mentality and consciousness.

Task Import

Task Material: The oil pressure warning light flashes when a Jetta car passes through a pit road.

Task Requirements: According to the fault phenomena of the car, consult relevant materials, select appropriate detection and diagnosis devices for fault diagnosis and repair, and fill in the task report.

Ⅰ. Fault Analysis

Low oil pressure means that the oil pressure is below the specified value at normal operating temperature and speed of the engine. The engine oil pressure warning light is now illuminated or flashing.

The main causes of low oil pressure are as follows:

(1) The oil pressure gauge or oil pressure sensor is misaligned, the sensor circuit is poorly connected or open-circuited.

(2) The oil is deteriorated, the viscosity is too low, and oil and water are mixed into the oil.

(3) The oil level is too low.

(4) The oil pump is severely worn and the oil supply capacity decreases.

(5) The oil collector and the oil filter are blocked.

(6) The oil pressure relief valve is not properly adjusted, closed tightly or the spring is broken.

(7) There is a leak in the oil circuit.

(8) The crankshaft main bearing, connecting rod bearing or cam bearing is worn, the bearing is loose, or the bearing alloy falls off or burns.

(9) The engine is overheated.

Ⅱ. Fault Diagnosis

(1) Check whether the oil level is too low, whether the oil is deteriorated and whether the viscosity is too low.

(2) Check whether the oil pressure indication system is normal. Check the connection between the oil pressure gauge and the sensor. If it is normal, remove the sensor wire and turn on the ignition switch to make the wire and the engine body grounded. If the pointer of the oil pressure gauge rises rapidly, it indicates that the oil pressure gauge is in good condition; If the pointer of the oil pressure gauge is stationary or slightly moved, it indicates that the oil pressure gauge fails.

(3) Check whether the filter element and bypass valve of the oil filter are blocked, whether the oil filter leaks, etc.

(4) For an externally mounted pressure relief valve, necessary checks and adjustments shall be made.

(5) Remove and inspect the oil pump, check the end face clearance, radial clearance and meshing clearance of the oil pump gear pairs, and conduct oil pressure and pump oil quantity and other performance tests.

(6) Check the mating clearance of crankshaft main bearing, connecting rod bearing, cam bearing, etc.

Ⅲ. Task Implementation

1. Inquiry

Know the time of fault from the owner; Check whether there is abnormal condition before the fault; The road condition of the car; Whether the car is maintained on time; Has it

been repaired after the fault occurred. Find out the situation before and after the fault and the specific information of the fault through the above inquiry, and complete the preliminary diagnosis of low oil pressure.

2. Test-drive and Basic Inspection

Start the engine, change the engine speed and observe whether the alarm light changes. In addition, observe whether the engine external components are abnormal; Observe for oil leakage.

3. Detection and Diagnosis

Firstly, pull off the oil dipstick and check the oil quantity and oil quality. It is found that the oil level is higher than the upper limit of the oil dipstick and the oil quality is normal. In addition, there is no abnormal sound when the engine is running at idle speed. On this basis, it is judged that there is little possibility of problems in the oil lubrication system. The oil pressure alarm switch or its circuit is suspected to be faulty at this time, so check the oil pressure alarm switch and its circuit with a multimeter and find that they are all normal, thus inferring that the cause of the fault is the oil pressure system. Considered that the owner said that the car was malfunctioned after the chassis touched the ground, and combined with the rose oil level, it is concluded that the root cause was probably in the oil pan. Then lift the car to check the oil pan and find that the oil pan was hit into a large pit after touching the ground, and the center of the pit faces the oil inlet of the oil pump.

4. Fault Elimination

After removing and repairing the oil pan, perform the test-drive and find the fault gone.

5. Inspection and Delivery

After troubleshooting, the oil pressure alarm display is normal during the test-drive without any other symptoms. Hand over the car to the owner.

IV. Task Summary

Because the automobile is driving on the pit road, the oil pan is deformed after the chassis touches the ground, the oil inlet of the oil collector of the oil pump is blocked and the oil inlet is not smooth, resulting in too low oil pressure and sparkling oil pressure alarm light.

V. Task Report

	Major		Class		Name	
	Task Name				Class Hours	2
	Model		Engine Model			
	Assessment Items	Assessment Contents			Maximum Score	Score
Task Completion Process	1. Description of fault symptoms				5	
	2. Possible causes and analysis of fault				25	
	3. Detection and diagnosis process				35	
	4. Fault Elimination				10	
	5. Summary of fault diagnosis				10	
Teacher Evaluation	Operation quality, operation efficiency, operation safety, etc.				15	
	Total Score				100	

VI. Knowledge Expansion

[Typical Case I] The oil pressure alarm light of a Buick CENTURY car was always on.

Fault Description: After a Buick Century GL car had been overhauled and replaced with pistons and other components, the oil pressure alarm light was always on after the engine was started.

Fault Diagnosis and Repair: Because it was a car that had been repaired by others, we should know what repairs and replacements had been done during the overhaul before diagnosis. It was known that the engine piston and piston ring had been replaced and all other components were normal. Therefore, all parts are cleaned and reassembled.

The engine was started, a metal knocking sound was heard, and the oil pressure indicator was on. The oil dipstick was pulled out and the liquid level and oil color were normal. The oil pressure alarm light was on, indicating that the oil pressure was low or the oil pressure sensor had a circuit fault. When the ignition switch was turned on for bulb detection, the oil pressure alarm light was automatically on. Then it went out. This proved that the fault was not on the line but still on the lubrication system.

According to the analysis, the oil circuit was initially suspected to be blocked. The oil filter was removed to drain the existing oil completely. Then the compressed air was filled from the oil filter to clean the entire oil circuit. This is the simplest cleaning method without disassembling the engine. After cleaning, the new oil was refilled to the specified amount, and the oil pressure alarm light was on after starting the car for a while. Then the oil pressure was detected. Low oil pressure was detected. Finally, it was decided to disassemble the engine for further inspection. After disassembling the engine for inspection, it was found that the engine crankshaft, crankshaft bearing, connecting rod bearing, piston, tappet, push rod and other components were basically normal. When the camshaft was removed for inspection, it was found that there was great wear on the cam and the bearing was seriously worn. After replacing the camshaft and its bearing and reassembling the engine, the fault was eliminated.

Summary: The fault was caused by heavy oil leakage due to severe wear of the camshaft, reducing the oil pressure normally supplied and causing the oil pressure alarm light on.

[Typical Case II] The oil pressure alarm light was on when the engine of a Sagitar car accelerated to 2, 000r/min.

Fault Description: The oil pressure alarm light was on when the engine of a 2011 Sagitar car accelerated to 2, 000r/min.

Fault Diagnosis and Repair: The repairman asked the user about the latest maintenance record, and learned that the last maintenance had not been maintained at the special service station. After the maintenance, the oil pressure alarm light was on after the car ran for a while.

Therefore, the repairman used the oil pressure detector VAG1342 to measure the oil pressure. He found that the idle oil pressure was only 40kPa, the oil pressure was obviously too low, and the oil pressure increased continuously with speed increase, but the pressure was always low. The pressure was only 160kPa at 2, 000r/min, and the oil pressure shall be

between 270~450kPa when the speed is 2,000r/min and the oil temperature is 80℃. Because the car had ran for a long distance after the oil pressure alarm light was on, the repairman removed the oil pan and checked all bearing shells and thrust gaskets for wear and found mo any abnormality. The oil filter was replaced again at the request of the user, and the fault remained, and the oil pressure was not improved again. There was no improvement after replacing the oil pump. A fault point was found when the oil filter base was removed. Foreign matter was found stuck on the pressure relief valve in the oil filter base, as shown in Figure 2-1.

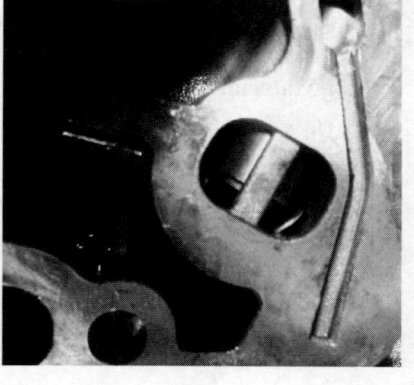

Figure 2-1　A Foreign Matter Stuck on the Pressure Relief Valve in the Oil Filter Base

　　The repairman removed the foreign matter and checked the pressure relief valve for no stagnation. The repairman remeasured the oil pressure after re-installation. The idle oil pressure was 400kPa. After operating the engine until the fan worked, the speed was increased to 2,000r/min and the oil pressure was 370kPa, which met the range of 270~450kPa. No alarm was given and the fault was eliminated.

　　Summary: The pressure relief valve of the oil filter base was stuck by a foreign matter, resulting in poor closing, and the oil flowed into the oil pan through the valve, causing low oil pressure. During automobile maintenance, communication with the user is very important. It is necessary to know whether the automobile is repaired and maintained at a regular service station. If the automobile fails after maintenance in an informal location, focus should be paid on checking whether the fault is caused by unqualified spare parts or non-standard operations.

Task Ⅱ　Fault Diagnosis and Repair of High Oil Pressure

 Learning Objectives

　　1. Be able to determine the direction and items of inquiry according to the fault phenomena of the automobile for repair.

　　2. Be able to prepare a correct fault diagnosis plan according to fault phenomena.

　　3. Be able to consult maintenance data skillfully, select appropriate detection and diagnosis devices according to fault phenomena and use them skillfully.

　　4. Be able to use suitable maintenance devices to detect high oil pressure fault according to the diagnosis plan.

　　5. Be able to correctly analyze the test results and determine the fault location and cause of high oil pressure.

　　6. Be able to repair the fault parts quickly and accurately and eliminate the hidden troubles.

Task Import

Task Material: A Volkswagen POLO 1.4L car, equipped with BCC engine, has serious valve rattle when running, severe jitter when running at idle speed. The engine power is obviously insufficient when driving.

Task Requirements: According to the fault phenomena of the car, consult relevant materials, select appropriate detection and diagnosis devices for fault diagnosis and repair, and fill in the task report.

I. Fault Analysis

High oil pressure fault occurs when the engine is operating at normal operating temperature and speed, the oil pressure is higher than the specified value. Oil filter seal gasket damage and oil leakage usually occur when the oil pressure is too high.

The main reasons for high oil pressure are as follows.

(1) The oil pressure gauge or oil pressure sensor is misaligned and the sensor circuit is faulty.

(2) The oil filter element is blocked and the pressure relief valve is stuck or improperly adjusted.

(3) The oil level of the oil pool is too high.

(4) The oil becomes thicker or the viscosity of the new oil is too high.

(5) There is blockage in the oil passage or the clearance of engine main bearing, connecting rod bearing and cam bearing is too small after overhaul.

II. Fault Diagnosis

(1) Check whether the oil level is too high, whether the oil viscosity is too high and whether the oil grade meets the requirements.

(2) Check whether the oil pressure indicator is faulty. If the indicator indicates pressure once the ignition switch is turned on, the oil pressure gauge or sensor is faulty.

(3) Check and adjust the pressure relief valve. For the pressure relief valve integrated with the oil pump, the oil pump shall be removed and inspected.

(4) Remove and inspect the engine, check and clean the lubricating oil passage, and blow it through with compressed air; Also check whether the mating clearances of crankshaft main bearing, connecting rod bearing and camshaft bearing are too small.

III. Task Implementation

1. Inquiry

Know the time of fault from the owner; Check whether there is abnormal condition before the fault; The road condition of the car; Whether the car is maintained on time; Has it been repaired after the fault occurred. Find out the situation before and after the fault and the specific information of the fault through the above inquiry, and complete the preliminary diagnosis of high oil pressure.

2. Test-drive and Basic Inspection

Start the engine, observe the running condition of the engine, and know whether the oil pressure alarm light displays normally; Change engine speed and observe for change. In addition, observe whether the engine external components are abnormal; Observe for oil leakage.

3. Detection and Diagnosis

Pull off the oil dipstick and check that the oil quantity and oil quality are completely normal. According to preliminary inspection, the cause of abnormal sound of valve is damage of hydraulic valve tappet, so replace the hydraulic valve tappet first. During replacement, a large amount of oil sludge deposit was found in the valve cover and the oil is dirty. After replacing the hydraulic valve tappet, clean the sludge in the valve cover and replace the oil and oil filter element. After the assembly and test-drive, the engine runs very quietly and smoothly in about 30s after the start-up, but after 30s, the engine starts to shake seriously and has insufficient power, but the abnormal valve sound disappears. Because of the special structure of BCC engine cylinder head (camshaft mounted on valve cover, valve, hydraulic tappet and other components installed on the cylinder head), according to the principle of simpleness to complexity, the engine electronic control system was tested with the scan tool 1552, and no fault code was found. Pulling out the injector plugs one by one for the cylinder disconnection test, it is found that the operation of each cylinder is not ideal, especially, the second cylinder is the worst. Then the spark plug, ignition coil and fuel injector are replaced. The fault remains. The cylinder pressure of each cylinder is checked with the cylinder pressure gauge, and the result is that the pressure display of each cylinder is normal. Therefore, it is considered that the cylinder pressure is sufficient. The intake manifold is then checked and no leaks are found, thus determining that there is a problem with the oil circuit or ignition control. Therefore, the oil circuit and the control system are checked. The gasoline pressure is also normal, and the ignition signal and fuel injection signal of each cylinder are normal. Ignition coil, spark plug, fuel injector, etc. are replaced and no problems are found. It is suspected that there is a gas timing error. The valve cover is disassembled and assembled twice and the gas timing is repeatedly checked and no abnormality is found. But one phenomenon is found: When the valve cover is removed and assembled each time, the engine runs smoothly within about 30s after starting. After about 30s, the engine starts to shake seriously.

Check that there are no problems with the timing and control parts through the above procedure. All the conditions associated with cylinder combustion work are normal, but the engine has obvious jitter. What exactly is the problem? Reanalysis is done for this fault. Engine shake and poor work should start with mechanical part and control part. Since the actuators such as ignition coil, spark plug and fuel injector have been replaced, the ignition, fuel injection and oil circuit have been checked, and no problems have been found (as these can be intuitively judged), the mechanical parts should be rechecked. As measured, the cylinder pressure display is normal and it seems to eliminate mechanical problems.

When the oil pressure is detected without clear diagnosis direction, it is found that the oil pressure is very high, and the oil pressure reaches 300kPa (higher than the specified value) at idle speed. So this time, the cylinder head is disassembled and inspected to find

out why the oil pressure is too high. When removing the valve, it is found that the valve seal is not very tight. There shall be a ring of bright annular belt at the port of the normal valve, which can basically see the color of metal, while all the ports of this automobile have partial slight blackening on the annular belt (the most obvious in cylinder 2), indicating that there is slight leakage at the port. Through careful inspection, it is found that the oil passage hole on the upper part of the valve rocker arm has been blocked by the oil sludge, which causes the oil in the hydraulic valve tappet to not be injected normally. The high oil pressure is related to this. After thorough cleaning and re-installation of the oil passage hole on the upper part of the valve rocker arm, the engine shake phenomenon has improved greatly, but there is still shake. The oil pressure is measured again at idle speed. Although it has dropped to 220kPa, it is still higher than the specified value. After checking the oil pump, it is found that the oil pan also has a thick oil sludge. It is concluded that there is also a large amount of oil sludge inside the oil pump, which cannot drain oil normally when the oil pressure is too high.

4. Fault Elimination

The oil pump is replaced and the oil pan and oil passage are cleaned. After re-installation, the engine is started, the shake disappears, the operation is stable, the test run on the route is accelerated vigorously, and the fault is completely eliminated.

5. Inspection and Delivery

After troubleshooting and without any other symptoms, hand over the car to the owner.

IV. Task Summary

Because the oil passage hole on the upper part of the rocker arm is completely blocked by sludge, the oil cannot drain normally, causing the oil pressure to rise continuously. After 30s, the valve hydraulic tappet is overstretched due to high oil pressure, combined with the pressure of combustion work in the cylinder, so that the already fragile seal is damaged, resulting in stable operation of the engine within about 30s after starting, but serious jitter after 30s.

V. Task Report

	Major		Class		Name	
	Task Name				Class Hours	2
	Model			Engine Model		
	Assessment Items	Assessment Contents			Maximum Score	Score
Task Completion Process	1. Description of fault symptoms				5	
	2. Possible causes and analysis of fault				25	
	3. Detection and diagnosis process				35	
	4. Fault Elimination				10	
	5. Summary of fault diagnosis				10	
Teacher Evaluation	Operation quality, operation efficiency, operation safety, etc.				15	
	Total Score				100	

VI. Knowledge Expansion

[Typical Case]　High oil pressure after overhaul of a Dongfeng EQ1091 engine.

Fault Description: In A Dongfeng EQ1091, 3 primary oil filter elements were damaged within 1 week after engine overhaul due to high oil pressure, and the bearing shell burnt twice.

Fault Diagnosis and Repair: The repairer who originally undertook to repair the engine thought that high oil pressure was not a fault, but that the bearing shell and the journal were slightly tight, in which case the engine had a longer service life. As long as the oil quantity was checked regularly, the oil pressure would be normal after the engine was run-in. After repairing the automobile, the repairman firstly checked the indication of the oil pressure gauge. When the ignition switch was set to ignition position, the engine was not running and the oil pressure was displayed as 250kPa, and when the engine was running at idle speed, the oil pressure was 700kPa. This indicated that the oil pressure sensor was misaligned. The repairman checked the oil pressure again after replacing the oil pressure sensor. The result was that the oil pressure gauge indicated that the oil pressure was 600kPa when the engine was running at idle speed, and the oil pressure was really too high. When disassembling the primary oil filter, it was found that the upper end face of the filter element had a hemispherical shape and kept dripping oil. When inspecting the oil pump, it was found that one screw and three spring washers (total thickness up to 8mm) were padded at one end of the pressure relief valve spring, but the spring length was significantly insufficient. The owner stated that they were padded before the engine overhaul due to low oil pressure and were not removed during the engine overhaul. Considering the insufficient spring length, the repairman removed the screw rod and 2 spring washers (one spring washer is remained) and reinstalled the oil pump, and then proceeded to the test run. At this time, the oil pressure returned to normal, and the primary oil filter element didn't leak any more. Because the primary oil filter element was damaged, it was replaced with a new one and the fault was eliminated.

Summary: Two insights can be drawn from the above troubleshooting: The idea of "slightly high oil pressure is beneficial and harmless" shall; Too high oil pressure does not help to improve the lubrication conditions of parts and prolong the life of the engine. On the contrary, it can increase oil leakage, resulting in increased oil consumption and damage of the primary oil filter element, and even accidents.

Task III Fault Diagnosis and Repair of Excessive Oil Consumption

Learning Objectives

1. Be able to determine the direction and items of inquiry according to the fault phenomena of the automobile for repair.

2. Be able to prepare a correct fault diagnosis plan according to fault phenomena.

3. Be able to consult maintenance data skillfully, select appropriate detection and diagnosis devices according to fault phenomena and use them skillfully.

4. Be able to use appropriate maintenance devices to detect the excessive oil consumption, according to the diagnosis plan.

5. Be able to correctly analyze the test results and determine the fault location and causes of excessive oil consumption.

6. Be able to repair the fault parts quickly and accurately and eliminate the hidden troubles.

Task Import

Task Material: The engine of a Shanghai Volkswagen Passat 1. 8T manual gear car with a distance of 201, 000 kilometers, after running 12, 000 kilometers upon overhaul, consumes more oil, and the exhaust pipe sometimes exhaust blue smoke at high speed.

Task Requirements: According to the fault phenomena of the car, consult relevant materials, select appropriate detection and diagnosis devices for fault diagnosis and repair, and fill in the task report.

I. Fault Analysis

GB/T 19055—2003 stipulates that the percentage of engine oil and fuel consumption shall be less than 0. 3% during full-speed full load test. The engines and automobiles meeting this standard shall have normal oil consumption.

There are two main aspects of reasons for excessive oil consumption: On the one hand, the engine "burns engine oil"; On the other hand, the engine "leaks oil". The "oil burning" can be clearly reflected from the exhaust of the engine. If the exhaust pipe of the engine is blue smoke, it indicates that the engine is burning oil. The "oil leakage" shall be mainly checked from the joints of each sealing surface and lubrication system pipeline. There will be obvious oil stains at the oil leakage.

There are 10 main reasons for engine "oil burning":

(1) Too much oil refilled causes the oil to burn.

(2) Engine cylinder "scuffing" causes oil to burn.

(3) Engine cylinder gaskets are ablated and oil enters the combustion chamber.

(4) The clearance between piston and cylinder wall is too large.

(5) The opening of the piston ring is not staggered.

(6) Piston ring sticks.

(7) The piston ring is not enough elastic.

(8) The "three clearances" of the piston ring are too large.

(9) The piston rings is assembled incorrectly.

(10) The valve stem oil seal is damaged and the valve guide is excessively worn.

The main parts of engine "oil leakage" are as follows:

(1) Engine front and rear crankshaft oil seals, timing gear chamber, joint surface of crankcase and oil pan, camshaft rear oil seal.

(2) Poor sealing of valve oil seal, large clearance between valve stem and valve guide.

(3) Exhaust turbocharger leaks.

(4) External leakage of components of the engine lubrication system.

Ⅱ. Fault Diagnosis

For the excessive oil consumption, the first thing is to determine whether the oil filling amount is normal, then distinguish whether the fault is caused by engine oil burning or oil leakage, and finally find out the specific position and cause of the fault according to the fault type.

1. The diagnostic method for "oil burning"

(1) If the exhaust pipe clearly emits blue smoke, it can be determined that excessive oil consumption is caused by engine oil burning. When the engine runs at heavy load and high speed, the exhaust pipe emits a lot of blue smoke. After pulling out the oil dipstick, if the blue smoke can also be seen from the oil filler, it means that the piston and piston ring are worn too much against the cylinder wall, or the end clearance, side clearance and back clearance of piston ring are too large, and the openings of multiple piston rings are faced to the same direction, the piston rings are attached to each other, the twisted ring or the conical ring is reverse, etc. , which makes the oil flow into the combustion chamber. The pistons and piston rings shall be replaced for such faults.

(2) If the exhaust pipe emits a large amount of blue smoke when the engine runs under heavy load, but the oil filler does not smoke, while the cylinder head cover is blowing smoke out, then the valve stem oil seal is damaged and the valve guide is worn too much, making the oil sucked into the combustion chamber. The valve stem oil seal or valve guide should be replaced for such faults.

(3) If the exhaust pipe emits a large amount of blue smoke after the engine is started, and the oil consumption is large, it is usually caused by the erosion of the engine cylinder gasket and the entry of oil into the combustion chamber. Such fault requires removing the cylinder head and replacing the cylinder gasket.

2. Diagnostic Method of "oil leakage"

(1) The first thing is to check the outside of the engine for leakage. Pay special attention to oil leakage at the oil seals at the front and rear ends of the crankshaft. Cracking, damage and aging of the front oil seal of crankshaft, or wear of contact surface between crankshaft pulley and oil seal may cause oil leakage at the front end of crankshaft. The cracking and damage of oil seal at the rear end of the crankshaft or too small oil return hole of the rear main bearing cover makes the oil return blocked, which may cause oil leakage at the rear end of the crankshaft. In addition, attention should be paid to the oil seal at the rear end of the camshaft for oil leakage. If the oil leakage is caused by aging or cracking of the oil seal, it should be replaced. In addition, the components of the engine lubrication system should be checked for leakage.

(2) If there is oil leakage at the front and rear oil seals of the engine, even oil leaks from front and rear cylinder head covers, front and rear valve tappet chambers, oil filters, oil pan gaskets, etc. , but no obvious oil leakage is found, the crankcase ventilation device should be checked and the crankcase ventilation pipe should be cleaned, especially checking whether the PCV valves are not working well due to carbon deposit and glue sticking. If the crankcase is poorly ventilated, it is likely that the pressure in the crankcase will increase, resulting in

multiple oil leaks.

(3) If the oil filter and the joints of some oil circuits are still leaking after being tightened, check whether the oil pressure is too high and the oil pressure relief valve is not working properly.

Ⅲ. Task Implementation

1. Inquiry

The repairman shall know the time of fault from the owner; Whether there are other abnormal conditions before the fault; Whether the symptoms change after finding the fault; Details of driving; Whether the automobile is maintained on time; Have other repairs been performed after the fault. The repairman may find out the situations before and after the fault and the specific information of the fault through the above inquiry, and complete the preliminary diagnosis of excessive oil consumption.

2. Test-drive and Basic Inspection

The repairman shall firstly check whether the amount of engine oil is normal, then start the engine, observe whether the exhaust pipe has blue smoke and the extent of blue smoke; Observe whether the engine operating condition changes and the symptoms change; Observe engine external components for obvious oil leakage.

3. Detection and Diagnosis

The repairman inspects the exterior of the engine and finds no leaks. The turbocharger has been replaced at the same time during overhaul, so the oil leakage at this part is preliminarily eliminated. An endoscope is used and placed deeply in the cylinder for inspection. It is found that there are more carbon deposits and glue on the back of the valve and significant oil marks on the valve stem. Based on the analysis of the present situation, it is concluded that the oil is infiltrated into the combustion chamber from the valve guide and the valve oil seal and burnt, but the same-directional openings of the piston rings can not be excluded. So the engine is disassembled. After disassembly of the engine, it is found that the openings of the piston rings of each cylinder are not in the same direction, the sealing performance is good, the cylinder diameter is not exceeded, the roundness and cylindricality of cylinder and the matching clearance between the cylinder and the piston are normal. After disassembling the cylinder head, it is found that the installation position of valve oil seal is normal, and the fitting clearance between valve and valve guide is normal. The above check determines that there should be no problems with the engine assembly during the last overhaul. According to the above inspection results and the main reasons for the large oil consumption, it may be that the crankcase pressure is too high. The main causes of crankcase pressure increase are: The sealing performance between piston ring and cylinder decreases, leading to blowdown gas; The positive crankcase ventilation line is blocked. According to the above inspection results, the first cause can be ruled out, with emphasis on checking the positive crankcase ventilation line. The engine of this model has two positive ventilation lines, namely, the ventilation line at idle speed (when the throttle valve is closed) and the ventilation line at load (when the throttle valve is open). All check valves in the ventilation lines are checked and no problem is found, but when checking under load, a blockage is found near the jet

pump. Because of carbon deposit here, the crankcase pressure rises when the engine is operating under load. When the pressure rises to a certain extent, the oil leaks into the combustion chamber from the valve guide and the valve oil seal, resulting in increased oil consumption and blue smoke in the exhaust pipe under heavy load.

4. Fault Elimination

After dredging the plugged parts and reinstalling the engine for test run, the fault is eliminated.

5. Inspection and Delivery

After troubleshooting and without any other symptoms, hand over the car to the owner.

IV. Task Summary

Be sure to pay attention to detail when repairing a car. Minor negligence can cause serious consequences. In this case, the fault is caused by the failure to thoroughly clean the positive ventilation lines during overhaul. When analyzing a fault, we must pay attention to logic and be familiar with relevant structures to find the fault location quickly and accurately.

V. Task Report

Major			Class		Name	
Task Name					Class Hours	2
Model				Engine Model		
	Assessment Items		Assessment Contents		Maximum Score	Score
Task Completion Process	1. Description of fault symptoms				5	
	2. Possible causes and analysis of fault				25	
	3. Detection and diagnosis process				35	
	4. Fault Elimination				10	
	5. Summary of fault diagnosis				10	
Teacher Evaluation	Operation quality, operation efficiency, operation safety, etc.				15	
Total Score					100	

VI. Knowledge Expansion

〔Typical Case Ⅰ〕 Abnormal oil consumption of a Toyota Crown car.

Fault Description: When the Toyota service technician checked the engine oil volume according to the procedure, he found that the oil level measured by the dipstick was only 2mm from the lowest point. Through communication with the owner, he knew that the automobile had been inspected for 3 times before, and the amount of oil had been abnormally reduced every time. These three times had been supplemented.

Fault Diagnosis and Repair: Through communication with the owner, he first added the oil to the full level line of the oil dipstick and delivered the car to the owner for normal use. After the car ran 500km, the owner returned to the factory to check, and it was found that the oil volume has been reduced. The service technician added oil to the full level line of the oil dipstick by a measuring cup gradually, and about 300mL was added in total. According to this, the oil consumption of the car every 5, 000km was calculated as 3L, completely beyond the normal range.

Item Ⅱ　Fault Diagnosis and Repair of Lubrication System

He checked all parts of the engine and found no signs of oil leakage, and he checked each vacuum, intake pipe and PCV valve and found no signs of abnormal oil leakage. There was no abnormality except that the cylinder 6 spark plug was slightly darker than other cylinders and the cylinder pressure was lower. Therefore, the reason for abnormal oil consumption was inside the engine. Therefore, he disassembled the engine assembly, checked the cylinder one by one and found that there was much carbon sludge deposited on the top of the piston. The piston rings 2 of cylinders 1, 4 and 5 coincided with the opening of the oil ring, the piston clearance of cylinders 1 and 6 exceeded the specified value, and the piston clearances of other cylinders also reached or approached the specified value. It was determined from the above that there was a problem with the engine body. As the car was under warranty, the engine is replaced with a new one. After installing the engine, there was no fault found after inspection, operation and road test, so the car was delivered to the owner. After half a month, the car was returned to the factory for inspection, and the oil volume was normal without reduction.

Summary: Because the openings of the piston rings coincided and the piston clearances of some cylinders are large, the engine burnt off the oil, which caused abnormal oil consumption. The oil consumption can be calculated by a certain detection method.

〔Typical Case Ⅱ〕 High engine oil consumption of a 2011 Changan Suzuki SX41. 8L car.

Fault Description: The engine oil fault alarm light was on during driving. Upon inspection, it was found that the oil level was too low, and the oil was added to the normal liquid level. After driving for a period of time, the oil fault alarm light was on again, and the oil level was still too low after inspection.

Fault Diagnosis and Repair:

1. The repairman checked the outside of the engine and found no leakage. Upon slam acceleration, it was found that the exhaust pipe had slight oil erosion smell.

2. He read out the fault code with a scan tool but no fault code was read out.

3. He checked the cylinder pressure of each cylinder and found no abnormality. He made preliminary judgment that the fault was caused by cylinder wear and piston ring fault. He mainly placed the fault area on: VVT system, camshaft oil seal, valve oil seal, valve, valve guide.

4. He checked the VVT system and associated pipes and found no leaks.

5. He checked the camshaft oil seal and found no abnormality.

6. He disassembled the cylinder head and checked the valve and valve oil seal and found no abnormality.

7. When inspecting the valve guide, he found that the cylinder head was cracked at the place where the cylinder head cylinder 3 intake valve was embedded in the valve guide, as shown in Figure 2-2. The crack caused engine oil to permeate into the com-

Figure 2-2　Crack of Cylinder Head Cylinder 3

bustion chamber, so during rapid acceleration, the exhaust pipe had a slight smell of oil erosion and the oil consumption was high. Then the cylinder head was replaced, and the car was normal during the test-drive. During the return visit after 3 days, the car was in normal condition and the fault was completely eliminated.

Summary: The fault is a typical fault with relatively small probability of occurrence. The fault point is concealed. Therefore, it is necessary to search one by one according to the possible causes of abnormal oil consumption and according to the characteristics and rules of the fault, to gradually narrow the fault range and finally find the fault point.

Task Ⅳ   Fault Diagnosis and Repair of Oil Deterioration

Learning Objectives

1. Be able to determine the direction and items of inquiry according to the fault phenomena of the automobile for repair.

2. Be able to prepare a correct fault diagnosis plan according to fault phenomena.

3. Be able to consult maintenance data skillfully, select appropriate detection and diagnosis devices according to fault phenomena and use them skillfully.

4. Be able to use suitable maintenance devices to test the oil deterioration according to the diagnosis plan.

5. Be able to correctly analyze the test results and determine the fault location and cause of oil deterioration.

6. Be able to repair the fault parts quickly and accurately and eliminate the hidden troubles.

Task Import

Task Material: A Haval CUV equipped with engine model 4G6454M, 2.4L. The owner said that the oil is deteriorated and the coolant consumption is abnormal. The owner wants to find out the cause.

Task Requirements: According to the fault phenomena of the car, consult relevant materials, select appropriate detection and diagnosis devices for fault diagnosis and repair, and fill in the task report.

Ⅰ. Fault Analysis

The so-called oil deterioration refers to that the engine oil is mixed with moisture, dust, fuel, or other mechanical substances, which changes the chemical composition of the oil, resulting in the oil lubrication performance degradation or disappearance.

The main reasons for oil deterioration are as follows:

(1) The component wear impurities are mixed into the oil, increasing the impurity content of the oil.

(2) The piston ring leaks, causing incomplete combustion to enter the crankcase and

mix with oil.

(3) Poor crankcase ventilation prevents harmful gases from being discharged in time.

(4) Gasoline and cooling water enter the oil pan due to leakage.

(5) Too much dust is mixed into the oil.

(6) Oxidation of the oil due to prolonged operation of the engine under overheating conditions.

II. Fault Diagnosis

When diagnosing oil deterioration, the first is to confirm whether the automobile is maintained on time, and then to determine the cause of the fault according to the characteristics of deteriorated oil under normal maintenance.

The diagnostic method of oil deterioration is as follows:

(1) Check whether the oil deteriorates due to excessive use time and not regularly replaced.

(2) If the oil is turbid emulsion and the oil level is raised, it means that the coolant enters the oil.

(3) Check the crankcase ventilation valve for failure.

(4) The oil is gray and smells of fuel, indicating that the oil has been diluted by fuel, usually due to air leaks in the cylinder piston bank, causing incompletely burnt fuel to flow into the oil pan.

III. Task Implementation

1. Inquiry

The repairman shall know the time of fault from the owner; Whether there are other abnormal conditions before the fault; Whether the symptoms change after finding the fault; Details of driving; Whether the automobile is maintained on time; Have other repairs been performed after the fault. The preliminary diagnosis of oil deterioration shall be completed by knowing the situation before and after the fault and the specific information of the fault.

2. Test-drive and Basic Inspection

The repairman checks whether the oil quantity and oil quality are normal, then starts the engine and observes whether the engine operates abnormally.

3. Detection and Diagnosis

The repairman checks the quality of the oil first, and finds that the engine oil is cloudy and emulsified, indicating that the coolant enters into the oil, and the consumed coolant enters into the oil pan.

When the car is cold, he opens the water tank cover and starts the engine. The coolant in the water tank violently sprays out when the engine starts, then he quickly closes the key door switch. Upon the analysis of the above situation, the cause may be that the cylinder gasket is damaged and the gas in the combustion chamber enters the cooling system. Therefore, he removes the cylinder gasket. After inspection, he found that the cylinder gasket is intact without any damage. He checks the cylinder block and the cylinder block is also intact. But there is antifreeze on the piston, which obviously enters the combustion chamber. He

checked the cylinder head, and found that the cylinder head is seriously corroded at several places near the combustion chamber, and each one can cause the combustion chamber to communicate with the water channel, so it can be determined that the cause of previous water leakage in the main water tank is here.

4. Fault Elimination

He replaces the cylinder head after determining that the cylinder head cannot be repaired. After replacing the cylinder head, he starts the engine again, and the antifreeze is no longer ejected from the water tank cover, and there is no bubble in the coolant, so the fault is gone.

5. Inspection and Delivery

After troubleshooting and without any other symptoms, hand over the car to the owner.

IV. Task Summary

The cause of this fault is that coolant enters the combustion chamber from the gap between the cylinder head and the cylinder gasket, and a portion of the coolant flows into the oil pan, eventually causing the oil to deteriorate.

The reason why the cylinder head is so seriously corroded should be caused by the water added by the owner or the antifreeze that fails to meet the standard. In short, it is caused by failure to pay attention to the correct maintenance. Therefore, when filling the automobile with coolant, antifreeze must be preferred. Even if water is added in case of no antifreeze, the antifreeze with quality guarantee shall be replaced in time under accessible case.

V. Task Report

Major			Class		Name	
Task Name					Class Hours	2
Model			Engine Model			
	Assessment Items		Assessment Contents		Maximum Score	Score
Task Completion Process	1. Description of fault symptoms				5	
	2. Possible causes and analysis of fault				25	
	3. Detection and diagnosis process				35	
	4. Fault Elimination				10	
	5. Summary of fault diagnosis				10	
Teacher Evaluation	Operation quality, operation efficiency, operation safety, etc.				15	
Total Score					100	

VI. Knowledge Expansion

[Typical Case] Oil deterioration of a Beijing Jeep.

Fault Description: A Beijing Jeep suddenly shut down during driving. After restarting, the engine ran unevenly with abnormal rattle. There was no oil pressure indication on the instrument, and the oil was found deteriorated.

Fault Diagnosis and Repair: The repairman firstly asked the owner and knew that the oil had not been changed according to the maintenance time. Therefore, he suspected that the oil was deteriorated due to excessive impurities in the oil caused by the oil not being changed for

a long time. Then he drained the oil from the oil pan and found that the oil collector was completely blocked by impurities.

Then he cleaned the oil collector and each lubricating oil passage, replaced it with new oil and replaced the filter, and found that the engine started normally, but the engine sounded abnormally. After further inspection, he found that the engine's abnormal rattle was caused by erosion of the fifth main bearing shell of the engine crankshaft. After replacement, he tested the engine again and found that the engine worked normally.

Summary: The engine oil was deteriorated and a large amount of impurities were stored in the engine oil for a long time because the car failed to be maintained on time, and the oil and the filter were not replaced according to regulations, so that the oil was dirty, so that the oil collector was blocked, so that the moving parts in the engine could not be fully lubricated and the bearing shell was burnt, so it suddenly turned off on the road.

Item III

Fault Diagnosis and Repair of Cooling System

The cooling system faults are mainly divided into two aspects: faults of coolant circulation system and faults of the cooling fan and its control circuit. Common fault characteristics of cooling system mainly include: engine overheating, abnormal consumption of coolant, etc.

Learning Objectives

1. Be able to determine the direction and items of inquiry according to the fault phenomena of the automobile for repair.

2. Be able to prepare a correct fault diagnosis plan according to fault phenomena.

3. Be able to consult maintenance data skillfully, select appropriate detection and diagnosis devices according to fault phenomena and use them skillfully.

4. Be able to use appropriate maintenance devices to test the engine overheating according to the diagnosis plan.

5. Be able to correctly analyze the test results and determine the fault location and cause of engine overheating.

6. Be able to repair the fault parts quickly and accurately and eliminate the hidden troubles.

7. Be able to have good service mentality and earnest work style, and to improve safety consciousness.

Task Import

Task Material: The owner of a Picasso car, driven for 120, 000 km, said that the engine water temperature indicator on the combination cluster showed a too high value, and the engine water temperature alarm light was on, and the STOP light was on.

Task Requirements: According to the fault phenomena of the car, consult relevant materials, select appropriate detection and diagnosis devices for fault diagnosis and repair, and fill in the task report.

Ⅰ. Fault Analysis

Engine overheating means that the water temperature is too high. The fault phenomena are that during the operation of the engine, the water temperature indicator displays the water temperature exceeding the normal range, the water temperature alarm light is on, even the radiator is accompanied by the "boiled" phenomenon, and the engine is liable to knock.

The main causes of engine overheating are as follows.

(1) The coolant is insufficient or deteriorated.

(2) The fan belt slips, the fan does not rotate or does not rotate at high speed.

(3) The thermostat cannot be opened or opened too late.

(4) The cooling water pipe is squeezed and concave.

(5) The radiator is blocked inside or is locked outside by dirt; There are too much scale deposited inside the radiator and jacket.

(6) The water pump does not work or works badly.

(7) The water temperature sensor or the temperature control switch do not work properly or the circuit is faulty.

(8) The fan control module or control circuit is faulty.

(9) Incorrect ignition timing prevents the engine from burning normally, generating excessive heat.

Ⅱ. Fault Diagnosis

(1) Check the coolant level and determine whether its specification and brand conform to the requirements. Check coolant for deterioration.

(2) Check whether the fan speed is normal; Check whether the fan belt is too loose, whether the blades are deformed, and whether the fan clutch fails, etc.

(3) Check the radiator for deformation, water leakage and excessive scale; Check whether the temperature of each part is uniform.

(4) Check whether the water pipe is abnormal, touch the radiator and the upper and lower water pipes. If the lower water pipe temperature is low, it indicates that the thermostat is faulty, and it should be removed and inspected.

(5) Check whether the water pump belt is too loose. Hold the water pipe from the top of the engine to the radiator by hand during inspection, then accelerate from idle speed to a certain high speed. If the flow velocity in the water pipe felt increases with the increase of engine speed, the water pump works normally; Otherwise, it indicates that the water pump is not working properly, and the water pump shall be dismantled and inspected.

(6) Check the technical condition of the water temperature sensor and the temperature control switch and confirm whether the technical condition is in good condition.

(7) Check the fan control module or control circuit for proper operation.

(8) Check the engine ignition system for fault.

Ⅲ. Task Implementation

1. Inquiry

Know the time of fault from the owner; Whether the symptoms change after the fault is

found, and whether there are other abnormal conditions before the fault; Details during driving; Whether the car is maintained on time; Have other repairs been performed after the fault. The preliminary diagnosis of high water temperature is completed by knowing the situation before and after the fault and the specific information of the fault through the above inquiry.

2. Test-drive and Basic Inspection

The repairman firstly checks the amount of engine coolant, which is completely normal, then starts the engine to observe the engine symptoms, and observes the cooling fan operation.

3. Detection and Diagnosis

He starts the engine to observe the cooling system operation. When the engine starts and runs for about 5min, it is found that the engine water temperature indicator reaches the highest point and the engine water temperature alarm light is on. At the same time, the electric cooling fan starts to operate at high speed. After several minutes of heat dissipation, the water temperature indication drops to the normal value (about 90℃), and the electric fan stops running.

The scan tool PROXIA3 is used to read out the fault message: water temperature indicator fault, temporary fault; High speed operation of electric fan fault, permanent failure. He clears the fault code but the fault remains.

According to the working principle of the cooling system, it is known that: When the engine temperature reaches 97℃, the engine control unit controls the cooling fan to start running at low speed for heat dissipation; When the engine temperature reaches 101℃, the engine control unit controls the cooling fan to start running at medium speed for heat dissipation; When the engine temperature reaches 105℃, the engine control unit controls the cooling fan to start running at high speed for heat dissipation; The thermostat opens at the engine temperature of 89℃ and fully opens when the engine temperature reaches 101℃.

The analysis shows that the high water temperature is probably caused by the thermostat fault or excessive scale in the water channel. Therefore, all the engine coolant is drained, and the thermostat and the radiator assembly are checked, and no abnormality is found. After replacing a new coolant, the fault remains.

Check whether the control circuit and relay of the engine cooling fan are normal.

Remove the engine water temperature sensor, measure its resistance value and compare it with the standard value. It is found that there is a large difference. It is suspected that the sensor is faulty.

4. Fault Elimination

After replacing a new engine water temperature sensor and conducting a test-drive, the fault disappears.

5. Inspection and Delivery

After troubleshooting and without any other symptoms, hand over the car to the owner.

Ⅳ. Task Summary

This fault is an engine temperature sensor fault that causes the engine control unit to

obtain incorrect water temperature information and a water temperature alarm. During such fault diagnosis, the data flow can be used to know whether the signal of the water temperature sensor is accurate, so as to avoid blind disassembly and replacement.

V. Task Report

Major			Class		Name		
Task Name					Class Hours		2
Model				Engine Model			
Task Completion Process	Assessment Items		Assessment Contents		Maximum Score		Score
	1. Description of fault symptoms				5		
	2. Possible causes and analysis of fault				25		
	3. Detection and diagnosis process				35		
	4. Fault Elimination				10		
	5. Summary of fault diagnosis				10		
Teacher Evaluation	Operation quality, operation efficiency, operation safety, etc.				15		
Total Score					100		

VI. Knowledge Expansion

〔Typical Case Ⅰ〕 Too High water temperature of a Santana 2000GSI engine.

Fault Description: A Santana 2000GSI car had a water temperature alarm and too high engine temperature during driving.

Fault Diagnosis and Repair: At first, the repairman touched the upper and lower pipes of the engine by hand respectively and found that the temperatures are basically the same, which indicated that the thermostat was open. After further inspection, he found that the engine cooling fan did not operate properly. Then he checked the fuse and temperature control switch of the cooling fan and found that the fuse of the cooling fan had burnt out. The engine's cooling fan could operate normally after replacing the fuse of the same model, but the same fault occurred again after 1 week. After replacing the fuse of the same model this time, the engine cooling fan did not work properly. After further inspection, he turned the blades of the active fan and the passive fan of the cooling fan respectively, and felt large resistance against the two fans, and both had jamming, which proved that the active fan and the passive fan had been damaged.

When replacing the cooling fan of the same specification and model, the high engine water temperature did not occur again.

Summary: Because the cooling fan was stuck, the rotating resistance was large, and the current load of the fan was increased, which caused the fuse of the engine cooling fan burnt out and the engine temperature too high. Normal operation after replacing the fuse is because that the cooling fan could still overcome the jamming resistance of the fan. However, after one week of operation, the engine cooling fan was stuck more seriously, which made the fan motor unable to rotate, so the cooling fan could not operate normally after replacing the fuse again, made the engine temperature too high.

〔Typical Case Ⅱ〕 High water temperature of Jetta CIX engine.

Fault Description: The engine of a Jetta CIX was running at a high temperature and the electric fan was not running at high speed.

Fault Diagnosis and Repair: After inspection, double temperature switch, electric fan, fan controller and thermostat were replaced successively, but the fault remained.

The control circuit of Jetta fan is shown in Figure 3-1. The double temperature switch is connected to the low gear at the engine water temperature of 95℃, and directly supplies 30V positive power from the fuse to the fan low speed coil, making the fan run at low speed.

When the engine water temperature is 105℃, the double temperature switch is connected to the high gear, transmits the signal to the fan controller, which supplies power to the fan high-speed coil, making the fan operate at high speed.

After short-circuiting the circuit of the double temperature switch, the low gear operated normally, while the high gear still did not rotate, it could be concluded that the problem was on the circuit of high gear.

The circuit from the plug line 3 of the double temperature switch to pin T10/7 of the fan controller was checked. The detected voltage was 12V, indicating the circuit was normal.

The fuse of S36 fan controller was checked with a voltage of 12V. The circuit of fan controller T10/9 was checked with a normal voltage.

The pin T10/6 and grounding of the fan controller were checked and the grounding was normal.

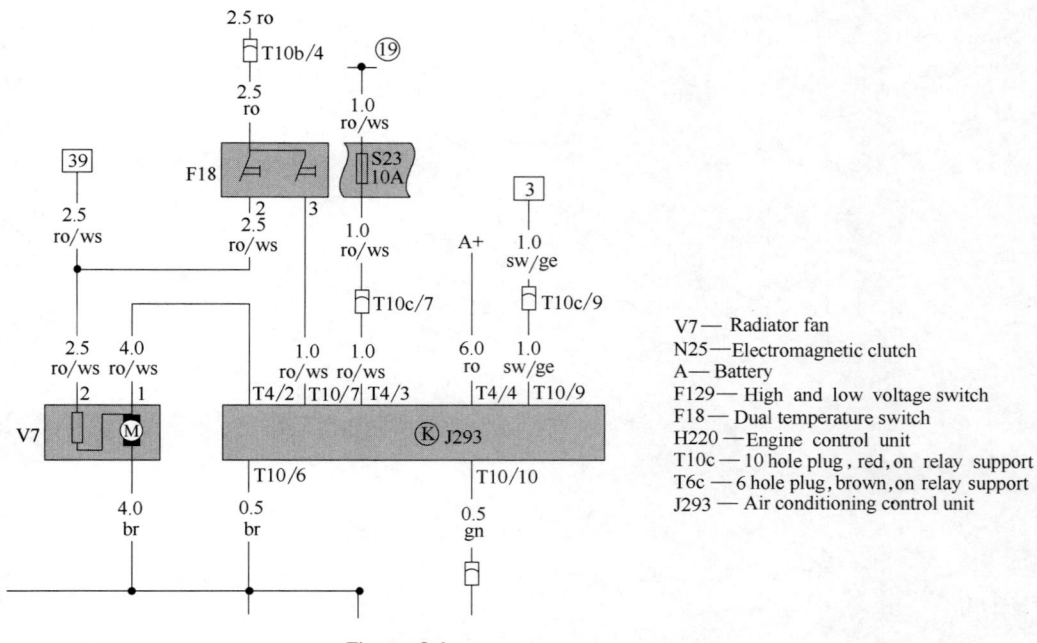

Figure 3-1 Control Circuit of Jetta Fan

At this point, it could be determined that the fan controller was not working.

After replacing another fan controller, the fault still remained. 30V positive power was separately led from the positive pole of the battery to the fan controller, and the fan high gear could work.

Finally, the fuse block was removed and it was found that the wiring harness behind fuse 36 had been broken, with little touch. There was a voltage during measurement, but current supplied was insufficient and the fan controller would not work. The fan worked nor-

mally after connecting this wire. The fault was gone.

Summary: This fault is a typical fault with too large line resistance. It is usually difficult to find the abnormality of the line by measuring the resistance of the line. If the replacement method is adopted, the fault location cannot be determined. The fault location can be determined by measuring the operating current of the fan circuit. In addition, the diagnosis must be combined with the working principle and circuit of the system.

Item IV

Fault Diagnosis and Repair of Abnormal Sound of Automobile

Abnormal sound of an automobile refers to abnormal sound produced by abnormal movement, wear and aging of running or moving parts. Abnormal sound is a common fault, including abnormal engine sound and abnormal chassis sound.

The abnormal sound is usually mixed with normal sound. The maintenance personnel must understand the characteristics and rules of abnormal sound during diagnosis, so as to quickly and accurately identify the fault source and find out the fault location.

 Task | Fault Diagnosis and Repair of Abnormal Engine Sound

Learning Objectives

1. Be able to determine the direction and items of inquiry according to the fault phenomena of the automobile for repair.

2. Be able to prepare a correct fault diagnosis plan according to fault phenomena.

3. Be able to consult maintenance data skillfully, select appropriate detection and diagnosis devices according to fault phenomena and use them skillfully.

4. Be able to use appropriate maintenance devices to test the engine abnormal sound according to the diagnosis plan.

5. Be able to correctly analyze the test results and determine the fault location and cause of abnormal engine rattle.

6. Be able to repair the fault parts quickly and accurately and eliminate the hidden troubles.

7. Be able to work rigorously and carefully, and have the spirit of artisans and craftsmen of excellence.

Task Import

Task Material: A 2011 Jetta engine rattles as it accelerates, with low noise when the car is cold and loud when it's hot.

Task Requirements: According to the fault phenomena of the car, consult relevant materials, select appropriate detection and diagnosis devices for fault diagnosis and repair, and fill in the task report.

Ⅰ. Fault Analysis

The abnormal engine sound refers to various abnormal sounds emitted by the engine during operation. The abnormal engine sounds can be divided into external and internal abnormal sounds. The external abnormal sounds refer to abnormal sounds from belt pulley assemblies, generators, water pump bearings, tension pulleys, etc.; The internal abnormal sounds refer to abnormal sounds from main bearing, connecting rod bearing, piston knocking, piston pin, etc.

The abnormal sound is related to engine speed, load, temperature, lubrication conditions and other factors. The different abnormal sound position has different sound characteristics, accompanying phenomena and occurrence time. Many abnormal sounds have obvious tone characteristics, which can help to determine the fault locations. The main abnormal sound characteristics include the following:

(1) Audio characteristics: Abnormal engine sounds have different tones, such as a dull "dang" sound from the main bearing, and a clear "click" sound from the valve foot. The frequency, amplitude and continuity of each sound can be observed by recording the sound waveform.

(2) Speed characteristics: Normally, abnormal sound varies with engine speed. With different abnormal sound, the speed range of the most obvious abnormal sound will be different. For example, the sounds of piston knocking, piston pin and valve foot are obvious at idle speed. The sounds of connecting rod bearing and valve seat are obvious at medium speed. The sounds of main bearing, connecting rod bearing and piston ring are obvious when accelerating rapidly.

(3) Load characteristics: Some abnormal sounds are related to the engine load, which increases or weakens when the load changes. For example, the sounds of crankshaft main bearing, connecting rod bearing, piston knocking and ignition knocking all increase with the increase of load (climbing, acceleration, full load, etc.) and weaken with the decrease of load. However, some abnormal sounds are irrelevant to the load, such as the valve sound, which does not change when the load changes.

(4) Temperature characteristics: Some abnormal sounds are related to engine temperature, and some sounds are independent from or not much related to engine temperature. For example, the piston knocking is obvious at low temperature, and the abnormal sound decreases or disappears after the temperature rises; Early combustion bursting noise caused by engine overheating, abnormal sound of cylinder knocking caused by deformation of piston and too small fitting clearance are not obvious at low temperature, and the abnormal sounds

50 | Automobile Integrated Fault Diagnosis and Repair |

are obvious or aggravated after temperature rise; Main bearing sound, connecting rod bearing sound and valve foot sound are less affected by temperature.

(5) Cylinder position characteristics: The abnormal sound with obvious variation during single cylinder flameout or refire is called engine upper cylinder or sound upper cylinder. For example, the sounds of connecting rod bearing, piston ring and piston knocking caused by too large fitting clearance of cylinder are relieved or disappeared during single cylinder flameout; There is no obvious change in the sound of crankshaft main bearing during single cylinder flameout, and the sound is reduced or disappeared when two adjacent cylinders are cut off; The sound of valve foot does not change or change obviously when the single cylinder are cut off.

(6) Working cycle characteristics: The abnormal engine sound is strongly related to the working cycle. For example, abnormal sound of crank connecting rod mechanism is sounded twice per working cycle, and abnormal sound of valve mechanism once per working cycle.

(7) Abnormal sound auscultation site and vibration area: The areas where abnormal sounds cause vibration on the engine are cylinder head, upper part of cylinder block, underside of cylinder block, interface between oil pan and crankcase, timing gear chamber and oil filling port (or crankcase ventilation pipe mouth).

(8) Concomitant phenomena: When the engine rattles, other malfunctions often occur. For example, the oil pressure is reduced, the exhaust gas color of the exhaust pipe is abnormal, the power drops, the operation is weak, the fuel consumption is too large, the individual cylinders do not work or work badly, shake, the operation is unstable, tempering, blasting, the engine oil deteriorates, the exhaust pipe has "chug" sound and the oil filler fluctuates and smokes.

II. Fault Diagnosis

The engine with good technical condition can only hear even exhaust sound and slight noise during operation. When abnormal sound occurs during engine operation, it indicates that the relevant parts are faulty. For an engine with abnormal sound, it is important to find out the characteristics and rules of the abnormal sound, analyze the causes and find out the abnormal sound position.

1. Fault Diagnosis of Crankshaft Main Bearing Sound

(1) Fault phenomenon

The main characteristic of crankshaft main bearing sound is that when the engine accelerates suddenly, it makes heavy and powerful "dang" or "gang" metal knocking sound, the engine body vibrates greatly if severe, and the sound increases with the increase of engine speed and increases with the increase of load. The sound is generated in the crankcase at the lower part of the cylinder block. There is no obvious change in the sound when the single cylinder cuts out. When two adjacent cylinders cut out at the same time, the sound will obviously weaken or disappear; when the temperature changes, there is no obvious change in the sound; if the sound is serious, the oil pressure will even decrease.

(2) Cause of failure

① The fixing screw of the main bearing cover is loose.

② The anti-friction alloy of the main bearing is burned or falls off.

③ The main bearing and the journal are worn too much, and the axial thrust device wears too much, resulting in excessive radial and axial clearance.

④ The crankshaft is bent.

⑤ Oil pressure is too low or oil viscosity is too low.

(3) Fault diagnosis

① Pull out the oil dipstick, auscultate from the nozzle of the oil dipstick, and repeatedly change the engine speed for test. If the main bearing sounds, the heavy and powerful metal knocking sound can be heard obviously.

② At low speed, shake the engine slightly by hand and repeatedly increase the throttle for test, listen carefully at the same time. If the sound increases with the increase of engine speed, and the sound is obvious at the moment of shaking the throttle, it is generally caused by loose main bearing; If the engine sounds obviously at idle speed or low speed and disordered at high speed, the crankshaft may be bent; If the engine body has great vibration at high speed and the oil pressure is obviously reduced, generally, the main bearing is severely loose, burned or the anti-friction alloy falls off.

③ Auscultate with an stethoscope. At the same time of constant change of throttle opening, contact the stethoscope or large flat-head screwdriver to the position where both sides of the crankcase are flush with the axis of the crankshaft for auscultation, and the loudest part is the main bearing sounded.

④ Cut-out test. If the sound obviously weakens after cylinder 1 cuts out, the first main bearing sounds; If the sound obviously weakens after the last cylinder cuts out, the last main bearing sounds; If the sound obviously weakens after any two adjacent cylinders cut out, the main bearing between the two cylinders sounds.

⑤ Depress clutch pedal for test. If it is suspected that the crankshaft moves in the axial direction and make sound, the clutch pedal can be depressed and held stationary. If the sound weakens or disappears, it will be the sound generated by axial movement of the crankshaft.

2. Fault Diagnosis of Connecting Rod Bearing Sound

(1) Fault phenomenon

When the engine accelerates suddenly, there is a continuous, obvious, light and short knocking sound, like "dang, dang, dang", which is the main characteristic of the connecting rod bearing sound; When the bearing is seriously loose, obvious sound can be heard during idle operation, and the oil pressure decreases; When the engine temperature changes, the sound does not change; When the engine load changes, the sound increases with the increase of the load; When the single cylinder is cut off, the sound obviously weakens or disappears, but immediately appears when the engine is re-ignited.

(2) Cause of failure

① The fixing bolt of connecting rod bearing cap is loose or broken.

② The anti-friction alloy of connecting rod bearing is burned or fell off.

③ The connecting rod bearing or journal is worn too much, resulting in excessive radial

clearance.

④ Oil pressure is too low or oil viscosity is too low.

(3) Fault diagnosis

① Auscultation. If we touch an stethoscope on the engine body for auscultation, it is often difficult to hear the sound clearly, but when we listen directly at the nozzle of the oil dipstick, we can hear clear connecting rod bearing sound.

② Change the engine speed. The sound is small at idle speed and obvious at medium speed. There will be continuous knocking sound when the throttle valve is slightly increased, and the knocking sound will increase with rapid acceleration, and it is not obvious due to other noise disturbance at high speed. Operate the engine at idle speed during diagnosis, then open the throttle from idle speed to low speed, from low speed to medium speed, and then from medium speed to high speed, at the same time, combine the single cylinder cutout method and auscultate at the nozzle of the oil dipstick. The sound increases with the increase of speed. When the throttle shakes, the abnormal sound is prominent at the moment of stepping on the accelerator. When the sound is severe, clear and obvious knocking sound can be heard at any speed.

③ When the single cylinder fires off, the sound obviously weakens or disappears, but immediately appears when it is re-ignited, it can be concluded that the connecting rod bearing of the cylinder sounds. However, when the connecting rod bearing is too loose, the sound has no obvious change when a single cylinder cuts out.

④ Connecting rod bearing sound is accompanied by a significant decrease in oil pressure. The engine body shakes when serious, which is different from piston pin sound and piston knocking. The screwdriver or stethoscope can be held against the lower part of the cylinder block or oil pan by hand, obvious vibration can be felt when touching the corresponding faulty cylinder position.

3. Fault Diagnosis of Piston Pin Sound

(1) Fault phenomenon

The engine shakes the throttle at idle speed, low speed and from idle speed to low speed, and brittle and coherent metal knocking sound of "click, click, click" can be heard; When the sound is serious, it increases with the increase of speed, and increases with the increase of load. When the engine temperature changes, it has little influence on the sound but not much. The oil pressure does not decrease; When the single cylinder is cut off, the sound obviously weakens or disappears, and the sound appears again or two sounds continuously at the moment of the re-ignition.

(2) Cause of failure

① The fit between piston pin and connecting rod small end bushing is loose.

② The fit between bushing and connecting rod small end hole is loose.

③ The fit between piston pin and the pin seat hole on the piston is loose.

(3) Fault diagnosis

① Auscultation. A brittle and coherent sound can be heard by touching the upper part of the cylinder sounded with a stethoscope when the engine speed is changed by a slight shake of the throttle. This sound can also be heard clearly by opening the oil filler cap for ausculta-

tion.

② Throttle shaking test. The engine runs at idle speed and then shakes the throttle from idle speed to low speed. The sound varies with the speed. Every time the throttle is shaken, if a brittle and coherent "click, click, click" sound can be heard, it may be the piston pin sound.

③ If the sound increases with the increase of the speed, but disordered when the single cylinder is disconnected, the fault is too large clearance between piston pin and bushing.

④ During idle speed operation, the sound is rhythmic and heavy. The sound does not decrease when increasing speed. At the same time, it is accompanied with slight engine vibration, and the sound increases during the cut-out test, which indicates that the piston pin moves freely.

⑤ Cut-out test. The engine shall be stabilized at the speed with obvious sound, and the cut-out test shall be carried out one by one. If the sound of a cylinder obviously weakens or disappears after the cut-out, and two sounds appear immediately or continuously at the moment of re-ignition, it can be concluded that the piston pin of the cylinder sounds.

4. Fault Diagnosis of Piston Knocking Sound

(1) Fault phenomenon

When the engine is running at idle speed or at low speed, the upper part of the cylinder emits clear and obvious metal knocking sound, "click, click, click", which weakens or disappears when operating at medium speed or above; Sound also changes when engine temperature changes; In most cases, the sound is obvious when the car is cold, while it weakens or disappears when the car is hot. There are also some cases where the piston knocking sound becomes louder when the temperature increases. The heavier the load, the louder the sound, but the oil pressure does not decrease; When a single cylinder cuts out, the sound weakens or disappears.

(2) Causes of fault

① The fitting clearance between piston and cylinder wall is too large.

② Lubrication condition between piston and cylinder wall is too poor.

③ The piston is not ellipse or the ellipse degree is too small at normal temperature.

④ The piston pin and piston pin seat hole are assembled too tightly.

⑤ The piston pin and connecting rod small end bushing are assembled too tightly.

⑥ The connecting rod bearing is too tight.

⑦ The piston cylinder is too large.

(3) Fault diagnosis

① Diagnose at different water temperatures. First diagnose when the car is cold. If there is knocking sound during cold car, and the sound disappears when the car is hot, it indicates that the fault is piston knocking, the fault is still light, and the car can continue running; If the engine is hot, the sound weakens but is still obvious, especially it is clear in the case of heavy load and low speed, it indicates that the sound is serious, and the car shall be stopped for maintenance.

② Cut-out test. Operate the engine at the speed with the most obvious knocking sound, and conduct cut-out test one by one. If the sound weakens or disappears after a cylinder cuts

out, the cylinder makes knocking sound.

③ Add oil to confirm the diagnosis. In order to further diagnose whether the piston knocks on the cylinder, the engine can be shut down, the spark plug (or fuel injector) of the cylinder with sound can be removed, a certain amount of oil can be injected into the cylinder, and the crankshaft can be rotated for several turns so that the oil is filled between the cylinder wall and the piston. Then install the spark plug (or fuel injector) to start the engine. If the sound weakens or disappears in a short time, but appears again, the piston knocking sound can be determined.

④ Auscultation. The stethoscope shall be touched on both sides of the upper part of cylinder for auscultation. Generally, the upper sound of the cylinder is strong and there is slight vibration. If "click, click, click" sound is heard, the clearance between cylinder and piston is too large; If "gang, gang, gang" sound is heard, it may be caused by poor lubrication of cylinder wall.

5. Fault Diagnosis of Valve Sound

(1) Fault phenomenon

The valve foot sound and valve seat sound are collectively referred to as valve sounds. The faults are: Continuous and rhythmic "click, click, click" (at valve foot) or "snap, snap, snap" (at valve seat) knocking sound when the engine is running at idle speed; When the speed rises, the sound increases, and the sound does not weaken with the temperature change and during the single cylinder cut-out; If several valves sound, the sounds are cluttered.

(2) Causes of fault

① The valve foot sounds are caused by the following causes.

a. The valve clearance is too large.

b. The valve clearance adjustment screw is loose or the contact surfaces at this clearance are uneven.

c. Excessive wear of valve cam results in reduced efficiency of buffer section, which increases the impact of tappet on valve.

d. The valve is poorly lubricated.

② The causes of valve seat sound are caused by the following causes.

a. The clearance between valve stem and its guide tube is too large.

b. The contact between the valve head and its seat ring is poor.

c. The valve seat ring is loose.

d. The valve foot clearance is too large.

(3) Fault diagnosis

① Auscultation. When the engine is running at idle speed, a rhythmic sound is heard. The sound increases with the increase of the speed, and does not weaken with the temperature change and the cut-out cylinder-by-cylinder. If the sound comes from the valve chamber, it can be diagnosed as the valve sound.

② The abnormal sound at the valve chamber or valve cover is obvious at idle speed. The valve foot sounds are clear and rhythmic, and clear sounds can be heard around the engine.

③ Check valve clearance. Open the valve cover and check the valve foot clearance with a

thickness gauge. The valve with biggest gap is often the loudest. For the engine in operation, when a thickness gauge is inserted into the valve foot clearance, the sound weakens or disappears, it can be determined that the valve sound is caused by too large clearance. If there is no change in the sound, it means the valve seat sound. If the valve seat sound is caused by loose seat ring, the sound is not as solid as the valve foot sound, with broken sound.

6. Fault Diagnosis of Cylinder Leakage Sound

(1) Fault phenomenon

When the engine is running, the leakage sound in the crankcase can be heard from the nozzle of the oil dipstick. The heavier the load, the louder the sound; the higher the speed, the smaller the sound. When the accelerator pedal is lifted or the single cylinder is cut off, the sound weakens or disappears. With the occurrence of sound, the oil filler emits smoke outward, and the times of smoke emission is the same as the frequency of sounding.

(2) Cause of failure

① The light leakage between piston ring and cylinder wall is excessive.

② The piston ring and the cylinder wall are severely worn.

③ The piston ring opening clearance is too large or the openings of piston rings coincide.

④ The elastic force of piston ring is too weak or the side clearance and back clearance are too small.

⑤ The piston ring is stuck in the ring groove.

⑥ The cylinder wall is strained and grooves appear.

(3) Fault diagnosis

① Cut-out test. Increase the engine speed until it is stable at the most obvious sound. Open the nozzle of the oil dipstick. If smoke emerges from the nozzle, it can be preliminarily diagnosed as cylinder leakage sound. If the sound weakens or disappears after a cylinder is cut off, and the amount of smoke emission at the oil filler is significantly reduced, it indicates that abnormal sound of air leakage is generated by the cylinder.

② Oil filling method. Remove the spark plug of the cylinder that may leak, inject a small amount of oil into the cylinder. After rotating the engine for several turns, install the spark plug and restart the engine. If the sound decreases obviously, it can be determined that the cylinder leaks.

7. Fault Diagnosis of Wear Abnormal Sound of Belt and Bearing

(1) Fault phenomenon

The accessories on the engine include generator, air conditioning compressor, power steering pump, water pump, etc. As the service time increases, the belt will wear and cause slipping, or the belt slips due to poor operation of the belt tensioner, making a sound of "squeak and squeak". Similarly, bearing parts such as compressor bearings, water pump bearings, generator bearings, etc. will have "sizzling" or "rustling" sound after a long time.

(2) Cause of failure

The abnormal sound of belt slipping is mainly due to increased wear after the belt is used for a long time, reduced elasticity of the belt, or too loose belt due to poor operation of the belt tensioner. Abnormal bearing sound is usually due to worn and loose bearing or poor

lubrication.

(3) Fault diagnosis

Belt slipping will make a "squeak, squeak" sound. During diagnosis, the engine can be turned off, and the belt can be pressed by hand or the tightness of the belt can be detected by a special testing device. The loose belt is the slipping belt.

Bearing fault usually has "sizzling" or "rustling" sound. Such sound tends to be harsh, loud, and noticeable in the cold car. During diagnosis, a stethoscope or a metal rod may be used to bear against the part that may have abnormal sound. If the sound is greater than elsewhere, the part may have abnormal sound.

III. Task Implementation

1. Inquiry

The repairman shall know the time of fault from the owner; Whether there are other abnormal conditions before the fault; Whether the symptoms change after finding the fault; Details of driving; Whether the automobile is maintained on time; Have other repairs been performed after the fault. Through the above-mentioned inquiry, the situation before and after the fault and the specific information of the fault can be known, and the preliminary diagnosis of abnormal sound fault of the engine is complete.

2. Test-drive and Basic Inspection

Carry out the test-drive to confirm the fault. Hear the location of abnormal sound to find out characteristics and rules of the abnormal sound.

3. Detection and Diagnosis

First use the scan tool for diagnosis. There is no fault code in the electronic control unit of the engine. Check whether the knock sensor data is normal, indicating that there is no cylinder knocking. Then make cylinder cut-out test to judge the source and position of abnormal sound.

Pull off the high-voltage wire of cylinder 1, 2 and 3, and the sound does not change.

When the high-voltage wire of cylinder 4 is unplugged, the abnormal sound disappears, indicating that the abnormal rattle comes from cylinder 4.

Check the engine cylinder pressure: 1.1MPa for cylinder 1, 1.15MPa for cylinder 2, 1.13MPa for cylinder 3 and 1.1MPa for cylinder 4. The pressure of the four cylinders is normal, indicating that the engine shall have no abnormal knocking sound due to cylinder wear.

Check the oil pressure. When the engine is idle, the pressure is lower than the normal value.

Combined with the above detection and analysis, the abnormal sound comes from crankshaft, piston, connecting rod, etc. , and then the cylinder block is disassembled, as shown in Figure 4-1. The piston pin and connecting rod bearing are normal, and the cylinder diameters all are within the standard range.

Check the clearance of the main bearing shell and find that the clearance of the fifth main bearing shell is greater than 0.76mm, so it is concluded that the fault may be caused by the fifth crank or the fifth main bearing shell. If the main shaft diameter is within the specified range, the fault shall be in the main bearing shell. The abnormal sound is made due

to large clearance caused by wear of the fifth main bearing shell.

4. Fault Elimination

After replacing the 5th main bearing shell, the abnormal sound is eliminated.

5. Inspection and Delivery

After troubleshooting, the engine is re-installed, and no any other abnormality is found during the test-drive, and the car is handed over to the owner.

IV. Task Summary

When making abnormal sound diagnosis, do not disassemble blindly, but understand the source of abnormal sound in detail, analyze the possible causes, and then diagnose and eliminate them item by item according to the steps. Note that the inspection standard must be subject to the maintenance manual.

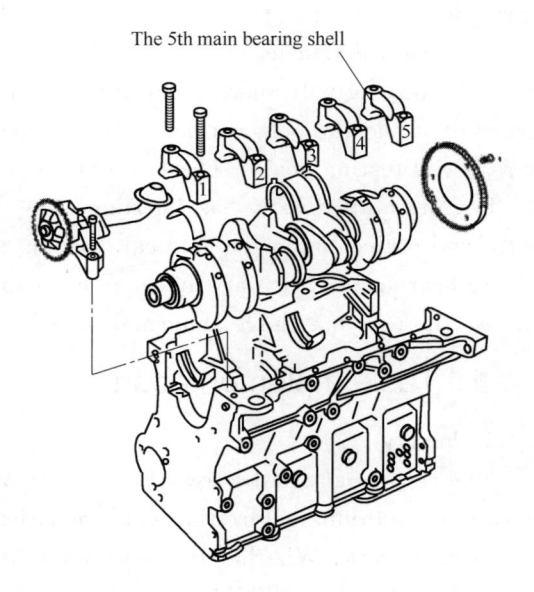

Figure 4-1 Disassembly of Cylinder Block

V. Task Report

Major			Class		Name	
Task Name					Class Hours	2
Model				Engine Model		
	Assessment Items		Assessment Contents		Maximum Score	Score
Task Completion Process	1. Description of fault symptoms				5	
	2. Possible causes and analysis of fault				25	
	3. Detection and diagnosis process				35	
	4. Fault Elimination				10	
	5. Summary of fault diagnosis				10	
Teacher Evaluation	Operation quality, operation efficiency, operation safety, etc.				15	
Total Score					100	

VI. Knowledge Expansion

〔Typical Case Ⅰ〕 Abnormal sound of a 2010 Sagitar 1. 6L engine when hot.

Fault Description: The engine sounds normally when the car is cold, but there is a 'squeak' sound at the front of the engine when it is hot.

Abnormal Engine Operation:

(1) The repairman asked the owner for any other repairs before. The owner said that after abnormal sound, the timing belt, tension pulley and water pump were replaced.

(2) He checked the car for signs of impact. After inspecting the chassis, engine and body, no traces of impact were found.

(3) He reviewed the sound source and found that this sound did not originate from the front wheel train. Because the abnormal sound of the belt is generally made when the car is

cold, while when it is hot, the sound is normal. The fault of this car was the opposite, so there were two possible reasons for analysis. One is abnormal sound of camshaft oil seal, and the other is abnormal sound caused by scratching camshaft at cylinder 1 with the connecting part of cylinder head or end cover. He removed the toothed belt protection cover for detailed inspection. Since the camshaft oil seal was visible on the outside at this time, it was first determined whether it is the abnormal sound of the camshaft oil seal.

The camshaft oil seal is made of plastic, nylon, etc. , so problems may occur due to heat. If it sounds, when we change its position, the sound should change. Then he reinstalled the oil seal with a special oil seal installation tool and changed its position. After adjustment and re-installation, the abnormal sound became significantly smaller, so it was basically determined that the fault was the abnormal sound caused by the camshaft oil seal.

(4) He removed the camshaft oil seal and checked that the journal at the installation of camshaft oil seal is correct, as shown in Figure 4-2, and then he installed the new oil seal. During installation, it shall be noted that the sealing lip of the oil seal shall not be immersed in oil, the installation piston shall not be located at the top dead center, and the camshaft journal must be free of oil. He reinstalled the oil seal into the wheel train and the fault was eliminated.

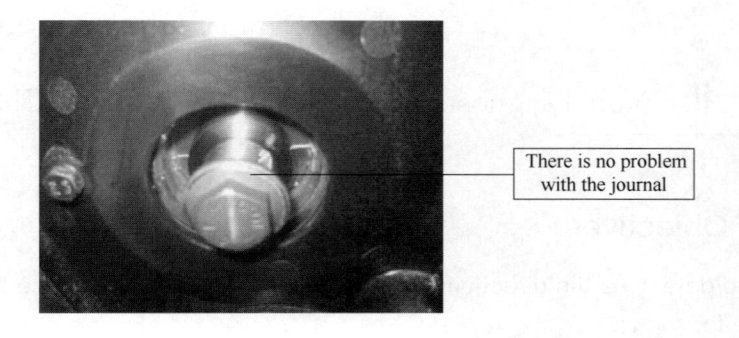

Figure 4-2　Camshaft Journal

Summary: The fault disappeared after replacing the camshaft oil seal. The abnormal sound may be caused by oil seal quality problem.

[Typical Case Ⅱ]　Abnormal sound of a Bora engine when hot.

Fault Description: A Bora with 1. 6L and manual transmission. The car made "murmur" sound in hot, and the sound was especially obvious after slam acceleration.

Fault Diagnosis and Repair: After the engine was hot, the timing belt made a "murmur" sound. The repairman considered that such sound was likely to occur in the following areas: generator; timing belt; tension pulley; water pump; mechanical engine.

He removed the generator belt and started the engine for inspection. The abnormal sound remained, so the abnormal sound of the generator was eliminated.

He assembled timing belt mechanism according to FAW-Volkswagen maintenance manual, and started the engine again. Abnormal sound still remained; He poured water onto the belt. The sound did not change. He raped the belt on the tension pulley for test run. The ab-

normal sound still existed; He replaced the tension pulley and timing belt for test, but the sound was still not eliminated.

He carefully listened to the water pump with a stethoscope and the sound was not obvious.

The oil level and pressure were normal. The oil pressure at idle speed was 340kPa (the standard is no less than 200kPa at idle speed) and 390kPa at 2, 000r/min (the standard is not higher than 700kPa at 2, 000r/min). The oil pressure was also normal.

He removed and inspected the cylinder head of the engine, and found that the camshaft had abnormal wear, and the second, third and fourth bearing shells were seriously worn. After careful inspection, he found that the bearing shell surface was relatively rough, resulting in abnormal wear of the camshaft, resulting in abnormal engine sound. After replacing with a new cylinder head, the fault was eliminated.

Summary: For faults where abnormal sound characteristics are not very obvious, it is necessary to check one by one from the parts that are prone to abnormal sound on the periphery of the engine. The determination of abnormal sound parts of the engine can depend on the stethoscope. For parts suspected to produce abnormal sound, changing friction coefficient by isolation or watering or adopting other relevant tests can be done for diagnosis. It shall be eliminated step by step according to the principle of "from easy to difficult" and " from outside to inside.

Task Ⅱ Fault Diagnosis and Repair of Abnormal Chassis Sound

Learning Objectives

1. Be able to determine the direction and items of inquiry according to the fault phenomena of the automobile for repair.

2. Be able to prepare a correct fault diagnosis plan according to fault phenomena.

3. Be able to consult maintenance data skillfully, select appropriate detection and diagnosis devices according to fault phenomena and use them skillfully.

4. Be able to detect abnormal chassis sound with appropriate maintenance devices according to the diagnosis plan.

5. Be able to correctly analyze the test results and determine the fault location and cause of abnormal chassis sound.

6. Be able to repair the fault parts quickly and accurately and eliminate the hidden troubles.

Task Import

Task Material: The owner of a 2007 Sagitar car with 1. 8T, driving 67, 000 km, said that the chassis "murmured" when the car is turning at low speed and large angle.

Task Requirements: According to the fault phenomena of the car, consult relevant materials, select appropriate detection and diagnosis devices for fault diagnosis and repair, and

fill in the task report.

Ⅰ. Fault Analysis

The abnormal chassis sound refers to the abnormal noise, sound and vibration sound from the components or mechanisms of the transmission system, driving system, steering system and brake system during driving. It is usually caused by wear or damage of car components, loose connection and poor quality or improper assembly of accessories.

The abnormal sound characteristics of the transmission mainly include: When the engine is running at idle speed and the transmission is in neutral, there is abnormal sound, but the sound disappears when stepping on the clutch pedal; There is abnormal sound when shifting gear or after moving into certain gear.

The abnormal sound produced when the clutch disengages and engages is usually the abnormal clutch sound.

When the drive shaft or drive axle rotates, a "click" or "clip-clop" impact sound occurs and the automobile shakes, it is usually the abnormal sound of the drive shaft or the drive axle.

Ⅱ. Fault Diagnosis

1. Fault Diagnosis of Abnormal Clutch Sound

(1) Causes of fault

① The release bearing is lack of oil or worn, and the return spring is too soft, broken or fell off.

② The screw of the release lever is broken or the supporting pin and pin hole are worn loose.

③ Clutch friction disc rivet is loose or rivet head is exposed.

④ The inner bore spline groove of clutch plate and the transmission driving shaft spline tooth are worn too much.

⑤ The steel plate of clutch plate is broken or the vibration damping spring is broken.

⑥ The return spring of pedal is too soft or breaks or falls off.

(2) Fault diagnosis

① No matter the clutch is disengaged and engaged, abnormal sound will be generated. Meanwhile, when the automobile shakes during driving, it is likely that the friction disc is cracked or rivets are exposed, or the driven disc and spline sleeve rivets are loose, etc.

② If there is no obvious abnormal sound when the clutch pedal is depressed but the sound is obvious when the pedal is lifted, it is likely that there is a major defect in the release bearing. There are two cases of abnormal sound from the release bearing. One is that the release bearing is jammed, and when it slides against the release lever head, it makes constant noises of "swish". The other is the unrhythmic "swoosh" sound of the release bearing due to lack of oil or damage.

③ If the pedal is depressed slightly, the "rustling" sound is emitted, and the sound disappears when the pedal is lifted, which is caused by the lack of lubricating oil on the

clutch bearing.

④ If the clutch sounds "click, click", the engine should be shut down immediately, which may be the sound of friction with the flywheel housing after the fixed screw of the clutch cover is released.

2. Fault Diagnosis of Abnormal Transmission Sound

(1) Causes of fault

① The backlash between the active and passive gears is too large; the gear wear too much; The gear teeth are broken.

② Bearing wear, fracture and poor lubrication.

③ Serious wear occurs on the inner side of the shift fork of the synchronizer sliding gear and the working face of the lower end of the gear lever.

(2) Fault diagnosis

When the gear lever is in neutral, the transmission has "knuckling" sound, but the sound disappears after depressing the clutch pedal. Check whether the rear bearing of the first shaft is worn or damaged. If the sound is even, the noise decreases or disappears after depressing the clutch pedal, it indicates that the normally engaged gear is not engaged properly.

When the gear lever is put into any gear, there is abnormal sound, but when entering the direct gear, the sound weakens or even disappears, or there is no sound in neutral. The cause of this fault is that the intermediate shaft is not parallel to the second shaft, or the second shaft bearing sounds.

There is abnormal sound when the gear lever is placed in the low gear, but the sound weakens in high gear. When "swoosh" sound is heard during sliding in the neutral, the drive axle can be supported to make the transmission run in low gear or reverse gear. If the sound is evident at the reverse gear, the rear bearing of the second shaft is loose or damaged. If the sound increases when the car speed changes abruptly and the sound is a continuous whine when the car speed is relatively stable, and increases with the increase of automobile speed, it indicates that the gear clearance is too large or too small, and the gear clearance shall be adjusted.

When the car is driving on uneven road surface, the gear lever vibrates and produces friction noise. When the gear lever is stabilized by hand, the sound disappears, which indicates that the shift fork is deformed, the fixing device is loose, or the shift fork and fork groove are worn seriously, which can be analyzed and handled in combination with the shake of the gear lever.

When the engine is running, if there is metal friction sound in the transmission, it may be caused by insufficient lubricating oil or deterioration of lubricating oil. At this time, add or replace the lubricating oil meeting the requirements.

When a gear is engaged during driving and abnormal sound is obvious, the cause is that the gear is worn too much, or the gear tooth profile is abnormal. Poor meshing of new and old gears and too long fixing bolts of side cover against the gear may cause abnormal sound.

3. Fault Diagnosis of Abnormal Sound of Drive Shaft

(1) Causes of fault

① The universal joint is short of oil for a long time, the universal joint cross shaft and the needle roller are worn loosely or the needle roller is broken.

② Drive shaft spline teeth and fork pipe spline grooves are worn loosely.

③ Transmission output shaft spline teeth and flange spline grooves wear too much.

④ Bolt at each connection part is loose.

⑤ The intermediate bearing is worn too much or even lacks lubricating oil.

⑥ The ball bearing is damaged.

⑦ The rubber sleeve of the intermediate bearing bracket is damaged or the position of the bracket is incorrect.

⑧ The bracket bolt is loose or the tightening is inconsistent.

⑨ The drive shaft is bent or the universal-joint forks at both ends of the drive shaft are installed incorrectly.

(2) Fault diagnosis

① When the car starts, it makes collision noise, and there is always abnormal sound during driving, which is caused by loose expansion spline, wear of transmission output shaft, loose universal joint or lack of oil.

② When the car is driving, it whines, indicating the sound from the middle bearing.

③ There is no abnormal sound when starting, abnormal sound is emitted during acceleration, and it is more obvious during coasting in neutral, which is caused by wrong installation of universal joint fork and bent drive shaft.

④ The abnormal sound disappears or lightens when pulling the handbrake, which means the handbrake shoe or the pin sleeve (disc) sounds.

4. Fault Diagnosis of Abnormal Sound of Drive Axle

(1) Causes of fault

① The backlash of each gear in the drive axle is too small or too large.

② The backlash of driving bevel gear and driven bevel gear is uneven or improperly assembled.

③ The bearing pretension is adjusted improperly.

④ Half-shaft tube is bent and deformed.

⑤ Gear is damaged or tooth surface is damaged.

⑥ The bearing is damaged.

(2) Fault diagnosis

① The drive axle sends out the sound of "choking". When sliding, it doesn't sound, which means that the gear of final reducer is engaged badly.

② When gear 1, gear 2 and gear 3 are engaged, it sounds, and even more serious at low speed gear, indicating that the passive gear or bearing of final reducer is loose, and driving bevel gear bearing or nut is loose; When gear 3, gear 4 and gear 5 are engaged, it sounds, and even more serious at high speed gear, indicating that the driving gear is damaged.

③ The sound when loosening the throttle is caused by loose gear or bearing of final reducer and loose bearing or nut of driving bevel gear. The sound when stepping on the throttle is caused by too tight gear or bearing of the reducer.

Ⅲ. Task Implementation

1. Inquiry

Know the time of the fault from the owner; Whether there is any abnormality before the fault; Whether the symptoms change after the fault; Details of automobile driving; Whether the automobile is maintained on time; Whether the car has been repaired after the fault. Find out the situation before and after the fault and the specific information of the fault through the above-mentioned inquiry, and complete the preliminary diagnosis of abnormal chassis sound.

2. Test-drive and Basic Inspection

Carry out the test drive and confirm the fault. When the faulty automobile turns at a speed of 20km/h, there is abnormal sound at the front. Listen to the general location of abnormal sound, characteristics and rules of abnormal sounds.

3. Detection and Diagnosis

After lifting the automobile, the driving wheel on either side brakes and the abnormal sound still exists, eliminating abnormal sound of wheel bearing and braking system.

After replacing the drive shaft, the abnormal sound still exists, excluding the drive shaft fault. Because the automobile only has abnormal sound when turning, it is judged to be differential sound.

Disassemble the transmission, measure the gear clearance and engagement marks of differential planetary gear, and find the meshing marks at the tooth root, as shown in Figure 4-3. Therefore, it is judged that the differential engages abnormally and produces abnormal sound.

The analysis shows that the abnormal wear of the spherical bushing of the differential causes the gear meshing part of the differential to reach the gear root (the middle gear meshing for normal case). Because the differential planetary gear only rotates when turning, this sound only occurs when turning, and the abnormal sound is obvious. In the process of judging whether the abnormal sound is from the differential, it is required to turn at a large angle (the steering wheel angle is greater than 180°) and accompanied by different acceleration and deceleration. If the abnormal sound can change with the starting speed, the probability of differential fault is higher.

Figure 4-3 Meshing Mark of Differential Gear

4. Fault Elimination

Replace the spherical bushing, reassemble, measure the backlash of the newly assembled differential planetary gear at about 0.4mm, while the actual measurement data of the differential with abnormal sound is about 0.6mm. The abnormal sound is eliminated during the test run.

5. Inspection and Delivery

After troubleshooting, hand over the automobile to the owner if there is no other abnormality.

Ⅳ. Task Summary

When making abnormal sound diagnosis, we need to listen repeatedly under the condition of abnormal sound, and also listen to whether there is any abnormality under other driving conditions. We should conduct corresponding disassembly after determining the source of the fault.

Ⅴ. Task Report

Major			Class		Name	
Task Name					Class Hours	2
Model				Engine Model		
Task Completion Process	Assessment Items		Assessment Contents		Maximum Score	Score
Task Completion Process	1. Description of fault symptoms				5	
Task Completion Process	2. Possible causes and analysis of fault				25	
Task Completion Process	3. Detection and diagnosis process				35	
Task Completion Process	4. Fault Elimination				10	
Task Completion Process	5. Summary of fault diagnosis				10	
Teacher Evaluation	Operation quality, operation efficiency, operation safety, etc.				15	
Total Score					100	

Ⅵ. Knowledge Expansion

〔Typical Case Ⅰ〕 Abnormal chassis sound of a POLO car.

Fault Description: A POLO 1.6L manual transmission car with a mileage of 86,000km. The chassis sometimes clattered when it was driving on a bumpy road or when it turned too sharply.

Fault Diagnosis and Repair: The repairman conducted test run, and no matter how he turned, turned the steering wheel without running, accelerated or reversed, the fault did not occur According to experience, the areas where such abnormal sound occurs on a POLO car are as follows: The inner and outer ball cages or drive shaft is worm; The front wheel bearing is loose; The big nut of outer ball cage is loose or falls off; The transverse stabilizer bar is deformed or the rubber bushing is worn; The ball head of stabilizer bar connecting rod is worn.

Then he lifted the automobile to carry out a thorough inspection of the above-mentioned parts. He found that the inner and outer ball cage dust boots on the left and right sides were in good condition without cracks, and all ball heads were well fastened without looseness;

He shook the tire with both hands and didn't found loose front wheel bearing and clearance on the ball head of steering tie rod; He fastened the big nut of outer ball cage and tire bolt, and found no looseness and the tightening torque conforms to the standard value; He shook the transverse stabilizer bar by hand and found no loose rubber bushing. No abnormal sound was found by inspection. It is generally very likely that abnormal sound during turning is caused by cage wear because the wear cannot be judged directly by appearance inspection. To confirm this judgment, he had a number of road tests with the owner, but the abnormal sound never appeared. It was therefore concluded that there could be wear inside the cage. For caution, the left and right outer cages were disassembled. Unexpectedly, there were no signs of wear.

Through communication with the owner, he knew that the car often made abnormal sound when driving on a relatively bumpy road. So he looked for similar road condition for fault simulation test. As the car bumped over the corner, he finally heard a few "clattering" sounds from the lower part of the right-hand suspension. The sound was generated only when the car turned right. The sound was dull, excluding the abnormal sound of the cage as well as that of the engine or transmission.

He lifted the automobile up and checked the right front suspension carefully. An invisible scratch was found at the right front half axis, but no foreign matter was found around it; The relevant components on the front right suspension did not show any traces of collision and maintained normal spacing. Theoretically there was no possibility of scratching each other. During further inspection, he found that although the transverse stabilizer bar of the car could keep tight, it moved a little left and right under the prying of the crow bar, and there was also a scratch difficult to detect at the end of the transverse stabilizer bar. After replacing the rubber bushing of the stabilizer bar, the fault was eliminated.

Summary: The sound generated when the automobile was turning on a bumpy road was caused by the collision between the transverse stabilizer bar and the right front half axle. During diagnosis, it is necessary to understand the conditions and road conditions of the fault from the automobile owner, so that the abnormal sounds can be quickly understood during the test-drive and eliminated.

[Typical Case Ⅱ] Abnormal chassis sound of a 2011 Sagitar car.

Fault Description: A 2011 Sagitar car with a mileage of 50, 000 kilometers. When the automobile was driving on a bumpy road, the right rear part made a "muttering" sound, similar to the sound of oil leakage from the shock absorber.

Fault Diagnosis and Repair: The repairman carried out the road test with the owner to confirm the fault phenomena, which were obvious.

After the automobile was raised, he checked the rear axle screws and tighten them to the standard torque. He checked the chassis visually and found there was oil leakage in the shock absorber. No additional issues were identified. The right rear shock absorber was replaced due to the sound similar to the sound when the shock absorber was damaged, but the fault remained during the test run.

After lifting the automobile again, he checked the lower control arm and other suspension connections, and found no problems with the handbrake cable, fuel tank, etc.

When shaking the two rear brake cylinders by hand, he found that the openness of the left and right cylinders is different, and the openness on the right side is relatively large. He compared this a other automobile and confirmed that the openness of the right rear cylinder of the automobile was abnormal.

He removed the right rear cylinder and the cylinder support for inspection and found that the guide bolt of the cylinder support was worn and the openness was relatively large. After replacing the right rear brake cylinder support, the fault was eliminated during the test-drive.

Summary: The abnormal sound of the car is concentrated at the rear right, where there are few relative moving parts. According to the principle of fault diagnosis, from simple to complex, the cylinder support and other components here should be checked firstly, instead of replacing the shock absorber first, which greatly increases the diagnosis time.

Item V

Fault Diagnosis and Repair of Abnormal Engine Operation

The abnormal engine operation includes abnormal engine starting, abnormal idle speed and insufficient power. During fault analysis, we should consider multiple systems related to faults comprehensively. On the basis of mastering fault diagnosis of engine oil circuit system, ignition system, etc., we should master comprehensive fault analysis and diagnosis. Only in this way can we work out a comprehensive and reasonable diagnosis scheme for the faults, and select appropriate diagnostic tools for scientific diagnosis.

 Task Ⅰ Fault Diagnosis and Repair of Engine Failure to Start

Engine failure to start is one of the common engine faults. Engine failure to start involves many systems such as engine system, anti-theft system and so on. The fault of engine system involves oil circuit system, ignition system and mechanical system. When diagnosing the engine failure to start, we should first analyze which system the fault occurs, then detect the fault position, finally find out the cause of the fault and fix it.

Learning Objectives

1. Be able to determine the direction and items of inquiry according to the fault phenomena of the automobile for repair.

2. Be able to prepare a correct fault diagnosis plan according to fault phenomena.

3. Be able to consult maintenance data skillfully, select appropriate detection and diagnosis devices according to fault phenomena and use them skillfully.

4. Be able to test the engine failure to start by appropriate maintenance devices according to the diagnosis plan.

5. Be able to correctly analyze the test results and determine the fault location and cause of engine failure to start.

6. Be able to repair the fault parts quickly and accurately and eliminate the hidden troubles.

7. Be able to have the spirit of artisans and craftsmen of excellence and rigorous and careful working attitude, and enhance environmental awareness.

Task Import

Task Material: The owner of a 2010 Sagitar car said that the car would not start in the morning after parking for one night.

Task Requirements: According to the fault phenomena of the car, consult relevant materials, select appropriate detection and diagnosis devices for fault diagnosis and repair, and fill in the task report.

I . Fault Analysis

1. Insufficient fuel

Insufficient fuel causes the oil circuit fail to establish normal oil pressure.

2. Engine starting system fault

(1) Insufficient battery power causes the starter to run weakly.

(2) Poor connection of battery terminal, poor connection of starter terminal or open circuit.

(3) Faulty start relay, start fuse and ignition switch starter, or open circuit or poor connection between them.

Special attention: If the starter does not rotate when starting the automatic transmission car, we should check whether the gear lever is in P or N (observe the gear indicator light on the instrument panel).

3. Anti-theft system fault

(1) The ignition key fails.

(2) The anti-theft electronic control unit or the anti-theft module fails.

(3) Reader coil fails (the name may vary with the automobile brand).

(4) The anti-theft system circuit is faulty.

4. Ignition system fault

(1) The spark plug is faulty, causing the spark plug to fail to ignite or become weak, causing the engine mixture unable to burn normally.

(2) The high voltage line is faulty, causing the spark plug sparking voltage too low or no voltage.

(3) The ignition coil is faulty, resulting in a failure to generate high voltage power.

(4) The high voltage power cannot be distributed to the spark plug of each cylinder due to the fault of the distributor.

(5) The electronic control unit or ignition module and its wiring fails, causing the ignition system to fail.

5. Oil Line System Fault

(1) The fuel injector is faulty. The fuel injector is blocked, the fuel injector circuit is faulty or the fuel injector is damaged, causing the fuel injection quantity too small or unable

Item V Fault Diagnosis and Repair of Abnormal Engine Operation | **69**

to be injected.

(2) The oil pump is faulty. The oil pump works poorly or is damaged, or the oil pump circuit fails, resulting in low oil pressure or no oil pressure in oil circuit.

(3) The oil pressure in the oil circuit is too low. Blockage of oil inlet filter of oil pump, poor operation of oil pump, poor connection of oil pump circuit or blockage of gasoline filter causes too low oil pressure in the oil circuit.

(4) The oil pressure in the oil circuit is too high. The oil pressure regulator fault causes too high oil pressure, rich mixture and the engine fail to burn normally.

6. Incorrect Ignition Timing

Excessive engine timing deviation due to loose timing belts, misalignment of timing marks, etc.

7. Crankshaft Position Sensor Fault

Crankshaft position sensor fault, circuit fault, signal tooth damage or the larger distance between signal tooth and sensor results in too weak signal.

8. Idle Speed Control System Fault

The idle control valve is stuck and cannot be opened, and the throttle body is too dirty, resulting in a serious shortage of intake air.

9. Engine Mechanical System Fault

The cylinder is worn too much and the intake and exhaust valves are not closed tightly, resulting in serious insufficient cylinder pressure.

10. Electronic Control Unit Or Circuit Fault

Internal fault of electronic control unit, fault of power supply circuit or grounding circuit of electronic control unit.

11. Poor Fuel Quality

The engine cannot burn normally due to poor fuel quality.

12. Sensor Fault

In addition to the crankshaft position sensor, the engine has multiple sensors that fail to function or work poorly, causing the engine to fail to function properly.

II. Fault Diagnosis

1. First, eliminate relevant faults by observing the instrument

(1) If insufficient fuel is indicated, add fuel first.

(2) If the anti-theft alarm light does not go off for several seconds, but flashes or stays on, it is preliminarily judged that the anti-theft system may be faulty.

Special Tips: In some models, such as Santana 2000, the engine can start normally when the anti-theft system fails, but it will automatically shut down a few seconds later after starting.

(3) If the engine fault alarm light does not go off after a few seconds, it is always on, indicating that fault information has been stored in the engine computer.

(4) If the engine fault alarm light is not on, it is likely that the power supply and grounding circuits of the engine electronic control unit are faulty, or it may be the fault of the electronic control unit.

2. Turn on the starter and observe the operation of the starter

（1）If the starter is unable to operate, the starting system should be detected. The battery may lose power, the starting circuit may be faulty, and the starter may be faulty.

（2）If the starter operates normally, the following tests should be done.

Special attention: When starting the starter, observe whether the engine speedometer swings. If the engine speedometer pointer is stationary, it is likely that the engine speed sensor fails. In this case, focus should be placed on detecting the engine speed sensor (crankshaft position sensor).

3. Use the scan tool to read out the fault code and view the data flow

Note: If the scan tool is unable to communicate with the engine electronic control unit but can access other electronic control systems such as ABS system and airbag system, the power supply circuit and grounding circuit of the engine electronic control unit should be checked, which are likely to be faulty.

（1）If there is a fault code in the engine electronic control unit, the fault code shall be analyzed and the fault shall be searched according to the fault code. Then the starting related data flow should be checked, such as water temperature sensor, throttle position sensor, etc.

（2）If there is no fault code in the engine electronic control unit, the following test shall be performed.

4. Check whether ignition is normal, fuel injector works normally and whether oil pump works

First turn on the starter (the oil pumps of some models will operate for several seconds after turning on the ignition switch) to check whether the oil pump is working.

（1）If the engine can be ignited and the fuel injector works, but the oil pump does not work, the oil pump and its corresponding circuit should be checked.

（2）If the fire is weak, the relevant parts of the ignition system should be found out. For example, we should check whether the spark plug is faulty or whether the high voltage wire has excessive resistance, etc.

（3）If there is no fire and the fuel injector works, the ignition module and circuit should be found out.

（4）If there is no fire and the fuel injector does not work, the crankshaft position sensor should be found, if necessary, we should check whether the timing is seriously wrong and whether the electronic control unit and circuit are faulty.

（5）If the fire is normal but the fuel injector does not operate, there may be a problem with the fuel injector circuit.

（6）If the fire is normal and the fuel injector operates normally, we should check whether the oil pressure in the oil circuit is abnormal. If the oil pressure is normal, we should check the idle control valve for faults, and also check whether the engine timing is faulty and the engine cylinder pressure is insufficient.

Special Tips: When the engine fails to start, don't forget to check for fuel deterioration.

III. Task Implementation

1. Inquiry

Ask the owner about symptoms before the engine failure to start; Under what circum-

stances the fault occurs; Whether maintenance has been carried out after the fault; Whether other repairs or additional equipment installation have been carried out before the fault; What is the automobile mileage; Whether the automobile is maintained on time, etc.

According to the automobile fault information obtained from the owner, the possibility of some faults shall be preliminarily eliminated and the scope of fault diagnosis shall be narrowed down.

2. Test-drive and Basic Inspection

Start the engine for fault confirmation. At the same time, observe the instrument fuel quantity display, and observe whether the engine starting speed is normal. Observe the swing amplitude of the pointer of the engine speedometer for deviation from the expected idle speed. Observe whether there is air leakage in the air inlet, whether the vacuum pipe is falling off or damaged, and whether the wire connector is loose. Observe whether there are four leakage phenomena, fuel leakage, water leakage, air leakage and electric leakage. Observe the throttle cable for proper adjustment.

3. Detection and Diagnosis

Use the scan tool VAS5052A to diagnose the automobile system, and find that each system has no fault code stored. Turn on the ignition key. The data flow is normal when the engine is not running.

Since the engine control unit can be diagnosed with VAS5052A, it is demonstrated that there are no issues with the engine control unit communication, power supply and grounding.

Check the engine ignition system: Remove the high voltage line, install the spark plug to test the ignition, and it is found that the ignition is normal, confirming that the engine ignition system and the speed sensor work normally.

Check the oil supply system: Check the pressure of the gasoline pump. After connecting the oil pressure gauge, start the automobile and find that the oil pressure can reach 280kPa, which proves that there is no problem with the gasoline pump and its control circuit.

Check the mechanical part of the engine: Check the cylinder pressure, connect the cylinder pressure gauge, measure the cylinder pressure to be 1.1MPa. The cylinder pressure is normal. When checking the cylinder pressure, it is found that the spark plugs are all dry, demonstrating too little gasoline entering the engine cylinders.

Check the fuel injector circuit: Connect a diode test light on top of the plug and the light flashes when starting the engine, indicating that the fuel injector control circuit is normal. Inject carburetor cleaner while starting the automobile, and the engine can be started.

It is concluded that: The engine mixture is too lean, causing the engine failure to start.

Use a VAS5051 oscilloscope to detect the fuel injection time when the fuel injector is started, as shown in Figure 5-1. The normal fuel injector working waveform is shown in Figure 5-2.

By comparing the two waveforms, it is obvious that the fuel injector injection time of the faulty car is too short, which makes the mixture too lean, making the engine unable to start.

The basic injection time of the engine depends on the engine load and speed.

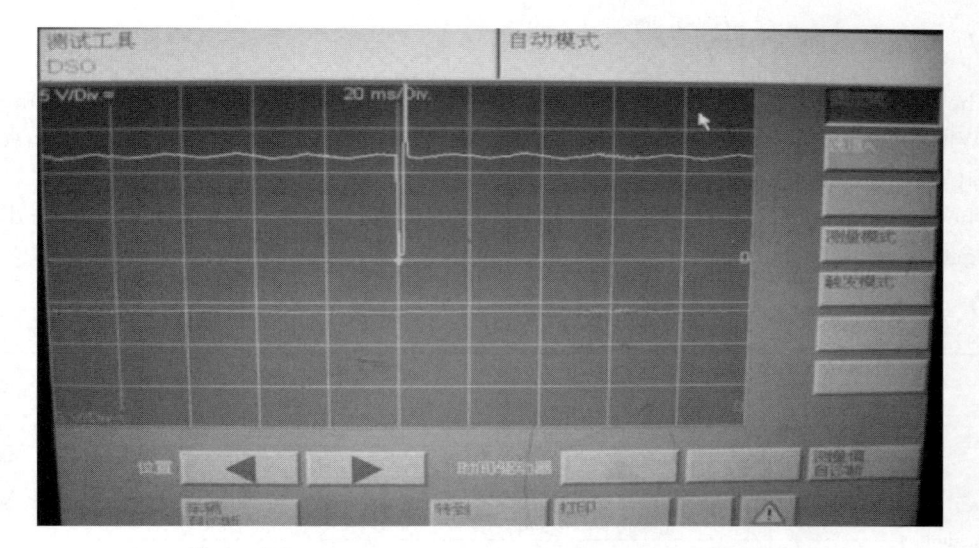

Figure 5-1 Fuel Injector Waveform at Start-up of a Faulty Car

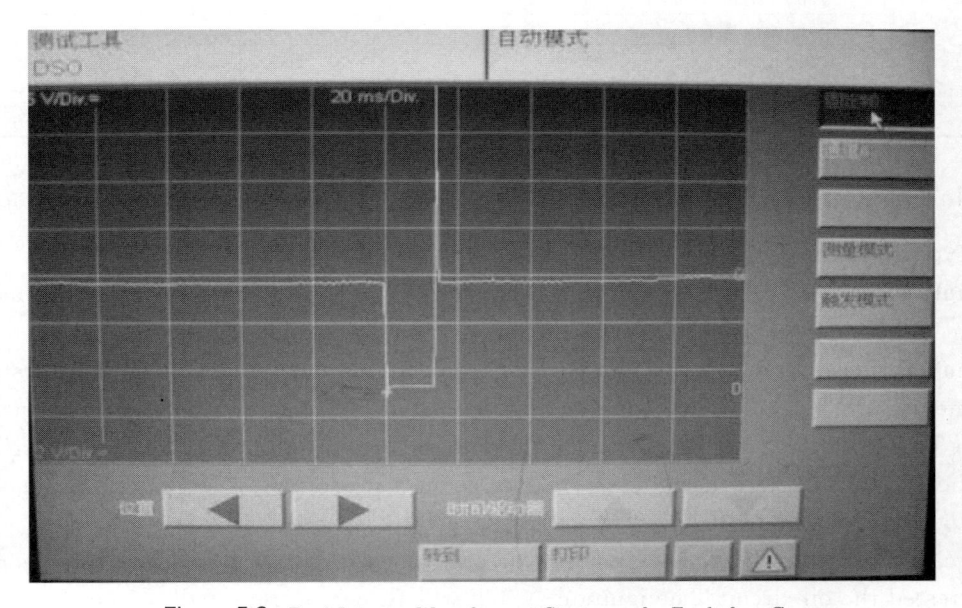

Figure 5-2 Fuel Injector Waveform at Start-up of a Fault-free Car

The engine speed sensor and intake pressure sensor are further detected and are normal.

Combined with the above detection and analysis, the fault is likely to be in the engine control unit.

4. Fault Elimination

Replace the engine control unit, use the scan tool for diagnosis, clear the fault codes in the electronic control unit, and check that all data flows are within the specified range. After troubleshooting, the fault is eliminated.

5. Inspection and Delivery

After troubleshooting, confirm that the engine has no other symptoms and hand over the car to the owner.

Ⅳ. Task Summary

The engine control unit receives engine speed and load signal to control the injection time. When the engine control unit fails, it can not control the fuel injection time correctly even if it can receive the signal normally.

The engine control unit itself is difficult to judge whether it is normal or not, and it can be judged whether it is normal by means of the easy-to-judge sensors and actuators.

Ⅴ. Task Report

Major			Class		Name	
Task Name					Class Hours	2
Model			Engine Model			
Task Completion Process	Assessment Items		Assessment Contents		Maximum Score	Score
	1. Description of fault symptoms				5	
	2. Possible causes and analysis of fault				25	
	3. Detection and diagnosis process				35	
	4. Fault Elimination				10	
	5. Summary of fault diagnosis				10	
Teacher Evaluation	Operation quality, operation efficiency, operation safety, etc.				15	
Total Score					100	

Ⅵ. Knowledge Expansion

【Typical Case Ⅰ】 Failure of a three-compartment fit to start.

Fault Description: The owner of a three-compartment Fit traveling 30, 000km, said that the car during the drive suddenly stalled and could not be started any more.

Fault Diagnosis and Repair: After turning on the ignition switch, the indicators on the instrument panel are normal. When starting the engine, the starter rotated vigorously and met the engine starting speed requirements, but the engine could not be started.

There are many reasons why the engine cannot be started, such as oil circuit system fault, ignition system fault, mechanical system fault, sensor fault, etc.

Because the engine has the function of oil pressure prefabrication, so the repairman firstly tested the oil circuit. The ignition switch was turned on repeatedly, and the fuel tank cover was opened at the same time. He listened to the operation of the fuel pump, and heard the "hiss" sound when the fuel pump was switched on. When the engine hood was opened, and the fuel inlet pipe clamp of fuel rail was released, there was fuel injected. He preliminarily judged that the fuel supply system was normal.

Then he checked the circuit for a fault. The ignition system uses Honda's latest I-DSI (Intellective Double Spark Plug Ignition) system with two ignition coils and spark plugs at the front and rear of each cylinder. He removed the front ignition coils and spark plugs of cylinders 1 and 2 and found that there was very wet fuel on the spark plug, indicating that the fuel had entered the cylinder. He inserted the spark plug into the ignition coil, placed it on the cylinder head and grounded it. He started the engine, but the spark plug had no spark, indicating that the ignition system was faulty. He pulled off the three-pin plug of the ignition

74 | Automobile Integrated Fault Diagnosis and Repair |

coil. The colors of the 3 wires are black/yellow, white and black respectively. He read the manual and knew that the 3 wires are power cord, computer control loop wire and grounding wire, respectively. He turned on the ignition switch and first measured the voltage of the black/yellow wire (power cord) with a multimeter, which shall be the battery voltage, but the result was no voltage. According to the circuit diagram, he found that the fuses No. 14 and No. 15 in the driver's side fuse box were blown. Fuse No. 14 is the front ignition coil fuse and Fuse No. 15 is the rear ignition coil fuse. After replacing a new fuse, the fuse was immediately blown when the ignition switch was turned on, indicating a short circuit in the ignition system. He used a multimeter to measure the resistance between No. 14 and No. 15 fuse sockets in the fuse box and ground. The measured value was 0Ω, indicating that the power supply was short-circuited to ground. He removed all ignition coil connectors and measured the resistance between No. 14 and No. 15 fuse sockets in fuse box and ground. The measured value was ∞, which indicated that the circuit was normal and the fault point should be in the ignition coil. Therefore, he removed and measured the eight ignition coils (4 at the front and 4 at the rear) one by one, and found that the ignition coils at the front and rear of cylinder 2 had internal short circuit faults. Then he reinstalled these ignition coils, all lines and fuses, and started the engine. The spark plug sparked strong, indicating that the ignition system fault had been eliminated. However, the engine was still unable to start. Because of multiple starts, the engine speed was obviously insufficient, indicating that the battery power had decreased significantly. He continued to start the engine after fully charging the battery. The engine had a "chug" sound that seemed to start, but it still could not be started. The engine cannot be started when there is oil and fire. Only mechanical and control system problems can be considered. The engine valve timing transmission adopts silent chain, which only ran 30, 000 km. The ignition timing should not be problematic. He used a scan tool to read out the engine fault information and the fault code was not stored in the electronic control unit.

He started the starter to read the data flow and found that the engine speed was only 60r/min, obviously lower than the actual value. Because the engine speed signal was obtained by the crankshaft position sensor, the crankshaft position sensor was suspected to be faulty. He measured the resistance of the crankshaft position sensor and it was completely normal. He then removed the sensor and found obvious wear at the end of the sensor. The car adopts electromagnetic induction crankshaft position sensor to obtain the engine speed through the rotation of crankshaft trigger wheel. Under normal circumstances, the sensor has certain clearance with the crankshaft trigger wheel and shall not be worn.

Therefore, the trigger wheel was suspected to be faulty and he was ready to remove the oil pan for inspection. When raising the car, he found that the oil pan had been collided and the oil pan had been removed for re-welding after the collision.

Then he removed the oil pan and found that there was a gear inside the oil pan. Then he checked the trigger wheel of the sensor and found that only a part of it was fixed on the crankshaft. The crankshaft trigger wheel had split into 2 pieces, one of which had fallen into the oil pan. The gear on the trigger wheel only gave the sensor a low engine speed signal and was not continuous, causing the engine to have a start sign but cannot be started.

After replacing the trigger gear, the engine started smoothly. He used the scan tool to check the data flow and everything was normal. The fault was eliminated.

He knew afterwards that the car had been repaired. It can be concluded that the ignition coil was damaged unreasonably by improper operation, while the trigger wheel was damaged by the small clearance between the oil pan and the crankshaft pulley and improper operation when removing the oil pan.

Summary: The fault that the engine cannot be started, but the engine is still supplying oil and the spark plug still sparks makes it easy for the repairmen to choose a wrong diagnosis direction, and think the fault should be in the mechanical part. For this type of fault, it is easier to find the cause of the fault if the repairman can continuously monitor the fuel injector or the sparks of the spark plug with the oscilloscope.

[Typical Case Ⅱ]　Failure of a Beijing Hyundai 2. 0 Tuscson car to start.

Fault Description: The owner of a Beijing Hyundai 2. 0 Tuscson car driving 58, 000 km said that the engine could not be started after parking for about 1 hour, and the instrument displayed normally.

Fault Diagnosis and Repair: The repairman knew that the automobile was under warranty, and the maintenance record of 4S store was normal. After arriving at the site, he checked that all kinds of oils were normal and did the test-drive, confirming the fault described by the owner.

He removed the spark plug, turned on the starter and checked that there was no high voltage.

With the scan tool, he checked the engine electronic control system and found that there was a fault code: P0335 The crankshaft angle sensor is abnormal.

He checked wire of crankshaft angle sensor and found that it connected well.

Power circuit check: He unplugged the sensor, placed the ignition switch at ON, and measured the voltage between the power terminal of the sensor harness connector and the ground of 12. 21V, as shown in Figure 5-3, consistent with the specified value. It indicated that the circuit and internal circuit of the electronic control unit were normal.

Ground circuit check: When the ignition switch was OFF, he measured the resistance between the ground terminal of the sensor harness connector and ground, and the resistance value was less than 0.5Ω, indicating that the circuit and the internal circuit of the electronic control unit are normal.

Signal circuit check: When the ignition switch was ON, he measured the voltage between the signal terminal of the sensor harness connector and ground as 4.95V (standard value is about 5V), as shown in Figure 5-4, indicating that the circuit and internal circuit of the electronic control unit were normal.

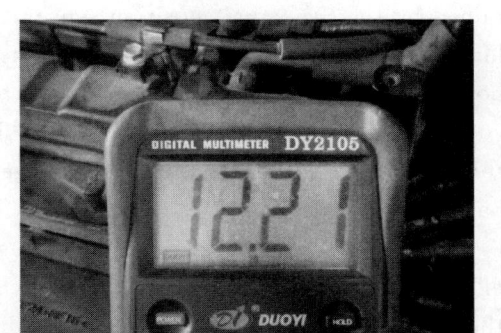

Figure 5-3　Voltage between Sensor Harness Connector Power Terminal and Ground

The sensor circuit and the control unit were normal through the checks above. Then,

76 | Automobile Integrated Fault Diagnosis and Repair |

the fault should be with the crankshaft position sensor itself. He replaced the crankshaft position sensor, tested the engine, found that the starting was normal, and used the scan tool to detect and got the normal result, as shown in Figure 5-5.

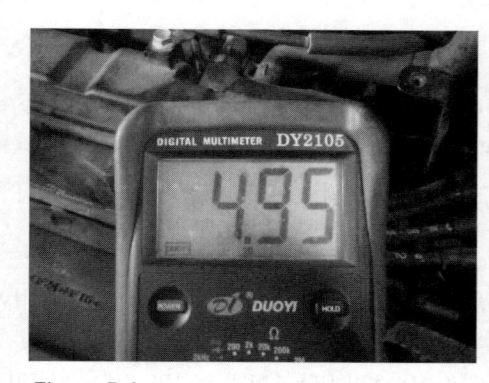

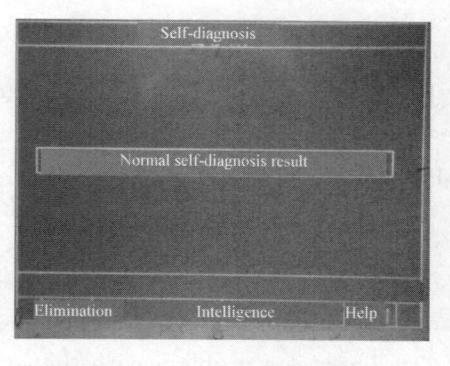

Figure 5-4 Voltage between Sensor Harness Connector Signal Terminal and Ground

Figure 5-5 Diagnosis Result of Scan Tool

Summary: The ECU calculates the engine speed according to the crankshaft position sensor signal to control fuel injection and ignition. The car could not start because the crankshaft position sensor was damaged and the ECU could not receive this signal.

During daily maintenance, the standard operation procedure should be strictly followed, which will reduce the diagnosis time and improve the efficiency of fault diagnosis.

Task **II** Fault Diagnosis and Repair of Engine with Signs of starting but Failing to Start

Learning Objectives

1. Be able to determine the direction and items of inquiry according to the fault phenomena of the automobile for repair.

2. Be able to prepare a correct fault diagnosis plan according to fault phenomena.

3. Be able to consult maintenance data skillfully, select appropriate detection and diagnosis devices according to fault phenomena and use them skillfully.

4. Be able to test the engine failure to start with appropriate maintenance devices according to the diagnosis plan.

5. Be able to correctly analyze the test results and determine the fault location and cause of engine failure to start.

6. Be able to repair the fault parts quickly and accurately and eliminate the hidden troubles.

Task Import

Task Material: The engine of a 2011 Bora 1.6L car, manual transmission car with a mileage of 78,000 km has signs of starting, but cannot be started.

Task Requirements: According to the fault phenomena of the car, consult relevant materials, select appropriate detection and diagnosis devices for fault diagnosis and repair, and fill in the task report.

Ⅰ. Fault Analysis

The fault symptom is that when starting the engine, the starter can drive the engine to rotate normally, that is, there are signs of starting, but it cannot be started. There are several possible reasons:

(1) There is an air leak in the intake pipe, causing the mixture to be too lean.

(2) Incorrect ignition timing causes the engine to fail to burn normally.

(3) The high-pressure spark is too weak, causing the mixture to fail to burn normally.

(4) The fuel pressure is too low, causing the mixture too lean.

(5) There is a problem with the coolant temperature sensor, causing the air-fuel ratio not to be offset.

(6) The air filter is blocked, causing insufficient intake air.

(7) There is a problem with the air flow meter, causing the air-fuel ratio to be offset.

(8) The fuel injector is blocked or leaking, causing the mixture to be too rich or lean.

(9) There is a problem with the fuel injection control system, causing the mixture to be too rich or lean.

(10) The cylinder pressure is too low, causing the mixture to fail to burn normally.

Ⅱ. Fault Diagnosis

There are signs of starting but the engine cannot be started, which means that the ignition system, fuel injection system and control system are faulty, but was not completely failed. The fault is usually checked with a scan tool, then the ignition system, intake system, fuel system, etc. can be checked in turn, and finally the engine cylinder pressure can be checked. The diagnostic procedure is as follows:

(1) Use the scan tool to check for fault codes: If there is a fault code, we can find the corresponding fault cause according to the displayed fault code. It should be noted that the displayed fault codes are not necessarily related to the engine failure to start, and intermittent faults will generally not affect the starting performance of the engine. The main components affecting the starting performance are: crankshaft position sensor, coolant temperature sensor, air flow meter, etc.

(2) Check high voltage sparks: In addition to checking whether the high voltage sparks on the high voltage bus of the distributor are normal, further check whether the high voltage sparks on the high voltage junction of each cylinder are normal. If the bus sparks are too weak, replace the high voltage coil; If the bus sparks are normal, but the junction sparks are weak or go off, it indicates that the distributor cover or distributor rotor is leaking and shall be replaced.

(3) Check air filter: If the filter element is too dirty and blocked, remove the filter element before starting the engine. Replace the filter element if it can start normally.

(4) Check whether there is air leakage in the intake system: Air leakage in the air inlet

pipe behind the air flow meter will affect the accuracy of the intake air quantity measurement and make the mixture lean. Severe leakage may cause the engine to fail to start. During inspection, carefully check whether the intake hose behind the air flow meter is cracked, whether the clamps of joints are loose, whether the resonance cavity is cracked, and whether the crankcase ventilation hose is connected properly. The fuel evaporation recovery system and the exhaust gas recirculation system are inoperative during start-up and idle operation. if they enter working state at start-up, the start-up performance will be affected. Block the fuel evaporation recovery hose or exhaust gas recirculation pipe, and then start the engine. If it can start normally, it indicates that the system is faulty and should be checked carefully.

(5) Check spark plugs: Too large or too small spark plug clearance, cracked spark plug or carbon deposit on it can affect the starting performance. Normal clearance of spark plugs is generally 0.8mm, and for some high energy electronic ignition systems, the spark plug clearance is large, up to 1.2mm. If the spark plug clearance is too large or too small, it shall be adjusted according to the standard value shown in the model service manual, and the spark plug shall be checked for carbon deposits and cracks.

(6) Check fuel pressure: If the fuel pressure is too low, check the fuel filter, oil pressure regulator and fuel pump for faults.

(7) If there is a large amount of wet gasoline on the spark plug surface, it indicates that the fuel injection volume is too large, remove all spark plugs, clean the surface of the spark plug and install the spark plug for restarting. If there is still excessive fuel injection, remove the fuel injector and check the fuel injector for oil leakage.

(8) Failure of the air flow meter or coolant temperature sensor can also cause excessive or low fuel injection. If this occurs, the two sensors should be measured against the data in the model service manual.

(9) Check ignition timing: If the ignition advance angle is incorrect, calibrate the ignition timing before starting the engine to check whether the fault is corrected.

(10) Check whether the cylinder compression pressure meets the standard.

Ⅲ. Task Implementation

1. Inquiry

Ask the owner about symptoms before the engine failure to start; Under what circumstances the fault occurs; Whether maintenance has been carried out after the fault; Whether other repairs or additional equipment installation have been carried out before the fault; Whether the automobile is maintained on time, etc.

According to the automobile fault information obtained from the owner, the possibility of some faults shall be preliminarily eliminated and the scope of fault diagnosis shall be narrowed down.

2. Test-drive and Basic Inspection

Start the engine and perform fault confirmation. At the same time, observe whether there is air leakage in the air inlet, whether the vacuum pipe is falling off or damaged, whether the wire connector is loose and whether there is oil leakage, water leakage, air leakage and electricity leakage.

Analyze the possible causes of fault symptoms according to the automobile's fault symptoms, basic inspection and experience.

3. Detection and Diagnosis

(1) This car cannot be started, it is dragged back to the maintenance station for inspection

① Use VAS5052 to detect engine and other systems-no fault codes.

② Check engine valve timing-normal.

③ Check ignition system and spark plugs-4 spark plug electrodes are wet and others are normal.

④ When further measuring gasoline pressure, the gasoline pressure is normal. Unplug the gasoline pump fuse and start the engine after multiple starts, but the engine shakes at idle speed.

⑤ After opening the oil filling cover, the engine can start normally, but it is found that there is a large amount of white smoke from the oil cover opening, and the engine idling jitter is serious.

(2) Based on the above test analysis, it is determined that the engine itself has mechanical problems After measuring the cylinder pressure, it is found that there is only 6kPa of cylinder 2 and the pressure is obviously low, as shown in Figure 5-6. The pressures of other cylinders are normal. There is no change in the cylinder pressure after adding oil into cylinder 2, so it can be determined that there is a problem with the piston ring of cylinder 2.

(3) Remove and inspect the piston of cylinder 2 It is found that the second air ring of the piston was fractured into 3 segments. See Figure 5-7.

Figure 5-6 Pressure Detection of Cylinder 2

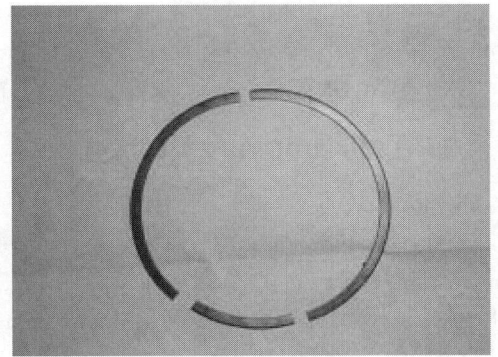

Figure 5-7 Damaged Air Ring

Cause analysis of fault: The piston air ring of cylinder 2 of the engine is broken, and a large amount of combustible mixture blows off from the fractured piston air ring into the crankcase. Through the crankcase ventilation system, the "blow-by" gas enters the back of throttle valve. The MAP sensor judges that the intake air quantity is large (low vacuum degree), which causes excessive fuel injection and spark plug drowning. The engine has starting signs but cannot be started.

80 | Automobile Integrated Fault Diagnosis and Repair |

After opening the oil filler cap, the "blow-by" gas in the crankcase is discharged from the oil cover opening, the gas pressure in the crankcase becomes smaller, so the membrane of the oil-gas separator cannot be pushed open. The "blow-by" gas cannot enter into the rear of the throttle valve through the crankcase ventilation system, so that the combustible gas mixture during starting is normal, and the engine can be started normally. The structure diagram of crankcase ventilation system is shown in Figure 5-8.

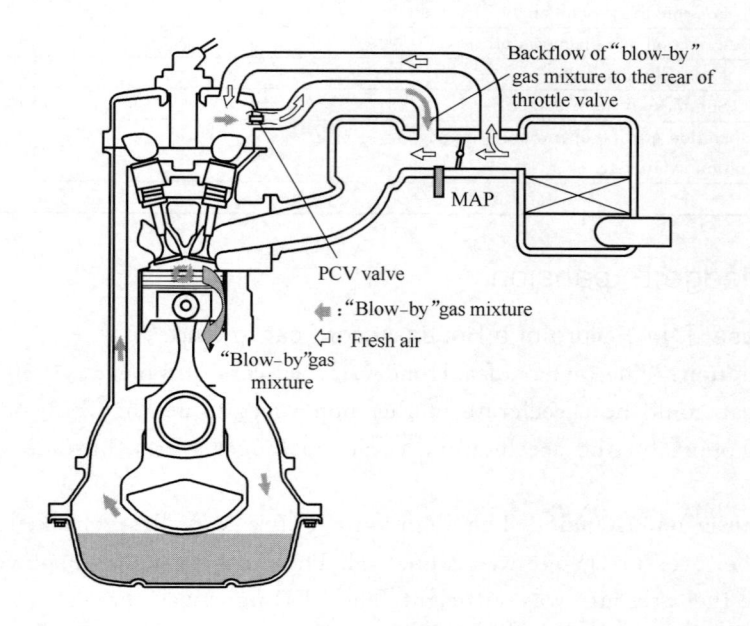

Figure 5-8 Structure Diagram of Crankcase Ventilation System

Pull out the fuse of gasoline pump and start the engine for many times, the gasoline pressure inside the fuel inlet pipe gradually decreases, so that the fuel injection quantity of the fuel injector decreases, and part of the combustible mixture in the combustion chamber is discharged. At this time, the engine can start normally.

4. Fault Elimination

After replacing the piston air ring of cylinder 2 for re-installation and test-drive, the fault is eliminated.

5. Inspection and Delivery

After troubleshooting, carry out test run to confirm that the engine starts normally without any other symptoms. Then use the scan tool to diagnose, clear the fault code in the electronic control unit, check that all data flows are within the specified range, and the troubleshooting is completed.

IV. Task Summary

When it is difficult to start the engine, the basic method should be used to formulate the maintenance technical scheme, and the cause of the fault should be analyzed step by step, and the problem should not be complicated by blind disassembly and assembly.

V. Task Report

Major		Class		Name	
Task Name				Class Hours	2
Model		Engine Model			
Task Completion Process	Assessment Items	Assessment Contents		Maximum Score	Score
	1. Description of fault symptoms			5	
	2. Possible causes and analysis of fault			25	
	3. Detection and diagnosis process			35	
	4. Fault Elimination			10	
	5. Summary of fault diagnosis			10	
Teacher Evaluation	Operation quality, operation efficiency, operation safety, etc.			15	
Total Score				100	

VI. Knowledge Expansion

〔Typical Case Ⅰ〕 Failure of a Honda Accord car to start.

Fault Description: The owner of a Honda Accord car, driving 90, 000 km, suddenly found that the car could not accelerate in the high speed, and then only idle, the engine stopped after stepping on the accelerator, could no longer start, but there were signs of starting.

Fault Diagnosis and Repair: The high-voltage fire was first checked and was normal. Then the fuel pressure gauge was connected. The pressure gauge displayed 295kPa, indicating that the fuel pressure was sufficient. The LED light was connected at the fuel injector plug and flashed when starting, indicating that the ECU sent the fuel injection signal to the actuator-fuel injector. The ignition advance angle was checked when starting with the ignition timing gun. It changed near the top dead center, was slightly late, indicating no obvious abnormality, at least not reaching the degree of failure to start. It was suspected that the air-fuel ratio at start-up was too rich, which may cause the spark plug to drown. Therefore, the accelerator pedal was pressed to the bottom to start, so that it entered the oil cut-off procedure, but could not be started, and no matter how to operate the throttle valve, it could not be started, but there were still signs of starting. The spark plugs of each cylinder were removed and the engine spark plug was found to be black, indicating that the mixture was rich. The spark plug was cleaned and the fuel injector plug was pulled off to keep it from fuel injection temporarily. The engine still could not start; The plug was plugged in to start, the starting signs seemed to be more obvious, but never started. In view of the sudden failure to start during driving and occasional reverse rotation of the crankshaft, although no obvious abnormality was found in the ignition timing gun, the valve cover was removed for safety reasons, the valve timing mark was observed, and the valve clearance was checked by accident. No abnormality was found. When the valve clearance is normal, it is impossible to occur starting failure due to insufficient compression pressure of 4 cylinders at the same time, so the reason of cylinder pressure may not be considered. The fault was thought to be caused by severe misalignment of the mixture or blockage of the exhaust pipe.

Ginde KT600 was used to check, and it was found that the system was normal without

fault code. The dynamic data flow was read during start-up. It was found that the fuel injection pulse width reached 17-18ms, the output voltage of the intake manifold absolute pressure sensor varied from 2. 4 to 2. 8V, while the exhaust pipe was blocked.

This caused a decrease in the intake manifold vacuum and an increase in the MAP voltage. When starting, the exhaust pressure at the exhaust port was felt by hand. The pressure was very low and the exhaust system was blocked. There were obvious signs to start when the spark plug of one cylinder was removed. When the accelerator pedal was pressed, the engine finally started, but it could be seen that a large amount of black exhaust gas was ejected from the spark plug gap. The data flow was observed, and the absolute pressure sensor was 2. 1V. It could be seen that the exhaust system was blocked. After removing the exhaust pipe, the starter accelerated very smoothly, indicating that there were no other faults. The MAP idle voltage was 1. 0V and the fuel injection pulse width was about 4ms. After installing the exhaust pipe, the engine could be started, idle speed was stable, and MAP was1. 2V. The three-way catalyst was removed and it was found that one third of its inner carrier was lost, sintered and attached to the carrier, and asbestos material fell off. After replacing the three-way catalyst, the engine started smoothly. The test drive was carried out, and the engine data flow was read and all within the normal range. The fault was eliminated completely. A week later, the user was visited and no fault was found.

Analysis of the fault causes shows that the vacuum degree of intake manifold decreased due to blockage of the three-way catalyst and unsmooth exhaust. Because the intake air quantity was detected by the absolute pressure sensor, the mixture was richer and the combustion was incomplete, which caused the temperature of the three-way catalyst to rise, accelerating its melting and being more blocked. Such a vicious cycle made the mixture richer, the temperature higher, the carrier melted away, and the asbestos material between the carrier and its casing dropped after some rapid acceleration, further blocking the exhaust pipe, resulting in difficulty in starting. After the spark plugs of each cylinder were removed, the exhaust gas accumulated in the exhaust pipe was ejected from the spark plug space with the opening of the exhaust valve of this cylinder. At this time, the spark plug gap of the cylinder acted as an exhaust pipe for intermittent exhaust, so the engine was easy to start.

Summary: In fact, the root cause of the three-way catalyst blockage was poor fuel. When a fault involves oil and fire, it is usually necessary to consider whether the inlet/exhaust system is faulty, such as, too lean or rich mixture; excessive exhaust resistance, etc. , which may cause the engine to fail to start.

[Typical Case II] Engine failure of a Bora car to start.

Fault Description: The engine of a Bora car automatic transmission car, driving 60, 000 km, had signs of starting, but could not start.

Fault Diagnosis and Repair: The basic inspection was done. The computer V. A. G5052 was used to check. The engine system was normal without fault code. The fuel pressure and cylinder pressure of the engine were within the normal range. The valve phase and ignition timing were normal.

When checking the spark plug, it was found that although the engine had been started several times, the spark plug did not show signs of flooding. From this point of view, was

this fault caused by too little fuel supply of the fuel injector and too lean mixture? But what caused the mixture to be too lean?

By reading the static engine data, it was found that the coolant temperature output by the engine ECU was 105℃, while the actual temperature of the engine was only about 5℃. Obviously, the water temperature signal received by the engine ECU was wrong, which indicated that the water temperature sensor was faulty. The circuit diagram of water temperature sensor is shown in Figure 5-9.

It was known after asking the owner carefully that the owner had flushed the engine at high engine temperature, which was exactly the key to this failure. To further confirm this, a new sensor was replaced for test drive and everything was OK. The analysis shows that the signal output from the water temperature sensor was distorted due to the wrong operation of the owner.

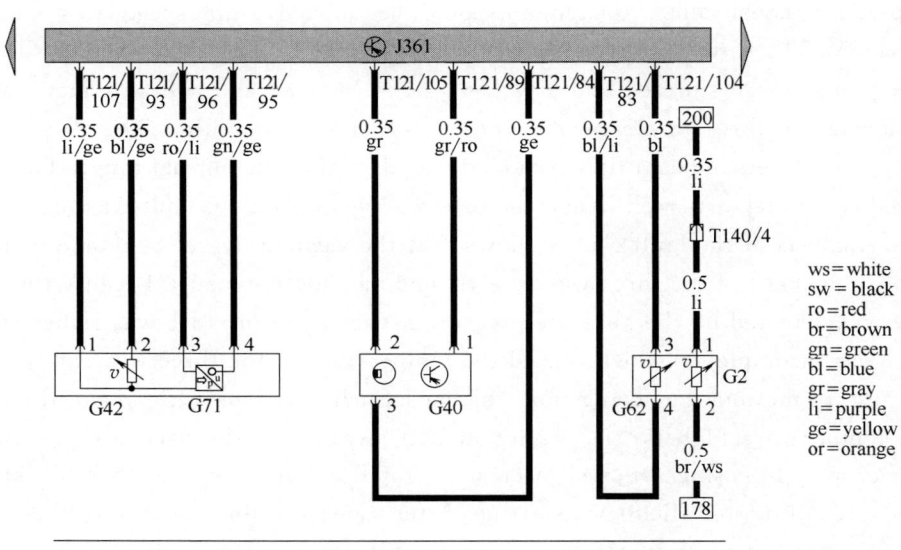

G2—Coolant temperature sensor
G40—Hall sensor
G42—Intake air temperature sensor
G62—Coolant temperature sensor
G71—Intake pressure sensor
J361—Simos multi-point injection control unit in the middle of the flow tank
T121—Plug,121-hole

Figure 5-9 Circuit Diagram of Water Temperature Sensor

Summary: This fault case is not practically complex, and experienced repairman may start directly with the water temperature sensor to find out the cause. However, this case shows that the ECU of the electronic control engine system does not memory some faults. For example, the water temperature sensor of the car had no open circuit or short circuit, only the signal was distorted, and the self-diagnosis function of the ECU would not be considered as fault. In this case, reading data blocks becomes the key to solving the problem. By reading the control unit data, the signal value sent to the ECU by each sensor could

84 | Automobile Integrated Fault Diagnosis and Repair |

be understood. The exact fault location could be found by comparison the signal value with the true value. It is also important for the ECU with fault code output to read the data of the control unit.

Task Ⅲ Fault Diagnosis and Repair of Engine Starting Difficulty

Learning Objectives

1. Be able to determine the direction and items of inquiry according to the fault phenomena of the automobile for repair.

2. Be able to prepare a correct fault diagnosis plan according to fault phenomena.

3. Be able to consult maintenance data skillfully, select appropriate detection and diagnosis devices according to fault phenomena and use them skillfully.

4. Be able to test start-up difficulty with appropriate maintenance devices according to the diagnosis plan.

5. Be able to correctly analyze the test result and determine the fault location and cause of difficult starting.

6. Be able to repair the fault parts quickly and accurately and eliminate the hidden troubles.

Task Import

Task Material: A 2009 Magotan 1. 8T car driving 90, 000 kilometers. The engine is difficult to start under cold car, and can start after multiple starts. After starting, idle speed is unstable, and the engine shakes.

Task Requirements: According to the fault phenomena of the car, consult relevant materials, select appropriate detection and diagnosis devices for fault diagnosis and repair, and fill in the task report.

Ⅰ. Fault Analysis

Engine starting difficulty means that the starter can drive the engine to rotate at normal speed, but it takes a long time to start, or it can start after several continuous starts.

Possible causes of the fault are as follows:

(1) The intake system is leaking.

(2) The fuel pressure is too low.

(3) The air filter element is blocked.

(4) The coolant temperature sensor is faulty.

(5) The air flow meter is faulty.

(6) The idle control valve or additional air valve is faulty.

(7) The fuel injector is faulty (inoperative, leaking, blocked).

(8) The ignition timing is incorrect.

(9) The cylinder compression pressure is too low.

Item Ⅴ Fault Diagnosis and Repair of Abnormal Engine Operation | **85**

(10) The electronic control unit is faulty.

II. Fault Diagnosis

Self-diagnosis of fault: If there is a fault code, find the corresponding fault cause according to the fault code.

Check vacuum of intake pipe at idle speed: If the vacuum is less than 66.7kPa, it indicates that there is air leakage in the intake system. Check all pipe joints, gaskets and vacuum hoses of the intake pipe, exhaust gas re-circulation system and fuel vapor recovery system.

Check the air filter: If the filter element is blocked, clean or replace it.

If the engine can start normally when the throttle valve is about 1/4 opening, and it is difficult to start when the throttle valve is fully closed, check whether the idle control valve and the additional air valve operate normally. In cold idle operation, pull off the wiring harness plug of the idle control valve, or clamp the intake hose of the additional air valve with pliers during cold idle operation. If the engine speed does not decrease, it indicates that the idle control valve is not working properly. Check the idle control valve and its control circuit.

Check fuel pressure: Short the two detection sockets of the electric fuel pump with a wire and turn on the ignition switch to allow the electric fuel pump to run. Under this condition, the fuel pressure shall reach about 300kPa. If the pressure is too low, check whether the oil pressure regulator and the fuel injector are leaking, whether the fuel filter is blocked and the maximum oil pressure of the fuel pump is normal.

Check the temperature sensor and the air flow meter: Pull off wiring harness plugs of the temperature sensor and the air flow meter, and measure resistance between temperature sensor and air flow meter terminals with the ohm gear of a multimeter. If the resistance does not meet the standard, replace it.

If it is not easy to start when cold, but the starting is normal during hot car, check whether the cold start fuel injector works normally. Check whether there is a voltage of about 12V at the wiring harness plug of cold start fuel injector when starting. If there is no voltage, the control circuit is faulty and the cold start temperature time switch and its control circuit shall be checked. If there is voltage at the harness plug during starting, check whether the resistance of the solenoid coil of the cold start fuel injector is normal and whether the nozzle hole is blocked, etc.

If it is difficult to start under hot state (starting in hot car state, starting after turning crankshaft by opening start switch for more than 3~4 turns can be considered as difficult to start), check whether the holding pressure of fuel system is normal after the ignition switch is turned off. After connecting the oil pressure gauge and turning off the ignition switch (engine is off), the fuel pressure should be kept not lower than 150kPa within 5 minutes. If the holding pressure is too low, check the oil pressure regulator, electric fuel pump, fuel injector, etc. for leaks.

Check ignition timing when the engine is running at idle speed: If it didn't meet the standard, it shall be adjusted.

Check whether the starting signal from the start switch to the electronic control unit is normal: If the electronic control unit fails to receive the starting signal of the starting

switch, the start enrichment control cannot be carried out, which will also cause difficulty in starting. For this, check whether there is a signal of start switch to the electronic control unit when starting from the wiring harness plug of the electronic control unit. If there is no signal, check the start switch and circuit.

Check the cylinder compression pressure: If the pressure is too low, remove and inspect the engine.

If the above checks are normal, a new ECU may be replaced. If the condition is improved, it indicates that the electronic control unit is faulty and the electronic control unit shall be replaced.

Ⅲ. Task Implementation

1. Inquiry

After receiving the car, the repairman shall first learn from the owner: time of the fault; the driving condition of the car; mileage; whether the car is maintained on time; whether maintenance has been carried out after the fault occurs; whether the car is equipped with sound and anti-theft devices. The reasons for the difficulty in starting can be judged by the above inquiry, and the examination time can be shortened and the diagnosis efficiency can be improved.

2. Test-drive and Basic Inspection

Carry out the test run, confirm the fault, test whether the car works normally under various working conditions, so as to comprehensively analyze the fault of the engine. Observe the characteristics and rules of the engine faults; Observe whether the ignition coil and fuel injector plug of each cylinder have obvious looseness, and whether there is obvious air leakage in the intake port.

3. Detection and Diagnosis

(1) Use VAS5052A to query the fault, and get the fault memory shown in Figure 5-10, Figure 5-11 and Figure 5-12.

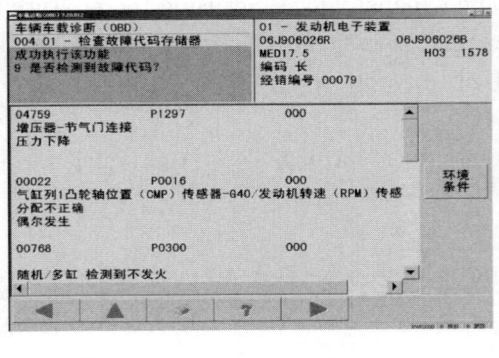

Figure 5-10 Read Fault Code (1)　　　　　　Figure 5-11 Read Fault Code (2)

(2) Analyze the possible cause of the fault 04759-Booster-Throttle pressure drop. The air flow meter is damaged; The booster pipeline behind the air flow meter is damaged and leaked; The booster pressure sensor is damaged.

(3) Analyze the possible cause of the fault 00022-Incorrect distribution of camshaft position

sensor G40/engine speed. The camshaft position sensor G40 and the engine speed sensor G28 are damaged; There is deviation in the actual adjusted value of intake camshaft.

(4) Analyze the possible cause of the fault 00017-Excessive camshaft position timing. The camshaft regulating valve N205 is damaged or N205 control circuit and control unit are damaged; The hydraulic control valve on the intake camshaft is damaged; The engine control unit is damaged.

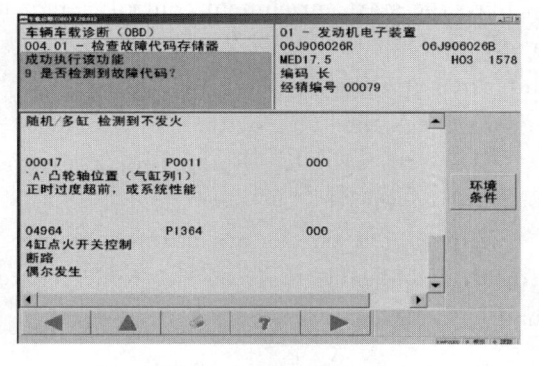

Figure 5-12　Read Fault Code（3）

(5) The intake system is free of pipeline damage and air leakage. During acceleration, the data of air flow meter of the third group data block and the booster pressure data of group 115 can change normally. Basically, the faults of air flow meter and booster system are excluded.

(6) Reading the Group 91 data block and comparing normal car data, it was found that the actual adjusted value of the camshaft differs too much from the rated value and this difference has been present since start-up.

(7) After disassembling N205, use VAS5052A to diagnose the actuator. The N205 solenoid valve can move freely, and N205 and its control circuit are normal.

(8) Toggle the camshaft adjustment control valve spool with a screwdriver and find that it cannot be moved, and that of a normal car shall be able to move easily. After checking, there are signs of disassembly and assembly of the control valve, and it feels tight when disassembling. Communication with the user shows that the engine timing system has been repaired due to accident. Therefore, it is concluded that the regulating valve is faulty.

The analysis shows that the valve core is stuck in the advance adjustment position due to deformed camshaft adjustment control valve caused by excessive tightening torque, which causes the intake cam to be in excessive advance state after the oil pressure is established, resulting in the excessive stacking angle of intake and exhaust valves, causing the mixture to be too lean, and the booster pressure to be discharged to the exhaust pipe when the intake and exhaust valves are stacked, thus generating fault memories.

4. Fault Elimination

After replacing the regulating valve and tightening it according to the tightening torque 35N・m, the fault is eliminated.

5. Inspection and Delivery

After troubleshooting, confirm that the engine has no other symptoms and hand over the car to the owner.

Ⅳ. Task Summary

The diagnosis of this fault makes full use of the scan tool to read the fault code and analyzes the meaning and conditions of the fault code, thus providing a good direction for diagnosis. At the same time, combined with data flow analysis, the fault range is locked more accurately, and then the specific parts can be disassembled and inspected to find the fault location.

V. Task Report

		Major		Class		Name	
		Task Name				Class Hours	2
		Model		Engine Model			
		Assessment Items	Assessment Contents			Maximum Score	Score
Task Completion Process		1. Description of fault symptoms				5	
		2. Possible causes and analysis of fault				25	
		3. Detection and diagnosis process				35	
		4. Fault Elimination				10	
		5. Summary of fault diagnosis				10	
Teacher Evaluation		Operation quality, operation efficiency, operation safety, etc.				15	
		Total Score				100	

VI. Knowledge Expansion

【Typical Case Ⅰ】 A 2008 Magotan 1.8TSI car not easy to start when hot.

Fault Description: A 2008 Magotan 1.8TSI car, running 192,000 kilometers. The car started normally in cold state. It was difficult to start when hot after stopping for a short time, but could start by pressing the accelerator pedal.

Fault Diagnosis and Repair:

(1) Read fault code: The fault codes stored in the engine control unit were read by VAS6150, as shown in Figure 5-13.

(2) Analyzed meaning of fault codes: Although the 08213 intake manifold sensor affects engine torque adjustment, it has little effect on the mixture regulation at start-up and idle speed.

The 00370 fuel adjustment system of cylinder bank 1 is too rich, indicating that the mixture is rich.

Figure 5-13 Read Fault Code (4)

00769 No ignition detected by cylinder 1 is an incidental fault.

The above fault codes cannot judge the actual state of the fault, so it is necessary to continue to collect key data of idle mixture status for analysis.

(3) Read data flow and analyzed it: It was found that the injection pulse width of 0.51ms was much lower than the normal value. The intake air quantity of 2.1g/s and engine load of 15% were also slightly lower than the normal value. Which indicated that the mixture was too rich.

(4) It was judged that the engine mixture was too rich according to the above data analysis.

The reasons causing too rich system mixture include: Large wear of fuel injector may cause oil leakage or oil dripping and poor atomization; The pressure of fuel oil supply system is high; The engine mixture is burned with additional oil vapor, for example, the fuel vapor

line is not closed tightly.

(5) Observed the idle running state of the engine, and found that the idle speed was relatively stable and there was no shake. Therefore, the fuel pressure and fuel vapor carbon canister solenoid valve were checked first. The fuel system pressure was normal. The fuel vapor connecting pipe connected with the carbon canister solenoid valve was blocked and the fuel injection pulse width data did not increase.

The pipeline of intake system was checked and found no leakage; When the nozzle was removed and cleaned, no oil dripping or bad atomization of the nozzle was found. The diagnosis was deadlocked.

After learning and sorting out, the diagnostic scheme was reworked out, focusing on the inspection of fuel injector and high-pressure pump. According to the scheme, the oil filler cap was unscrewed after the hot car was turned off and a strong smell of fuel vapor was smelt, indicating that the crankcase was mixed with fuel and the fault point was directly related to the high-pressure oil pump. Therefore, the high-pressure oil pump, engine oil and filter was replaced, and the fault was eliminated.

The analysis shows that because of the leakage of fuel from the plunger of the high-pressure oil pump into the crankcase oil, the crankcase fuel vapor was too rich after the hot car, and the engine air-fuel ratio was always in the rich state, and the pulse width of the engine control unit was reduced but could not reach the normal value.

Summary: At present, the control system and structure of middle and high-end cars are complicated, so it is time-consuming and it increases the labor intensity to find out faults by replacing parts. The car operation data can accurately reflect its working conditions, and the fault range of the car can be judged and analyzed through the data, which can achieve high efficiency.

[Typical Case Ⅱ] A 2011 Bora car not easy to start when hot.

Fault Description: A 2011 Bora car, driving 30,000 km. The owner described that the hot car was not easy to start, could only be started by stepping on the accelerator.

Troubleshooting process: After the test drive, it was proved that the car was not easy to start, even if it could start, the idle speed was very low at first, and it was normal to start by pressing the accelerator.

(1) According to the experience, the poor start of hot car generally means that the water temperature sensor is faulty, but the computer was used to detect that the component was not faulty and the read data block was normal. The water temperature display was normal when the water temperature sensor was shaken and the engine speed sensor was not faulty.

(2) The fuel pressure was checked, and the result was that the oil pressure was normal, 250kPa at idle speed and 300 kPa during slam acceleration. At this time, it was suspected that the fuel injector may leak oil, resulting in poor starting due to over-rich mixture. The oil inlet pipe and return pipe were clamped with water pipe clamps, and the oil pressure was always maintained at 200kPa after maintaining pressure for 30min, indicating that there was no obvious oil leakage from the fuel injector.

(3) There was no air leakage in each vacuum pipeline, spark plug and cylinder line were normal.

According to the experience, when the throttle valve of Bora car is dirty, this phenomenon will occur. However, the throttle valve of this car was not very dirty and the opening was 1. 9. But the repairman cleaned the throttle valve of the car with a try. Through a test-drive, the car started normally.

Summary: During the automobile diagnosis, it is very important not only to have good diagnosis devices and correct maintenance methods, but also to accumulate experience. If there is no fault code and the fault location cannot be clearly seen from the data flow, the solution can be sought by referring to similar faults of similar automobiles.

Task Ⅳ Fault Diagnosis and Repair of Engine Idle Unsteady

Unsteady idle speed is one of the most common faults in engines. There are many reasons for unstable idle speed, which may be caused by malfunction of oil circuit system, ignition system and mechanical system. During the diagnosis of unstable idle speed, the characteristics and rules of unstable idle speed should be analyzed, and the diagnosis scheme should be determined according to the specific characteristics of the fault. In particular, it is necessary to learn about the use, maintenance and repair of faulty automobiles.

Learning Objectives

1. Be able to determine the direction and items of inquiry according to the fault phenomena of the automobile for repair.

2. Be able to prepare a correct fault diagnosis plan according to fault phenomena.

3. Be able to consult maintenance data skillfully, select appropriate detection and diagnosis devices according to fault phenomena and use them skillfully.

4. Be able to test the cold unstable idle speed with suitable maintenance devices according to the diagnostic scheme.

5. Be able to correctly analyze the test results and determine the fault location and cause of the cold idle instability.

6. Be able to repair the fault parts quickly and accurately and eliminate the hidden troubles.

Task Import

Task Material: A 2008 Magotan 1. 8T car, driving 160, 000 km. The user said that after the engine started, it shook at idle speed, and the power dropped.

Task Requirements: According to the fault phenomena of the car, consult relevant materials, select appropriate detection and diagnosis devices for fault diagnosis and repair, and fill in the task report.

Ⅰ. Fault Analysis

1. Intake system failure

(1) Leakage of intake port or gas line and valve body connected with it   Excess air en-

tering the intake port or intake manifold will lean the engine mixture, causing unstable engine idle. Similarly, when the engine is idle, if the exhaust gas recirculation system fails, allowing the exhaust gas to enter the engine, it will cause unstable engine idle speed. Common causes of failure are: The clamp of intake manifold is loose or the hose is cracked; The intake manifold gasket is leaking; The seal ring of fuel injector is leaking; The vacuum pipe plug falls off and is broken; The opening of positive crankcase ventilation (PCV) valve is large; The solenoid valve of the activated carbon tank is not closed tightly or normally open; The exhaust gas recirculation (EGR) valve is not closed tightly, etc.

(2) Excessive scaling of throttle valve or intake port   There is too much carbon deposit and dirt in the throttle valve or surrounding intake port, and the cross-sectional area of the air passage changes, which makes the electronic control unit unable to accurately control the idle intake air quantity, causing unstable idle speed.

(3) Failure of idle air control element   The idle air control element is the idle solenoid valve or idle motor that controls the idle speed of the engine. Failure of these idle air control elements, poor operation, or presence of oil and carbon deposits on the valve body will result in inaccurate idle air control and unstable engine idle speed.

(4) Misalignment of intake air quantity control   If the engine water temperature sensor, intake air pressure sensor, air flow meter and other sensors or their circuits fail, the electronic control unit will receive an error signal and perform wrong idle control, causing misalignment of engine idle air intake amount control.

2. Failure of fuel system

(1) Failure of fuel injector   The fuel injectors of individual cylinders of the engine do not work or work badly, and the fuel injection quantity of each cylinder is uneven and the atomization is not good, which may cause the power emitted by each cylinder to be inconsistent, thus causing the engine to be unstable at idle speed.

(2) Fuel pressure fault   Too low fuel pressure will cause poor atomization of fuel ejected from fuel injector, and reduce fuel injection volume and lead to excessive lean gas mixture; The too high fuel pressure will increase the actual fuel injection volume, make the mixture rich. Both of the two cases can lead to unstable idle speed of the engine. Common causes of fuel pressure failure are: The fuel filter is blocked, the fuel pump strainer is blocked, the fuel pump is not working properly, the tubing is deformed, the fuel pressure regulator is faulty, etc.

(3) Misalignment of fuel injection quantity   If the engine water temperature sensor, intake air pressure sensor, air flow meter and other sensors or their circuits fail, the electronic control unit will receive an error signal and perform wrong idle control, causing misalignment of engine idle fuel injection amount control.

3. Ignition system failure

(1) Ignition module and ignition coil fault   For the independently ignited engine, the ignition module or ignition coil of individual cylinder does not work or works badly, resulting in the inoperative or poor operation of individual cylinder, causing unstable engine idle speed. For example, the ignition module is damaged, the power circuit and signal circuit of the ignition module are faulty; the ignition coil is damaged or works unstably, etc. For the

non-independently ignited engine, if the ignition module or ignition coil is unstable, the engine will also be unstable at idle speed.

In recent years, ignition modules and ignition coils have been made into one in most models. The failure of ignition module or ignition coil is mainly characterized by weak high-voltage sparks or non-ignition of spark plugs. Common reasons are: Loss of ignition trigger signal; Failure of ignition module; Loose connection and poor contact of power supply or grounding wire of ignition module; Faulty primary coil or secondary coil, etc.

(2) Failure of spark plugs and high voltage wires   Failure of spark plugs and high voltage wires may cause spark energy loss or misfire. Common reasons are: Incorrect spark plug clearance; Ablation or damage of spark plug electrode; Carbon deposit on the spark plug electrode; Crack in magnetic insulator of spark plug; Too large resistance of high voltage wire; Leakage of insulation sheath or plug of high voltage wire; Ablation or poor insulation of distributor rotor electrode.

(3) Misalignment of ignition advance angle   Because of faulty engine crankshaft position sensor, camshaft position sensor and circuit, the electronic control unit receives an error signal, which causes the ignition advance angle to be incorrect.

4. Failure of mechanical parts

(1) Failure of valve train   Failure of the valve train causes excessive power drop of individual cylinders, resulting in unbalanced power for each cylinder. Common reasons are: Incorrect installation position of timing belt causes the opening/closing time of each cylinder valve to change, resulting in misalignment of valve phase and abnormal combustion of each cylinder; There is too much carbon deposit between the valve working face and the valve seat ring, and the valve seal is not tight, so that the compression pressure of each cylinder is inconsistent; The cam of camshaft is worn, and the abrasion of the cam of each cylinder is inconsistent, resulting in inconsistent amount of air entering into each cylinder; Valve related parts are faulty, such as valve push rod worn or bent, rocker arm worn, valve jammed or leaked, valve spring broken, etc.

If there is a large amount of carbon deposit on that back of the intake valve, the carbon deposit after cold start will absorb the fuel just injected, reduce the amount of fuel entering the cylinder, and make the mixture too lean, thus causing the idle speed to be unstable when the cold car is started.

In addition, an engine equipped with a hydraulic tappet is fitted with a relief valve on the oil passage to the cylinder head. When the pressure is higher than 300kPa, the valve opens. If the valve is plugged, excessive oil pressure causes the hydraulic tappet to extend too much, causing the valve to close poorly.

(2) Failure of engine block and piston connecting rod mechanism   Common faults in the engine block include: The cylinder liner is ablated or damaged, resulting in single cylinder leakage or air leakage between two cylinders; The piston and the cylinder are worn, and the cylinder roundness and cylindricality are out of tolerance; When the cylinder enters water, the connecting rod bends and the compression ratio is changed.

Common faults in the piston connecting rod mechanism are: The piston ring end clearance is too large, butt or fractured, and the piston ring loses elasticity; There is too much

Item V   Fault Diagnosis and Repair of Abnormal Engine Operation   **93**

carbon deposit in piston ring grooves.

These faults of the engine block and piston connecting rod mechanism will cause the power of individual cylinders to drop too much, thus making the power of each cylinder unbalanced.

(3) Other reasons For an engine equipped with exhaust gas recirculation system, if the EGR valve becomes stuck due to carbon deposit and opens at idle speed, part of the exhaust gas will enter the combustion chamber, causing the combustion of the engine to become unstable and thus the idle speed becomes unstable.

Unqualified dynamic balance of rotating parts such as engine crankshaft and flywheel, damage and looseness of engine support rubber pad will also cause unstable engine idle speed.

II. Fault Diagnosis

There are many fault points involved in the instability of idle speed. The scan tool should be fully used in fault diagnosis, combined with other detection and diagnosis devices, and a reasonable diagnosis scheme should be made according to the characteristics and rules of the fault. Only by scientific detection and analysis can the fault be eliminated quickly and accurately.

1. Diagnosis with a scan tool

The engine electronic control unit has a self-diagnosis function, so the self-diagnosis function of the electronic control unit shall be used firstly to check whether there is fault information record, so as to provide diagnosis direction for maintenance personnel.

First read out the fault code to see if there are permanent or incidental fault codes. If there are fault codes, analyze which fault codes are related to unstable idle speed. If there are more than one fault code, it is necessary to analyze the fault codes, analyze whether there are correlations among fault codes, and understand the cause and influencing factors of the fault codes. Once the analysis is completed, the next overhaul can be carried out according to the fault codes. If there is no fault code, diagnosis shall be carried out according to the routine method, focusing on the parts that fail but the electronic control unit cannot monitor and record the fault code.

Second, review and analyze data flow. A data flow may provide real-time data during engine operation. Check the engine speed, throttle opening, idle air flow learning value, idle air adjustment value, suction air quantity, ignition advance angle, coolant temperature and other data when the engine is unstable at idle speed. Data real-time value, learning value and adjustment value are expressed as actual value or percentage, and working condition is expressed in words. If the actual value of which data flow is found to be outside the specified range, the cause of the numerical deviation shall be analyzed and the corresponding components and lines shall be overhauled.

In addition, it is also possible to use the active test function of the scan tool to dynamically test possible faulty components, such as the fuel injector, the fuel pump, etc. , so as to observe whether they can operate, so as to determine whether they and their circuits are faulty or not.

2. Other detection and diagnosis

The detection content shall be determined according to the fault phenomenon, fault code content and data flow value. Multimeter, exhaust detector, fuel pressure gauge, vacuum gauge, cylinder pressure gauge, oscilloscope and other testing devices shall be selected according to the test items. Exhaust detection and waveform analysis are very important. Engines with non-independent ignition can also quickly the cylinders with low output power by cylinder cut-off method. The vacuum gauge can be used to analyze the specific reasons affecting vacuum degree. The detection principle is usually from electric to mechanical, from simple to complicated, and the fault location shall be determined without disassembly or less disassembly.

Diagnosis Tips: During the fault diagnosis of unstable idle speed of the engine, it shall be paid attention to check whether the engine still has abnormal conditions under other working conditions, such as poor starting, poor acceleration, insufficient power and flameout by deceleration. If the engine is only unstable at idle speed, the fault cause that affect the unstable idle speed of the engine should be considered in the diagnosis; If there are other symptoms, it is necessary to comprehensively consider the fault parts which may cause abnormal operation under multiple working conditions simultaneously.

Ⅲ. Task Implementation

1. Inquiry

After receiving the car, the repairman shall learn from the owner: Time of unstable idle speed; The driving condition of the car under unstable idle speed; Whether the car is maintained on time; Whether maintenance has been carried out after the fault occurs; Whether the car is equipped with sound and anti-theft devices. The preliminary judgment of idle speed instability is completed through the above inquiry, which can shorten the inspection time and improve the diagnosis efficiency.

2. Test-drive and Basic Inspection

Carry out the test run to confirm the fault, test whether the car works normally under the working condition outside idle speed, so as to comprehensively analyze the fault of the engine. Observe the characteristics and rules of engine jitter; Observe that the ignition coil and fuel injector plug of each cylinder have no obvious looseness, and the intake port has no obvious leakage.

3. Detection and Diagnosis

Use the scan tool 5052 to diagnose and query the fault message display: Cylinder 2 misfire.

According to fault phenomenon and diagnosis result, consider whether cylinder 2 does not fire first. Check the spark plug and find that the spark plug of cylinder 2 is ablated and a part of the side electrode is lost after ablation.

The analysis shows that the spark plug is seriously damaged by ablated. The misfire of cylinder 2 may be caused by poor operation of spark plug. The engine jitter should be caused by it. In addition, according to the user's report, the spark plug has not been replaced, and the status quo of other 3 spark plugs is obviously not very good, indicating that there are carbon deposits and erosion conditions to varying degrees. Then a new set of spark plugs are

changed and the test run is done, the engine is still as unstable as it used to be. This temporarily eliminates the fault of the ignition system.

Problems in the oil circuit, such as blocked fuel injector and inoperative fuel injector solenoid valve, can also cause unstable idle speed. Therefore, the fuel injection guide rail and the fuel injector is removed for inspection. The fuel injector has no abnormality. It is normal that there is slight carbon deposit around the fuel injector orifice. The fuel injector is installed on the guide rail and the motor is started to visually test the fuel injection. The fuel injection of the four fuel injectors is normal. This means there is no problem with the oil circuit.

It is suspected that ignition failure may be caused by failure of ignition coil. The ignition coil is replaced and the engine is tested. The engine situation is still not improved, and a new spark plug is installed on the ignition coil to test the spark plug fire. The result is also normal. This indicates that the ignition coil has no problem.

There is no problem with the oil circuit and there is no problem with the circuit, so the fault analysis should be the cylinder pressure problem. After removing the spark plug, the cylinder pressure is measured by the cylinder pressure gauge. It is found that the cylinder pressure of cylinder 2 is close to "0". The reason of low cylinder pressure may be valve problem or poor cylinder seal. The assembly of crankshaft and camshaft of the car should be no problem, because other cylinders work normally, only cylinder 2 misfires. To find the true fault, the cylinder head must be removed and inspected.

After disassembling the cylinder head, it is found that the cylinder surface was worn normally and the piston top is intact, but one exhaust valve of cylinder 2 is burnt out, as shown in Figure 5-14.

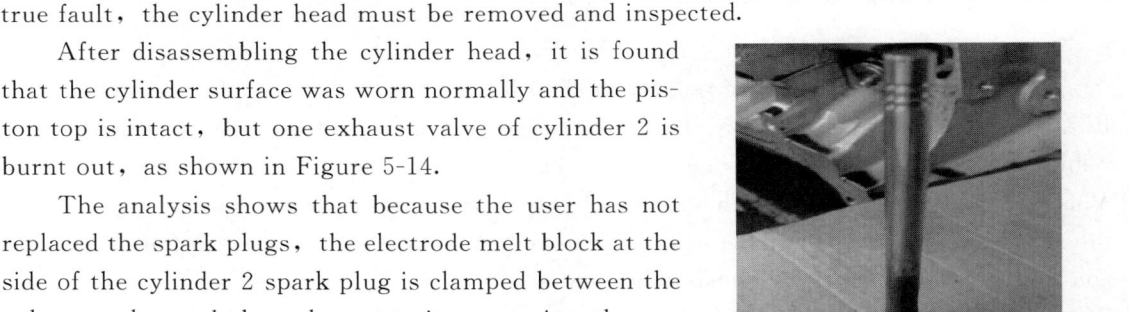

The analysis shows that because the user has not replaced the spark plugs, the electrode melt block at the side of the cylinder 2 spark plug is clamped between the exhaust valve and the valve seat ring, causing the exhaust valve not to close tightly and leak. Under this condition, the burning high temperature flame flows through the gap formed between the valve and the seat ring, which causes local high temperature ablation of

Figure 5-14 Damaged Exhaust Valve

the exhaust valve and serious damage, resulting in unstable engine idle speed.

4. Fault Elimination

After replacing all spark plugs and exhaust valve of cylinder 2 and assembling the engine, the engine runs smoothly. The scan tool is used for diagnosis, the fault code in the electronic control unit is cleared and the troubleshooting is completed.

5. Inspection and Delivery

After troubleshooting, confirm that the engine has no other symptoms and hand over the car to the owner.

IV. Task Summary

When diagnosing the unstable idle speed of the engine and when the electronic control

unit reports a cylinder misfire, it is necessary to consider not only faults in the ignition system and the oil circuit system, but also faults in the mechanical system. The airtightness of the piston cylinder and the valve tightness can be determined by detecting the cylinder pressure, and an endoscope may be used to check the conditions in the combustion chamber.

V. Task Report

Major			Class		Name	
Task Name					Class Hours	2
Model			Engine Model			
Task Completion Process	Assessment Items		Assessment Contents		Maximum Score	Score
	1. Description of fault symptoms				5	
	2. Possible causes and analysis of fault				25	
	3. Detection and diagnosis process				35	
	4. Fault Elimination				10	
	5. Summary of fault diagnosis				10	
Teacher Evaluation	Operation quality, operation efficiency, operation safety, etc.				15	
Total Score					100	

VI. Knowledge Expansion

〔Typical Case Ⅰ〕 Engine idle unsteady of a 2010 Jetta.

Fault Description: The engine of a 2010 Jetta, traveling 180, 000 km, was found unstable at idle speed while driving.

Fault Diagnosis and Repair: The Volkswagen special scan tool VAS5052 was used and displayed a throttle fault. The fuel pressure, start-up and idle pressure were normal.

The spark plugs were removed and inspected, and the high-voltage fire and the sparks were normal.

The cylinder pressure was tested, 1.13MPa for cylinder 1, 1.16MPa for cylinder 2, 1.09MPa for cylinder 3 and 1.12MPa for cylinder 4. The pressure of all cylinders is within normal range.

The fuel injector was removed and inspected, the fuel injection quantity and atomization were good and there was no oil dripping.

The ignition timing was checked and was completely normal.

The cylinder head was removed and inspected and the valve mechanism was checked and the intake valve spring of cylinder 1 was broken.

The analysis shows that the motor speed was low during starting, and when the piston was compressed, the compressed gas force could close the intake valve, so the cylinder pressure detected by low speed was normal. The speed rose after starting, and the intake valve was not controlled by cam and could not be closed in time. Therefore, the cylinder pressure was insufficient during normal operation of engine, resulting in poor operation of cylinder 1 and unstable idle speed.

After replacing the valve spring, the fault was eliminated.

Summary: There are many fault parts and causes of unstable idle speed, which makes it difficult to diagnose. When diagnosis, scientific and reasonable analysis must be carried out according to

the working principle of each system to eliminate the fault quickly and accurately.

[Typical Case Ⅱ] Engine idle jitter of a Beijing Hyundai Sonata 2. 4L car.

Fault Description: The owner of a Beijing Hyundai Sonata 2. 4L car said that the engine fault light was on, the car shook at idle speed, and occasionally appeared flameout when waiting for the red light.

Fault Diagnosis and Repair: The repairman carried out the test run and found the fault as the owner said, the car was jittering seriously when the engine was idle, but the acceleration was normal. He read out the fault codes with a scan tool: P0170—Fuel correction fault; P2187—System too lean at idle (existing fault).

The meaning of fault codes is analyzed as follows.

① Cause of fault code P0170: When the air-fuel ratio control reaches the maximum or minimum limit, the system will not be able to perform air-fuel ratio control and record DTC P0170.

② Cause of fault code P2187: After the air-fuel ratio control reaches the maximum limit at idle speed, the system will record DTCP2187.

There are several possible causes for the failure of the above two fault codes.

① Failure of front oxygen sensor and intake air flow sensor.

② Failure of carbon canister solenoid valve and intake system.

③ Corresponding line fault.

The troubleshooting procedure is as follows.

① The data flow was checked with the detector, and the data waveform of the front oxygen sensor had no obvious change at the low level of 0. 01V. The engine jitter did not improve after disconnecting the front oxygen sensor plug. Normally, if there is a front oxygen sensor failure, the engine tends to smooth when the plug is disengaged.

② The intake air flow sensor was checked and no abnormality was found. After cleaning the throttle, the fault was not eliminated. Because there was no fault code of the corresponding sensor and the probability of failure of each sensor itself was small, the intake system was checked directly.

③ The carbon canister solenoid valve was checked. The engine was started and the hose on the discharge side of the carbon canister solenoid valve was pinched with the pointed-nose pliers. There was no change in the engine and no leakage was found. The fuel injector was found to have been removed during inspection of the intake system. Injection of carburetor cleaning agent into the connection between the intake manifold and the fuel injector found that there was a significant increase in idle speed when each fuel injector was injected. After removing the fuel injector, it was found that the sealing rings of the four fuel injectors were smaller than the original ones and could not play a role in sealing. It was determined that the fuel injector sealing ring was installed incorrectly, causing the above fault.

Engine jitter disappeared after replacing the fuel injector sealing rings. The variation of the front oxygen sensor data waveform from 0. 1V to 0. 9V was checked and recovered to normal, and the fault code did not appear again. The fault was eliminated.

Summary: The poor seal of the fuel injector, increased air intake, causing the air-fuel ratio to be too lean and beyond the maximum adjustment limit. The ECM confirmed that it

could not be repaired according to the signal feedback from the oxygen sensor, stopped the air-fuel ratio control, and recorded the fault codes DTC P0170 and P2187. At idle speed, when the fuel injection quantity is constant, the additional increase of intake air will cause the engine to shake.

Task V Fault Diagnosis and Repair of Engine Power Shortage

Learning Objectives

1. Be able to determine the direction and items of inquiry according to the fault phenomena of the automobile for repair.

2. Be able to prepare a correct fault diagnosis plan according to fault phenomena.

3. Be able to consult maintenance data skillfully, select appropriate detection and diagnosis devices according to fault phenomena and use them skillfully.

4. Be able to test the engine power shortage with appropriate maintenance devices according to the diagnosis plan.

5. Be able to correctly analyze the test results and determine the fault location and cause of engine power shortage.

6. Be able to repair the fault parts quickly and accurately and eliminate the hidden troubles.

Task Import

Task Material: For a Magotan 1. 8TSI car, its engine can start normally but the speed can only reach 80km/h.

Task Requirements: According to the fault phenomena of the car, consult relevant materials, select appropriate detection and diagnosis devices for fault diagnosis and repair, and fill in the task report.

I. Fault Analysis

Engine power shortage means that the engine is basically normal when running without load, but the acceleration is slow when running on load, and the uphill is weak; when the accelerator pedal is pressed to the end, it still feels insufficient power, and the speed rises slowly and cannot reach the maximum speed.

Common fault causes of engine power shortage mainly include the following.

(1) The intake and exhaust systems of the engine is blocked.

(2) The throttle is not adjusted properly and cannot be fully opened.

(3) The fuel pressure is too low.

(4) The fuel injector is blocked or poorly atomized.

(5) The coolant temperature sensor is faulty.

(6) The gas flow meter is faulty.

(7) The ignition timing is incorrect or the high voltage fire is low.

(8) The compression pressure of the engine cylinder is insufficient.

(9) The turbocharger does not work or works badly.

(10) The intake or exhaust system does not work or works badly.

II. Fault Diagnosis

(1) Press the accelerator pedal to the bottom and check whether the throttle valve is stuck and fully opened.

(2) Check the air filter for blockage: Replace it if it is blocked.

(3) Perform fault self-diagnosis and check whether there is a fault code: Sensors and actuators that affect engine power include coolant temperature sensor, air flow meter or intake manifold absolute pressure sensor, igniter, fuel injector, etc. Find the cause of the fault according to the displayed fault code.

(4) Check that the idle switch and full load switch of the throttle position sensor are adjusted correctly: If it is incorrect, it shall be readjusted according to the standard.

(5) Check the ignition timing: When the engine temperature is normal, both the ignition advance angle at idle speed and the ignition advance angle during acceleration shall comply with the requirements. If the ignition advance angle at idle speed is incorrect, the initial ignition advance angle should be adjusted; If the ignition advance angle during acceleration is abnormal, the ignition advance control circuit, crankshaft position sensor, igniter, etc., should be checked.

(6) Check the coolant temperature sensor: The resistance of the coolant temperature sensor shall vary according to the specified standard value at different temperatures. If the resistance does meet the standard value, the coolant temperature sensor should be replaced.

(7) Check the air flow meter or intake manifold pressure sensor: Replace if there is any abnormality.

(8) Check spark plugs, high voltage wires, ignition coils, igniters, etc. of cylinders: Replace if there is any abnormality.

(9) Check fuel pressure: If the pressure is too low, the electric fuel pump, oil pressure regulator, fuel filter, etc., should be further checked.

(10) Remove the fuel injector and check whether the fuel injection quantity is normal: If the fuel injection quantity is abnormal or the fuel injection atomization is poor, the fuel injector should be cleaned or replaced.

(11) Measure cylinder compression pressure: If the pressure is too low, remove and inspect the engine.

III. Task Implementation

1. Inquiry

Know the time of fault from the owner; Check whether there is abnormal condition before the fault; The road condition of the car; Whether the car is maintained on time; Has it been repaired after the fault occurred. The preliminary diagnosis of engine power shortage can be completed by knowing the situation before and after the fault and the specific informa-

tion of the fault.

2. Test-drive and Basic Inspection

Firstly, carry out the test-drive to confirm the fault. Check whether there is air leakage in the intake pipeline and check whether the fuel injector plug and ignition module plug are connected properly.

3. Detection and Diagnosis

Use the scan tool VAS5051 to read out the fault code and find the fault code "17957 P1549 Booster pressure limit solenoid valve-N75 Open circuited/Short circuited to Ground". Possible causes of the fault are: Failure of wiring harness or harness connector of booster pressure limit solenoid valve; Failure of the booster pressure limit solenoid valve.

Check the data flow to enter Engine Address 01-08-115 Group Data Group Areas 3 and 4. The specified value and the actual value of intake pressure are 80kPa at idle speed. The specified value is 160kPa during rapid acceleration and the actual value is 78kPa. The actual value is much smaller than the specified value, indicating that the booster has no boosting effect.

Possible reasons for no boosting are: Blocked intake system; Blocked exhaust system; Turbocharger failure.

After disconnecting the pressure hose of the turbocharger pressure unit, the problem remains.

After disconnecting the plug of booster pressure limit solenoid valve, the voltage of line 1 is measured as 12.2V by a multimeter, and the voltage value is normal. The plug and the wiring harness are normal. After interchanging the turbocharger pressure limit valves, the problem remains. It indicates that the solenoid valve and the circuit are normal.

The connections of air filter, intake manifold and intercooler are disassembled and inspected and no foreign matter is found to block the intake port.

After removing the air circulation valve of the turbocharger, a voltage of 12.2Vis measured from the plug end, and the voltage is normal. The power-on test on the air circulation valve is done, and the solenoid valve can be sucked normally. It indicates that the solenoid valve and its circuit are normal.

After removing the oxygen sensor and increasing the exhaust volume, the fault remains, indicating that the three-way catalyst is not blocked.

After removing the turbocharger, it is found that the adjusting gasket of the turbine shaft on the exhaust side is broken and the turbine shaft at the exhaust side is stuck, and the exhaust gas turbine cannot rotate, so there is no turbocharging.

4. Fault Elimination

The turbocharger assembly is replaced. After assembly, the test-drive is conducted. The fault is eliminated.

5. Inspection and Delivery

After troubleshooting, the test-drive is conducted, and the gear shift is normal without any other symptoms. The car is handed over to the owner.

IV. Task Summary

The engine power shortage is a common problem encountered in maintenance. During

maintenance, analysis should be made according to the actual failure performance, and more attention should be paid to the diagnosis of engine related data flow.

For Volkswagen exhaust turbocharger series engines, attention should be paid to the influence of turbocharger failure when engine power shortage occurs.

V. Task Report

	Major			Class		Name	
	Task Name					Class Hours	2
	Model			Engine Model			
		Assessment Items		Assessment Contents		Maximum Score	Score
Task Completion Process		1. Description of fault symptoms				5	
		2. Possible causes and analysis of fault				25	
		3. Detection and diagnosis process				35	
		4. Fault Elimination				10	
		5. Summary of fault diagnosis				10	
Teacher Evaluation		Operation quality, operation efficiency, operation safety, etc.				15	
		Total Score				100	

VI. Knowledge Expansion

[Typical Case Ⅰ] Weak acceleration of a 2011 Jetta car.

Fault Description: The engine was running normally at idle speed, but the acceleration was weak and the engine shook seriously during acceleration.

Fault Diagnosis and Repair:

(1) A Volkswagen special scan tool was used for detection, and the engine had no fault code.

(2) The engine data flow was checked, the engine was stable at 750r/min at the idle speed, and the throttle opening was 2.2, which were normal.

(3) The pressure of the engine intake system was checked. When there was no load at idle speed, it was 30kPa and normal.

(4) The fuel pressure was checked with an oil pressure detector as 0.28MPa, which was normal; The fuel injection test was carried out after cleaning the fuel injector. The fuel injection atomization was normal without dripping and leakage, indicating that the fuel injector worked normally.

(5) The ignition waveform of high voltage wire was normal; The spark plug was removed, the spark plug electrode clearance was normal. After inserting the high-voltage wire into the spark plug, the spark plug sparks normally, indicating that the ignition system was working normally.

(6) It was judged that the ignition coil may have thermal stability failure, causing high-temperature flameout, and then the ignition coil was replaced for test drive; The problem remained.

(7) It was suspected that there was a fault inside the engine electronic control unit, so the engine control unit was replaced, but the fault remained.

(8) During acceleration, it was found that the exhaust emission was less than that of

102 | Automobile Integrated Fault Diagnosis and Repair |

the normal cars. It was analyzed that the engine was not exhausted smoothly.

(9) The three-way catalyst was replaced for test run, the fault was eliminated.

Summary: Engine power shortage caused by blockage of the three-way catalyst in the exhaust pipe is easy to be neglected in fault diagnosis, especially for maintenance personnel with insufficient experience. When there is no fault found in the ignition system and the oil circuit system with relatively high failure rate, the blockage of the three-way catalyst shall be considered. The simplest and effective method to detect the blockage of the three-way catalyst is to use an infrared thermometer to detect. When the three-way catalyst is blocked, its inlet temperature is higher than the outlet temperature, and under normal conditions, the outlet temperature is more than 20 ℃ higher than the inlet.

[Typical Case Ⅱ] Weak acceleration of a Beijing Hyundai Sonata 2. 0GLSAT car.

Fault Description: The owner of a Beijing Hyundai Sonata 2. 0GLSAT car, driving 130,000 kilometers, said that the speed rose weakly and could not reach the maximum speed.

Fault Diagnosis and Repair: Through communication with the owner, it was known that the automobile had been thoroughly inspected in a automobile repair plant, replaced the spark plug and the cylinder line but not helpful, and there was a fault code P0340-Camshaft position sensor circuit fault. The repairman at the automobile repair plant recommend replacing the engine module.

The test run was carried out. During driving, it was found that the speed increased slowly when accelerating, and the maximum speed was only 120km/h.

The decoder was used to enter the engine and the transmission for inspection. Except for fault code P0340, the data flow of the engine and the transmission was normal. The engine was started after clearing the fault code, but the fault code appeared again.

The diagnosis was made according to the fault code P0340.

The ignition switch was turned off and the camshaft position sensor plug was pulled off. The ignition switch was turned on, it was measured that the sensor terminal 1 had a power supply voltage of 12. 5V, terminal 2 had a signal voltage of 4. 8V, and terminal 3 was grounded normally. Through the above checks, it was confirmed that there was no problem with the CMP circuit, probably there was short circuit or open circuit in the internal circuit of the camshaft position sensor. The sensor was replaced for test-drive, but the fault symptoms remained and the fault code still could not be cleared. The fault diagnosis was stuck here. Therefore, the thinking was reorganized and the phenomenon of engine weakness was considered.

The spark plug and high voltage wire were completely normal. The fuel pressure was 350 kPa and normal. The cylinder pressures normal. The three-way catalyst was not blocked.

The fuel quality problem could also be eliminated because the fuel inside the fuel tank had been replaced during the inspection by the other repair shop. What else can cause engine weakness? Only the engine timing system and valve phase are the faults that can cause engine acceleration weakness. Then the engine timing was checked.

The upper housing of the camshaft pulley was opened, the crankshaft pulley was rotated to make cylinder 1 stay at the top dead center position of compression stroke. The valve timing was checked, and it was found that the camshaft pulley missed a tooth against the

timing mark.

The timing belt was removed to re-align the timing. After the scan tool cleared the fault code, the test run was carried out, the engine power returned to normal, and the fault code P0340 no longer appeared after checking.

Summary: Be careful and comprehensive in the process of communicating car failures with customers, and try to know exactly the time, phenomenon, location of the faults and items that have been repaired. In this way, it is possible to reduce the maintenance time and improve the maintenance efficiency.

In addition, it is necessary to have the ability of comprehensive analysis on the engine faults and understand the characteristics and rules of faults. In fact, the cause of making the electronic control unit generate a fault code about the CMP and causing the engine to run weakly is usually an error in the timing of the engine.

Item VI

Fault Diagnosis and Repair of Transmission System

Task I Fault Diagnosis and Repair of Clutch Slipping

Learning Objectives

1. Be able to determine the direction and items of inquiry according to the fault phenomena of the automobile for repair.

2. Be able to prepare a correct fault diagnosis plan according to fault phenomena.

3. Be able to consult maintenance data skillfully, select appropriate detection and diagnosis devices according to fault phenomena and use them skillfully.

4. Be able to test clutch slipping faults with appropriate maintenance devices according to the diagnosis plan.

5. Be able to correctly analyze the test results and determine the fault location and causes of clutch slipping.

6. Be able to repair the fault parts quickly and accurately and eliminate the hidden troubles.

7. Be able to strengthen the consciousness of norm and have the spirit of artisans and craftsmen of excellence.

Task Import

Task Material: For a Sagitar 2.0 car with a driving mileage of 90,000 km, when the speed reaches 3,000r/min, the fifth gear speed can only reach 45km/h.

Task Requirements: According to the fault phenomena of the car, consult relevant materials, select appropriate detection and diagnosis devices for fault diagnosis and repair, and fill in the task report.

I. Fault Analysis

Failure analysis of clutch slipping: A car can only start when the clutch pedal is nearly

completely relaxed. After the clutch is engaged, the engine power cannot be transmitted to the driving wheel completely, which may cause the car to start difficultly, fuel consumption rises, the engine speed is too high during driving or acceleration, but the automobile speed increases slowly.

(1) The car can only start when the clutch pedal is nearly completely released, i. e. difficult to start.

(2) When the car accelerates during driving, the engine speed rises, but the speed cannot be increased synchronously, i. e. poor acceleration and weak driving.

In addition, clutch slipping will also appear increased fuel consumption, failure to reach the maximum speed, even burning smell when uphill or under heavy load.

The main reasons for clutch slipping are as follows:

① Clutch has no free stroke or free stroke is too small.

② The friction disc of driven disc is excessively worn or rivets are exposed, and the friction disc is viscous, carbonized, burnt and damaged.

③ The clutch pressure plate spring is too soft or broken, the diaphragm spring is damaged, the working end face of the pressure plate is worn more than 0. 3mm and deformed, the installation screw is loose, and the separation finger tip jumps more than 1mm.

④ Flywheel working face is worn greatly, exceeding 0. 5mm.

⑤ There is no running allowance for the release fork or release bearing.

⑥ The oil return hole of clutch master cylinder is blocked.

⑦ Clutch slave cylinder does not return.

II. Fault Diagnosis

Tighten the parking brake, start the engine, step on the clutch pedal, put on the first gear, loosen the clutch pedal and depress the accelerator pedal. If the engine shuts down quickly, it is proved that the clutch does not slip; If the engine stalls slowly or not, it is confirmed that the clutch slips.

III. Task Implementation

1. Inquiry

After receiving the car, the repairman shall first learn from the owner: Clutch slipping time; Driving condition of the car when the clutch slips; Mileage; Whether the car is maintained on time; Whether maintenance has been carried out after the fault occurs; Whether the car is equipped with sound and anti-theft devices. The preliminary judgment of clutch slipping failure can be completed through the above inquiry, which can shorten the inspection time and improve the diagnosis efficiency.

2. Test-drive and Basic Inspection

Conduct the test run, confirm the fault, and confirm whether there is burnt smell near the clutch after shutdown.

3. Detection and Diagnosis

Check that the clutch pedal free stroke is too small, and the can only start when the clutch is depressed to the bottom and then released to a high degree. Remove the clutch slave

cylinder and gently press the push rod of the clutch slave cylinder, which can be pressed to the bottom and return. Press the clutch pedal gently, the push rod of the slave cylinder can extend, release the clutch pedal, and the push rod of the slave cylinder can return to position. This is the same as a new car, and it is roughly judged that the clutch hydraulic system is normal. At this time, shake the release fork by hand, and find that there is no movement allowance for the fork. Meanwhile, the fork is hot and cannot be returned.

In most cases, clutch plates, pressure plates and flywheels are combined to ensure maximum transmission of power. At this time, the release fork and the release bearing are free and do not participate in the work. Only when the clutch slips, the clutch plate rubs and generates heat. The heat generated can be transmitted to the release fork through the pressure plate and the release bearing, causing abnormal temperature of the release fork. Why does the release fork have no clearance? With this question, through careful inspection, it is found that the fixing bolt of the fixed gearshift bracket is screwed into the transmission housing too much, which just blocks the release fork, so that the release fork cannot be returned. This is the root cause of the clutch slipping. Through comparison with a new car, it is found that there should be an iron sleeve in the rubber of the fixed bracket, and there is no iron sleeve on the repaired car, which leads to excessive screwing of the bolt and blocking the release fork to make it unable to return, causing the clutch to slip.

4. Fault Elimination

After installing an iron sleeve of the same specification and reassembling, the test-drive is done and the fault is gone.

5. Inspection and Delivery

After troubleshooting, the test-drive speed is normal without any other symptoms, and the car is handed over to the owner.

IV. Task Summary

The efficiency of fault diagnosis can be improved by doing every inspection and analysis according to the fault phenomena. In the fault diagnosis, analysis should be done according to the working principle of the mechanism. Do not rely excessively on maintenance experience.

V. Task Report

Major				Class		Name	
Task Name						Class Hours	2
Model				Engine Model			
		Assessment Items		Assessment Contents		Maximum Score	Score
Task Completion Process		1. Description of fault symptoms				5	
		2. Possible causes and analysis of fault				25	
		3. Detection and diagnosis process				35	
		4. Fault Elimination				10	
		5. Summary of fault diagnosis				10	
Teacher Evaluation		Operation quality, operation efficiency, operation safety, etc.				15	
Total Score						100	

VI. Knowledge Expansion

[Typical Case I]　Poor acceleration of a Dongfeng Peugeot 307 car.

Fault Description: A Dongfeng Peugeot 307 car, manual transmission, driving 120,000 kilometers, when the car accelerated rapidly, the engine speed could reach 5,000r/min instantly, but the speed increased slowly.

Fault Diagnosis and Repair: The test run was carried out and the fault was completely as described by the owner. It was considered likely that the clutch plate was too thin. Therefore, the clutch plate was replaced, and the test run was carried out after re-installation, and the fault disappeared and the car was handed over to the owner.

A few days later, the owner came back and said that clutch slipping occurred, and the failure was the same as last time. Then the test run was conducted again. When the car accelerated rapidly in 3rd gear, the engine speed rose from 2,000r/min to 5,000r/min instantly. For causes of clutch slipping, besides the clutch plate too thin, the clutch pressure plate cannot fully press the clutch plate after the clutch pedal is released due to stuck clutch slave cylinder or master cylinder. What causes the clutch slave cylinder or master cylinder to get stuck? There are two specific reasons, on the one hand, the clutch operating fluid is too dirty, and on the other hand, the clutch slave cylinder or master cylinder is damaged. After inspection, it was found that the clutch fluid of the car was very dirty. After replacement, the test run was carried out, and the fault remained.

The clutch slave cylinder was removed for inspection. One person pressed the clutch pedal on the car and the other person pressed the slave cylinder with his hand. When the clutch pedal was depressed, the clutch slave cylinder could be ejected normally. When the clutch pedal was released, the person could pressed the clutch slave cylinder back into position, which indicated that the clutch slave cylinder or master cylinder had no jamming phenomenon.

To find out which one of the clutch operating mechanism or clutch pressure plate or the clutch plate is faulty, the clutch slave cylinder was removed to completely separate the clutch operating mechanism from the clutch plate and the clutch pressure plate. Then a test run for 5 km was done after removal; after rapid acceleration, the engine was no longer idling, and the clutch work returned to normal. So far, it could be determined that the fault was in the clutch slave cylinder or the master cylinder. After replacing the clutch slave cylinder, the fault remained during the test-drive. Then the clutch master cylinder was replaced and the fault was completely gone during the test-drive. Then the car was handed over to the owner.

Summary: Clutch slipping is a common fault of poor acceleration of a car. Most faults are caused by excessive wear of clutch plate, which will be eliminated immediately after replacement. The faulty car is a clutch controlled by hydraulic pressure, and the fault occurs in the clutch master cylinder. It is considered that the clutch master cylinder was faulty due to too dirty clutch oil, and finally caused the clutch plate to slip due to insufficient pressing force. When judging whether the clutch operating mechanism is faulty, it is better to adopt the isolation method, that is, the test run is carried out after cutting off the clutch operat-

ing mechanism. If the fault disappears, it is the fault of this part.

Task II Fault Diagnosis and Repair of Shifting Difficulty of Manual Transmission

Learning Objectives

1. Be able to determine the direction and items of inquiry according to the fault phenomena of the automobile for repair.

2. Be able to prepare a correct fault diagnosis plan according to fault phenomena.

3. Be able to consult maintenance data skillfully, select appropriate detection and diagnosis devices according to fault phenomena and use them skillfully.

4. Be able to test shifting difficulty of manual transmission with suitable maintenance devices according to the diagnosis plan.

5. Be able to correctly analyze the test results and determine the fault location and cause of shifting difficulty of manual transmission.

6. Be able to repair the fault parts quickly and accurately and eliminate the hidden troubles.

Task Import

Task Material: The owner of a 2011 Volkswagen Bora 1.6L car, driving mileage of 120,000 kilometers, said that the car was easy to engage the 1st and the 2nd gears when parking, but during driving, it was difficult to shift from the 1st gear to the 2nd gear or from the 2nd gear to the 1st gear.

Task Requirements: According to the fault phenomena of the car, consult relevant materials, select appropriate detection and diagnosis devices for fault diagnosis and repair, and fill in the task report.

I. Fault Analysis

Shifting difficulty means that the transmission does not move smoothly into the required gear when shifting and usually produces a gear impact sound.

The reasons of shifting difficulty mainly come from two parts: transmission control mechanism and gear transmission mechanism.

1. Reasons for transmission control mechanism

(1) Transmission lever of remote control mechanism does not work reliably.

(2) The sift fork shaft is bent and deformed.

(3) The shift fork is bent and deformed, the fixing pin is loose, and the lower end face of the shift fork is seriously worn.

(4) Gear lever ball bearing hinge is worn too much.

(5) The shift block is worn too much.

Item VI Fault Diagnosis and Repair of Transmission System **109**

2. Reasons for gear transmission mechanism

(1) The transmission self-locking and interlocking devices are faulty.

(2) The synchronizer is worn too much and the fitting is loose and faulty.

3. Other reasons

(1) The connecting bolt of the transmission housing is loose.

(2) In severe cold areas, the gear oil grade is incorrect, resulting in solidification.

(3) Foreign matter blocks the normal engagement of the gear.

II. Fault Diagnosis

Do not disassemble blindly in case of shifting difficulty. Find out the causes in a reasonable order in combination with the working principles, and then take corresponding measures.

(1) If there is gear impact sound in all gears during shifting, it is possible that the engine power cannot be cut off temporarily. Check whether the clutch can not be disengaged fully. Check whether the free stroke of clutch and the height of release lever are normal.

(2) If the clutch is normal, check whether the quality and oil quantity of the transmission gear oil meet the requirements. Select qualified gear oil according to season, speed and load.

(3) If some cars adopt remotely operated transmission control mechanism, check whether the adjustment of the remote control mechanism is suitable and whether the lever is deformed or stuck. In case of abnormality, it shall be removed for correction, fastening or repair.

(4) If the above checks are normal, check whether the first shaft of the transmission is deformed and the spline is worn. If it is abnormal, remove it for correction, welding or replacement.

The troubleshooting flow of shifting difficulty of transmission is shown in Figure 6-1.

III. Task Implementation

1. Inquiry

After receiving the car, the repairman shall first know the time when the shifting difficulty occurs from the owner; Whether the car is maintained on time; whether it has been repaired after the fault. The preliminary judgment on clutch shifting difficulty can be made through the inquiry, which can shorten inspection time and improve diagnosis efficiency.

2. Test-drive and Basic Inspection

Carry out a test drive to confirm the fault. Through the test drive, it is found that there is difficulty in shifting between the 1st gear and the 2nd gear, but other gear shifts are smooth.

3. Detection and Diagnosis

It is thought that the car has a difficulty in shifting between individual gears during driving, and the fault caused by clutch, connecting bolt and lubricating oil can be excluded basically.

110 | Automobile Integrated Fault Diagnosis and Repair |

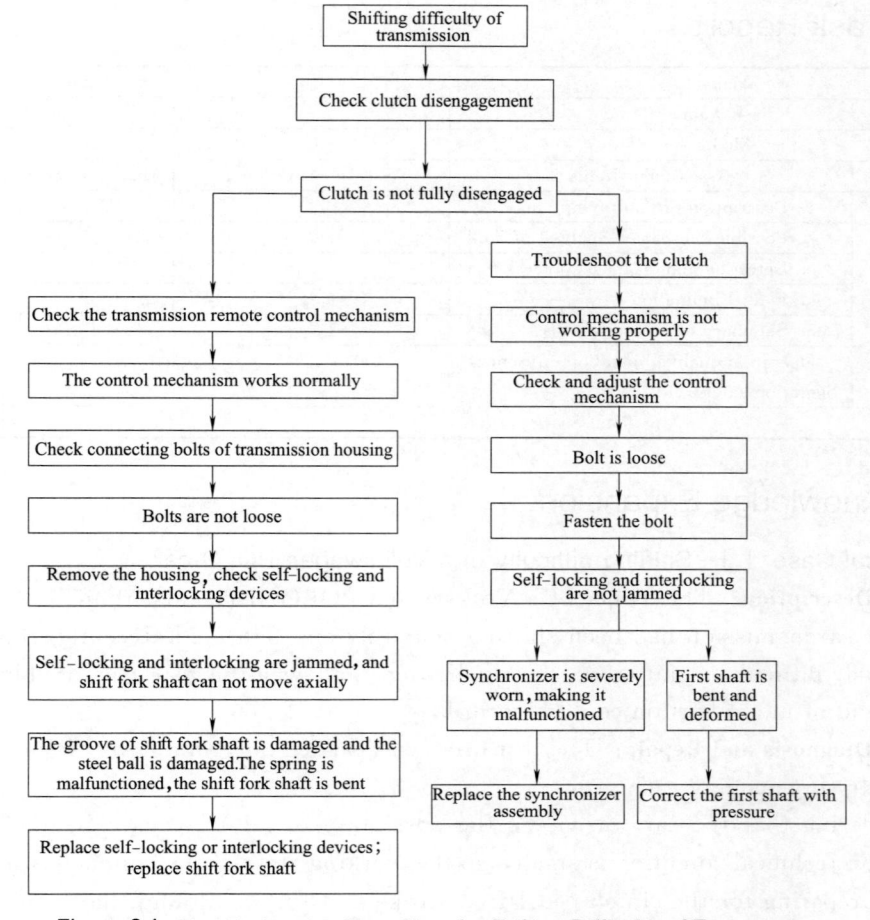

Figure 6-1 Troubleshooting Flow Chart for Shifting Difficulty of Transmission

According to the troubleshooting flow, check the transmission control mechanism first, and check whether there is deformation or jamming of the lever.

Then remove the transmission cover, check the transmission shift fork, self-locking and interlocking mechanism, etc. and find these components in good technical condition. Check the transmission mechanism and find that the synchronizing cone ring of the 1st gear and the 2nd gear synchronizer is seriously worn.

4. Fault Elimination

Replace the synchronizer, reassemble and retest. The fault is eliminated.

5. Inspection and Delivery

After troubleshooting, the test-drive speed is normal without any other symptoms, and the car is handed over to the owner.

IV. Task Summary

In case of shifting difficulty of transmission, the car must be fully tested to understand the scope and characteristics of the fault. When a transmission is difficult to shift between individual gears, the relevant components of these gears shall be subject to technical inspection without blind disassembly and assembly, so as to avoid more inspections.

Item VI Fault Diagnosis and Repair of Transmission System | **111**

V. Task Report

Major		Class		Name	
Task Name				Class Hours	2
Model			Engine Model		
	Assessment Items	Assessment Contents		Maximum Score	Score
Task Completion Process	1. Description of fault symptoms			5	
	2. Possible causes and analysis of fault			25	
	3. Detection and diagnosis process			35	
	4. Fault Elimination			10	
	5. Summary of fault diagnosis			10	
Teacher Evaluation	Operation quality, operation efficiency, operation safety, etc.			15	
	Total Score			100	

VI. Knowledge Expansion

【Typical Case Ⅰ】 Shifting difficulty of a Volkswagen POLO car.

Fault Description: The owner of a Volkswagen POLO 1.4L car, running 2,000 km, said that the transmission had been shifting smoothly and felt good. Recently, however, it was obviously difficult to shift gears during driving, and even the gear was forcibly engaged, "click" sound of metal friction could be heard.

Fault Diagnosis and Repair: The test drive was carried out, and it was found that there was difficulty in engaging each gear.

Considering that the car was new, the possibility of failure caused by the decline of transmission technical condition is small, so the working state of the clutch was tested firstly. Before preparing for the clutch pedal free stroke test, it was found that a thick layer of carpet was laid on the interior of the car by the owner, resulting in reduced clutch pedal travel. Then the carpet was removed from the driver's side, the test drive was carried out and the fault was eliminated.

Summary: It is necessary to detect the external structure of transmission and the technical condition of clutch when transmission-related fault diagnosis is carried out, and the transmission cannot be disassembled blindly. When it is determined that the fault is not caused by external causes, then the transmission may be disassembled. At the same time, it is necessary to prompt the owner that during the interior decoration of the car, do not lay thick carpet or floor glue on the clutch and brake pedal, which may easily lead to the clutch pedal unable to step down to the bottom, resulting in incomplete clutch disengagement, leading to difficulties in shifting and other faults.

【Typical Case Ⅱ】 Shifting difficulty of a Chery Cowin car.

Fault Description: The owner of a Chery Cowin car, driving 120,000 km, said that it was difficult to engage the third gear whether on driving or in place.

Fault Diagnosis and Repair: It was learned from communication with the owner that the transmission housing had broken and replaced at other Chery maintenance station, but there was a difficulty in engaging the 3rd gear on the way back after the service.

It was found that engaging the 3rd gear was difficult whether the engine started or

not. However, other gears, especially the 4th gear, which shares a set of synchronizer and a shift fork with the 3rd gear, could be easily engaged. The 3rd gear could be shifted smoothly under the following conditions: When the engine did not start, the 3rd gear could be incidentally engaged with no more shifts, at this time, it was easy to engage the 3rd gear repeatedly. When the engine was running, sometimes, the 3rd gear may be engaged smoothly. It was thought that the fault location should concentrate on the sliding sleeve (outer sleeve) and synchronizing ring of the 3rd and 4th gear synchronizer.

The transmission was disassembled. It was found that the tooth end of the internal teeth of the 3rd and 4th gear synchronizer sliding sleeve was chamfered at one side, and the end was sharp; but the other side was not chamfered and the end was flat. The unchamfered side was just the end of engagement with the 2rd gear, and the cause of the failure was finally clear. At the chamfered side (the 4th gear), when shifting, at the moment when the sliding sleeve synchronized with the peripheral speed of the gear, the synchronous sliding sleeve was subjected to the axial force of shifting and the reverse force of synchronizing ring and corresponding gear. The contact of two sharp angles could break down a part of the axial force of the shifting into two rotation forces in opposite directions, so as to make the synchronous sliding sleeve rotate relative to the gear to be engaged, so as to realize smooth meshing between the sliding sleeve and the gear and easy shifting. The sliding sleeve at the unchamfered side (the 3rd gear) contacted the plane of the internal teeth of the sliding sleeve with the sharp angle of the 3rd gear. When the sharp angle of the 3rd gear was against the plane of the sliding sleeve, the axial force of the shifting could not be divided into two opposite forces, and the sliding sleeve did not rotate relative to the gear, so it was difficult to realize the shifting. Only when the internal teeth of the sliding sleeve and the backlash of the gear were exactly aligned, the 3rd gear could be smoothly engaged.

According to the user, there was no such phenomenon before changing the transmission housing, but there was no doubt that the internal tooth end of the synchronizer sliding sleeve should be chamfered. With this problem for further observation, it was found that the 5th gear synchronous sliding sleeve was basically consistent with the shape geometry of the sliding sleeve of the 3rd and 4th gear synchronizer. Was it installed in a wrong position? The repairman did not agree with this assumption: When replacing the transmission housing, the above-mentioned components should not be disassembled, and it was impossible to install wrongly. Where were the unqualified 3rd and 4th gear sliding sleeve from? According to the fact that the geometry of the sliding sleeve of the 3rd and 4th gear synchronizer was basically the same as that of the 5th gear synchronizer, it was decided to disassemble the 5th gear synchronizer and compare the two synchronizer sliding sleeves. It was found that they not only had the same geometry, but also had the same geometric dimension, but also had chamfers at both ends. According to this feature, the two sliding sleeves were interchanged in position, reinstalled and tested and the fault was eliminated.

Summary: The 3rd and 4th gear synchronizer sliding sleeve of Chery Cowin transmission and the 5th gear synchronizer sliding sleeve cannot be interchanged. The maintenance personnel should understand the characteristics, performances and working principles of various mechanical structures so as to make accurate judgments on various abnormal faults during the repair.

Item Ⅶ

Fault Diagnosis and Repair of Automatic Transmission

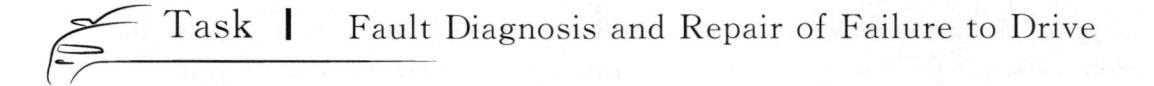

Task Ⅰ   Fault Diagnosis and Repair of Failure to Drive

Learning Objectives

1. Be able to determine the direction and items of inquiry according to the fault phenomena of the automobile for repair.

2. Be able to prepare a correct fault diagnosis plan according to fault phenomena.

3. Be able to consult maintenance data skillfully, select appropriate detection and diagnosis devices according to fault phenomena and use them skillfully.

4. Be able to test the failure to drive with suitable maintenance devices according to the diagnosis plan.

5. Be able to correctly analyze the test results and determine the location and cause of failure to drive.

6. Be able to repair the fault parts quickly and accurately and eliminate the hidden troubles.

7. Be able to keep pursuing perfection, be brave to innovate, and improve teamwork ability.

Task Import

Task Material: A Buick GL8 business vehicle, driving distance of 130, 000 km, with automatic transmission model 4T-65E, suddenly lost power when driving uphill, failed to engage again, at the same time, could not drive no matter where the gear lever was.

Task Requirements: According to the fault phenomena of the car, consult relevant materials, select appropriate detection and diagnosis devices for fault diagnosis and repair, and fill in the task report.

Ⅰ. Fault Analysis

Whether the gear lever was in D gear, L gear or R gear, the car could not drive, or the

car could not drive after a long distance. The causes of failure mainly include the following.

(1) Automatic transmission oil leaks, causing serious oil shortage.

(2) The connecting rod or cable between the gear lever and the rocker arm of the manual valve is loosened to keep the manual valve in the N or P position.

(3) Failure of the oil pump or severe blockage of the filter results in the failure of the main oil circuit to establish normal oil pressure.

(4) The automatic transmission has mechanical failure, such as severe wear of turbine spline hub, damage to planetary gear system, etc.

II. Fault Diagnosis

(1) Check the fluid level of the automatic transmission. If the fluid level is too low or there is no oil, check the ATF pan, transmission oil radiator, oil pipe, etc. for damage and oil leakage. If there is any oil leakage, it should be repaired and refueled.

(2) Check whether the connecting rod or cable between the gear lever and the manual valve rocker arm is loose. If loose, reinstall and adjust the position of the gear lever.

(3) Detect oil pressure of main oil circuit. If the oil pressure is too low, open the oil pan and check the filter for blockage. If the filter screen is not blocked, it indicates that the oil pump is faulty or the main oil circuit is seriously leaking. For this, the automatic transmission should be disassembled for further inspection. If the oil pressure in the main oil circuit is normal, the fault shall be mechanical failures such as severe wear of the turbine spline hub, damage to the planetary gear system, etc. If there is certain oil pressure in the main oil circuit during cold starting, but the oil pressure after the hot car decreases significantly, it means that the oil pump is worn too much or the filter is blocked.

Special Tips: When the car can travel a short distance after cold starting, and can't travel under hot conditions, commonly, the fault shall be that the filter is blocked. The reason is that the filter blockage is not serious when the car is cold, so the car can drive. The impurities adsorbed on the filter gradually increase after the car is hot. The suction of the oil pump will make the interlayer of the filter screen tightly sucked together, finally, the transmission oil cannot pass through the filter screen, thus causing the failure of driving after hot car.

III. Task Implementation

1. Inquiry

Know the time of fault from the owner; Check whether there is abnormal condition before the fault; The road condition of the car; mileage; Whether the car is maintained on time; Has it been repaired after the fault occurred. Find out the situation before and after the fault and the specific information of the fault through the above inquiry, and complete the preliminary diagnosis of the failure.

2. Test-drive and Basic Inspection

First carry out a test drive to confirm the fault, check whether the ATF liquid level is normal. It is found that the oil color has become black, and the ATF oil has burning smell.

3. Detection and Diagnosis

Start the engine. No abnormal sound is found when running in each gear. Then open the

oil pan and find more metal particles on the oil pan. So remove the transmission, disassemble and check the one-way roller clutch at the valve body, forward brake belt, and find no abnormality. It is found that the filter screen of the transmission has been seriously plugged with dirt and glued. It is thought that the reason why the power of the drive wheel assembly cannot be output is that the automatic transmission filter screen is seriously blocked, which makes the ATF oil cannot be sucked into the oil pump, making the hydraulic oil in the oil circuit from insufficient to almost no finally. This process is actually a gradual, slow process, but the owner does not notice the driving change. When the disassembly continues, it is noted that the copper sleeve at the drive sun gear shaft falls off and is cracked. In addition, the drive assembly sun gear shaft has cracked axially and both ends have fractured, which is the source of metal particles.

4. Fault Elimination

Replace the damaged drive wheel assembly, worn clutch plate and filter, thoroughly clean the torque converter, radiator and valve body before assembly, reassemble and re-test. The fault is eliminated.

5. Inspection and Delivery

After troubleshooting, the test-drive is conducted, and the gear shift is normal without any other symptoms. The car is handed over to the owner.

IV. Task Summary

After inquiring the owner, it is known that the transmission oil has not been replaced, and the car often runs under high speed and heavy load conditions. Therefore, the transmission oil is damaged because the transmission oil has been used, not replaced for a long time and deteriorated. When the performance of oil deteriorates, some friction elements appear slipping and heating due to poor lubrication, which accelerates the wear of corresponding friction elements. However, the slippage and wear of the clutch and the brake make a large amount of wear debris enter into the oil, which accelerates the deterioration and pollution of transmission oil. The deteriorated and polluted ATF oil scale eventually blocks the filter screen seriously, causing the failure of sudden loss of power during driving.

V. Task Report

			Class		Name	
	Major					
	Task Name				Class Hours	2
	Model		Engine Model			
		Assessment Items	Assessment Contents		Maximum Score	Score
Task Completion Process		1. Description of fault symptoms			5	
		2. Possible causes and analysis of fault			25	
		3. Detection and diagnosis process			35	
		4. Fault Elimination			10	
		5. Summary of fault diagnosis			10	
Teacher Evaluation		Operation quality, operation efficiency, operation safety, etc.			15	
	Total Score				100	

VI. Knowledge Expansion

[Typical Case] Failure to drive of a new Passat.

Fault Description: A new Passat encountered a stone on the road while driving. Due to improper avoidance, the stone was dragged into the car bottom, and then the speed dropped, and the car could not drive regardless of the gear.

Fault Diagnosis and Repair: When the car was towed to the repair shop for inspection, it was found that the fault light was on. The VAG1552 scan tool was used to detect and displayed the open circuit or short circuit between the transmission speed sensor and the N89 shift solenoid valve. The car was lifted up. It was found that the transmission oil pan was heavily collapsed. The oil pan was opened and it was found that the terminal of N89 shift solenoid valve had been disconnected, the appearance of transmission speed sensor was normal, and the transmission oil filter element was deformed. The wiring harnesses of the electronic control unit, the transmission speed sensor and the N89 shift solenoid valve were checked with a digital multimeter. The resistance values all were less than 1Ω, and the resistance between lines and ground was infinite, indicating that the harnesses were normal. The resistance value of transmission speed sensor and N89 shift solenoid valve was measured with a multimeter as ∞, indicating that transmission speed sensor and N89 shift solenoid valve were damaged. When the self-diagnosis system of the electronic control unit of Volkswagen automatic transmission finds that the sensor or solenoid valve is open-circuited or short circuited, it will enter the failure protection program. There will be a 3rd gear at position "D", and the maximum speed can reach 150km/h, but the car cannot drive. Therefore, after further checking the filter, it is found that the filter cannot be overoiled, so the solenoid valve, transmission speed sensor, transmission oil pan and filter were replaced. The test run was normal and the fault was eliminated.

Summary: The cause of this fault is that the oil pan of automatic transmission was touched against the ground and the oil pan was deformed to block the oil inlet of the oil filter of automatic transmission. Meanwhile, the solenoid valve was damaged. Finally, the car cannot drive. When diagnosing cars with such accident, the location of the accident and the possible influence on the transmission shall be analyzed to determine the fault diagnosis direction more accurately.

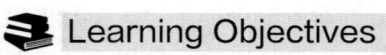

Task Ⅱ Fault Diagnosis and Repair of Shifting Shock

Learning Objectives

1. Be able to determine the direction and items of inquiry according to the fault phenomena of the automobile for repair.

2. Be able to prepare a correct fault diagnosis plan according to fault phenomena.

3. Be able to consult maintenance data skillfully, select appropriate detection and diagnosis devices according to fault phenomena and use them skillfully.

4. Be able to test shifting shock with appropriate maintenance devices according to the diagnosis plan.

5. Be able to correctly analyze the test results and determine the position and cause of shift shock.

6. Be able to repair the fault parts quickly and accurately and eliminate the hidden troubles.

Task Import

Task Material: A 2011 Sagitar car driving 80,000 km. The owner said that in D gear, when starting and accelerating, the car shrugged and had great shifting shock during shifting the 1st gear to the 2nd gear, and this phenomenon occurred every time when starting from D gear. The shift process between the 3rd gear, 4th gear and 5th gear was normal.

Task Requirements: According to the fault phenomena of the car, consult relevant materials, select appropriate detection and diagnosis devices for fault diagnosis and repair, and fill in the task report.

I. Fault Analysis

Shifting shock refers to gear engagement shock when the car is shifted from P gear or N gear to D gear or R gear when starting; obvious shock of automatic transmission at the moment of up-shifting or down-shifting or severe shifting shock in individual gears during driving.

1. Gear engagement shock in all gears

When all gears have gear engagement shocks, it is usually caused by excessive engine idle speed, high transmission oil level, too tight throttle cable or abnormal throttle position sensor signal, and the failure protection program of the electronic control unit.

2. Shifting shock in all gears

All gears have shift shock, usually due to high main oil pressure.

3. Severe shifting shock in some gears

Some gears have severe shift shock, usually caused by poor operation of relevant parts of oil pressure buffer system of corresponding gear or poor sealing of clutch and brake piston.

II. Fault Diagnosis

There are many reasons for the shifting shock of automatic transmission. In the course of fault diagnosis, we should follow the principle of from outside to inside, from simple to complicated, and make careful inspection on each part of automatic transmission. On the basis of basic inspection, the transmission shall be disassembled and repaired in a targeted manner, and shall not be disassembled and repaired blindly. If the fault is caused by improper adjustment, it can be eliminated only by slight adjustment; If the internal control valve, accumulator or shift actuator of automatic transmission is faulty, the valve body was first disassembled and then the automatic transmission is disassembled for repair; If the electronic control system is faulty, the electronic control system shall be tested to find out the specific reasons and eliminate it. The specific diagnosis and repair process is as follows.

1. Diagnosis and repair of gear engagement shock in all gears

In case of this fault, first check whether the engine idle speed is too high. If the idle speed is high, check the engine to find out the cause of high idle speed; Check whether the throttle cable is too tight or whether the throttle position sensor signal is abnormal. If there is any problem, repair it; Check whether the oil level of transmission is too high. If the oil level is too high, drain off the excess oil to make the oil level reach the specified range; With the scan tool, check whether the transmission is in failure protection state, and if it does, further check the cause of the failure protection.

2. Diagnosis and repair of shifting shock in all gears

When this fault occurs, first check the oil pressure of the main oil circuit. If the oil pressure is too high, it can be determined that the fault occurs in the pressure regulating solenoid valve of the main oil circuit or the pressure regulating valve of the main oil circuit. At this time, check whether the circuit of oil pressure regulating solenoid valve and oil pressure solenoid valve work normally, and whether the computer sends control signal to oil pressure solenoid valve at the moment of shifting. If the solenoid valve circuit is faulty, it shall be repaired; If the solenoid valve is damaged, replace the solenoid valve; If the computer does not send a control signal to the oil pressure solenoid valve at the moment of shifting, it indicates that the computer is faulty, replace the computer. If the solenoid valve is operating properly, it is usually necessary to disassemble the automatic transmission valve body and check whether the pressure regulating valve of the main oil circuit is stuck. If stuck, use fine sandpaper No. 1200 to grind along the circular arc direction, and replace if the valve body is seriously damaged and cannot be repaired.

3. Diagnosis and repair of severe shifting shock in some gears

In case of serious shifting shock in some gears, road test shall be carried out firstly. If some gears are found to be too late for up-shifting, it indicates that the fault with large shifting shock is caused by too late up-shifting. If the engine speed rises abnormally before the up-shifting, resulting in a large shifting shock at the moment of up-shifting, it indicates that the clutch or brake is slipping. Check whether the oil pressure in the gear oil circuit is normal. If necessary, disassemble the automatic transmission and repair it.

Secondly, the shifting oil pressure of gear with shifting shock shall be tested. If the oil pressure of a gear is found to be stable during gear shifting, it indicates that the relevant components of the oil pressure buffer system in charge of this gear fail. On the transmission equipped with accumulator in each gear, if the accumulator piston sealing ring leaks, the shifting shock will be severe when the car is hot; If the accumulator piston is stuck, it cannot also act as oil pressure buffer, which will cause shifting shock. On the transmission equipped with the coasting regulating valve, the valve reduces the passage of hydraulic oil at the moment of shifting, allowing the clutch or brake to slowly engage. If the valve is stuck, the shifting shock will occur in the corresponding gear. In addition, on the transmission equipped with a one-way ball valve, if the ball valve is worn, misassembled or missed, it will cause too fast coupling of the clutch and/or the brake and also cause serious shifting shock.

In addition, a poor seal of the clutch or the brake piston will delay its engagement time,

and shifting shock will occur in the gears for which the clutch or brake piston is responsible. The tightness of the clutch or brake piston can be tested by pressure.

Ⅲ. Task Implementation

1. Inquiry

Know the time of fault from the owner; Check whether there is abnormal condition before the fault; The road condition of the car; mileage; Whether the car is maintained on time; Has it been repaired after the fault occurred. Find out the situation before and after the fault and the specific information of the fault through the above inquiry, and complete the preliminary diagnosis of shifting shock.

2. Test-drive and Basic Inspection

Carry out the test run, confirm the fault, and then check whether there is oil leakage or damage on the outer surface of the transmission. Check whether the oil level and oil quality of automatic transmission are normal, without obvious color change (normally dark red) and burning smell.

3. Detection and Diagnosis

Enter gateway installation list with VAS5051 for query, no fault storage, enter 02 (automatic transmission system) to read automatic transmission measurement data block, with normal display. The automatic transmission control unit is coded correctly.

The automatic transmission stall test shows that the engine speed is about 2,000r/min, within normal range. It proves that the friction elements such as internal clutch and brake of automatic transmission are normal.

According to the working principle of 09G automatic transmission up-shifting: During up-shifting from the 1st gear to 2nd gear, the actuators involved when the automatic transmission shifts between the 1st and 2nd gear are K1 and B1, and the corresponding solenoid valves are N92 and N283. Check the line between solenoid valve N92 and N283 and find no short circuit and open circuit.

Remove the slide valve box of the automatic transmission: Check the operating performance of the N283 solenoid valve, including whether there is blockage and jamming, which is completely normal after inspection. The mechanical valve connected to the N283 solenoid valve is disassembled and inspected. The spring of the mechanical valve is found to be broken into two sections, as shown in Figure 7-1.

In the automatic transmission valve plate, the mechanical valve spring connected with the N283 solenoid valve itself is defective. After a period of normal use, the mechanical valve spring breaks into two sections and the total spring force is less than the original value. After the duty cycle signal is input by the N283 solenoid valve, the mechanical valve spring cannot push the mechanical valve to move quickly to switch

Figure 7-1 Damaged Mechanical Valve Spring

the oil passage, resulting in the piston of B1 (brake) unable to move rapidly, and the engagement is slow, causing the body to rise from the 1st gear to the 2nd gear, and great shifting shock.

4. Fault Elimination

Replace a new 09G automatic transmission valve plate, and conduct the test-drive after assembly. The fault was eliminated

5. Inspection and Delivery

After troubleshooting, the test-drive is conducted, and the gear shift is normal without any other symptoms. The car is handed over to the owner.

Ⅳ. Task Summary

When diagnosing this kind of fault, we should first understand the characteristics and rules of shock, then analyze according to the working principle of transmission shifting control, and then eliminate it one by one to find out the cause of failure.

Ⅴ. Task Report

Major			Class		Name	
Task Name					Class Hours	2
Model				Engine Model		
Task Completion Process	Assessment Items		Assessment Contents		Maximum Score	Score
	1. Description of fault symptoms				5	
	2. Possible causes and analysis of fault				25	
	3. Detection and diagnosis process				35	
	4. Fault Elimination				10	
	5. Summary of fault diagnosis				10	
Teacher Evaluation	Operation quality, operation efficiency, operation safety, etc.				15	
Total Score					100	

Ⅵ. Knowledge Expansion

〔Typical Case Ⅰ〕 Shifting shock of a Passat car.

Fault Description: The owner of a Passat car (01N automatic transmission) said the car had been wading when it rained last year. From then on, after about two months, the car gradually became unstable, with obvious shock when shifting gears.

Fault Diagnosis and Repair: During the test run, it was found that the car had shock in the D gear and R gear every time the gear was engaged. When the accelerator pedal was accelerated to 2, 000~3, 000r/min, the car could drive slowly after obvious shock. When the car was cold, the car could shift freely. When the oil temperature reached the normal temperature, the car would be idled in the 2nd gear and the 3rd gear, and the car was unable to raise the speed easily. The maximum speed could only reach about 80km/h, but the engine speed had reached 4, 000r/min.

(1) The Shanghai Volkswagen special scan tool 5051B was connected and entered the automatic transmission system 02 to detect the fault codes as follows: P0735-Unreliable gear signal detected; P0712-Transmission oil temperature sensor fault; P0741—Lockup clutch

mechanical failure.

(2) The phenomenon of the test run was slipping in the 2nd gear to the 3rd gear. According to the wading experience of the car, it was considered that water may enter into the transmission, and the transmission ATF oil was mixed with water, resulting in the loss of buffering, lubrication, heat dissipation and driving functions of the transmission oil. Transmission oil driving is required for transmission gear shifting, and clutch friction disc also needs lubrication and heat dissipation of transmission oil. However, transmission oil lost the above functions and valve body pressure regulation was abnormal. At the beginning of the fault, only the transmission impact was caused. However, due to failure in timely maintenance, the pressure regulating valve of the main oil circuit was partially stuck, which made the clutch in the semi-clutch working state for a long time, causing the oil temperature of the transmission to rise. High temperature ablated the most commonly used 3rd gear clutch friction disc inside, causing an error in the transmission input to the output detected by the speed sensor. This error signal was transmitted to the transmission ECU, and the electronic control unit compared the signal with the correct data inside the transmission electronic control unit and determined that it was inconsistent with the correct signal, so that the transmission gear signal was unreliable.

(3) The locking system settings are different from other models. In most cases, the hydraulic oil inside the torque converter shall be radiated after locking operation. The locking system of this automobile is that after the oil pump builds pressure, the oil pressure is released to each pressure regulating valve and the pressure regulating valve of the torque converter, radiates through the radiator, reaches the TCC valve and finally reaches the lockup clutch. At this time, the internal wear of the transmission had produced many iron chips. They flew into the radiator together with the transmission oil and finally reached the locking valve inside the valve body, causing the lockup valve core to become stuck, causing the lockup clutch to not normally establish the working pressure and make the lockup clutch slip. The transmission electronic control unit detected that the lockup clutch was idle and stored the phenomenon in the fault memory of the electronic control unit.

(4) Hydraulic test: The pressure gauge was connected to the pressure test port of the transmission oil circuit to detect the transmission oil circuit pressure. The pressure gauge displayed that the system pressure was low (idling speed: D-2.5 kPa, R-3 kPa, stall: D-6 kPa, R-6 kPa, normal pressure should be 3.8 kPa for D at idle speed, 11.5 kPa for D at stall, 5.8 kPa for R at idle speed, 24.5 kPa for R at stall). Therefore, it could be concluded that the hydraulic system in the transmission was stuck and the pressure regulation of the main oil circuit was out of order, and the pressure required by the clutch and brake could not be adjusted, so that the transmission could not work normally.

(5) After the above tests and analyses, it was determined that the transmission would be overhauled. With the approval of the owner, the transmission was removed from the car and disassembled. It was found that the interior had been seriously damaged and all clutch brake friction discs had been damaged. After disassembling the valve body, it was found that the main oil pressure regulating valve and locking valve in the valve body were stuck. The cause of the transmission failure had been determined, followed by an overhaul of the trans-

mission, replacement of internal damaged components, a pressurization test of the clutch piston, a readjustment of the clutch clearance, and then reassembly of the transmission. The Shanghai Volkswagen special scan tool was connected to clear the fault information stored in the electronic control unit of the transmission, the test-drive was carried out and the fault was eliminated.

Summary: Automatic transmission is driven, radiated and lubricated by ATF oil, so it is necessary to regularly detect and replace ATF oil to ensure normal operation of automatic transmission.

For the fault diagnosis of automatic transmission, detecting and determining the fault position must be done before disassembly, so as to avoid more invalid inspections or failure to find real cause of failure.

[Typical Case Ⅱ] Shifting shock of a Volkswagen 2010 Bora car.

Fault Description: A Volkswagen 2010 Bora car, equipped with 01M automatic transmission. The car had obvious shock at all shifting points when operating at D gear, the 3rd gear and the 2nd gear.

Fault Diagnosis and Repair: Firstly, the fault code was read with the scan tool, but no fault code was read out, and then the data flow was read, showing that the actual current value of the oil pressure regulating solenoid valve was consistent with the rated current value.

There are many causes of shifting shock, mainly including high oil pressure, shift solenoid valve fault, clutch and brake failure. Each shift point of the automatic transmission had impact, and the main oil pressure was likely to be too high. The oil pressure gauge was connected to detect the main oil pressure of the transmission, and the main oil pressure of N gear at idle speed was 550kPa (the specified value is 450 kPa), significantly higher than the specified value. Because the oil pressure regulating solenoid valve had been replaced during previous service and the data flow was considered normal, the fault may occur in the main pressure regulating valve. The valve plate was removed and the main pressure regulating valve was checked. It was found that the valve hole on the spring side of the main pressure regulating valve had been seriously worn. The wear and leakage here would increase the oil pressure at the right end of the valve core of the main pressure regulating valve, resulting in excessively high main oil pressure, and finally causing shifting shock of each gear.

Summary: The up-shifting shock of the automatic transmission is usually caused by the fault of shift solenoid valve and excessive oil pressure. Firstly, the fault finding shall be carried out with the scan tool, and then analysis shall be done from the causes affecting the excessive oil pressure.

Task Ⅲ Fault Diagnosis and Repair of Abnormal Sound of Automatic Transmission

Learning Objectives

1. Be able to determine the direction and items of inquiry according to the fault phenomena

of the automobile for repair.

2. Be able to prepare a correct fault diagnosis plan according to fault phenomena.

3. Be able to consult maintenance data skillfully, select appropriate detection and diagnosis devices according to fault phenomena and use them skillfully.

4. Be able to test abnormal sound of transmission with appropriate maintenance devices according to diagnosis plan.

5. Be able to correctly analyze the test results and determine the location and cause of abnormal sound of transmission.

6. Be able to repair the fault parts quickly and accurately and eliminate the hidden troubles.

Task Import

Task Material: In a Bora 1. 6 L car, the automatic transmission is accompanied with a "buzz" sound during driving, and the sound increases with increasing speed.

Task Requirements: According to the fault phenomena of the car, consult relevant materials, select appropriate detection and diagnosis devices for fault diagnosis and repair, and fill in the task report.

I. Fault Analysis

1. There is always a sound in the automatic transmission while the engine is running

When the engine is running, there is always abnormal sound in the automatic transmission. When the shift lever is shifted from P or N to other gears, the abnormal sound disappears, usually the oil pump or torque converter is faulty.

2. The automatic transmission has abnormal sound while the car is driving, while the sound disappears when the shift lever is at P or N

The automatic transmission has abnormal sound during driving, while the abnormal noise disappears at P or N, which is usually caused by wear and breakage of planetary gear mechanism or excessive axial clearance between planetary gear and planetary carrier.

II. Fault Diagnosis

1. There is always a sound in the automatic transmission while the engine is running

If there is always a continuous sound in the automatic transmission in any gear, normally the oil pump and the torque converter should be removed to check the oil pump for wear and the torque converter for a large amount of friction powder. The oil pump or torque converter should be replaced if there is an abnormality.

2. The automatic transmission has abnormal sound while the car is driving, while the sound disappears when the shift lever is at P or N

If the automatic transmission has abnormal sound only during driving and there is no abnormal rattle in the P or N, the abnormal sound should be made in the planetary gear mechanism. Therefore, the automatic transmission should be disassembled to check whether the parts of the planetary row have wear traces, whether the gear is broken, whether the oneway roller clutch is worn or stuck, whether the bearing or thrust gasket is damaged, and

whether the axial clearance between the planetary gear and the planetary carrier is too large. Replace if there is any abnormality.

Special Tips: If the automatic transmission has no abnormal sound in direct gear and there is abnormal sound in other gears, the fault usually lies in the planetary gear mechanism. On the contrary, if there is no abnormal sound in other gears and there is a abnormal sound in the direct gear, the fault will not be in the planetary gear mechanism. If there is a change in abnormal sound when changing the speed or shifting but the sound always exists, the fault is likely to be in the hydraulic system.

Ⅲ. Task Implementation

1. Inquiry

Know the time of failure from the owner; Whether there are other abnormal conditions before failure; Does the symptom change after the fault is found: Details of car driving; Whether the car is maintained on time; Have other repairs been performed after the failure. Find out the situation before and after the fault and the specific information of the fault through the above inquiry, and complete the preliminary diagnosis of abnormal sound of transmission.

2. Test-drive and Basic Inspection

First carry out a test drive to verify that the "buzz" sound does come from the inside of the transmission and increases with the speed increase. Check the transmission oil quantity and oil quality and find no obvious abnormality.

3. Detection and Diagnosis

Put the gear lever at "1", and the "buzz" sound is not obvious during acceleration; At the "2" position, the sound increases when the car is driving at 2nd gear speed. When the gear lever is placed at "3", the sound is obvious when the speed is about 50km/h. At this time, the accelerator pedal is loosened slightly and the accelerator pedal is compressed, the sound has no obvious change. If the car is driving in 4th gear, the sound increases significantly.

Throughout the test run, it can be judged that it is not the sound of a gear. Because there is no relative rotation between the internal Lavigneaux planetary gears of the transmission in 3rd gear (direct gear), it can be judged that the fault position must be the component that participates in the operation in 1st, 2nd, 3rd and 4th gears.

There are only two possible causes of failure: Gear sound or bearing sound.

Lift the automobile, engage in "D" and keep it in driving position, and use a stethoscope to hear under the car and hear that the sound is from the rear cover of the transmission. From the characteristics of the sound, it can be judged that the "buzz" sound is from the bearing, not the "click, click" sound from the gear. Remove the rear cover and check the active gear and the passive gear and find that the passive gear bearing has been pinned out.

4. Fault Elimination

After replacing the passive gear bearing, the fault .

5. Inspection and Delivery

After troubleshooting and without any other symptoms, hand over the car to the owner.

Ⅳ. Task Summary

Rattle faults are difficult to diagnose. S eliminated The test run shall be carried out at different gears, different loads and speeds during diagnosis to understand the characteristics and rules of abnormal sound; We may reduce the fault range of abnormal sound by listening carefully; Finally, we can disassemble and inspect the abnormal sound parts to find out the faulty parts.

Ⅴ. Task Report

Major			Class		Name	
Task Name					Class Hours	2
Model			Engine Model			
	Assessment Items		Assessment Contents		Maximum Score	Score
Task Completion Process	1. Description of fault symptoms				5	
	2. Possible causes and analysis of fault				25	
	3. Detection and diagnosis process				35	
	4. Fault Elimination				10	
	5. Summary of fault diagnosis				10	
Teacher Evaluation	Operation quality, operation efficiency, operation safety, etc.				15	
Total Score					100	

Ⅵ. Knowledge Expansion

【Typical Case Ⅰ】 Abnormal sound at the side of the transmission when a Buick Regal car reached a certain speed.

Fault Description: A Buick Regal car, equipped with a 4T65E automatic transmission. Abnormal sound was mode from the side of the transmission when the automobile reached a certain speed. With the engine running, the abnormal sound disappeared when the brake pedal was pressed.

Fault Diagnosis and Repair: Firstly, the test drive was carried out. The phenomena was basically the same as the owner said. It was thought that the abnormal sound may come from the hydraulic torque converter turbine, drive sprocket, drive chain, driven sprocket, input clutch, input strut one-way clutch, and planetary gear set. Because the above elements operated in "P" or "N" gears. Engaging "R" gear or "D" gear, when the brake pedal was pressed, there was no abnormal sound. When the car reached a certain speed per hour, that is, when the engine was running at a certain speed, abnormal rattle occurred. Because the abnormal sound was emitted from the side position, it was judged that the abnormal sound was from the drive sprocket, the drive chain and the driven sprocket. Then the transmission was disassembled. The drive sprocket, the drive chain and the driven sprocket were checked carefully. It was found that the chain was worn and the distance between the transmission and the drive chain was less than the 3.2mm standard given by the manufacturer. After replacing the drive sprocket, the drive chain and the driven sprocket, the fault was eliminated

Summary: When making abnormal sound diagnosis, we should start with the state (stationary or running) of each element under different working conditions. Generally,

126 | Automobile Integrated Fault Diagnosis and Repair |

moving element is likely to produce abnormal sound. Then we should start with the abnormal sound position, which requires a clear understanding of the spatial positions of the components inside the automatic transmission. If we are not familiar with its internal structure, it is difficult for us to make an accurate judgment. When confirming the fault, if we can find technical data, the technical parameters provided by the manufacturer should prevail, to avoid subjective assumption and wrong replacement. Such abnormal sound due to wear is difficult to confirm without technical parameters provided by the manufacturer.

[Typical Case Ⅱ]　Abnormal sound of a Honda Accord in R gear.

Fault Description： A repaired Honda Accord, equipped with MPOA transmission. After being repaired, it was tested and it was found that it was normal in D gear and had abnormal sound in R gear.

Fault Diagnosis and Repair： The oil level and oil quality of the automatic transmission was checked first, and no abnormality was found. Then no fault code was called out. During the test drive, the sound was heard as the sound of gear friction. It was thought that the gear could not be engaged in place. Then the car was lifted, the gear lever cable was removed, the engine was started and the manual valve was shifted by hand to engage. At this time, it was shifted from P to R, from N to R, and the engine speed was constantly changed. The N was shifted but no abnormal sound was heard. The cable of the gear lever was installed again. When R was engaged, the abnormal sound of the transmission appeared again. It was basically certain that the abnormal sound was not inside the automatic transmission. The gear lever and the cable were further checked, and it was found that the adjusting nut was loose. The cable was adjusted and the adjusting nut was tightened. After the test drive, the abnormal sound of the transmission disappeared. The fault of this car was caused by the change of cable length, which made the R gear unable to be engaged in place.

Summary： Honda Accord MPOA automatic transmission is of parallel shaft type, and the R gear is realized by means of meshing between the shift fork sliding sleeve and the driven gear. Because the gear lever adjusting nut was loose, the R gear sliding sleeve could not fully mesh with the driven gear, resulting in abnormal sound in R gear (the working principle is basically the same as that of manual transmission). When overhauling an automatic transmission, we should know the basic structural features of transmission firstly, and then conduct external inspection and adjustment. We should conduct the maintenance in order from outside to inside and from simple to complicated, so as to achieve the rapid maintenance.

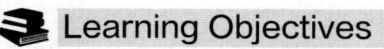 Task Ⅳ　Fault Diagnosis and Repair of Upshifting Hysteresis

Learning Objectives

1. Be able to determine the direction and items of inquiry according to the fault phenomena of the automobile for repair.

2. Be able to prepare a correct fault diagnosis plan according to fault phenomena.

3. Be able to consult maintenance data skillfully, select appropriate detection and diagnosis devices according to fault phenomena and use them skillfully.

4. Be able to test upshifting hysteresis with appropriate maintenance devices according to the diagnosis plan.

5. Be able to correctly analyze the test results and determine the fault location and cause of upshifting hysteresis.

6. Be able to repair the fault parts quickly and accurately and eliminate the hidden troubles.

Task Import

Task Material: A FAW-Volkswagen Bora 1. 6L car, automatic transmission model of 01M, driving mileage of 60, 000km. When the car accelerates steadily, it is delayed each upshifting from the 1st gear to the 4th gear. The engine speed obviously exceeds the normal speed range during upshifting.

Task Requirements: According to the fault phenomena of the car, consult relevant materials, select appropriate detection and diagnosis devices for fault diagnosis and repair, and fill in the task report.

I. Fault Analysis

The upshifting hysteresis usually shows that the upshifting is not achieved, even reaching the range of upshifting speed, and the upshifting can only be upshifted with higher car speed and engine speed, which is also called too late upshifting. The causes of upshifting hysteresis are as follows:

(1) The throttle position sensor or car speed sensor has a poor signal or the circuit is faulty.

(2) Automatic transmission oil quantity is insufficient, deteriorated, etc.

(3) Hydraulic actuators such as clutch or brake slip.

(4) The main pressure regulating valve or manual control valve is faulty.

(5) The oil pressure in the main oil circuit is too low due to leakage of oil circuit or blockage of the collector.

(6) The electronic control unit or its circuit is faulty.

(7) The hydraulic torque converter does not work properly.

(8) The turbine shaft or planetary gear set has mechanical damage.

II. Fault Diagnosis

First check the automatic transmission for sufficient oil quantity and for oil deterioration.

Then use the scan tool to read out the fault code storage and also view the data flow affecting the upshifting hysteresis, such as engine water temperature, transmission oil temperature, throttle opening, etc.

Check the oil pressure in the oil circuit and judge whether the fault is in the hydraulic system or the mechanical system by detecting the oil pressure.

If the oil pressure is low, the fault is in the hydraulic system. Further check whether the oil pump and the oil pressure regulating valve are faulty.

If the oil pressure is normal, the fault is in the mechanical system and further inspection shall be carried out on the mechanical parts that may fail.

Ⅲ. Task Implementation

1. Inquiry

Know the time of the fault from the owner; Whether the symptoms change after finding the fault; Whether there are other abnormal conditions before the fault; Details of driving; Whether the car is maintained on time; Have other repairs been performed after the fault. Find out the situation before and after the fault and the specific information of the fault through the above inquiry, and complete the preliminary diagnosis of too late upshifting.

2. Test-drive and Basic Inspection

During the trial run, it is found that when advancing the throttle stably, it is delayed from the 1st gear to the 2nd gear, the engine speed exceeds 3, 000r/min from the 2nd gear to the 3rd gear, and the engine speed exceeds 3, 500r/min from the 3rd gear rises to the 4th gear, and the speed values all are far beyond the normal range.

By checking the ATF level and oil quality, no abnormality was found.

3. Detection and Diagnosis

First check with VAS5051 and find no fault code. Check data flow affecting upshifting hysteresis: The oil temperature is usually lower than 105℃ and occasionally reaches 120℃; Engine load is within $10\%\sim150\%$ and $0\sim260$N·m during full speed test run; At full speed test run, the throttle position is within $0\sim100\%$, the throttle angle G188 is within $97\%\sim3\%$ and G187 is within $3\%\sim93\%$; The water temperature is within $80\sim105$℃.

The test results show that the above data are basically normal, except that the oil temperature is occasionally slightly higher, which indicates that the clutch and the brake may slip due to poor heat dissipation. Therefore, the radiator was cleaned, but the fault remains.

Judging from the above checks, the fault is likely to be in the hydraulic system or mechanical system. The oil pressure is then tested: When the oil temperature rises to 60℃, the oil pressure of the D gear is 370kPa at idle speed and the normal value is within $340\sim380$kPa, and the oil pressure is normal. When the clutch slips under normal oil pressure, it can be inferred that the fault point is the clutch.

The analysis of shifting actuator worksheet (Figure 7-2) shows that there is no fault in the 1st gear and R gear, indicating that K1, B1 and K2 are normal, and the fault may be B2 and K3.

By simulating the stall test for the 3rd gear (plugging off the solenoid valve plug), compared with the same model, it is found that the engine

		B1	B2	K1	K2	K3	F	LC
R		✕			✕			
1	H			✕			✕	
	M			✕			✕	✕
2	H		✕	✕				
	M		✕	✕				✕
3	H			✕		✕		
	M			✕		✕		✕
4	H		✕			✕		
	M		✕			✕		✕

Figure 7-2 Shifting Actuator Worksheet

speed of the car is high and the cause of the fault may be K3 slipping.

The automatic transmission is disassembled, the K3 clutch and B2 brake are checked, and it is found that the clearance is too large.

4. Fault Elimination

After replacing friction discs for clutch K3 and brake B2 the fault is eliminated.

5. Inspection and Delivery

After troubleshooting, re-installation and test run are conducted without any other symptoms, and the car is handed over to the owner.

IV. Task Summary

Transmission upshifting hysteresis is caused due to slipping caused by excessive clearance between clutch K3 and brake B2. Because both components are involved in up-shifting from the 1st gear to the 4th gear, each up-shifting slips.

Be sure to fully use the scan tool during diagnosis, read the fault information and view the relevant data flow. Combined with the corresponding detection and information from all aspects, the efficiency of diagnosis can be improved according to the fault diagnosis flow, and the fault location can be found smoothly.

V. Task Report

Major			Class		Name	
Task Name					Class Hours	2
Model			Engine Model			
	Assessment Items		Assessment Contents		Maximum Score	Score
Task Completion Process	1. Description of fault symptoms				5	
	2. Possible causes and analysis of fault				25	
	3. Detection and diagnosis process				35	
	4. Fault Elimination				10	
	5. Summary of fault diagnosis				10	
Teacher Evaluation	Operation quality, operation efficiency, operation safety, etc.				15	
	Total Score				100	

VI. Knowledge Expansion

[Typical Case I] Too high engine speed of a Toyota Camry 2.0L car during up-shifting from the 2nd gear to the 3rd gear

Fault Description: A Toyota Camry 2.0L car, equipped with A140E automatic transmission. The transmission up-shifted the 1st gear and the 2nd gear normally, but when up-shifting to the 3rd gear, it could be up-shifted when the engine speed was high, and there was no OVER DRIVE. Meanwhile, the "OD OFF" indicator light always flashed.

Fault Diagnosis and Repair: The test run was carried out, and it was found that the failure phenomenon was basically the same as the owner said. The 1st and 2nd gears of the automatic transmission were basically normal, but it was very slow from the 2nd gear to the 3rd gear and the OVER DRIVE could not be engaged, and the engine speed was higher in high gear. The "OD OFF" indicator light always flashed. There was no abnormality found

through basic inspection, which indicated that the electronic control system of automatic transmission was likely to fail. The decoder was connected, the fault code "62" was read out, namely solenoid valve 1 or line were faulty. The circuit from the electronic control unit to the solenoid valve was checked, and no wiring damage, grounding and short circuit was found. The circuit was normal. The conductive resistance of two shift solenoid valves was measured. The resistance value of solenoid valve 1 was 4.5Ω, the resistance value of solenoid valve 2 was 15.2Ω, and the normal resistance value of A140E automatic transmission shift solenoid valve was $14\sim16\Omega$. Obviously, the resistance value of solenoid valve 1 was too small, indicating the short circuit between the turns of the electromagnetic coil. A new solenoid valve 1 was replaced and reassembled into the car. During the test run, the fault was eliminated.

Summary: The fault of shift solenoid valve 1 was checked with the decoder. Because when the A140E automatic transmission operated in 1st gear, the solenoid valve 1 was energized and the solenoid valve 2 was de-energized; When working in 2nd gear, both solenoid valves were energized; When working in 3rd gear, the solenoid valve 1 was powered off and the solenoid valve 2 was energized; When operating in 4th gear, both solenoid valves were de-energized. According to the control principle and fault phenomenon of this car, it was judged that the solenoid valve 1 was faulty. The combination of inspection and maintenance manual is helpful for diagnosis and elimination of faults.

[Typical Case Ⅱ] Too Late Up-shifting of a Honda Accord.

Fault Description: The owner of a Honda Accord 2.0L said that the automatic transmission was too late to upshift, the engine was running idly during the up-shifting, and the fault was not obvious when the car was cold, but after several thousand meters of driving, the above-mentioned fault was obvious.

Fault Diagnosis and Repair: Firstly, the test run was conducted. It was found that the automatic transmission was obviously too late to upshift. The accelerator pedal was pressed slightly, the up-shifting could be done when the engine speed reached above 2,300r/min. When the accelerator pedal was pressed quickly and the engine speed reached 3,000r/min, the up-shifting could be achieved. The engine would idle from the 3rd gear to the 4th gear. The speed would suddenly rise above 3,500r/min and then dropped to about 2,800r/min, which means that there was obvious instantaneous slipping.

The oil quantity of automatic transmission met the requirements, but there was a burning smell in the oil, and no impurities were found; the tightness of throttle cable was moderate; The "S" indicator on the instrument panel did not flash, indicating that the PCM did not detect the automatic transmission system electrical failure; The speedometer display was normal when the car was driving, indicating that the speed sensor was normal.

The stall test was carried out. When the gear lever was placed in D4, D3, 1 and R, the stall speed was about 2,400r/min, which was completely normal; The stall speed was also within the normal range when placed in 2. The connector at the wire side of the shift solenoid valve was disconnected, and the stall test was done at D4 and D3, and the stall speed was also normal. The above tests indicated that each clutch did not slip.

The signal voltage of the throttle position sensor was measured. Measured at the throttle position sensor, when the engine was idle, its signal voltage was 0.45V, when the throttle

was fully open, its signal voltage was about 4.4V, and the signal voltage changed smoothly with the throttle opening.

The resistance of the spindle speed sensor and the auxiliary shaft speed sensor was checked and within normal range. The "S" shift program switch was checked and normal. The PCM cover plate was removed for inspection and no obvious problems were noted. The two front wheels were lifted, the engine was started, and the gear lever was engaged at D4 for test run. It was found that gear shifting was too late and it slipped instantly from the 3rd gear to the 4th gear. The gear lever was engaged at D3, when accelerating to 70km/h, then the gear lever was engaged to D4, but it still slipped at the moment of shifting into the 4th gear. The gear lever was engaged at D4, the transmission was kept running in the 3rd gear, and the wire side connector of the shift solenoid valve was quickly disconnected. The automatic transmission could be switched into 4th gear quickly without instantaneous slipping. Therefore, it could be concluded that the fault location was still in the automatic transmission electronic control part. Because the coolant temperature signal, throttle position signal, automobile speed signal, speed signal, solenoid valve circuit, PCM power supply and grounding condition were all normal, it was suspected that the PCM fault caused the automatic transmission to shift lately and the automatic transmission to slip at the moment of shifting.

Therefore, the PCM was replaced, and the test drive was carried out. The automatic transmission could be up-shifted around 2,000r/min, and the instantaneous slipping phenomenon disappeared when shifting.

Summary: This fault was caused by the failure of the automatic transmission electronic control unit, which made the shifting control abnormal and the shifting hysteresis occur. Because the fault had no fault code and the automatic transmission fluid had a burning smell, when the transmission slipping was determined during diagnosis, analysis could only be conducted according to the causes of the automatic transmission slipping one by one. When the fault other than the electronic control unit was eliminated, it could be judged as the fault of the electronic control unit, and the cause of the failure could be determined by replacing the electronic control unit for test.

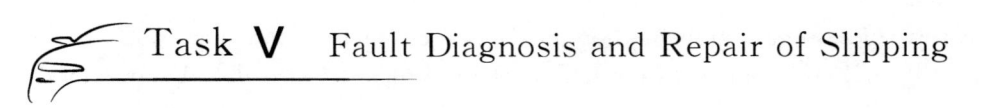

Task V Fault Diagnosis and Repair of Slipping

Learning Objectives

1. Be able to determine the direction and items of inquiry according to the fault phenomena of the automobile for repair.

2. Be able to prepare a correct fault diagnosis plan according to fault phenomena.

3. Be able to consult maintenance data skillfully, select appropriate detection and diagnosis devices according to fault phenomena and use them skillfully.

4. Be able to test slipping fault with appropriate maintenance devices according to the diagnosis plan.

5. Be able to correctly analyze the test results and determine the fault location and cause of slipping.

6. Be able to repair the fault parts quickly and accurately and eliminate the hidden troubles.

Task Import

Task Material: A Shanghai Buick Century GL is equipped with 4T65-E automatic transmission. The automatic transmission slipping due to several burnouts of the brake belts. After several repairs and replacements of some important components such as valve body, it will be difficult to start without reverse gear after each maintenance. After starting, the car speed can rise normally, but when the car speed exceeds 120km/h for acceleration, the engine speed rises but the car speed cannot be increased accordingly.

Task Requirements: According to the fault phenomena of the car, consult relevant materials, select appropriate detection and diagnosis devices for fault diagnosis and repair, and fill in the task report.

Ⅰ. Fault Analysis

Automatic transmission skip has one or more of the following characteristics:

(1) When the car starts and the accelerator pedal is pressed, the engine speed increases quickly, but the car speed rises slowly.

(2) The car's up-shifting speed is high during driving. The engine speed rises during the up-shifting, but the car speed does not increase quickly.

(3) When the car is moving, the engine speed suddenly increases while engaging into a gear, but the car speed increases slowly.

(4) The engine speed rises rapidly when the automobile is uphill or rapidly accelerated, but the car is running slowly.

(5) Automatic transmission oil temperature rises easily, burnt smell of the automatic transmission may be smelt.

The main causes of automatic transmission slipping are as follows:

(1) Automatic transmission fluid level is too low or too high.

(2) The variety of transmission oil is poor.

(3) The valve body is leaking (including solenoid valve).

(4) The clutch, the brake, or the one-way clutch itself is severely worn, causing slipping. In the case of a newly overhauled automatic transmission, whether the clutch plate set clearance is correct or whether the brake belt clearance is adjusted correctly should be considered.

(5) The clutch or brake piston sealing ring is damaged, causing oil leakage.

(6) The main oil pressure is too low, causing slipping. Too low oil level of automatic transmission, blockage of filter, serious wear of oil pump, leakage of main oil circuit, failure of main pressure regulating valve or pressure control solenoid valve, etc. will cause low main oil pressure, resulting in slipping and burnout of multiple actuators.

(7) The operating oil pressure of the individual actuator is too low. Damage of piston

Item Ⅶ Fault Diagnosis and Repair of Automatic Transmission **133**

sealing ring of actuator, damage of oil circuit sealing ring, leakage of pressure accumulator, blockage of throttle device, etc. will cause slipping and burnout of actuator, which is shown as slid in corresponding gear, which is often accompanied by impact, i. e. first slid and then impact.

II. Fault Diagnosis

Automatic transmission slipping is one of the most common faults. Automatic transmission slipping is often accompanied by severe wear and even burning of clutch or brake friction disc. However, if it simply replaces the worn friction disc without finding out the real cause of slipping, it will cause the automatic transmission after repair for a period of time to slip again. Therefore, for automatic transmission with slippage, do not rush to disassemble it. We should carry out various inspection tests first, to find out the true cause of slipping.

1. Check hydraulic oil height

If the hydraulic shaft is too low or too high, find out the cause and adjust it to the normal position after repair.

2. Check automatic transmission fluid (ATF) quality

If the ATF is discolored and has a burning smell, it indicates that clutch inside the automatic transmission or the brake friction disc is burnt out, and the test run shall be carefully carried out to avoid stall test and to avoid further damage to the components. The ATF can be drained first and the ATF pan can be removed to check for excessive wear debris. The black and brown particles in the wear debris are fallen friction materials; Silver powders are ground steel sheet or metal shell materials; The red and brown powders are ground copper sheath materials. In the above cases, the automatic transmission shall be disassembled for overhaul.

3. Measure oil pressure

Most automatic transmissions are equipped with main oil pressure test ports, and some automatic transmissions have oil pressure test ports for each clutch or brake. Oil pressure test is the most direct and most effective method to judge automatic transmission slipping.

See corresponding data for the position of oil pressure test port and oil pressure standard value. If the main oil circuit pressure is normal, simply replace the worn or burnt friction element. If low oil pressure is measured, remove the ATF pan first and check if the ATF filter is blocked. Some types of automatic transmission filters are not bolted and often cause the filter to fall off if equipped with poor quality fittings. If the filter is normal, remove the valve body for inspection, clean the oil circuit, check or replace the oil pressure regulating valve. If the above treatment has no effect, disassemble the automatic transmission, check whether the oil pump and all seals are in good condition, and replace the seal and sealing ring as required.

4. Conduct road test

A road test can determine whether the automatic transmission is slipping and determine the gear and degree of slippage. When conducting the road test for the slipping automatic transmission, be careful not to accelerate rapidly or perform stall test to avoid further damage of automatic transmission.

Turn the gear lever into different positions during driving. If the engine speed suddenly increases when the automatic transmission rises to a certain gear, but the automobile speed does not increase correspondingly, the gear slips. The faster the engine speed rises when slipping, the more severe the slipping. According to the law of slipping, the actuator of slipping can be judged.

III. Task Implementation

1. Inquiry

The repairman shall know the time of fault from the owner; Whether there are other abnormal conditions before the fault; Whether the symptoms change after finding the fault; Details of driving; Whether the automobile is maintained on time; Have other repairs been performed after the fault. Know the situation before and after the fault and the specific information of the fault and complete the preliminary diagnosis of automatic transmission slipping.

2. Test-drive and Basic Inspection

Conduct a test-drive to confirm the fault, check the oil level and oil quality of automatic transmission and find no abnormality.

3. Detection and Diagnosis

Read out the fault code of automatic transmission with the Buick scan tool TECH2, and there is no fault code displayed. Shift the gear lever to N (neutral) gear, and increase the throttle. The engine speed can reach 5, 000~6, 000r/min, and the engine running sound is normal, indicating that the engine is free of fault. Connect the oil pressure gauge to detect the pipeline pressure of automatic transmission. When the gear lever is in the D position, the oil circuit pressure of D1 gear and D4 is low. When the gear lever is in R, the oil circuit pressure is only 830kPa, which is far lower than the standard value of 1, 540~1, 869kPa. This indicates that there is leakage in the D1, D4 and R oil circuits. Because the transmission of this car has been repaired many times, and it is repaired because of the same fault. Before finding out the real cause of the fault, we did not disassemble and repair the transmission, but first analyzed the structure of 4T65-E automatic transmission.

The planetary gears of 4T65-E automatic transmission adopt Simpson II planetary gear train. The planetary gear train has only two planetary rows at the front and rear. The planetary gear transmission with 4 forward gears and 1 reverse gear is composed of 3 clutches, 4 brakes (3 belt brakes, 1 disc brakes) and 3 one-way clutches controlled by 10 shift actuators.

The transmission route of 4T65-E automatic transmission is shown in Figure 7-3. The operation of clutches and brakes in each gear is shown in Table 7-1.

According to Figure 7-3 and Table 7-1, the transmission route of each gear of 4T65-E automatic transmission can be analyzed.

In D1, the actuators involved include input clutch C3 and forward brake B4, and because the reverse gear of the car is not working properly and the input clutch C3 is also involved in the operation of reverse gear, we assume that the input clutch C3 is faulty. It can also be seen from Figure 7-3 and Table 7-1 that if forward brake B4 cannot realize braking during normal operation of D1, the rear sun gears can rotate freely to make power output

Item VII   Fault Diagnosis and Repair of Automatic Transmission   **135**

impossible. The automatic transmission must have no D1. Therefore, we think that the piston seal for the forward brake B4 is not good and the control oil circuit may also be problematic. To check the operation of the input clutch C3 and the forward brake B4, the automatic transmission must be disassembled. Therefore, before disassembling the automatic transmission, we analyze the possibility of a failure in the control oil circuit so as to avoid unnecessary disassembly of the automatic transmission.

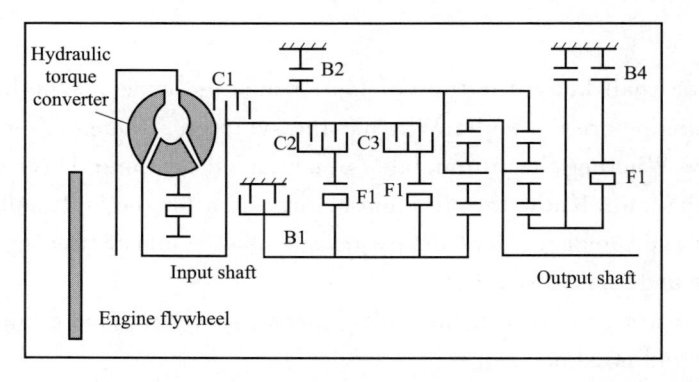

Figure 7-3 Transmission Circuit Diagram of 4T65-E Automatic Transmission

Table 7-1　Operation of Clutch and Brake

	Gear	S1	S2	C1	C2	C3	B1	B2	B3	B4	F1	F2	F3
P	P	ON	ON			A*						H*	
R	R	ON	ON			A		A				H	
N	N	ON	ON			A*						H	
D	1st gear	ON	ON			A				A		H	H
	2nd gear	OFF	ON	A		A*				A		O	H
	3rd gear	OFF	OFF	A	A					A*	H		O
	4th gear	ON	OFF	A	A*		A			A*	O		O
3	1st gear	ON	ON			A				A		H	H
	2nd gear	OFF	ON	A		A*				A		O	H
	3rd gear	OFF	OFF	A	A	A				A*	H	H	O
2	1st gear	ON	ON			A				A		H	H
	2nd gear	OFF	ON	A		A*				A		O	H
1	1st gear	ON	ON		A	A				A	H	H	H

Note: ON, the solenoid valve is energized; OFF, the solenoid valve is not energized; A, Applied; H, Holding; *, applied or holding without load; O, Overrun; S1, 1-2/3-4 shift solenoid valve; S2, 2-3 shift solenoid valve.

Two shift solenoid valves are used for the 4T65-E automatic transmission. The 1-2/3-4 shift solenoid valve (shift solenoid valve S1) controls 1-2/3-4 shift and the 2-3 shift solenoid valve (shift solenoid valve S2) controls 2-3 shift. The shift solenoid valve is controlled by PCM according to car speed and transmission ratio. In case of power failure, the shift solenoid valve will release the oil circuit pressure from the oil pump. When powered on, the shift solenoid valve closes the pressure relief port, so that the oil circuit pressure from the oil pump is transmitted to the shift valve to realize the shifting. There are two possibilities for failure of the shift solenoid valve: Electronic fault and mechanical fault. When any shift sole-

136 | Automobile Integrated Fault Diagnosis and Repair

noid valve has an electronic fault, the automatic transmission malfunction indicator light (MIL) shall flash, and the automatic transmission enters into the forced D3 emergency mode. However, according to the fault phenomenon of the car, the car does not enter the forced D3 emergency mode when it fails, and the fault code is not read by the TECH2 scan tool. Thus, it can be preliminarily concluded that there is little possibility of electronic fault of the shift solenoid valve, and the "mechanical" problem of the shift solenoid valve shall be checked. When there is a mechanical fault of the shift solenoid valve, the shift solenoid valve acts under the control of the PCM but does not function as a control fluid, so it is determined that the shift solenoid valve should have a fault in its sealing performance in the event of a mechanical fault.

It can be seen from the above structural analysis that the fault should focus on the piston seal conditions of the forward brake B4, the input clutch C3 and the seal condition of the shift solenoid valve. Because the shift solenoid valve is located on the oil circuit board, it is easy to remove and inspect, so it is decided to check the sealing condition of the shift solenoid valve first. Remove the shift solenoid valve and carefully inspect all parts of the shift solenoid valve. It is found that the working surface of the slide valve of the 1-2/3-4 shift solenoid valve (shift solenoid valve S1) has been seriously worn.

4. Fault Elimination

Replace the 1-2/3-4 shift solenoid valve and conduct a test run. The fault is eliminated completely.

5. Inspection and Delivery

After troubleshooting and without any other symptoms, hand over the car to the owner.

IV. Task Summary

In D-1 gear, after 1-2/3-4 shift solenoid valve (shift solenoid valve S2) receives the ON command from PCM, the pressure relief port shall close to maintain oil pressure. However, the ATF leaks at the slide valve due to severe wear on the slide valve surface of the shift solenoid valve, resulting in too low oil pressure in the oil circuit. Under the action of low oil pressure, the 1-2/3-4 shift solenoid valve cannot operate, causing the forward brake B4 piston to be driven without oil pressure, and the sun gear of the rear planetary gear mechanism cannot realize braking, resulting in no D1 gear, so it is difficult to start. In D4 gear, the valve does not operate, causing the 4th gear brake B1 piston to be driven without oil pressure and the sun gear of the front planetary gear mechanism unable to brake, resulting in no overdrive. In reverse gear, the valve does not operate, causing the reverse brake (belt type) B2 piston to be hydraulically driven and the front planetary carrier and rear ring gear cannot be fixed, thus causing no reverse gear. However, in D2 and D3, the 1-2/3-4 shift solenoid valve does not work, so the 2-3 shift valve can operate normally.

It can be seen from the elimination of this fault that it is very important to combine the transmission route and the automatic transmission execution worksheet to diagnose the fault during fault diagnosis of automatic transmission, which can improve the diagnostic efficiency and avoid blind disassembly and assembly.

V. Task Report

	Major		Class		Name	
	Task Name				Class Hours	2
	Model		Engine Model			
	Assessment Items	Assessment Contents		Maximum Score		Score
Task Completion Process	1. Description of fault symptoms			5		
	2. Possible causes and analysis of fault			25		
	3. Detection and diagnosis process			35		
	4. Fault Elimination			10		
	5. Summary of fault diagnosis			10		
Teacher Evaluation	Operation quality, operation efficiency, operation safety, etc.			15		
	Total Score			100		

VI. Knowledge Expansion

〔Typical Case Ⅰ〕 Automatic transmission slipping of a Peugeot.

Fault Description: A Peugeot with 4HP14 automatic transmission. The car first slipped with an automatic transmission while driving, then smoked under the car, and then could not drive.

Fault Diagnosis and Repair: The oil level of the automatic transmission was checked. It was found that the oil level was 1.5cm higher than the MAX during the cold engine, and the oil was dirty and smelt burning. An operation test was done to raise the temperature of the ATF. When the car entered the 4th gear, the engine accelerated while the automatic transmission began to slip. The gear lever was set to the "3" and the automatic transmission returned to normal state in the 3rd gear. The stall test was done and the engine stall speed was 2,100r/min, whether forward or backward, which was normal. The car was lifted for inspection and it was found that there was a lot of leaking ATF in the area between the automatic transmission and the engine, between the sub-frame and the power steering pump. The automatic transmission oil pan was removed and it was found that there were a large amount of clutch debris inside the oil pan. In view of this situation, the automatic transmission had to be disassembled for inspection.

Firstly the E clutch was taken out and it was found that the brake drum was discolored due to heat, the friction disc was severely worn, and the steel plate was exposed. The piston seal hardened due to heat. The remaining clutches A, B, C and D were checked, and there was no internal abnormality. The inspection was conducted along the pressure oil supply passage of the clutch E, it was found that the pressure oil flew from the bore inside the pump housing through the bore of the turbine shaft into the inside of the piston of the clutch E. With the touch of hand, it felt obvious wear steps and had formed a groove, which may be the cause of wear of the clutch E. The steel ring, the friction disc and the seal kit were replaced, the axial clearance was adjusted, and the automatic transmission body and the torque converter were cleaned After installing the automatic transmission, the driving test was conducted under the condition of connecting the oil pressure gauge. The result showed that the up-shifting point was good, there was no vibration when the automatic limit kicked

down and during down-shifting, and the engine braked well.

The faults of the car were that the automatic transmission leaked oil and the oil level was high when the car was cold. If fluid is replenished at low oil temperature, the oil level shall be controlled at 1.5 cm below the MIN. In some imported models, there are oiling horizontal lines in cold and hot states, while others are only carved with two lines of MIN (minimum) and MAX (maximum). This car belongs to the latter. Therefore, when the oil temperature does not reach above 60℃, it is difficult to judge how much oil should be filled. The ATF of the car was added too much. During the high speed driving, the fluid expanded due to the temperature rise, and finally overflowed from the cooler and fell on the exhaust pipe, so there was smoke. At the same time, when the oil temperature rose and the sleeve was worn, which caused too low oil pressure. When driving at high speed, the clutch burned out due to excessive load, so the car could not drive.

Summary: There are many reasons for automatic transmission slipping, which is difficult to diagnose. However, as long as we master the basic structure and principle of automatic transmission, check and analyze around brake, clutch and oil circuit, we can find out the fault position and analyze the cause smoothly.

〔Typical Case Ⅱ〕 Instant slipping of a Honda Accord 2.0L from 3rd gear to 4th gear.

Fault Description: The owner of a Honda Accord 2.0L said that the automatic transmission was too late to up-shift, the engine when up-shifting had idling, it would appear slow up-shifting after driving thousands of meters.

Fault Diagnosis and Repair: Firstly, the test run was carried out. When accelerating under the small throttle, it was found that the engine could only up-shift above 2,300r/min, and when the throttle is larger, it would achieve the up-shifting above 3,000r/min; At the moment of 3rd gear to 4th gear, the engine idled, and the speed suddenly rose to 3,500r/min or even higher, and then dropped to about 2,800r/min, which showed obvious instantaneous slippage. The engine speed was basically consistent with the automobile speed during the remaining working hours, indicating no slippage.

The oil content of automatic transmission was normal, the oil quality was a little scorched, but there was no obvious impurity. It was basically normal because it had not been replaced for a long time. The throttle cable was normal and the time lag test was normal. The fault light did not flash, indicating that the computer did not detect the fault, and the speedometer indicated normal while driving, indicating that the speed sensor was normal. The stall speed of D4, D1, 1st gear and R all were about 2,400r/min for stall test, all of which were normal, and the stall speed of 2nd gear was normal. The plug of shift solenoid valve was disengaged, the stall test was done in D4 or D3, and the stall speed was also normal. This indicated that the clutches in gears were not slipping.

Because too late shifting occurred when the speedometer indication was normal, the throttle position sensor signal was checked and measured at throttle position sensor, signal voltage at idle speed was 0.45V, full opening was about 4.4V, and it changed smoothly with throttle opening and was normal. The resistance value of solenoid valve was checked, and the spindle speed sensor and the auxiliary shaft speed sensor were all normal. The "S" shift program switch was also normal. The transmission control computer cover was removed

and any signs of malfunction was not found visually.

The two front wheels were lifted, the engine was started and operated in the "D1", and the result was too late up-shifting as the test drive. The instant slipping of 3rd gear and 4th gear was still remained. When operating in the "D3", accelerating to about 70km/h and pushing the gear lever quickly to the "D4". The result was that there was still slipping at the moment of shifting into 4th gear. When operating in the "D1", keeping it in 3rd gear and quickly disconnecting the plugs of the two shift solenoid valves, the automatic transmission could be quickly shifted into 4th gear without instantaneous slippage. Therefore, it could be basically concluded that the fault was still in the electronic control part, not caused by the slow action of the shift solenoid valve and its oil circuit control valve body and actuator element.

Because the automatic transmission electronic control circuit part, including water temperature signal, throttle position signal, automobile speed signal, engine speed signal, solenoid valve circuit, computer power supply, ground circuit, etc. were all in good condition, so it was concluded that the computer was faulty. The automatic transmission computer was replaced for test run, at about 2, 000 r/min, the up-shifting was done with no instantaneous slipping. The good shifting quality confirmed that too late shifting and instant slipping was really caused by computer failure.

Summary: The up-shifting instantaneous slipping caused by the automatic transmission electronic control unit is rare, and the diagnosis is more difficult. Slipping at the moment of up-shifting is usually considered to be caused by poor operation of the internal shift valve or shift actuator of the transmission. When diagnosing such fault, it is necessary to carry out tests such as simulated shifting test and manual shifting test to distinguish the cause is circuit failure or mechanical failure, rather than easily disassembling the automatic transmission to find out the fault location.

Item VIII

Fault Diagnosis and Repair of Steering System

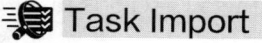

Task I Fault Diagnosis and Repair of Heavy Steering of Hydraulic Power Steering System

Learning Objectives

1. Be able to determine the direction and items of inquiry according to the fault phenomena of the automobile for repair.

2. Be able to prepare a correct fault diagnosis plan according to fault phenomena.

3. Be able to consult maintenance data skillfully, select appropriate detection and diagnosis devices according to fault phenomena and use them skillfully.

4. Be able to test heavy steering of hydraulic power steering system with appropriate maintenance devices according to the diagnosis plan.

5. Be able to correctly analyze the test results and determine the fault location and cause of heavy steering of hydraulic power steering system.

6. Be able to repair the fault parts quickly and accurately and eliminate the hidden troubles.

7. Be able to have strong sense of responsibility, rigorous and careful working attitude, improve team cooperation ability.

Task Import

Task Material: The owner of a Volkswagen Jetta GT said that the car had been turning relatively heavy and after inspection, it was found that the tank lacked power steering fluid. After refueling according to regulations and conducting the test run, the steering was more heavy, seemed to have no power.

Task Requirements: According to the fault phenomena of the car, consult relevant materials, select appropriate detection and diagnosis devices for fault diagnosis and repair, and fill in the task report.

Ⅰ. Fault Analysis

Heavy steering refers to that turning the steering wheel left and right during driving, it feels heavy, after turning, the steering wheel can not be returned timely.

The main reasons for heavy steering are as follows:

(1) Too low tire pressure　Too low tire pressure results in increased steering torque.

(2) Incorrect four-wheel positioning　The four-wheel positioning is inaccurate, such as too large kingpin caster angle and improper kingpin inclination angle, etc.

(3) Failure of mechanical parts

① Each connection fits too tightly, for example: The ball of the drag link is rusted and lacks oil, making the matching clearance too tight, so that the resistance applied to the steering wheel overcoming the steering knuckle rotation increases, so that the steering is not easy.

② Frame deformation and drag link bending make the front wheel positioning parameters incorrect. For example, the frame is deformed and makes the kingpin inclination angle and the kingpin caster angle changed, so that the steering is heavy; The drag link bending makes the front wheel toe-in and front wheel camber larger or smaller, thus increasing the frictional resistance between tire and ground, making the steering heavy.

③ The friction inside the steering gear is increased due to lack of oil and jamming, thus increasing the resistance of overcoming the steering gear and making the steering heavy.

(4) Power steering system failure　The power steering fluid is insufficient; The oil is too dirty and there is air in the oil passage; The drive belt of oil pump slips and the oil pump is seriously worn; The safety valve leaks seriously; The flow control valve is not sealed and leaks seriously, resulting in insufficient pump oil pressure; The sealing ring of steering control valve is not sealed, causing leakage between oil passages; Leakage caused by unsealed steering power cylinder causes insufficient pressure.

Ⅱ. Fault Diagnosis

1. Check tire and fit

First, consider whether the tire pressure is too low and whether the tire specifications meet the requirements. In the case of a newly repaired car, consideration shall be given to whether the assembly of the kingpin and the bushing is too tight, and whether the ball of the drag link is assembled too tightly.

2. Check whether the oil pump drive belt is too loose

If the belt is too loose, the slipping will occur and the pressure of the oil pump is insufficient.

3. Check the quantity and quality of power steering fluid

When the engine is running at idle speed, turn the steering wheel in situ for several times to raise the temperature of hydraulic oil to about 80℃. The oil level shall be at the normal mark of the oil dipstick (when the oil temperature is 80℃, it shall be on the hot scribe line of the oil dipstick and cold scribe line at normal temperature), and check whether the oil in the tank has bubbles and oil is cloudy.

If the oil quantity is insufficient, check whether the bolts of pipe joints and joint sur-

faces are loose, whether the seal is damaged, the oil pipe is cracked. The leaked parts shall be trimmed or replaced.

If there is foam in the oil, the hydraulic system is mixed with air. Exhaust first when the air is mixed in the hydraulic system.

4. Test oil pressure of oil pump

Connect the pressure gauge to the circuit of the power steering unit to raise the oil to 80℃ and keep the engine running at idle speed. If the oil pressure does not reach the specified value and the oil pressure does not rise when the manual valve is gradually closed, it can be judged that the oil pump is faulty or the safety valve is not adjusted properly. It should be disassembled and repaired and the oil pressure shall be adjusted again, and new parts shall be replaced if necessary.

5. Check failure of mechanical parts

Lift the front axle and turn the steering wheel. If the steering is not heavy at this time, it can be judged that the fault is caused by the improper positioning of the front wheels (for example: The kingpin caster angle is too large, the kingpin inclination angle is too small or too large, the front wheel toe-in and front wheel camber is larger or smaller), the four-wheel positioning shall be carried out first. If the steering is heavy at this time, the connection fit is too tight (for example: The drag link ball coordination or kingpin plane bearing fit clearance is too tight) or the steering gear lacks oil or is jammed, the steering shaft/column is bent.

Check whether the drag link is bent and deformed (affecting the kingpin caster angle and the kingpin inclination angle).

Check whether the frame is bent or deformed (which affects the kingpin caster angle and the kingpin inclination angle). If bent or deformed, correct or replace the parts; If not, check whether the steering knuckle is bent (which affects the kingpin caster angle and the kingpin inclination angle); If bent, correct or replace the piece. The inspection shall be carried out in accordance with the principle from easy to difficult.

If the steering is heavy due to too tight connection, check whether the steering ball is too tight, rusted or lack of oil; if it is too tight, rusty or lack of oil, replace the kingpin plane bearing; If it is normal, check whether the kingpin plane bearing is rusted; Replace the kingpin plane bearing if it is rusted; If normal, check the steering shaft for fault.

If the heavy steering is not caused by too tight connection, check whether the steering shaft is bent, and correct or replace the steering shaft in case of bending; If it not bent, check whether the column is concavely bent, and if it is concavely bent, correct or replace it; If not, check the steering gear for lack of oil, jamming, etc.

Ⅲ. Task Implementation

1. Inquiry

The repairman shall know the time of fault from the owner; Whether there are other abnormal conditions before the fault; Whether the symptoms change after finding the fault; Details of driving; Whether the automobile is maintained on time; Have other repairs been performed after the fault. The preliminary diagnosis of heavy steering can be completed by

knowing the situation before and after the fault and the specific information of the fault through the above inquiry.

2. Test-drive and Basic Inspection

Firstly, carry out the test-drive to confirm the fault. Then check whether the tire pressure meets the specified value, check whether the power steering fluid is sufficient and the brake pipeline has obvious oil leakage. No fault is found through the above inspections.

3. Detection and Diagnosis

First check the belt tightness of the power steering pump, which is completely normal. Therefore, it is suspected that the power steering pump is damaged. The test run is conducted after replacing one power steering pump, but the problem is not solved. Turn in place. After observation, it is found that the oil return of power steering pipeline is not good. The oil pipe and the tank are removed and a plastic sheet is found in the tank, which blocks the oil outlet. When the oil level is low, the pressure is small, and the power steering fluid can pass through some, so there is some power action; When the oil is filled up, the pressure is high. Press the plastic sheet on the oil outlet, and the power steering fluid cannot pass through, so it cannot reach the power steering pump and the steering gear, causing no power steering. Why is there a plastic sheet inside the tank? With doubt, check the locking cap carefully and find that a layer of plastic sheet inside the locking cap which acts as oil-proofing falls off, causing the fault.

4. Fault Elimination

Remove the plastic sheet, replace the original power steering pump, replace the tank with a new one, fill the power steering fluid according to the regulations, and then conduct the test run The fault is eliminated.

5. Inspection and Delivery

After troubleshooting and without any other symptoms, hand over the car to the owner.

IV. Task Summary

Usually, when the power steering system fails, we are always to suspect parts such as power steering pump and steering gear first, but rarely carefully inspect pipeline, tank and other small parts. However, sometimes small parts can cause major failures, which requires our attention in future maintenance.

V. Task Report

Major			Class		Name	
Task Name					Class Hours	2
Model			Engine Model			
	Assessment Items		Assessment Contents		Maximum Score	Score
Task Completion Process	1. Description of fault symptoms				5	
	2. Possible causes and analysis of fault				25	
	3. Detection and diagnosis process				35	
	4. Fault Elimination				10	
	5. Summary of fault diagnosis				10	
Teacher Evaluation	Operation quality, operation efficiency, operation safety, etc.				15	
Total Score					100	

VI. Knowledge Expansion

【Typical Case Ⅰ】 Heavy steering of a Toyota Crown 2.8L car.

Fault Description: A Toyota Crown 2.8L car turned heavily, whose wheels could be deflected under more force.

Fault Diagnosis and Repair: Upon inquiry, the owner said that steering during driving was more and more laborious until he felt heavier. It was therefore suspected that there was a problem with the power steering system. Visual inspection was carried out first, and no oil leakage was found; The oil level was checked and the height was normal. Then the oil pump was checked. An oil pressure gauge was connected at the output end of the oil pump and the input terminal of the steering booster. The measured oil pressure was 3.5MPa (the standard value is greater than 7.0MPa), indicating that the oil pressure was too low. The steering wheel was turned to the left or right extreme position, the oil pressure was respectively measured, which was still 3.5MPa, which indicated that the steering booster, safety valve and overflow valve were all normal, and the fault may be in the oil pump. The vane pump was removed and inspected and it was found that the surface of each slide of the vane pump was seriously worn, and the thickness was only 1.35mm (standard value is 1.55mm). The blade was worn, resulting in insufficient oil pressure of oil pump, significantly weakening of power effect and heavy steering. After replacing a set of slides (6 pairs), springs and spring seats, the pump oil pressure was returned to normal and the fault was eliminated.

Summary: During the fault diagnosis, when confirming whether the oil pump is faulty, the method of detecting the oil pressure in the oil circuit during steering is selected for judgment rather than the method of changing parts, which conforms to the diagnosis idea. It should be noted that the values specified in the maintenance manual must be referred when using the test method.

【Typical Case Ⅱ】 Heavy steering of a Santana.

Fault Description: A Santana suddenly appeared heavy steering while the steering wheel was turned during driving.

Fault Diagnosis and Repair: After lifting the front axle and turning the steering wheel, it was felt that the steering wheel rotated heavily, indicating that the fault was not in the front-wheel positioning. When the engine was off, the comparison between the steering wheel rotating in situ and the steering wheel rotating in situ after starting the engine showed that both steering wheels were heavy, which indicated that the fault position was in the hydraulic power steering mechanism. The tightness of drive belt of the power steering pump was checked with proper tightness. The engine was started, and the liquid level of transmission fluid was checked. It was found that the liquid level was low. Then the transmission fluid was filled to the normal liquid level. After test run, it was found that the fault was slightly improved, but the steering was still heavy. It indicated that the heavy steering was not only caused by insufficient transmission fluid, but also for other reasons.

It was thought that there was probably air in the transmission fluid, and there were bubbles in the liquid surface after the large steering test in situ. At the same time, combined with the low liquid level, it indicated that there was leakage in the hydraulic system. Then

the engine was started, the steering wheel was turned to the left or right extreme position and fixed, so that the oil pressure in the pipe reached the maximum value. The distribution valve, rack seal and inlet and return pipe joints were carefully inspected and it was found that there was oil leakage at the oil inlet pipe joint. After replacing the sealing ring of oil inlet pipe joint and fastening the sealing ring bolt, the steering wheel was continuously turned to the left and right extreme positions until the liquid level was stable and no bubbles emerged. Through road test, the steering wheel can be turned lightly and freely.

Summary: When oil leakage occurs in the pipeline of power steering mechanism, there will be air in the transmission fluid in the pipeline, affecting the transmission of power. At the same time, since the pipeline leaks when turning the steering wheel, it also causes insufficient pressure in the pipeline, so there is a heavy feeling when turning the steering wheel.

Task II Fault Diagnosis and Repair of Heavy Steering of Electronic Power Steering System

Learning Objectives

1. Be able to determine the direction and items of inquiry according to the fault phenomena of the automobile for repair.

2. Be able to prepare a correct fault diagnosis plan according to fault phenomena.

3. Be able to consult maintenance data skillfully, select appropriate detection and diagnosis devices according to fault phenomena and use them skillfully.

4. Be able to test heavy steering of the electronic power steering system with appropriate maintenance devices according to the diagnosis plan.

5. Be able to analyze the test results correctly and determine the fault location and cause of the heavy steering of the electronic power steering system.

6. Be able to repair the fault parts quickly and accurately and eliminate the hidden troubles.

Task Import

Task Material: A 2011 Magotan car, while driving, the electronic power steering wheel light occurred red alarm, the steering was heavy instantly, and it was unable to drive normally. After the fault occurred, the owner, to recover the car under emergency, turned off the key, removed the negative electrode of the battery, and tried to remove the fault by power-off test. After reinstalling the negative electrode of the battery, the fault remained.

Task Requirements: According to the fault phenomena of the car, consult relevant materials, select appropriate detection and diagnosis devices for fault diagnosis and repair, and fill in the task report.

I. Fault Analysis

There are several reasons for the heavy steering of the electronic power steering system:

（1）Failure of CAN line causes signal communication failure.

（2）Failure of steering gear circuit, such as open fuse or false connection, poor grounding, etc.

（3）Open circuit or false connection of power supply and ground wire of steering gear control unit.

（4）The signal of the steering angle sensor is poor.

（5）Internal failure of steering gear control unit.

II. Fault Diagnosis

First, use the scan tool to read the fault code, and determine the direction of fault detection by analyzing the fault code. If the CAN line fault causes the failure of signal communication, the fault code will be stored in the electronic control unit. Then use the multimeter for circuit detection, check whether the signal of the steering angle sensor is normal, and check whether there is mechanical failure of the steering gear. If all parts of the steering system are checked to be normal, the fault will be in the electronic control unit.

III. Task Implementation

1. Inquiry

The repairman shall know the time of fault from the owner; Whether there are other abnormal conditions before the fault; Whether the symptoms change after finding the fault; Details of driving; Whether the automobile is maintained on time; Have other repairs been performed after the fault. Find out the situation before and after the fault and the specific information of the fault through the above inquiry, and complete the preliminary diagnosis of high oil pressure.

2. Test-drive and Basic Inspection

The repairman shall firstly check whether the amount of engine oil is normal, then start the engine, observe whether the exhaust pipe has blue smoke and the extent of blue smoke; Observe whether the engine operating condition changes and the symptoms change; Observe engine external components for obvious oil leakage.

3. Detection and Diagnosis

For normal cars, after the battery line is removed and the ignition switch is turned on, the electronic power steering wheel light shall display yellow, but the car is red when the battery line is removed. See Figure 8-1.

Figure 8-1 Electronic Power Steering Wheel Light Shows Red

（1）Use VAS5051 to enter gateway list detection and display address code 44 Power steering system malfunction.

（2）Enter 44-02 address code, detect fault code of 00569, meaning current, power steering motor exceeds upper limit.

Enter the 44-05 fault clearing function, the fault code can be cleared and the steering

wheel red alarm light can be turned off, but the steering wheel is still heavy. After ignition, the red alarm light is on again, and the fault code is still 00569.

(3) Go to 44-08 to view the data flow. It can be seen from data flow 08-02 that the power supply is normal; The engine running state can be identified in the control unit and the engine speed is normal as seen in 08-03.

The precondition for power steering operation is positive No. 15 and normal engine speed, and the above data indicates that the precondition is normal.

Read data 08-04. It can be seen from the 08-04 data that the display 6 in the data area Ⅰ belongs to the fault state (the normal power steering system data shall be 3, i. e. the system is normal). Data area Ⅱ indicates that the ignition switch is on.

Read data flow 08-05. For a working steering gear, the 08-05 data flow shall be constantly changing during steering. The data shall be area Ⅰ: theoretical value of power steering torque of $\pm 5 \mathrm{N} \cdot \mathrm{m}$; area Ⅱ: $\pm 5 \mathrm{N} \cdot \mathrm{m}$; area Ⅲ: Output torque of power steering motor $\mathrm{MAX} = 4.375 \mathrm{N} \cdot \mathrm{m}$; area Ⅳ: Torque of torsion bar $\mathrm{MAX} = 11 \mathrm{N} \cdot \mathrm{m}$. The four areas of the car display $0.000 \mathrm{N} \cdot \mathrm{m}$, according to which it can be seen that torque sensor G269 has no torque output.

Read data 08-06. Normally operating power steering system, area Ⅱ shows: On. However, the area Ⅱ of the car is shown as: Off, indicating that the steering gear is not working at all.

Read data 08-07. It can be seen from the data that the steering angle sensor G85 is working normally, which indicates that the fault cause of the car is independent of G85.

Read data 08-125 and 08-126, indicating that communication between the control units is normal.

According to the comprehensive analysis of the above data, the steering auxiliary control unit J500 does not control the booster motor of the steering gear to operate.

(4) To further analyze the reason why the booster motor is not working, analyze the circuit diagram and check the circuit.

Check SA2 and SC3 fuses, normal. Check and find that the grounding wire under the air filter housing (i. e. grounding point 2) and plug contact are normal.

(5) Comprehensively judge that steering auxiliary control unit J500 does not control the booster motor of the steering gear to operate. Since the steering auxiliary control unit J500 and the steering gear mechanism are an assembly, the steering gear assembly should be replaced.

4. Fault Elimination

After replacing the steering gear assembly, turn on the ignition switch, and the steering wheel red light turns yellow immediately. Turn the steering wheel to the left/right extreme position, and return to the middle position. After starting for 20m, the ESP light and the steering wheel light go out simultaneously. The fault code in 44-02 is eliminated automatically, and the steering wheel power steering is returned to normal.

So far, the heavy steering of the steering wheel is eliminated and the car resumes normal operation.

5. Inspection and Delivery

After troubleshooting and without any other symptoms, hand over the car to the owner.

IV. Task Summary

(1) For the new Volkswagen models (PQ35, PQ46), it is almost ineffective to eliminate the fault memory by disconnecting the battery line.

(2) Fault diagnosis of this car is easier because of fault code prompt. The key is to note that after replacing the steering gear assembly, it feels that the steering gear assists and the electronic power steering wheel light is off, and the fault is not completely eliminated at this time. It is necessary to enter the steering auxiliary device 44 address code for the activation setting of the new steering wheel assembly, change 1 to 0 in 44-10-03, store it and clear the fault code 03 ABS. In the gateway list check, after each system is completely normal, the fault is completely eliminated and the car returns to normal.

V. Task Report

Major			Class		Name	
Task Name					Class Hours	2
Model			Engine Model			
		Assessment Items	Assessment Contents		Maximum Score	Score
Task Completion Process		1. Description of fault symptoms			5	
		2. Possible causes and analysis of fault			25	
		3. Detection and diagnosis process			35	
		4. Fault Elimination			10	
		5. Summary of fault diagnosis			10	
Teacher Evaluation		Operation quality, operation efficiency, operation safety, etc.			15	
Total Score					100	

VI. Knowledge Expansion

【Typical Case Ⅰ】 Heavy steering of a Volkswagen CC car.

Fault Description: The owner of a 2010 Volkswagen CC car, driving 120, 000 km, said that the car turned heavily while driving and the indicator red light alarmed.

Fault Diagnosis and Repair: The causes of heavy steering was analyzed, and the main causes of the fault are as follows:

(1) CAN line system failure.

(2) The fuses SC3 and SA2 are open-circuited or falsely connected.

(3) The ground wire of the steering gear control unit is open-circuited or falsely connected.

(4) The power plug of steering gear is loose.

(5) Internal failure of steering gear control unit.

For the electronic power steering of the Volkswagen CC car, steering power is controlled by power steering control unit, so the system self-diagnosis is first used for analysis.

The gateway list was detected by the Volkswagen special scan tool VAS5052, and the systems of other units except address 44 were normal. The address 44 fault code is shown in

Figure 8-2.

Based on reading the gateway list, the systems other than address 44 were normal, and the fault code of address 44 could be read, the CAN bus system fault was first eliminated.

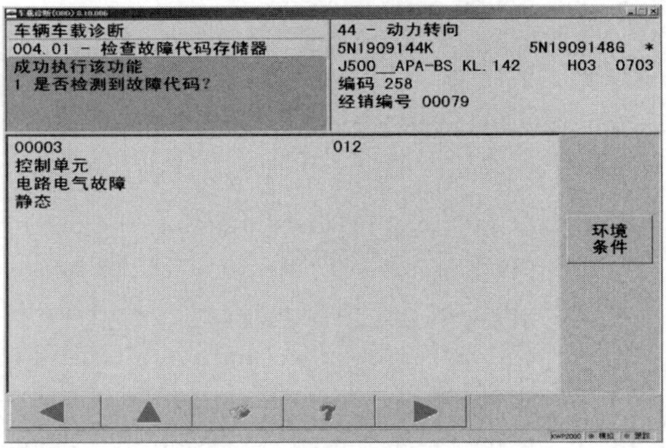

Based on the circuit diagram analysis, the following results were obtained:

(1) The SA2 and SC3 fuses had open circuit or false connection.

(2) The grounding point and circuit of steering gear control unit were free of false connection.

Figure 8-2　Address 44 Fault Code

(3) After removing the plug of steering gear control unit for inspection, no looseness was found. Its voltage measured with a multimeter was 12.65V (power supply was normal).

(4) After excluding the above possible factors, it may be an internal problem with the steering gear control unit.

Therefore, the steering gear was replaced and matched. then the car was running uniformly at a speed lower than 20km/h, the steering wheel was turned to the left to the bottom and then the brake was applied. After hearing three alarm sounds, the steering wheel was turned to the right to the bottom and then the brake was applied. After hearing three alarm sounds, the steering wheel was returned to straight. At this time, the yellow indicator light went out. The system fault code was cleared and the test-drive was done. The fault was eliminated.

Summary: The fault diagnosis process combines the diagnosis of the scan tool with the use of the circuit diagram, and conducts an analysis based on the working principle of the power steering system. The diagnosis process is relatively logical. We should pay attention to diagnosis and analysis, avoid relying on experience to disassemble and replace parts blindly, which is the basic capability required for diagnosis of the electronic control system.

[Typical Case Ⅱ]　Heavy steering of a Volkswagen POLO car.

Fault Description: A Volkswagen POLO car, manual transmission, driving 150,000 km, turned heavily while driving, and occasionally, all fault warning lights on the instrument panel flashed and alarmed.

Fault Diagnosis and Repair: The test run was conducted, the ignition switch was turned on, and the instrument indicators display normally. After starting, it was found that the steering was really heavy. The power steering malfunction indicator on the instrument panel was on after a long drive. The scan tool was used to enter the "power steering" system to read out the fault code and the fault code was 01309 power steering (J500) control unit. After clearing the fault code and starting the engine, all the fault warning lights on the instrument panel flashed and alarmed. The scan tool was connected again but it could not enter the "power steering" system. The scan tool was used to enter the engine system for detection and the result showed that the system was normal. After entering the onboard network

control unit, 2 fault codes were found: 01312 Powertrain data bus; 01760 Power steering control unit (J500) no communication. After entering the gateway (J533) data bus, two identical fault codes were detected. The circuit and wire of the power steering control unit were checked according to the circuit diagram, which were normal. Next gateway J533 was checked. Because the gateway J533 is integrated with the onboard network control unit J519, only the onboard network control unit J519 could be replaced. After replacement, the fault still remained. The fault may also be related to the power steering control unit according to the warning of the previously detected fault codes. Then the plug on the power steering control unit J500 was pulled off. After seeing the instrument panel, it was found that the alarm lights were off except for the power steering alarm light. At this point, when the fault was found and the power steering control unit was replaced, the power steering control unit was coded with a scan tool and the fault was eliminated.

Summary: This car adopts a new generation of CAN-BUS system to exchange data between controllers of the car. The control units in the system adopt copper cable (twisted pair) serial connection mode, that is, each control unit is connected serially. The failure of the other control units to communicate due to damage to the power steering control unit is a short circuit in the CAN-BUS system wiring in the control unit.

Item IX

Fault Diagnosis and Repair of Brake System

Brake system failures can be divided into poor braking, braking failure, braking deviation, braking dragging and parking brake failure.

Because the structure and working principle of various types of braking systems are different, although the failure phenomena of brake systems are basically the same, the causes of failure are different, so the fault diagnosis should be different. It should also be noted that the cause of brake system failure shall not be limited to the braking device. System failures such as frame, suspension, traveling mechanism, road conditions, loading conditions and other external conditions can also affect the effectiveness of brake system. Using the brake test bench to test the automobile brake is very helpful for fault diagnosis and elimination.

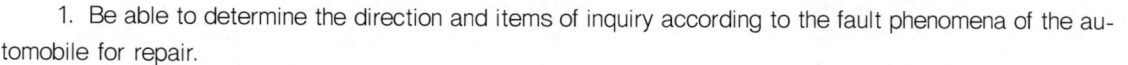

Task I Fault Diagnosis and Repair of Insufficient Braking Force

Learning Objectives

1. Be able to determine the direction and items of inquiry according to the fault phenomena of the automobile for repair.

2. Be able to prepare a correct fault diagnosis plan according to fault phenomena.

3. Be able to consult maintenance data skillfully, select appropriate detection and diagnosis devices according to fault phenomena and use them skillfully.

4. Be able to detect the insufficient braking force with appropriate maintenance devices according to the diagnosis plan.

5. Be able to correctly analyze the detection results and determine the fault location and cause of insufficient braking force.

6. Be able to repair the fault parts quickly and accurately and eliminate the hidden troubles.

7. Be able to work rigorously and carefully, and improve safety and service awareness.

Task Import

Task Material: A Toyota VIOS 1.5L, driving 160, 000 kilometers. The owner said

that the car's braking force was insufficient, and the symptoms were getting worse.

Task Requirements: According to the fault phenomena of the car, consult relevant materials, select appropriate detection and diagnosis devices for fault diagnosis and repair, and fill in the task report.

I. Fault Analysis

Insufficient braking force means that the braking efficiency decreases significantly, the braking deceleration is insufficient and the braking distance becomes longer. There are no tire trails or short trails on the ground (except for automobiles with ABS).

The main reasons for insufficient braking force are as follows:

(1) The brake fluid in the brake system is insufficient or deteriorated.

(2) There is gas in the brake lines.

(3) The brake friction disks are worn too much.

(4) The brake pedal free stroke is too large and the pedal drive mechanism is loose.

(5) Failure of brake master cylinder: The piston and cylinder wall of hydraulic master cylinder wear too much, resulting in loose fit and oil leakage; The oil outlet valve spring of hydraulic master cylinder is too soft or broken, or the sealing of oil outlet valve is not tight; The oil return valve of hydraulic master valve is not sealed tightly; The oil return hole of hydraulic master valve is blocked.

(6) Fault of brake cylinder: Aging, swelling, wear, or deformation of the cup or collar of the hydraulic cylinder; The piston and cylinder wall of hydraulic cylinder wear too much, resulting in loose fit and oil leakage; The piston return spring of hydraulic cylinder is too soft or broken.

(7) Brake line fault: The brake pipeline is concave, damaged and leaks oil, and the brake hose is aged and expanded; Damage, looseness and poor sealing of brake pipe joint lead to oil leakage.

(8) Vacuum servo brake failure: The vacuum pipe joints are damaged or loose, leading to air leakage; Vacuum tubes are broken, concave and twisted, leading to air leakage; The one-way valve of vacuum gas tank is not sealed tightly; The air valve or vacuum valve in control valves is not sealed tightly; The diaphragm of control valve is damaged; The piston and collar of the control valve are worn, and the seal is poor; The diaphragm of the afterburner chamber is broken; The piston of the booster cylinder wears too much, and the wear of the collar causes oil leakage; The piston return spring of the booster cylinder is too soft; The sealing of piston ball valve of booster cylinder is poor.

II. Fault Diagnosis

(1) Check whether brake system leaks, brake fluid level and oil quality are normal.

(2) Check whether the brake friction disc is too thin.

(3) Check whether the pedal free stroke and brake stroke are normal.

(4) Check whether the brake vacuum booster operates normally.

(5) Check brake lines for abnormalities.

(6) Replace brake fluid and bleed.

（7）Check brake oil pressure during braking and judge whether brake master cylinder is normal.

Ⅲ. Task Implementation

1. Inquiry

Know the time of fault from the owner; Check whether there is abnormal condition before the fault; The road condition of the car; mileage; Whether the car is maintained on time; Has it been repaired after the fault occurred. Find out the situation before and after the fault and the specific information of the fault through the above inquiry, and complete the preliminary diagnosis of insufficient braking force.

2. Test-drive and Basic Inspection

Carry out the test drive, confirm the fault, and check whether the brake fluid level and oil quality are normal.

3. Detection and Diagnosis

It is known from communication with the owner that the brake friction disk has been replaced shortly, so the excessive wear of friction disc is temporarily eliminated. Check whether the pedal free stroke and brake stroke are normal. Check whether the vacuum booster operates normally. Check whether the brake pipeline is abnormal such as concave and flat. Replace the brake fluid and carry out exhaust test run, and the problem remains. When the brake oil pressure is detected during braking, it is found that the brake oil pressure is obviously lower than the normal value, thus judging that the brake master cylinder is faulty.

4. Fault Elimination

The fault is eliminated after replacing the brake master cylinder.

5. Inspection and Delivery

After troubleshooting, the brake is completely normal, and the car is handed over to the owner.

Ⅳ. Task Summary

In a conventional fault diagnosis such as insufficient braking force, it is sufficient to perform that diagnosis from large to small according to the probability that the braking force is insufficient, and the diagnosis is not carried out completely according to the experience. Especially for the fault judgment of master cylinder, it must be judged through the detection of brake oil pressure, and the replacement test shall not be carried out blindly.

Ⅴ. Task Report

Major			Class		Name	
Task Name					Class Hours	2
Model			Engine Model			
	Assessment Items		Assessment Contents		Maximum Score	Score
Task Completion Process	1. Description of fault symptoms				5	
	2. Possible causes and analysis of fault				25	
	3. Detection and diagnosis process				35	
	4. Fault Elimination				10	
	5. Summary of fault diagnosis				10	
Teacher Evaluation	Operation quality, operation efficiency, operation safety, etc.				15	
Total Score					100	

VI. Knowledge Expansion

[Typical Case Ⅰ] Insufficient braking force of a Beijing Hyundai Elantra.

Fault Description: The owner of a Beijing Hyundai Elantra, traveling 160, 000 kilometers, said that the car had insufficient braking force.

Fault Diagnosis and Repair: Firstly, the brake fluid was checked and it was found that the brake fluid was insufficient, and the brake fluid was somewhat deteriorated. It was known from communication with the owner that the brake fluid had never been replaced.

The brake fluid was replaced and the brake fluid was bled. The brake friction disc was not worn and not replaced. The fault was still found after the test run.

The brake pipeline had concave and deformed parts.

When the brake oil pressure is detected during braking, it is found that the brake oil pressure is obviously lower than the normal value, thus judging that the brake master cylinder is faulty. The brake master cylinder was replaced and the fault was found to remain after the test run.

It was thought that the fault could only occur in the ABS pump. Therefore, the ABS pump was replaced and the fault was eliminated after the test drive.

Summary: In case of such faults, the brake oil pressure shall be detected when no fault was found by the routine inspection, so as to avoid repeated disassembly and assembly and save diagnosis time. Attention shall be paid to connecting the oil pressure gauge to the brake header during oil pressure detection.

[Typical Case Ⅱ] Insufficient braking force of a PASSAT 1. 8T car.

Fault Description: A PASSAT 1. 8T manual transmission car, driving 80, 000 kilometers. The owner said that he felt the brake was soft when braking and seemed that it could not make the car to stop.

Fault Diagnosis and Repair: The test run was carried out first and the failure was found to be exactly as described by the owner. Reasons for poor braking and long braking distance include: Insufficient brake fluid; The brake master cylinder is faulty; The brake cylinder is faulty; Excessive wear of brake block and brake disc; There is air in the brake pipeline; Poor brake fluid performance.

The above were checked item by Item according to the above analysis. Firstly the brake fluid was checked and was within the specified range, the brake pipeline and oil pipe joints were well fastened without looseness and leakage, and the oil pipe was free of aging and deformation; Brake cylinder cup was in good condition without brake fluid leakage; Brake disc and brake block were worn normally; The color of brake fluid was clear and transparent.

The brake system was bled without air in the line. According to past experience, the brake master cylinder causes the most of this failure. Therefore the brake master cylinder was replaced. The fault was gone after the test drive. So the car was delivered to the owner. After a week, the owner came back and said the same fault. Therefore, the brake fluid, pipeline and other components were thoroughly inspected again, and no abnormality was found. So it was known after carefully asking the owner that, only after a long period of driving, and when driving in the city and frequently braking, the failure occurred, and the

Item IX　Fault Diagnosis and Repair of Brake System　**155**

probability of appearing in the morning was small, the probability of appearance in the afternoon was large. Based on the situation said by the owner, a further careful analysis was made, suspecting that the brake performance was degraded by thermal decay. However, frequently used brakes do not affect braking by overheating the brakes, and this had not occurred in other car. It was thought that the failure was probably caused by poorer brake disc ventilation and heat dissipation performance. The front brake disc was removed for inspection and it was found that there was a lot of dirt in the vent slot in the middle of the brake disc, so it was determined that the cause of the fault was on the front brake disc. Because there was dirt blockage in the vent slot of the brake disc, the heat dissipation of the brake was poor, affecting the braking performance. Therefore, the two front brake discs were cleaned and reinstalled. After the test drive, everything was normal. This fault has not occurred again.

Summary: The reason for this failure is that the brake performance was reduced due to thermal decay due to poor brake disc ventilation and heat dissipation, which is rarely encountered in maintenance. The only factors affecting the insufficient braking force are the relevant components in the braking system. The maintenance personnel should understand the working principle of braking system, and need to do full inquiry to understand the conditions, environment and rules of failure, etc. This information can help the maintenance personnel determine the direction of fault diagnosis.

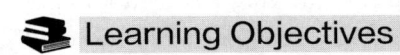

Task II Fault Diagnosis and Repair of Brake Deviation

Learning Objectives

1. Be able to determine the direction and items of inquiry according to the fault phenomena of the automobile for repair.

2. Be able to prepare a correct fault diagnosis plan according to fault phenomena.

3. Be able to consult maintenance data skillfully, select appropriate detection and diagnosis devices according to fault phenomena and use them skillfully.

4. Be able to detect the brake deviation with suitable maintenance devices according to the diagnosis plan.

5. Be able to correctly analyze the detection results and determine the fault position and cause of brake deviation.

6. Be able to repair the fault parts quickly and accurately and eliminate the hidden troubles.

Task Import

Task Material: The owner of a 2011 Jetta, driving 90, 000 kilometers, said the car slightly drifted when braking.

Task Requirements: According to the fault phenomena of the car, consult relevant materials, select appropriate detection and diagnosis devices for fault diagnosis and repair, and fill in the task report.

Ⅰ. Fault Analysis

The braking deviation means that when braking, the car's ability to maintain straight driving becomes poor, and it cannot stop along the straight line, but deviates to the side of the road.

The main factors affecting car braking deviation include brake, suspension system, front wheel positioning and tire etc.

1. Effect of brake

(1) Coaxial left and right braking forces are not equal. During the test drive, this phenomenon mainly shows that when the emergency braking occurs, the wheel on one side is locked, and the other wheel only slows down without locking. The car deflected towards the side of the wheel that was locked. From the drag between the brake wheels and the ground, one side has a deep trail, while the other side has a shallow, even no trail. The main causes of this failure are: The diaphragm of certain brake air chamber is broken or the sealing ring of the brake cylinder is damaged, and the brake air pipe or oil pipe leaks air or leaks oil; When a brake air chamber push rod is deformed or stuck, the piston of the brake cylinder bites; A certain brake camshaft is rusty, the action is not flexible, and the regulator is damaged; The brake shoe bearing pin is rusty and bites; Clearance between left and right brakes and shoes varies; The friction discs of the left and right brakes have different materials, uneven thickness and different friction coefficients; A brake friction disc has oil stain.

(2) Coaxial left and right braking forces increase inconsistently. This phenomenon manifested in a test run is that the wheel on one side decelerates quickly while wheel on the other side decelerates slowly, when the car brakes, the car obviously deviates to the side where the wheel decelerates fast during the deceleration. The main causes of this failure are: The tension of return springs of left and right brakes varies; Length of push rods of left and right brake air chambers is inconsistent; Individual brake drums are seriously worn or out of round; The camshaft bushing and the shoe bearing pin of individual wheels are loose, etc.

2. Effect of suspension system

Car frame deformation and suspension system failure will cause uneven wheel load distribution, incorrect front wheel positioning, front and rear axle displacement, etc., which will lead to brake deviation. When braking, under the condition that the braking force of the left and right wheels is equal and the braking force increase is consistent, the wheel bearing the small load must be locked first, and the wheel with large load must be locked afterwards due to the action of inertia, so the brake deviation occurs. This phenomenon is obvious only when the car is loaded, and generally does not occur under no-load condition. There is also no apparent response to inspection on the brake test bench. The main causes of this failure are: Deformation of frame; Damage of shock absorber; Deformation, fracture and fatigue of leaf spring; Deformation of guide bar or balance bar of suspension system, etc. The uneven stacking of goods during loading will also result in uneven distribution of left and right wheel loads, leading to brake deviation.

3. Front wheel positioning

Incorrect front wheel positioning will cause "swing" of steering wheel, automatic "devi-

ation" of steering wheel, abnormal wear of tires, etc., which will damage the stability of car driving, and also cause brake deviation during braking, mainly deviation during front braking. During the test drive, it can be found that the direction of brake deviation is not constant, but sometimes left sometimes right. There is no apparent reaction when tested on the brake test bench. The main causes of this failure are: Deformation of frame; Damage and deformation of suspension system; Deformation of front axle; Loose steering knuckle and improper toe-in adjustment, etc.

In addition, when the car is seriously overloaded, the frame is deformed and the radian of the spring steel plate changes greatly, which will also lead to incorrect positioning of the front wheel, causing the brake deviation. This phenomenon should be highly valued by the driver to avoid safety accidents. Displacement of front and rear axles (large left and right wheelbase differences), deformation of frame, loosening of U-shaped bolts of front and rear axle spring steel plates, fracture of central bolts of spring steel plates may cause displacement of front and rear axles (excessive left and right wheelbase differences), leading to running deviation during straight driving and braking.

4. Effect of tire

To realize braking, the car needs not only enough braking force, but also enough adhesion coefficient between tire and ground. If the air pressure, pattern and wear degree of the coaxial tires are inconsistent, the adhesion coefficients of the tires will be different, which may cause the brake deviation. Unequal tire sizes on the same axle (diameters are not equal) will result in unequal braking forces generated by the left and right wheels and also lead to brake deviation. During the road test, it can be found that the brake deviation caused by the tire is also irregular, sometimes left sometimes right. Therefore, when repairing the car, the tires shall be properly allocated and replaced in time according to the regulations to avoid abnormal wear. Because of the muddy road surface, unevenness and deflection, the brake deviation will also occur when the car brakes, which requires that the road test must be done on a straight, dry and clean cement or asphalt pavement with high adhesion coefficient, to eliminate the influence of road factors on the brake deviation.

II. Fault Diagnosis

(1) Check whether the pressures and specifications of left and right tires are the same.

(2) Check whether the frame and the suspension system are deformed.

(3) Carry out the road test (the function of ABS system is canceled), make emergency braking, observe the road tire trailing mark. The brake on the side where there is no drag mark or short drag marks is faulty, should be carefully inspected, such as thickness of friction disc, wear degree of brake drum, working condition of brake cylinder, etc.

4. Perform four-wheel positioning test to see if the front wheel positioning angle is abnormal.

III. Task Implementation

1. Inquiry

Know the time of fault from the owner; Check whether there is abnormal condition be-

fore the fault; The road condition of the car; mileage; Whether the car is maintained on time; Has it been repaired after the fault occurred. Find out the situation before and after the fault and the specific information of the fault through the above inquiry, and complete the preliminary diagnosis of brake deviation.

2. Test-drive and Basic Inspection

Carry out test run to confirm the fault, check whether the tire pressure and specifications are consistent, whether the car body is tilted, etc.

3. Detection and Diagnosis

(1) Remove the ABS computer plug for the test drive. When the car speed reaches 45km/h, pull the handbrake. It is found that the right rear wheel brake brakes normally, and the left rear wheel does not brake, which is abnormal.

(2) The test drive indicates that the left rear wheel has insufficient braking force. It may be that the brake drum and the brake disc are poorly fitted and the braking force is low.

(3) Remove the left rear wheel brake drum and check. It is found that there is no oil stain and installation problem and the brake discs are normal. It is judged that the fit clearance between the brake drum and the brake disc is too large.

4. Fault Elimination

Remove the left rear brake disc and replace it. During the test run, it can brakes normally without drifting. The fault is eliminated.

5. Inspection and Delivery

After troubleshooting, the brake is normal without any other symptoms. Hand over the car to the owner.

Ⅳ. Task Summary

This fault is that the left rear wheel brake drum is worn too much and the braking force is significantly lower than the right rear wheel. After replacing the left and right brake discs, the left and right braking forces are equal, and the brake drifting fault disappears. The fault is relatively simple and can be eliminated by using the routine brake deviation fault diagnosis process.

Ⅴ. Task Report

Major			Class		Name	
Task Name					Class Hours	2
Model				Engine Model		
		Assessment Items	Assessment Contents		Maximum Score	Score
Task Completion Process		1. Description of fault symptoms			5	
		2. Possible causes and analysis of fault			25	
		3. Detection and diagnosis process			35	
		4. Fault Elimination			10	
		5. Summary of fault diagnosis			10	
Teacher Evaluation		Operation quality, operation efficiency, operation safety, etc.			15	
Total Score					100	

Item Ⅸ Fault Diagnosis and Repair of Brake System

VI. Knowledge Expansion

【Typical Case Ⅰ】 Brake deviation of a Beijing BJ2022 "Yongshi".

Fault Description: A Beijing BJ2022 "Yongshi", when braking, the right front wheel had no drag mark, and the direction deviates to left too much.

Fault Diagnosis and Repair: The test run was carried out. It was found that the braking force of the right front wheel was insufficient. The right front tire was removed. The clearance between the brake shoe of the right front wheel and the brake drum was too large, but after being adjusted according to the standard, the fault could not be eliminated. The drive mechanism of the front brake of the car was checked. When stepping on the brake pedal, it was found that the deformation of the right front wheel brake air chamber bracket was larger than that of the left front wheel, and the return spring of the brake air chamber was skewed, and the connecting fork of push rod could not reach the corresponding position. After replacing the right front brake air chamber and the brake arm adjustment assembly, the fault was eliminated.

Summary: Because the right front wheel brake air chamber bracket deformed too much, the return spring of brake air chamber was skewed, and the connecting fork of push rod could not be in place, which caused the effective working stroke of the brake air chamber push rod to decrease, the braking force of the right front wheel to decline, causing brake deviation.

【Typical Case Ⅱ】 Drifting of a Volkswagen Sagitar 1. 8TSI under emergency brake.

Fault Description: A Volkswagen Sagitar 1. 8TSI, driving 79, 000 km. During emergency braking, the car drifted. At this time, ABS worked normally.

Fault Diagnosis and Repair: Through inspection, it was found that the drifting was serious during emergency braking, and the left front wheel had no braking force.

The left front wheel was removed and inspected to check the brake disc and the brake caliper. No leakage or other problems were found. After bleeding the brake system according to "Sagitar2006 brake device", there was no braking force on the left front wheel after the test drive and the drifting during braking remained.

The brake system was checked and no abnormal deformation or crushing traces of the brake pipeline were found. Then the brake system detection device V. A. G1310A and adaptor V. A. G1310/6 were connected to conduct the sealing test under pressure, and the test result complied with the requirements of maintenance manual: The brake pedal was pre-pressed, the pressure drop did not exceed 400 kPa during the test period of 45 seconds. Pressure drop met the standard.

When the left front wheel was connected with V. A. G1310A and the brake pedal was stepped down quickly, the left front wheel pressure gauge rose slowly (the right front wheel could reach 10MPa quickly). It turned out that the braking force of left front wheel came too late, which resulted in unbalanced braking force, and drifting when braking. The fault was eliminated after replacing the ABS pump.

Summary: The braking system is at the stage of pressure build-up during braking. If the increase of wheel braking forces on both sides is different, the car will deviate or

drift. Measuring the brake pressure during braking is a better way to judge whether the braking system is faulty.

Task Ⅲ   Fault Diagnosis and Repair of ABS System

Learning Objectives

1. Be able to determine the direction and items of inquiry according to the fault phenomena of the automobile for repair.

2. Be able to prepare a correct fault diagnosis plan according to fault phenomena.

3. Be able to consult maintenance data skillfully, select appropriate detection and diagnosis devices according to fault phenomena and use them skillfully.

4. Be able to detect ABS system failure with appropriate maintenance devices according to the diagnosis plan.

5. Be able to correctly analyze the detection results and determine the fault location and cause of ABS system.

6. Be able to repair the fault parts quickly and accurately and eliminate the hidden troubles.

Task Import

Task Material: A 2010 Sagitar 1.6L manual transmission sedan, whose ABS warning light is on and can't be extinguished.

Task Requirements: According to the fault phenomena of the car, consult relevant materials, select appropriate detection and diagnosis devices for fault diagnosis and repair, and fill in the task report.

Ⅰ. Fault Analysis

The electronic control unit of ABS system has self-diagnosis function. When the electronic control unit detects the system failure, the electronic control unit will illuminate the fault indicator light and store the fault code in the electronic control unit.

Common ABS system failure causes are as follows:

(1) Failure of the wheel speed sensor results in no signal or poor signal.

(2) The ABS system circuit is faulty.

(3) The electronic control unit is faulty.

(4) The hydraulic control unit is faulty.

Ⅱ. Fault Diagnosis

The scan tool is used to read the fault code and to determine the detection direction of fault by analyzing the fault code. Then a multimeter is used for detection, including the wheel speed sensor plug, signal and wiring; Electric control unit power supply, grounding, signal circuit, etc. In addition, it can be judged whether the ABS hydraulic control unit operates normally by detecting the brake oil pressure.

Item Ⅸ   Fault Diagnosis and Repair of Brake System   **161**

If all parts of the system are checked to be normal, the fault will be in the electronic control unit.

III. Task Implementation

1. Inquiry

Know the time of fault from the owner; Check whether there is abnormal condition before the fault; The road condition of the car; mileage; Whether the car is maintained on time; Has it been repaired after the fault occurred. The preliminary diagnosis of ABS system fault shall be completed by knowing the situation before and after the fault and the specific information of the fault.

2. Test-drive and Basic Inspection

First conduct the test-drive to confirm the fault, and check whether the brake fluid oil level and oil quality are normal.

3. Detection and Diagnosis

Use the Volkswagen special scan tool VAS5051 to detect and find a fault with signal error of the right rear wheel speed sensor, which can not be cleared. Enter the ABS control unit to read the data block, look at group 001. It is found that Groups 1, 2 and 4 change back and forth between ON and OFF, and only group 3 is always ON. Therefore, it is judged that the failure may be caused by the following aspects:

(1) Right rear wheel speed sensor is faulty.

(2) There is a short circuit or an open circuit in the right rear wheel speed sensor wire.

(3) The right rear target wheel is damaged or there is foreign matter between it with the sensor.

(4) The ABS control unit has internal failure.

Firstly, check the right rear wheel speed sensor. No damage is found from the external appearance. Measure the resistance of two internal plugs. No accurate values are obtained. Compare it with the wheel speed sensor on the left side and find that the two sensors are consistent. Basically judge that the wheel speed sensor is normal.

To further determine the judgment just now, replace the new wheel speed sensor. The fault code can be cleared after replacement, but the ABS alarm light is still on. After the road test is conducted for a while, and then 5051 is used to detect, the result is the same. It is determined that the wheel speed sensor is normal.

Check the connecting wire from ABS pump to the wheel speed sensor, and measure with a multimeter and find no short circuit or open circuit.

Next check the target wheel of the wheel speed sensor. Remove the external brake cylinder bracket and other components and find that the target wheel is integrated with the bearing, and some iron chips are sucked on the magnetic surface. It is suspected that this is the cause of the failure.

4. Fault Elimination

Clean the surfaces of the target wheel and the bearing. After they are reinstalled, the test drive is carried out and the fault is eliminated.

5. Inspection and Delivery

After troubleshooting, the test drive is done, and the ABS warning light is off, the braking was normal without any other symptoms, and the car is handed over to the owner.

Ⅳ. Task Summary

The wheel speed sensor and target wheel of this car adopt similar structure to Jetta SDI engine speed sensor. The target wheel and the rear wheel bearing are integrated together with spaced magnetic poles, which lead to abnormal sensor signal after absorbing iron chips, which turns on the fault light.

The fault memory and data block read by 5051 basically determine the possible factors causing the fault, and the fault is eliminated step by step according to the principle of simple to difficult.

Ⅴ. Task Report

Major		Class		Name	
Task Name				Class Hours	2
Model		Engine Model			
	Assessment Items	Assessment Contents		Maximum Score	Score
Task Completion Process	1. Description of fault symptoms			5	
	2. Possible causes and analysis of fault			25	
	3. Detection and diagnosis process			35	
	4. Fault Elimination			10	
	5. Summary of fault diagnosis			10	
Teacher Evaluation	Operation quality, operation efficiency, operation safety, etc.			15	
Total Score				100	

Ⅵ. Knowledge Expansion

[Typical Case Ⅰ]　The ABS light of a Jetta is always on when braking.

Fault Description: The ABS light of a Jetta, traveling 120,000 km, is always on when braking.

Fault Diagnosis and Repair: The ABS system was tested with VAS5051 and it was found that the fault is 00290 left rear wheel unreliable signal. The computer VAG1552 was used to read the data, the ABS data was normal when the brake was not applied, and there is error between the left rear wheel data and other wheel data when braking slightly.

After checking, it was found that the left rear wheel ABS sensor resistance value was within the normal range. After measuring the working voltage, it was found that the left rear wheel voltage was too high as the battery voltage.

The circuit was checked and it was found that the ABS and body wiring harness plug were corroded. The brake switch wire in the plug and the ABS left rear wheel sensor wire are short circuited, causing the brake ABS light on.

After cleaning the wiring harness plug and conducting the road test, the fault was eliminated.

Summary: The fault diagnosis started with the fault code reported by the electronic con-

trol unit, read the dynamic data flow in the working state, then combined with the multimeter detection, finally found the fault point. For this kind of system which does not display fault in static state, but reports fault in working state, it is necessary to detect the fault position quickly and accurately when the system is working.

[Typical Case II] ABS of a new Bora car worked under low speed and slight braking.

Fault Description: The ABS of a new Bora car, driving 100, 000 km, worked under low speed and slight braking.

Fault Diagnosis and Repair: The test run was done to confirm the fault phenomenon. When stepping on the brake, the ABS started working whenever the speed dropped to 10km/h. The data flow was read and it was found that the right front wheel was 0 when the left front/left rear/right rear wheel speed was about 10km/h. Disassembling the right front wheel found that the ABS sensor had a large clearance with the ring gear.

After replacing the flange, adjusting the clearance between sensor and ring gear, conducting the test run and reading the data, the four wheels had the same speed, when stepping on the brake lightly, ABS did not work wrongly and the fault was eliminated.

Summary: This car is an accident car, whose original flange was replaced by a non-original one, resulting in too large clearance between sensor and ring gear, causing little change in magnetic flux of ABS sensor at low speed. Therefore, the control unit mistakenly thought that the wheel locked and drove ABS to work incorrectly. This fault is not difficult to repair, but it is important to pinpoint the fault. The purpose of ABS operation is to control wheel locking and restrain lateral slip. Therefore, when ABS operates, it must be considered by the control unit that a wheel is locked, so it is necessary to read the wheel speed difference first. The diagnosis speed can be improved by confirming the fault starting point.

Item X

Fault Diagnosis and Repair of Driving System

Task I Fault Diagnosis and Repair of Vehicle Running Deviation

 Learning Objectives

1. Be able to determine the direction and items of inquiry according to the fault phenomena of the automobile for repair.

2. Be able to prepare a correct fault diagnosis plan according to fault phenomena.

3. Be able to consult maintenance data skillfully, select appropriate detection and diagnosis devices according to fault phenomena and use them skillfully.

4. Be able to detect the running deviation with suitable maintenance devices according to the diagnosis plan.

5. Be able to correctly analyze the detection results and determine the fault location and cause of running deviation.

6. Be able to repair the fault parts quickly and accurately and eliminate the hidden troubles.

7. Be able to work hard and have strong sense of responsibility, rigorous and careful working attitude.

 **Task Import**

Task Material: A 2011 Magotan 2.0, with engine numbered BYJ. The owner said that the car was running in a biased direction, sometimes running left and sometimes running right, and had been repaired twice. The left and right suspensions and steering gears of the front wheels had been replaced, without any improvement.

Task Requirements: According to the fault phenomena of the car, consult relevant materials, select appropriate detection and diagnosis devices for fault diagnosis and repair, and fill in the task report.

Ⅰ. Fault Analysis

After a straight-line running for a while, when the steering wheel is stationary, the driving direction of the car deviates to one side, which is called the running deviation. Vehicle running deviation causes the ability to maintain straight-line driving to decline. Drivers need to constantly revise the driving direction to keep the car running normally.

(1) Driving system failure   Unequal tyre pressure or inconsistent tire specifications between two front wheels; The camber angle or wheel camber of two front wheels are not equal; Toe-in value of front wheel is too large or too small; The front suspension spring is broken, the leaf spring is misplaced or the force of the left and right springs is inconsistent; Frame deformation or front axle deformation; Displacement of axle or deformation of drive axle; The left and right wheelbases of front and rear axles are too large (thrust angle occurs); The adjustment of pre-tightness of left and right hub bearings of front and rear axles is inconsistent, and the difference is too large.

(2) Steering system failure   Incorrect adjustment of steering gear, too tight worm bearing, too tight meshing and jamming; The clearance between steering knuckle kingpin and independently suspended ball pin is too large or too small, which may cause loose or inflexible operation; Left and right steering knuckle trapezoid arms are inconsistent, and one side of steering trapezoid arm is deformed; Left and right tie rods of independent suspension are unequal in length and improperly adjusted; The vertical arm of steering gear is not in the middle position and the installation mark is not aligned.

In addition, if a car with hydraulic steering booster is deflected during driving, this is usually caused by failure of control valve, which causes pressure difference on both sides of the piston of the power cylinder to automatically generate boosting action.

(3) Brake system failure   The brake clearance adjustment of wheel brake on one side is too small; One side of the wheel brake does not return; The wheel hub bearing clearance on one side of the wheel is too large, causing the brake drum to deflect and drag.

(4) Other faults   The car is seriously overloaded; The adhesion of left and right drive wheels is different due to road surface or uneven wear of tire patterns; The differential is improperly assembled and adjusted to make the rotation speed of the left and right drive wheels differ; The pavement slopes to one side.

Ⅱ. Fault Diagnosis

First check whether the air pressure of the left and right tires (focusing on the front wheels) is consistent and whether the tire specifications are consistent.

If the tires meet the requirements, tough the brake drum (disc) or wheel hub on the deviation side by hand for heating, and compare it with the brake drum (disc) and wheel hub on the other side.

If the temperature of the brake drum on the deviation side is higher than that of the brake drum on the other side, it indicates that there is braking drag phenomenon on the side, and the wheel brake on this side shall be removed and inspected.

If the temperature of the wheel hub on the deviation side is higher than the temperature

of the hub on the other side, it indicates that the adjustment of the hub bearing on the side is too tight and lack of oil, so it needs maintenance and adjustment.

If the temperature of brake drum and hub is normal, check whether the suspension spring is misaligned or broken, and check whether the elastic force of left and right springs is consistent. If they do not meet the requirements, they should be repaired or replaced.

Check whether the car body is skewed in front of the car. Pay attention to make the car unloaded or evenly loaded during inspection, and park it on a flat, dry and hard ground.

If the above items meet the requirements after inspection, the following items shall be checked:

(1) Check whether the front wheel positioning parameters are correct, and if they do not meet the requirements, they shall be adjusted again.

(2) Check whether the front and rear axles are deformed or displaced, and repair or replace them if any.

(3) Check the installation and adjustment of steering system mechanism.

(4) Check whether the left and right wheelbases of front and rear axles are consistent.

Ⅲ. Task Implementation

1. Inquiry

Know the time of the fault from the owner; Check whether there is abnormal condition before the fault; Road condition; mileage; Repair after the fault occurred. Find out the situation before and after the fault and the specific information of the fault through the above inquiry, and complete the preliminary diagnosis of driving deviation.

2. Test-drive and Basic Inspection

Firstly, carry out the test-drive to confirm the fault. After the test run, it is found that the car is not only deflected when driving, but also the steering wheel feels bad during driving. It is light when turning to the left but heavy when turning to the right.

Then check whether there is any collision on the chassis and check whether there is any bump on the chassis. Check the tire model. All four tires are of the same model.

3. Detection and Diagnosis

Test tire pressure. Coaxial tire pressure is basically the same.

Check the tire wear and find that there is abnormal wear on the left rear wheel, the left and right wear surfaces of the tire are inconsistent, and the wear surface of the entire tire is seriously shifted to the right, and the wear degree is serious, as shown in Figure 10-1, which indicates that the positioning of the car is problematic. It is learned from the owner that four-wheel positioning had been done twice but the problem wasn't solved. Look at the print reports of the four-wheel positioning, the two positioning data differ greatly, even standard data

Figure 10-1　Abnormally Worn Tire

of one copy are wrong, so these two positioning operations are not completely credible.

Remove four tires and replace them with new ones for test run. The symptoms are improved slightly.

When the car is lifted, the ball head of the steering tie rod is not loose, and the steering gear clearance is normal.

The rubber sleeves of sub-frame and steering knuckle have no obvious wear and looseness.

4. Fault Elimination

Finally, it is decided to make four-wheel positioning for the car again. After calibration of the four-wheel positioning and hoisting machine, the four wheels is positioned according to the standard operation. During the positioning process, it is found that the toe-in value of the rear wheel and the camber angle have great deviation, and the wheel positioning angle is adjusted to the specified range. After positioning, check "additional detection value" to see if there is deformation of the car body, and the additional detection value reflects that the car body is in good condition without deformation. After completion of positioning, the test drive is conducted, the car can run normally and the fault is eliminated.

5. Inspection and Delivery

After troubleshooting, the car runs smoothly without deviation and is handed over to the owner.

IV. Task Summary

When diagnosing car running deviation, we cannot simply replace parts, but determine the possible cause of failure according to the characteristics of car running deviation, and then diagnose it item by item. The positioning device must be accurate during four-wheel positioning, and the operation shall be standardized at the same time. In fact, many running deviation failures may only be caused by incorrect positioning data.

V. Task Report

Major			Class		Name	
Task Name					Class Hours	2
Model			Engine Model			
	Assessment Items		Assessment Contents		Maximum Score	Score
Task Completion Process	1. Description of fault symptoms				5	
	2. Possible causes and analysis of fault				25	
	3. Detection and diagnosis process				35	
	4. Fault Elimination				10	
	5. Summary of fault diagnosis				10	
Teacher Evaluation	Operation quality, operation efficiency, operation safety, etc.				15	
Total Score					100	

VI. Knowledge Expansion

【Typical Case I】 A Sagitar 1. 8T car ran leftward while driving.

168 | Automobile Integrated Fault Diagnosis and Repair

Fault Description: A Volkswagen Sagitar 1.8T car, equipped with a manual transmission, ran to the left when the steering wheel was released while traveling straight.

Fault Diagnosis and Repair: The test drive was conducted to confirm that the fault phenomenon was true, but the steering wheel position was correct when the car ran straightly. The owner said that the car was an accident car just repaired at a comprehensive car repair shop. The accident location was on the left front suspension. Most parts of the left front suspension, main airbag, auxiliary airbag and instrument panel assembly had been replaced and four-wheel positioning had been performed. Reasons for general running deviation of cars include: The four-wheel positioning is not correct, the left and right wheelbases of the car are inconsistent, the pressure of the left and right tires is inconsistent, or the brands or patterns of the left and right tires are inconsistent. The car had done four-wheel positioning, and the four-wheel positioning print data provided by the owner were within the standard range; The left and right wheelbases of the car were measured and same; The pressure of left and right tires is also normal. To excluding the reasons of tires, the left and right front tires of the car were tested after exchange, and the fault remained.

Then the cause of the fault was analyzed from the power steering system. The power steering system of a Sagitar is different from that of ordinary cars. Its power steering mode is double-gear mechanical electric power steering type. Its functions include the electronic power steering (EPS) function and active return function. There is a steering angle sensor (G85) in the power steering system, which can recognize the rotational angular velocity and angular position of the steering wheel. When the steering wheel of the car is not forced, if it recognizes that the steering wheel is not in the center position (the steering wheel angle is 0°), the power steering control unit (J500) will control the steering motor (V187) to operate according to the signal of G85. It returns the steering wheel to the center by providing an return torque to the steering wheel via the steering gear. The steering wheel angle identified by G85 can be read out using VAS5052 (Group 1 data in Area 44-08-007).

The steering wheel was turned to the straight driving direction of the car (center position of steering wheel) and the data of G85 (angle of steering wheel) was read with VAS5052, which was $-7.52°$. The data of G85 would be 0° only after turning the steering wheel to the left at a certain angle. So far, the cause of the fault was found. Although the steering wheel position was correct when the car ran straightly, the steering wheel angle recognized by G85 was not 0°, so J500 gave the steering wheel a left return moment through the steering gear, resulting in the car running to the left.

After using the VAS5052 function boot program to make the basic setting of the zero point of G85 and conducting the test run, the fault was eliminated. VAS5052 was used again to read the data of G85 at the steering wheel center position, it was 0°

Summary: This fault was caused by the error of basic zero setting of power steering control unit. The electronic control unit would receive the wrong signal to carry out wrong control.

[Typical Case Ⅱ] A Toyota Previa ran to the right while driving.

Fault Description: A Toyota Previa ran to the right when it traveled on the urban ring

road at 60km/h. The steering wheel must be pulled counterclockwise by hand to make the car run straightly.

Fault Diagnosis and Repair: The tires were checked. The four tires were 215/55R17 94V, tires with good appearance and no abnormal wear. The tire pressure was adjusted to 280kPa. The left and right heights of the car were checked, the left side was slightly higher than the right side by 3mm, which should not be a major problem. The left and right wheelbases were identical.

The front wheel positioning was as follows.

① Toe-in. The difference between short front and long rear was 1mm, standard value: 1.0±2.0mm.

② Camber angle. Left: −0°15"; Right: 0°20"; Standard value: −0°10" ±45".

③ Caster angle. Left: 5°15"; Right: 5°55"; Standard value: 5°45" ±45".

④ Inclination angle of steering axis. Left: 12°45"; Right: 12°36"; Standard value: 11°22" ±45".

Upon check, the front-wheel positioning basically complied with the maintenance data provided in the maintenance manual.

According to previous repair experience, the two front wheel tires were switched, but the fault remained

Considering that when checking the front wheel positioning, the camber angle (Left: −0°15" Right: +0°20"), although they met the standard, the left and right camber angles were tilted to the right, which was suspected to be related to car failure. Therefore, the left camber angle was adjusted to +0°10" and the right camber angle to −0°15" . After the test run, the fault was eliminated and the car returned to normal condition. Three days later, the automobile was visited and the owner said that the car was in good condition.

Summary: The fault of running deviation of the car was finally eliminated by adjusting the front wheel positioning. Although the data of the front wheel positioning of the car conformed to the data in the maintenance manual, the data had certain adjustment space within the specified deviation range. The left wheel positioning value was negative and the right wheel positioning wheel was positive, and the deviation between the two wheels was large, thus causing the car to run rightward, that is, the positioning value within the specified range may also cause the car to deviate.

Task II   Fault Diagnosis and Repair of Abnormal Tire Wear

Learning Objectives

1. Be able to determine the direction and items of inquiry according to the fault phenomena of the automobile for repair.

2. Be able to prepare a correct fault diagnosis plan according to fault phenomena.

3. Be able to consult maintenance data skillfully, select appropriate detection and diagno-

sis devices according to fault phenomena and use them skillfully.

4. Be able to test the abnormal tire wear with appropriate maintenance devices according to the diagnosis plan.

5. Be able to correctly analyze the test results and determine the fault location and cause of abnormal tire wear.

6. Be able to repair the fault parts quickly and accurately and eliminate the hidden troubles.

Task Import

Task Material: In a Nissan Bluebird car, two front tires are seriously worn on the outside, and the inside edge pattern grooves are worn in feather-like shape. The wear marks are gradually aggravated from the inside to the outside, crossing the tread, and the wear on the outside of the right front wheel is particularly severe.

Task Requirements: According to the fault phenomena of the car, consult relevant materials, select appropriate detection and diagnosis devices for fault diagnosis and repair, and fill in the task report.

I. Fault Analysis

(1) Inaccurate front-wheel positioning. When the toe-in value is too large, the steering wheel will float. The outer side of the front wheel is worn and the inner patter groove edge is feather-shaped. The toe-in value is too low, the steering is heavy, the inside of the wheel is seriously worn, and the outer pattern groove edge is feather-like wear. When the kingpin caster angle is too much, the automatic return resistance is too large after the wheel is turned. The tire will shake excessively at low speed, while at high speed it will drift, increasing impact on the road surface and causing serious wear of tread. When the kingpin caster angle is incorrect, the two front wheels will drag unevenly during braking, the braking performance will be deteriorated, and the tires will be worn. The kingpin caster angle and the kingpin inclination angle are generally determined by the car body itself, which does not directly cause abnormal tire wear, but is the main induction cause of tire abnormal wear.

(2) Poor driving skills. Fast starting, frequent emergency braking, turning too fast, passing obstacles at high speed, etc., can make the tires suffer severe impact and damage.

(3) Deformation of rear axle and frame. Traffic accidents, long-term overload and unbalance load will cause deformation of front and rear axles and frame, causing abnormal wheel swinging, increased sliding wear of steering wheels, and regular interval diagonal wear on tire tread.

(4) Unfavorable suspension technical condition, improper installation of steel plate assembly and different stiffness of left and right leaf springs lead to alternating dynamic load change and bad swing phenomenon of axle, which may lead to uneven tire wear.

(5) Poor brake working. Excessive wear of brake drum causes uneven braking, braking stagnation and deadness and tire dragging, thus aggravating tire wear.

(6) The wheelbases vary. Distortion or displacement of front and rear axles, deformation of frame, loosening or falling of rivets of leaf spring lifting lugs, bending or breaking of

central bolts of leaf spring, etc. will change the wheelbases, making tires running not on a straight line, resulting in tire injury caused by tire eccentric wear.

II. Fault Diagnosis

(1) Both shoulder patterns of the tread are worn. Due to low tire pressure, long-term lack of air or compression deformation due to frequent overloading, the middle part of the tread bends inward, and the load on the tread edge increases dramatically, making the tread unevenly worn.

(2) The middle of the tread is worn. Because the tire pressure is too high for a long time, the cord is stretched excessively, and the carcass fatigue process is too fast, thus reducing the contact area of tire, increasing the unit pressure load and causing wear of the middle part of the tread.

(3) Side wear, i. e. eccentric wear on the outside of the tire, most of which is caused by different specifications and dimensions of tires and different loads; Or driving on arched pavement for a long time; Or tires are not shifted regularly.

(4) The sidewall is serrated. Due to long-term overloaded operation or lack of air travel, tires are not replaced in time, and braking is too frequent, so that tires often friction with road surface in one direction under braking force, causing irregular wear.

(5) The inner side of the tire is severely worn, and the outer pattern groove edge is roughened. It is mainly camber wear and drag wear due to incorrect front wheel positioning caused by deformation of steering tie rod, bending of steering arm, distortion of front axle and deformation of front end of frame.

(6) The tread is wavy worn. This is caused by pressing and deformation of the front end of the pattern block immediately when the tread is in contact with the hard road surface, sliding abrasion of the rear end when it is off the ground, poor tire balance, loose hub, curved wheel rim or frequent use of emergency braking.

III. Task Implementation

1. Inquiry

Know the time of fault from the owner; Whether the symptoms change after the fault is found, and whether there are other abnormal conditions before the fault; Details during driving; Whether the car is maintained on time; Have other repairs been performed after the fault. Through the above inquiry, understand the situation before and after the fault and the specific information of the fault, and complete the preliminary diagnosis of abnormal tire wear.

2. Test-drive and Basic Inspection

Observe the pressure and specifications of the left and right tires, which are in full compliance with the requirements, and visually observe the car body without and find no obvious inclination. Conduct a test drive to test the car for running deviation, steering wheel swing, etc.

3. Detection and Diagnosis

Based on the observation of abnormal tire wear and the comprehensive analysis of the a-

bove causes, it can be preliminarily judged that the fault is caused by improper front-wheel positioning parameters.

According to the different influence of four parameters of front wheel positioning on abnormal tire wear, improper toe-in and camber angle of front wheel will lead to single shoulder side wear of tire, and too large toe-in and camber angle will cause excessive wear of the outer sidewall, which is consistent with the actual situation of the car. Through careful observation of the car, it is found that the steering wheel floats and the steering is unstable when driving. Therefore, it is basically determined that the toe-in and camber angle of the front wheels of the car may be too large. However, other reasons, such as improper kingpin caster angle and kingpin inclination angle, the looseness of steering gear and steering gear mechanism, loose suspension support and shock absorber, tire imbalance and improper air pressure, deformation of wheel rim, improper driving technique, etc., will mainly cause the vibration of the car during driving, resulting in abnormal radial wave wear of tire. This is inconsistent with the actual situation of car, and its influence can basically be excluded. The fault is likely due to incorrect toe-in and camber angle of the front wheels.

The front wheel positioning and toe-in is tested with the four-wheel aligner. The measured result is the toe-in of the front wheel: +8mm; Front wheel camber angle: 1°08′; Kingpin caster angle: 3°30′; Kingpin inclination angle: 10°30′. According to the above measurement data, the front wheel camber angle, the kingpin inclination angle and the kingpin caster angle are all normal and need not be adjusted. The measurement also shows that the toe-in is too large.

Check the parts affecting the front wheel toe-in, i. e. check whether the front axle assembly and steering mechanism components are damaged or deformed. Upon inspection, the steering rod, ball pin, pin seat and steering knuckle are normal, the front wheel bearing is not loose, and the frame and suspension are free from deformation.

Check before toe-in adjustment of front wheel: Inflate tires according to standards; Check the shock absorber for oil leakage and damage; The frame has been correctly calibrated and the suspension is free to move; The steering gear is adjusted correctly without large clearance and damage to the front suspension.

4. Fault elimination

After adjusting the toe-in, the test drive is conducted. After a period, feedback shows there is no abnormal tire wear. The fault is eliminated

5. Inspection and delivery

After troubleshooting, if there is no any other symptom, the car should be handed over to the owner.

IV. Task Summary

The abnormal tire wear of the car is caused by the abnormal front wheel toe-in, which is eliminated after four-wheel positioning detection and adjustment. The inspection of basic items, such as tire specifications, air pressure, automobile body, suspension, etc., shall not be neglected during inspection. Only in this way can the cause of the fault be accurately

analyzed and eliminated.

V. Task Report

	Major		Class		Name	
	Task Name				Class Hours	2
	Model		Engine Model			
	Assessment Items	Assessment Contents			Maximum Score	Score
Task Completion Process	1. Description of fault symptoms				5	
	2. Possible causes and analysis of fault				25	
	3. Detection and diagnosis process				35	
	4. Fault Elimination				10	
	5. Summary of fault diagnosis				10	
Teacher Evaluation	Operation quality, operation efficiency, operation safety, etc.				15	
	Total Score				100	

Item XI

Fault Diagnosis and Repair
of Airbag System

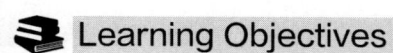

Learning Objectives

1. Be able to determine the direction and items of inquiry according to the fault phenomena of the automobile for repair.

2. Be able to prepare a correct fault diagnosis plan according to fault phenomena.

3. Be able to consult maintenance data skillfully, select appropriate detection and diagnosis devices according to fault phenomena and use them skillfully.

4. Be able to detect the airbag system failure with appropriate maintenance devices according to the diagnosis plan.

5. Be able to correctly analyze the detection results and determine the fault location and cause of the airbag system.

6. Be able to repair the fault parts quickly and accurately and eliminate the hidden troubles.

7. Be able to work rigorously and carefully, improve safety awareness and teamwork ability.

Task Import

Task Material: The owner of a 2010 Volkswagen CC car said that the airbag fault light on the instrument panel was on during driving.

Task Requirements: According to the fault phenomena of the car, consult relevant materials, select appropriate detection and diagnosis devices for fault diagnosis and repair, and fill in the task report.

Ⅰ. Fault Analysis

The electronic control unit of airbag system has self-diagnosis function. When the electronic control unit detects system failure, the electronic control unit will illuminate the fault indicator light and store the fault code in the electronic control unit.

Common causes of airbag failure include the following:

(1) The crash sensor is faulty.

(2) The airbag system line is faulty, including spiral harness and other lines.

(3) The electronic control unit is faulty.

II. Fault Diagnosis

Firstly, the scan tool is used to read the fault code and to determine the detection direction of fault by analyzing the fault code. A multimeter is then used for line detection. The crash sensor cannot be detected. It can be confirmed by a replacement method.

If all parts of the system are checked to be normal, the fault will be in the electronic control unit.

III. Task Implementation

1. Inquiry

Know the time of the fault from the owner; Check whether there is abnormal condition before the fault; Road condition; mileage; Repair after the fault occurred. Find out the situation before and after the fault and the specific information of the fault through the above inquiry, and complete the preliminary diagnosis of the fault.

2. Test-drive and Basic Inspection

Carry out the test-drive to confirm the fault.

3. Detection and Diagnosis

Read the fault code with the Volkswagen special scan tool 5051, as shown in Figure 11-

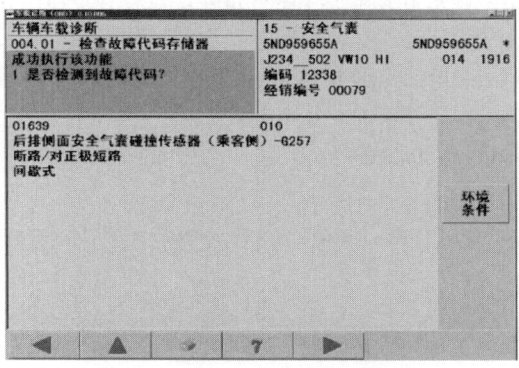

Figure 11-1 Fault Code Read by 5051

1. The fault code displays "01639 Rear Side Airbag Crash Sensor (Passenger Side) G257 Open/Short to Positive Electrode Intermittent". After clearing the fault code, the fault light goes off, and the fault is reproduced for a period of test run.

According to the fault code content, it can be judged that the possible causes of the fault are as follows:

(1) J234 airbag control unit is damaged.

(2) G257 rear side airbag crash sensor (passenger side) is faulty.

(3) The circuit between J234 and G257 is faulty.

It is thought that the crash sensor may be damaged, so the G257 rear side airbag crash sensor (passenger side) is replaced first, and the fault is reproduced after the test run.

Check the wiring from the sensor to the airbag control unit with a multimeter, as shown in Figure 11-2. The resistance value from sensor pin 1 (green wire) to airbag control unit is 0.3Ω, and the circuit is completely normal; The resistance from pin 2 (brown wire) to airbag control unit is 0.2Ω without short circuit or open circuit.

Install the airbag control unit and harness interface, read the fault code, and find that the fault code is changed from "intermittent" to "static", which cannot be removed. There-

176 Automobile Integrated Fault Diagnosis and Repair

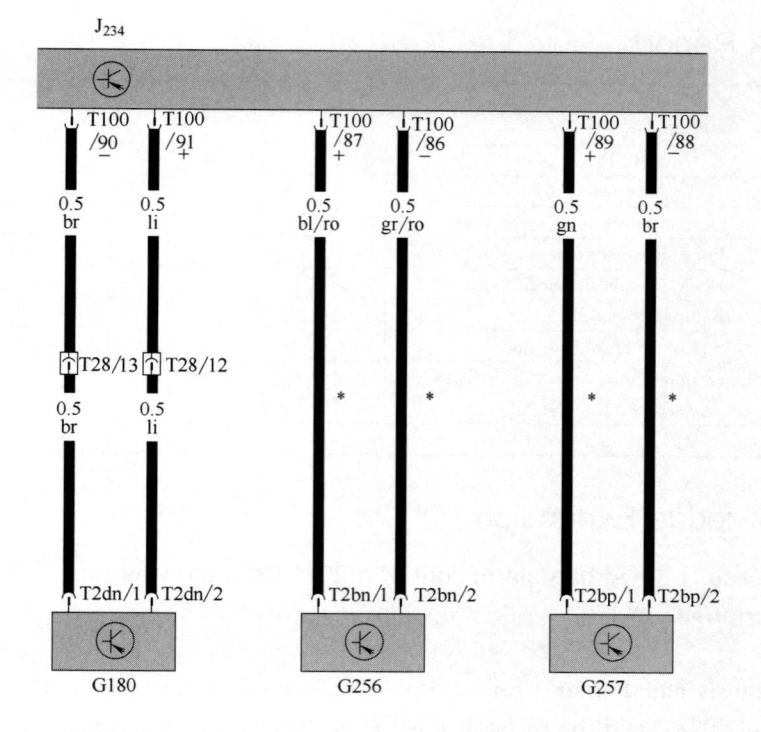

Figure 11-2 Circuit Diagram of Volkswagen CC Airbag System

fore, it is judged that there is probably poor contact between airbag control unit and harness interface.

Withdraw the pins T100/8 and T100/88 of airbag control unit, clamp the interface with pliers, and the fault code after re-installation is defined as incidental. After clearing the fault code, the airbag light is not on again during the test drive. After several days of follow-up tracking, the fault is not reproduced.

Intermittent failure of G257 is caused by poor contact between T100/8 or T100/88 pin on airbag control unit plug and lead.

4. Fault Elimination

Tighten the pins again with pliers. The fault is eliminated.

5. Inspection and Delivery

After troubleshooting, if there is no any other symptom, the car should be handed over to the owner.

IV. Task Summary

（1）According to the definition analysis of fault code, combining with the circuit diagram to measure and diagnose the circuit is the common idea of troubleshooting.

（2）When checking the on/off of the circuit, we should have patience and a clear mind.

（3）We can understand the definitions of the fault code type "Intermittent" and "Static" through the case. These two fault code type definition prompts can help us diagnose faults.

Item XI Fault Diagnosis and Repair of Airbag System | **177**

V. Task Report

Major			Class		Name	
Task Name					Class Hours	2
Model				Engine Model		
	Assessment Items		Assessment Contents		Maximum Score	Score
Task Completion Process	1. Description of fault symptoms				5	
	2. Possible causes and analysis of fault				25	
	3. Detection and diagnosis process				35	
	4. Fault Elimination				10	
	5. Summary of fault diagnosis				10	
Teacher Evaluation	Operation quality, operation efficiency, operation safety, etc.				15	
Total Score					100	

VI. Knowledge Expansion

〔Typical Case Ⅰ〕 Airbag alarm light of a 2011 Bora car was on.

Fault Description: A 2011 Volkswagen Bora car, while driving, the airbag alarm light was on.

Fault Diagnosis and Repair: First, the fault code was read out with the Volkswagen special scan tool 5052, and the resistance value of the airbag detonator on the driver side was too large (incidental), after clearing the fault code, and then checking, everything was normal. The owner agreed to drive the car away first and then the alarm light was on again after several days of driving.

The airbag fault code was read again as follows: The resistance value of the airbag detonator on the driver side was too large (incidental).

In consideration of the particularity of the airbag circuit, the relevant components were replaced for testing. The airbag slip ring, main airbag and airbag control unit were replaced successively. The fault was not solved.

The relevant lines could only be rechecked according to the wiring diagram. The circuit is shown in Figure 11-3. When checking the wiring and plug between the control unit and the main airbag, it is found that the airbag reset ring was broken and falsely connected to pin 4 of the plug of harness T5, as shown in Figure 11-4.

After replacing the harness pins of the same model with a special tool, the connection points were connected with heat shrinkable tubes to ensure that the connection points were firmly connected. The fault was eliminated.

Summary: This fault is airbag light alarm caused by false connection after the line was broken. It is recommended to use simulated fault occurrence state (vibration/shaking wiring harness) as far as possible when handling similar incidental failures, and observe the requirements of airbag circuit maintenance operation, be patient and careful during maintenance to avoid blind replacement test run.

〔Typical Case Ⅱ〕 Airbag alarm light of a 2011 Bora was on car.

Fault Description: The owner of a 2011 Volkswagen Bora car said that the airbag alarm light was on.

Fault Diagnosis and Repair: Firstly, VAS5051 was used for fault inquiry and fault code 01217-029 was found, i. e. short circuit to ground of driver side airbag detonator N199, incidental. After clearing the fault code, the fault disappeared. Meanwhile, the wiring harness and plug of the side airbag under the seat were not loose or improperly fixed (because many cars may be equipped with floor glue or rear seat foot cushion, which may cause the plug to fall off and the wiring harness is not fixed and the airbag light is on, so the car was handed over to the owner).

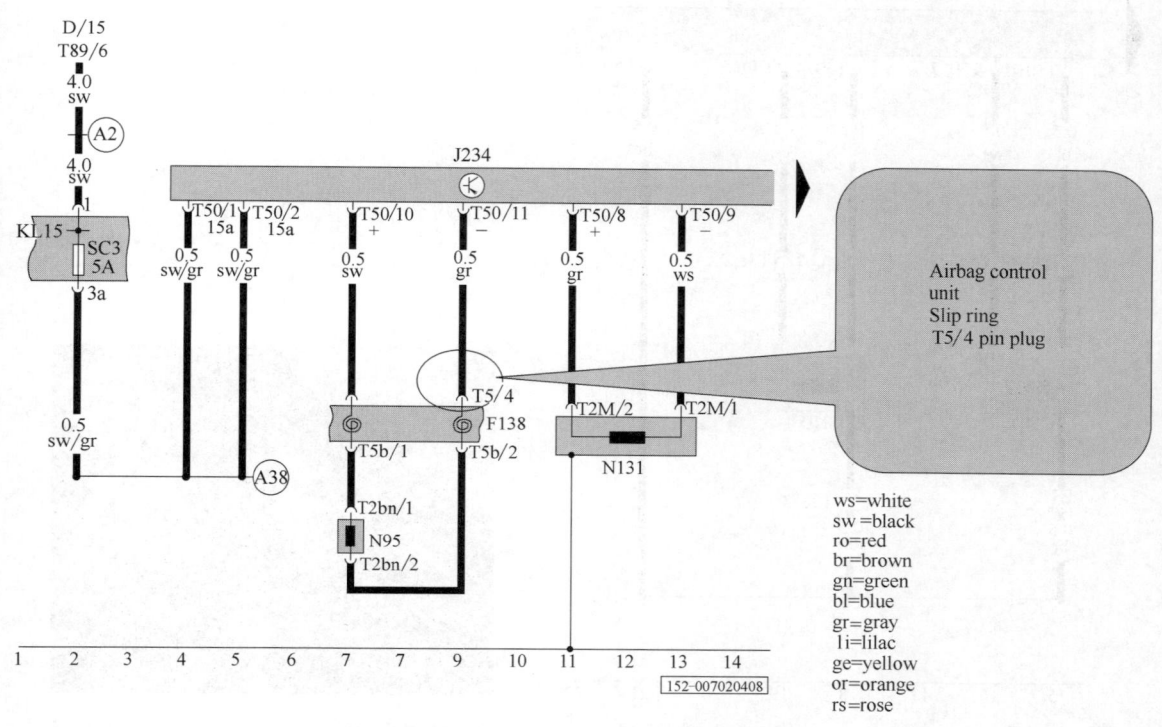

Figure 11-3 Circuit Diagram of Airbag System

However, the airbag light was on again after a few days of driving. The fault was checked again. The fault code was still 01217-029, and the car returned to normal after eliminating the fault. However, considering that the fault occurred frequently. Therefore, the seat was disassembled and the circuit of the airbag system was further checked according to the circuit diagram of the airbag system (as shown in Figure 11-5). After inspection, the wiring harness or plug was not installed loosely. No abnormality was found in the wiring harness at the side of airbag computer detected by the

Figure 11-4 Damaged Terminal

multimeter.

When turning over the seat and looking into the seat along the wiring harness of the side

Item XI Fault Diagnosis and Repair of Airbag System **179**

airbag，it was found that the wiring harness came out of the manual adjusting pressure bar，so it was suspected that the wiring harness of the side airbag was squeezed here，so the side trim panel of the seat was removed for inspection. The airbag wiring harness at the gear at the end of the pressure bar was found to be damaged after disassembling the seat adjusting pressure bar. The fault point was no doubt here，as shown in Figure 11-6. After replacing the side airbag assembly on the driver side，the fault was eliminated.

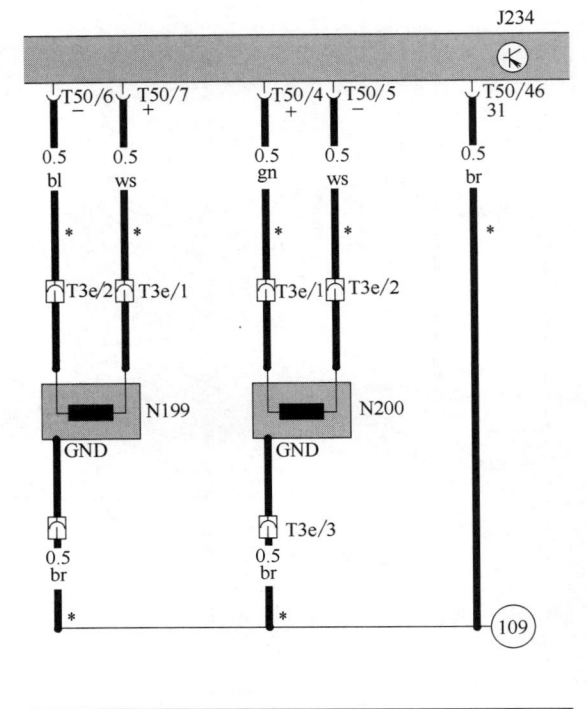

Figure 11-5　Circuit Diagram of New Bora Airbag System

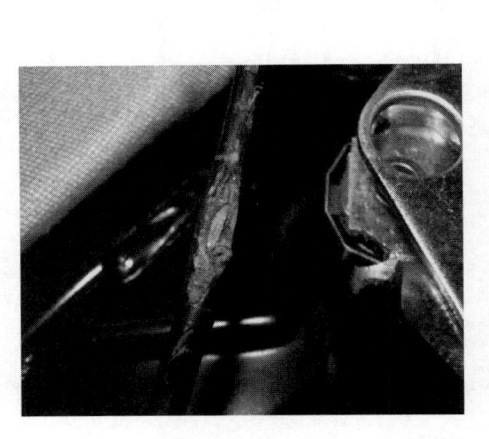

Figure 11-6　Damaged Airbag Wiring Harness

Summary：Firstly，the meaning of fault code was analyzed. Most of the faults are caused by that the plug is unplugged or loose，and a few are caused by airbag body faults. The other fault was that the resistance of the N199 detonator was too small，and this kind of fault is rarely caused by short circuit between the control unit and the airbag（which rarely happens）. The fault with too small resistance is mostly caused by the airbag body fault. This fault showed that the short circuit of N199 to ground should be a short circuit to ground in the positive wire between the airbag control unit and N199，so the wire between the control unit and N199 should be carefully inspected.

We should be careful and responsible when repairing the fault of airbag. Do not simply clear the fault or replace the parts blindly，so as to avoid the loss caused by the failure of airbag to detonate normally in case of an accident.

Item XII

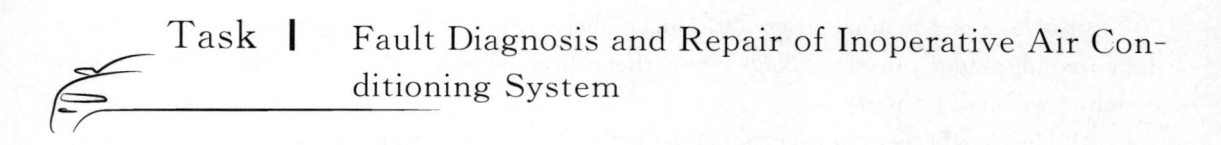

Fault Diagnosis and Repair of Automotive Air Conditioning System

Task I Fault Diagnosis and Repair of Inoperative Air Conditioning System

Learning Objectives

1. Be able to determine the direction and items of inquiry according to the fault phenomena of the automobile for repair.

2. Be able to prepare a correct fault diagnosis plan according to fault phenomena.

3. Be able to consult maintenance data skillfully, select appropriate detection and diagnosis devices according to fault phenomena and use them skillfully.

4. Be able to test the inoperative air conditioning system with appropriate maintenance devices according to the diagnosis plan.

5. Be able to correctly analyze the test results and determine the fault location and cause of the inoperative air conditioning system.

6. Be able to repair the fault parts quickly and accurately and eliminate the hidden troubles.

7. Be able to work rigorously and carefully and improve service consciousness.

Task Import

Task Material: A Santana 3000 car with automatic air conditioning. After the car's air conditioning is turned on, the compressor does not work and cannot be cooled, and its other functions are normal.

Task Requirements: According to the fault phenomena of the car, consult relevant materials, select appropriate detection and diagnosis devices for fault diagnosis and repair, and fill in the task report.

I. Fault Analysis

Inoperative air conditioning means that the air conditioning compressor does not operate

after the air conditioning switch is turned on.

The main reasons why the air conditioning system does not operate include the following:

(1) The air conditioning compressor or circuit is faulty.

(2) There is insufficient refrigerant in the air conditioning system.

(3) The air conditioning A/C switch is damaged.

(4) The A/C amplifier or its wiring is faulty.

(5) The evaporator surface temperature sensor or temperature control switch is faulty.

(6) The engine water temperature is too high.

(7) The external temperature is too low and the set temperature is too high.

(8) The electronic control unit of air conditioning or its circuit is faulty.

II. Fault Diagnosis

(1) For an automatic air conditioning first read fault code with a scan tool. If there is a fault code, check it according to fault code. If there is no fault code, read data flow to check whether sensor and switch related to compressor start are normal.

In the case of a manual air conditioning, check whether the refrigerant is sufficient with the air-conditioning pressure gauge, and then check whether the air-conditioning pressure switch is working properly.

(2) Check whether the electromagnetic clutch and its wiring are normal.

(3) Check whether the evaporator surface temperature sensor or the thermal switch is normal.

(4) Check the compressor if the switches and electromagnetic clutches work normally while the compressor does not rotate.

(5) If the scan tool does not communicate properly with the AC electronic control unit or the AC control unit cannot control the actuator to operate, the AC control unit fails.

III. Task Implementation

1. Inquiry

The repairman shall know the time of fault from the owner; Whether there are other abnormal conditions before the fault; Whether the symptoms change after finding the fault; Details of driving; Whether the automobile is maintained on time; Have other repairs been performed after the fault. Find out the situation before and after the fault and the specific information of the fault through the above inquiry, and complete the preliminary diagnosis of inoperative air conditioning.

2. Test-drive and Basic Inspection

Carry out the test-drive to confirm the fault. After shutdown, check whether there is oil stain on the air-conditioning pipeline and whether the plugs of electromagnetic clutch, pressure sensor or pressure switch are firmly connected. In addition, it is necessary to determine the structure characteristics and wire connection mode of the air conditioning system.

3. Detection and Diagnosis

Check the pressure of the refrigerant in the air conditioning system and find that the

pressure is normal and the refrigerant is sufficient. Conduct preliminary inspection on some connectors related to air conditioning in the engine compartment, and find no looseness or falling off. Start the car immediately, turn on the air conditioning and carry out further inspection. Open the "Relay-Fuse Block" located on the left side of the engine compartment, pull off the electromagnetic clutch relay J44 at RL2 position and use a test pen to measure that pin 2/30 on the relay holder is not powered. A wire is used to supply power directly from the battery to pin 5/87a of the socket. The compressor works normally for cooling. This indicates that the circuit from the 147B relay to the compressor is normal, and the air conditioning system itself has no problem, and the fault is on the control circuit. Continue checking the wiring and pin 2/30 of the 147B relay is powered through the air conditioning pressure switch F129 located on the dryer. Remove plug T4at and measure pin 2 and pin 2 is not powered. Since this line leads to pin T32e/23 of air conditioning control unit J127, J127 is checked first. During the inspection, it is found that all the statuses displayed on the control panel are normal and the data block reading function of the automatic air conditioning is activated to view it. Check and find that the internal and external temperature, evaporator temperature, water temperature, solar radiation (sampling value 1/20), inlet temperature and automobile speed (sampling value 1/5) are all normal.

Then the self-diagnosis function of the air conditioning is activated. No fault indications are found after inspection. Remove the air conditioning control unit, and when the air conditioning control unit is unintentionally shaken, the foreign matter sounds inside as if something falls off inside. Therefore, the control unit J127 is disassembled, and it is found that the fallen foreign matter is a patch resistor on a circuit board. After installing the new air conditioning control unit, the air conditioning still does not work. Remove the air conditioning control unit again, directly supply power to pin T32e/23 with 12V power (a pin is inserted into pin T32e/23), the compressor starts to work and cools normally. It is suspected that there is a problem with the circuit. Once again, the power supply to pin T32e/23 is supplied directly, and huge sparks appear at the moment of connection, and the pin inserted into the pin T32e/23 is melted, which indicates that there is a serious grounding short circuit in the circuit. Then remove the lower trim panel of the instrument panel and carefully inspect the wiring harness of the air conditioning. Finally, after removing the central fuse box, it is found that the wiring harness of the air conditioning is wrapped into the shaft on the clutch pedal bracket, and the wiring harness has been squeezed into serious damage.

4. Fault Elimination

After taking out the wiring harness and wrapping it up, start the air conditioning. The air conditioning system works normally and the fault is eliminated.

5. Inspection and Delivery

After troubleshooting, re-installation and test run are conducted without any other symptoms, and the car is handed over to the owner.

IV. Task Summary

In the automobile maintenance work, it is very important to make a maintenance scheme. A reasonable scheme can improve the work efficiency and the formulation of a rea-

sonable scheme is based on a comprehensive analysis of the cause of the failure. This shall not only consider the primary and secondary relationship of fault causes, but also consider the difficulty of troubleshooting, i. e., to follow the maintenance principle of "from primary to secondary, from simple to complicated".

V. Task Report

					Major			Class		Name		
			Task Name							Class Hours		2
			Model						Engine Model			
			Assessment Items			Assessment Contents				Maximum Score		Score
Task Completion Process			1. Description of fault symptoms							5		
			2. Possible causes and analysis of fault							25		
			3. Detection and diagnosis process							35		
			4. Fault Elimination							10		
			5. Summary of fault diagnosis							10		
Teacher Evaluation			Operation quality, operation efficiency, operation safety, etc.							15		
			Total Score							100		

VI. Knowledge Expansion

【Typical Case Ⅰ】 The air conditioning of A Volkswagen Sagitar 1. 8T car did not cool.

Fault Description: A 2010 Volkswagen Sagitar 1. 8T car, driving 50, 000 km. The owner said that during high speed driving, the air conditioning suddenly did not cool.

Fault Diagnosis and Repair: At first, the computer (5052A) was used to test the air conditioning system, and there was no fault record. The air conditioning fuse and refrigerant filling amount were normal upon inspection.

The other systems were read and two faults in the 09 system were found: 01333 Door Control Unit-Left Rear-J388 No Signal/Communication (Incidental); Alternator Terminal DF Load Signal, Unreliable Signal (Incidental).

This indicates that the fault should occur in the control part. Therefore, the power generation was measured by the multimeter, varying from 11. 8V to 12. 0V. The magnetic field voltage of the generator was 0V. This determines that the fault point was the car power supply. The positive and negative connection points of the whole car were normal upon inspection.

Inspection was conducted according to relevant circuit diagrams (as shown in Figure 12-1 and Figure 12-2), and it was found that: Wire from generator T2/1 to J519F/4 was not connected. Then the 4-pin connection plug of T4t/2 was checked and it was found that the secondary plug fell off. After re-installation and plugging, the power generation was normal, and the air conditioning worked normally. The fault was eliminated.

Summary: This fault was caused by the disconnection of the plug causing a failure of multiple systems such as the generator, door, air conditioning, etc., and the plug is involved in these system wires. When solving such faults, the fault codes can be read firstly, and through comprehensive analysis of multiple fault codes, it can be judged that the plug involved in these multiple systems has a fault.

184 | Automobile Integrated Fault Diagnosis and Repair |

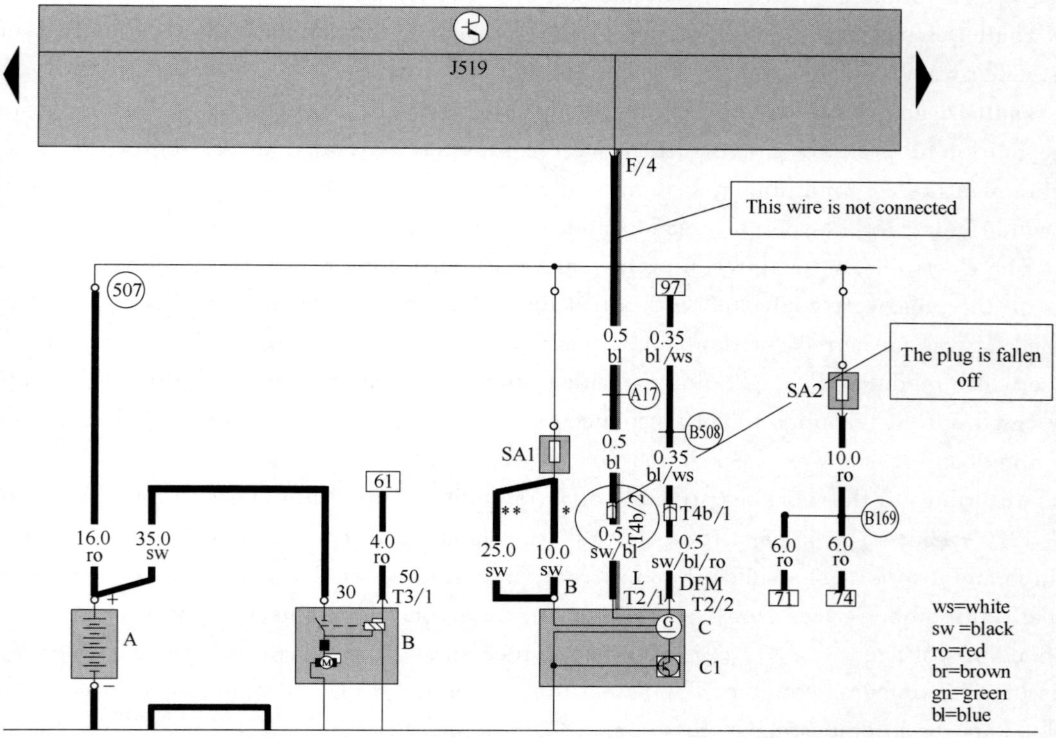

Figure 12-1 Circuit Diagram of Air Conditioning System（1）

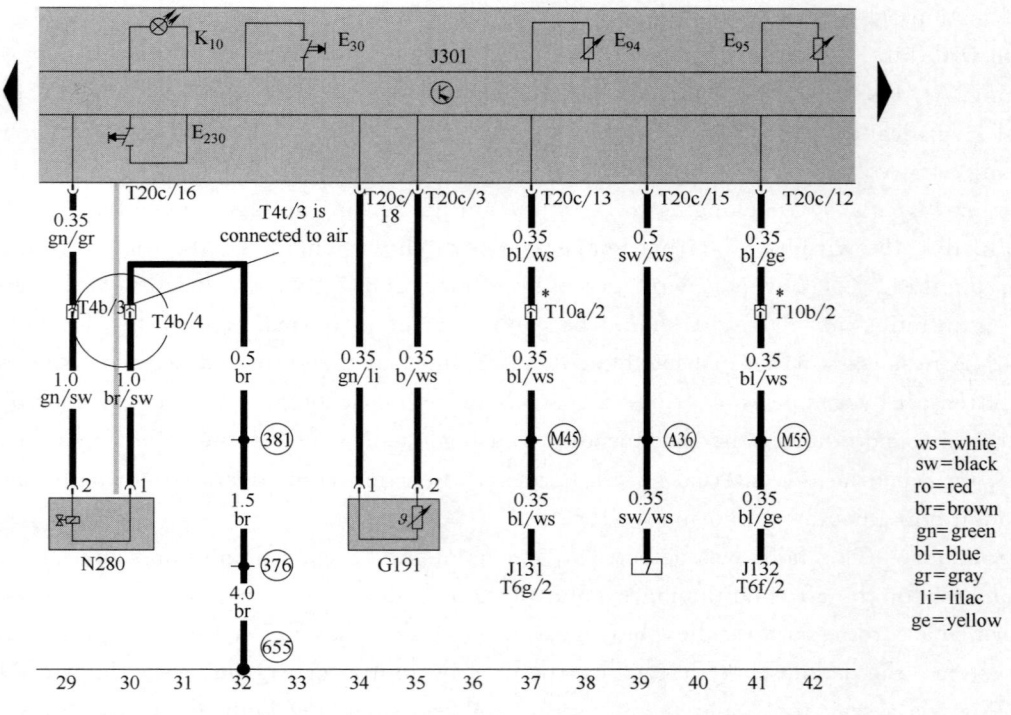

Figure 12-2 Circuit Diagram of Air Conditioning System（2）

[Typical Case Ⅱ]　The air conditioning of a Volkswagen Bora 1. 6 car did not work .

Fault Description: A Volkswagen Bora 1. 6 car, with a mileage of 90, 000 kilometers. The owner said that the air conditioning did not work.

Fault Diagnosis and Repair: The high and low pressure pipelines were checked with an air conditioning pressure gauge, which were completely normal. The possibility that no refrigerant in the air conditioning system or the refrigerant was insufficient, which caused the air conditioning to not operate, was excluded.

The electromagnetic clutch plug of air conditioning compressor was removed. The two pins on the plug were connected with a test light. The voltage when the air conditioning was turned on was measured, without light flashing (the control voltage of Bora compressor is pulse width modulated signal voltage, which cannot be measured with a multimeter). Then the signal output terminal T14/10 (connected with green/black wire) of J293 air conditioning relay compressor was checked and not powered.

According to the working principle of Bora engine air conditioning system, the control unit J220 receives the signals from sensors (the signal of air conditioning switch, the signal of high and low voltage switch, F38 external temperature switch, water temperature sensor signal, automobile speed signal and special working condition signal), and outputs the corresponding voltage to J293 after analysis and processing, so as to control the suction of compressor electromagnetic clutch. The signal input terminal T14/3 (connected to green wire) of J293 air conditioning relay control unit J220 was measured and not powered. This indicates that the air conditioning did not work due to abnormal sensor signal.

According to the maintenance principle from simple to complicated, firstly, the signal identification status of air conditioning switch was checked, i. e. pin T14/8 of J293 (connected with blue/red line). The air conditioning switch was turned on when the engine was working. At this time, the voltage was 12V, and the off AC switch turned to 0V. Then the signal identification status of high and low voltage switch was checked. When the engine was working, the voltage in the high-voltage pipe sensed by pin T14/2 of J293 (connected with white line) was 2. 9V, belonging to the static normal sensing voltage range of air conditioning. Finally, the wiring of external temperature switch was checked, and the resistance between pin T14/14 (connected with green/blue line) and T14/5 (connected with blue/red line) is infinite (normally, it should be connected under normal temperature). The F38 wiring harness was further inspected and it was found that the wiring harness near the switch was bitten off by a mouse, causing an open circuit, thus sending a signal to the control unit that the air conditioning was disconnected, causing the air conditioning to not operate.

After repairing the external switch harness, the compressor operated normally and the air conditioning could cool normally.

Summary: This fault was detected by means of the air conditioning pressure gauge and multimeter for the air-conditioning system pressure and circuit, and the fault analysis was performed according to principle, but the scan tool was not used. For this Bora air conditioning system, the diagnostic efficiency can be greatly improved by reading the fault code and data flow via a scan tool, and then checking the corresponding fault according to the fault code information.

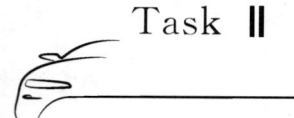

Task Ⅱ Fault Diagnosis and Repair of Insufficient Cooling of Air Conditioning System

Learning Objectives

1. Be able to determine the direction and items of inquiry according to the fault phenomena of the automobile for repair.

2. Be able to prepare a correct fault diagnosis plan according to fault phenomena.

3. Be able to consult maintenance data skillfully, select appropriate detection and diagnosis devices according to fault phenomena and use them skillfully.

4. Be able to detect insufficient cooling of air conditioning with appropriate maintenance devices according to the diagnosis plan.

5. Be able to correctly analyze the detection results and determine the fault location and cause of insufficient cooling of air conditioning.

6. Be able to repair the fault parts quickly and accurately and eliminate the hidden troubles.

Task Import

Task Material: A Honda Accord, driving 160, 000 kilometers. The owner said that the air conditioning cooling effect was poor.

Task Requirements: According to the fault phenomena of the car, consult relevant materials, select appropriate detection and diagnosis devices for fault diagnosis and repair, and fill in the task report.

Ⅰ. Fault Analysis

The so-called insufficient cooling means that the compressor operates normally, but the cold air out of the air outlet is insufficient, and the cooling effect is poor.

There are several reasons for the insufficient cooling:

(1) Too low power supply and voltage reduce the suction of electric clutch of compressor or oil stain exists between pressure plate of electric clutch and belt plate.

(2) The compressor drive belt is too loose.

(3) The refrigerant is too much, which is usually caused by excessive refrigerant filling during maintenance.

(4) The refrigerant is too little, which is mostly due to micro-leakage of refrigerant in the system.

(5) There are excessive impurities in refrigerant and refrigeration oil, causing a little blockage.

(6) There is moisture penetration in the air conditioning refrigeration system.

(7) There is air in the system.

(8) The heat dissipation capacity of condenser is reduced.

Item Ⅻ Fault Diagnosis and Repair of Automotive Air Conditioning System **187**

(9) The expansion valve is damaged.

II. Fault Diagnosis

1. Check whether the compressor belt is too loose

When the engine is shut down, manually move the belt at the middle position of the belt. If the belt can be turned over by about 90°, it indicates proper tightness; Too much rotation means that the belt is too loose and should be tightened. Replace the belt if the tightening is invalid or if the belt has cracks and is aging.

2. Check if there is too much or too little refrigerant

It can be seen from the liquid sight glass above the receiver-dryer. If no air bubbles can be seen from the liquid sight glass during the operation of the automobile air conditioning and there is no bubble after the compressor stops, which means too much refrigerant.

If there is too much refrigerant, it can slowly discharge some at the service opening on the low pressure side of the air conditioning system. In the normal operation of the air conditioning, if there are continuous slow bubbles in the liquid sight glass, it indicates that the refrigerant is insufficient. Significant bubble reversal indicates a serious shortage of refrigerant. If the refrigerant is insufficient, add refrigerant. If the amount of pressurized cooling oil is excessive, the more cloudy air bubbles can be seen from the liquid sight glass when the air conditioning system is operating normally.

3. Check for impurities in refrigerant and refrigeration oil

It can be observed from the liquid sight glass above the dryer. When the air conditioning system operates normally, the relatively turbid bubbles can be seen from the liquid sight glass, which indicates that there are too many impurities in the system, and the refrigerant shall be replaced.

4. Check for water penetration in the refrigeration system

When the cooling effect of the air conditioning becomes poor, the refrigeration system will be in normal condition again after shutdown for a while, which indicates that there is water in the system. At the same time, to better detect the amount of water in the system, the desiccant used in some cars is blue when it does not contain water. Once there is too much water, the desiccant becomes red. If the refrigerant has too much water, replace the desiccant or the dryer, vacuum the system again, and refill with new and right amount of refrigerant.

5. Check heat dissipation capacity of the condenser

First check whether there is oily soil or sundries on the surface of condenser installed in front of car engine, if any, remove the soil or sundries on condenser surface with a soft brush. Then check whether the cooling fan is working properly, such as loose drive belt and reduced fan speed, which will also result in reduced heat dissipation capacity of condenser. If there is a problem with the fan, repair or replace the electric fan.

6. Check other conditions of the refrigeration system

Check the refrigeration system for blockage, leaks and air in the system.

Ⅲ. Task Implementation

1. Inquiry

The repairman shall know the time of fault from the owner; Whether there are other abnormal conditions before the fault; Whether the symptoms change after finding the fault; Details of driving; Whether the automobile is maintained on time; Have other repairs been performed after the fault. Through the above inquiry, understand the situation before and after the fault and the specific information of the fault, and complete the preliminary diagnosis of insufficient cooling.

2. Test-drive and Basic Inspection

Carry out the test-drive to confirm the fault. After shutdown, check whether the air conditioning pipeline has oil stains, whether the condenser surface is too dirty, and whether the cooling fan works normally.

3. Detection and Diagnosis

Upon inspection, compressor and clutch work normally.

After the engine runs for a period of time, keep idle running. Turn on the air conditioning switch. Continuous bubbles can be seen from the observation window of reservoir. The low pressure pipeline is not cold enough and there is no water bead on the surface. The air at the air outlet of the air conditioning is not cold. The preliminary diagnosis is lack of refrigerant.

A manifold pressure gauge is used to detect the high and low pressure ends, whose pressure values are both low, which verifies the judgment of lack of refrigerant. Lack of refrigerant is often caused by leaks in the refrigeration system. After inspection, leaks are found at the joint of the reservoir.

4. Fault Elimination

Replace the washer and tighten the nut according to the specified torque. Fill refrigerant until the pressure on the high pressure gauge reaches the normal value, and then conduct gas leakage detection to confirm that there is no leakage. During the engine running, no bubbles of the refrigerant are observed from the observation window, and the air at the outlet is cold, which indicates that the refrigerant quantity is appropriate, the cooling effect is good, and the fault is eliminated.

5. Inspection and Delivery

After troubleshooting, re-installation and test run are conducted without any other symptoms, and the car is handed over to the owner.

Ⅳ. Task Summary

The fault belongs to a common fault of refrigerant shortage caused by leakage of the refrigeration system, so it can be judged that the cause of the failure is refrigerant leakage by performing the pressure detection of the air conditioning system. The key point is to find out the root cause of refrigerant leakage and solve it and eliminate the hidden trouble.

Ⅴ. Task Report

Major			Class		Name	
Task Name					Class Hours	2
Model				Engine Model		
	Assessment Items		Assessment Contents		Maximum Score	Score
Task Completion Process	1. Description of fault symptoms				5	
	2. Possible causes and analysis of fault				25	
	3. Detection and diagnosis process				35	
	4. Fault Elimination				10	
	5. Summary of fault diagnosis				10	
Teacher Evaluation	Operation quality, operation efficiency, operation safety, etc.				15	
	Total Score				100	

Ⅵ. Knowledge Expansion

[Typical Case Ⅰ]　Poor cooling of the air conditioning in a Volkswagen Jetta car.

Fault Description: A Volkswagen Jetta 1.6L car had poor cooling of air conditioning.

Fault Diagnosis and Repair: Firstly, the air-conditioning pipeline connector was observed without obvious oil stain, indicating no obvious leakage. There was no abnormal sound when the compressor was running.

Then the air conditioning system pressure was measured with a pressure gauge as follows.

Measured operating conditions. Engine speed: 1,500~2,000r/min; Ambient temperature: 25℃ to 30℃.

Measured actual pressure. Low pressure: 0.33MPa; High pressure: 1.1MPa.

Normal system low pressure: 0.15~0.25MPa; High pressure: 1.2~1.5MPa.

According to comparison between low pressure and high pressure and corresponding normal system pressure, low pressure was obviously higher than normal value.

If the low pressure is high and the high pressure is low, the fault location is usually the compressor.

After replacing the expansion valve, the test drive was conducted and the fault remained. After replacing the compressor, the test drive was conducted and the fault was eliminated.

Summary: The diagnosis direction of the fault was determined by detecting the pressure of the air conditioning system. The fault location is usually in the compressor, and the probability of failure of the expansion valve is relatively small. When troubleshooting, the compressor should have been replaced instead of the expansion valve, and the repair took a wrong path.

[Typical Case Ⅱ]　Insufficient refrigeration capacity of air conditioning in a Shanghai Volkswagen Lavida car.

Fault Description: A 2011 Shanghai Volkswagen Lavida car, equipped with 1.6L CDE engine, manual air conditioning, driving 25,000 km. The owner said after turning on the air conditioning refrigeration system, it felt that the cooling capacity was insufficient.

190　Automobile Integrated Fault Diagnosis and Repair

Fault Diagnosis and Repair: After taking over the car, the repairman firstly confirmed whether there was insufficient cooling capacity of air conditioning system. He started the engine, turned on the cooling function of air conditioning, turned on the wind speed to 2nd gear and the wind direction to the middle air outlet. He measured the air outlet temperature with a thermometer. After 5 minutes, the thermometer displayed 16.7℃, which was much higher than the standard value of "air outlet temperature ＜11℃". There was a obvious fault.

The air conditioning system of this car consists of refrigeration system, heating system, air supply system and electronic control system. The heating system could not be considered as it was a cooling issue. Firstly, the refrigerant analyzer 16900 was used to analyze the purity of the refrigerant in the pipeline, and the analysis result was qualified; Then the pressure gauge was connected, and the indexes of high and low pressure were within the normal range; The condenser was checked and was clean and free from dirt; There was dew on low-pressure pipe via visual inspection. The pipe was very cold. These preliminary inspections showed that there was no problem with the cooling capacity, and the refrigeration system problem can basically be ruled out. Since the refrigeration system compressor worked properly, it proved that the control system of the air conditioning worked properly, and only the air supply system was the remaining suspicious part. Then the console was removed to check the blower housing. It was found that the plastic skin on the cold and hot air doors inside the blower had been seriously peeled off and wrinkled, as shown in Figure 12-3. This made the cold and hot air doors unable to close completely, so that part of the hot air mixed with the cooled air, and sent out the air outlet, causing the air outlet temperature could not reach the normal range.

Although significant problems were noted with the cold and hot air doors, the entire lower assembly was replaced because no separate door fittings were availa-

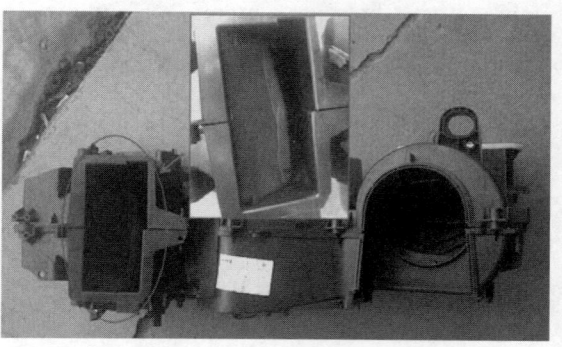

Figure 12-3 Wrinkled Cold and Hot Air Door

ble. After replacement, the engine was operated, the air conditioning was turned on, the wind speed was set to 2nd gear, the wind direction was selected as the middle air outlet, and the temperature of the air outlet was measured. After 5min, the thermometer displayed 12.2℃. The temperature dropped but was still higher than the normal range. The temperature of the low pressure pipe of air conditioning was also very low through hand feeling, which means that the cooling was OK. What will be the reason why the air outlet temperature can not be lowered? There are other factors affecting the temperature of the air outlet except that the cold and hot air doors are not closed tightly.

If the evaporator cools the air insufficiently, the air passing through the evaporator will not be sufficiently cooled, so the temperature of the air sent out from the air outlet will become higher. The working mode of the evaporator is shown in Figure 12-4. After passing through the evaporator, the hot air will be cooled to cold air. Therefore, the blower was re-

moved and the evaporator shell in the blower was touched by hand. It was found that the temperature of the shell was obviously higher than that of the low-pressure pipe of the air conditioning, but it was slightly cool, not like the low-pressure pipe, which was obviously abnormal. Therefore, it was judged that the inside of evaporator was blocked, causing poor

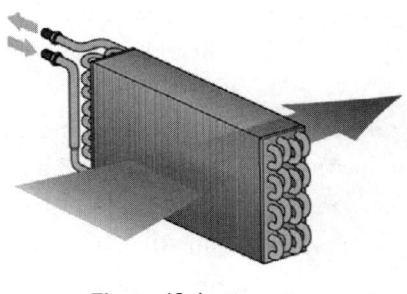

Figure 12-4　Operating
Diagram of Evaporator

heat exchange. The blower was removed again, the evaporator was replaced. Then the blower was installed and the test drive was conducted. After testing, the temperature of air outlet was reduced to 4℃, which met the standard of air outlet temperature. The fault, insufficient cooling capacity of air conditioning, was eliminated.

Summary: The fault was a comprehensive fault. The root cause was the blockage inside the evaporator, which caused the air passing through the evaporator not to be sufficiently cooled. Meanwhile, the cold and hot air doors of the air supply system was not closed tightly, which caused the air with higher temperature to mix with the hot air and then sent it out, and finally the air supply temperature at the air outlet was too high. For the fault of the air conditioning system, it is better to diagnose the sub-system according to the composition of the air conditioning system according to the order of refrigeration system, heating system, air supply system and electronic control system, which can greatly simplify the diagnosis flow and improve the diagnosis efficiency.

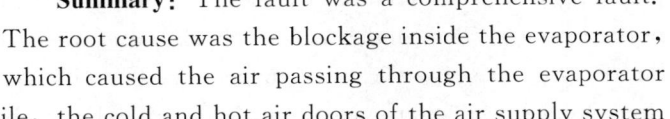

Task Ⅲ　Fault Diagnosis and Repair of Air Conditioning Easy to Ice

Learning Objectives

1. Be able to determine the direction and items of inquiry according to the fault phenomena of the automobile for repair.

2. Be able to prepare a correct fault diagnosis plan according to fault phenomena.

3. Be able to consult maintenance data skillfully, select appropriate detection and diagnosis devices according to fault phenomena and use them skillfully.

4. Be able to test the fault of the air conditioning easy to ice with appropriate maintenance devices according to the diagnosis plan.

5. Be able to correctly analyze the test results and determine the fault location and reason of air conditioning easy to ice.

6. Be able to repair the fault parts quickly and accurately and eliminate the hidden troubles.

Task Import

Task Material: A Magotan 1. 8TSI car, driving mileage of 65, 000 km. When the air

conditioning is in cooling state, and after driving at high speed for more than 30 minutes, the air outlet of the air conditioning does not blow air out and the cooling function fails.

Task Requirements: According to the fault phenomena of the car, consult relevant materials, select appropriate detection and diagnosis devices for fault diagnosis and repair, and fill in the task report.

I. Fault Analysis

The failure shows that after turning on the air conditioning for a period of time, the cooling effect of the air conditioning is obviously reduced, and at the same time, frost is formed on the inlet and outlet pipes of the evaporator. After removing the frost, the cooling effect recovers.

The causes of this failure are as follows:

(1) The evaporator surface temperature sensor or temperature switch does not work properly.

(2) The amount of refrigerant filled is incorrect.

(3) The pipe of the system is blocked.

(4) There is moisture in the system.

(5) The expansion valve does not work properly.

(6) The adjustment function of the compressor itself fails.

II. Fault Diagnosis

(1) Check the refrigerant filling amount. Observe from the liquid sight glass above the dryer. During the running of the air conditioning, if no bubbles can not be seen from the liquid sight glass, and there is no bubble after the compressor stops, that means excessive refrigerant.

(2) Read out the fault code with the scan tool. If there is a fault code, eliminate the fault according to the fault code. Read whether the data flow of the evaporator surface temperature sensor is normal and whether the temperature switch opens or closes normally.

(3) Use the air conditioning pressure gauge to detect the pressure of high and low pressure pipelines, and compare the detected pressure values with the normal values to judge the fault location.

(4) The refrigerant in the air conditioning system can be recovered and refilled with the specified quantity to eliminate moisture in the system.

III. Task Implementation

1. Inquiry

The repairman shall know the time of fault from the owner; Whether there are other abnormal conditions before the fault; Whether the symptoms change after finding the fault; Details of driving; Whether the automobile is maintained on time; Have other repairs been performed after the fault. Through the above inquiry, understand the situation before and after the fault and the specific information of the fault, and complete the preliminary diagnosis of the air conditioning easy to ice.

Item XII　Fault Diagnosis and Repair of Automotive Air Conditioning System

2. Test-drive and Basic Inspection

Carry out the test-drive to confirm the fault. Check the air-conditioning pipeline after stopping, and find that there is ice formation in the low-pressure pipe of the air conditioning.

3. Detection and Diagnosis

Use the scan tool VAS5052A to read out the fault code. No fault code is displayed, go to 08-08 to read the air-conditioning system data flow and find that the Group 6 data flow displays abnormally.

For a normal car, the Group 6 data—Area 1: The temperature behind the evaporator is shown as 1~2℃.

For the faulty car, the Group 6 data—Area 1: The temperature behind the evaporator is displayed as 5~10℃.

The temperature behind the evaporator is detected by the outlet air temperature sensor behind the evaporator.

There is no fault code because the sensor data changes dynamically with the change of working state of the air conditioning. Combined with the abnormal display of data flow, it can be basically judged that the outlet air temperature sensor behind the evaporator is abnormal.

Therefore, the sensor located at the passenger's evaporator is removed for inspection, and it is found that the sensor is installed incorrectly, and the outlet air temperature sensor behind the evaporator of the Sagitar manual air conditioning is mistakenly installed on the Sagitar automatic air conditioning. The outlet air temperature sensor behind the evaporator of the Sagitar automatic air conditioning is longer than that of the Sagitar manual air conditioning.

Since the outlet air temperature sensor behind the evaporator of the Sagitar manual air conditioning is shorter than that of the Sagitar automatic air conditioning, the actual temperature of evaporator cannot be sensed. When the outlet temperature of evaporator is close to 1~2℃, the reflected temperature is 5~10℃. According to this signal, the air conditioning electronic control system controls the compressor to operate at a large displacement, causing the evaporator to freeze. When the evaporator freezes, there is no cold air blowing out of the air conditioning, and the temperature reflected by the outlet air temperature sensor behind the evaporator continues to rise, and the air conditioning control system will operate at greater displacement according to the signal, so that the air conditioning evaporator accelerates ice formation, and the cold air cannot be blown out, and the low pressure pipe of the air conditioning is frosted.

4. Fault Elimination

After replacing the outlet air temperature sensor behind the evaporator, the fault is eliminated.

5. Inspection and Delivery

After troubleshooting, re-installation and test run are conducted without any other symptoms, and the car is handed over to the owner.

IV. Task Summary

The failure analysis of this case is mainly to find out the cause of failure from the data flow. The evaporator outlet temperature sensor data in Group 6 Area 1 is higher than normal and the fault is due to an incorrectly assembled evaporator outlet temperature sensor. This kind of fault diagnosis requires not only knowledge of diagnosis, but also familiarity with auto parts.

V. Task Report

Major			Class		Name	
Task Name					Class Hours	2
Model				Engine Model		
Task Completion Process	Assessment Items		Assessment Contents		Maximum Score	Score
Task Completion Process	1. Description of fault symptoms				5	
Task Completion Process	2. Possible causes and analysis of fault				25	
Task Completion Process	3. Detection and diagnosis process				35	
Task Completion Process	4. Fault Elimination				10	
Task Completion Process	5. Summary of fault diagnosis				10	
Teacher Evaluation	Operation quality, operation efficiency, operation safety, etc.				15	
Total Score					100	

VI. Knowledge Expansion

【Typical Case Ⅰ】 Air conditioning evaporator icing of a 2004 Audi A6 2. 4L car.

Fault Description: The owner of an Audi A6 2. 4L car said that after long-distance driving, the air conditioner was poorly cooled and the air volume at the air outlet decreased. After stopping for a while or turning off the air conditioning for a while, the air conditioning was turned on and returned to normal, and there was a large amount of air conditioning water on the floor on the driver's side.

Fault Diagnosis and Repair: According to the description of the owner, it was preliminarily judged that the fault phenomenon was caused by the ice formation of the evaporator of the air conditioning system. Firstly, the pressure of the air conditioning system was checked. When turning on the air conditioning, the pressure at the high and low pressure ends was normal upon inspection, high pressure 1,600kPa and low pressure 280kPa. System pressure was OK.

The air conditioning control unit was checked with VAS5052, and no fault code was detected. The value of each air outlet sensor of the air conditioning control unit was checked with data block and was normal.

Audi A6 adopts variable displacement compressor. It was preliminarily judged that the evaporator icing of the air conditioning system was caused by the adjustment function malfunction of the compressor during long-distance driving, and the air conditioning system was at the cooling state with large load all the time. Possible causes of evaporator ice formation are: The adjustment function of compressor itself fails; Incorrect refrigerant filling amount; There is moisture in the system; The pipe of the system is blocked. Although the

pressure of the system was normal during operation, the normal pressure value did not mean that the refrigerant filling amount of the air conditioning system was normal. When recovering the refrigerant from the air conditioning system of the car, it was found that the refrigerant quantity of the air conditioning system of the car was 510g, and the normal value should be (650±50)g. After vacuumizing and system leakage detection, 650g of refrigerant was refilled, the test run was conducted and the ice formation of evaporator was eliminated.

Summary: The maintenance personnel must confirm the fault phenomenon and fault representation of the automobile when judging the automobile fault, and shall make judgment through actual detection not through guessing. Through this fault, we know that the refrigerant amount of the air conditioning system must be filled according to the original data given by the automobile, not too much or too little. In addition, the maintenance personnel must understand the working principle of the system in detail, and analyze the cause of failure according to the working conditions, so as to quickly and accurately judge the fault and find out the cause of the failure.

Item XIII

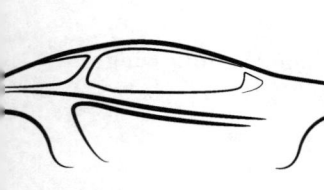

Fault Diagnosis and Repair of Body Electrical Apparatus

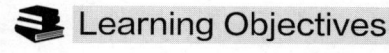

Task I Fault Diagnosis and Repair of Central Control Door Lock

Learning Objectives

1. Be able to determine the direction and items of inquiry according to the fault phenomena of the automobile for repair.

2. Be able to prepare a correct fault diagnosis plan according to fault phenomena.

3. Be able to consult maintenance data skillfully, select appropriate detection and diagnosis devices according to fault phenomena and use them skillfully.

4. Be able to detect the central control door lock fault with appropriate maintenance devices according to the diagnosis plan.

5. Be able to correctly analyze the detection results and determine the fault position and cause of the central control door lock.

6. Be able to repair the fault parts quickly and accurately and eliminate the hidden troubles.

7. Be able to work rigorously and carefully, and improve safety and service awareness.

Task Import

Task Material: A 2010 Jetta car with a driving mileage of 130,000 km. The owner said that the four-door window regulator could not be lifted or lowered. It was repaired many times outside and replaced the regulator fuse. It was easy to use at that time, but after a period of time the fault appeared again.

Task Requirements: According to the fault phenomena of the car, consult relevant materials, select appropriate detection and diagnosis devices for fault diagnosis and repair, and fill in the task report.

Ⅰ. Fault Analysis

The working mode of central control door lock is mainly divided into two categories: one is the direct control of switch or module; The other is controlled by onboard network transmission signal and electronic control unit. The first type of fault diagnosis is relatively simple, it does not involve the onboard network circuit, and the working circuit is only ordinary wire. Only the central control door locks which are controlled by onboard network transmission signal and electronic control unit are analyzed here. This kind of control method involves multiple electronic control units, and the working circuit has not only common wires, but also CAN or Lin bus, so the working principle is complicated.

The main reasons why a central control door lock does not work include the following:

(1) The lock control switch is faulty.

(2) The control unit and its wiring are faulty.

(3) The lock motor and its circuit are faulty.

(4) The lock CAN or Lin signal circuit is faulty.

(5) The network control unit is faulty.

(6) The lock is mechanically faulty.

Ⅱ. Fault Diagnosis

(1) If the central control door lock of the door is not working, firstly, we should read out the fault code with a scan tool. If there is a fault code, find out the fault location according to the fault code. We can also use the scan tool for active test. If it works during the active test, the fault location is in the circuit and plug in the switch and from switch to its control unit. If it doesn't work during the active test, the fault location is likely to be: central control door lock control unit and its power ground circuit; CAN or Lin signal line between the control unit and its upper-level control unit; Central control door lock; Mechanical part of central control door lock.

(2) All central control door locks do not work. Firstly, we should read out the fault code with the scan tool. If there is a fault code, find out the fault location according to the fault code. In addition, the upper-level master control unit and its CAN or Lin signal line shall be detected for all central control door lock control units.

Ⅲ. Task Implementation

1. Inquiry

The repairman shall know the time of fault from the owner; Whether there are other abnormal conditions before the fault; Whether the symptoms change after finding the fault; Details of driving; Whether the automobile is maintained on time; Have other repairs been performed after the fault. Find out the situation before and after the fault and the specific information of the fault through the above inquiry, and complete the preliminary diagnosis of the central control door lock fault.

2. Test-drive and Basic Inspection

Perform the door lock function test to understand the fault characteristics and confirm

the fault. In addition, the structural features and wiring connection mode of the central control door lock of the car shall be determined.

3. Detection and Diagnosis

Measure the fuse (S111) for power and when measuring it is found to be very hot. Part of the Jetta car window regulator fuses are thermally protected. In case of excessive power consumption or short circuit of positive electrode to ground, the fuses will be disconnected automatically.

Therefore, it can be judged that the electric appliance behind the fuse is abnormal. Looking at the circuit diagram of the window regulator, it can be seen that the fuse supplies power to the motor of the four doors, so the circuit behind the fuse is further tested.

There are the following methods of detection:

(1) Disassemble the four door inner panel and disconnect the motor plug to see if the fuse is still hot.

(2) Find the four-door positive connection points and disconnect them one by one.

(3) Use the current sensing clamp to sense four-door discharge.

The second method is used here to disconnect the power supply lines of the four doors one by one.

It is observed that when the right front door is disconnected, the discharge quantity disappears and the fuse is no longer overheated, so it can be judged that the fault point is inside the right front door harness or motor. Disassemble the inner panel of right front door and inspect the motor and wiring harness, and find the wiring harness at the folded part of right front door is worn, and the positive wire is exposed and grounded. The fault point is shown in Figure 13-1.

Figure 13-1 Broken Wiring Harness

4. Fault Elimination

After re-wrapping the wiring harness, a test run is done and the fault is eliminated.

5. Inspection and Delivery

After troubleshooting, re-installation and test run are conducted without any other symptoms, and the car is handed over to the owner.

IV. Task Summary

From this fault case, we realize that we can list several feasible solutions and find an

easy way to troubleshoot when repairing the fault, which allows us to find the fault point faster and more accurately.

V. Task Report

	Major		Class		Name	
	Task Name				Class Hours	2
	Model		Engine Model			
	Assessment Items	Assessment Contents			Maximum Score	Score
Task Completion Process	1. Description of fault symptoms				5	
	2. Possible causes and analysis of fault				25	
	3. Detection and diagnosis process				35	
	4. Fault Elimination				10	
	5. Summary of fault diagnosis				10	
Teacher Evaluation	Operation quality, operation efficiency, operation safety, etc.				15	
	Total Score				100	

VI. Knowledge Expansion

〔Typical Case Ⅰ〕 Only the left front door of a Chevrolet SAIL car could be opened.

Fault Description: A Chevrolet New SAIL car, manual transmission, 62, 000 kilometers. The owner said that the central control lock system failed, from inside or outside, only the left front door could be opened.

Fault Diagnosis and Repair: The car has the anti-theft locking function, i. e. when the car is in the electronic anti-theft locking state, unless the lock is opened at the left front door with the key, no other means can unlock it.

According to the fault phenomenon, the suspected possible causes included wiring problem, central control module fault and S41 switch fault, etc. During detection, based on the principle from simpleness to complexity and from periphery to interior, firstly, the circuit was tested, then the central control module was tested, and finally the S41 switch was detected.

Firstly, the key was used to unlock and lock the trunk, and the result was that the trunk lock worked normally. The left front door was opened, and the central control module was removed. According to the circuit diagram of the central control door lock system, a test light was used to connect with the 12V power supply at one end, and to connect with terminal 7 of the central control module at the other end. When the key rotated the left front door lock cylinder at unlocking position, the test light was on, and the test light was off when the key was turned back. After repeating the above test on the right front door, the result was same, indicating that an unlocking signal was transmitted to the central control door lock module. The terminal 8 of the central control module was tested with the test light. One end of the test light was grounded and the other end was connected to terminal 8. The result was that the test light was not on, indicating that the central control module had no correct unlocking signal input. There were two possible reasons: Firstly, there was an internal fault of the central control module. The fault still remained after replacing the central control module, so the fault of the central control module was excluded; Secondly, the central con-

trol system entered the anti-theft mode and did not respond to any input signal. The anti-theft of the left front door lock only depends on mechanical theft and does not have electronic locking anti-theft, so the lock on this side could still be unlocked and locked freely. The way to bring the central control door lock into the anti-theft setting and maintain this state is by turning on terminals 1 and 2 of switch S41. So it was likely that the S41 switch was faulty. After removing the connecting plug of S41 switch on the interlocking core assembly of the outside handle of left front door, the key was used to unlock, all the doors were opened and the central control system returned to normal. When the plug was plugged back, the central control system repeated the previous fault.

After removing the anti-theft deadlock switch, it was found that terminals 1 and 2 of the switch were glued together upon measurement, resulting in the central control module in the anti-theft deadlock state for a long time. Even if the unlocking signal was received, the signal would be ignored due to the execution of internal procedures, so the remaining 3 doors were locked. After replacing the anti-theft deadlock switch, the fault was thoroughly eliminated.

Summary: The cause of this fault was on the main driver's anti-theft deadlock switch, which is mainly due to the particularity of the deadlock function of the door lock of SAIL. During automobile maintenance, we must carefully analyze the system circuit and internal control characteristics, so as to find out the cause of fault and eliminate the fault accurately.

[Typical Case II] The lock indicator of central control lock of a 2010 Golf 6 car was not on.

Fault Description: A 2010 Golf 6 car, an accident automobile. During inspection and delivery after maintenance, it was found that the lock indicator of central control lock was not on, and during the locking process, the lock block part emitted 2~3 sounds of action.

Fault Diagnosis and Repair: Firstly, the fault diagnosis was performed by using Volkswagen special scan tool. There were two fault codes, namely, the driver side of the locking unit of the central control lock-F220 unreliable signal and the driver side central control lock fuse/lock signal unreliable signal, as shown in Figure 13-2.

Because the car was an accident repaired car and the left front door and all accessory components had been replaced, other lines may be damaged during the initial diagnosis, resulting in this fault (because the parts of the central control door lock were new). The corresponding circuit was checked according to the circuit diagram shown in Figure 13-3. No short circuit or open circuit was found. Therefore, the problem was locked on the replaced spare parts. Inadvertently, the lock block plug was pulled off, the indicator was on after pressing the lock key. If the wiring harness of the lock block was suspected to be faulty, the circuit of the lock block was checked again. After the ground wire of the lock block was disconnected, the indicator was on through pressing the lock key. Because the lock block installed on the car was new, the spare parts of the car were checked and two kinds of lock blocks were found, one of which has part number: L5K1 837 015C, the other has the part number without tail C, the former is used by Golf and new Sagitar, and the latter is used by Golf. Because it was an accident car, the original part number could not be confirmed, and the circuit of the car was checked to be in good condition. At the same time, the computer indicated that there was a problem with the lock block. After replacing the lock block with

Item XIII   Fault Diagnosis and Repair of Body Electrical Apparatus   **201**

the tail C, and the fault became incidental. It was determined that the fault point was that the model of the internal lock block was incorrect. Therefore, the lock block was replaced and the fault was eliminated completely.

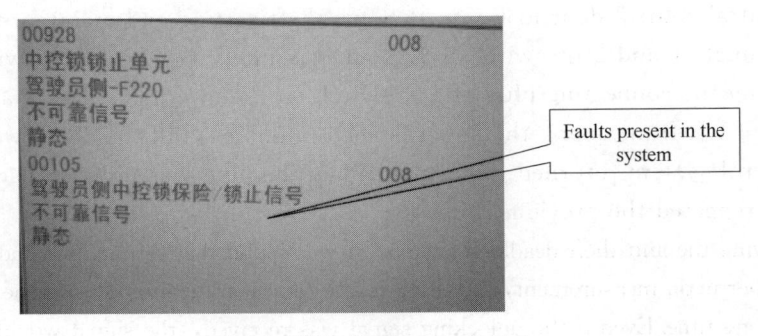

Figure 13-2 Reading Fault Codes

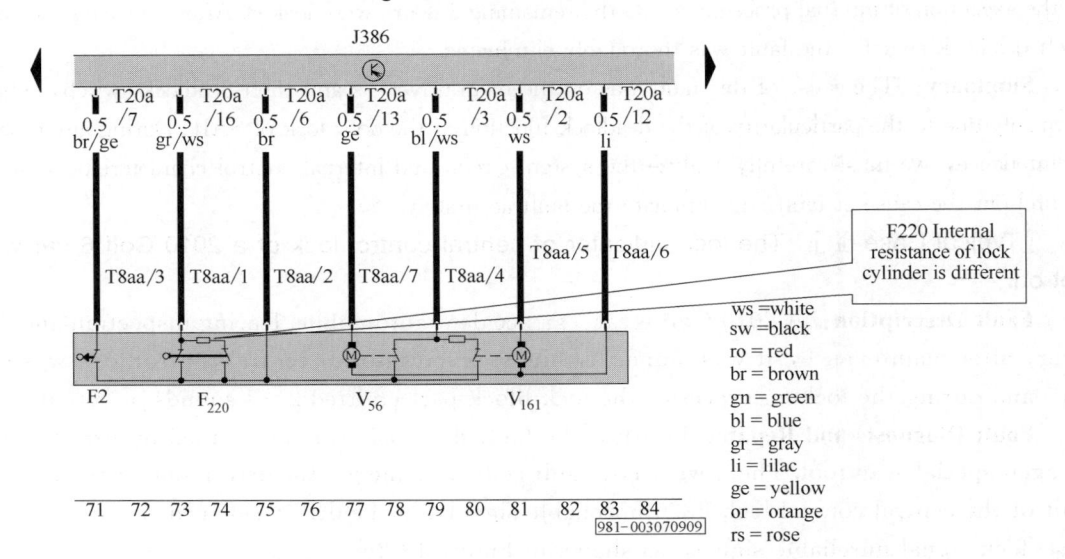

Figure 13-3 Circuit Diagram of Golf 6 Central Control Door Lock System

Summary: Different spare parts have different internal structures. Although they can be installed and used, they may result in limitations of some functions. Replacement of spare parts, especially general spare parts, may cause different internal structure. Spare part L5K1 837 015 is a lock block installed on Golf, but the car was equipped with spare part with tail C, and the internal resistance of the two lock blocks is different, resulting in the indicator light not on and the function limited.

Task Ⅱ Fault Diagnosis and Repair of Electric Window Regulator

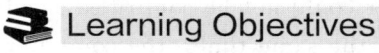

Learning Objectives

1. Be able to determine the direction and items of inquiry according to the fault phenomena

202 | Automobile Integrated Fault Diagnosis and Repair |

of the automobile for repair.

2. Be able to prepare a correct fault diagnosis plan according to fault phenomena.

3. Be able to consult maintenance data skillfully, select appropriate detection and diagnosis devices according to fault phenomena and use them skillfully.

4. Be able to test the fault of the electric window regulator with appropriate maintenance devices according to the diagnosis plan.

5. Be able to correctly analyze the test results and determine the fault location and cause of electric window regulator.

6. Be able to repair the fault parts quickly and accurately and eliminate the hidden troubles.

Task Import

Task Material: A 2010 Jetta car, driving 70, 000 km. The owner said that the four door regulators did not have automatic window lifting function after locking.

Task Requirements: According to the fault phenomena of the car, consult relevant materials, select appropriate detection and diagnosis devices for fault diagnosis and repair, and fill in the task report.

I. Fault Analysis

The working mode of electric window regulator is mainly divided into two categories: one is the direct control of switch or module; The other type is controlled by onboard network transmission signal and electronic control unit. The first type of fault diagnosis is relatively simple, it does not involve the onboard network circuit, and the working circuit is only ordinary wire. Only the electric window regulator which is controlled by onboard network transmission signal and electronic control unit is analyzed here. This kind of control method involves multiple electronic control units, and the working circuit has not only common wires, but also CAN or Lin bus, so the working principle is complicated.

The main reasons why an electric window regulator does not work include the following:

(1) The control switch of electric window regulator is faulty.

(2) The electric window regulator control unit and circuit are faulty.

(3) The electric window regulator motor and circuit are faulty.

(4) The CAN or Lin signal circuit of electric window regulator is faulty.

(5) The onboard grid control unit is faulty.

(6) The electric window regulator is mechanically faulty.

II. Fault Diagnosis

(1) If the individual door electric window regulator is not working, the fault code should be read firstly with the scan tool. If there is a fault code, find out the fault location according to the fault code. In addition, the scan tool can be used for active test. If it can work during the active test, the fault position is in the circuit and plug in the switch and from the switch to its control unit; If it does not work during the active test, it is likely that the fault location is: electric window regulator control unit and its power ground circuit;

Item XIII Fault Diagnosis and Repair of Body Electrical Apparatus | **203**

CAN or Lin signal line between the control unit and its upper level control unit; electric window regulator motor; mechanical part of electric window regulator.

(2) If all door electric window regulators do not work, the fault code should be first read out with the scan tool. If there is a fault code, the fault location should be found out according to the fault code. In addition, check the upper-level main control unit and its CAN or Lin signal lines for all electric window regulator control units.

Ⅲ. Task Implementation

1. Inquiry

The repairman shall know the time of fault from the owner; Whether there are other abnormal conditions before the fault; Whether the symptoms change after finding the fault; Details of driving; Whether the automobile is maintained on time; Have other repairs been performed after the fault. Through the above inquiry, understand the situation before and after the fault and the specific information of the fault, and complete the preliminary diagnosis of the fault of the electric window regulator.

2. Test-drive and Basic Inspection

Carry out the function test of the electric window regulator, understand the fault characteristics, confirm the fault, and determine the control mode and circuit connection mode of the electric glass regulator of the car.

3. Detection and Diagnosis

Check the four door regulators. They are in normal conditions in case of single control and the central control lock works normally, but the left front main control switch cannot control the right rear door, and the right rear door switch can control it independently. Because the car was manufactured after February 22, 2005, it has the function of locking and raising the windows. The car has Lin bus communication function and K-line diagnosis function, so it enters the address 46-Comfort System with 5051 for fault inquiry. The fault is the fault of V27 right rear door window regulator motor. According to the above analysis, the fault point may be a short circuit in the wiring harness or damage to the control unit.

Measure the harness according to the circuit diagram (as shown in Figure 13-4) and find the open circuit between T23/3 pin and T69-2Lin wire. It is found that the Lin wire is worn out under the driver's seat. After repair, the right rear regulator works normally, but still can not raise the window when the car is locked.

So it is thought that the control unit is faulty.

4. Fault Elimination

After replacing the control unit, a test run is done and the fault is eliminated.

5. Inspection and Delivery

After troubleshooting, re-installation and test run are conducted without any other symptoms, and the car is handed over to the owner.

Ⅳ. Task Summary

There are two fault points in this fault, and the electronic control unit is also damaged due to line failure. When troubleshooting, we should know how the system works, and at

the same time, we should perform fault analysis by means of the circuit. It is important to note that Jetta cars manufactured after February 22, 2005 have the function of locking and raising windows, and pay attention to the computer appearance part number.

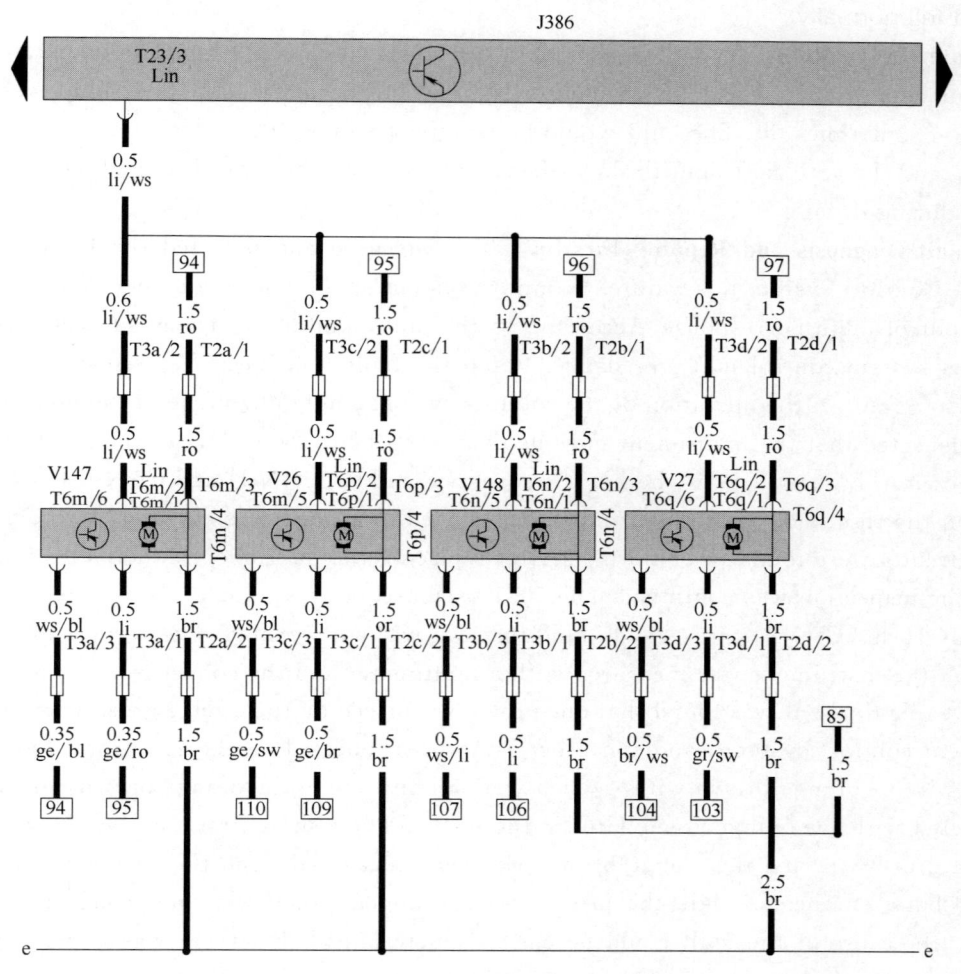

Figure 13-4 Circuit Diagram of Electric Window Regulator

V. Task Report

		Major		Class		Name	
		Task Name				Class Hours	2
		Model		Engine Model			
		Assessment Items	Assessment Contents			Maximum Score	Score
Task Completion Process		1. Description of fault symptoms				5	
		2. Possible causes and analysis of fault				25	
		3. Detection and diagnosis process				35	
		4. Fault Elimination				10	
		5. Summary of fault diagnosis				10	
Teacher Evaluation		Operation quality, operation efficiency, operation safety, etc.				15	
		Total Score				100	

Item XIII   Fault Diagnosis and Repair of Body Electrical Apparatus | **205**

VI. Knowledge Expansion

[Typical Case Ⅰ] The four door glass regulators of a Volkswagen Bora car could not lift and fall normally.

Fault Description: A Volkswagen Bora car travelled 62,000 km. The owner said that the four door window regulators could not rise and fall normally, the door light was sometimes on sometimes off. The light would be on after pressing the central control lock several times, and the anti-theft light flashed when it was not on. The central control lock jumped around during driving.

Fault Diagnosis and Repair: Firstly, 5051 was used and detected the following fault codes: Comfort system bus failure; Comfort system single-line mode operation; The four door control units no response. According to the fault condition, it was suspected that the comfort system control unit was damaged and the fault remained after replacement. There was also a fault in the operation of the comfort system single-line mode in the instrument. It was suspected that the instrument may also have problems. According to the circuit diagram (as shown in Figure 13-5), whether the corners 8 and 9 (CAN-H and CAN-L lines) of the plug on the right side of the instrument are shorted to ground was checked. After checking, both circuits were found to be normal. After replacing the instrument, the fault remained.

The inspection was continued. The 5051 oscilloscope was used to detect the waveforms of CAN-H and CAN-L wires, and found that one was not working. The harness of left front door on the instrument was measured with a multimeter and the connection was normal.

At this time, it was found that one probe was placed on the orange green wire of the instrument comfort system, and the other end was connected to the left front door orange green wire or orange brown wire, which were all on, while the orange brown wire was not connected with the orange green wire. So there should be a short circuit in the two wires. The orange-green wire and the orange-brown wire were measured, and the two wires were connected between them, while the probe was exchanged, they were not connected. At this point, the cause of the fault could be basically determined that there was a short-circuited connection between the buses, like with a diode.

The control units of doors were pulled off one by one and the orange green wire and the orange brown wire were conductive upon inspection.

The car has power seats controlled by the control unit and the fault disappeared when the seat control unit was removed and the fault code was cleared.

Each transmission line of the control unit converged in star form, so that if one control unit fails, the other control units can still transmit their respective data.

In case of short circuit to ground, short circuit to positive or open circuit in some part of the system circuit, the CAN system will immediately switch to emergency mode or single pin mode for operation.

The fault of this car was caused by internal damage of seat control unit, which led to short circuit connection between comfort CAN-H and CAN-L wires like with a diode, which led to orange green wire and orange brown wire conduction, and vice versa. The fault caused the comfort system CAN bus to operate in single wire mode.

After replacing the seat control unit, the function test was done to the four door window regulators and they returned to normal.

Summary: In this case, due to an internal failure of the seat control unit in the onboard network system, the network transmission circuit was faulty and the four door window regu-

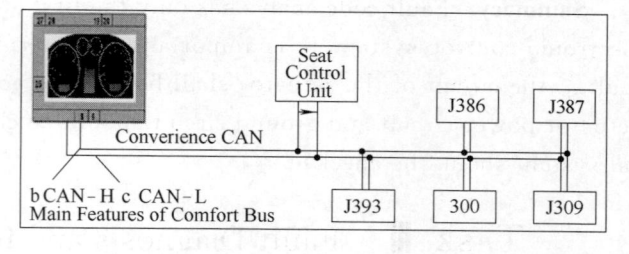

Figure 13-5　CAN Bus Circuit Diagram of Comfort System

lators failed. This kind of fault is the typical fault that is common in cars with onboard network control at present, that is, when the function of a certain system is abnormal, not only the fault of the system components and the circuit, but also the network system fault should be considered.

〔Typical Case Ⅱ〕 The left front door window regulator of a 2010 Volkswagen Sagitar car failed to be lifted or lowered.

Fault Description: A 2010 Volkswagen Sagitar car, driving 58,000 kilometers. The owner said that the left front door window regulator could not lift and lower, the rest window regulators functioned normally.

Fault Diagnosis and Repair:

(1) The fault code was read out with VAS5052A, as shown in Figure 13-6. There were two fault memories found.

① 00932 Driver Side Window Regulator Motor-V147 Circuit Electrical Failure (Static).

② 00120 Driver Side Exterior Alarm Light/Door Light Circuit Electrical Failure (Static).

(2) The following inspections were done by referring to the circuit diagram.

① Actuator power supply-fuse SC12 was checked with a voltage of 12V, normal.

② The voltage at the connector terminal T20a/12 of the left front door control unit J386 was measured and was zero.

③ The left front door connection plug T28 was disconnected, the voltage of terminal T28/1 was 12V, and it was determined that there was open circuit in the internal circuit of the door. The detection of stripping the wiring harness found open circuit in the wiring harness, as shown in Figure 13-7. After repairing the wire harness, the fault was eliminated.

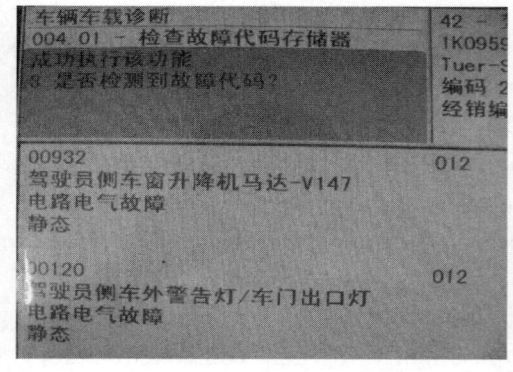

Figure 13-6　Reading Fault Codes

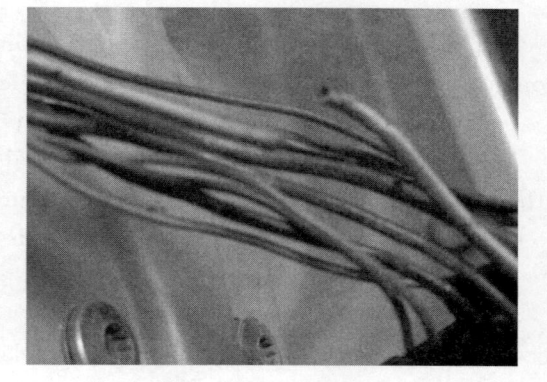

Figure 13-7　Damaged Wiring Harness

Summary: Fault code analysis is only the first step in diagnosing the fault of automobile electronic control system. It is important to determine the cause of fault code. For such faults, the circuit of the actuator shall be checked according to the circuit diagram, i. e. the actuator power circuit and ground circuit should be checked, and then the associated electrical system should be checked.

Task Ⅲ Fault Diagnosis and Repair of Automobile Lighting System

Learning Objectives

1. Be able to determine the direction and items of inquiry according to the fault phenomena of the automobile for repair.

2. Be able to prepare a correct fault diagnosis plan according to fault phenomena.

3. Be able to consult maintenance data skillfully, select appropriate detection and diagnosis devices according to fault phenomena and use them skillfully.

4. Be able to test the automobile lighting system failure with appropriate maintenance devices according to the diagnosis plan.

5. Be able to analyze the test results correctly and determine the fault location and cause of automobile lighting system.

6. Be able to repair the fault parts quickly and accurately and eliminate the hidden troubles.

Task Import

Task Material: A 2012 Beijing Hyundai ELANTRA car, driving 70, 000 km. The owner said that the brightness of headlights on both sides was inconsistent, right front brightness was normal, while left front brightness was insufficient. Task Requirements: According to the fault phenomena of the car, consult relevant materials, select appropriate detection and diagnosis devices for fault diagnosis and repair, and fill in the task report.

Ⅰ. Fault Analysis

The working mode of automobile lighting system is mainly divided into two categories: one is direct switch control; The other is electronic control unit control.

1. Fault Analysis of Automobile Lighting System with Direct Switch Control

For a switch-directly controlled automobile lighting system, when the switch is closed, the power supply circuits of all lights are turned on and all lights shall be illuminated.

(1) When the lighting system switch is turned on, all the lights controlled are not on

① Switch failure;

② Fuse failure;

③ Relay failure (most models have relays in headlight, fog light control circuits);

④ Power supply line fault.

（2）Some of the lights controlled when the lighting system switch is turned on does not illuminate

① Bulb Failure;

② Failure of light plug terminal or its power supply circuit;

③ Light ground circuit fault.

The fault diagnosis of the lighting system directly controlled by a switch is relatively simple. It does not involve the onboard network and electronic control unit, and the working circuit is only ordinary wire.

2. Fault Analysis of Lighting System Controlled by Electronic Control Unit

In the lighting system controlled by the electronic control unit, the electronic control unit receives the closing signal of the light switch, and then the electronic control unit supplies power to each bulb respectively. The grounding circuit of the light is directly grounded, and all lights are on.

（1）When the lighting system switch controlled by the electronic control unit is turned on, all the lights controlled are not on

① Switch failure;

② Faulty signal circuit in which the switch is located;

③ Local fault of electronic control unit;

④ Automotive network circuit fault (some light switch signals need to be transmitted via network).

（2）After the lighting system switch controlled by the electronic control unit is turned on, some of the lights controlled are not on

① Bulb Failure;

② Failure of light plug terminal or its power supply circuit;

③ Light ground circuit fault;

④ Local fault of electronic control unit.

II. Fault Diagnosis

1. Fault diagnosis of automobile lighting system under direct switch control

（1）When the lighting system switch is turned on, all the lights controlled are not on

① First check whether the fuse is blown, replace with the new fuse if it is blown, and if the fuse is normal, carry out the next test.

② Check the light control relay (some light controls have no relay). Replace the relay if it is damaged. If the relay is normal, carry out the next test.

③ Check whether the light switch is connected normally. If the switch cannot be connected normally, replace the switch with a new one. If the switch is normal, carry out the next test.

④ Inspect the power supply circuit for open circuit or false connection. If the circuit fails, repair it or replace the wiring harness.

（2）Some of the lights controlled after the lighting system switch is turned on are not on

① First check whether the light plug connection is normal. If the contact is poor, repair

it; if it is normal, carry out the next test.

② Check whether the bulb is damaged, replace it with a new one if it is damaged, and conduct the next test if it is normal.

③ Check whether there is open circuit, short circuit or false connection in the power supply circuit of the light. If the circuit fails, repair it or replace the wiring harness.

④ Check whether there is open circuit or false connection in the grounding circuit of the light. If the circuit fails, repair it or replace the wiring harness.

2. Fault diagnosis of lighting system controlled by electronic control unit

When the lighting system switch controlled by the electronic control unit is turned on, all the lights controlled are not on:

① First read out the fault code with the scan tool. If there is a fault code (the electronic control units of some cars can monitor all lights and their circuits, and will generate a fault code if there is a fault), find out the fault location according to the fault code.

② Use the scan tool to read the data flow of switch status. If the scan tool fails to display the corresponding data flow normally when the switch is turned on and off, further check the light switch and its signal circuit, even check the onboard network circuit, etc. If the scan tool can normally display the corresponding data flow when the switch is turned on and off, it indicates that the switch and signal circuit are normal.

③ Carry out the actuator test with the scan tool. If the light is still not on during the test, check whether the light, power supply and grounding circuit are faulty, and if there are faults, eliminate them; if there are no faults, the fault location shall be inside the control unit; If the light illuminates normally during the test, the fault is also inside the control unit.

Ⅲ. Task Implementation

1. Inquiry

The repairman shall know the time of fault from the owner; Whether there are other abnormal conditions before the fault; Whether the symptoms change after finding the fault; Details of driving; Whether the automobile is maintained on time; Have other repairs been performed after the fault. Through the above inquiry, we can understand the situation before and after the fault and the specific information of the fault, and complete the preliminary diagnosis of automobile lighting system fault.

2. Test-drive and Basic Inspection

Carry out the car fault test to understand the fault characteristics and confirm the fault. In addition, the structure characteristics and wiring connection mode of the lighting system of the car are determined.

3. Detection and Diagnosis

Check the plug connection of the left front headlight high-low beam. The connection is normal. Check the fuse of the left low beam light. It is plugged properly and has no false connection. Since the left and right high beam lights share one fuse and the right headlight works normally, the headlight high beam fuse shall be normal. Pull off the plug of the left high-low beam light, detect terminal 3 with voltage of 12V and normal voltage. Check the high-low

beam bulb and bulb is normal. Insert the plug properly. Measure the voltage between terminal 3 and terminal 4 again as 8V, and normally it should be 12V. Disconnect the plug to detect the resistance between ground terminal 4 and the automobile body is 2Ω, and the normal resistance shall be close to zero. Therefore, it is judged that the grounding of the left headlight circuit should be faulty. Look up the circuit diagram (Figure 13-8), find the grounding point GE11 position, check the fixing bolt of the grounding point. It is found that the bolt is tightened normally, but the surface of the bolt is seriously rusted. After removing the grounding point and the bolt, it is found that there is serious corrosion around the bolt.

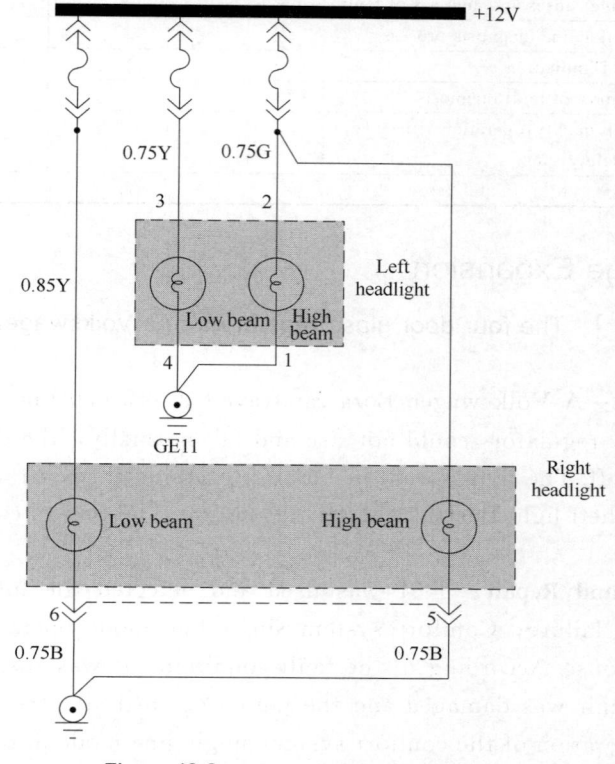

Figure 13-8 Circuit Diagram of Headlight

4. Fault Elimination

Derust the grounding point, grounding bolt and grounding wire terminal, and re-fix the grounding wire. Then the fault is eliminated

5. Inspection and Delivery

After troubleshooting, re-installation and test run are conducted without any other symptoms, and the car is handed over to the owner.

IV. Task Summary

The serious corrosion of the thread of the grounding bolt caused poor grounding, resulting in excessive grounding resistance of the wire and reduced circuit current, resulting in insufficient brightness of the bulb. The voltage at both ends of the bulb was lower than the normal voltage. After determining the fault phenomenon, we should first check the circuit diagram, find out the circuit characteristics of the headlights on the left and right sides, and

then make a comprehensive analysis, so that the key parts can be detected purposefully and the maintenance efficiency can be improved.

V. Task Report

Major			Class		Name	
Task Name					Class Hours	2
Model			Engine Model			
	Assessment Items		Assessment Contents		Maximum Score	Score
Task Completion Process	1. Description of fault symptoms				5	
	2. Possible causes and analysis of fault				25	
	3. Detection and diagnosis process				35	
	4. Fault Elimination				10	
	5. Summary of fault diagnosis				10	
Teacher Evaluation	Operation quality, operation efficiency, operation safety, etc.				15	
	Total Score				100	

VI. Knowledge Expansion

〔Typical Case Ⅰ〕 The four door glass regulators of a Volkswagen Bora car could not lift and fall normally.

Fault Description: A Volkswagen Bora car travelled 62,000 km. The owner said that the four door window regulators could not rise and fall normally, the door light was sometimes on sometimes off. The light would be on after pressing the central control lock several times, and the anti-theft light flashed when it was not on. The central control lock jumped around during driving.

Fault Diagnosis and Repair: 5051 was used and detected the following fault codes: Comfort system bus failure; Comfort system single-line mode operation; The four door control units no response. According to the fault condition, it was suspected that the comfort system control unit was damaged and the fault remained after replacement. There was also a fault in the operation of the comfort system single-line mode in the instrument. It was suspected that the instrument may also have problems. According to the circuit diagram (as shown in Figure 13-9), check whether the corners 8 and 9 (CAN-H and CAN-L lines) of the plug on the right side of the instrument are short-circuited to ground. After inspection, both lines are found to be normal. After replacing the instrument, the fault remained.

The inspection was continued. The 5051 oscilloscope was used to detect the waveforms of CAN-H and CAN-L wires, and found that one was not working. The harness of left front door on the instrument was measured with a multimeter and the connection was normal.

At this time, it was found that one probe was placed on the orange green wire of the instrument comfort system, and the other end was connected to the left front door orange green wire or orange brown wire, which were all on, while the orange brown wire was not connected with the orange green wire. So there should be a short circuit in the two wires. The orange-green wire and the orange-brown wire were measured, and the two wires were connected between them, while the probe was exchanged, they were not connected. At this point, the cause of the fault could be basically determined that there was a short-circuited

connection between the buses, like with a diode.

The control units of doors were pulled off one by one and the orange green wire and the orange brown wire were conductive upon inspection.

The car has power seats controlled by the control unit and the fault disappeared when the seat control unit was removed and the fault code was cleared.

Each transmission line of the control unit converged in star form, so that if one control unit fails, the other control units can still transmit their respective data.

In case of short circuit to ground, short circuit to positive or open circuit in some part of the system circuit, the CAN system will immediately switch to emergency mode or single pin mode for operation.

The fault of this car was caused by internal damage of seat control unit,

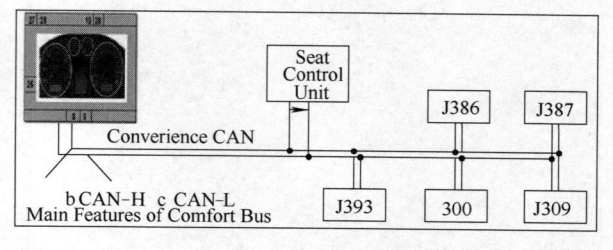

Figure 13-9 CAN Bus Circuit Diagram of Comfort System

which led to short circuit connection between comfort CAN-H and CAN-L wires like with a diode, which led to orange green wire and orange brown wire conduction, and vice versa. The fault caused the comfort system CAN bus to operate in single wire mode.

After replacing the seat control unit, the function test was done to the four door window regulators and they returned to normal.

Summary: In this case, due to an internal failure of the seat control unit in the onboard network system, the network transmission circuit was faulty and the four door window regulators failed. This kind of fault is the typical fault that is common in cars with onboard network control at present, that is, when the function of a certain system is abnormal, not only the fault of the system components and the circuit, but also the network system fault should be considered.

[Typical Case Ⅱ]   The left front door window regulator of a 2010 Volkswagen Sagitar car failed to be lifted or lowered.

Fault Description: A 2010 Volkswagen Sagitar car, driving 58, 000 km. The owner said that the left front door window regulator could not lift and lower, the rest window regulators functioned normally.

Fault Diagnosis and Repair:

(1) Read out the fault code with VAS5052A, as shown in Figure 13-10. There were two fault memories found.

① 00932 Driver Side Window Regulator Motor-V147 Circuit Electrical Failure (Static).

② 00120 Driver Side Exterior Alarm Light/Door Light Circuit Electrical Failure (Static).

(2) The following inspections were done by referring to the circuit diagram.

① The voltage of the actuator power supply-fuse SC12 was measured as 12V, which was normal.

② The voltage at the plug terminal T20a/12 of the left front door control unit J386 was

Item Ⅷ Fault Diagnosis and Repair of Body Electrical Apparatus **213**

measured as zero.

③ The left front door connection plug T28D was disconnected，the voltage of terminal T28/1 was measured as 12V，so it was determined that there was open circuit in the internal circuit of the door. The wiring harness was peeled off for detection and it was found that the wiring harness was open circuited，as shown in Figure 13-11. After repairing the wire harness，the fault was eliminated.

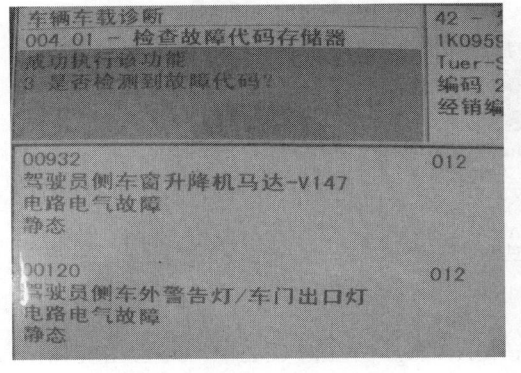

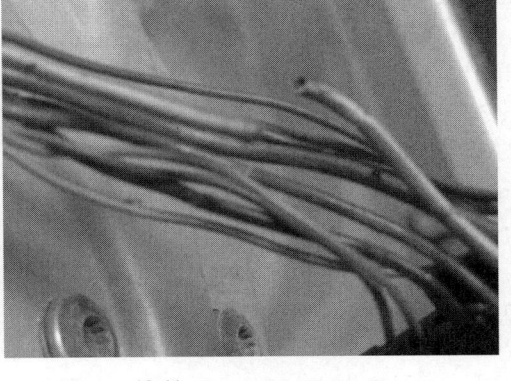

Figure 13-10　Reading Fault Codes　　　　　　**Figure 13-11**　Damaged Wiring Harness

Summary： Fault code analysis is only the first step in diagnosing the fault of automobile electronic control system. It is important to determine the cause of fault code. For such faults，the circuit of the actuator shall be checked according to the circuit diagram，i. e. the actuator power circuit and ground circuit should be checked，and then the associated electrical system should be checked.

Item XIV

Fault Diagnosis and Repair of Automobile Onboard Network System

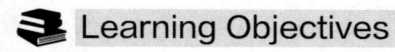

Learning Objectives

1. Be able to determine the direction and items of inquiry according to the fault phenomena of the automobile for repair.

2. Be able to prepare a correct fault diagnosis plan according to fault phenomena.

3. Be able to consult maintenance data skillfully, select appropriate detection and diagnosis devices according to fault phenomena and use them skillfully.

4. Be able to test the automobile onboard network system failure with appropriate maintenance devices according to the diagnosis plan.

5. Be able to correctly analyze the test results and determine the fault location and cause of the automobile onboard network system.

6. Be able to repair the fault parts quickly and accurately and eliminate the hidden troubles.

7. Be able to keep pursuing perfection, be brave to innovate and work rigorously and carefully.

Task Import

Task Material: In a Volkswagen Passat, occasional airbag yellow light alarm and oil light alarm occurred.

Task Requirements: According to the fault phenomena of the car, consult relevant materials, select appropriate detection and diagnosis devices for fault diagnosis and repair, and fill in the task report.

I. Fault Analysis

Through the car network topology diagram, we can understand the automobile network information transmission mode. For example, at present, Volkswagen Audi and other auto-

mobile systems generally adopt CAN data bus, including an independent gateway, as well as the power network, comfort network, infotainment network and other multi-channel networks connected with the gateway.

CAN data bus realizes real-time exchange, transmission and sharing of data and information among various electronic control systems, which makes a certain fault not only affect the electronic control system, but also affect the related electronic control systems, thus causing more faults.

Failures in the automobile CAN data bus system include two categories: One is the failure of electronic control unit itself, which is the node of information transmission of CAN data bus system; The other is the failure of CAN data bus information transmission line.

If the CAN data bus system fails, the relevant fault code information must be stored in the memory of the relevant control unit.

II. Fault Diagnosis

(1) Read the fault code and analyze the meaning of the fault code.

(2) If the scan tool fails to communicate with all electrical control units, the CAN line between the diagnosis interface and the gateway, the power supply line of the gateway and the gateway itself shall be checked for faults.

(3) If the scan tool fails to communicate with individual electronic control units, it is necessary to focus on checking whether the power supply circuit of the electronic control unit and its itself are faulty, or whether there is a open circuit between the CAN line of the electronic control unit and the network node.

(4) If the scan tool cannot communicate with all electrical control units of a certain bus, and the communication with all electronic control units of other buses is normal, it is necessary to focus on checking whether there is line fault on the bus, or whether there is a short circuit and other faults inside an electronic control unit on the bus.

Note that the power bus in the CAN data bus is usually unable to transmit information on a single wire, but the comfort bus can transmit information on a single wire, and there is no obvious fault phenomenon on the car (the fault characteristics are also obvious after some high-speed transmission comfort buses fail).

If the internal fault of individual electronic control unit causes fault of a certain bus system, the fault can be found by disconnecting each control unit one by one. When a certain control unit is disconnected, its bus system returns to normal, which indicates that there is fault inside the control unit.

If there is fault in the network circuit, the bus waveform can be detected through a dual-channel oscilloscope, and the fault type can be determined by analyzing waveform characteristics, and then the bus can be searched section by section to finally determine the fault point.

III. Task Implementation

1. Inquiry

Know the time of the fault from the owner; Check whether there is abnormal condition

before the fault; Road condition; mileage; Repair after the fault occurred. Find out the situation before and after the fault and the specific information of the fault through the above inquiry, and complete the preliminary diagnosis of the fault. According to the owner, the fault has been repaired several times and has not been resolved.

2. Test Drive and Basic Inspection

Carry out the car fault test to understand the fault characteristics and confirm the fault. In addition, the characteristics of the automobile onboard network and the connection mode of the line shall be determined.

3. Detection and Diagnosis

Use the Volkswagen special scan tool to enter the function of "guidance fault search" and to fully detect all fault information of electronic control system. The test data are as follows.

Fault code memory content:

The data bus drive chain lacks information from the airbag control module. Occasional failure; There is no information from the instrument panel in the data bus drive chain Occasional failure; There is no communication on the diagnostic interface of the data bus Occasional failure; The data bus of the drive chain is damaged; Engine control unit has no information exchange; The airbag control unit J234 has no information exchange.

Analysis of the entire test data:

In the electronic control systems of airbag, instrument and engine, there are fault information prompts of data bus, of which there are fault information of the airbag control module and data communication interface on each system.

Common failure points here are: The communication information of airbag data bus is abnormal in all fault information, together with fault information of communication between instrument system and electronic control system of engine.

Considering that the airbag light is always on, the fault cause and fault code information in the airbag system are analyzed, and the airbag electronic control system is further checked, especially the CAN data bus of airbag.

The airbag CAN data bus and airbag computer are located under the rubber floor of the cab. When checking the wiring harness, it is necessary to remove the instrument panel and the inner bracket of the instrument panel, disassemble the heating water tank, evaporation box and main fuse box wiring harness at the lower part of the instrument panel, remove all seats, remove the middle guard of gear lever, remove the lower guard plates of front and left door frames, and finally lift the entire rubber floor. Once the floor has been removed, the multiple wiring harnesses at the bottom connecting the comfort computer and the airbag computer are exposed.

Check the airbag computer and it is normal, and check the wiring harness and it has no obvious damage or poor contact.

Analyze carefully, fault code: 01299 049 The diagnostic interface of the data bus has no communication, which means that no data is transferred to the diagnostic interface, which includes the inability to transfer due to the line; The data bus of the drive chain is corrupted, which means a problem with the data link bus itself. Both point to a failure of the data link, so it is judged that the problem is still on the CAN data wiring harness.

Item XIV Fault Diagnosis and Repair of Automobile Onboard Network System | **217**

Repeatedly check the airbag computer wiring harness based on this analysis, paying particular attention to the twisted pair of the CAN data bus. The wiring harness is located on the floor at the rear of the gear lever bracket. Careful inspection shows that there is a very thin gap on the insulation rubber of CAN twisted pair of airbag. Under the condition of not being squeezed by external force, there is no gap visible on the rubber of the wire. Only when the wire is bent will the gap appear. This wire is cut by the plate of the sharp U-shaped bracket behind the manual transmission handle bracket.

4. Troubleshooting

After handling the exposed twisted-pair with insulating tape, wrap the entire wiring harness and secure it to the rear of the U-shaped bracket.

5. Inspection and delivery

After troubleshooting, re-installation and test drive, the fault phenomenon disappears without any other symptoms, and the car is handed over to the owner.

IV. Task Summary

The fault cause is that after the insulation layer of the twisted pair of CAN data bus of airbag is cut off, sometimes the data bus is grounded at the same time, and sometimes the data bus is disconnected from the ground when the automobile bumps, thus forming the intermittent failure of the car. When the bus is grounded, its potential is pulled down, causing abnormal transmission of CAN data bus information. The airbag computer first detects and records the fault, and transmits the information to the engine electronic control unit and instrument electronic control unit through CAN data bus. In a word, for the fault diagnosis of CAN data bus system, it is necessary to find out the common information in many systems by analyzing the fault code information, and determine the source fault electronic control system; On this basis, the specific fault points of source fault information system shall be analyzed. With regards to the judgment thinking, on the basis of logic reasoning, the fault information and each system shall be analyzed comprehensively, from multiple systems to single system, and then the fault range of single system shall be tested, reasoned, analyzed and judged to finally determine the fault point.

Major			Class		Name	
Task Name					Class Hours	2
Model			Engine Model			
Task Completion Process	Assessment Items		Assessment Contents		Maximum Score	Score
	1. Description of fault symptoms				5	
	2. Possible causes and analysis of fault				25	
	3. Detection and diagnosis process				35	
	4. Fault Elimination				10	
	5. Summary of fault diagnosis				10	
Teacher Evaluation	Operation quality, operation efficiency, operation safety, etc.				15	
Total Score					100	

VI. Knowledge Expansion

〔Typical Case Ⅰ〕 A Magotan B7L car cannot be automatically locked.

218 | Automobile Integrated Fault Diagnosis and Repair

Fault Description：A Magotan B7L 1.8T car frequently failed to be locked automatically.

Fault Diagnosis and Repair：

（1）The guiding function of the Volkswagen special scan tool was used to enable the automatic locking function of the car，but the car could not be locked automatically.

（2）The Volkswagen special scan tool was used to access the gateway list：All comfort system control units displayed "Failure" or "Failure to access"，as shown in Figure 14-1.

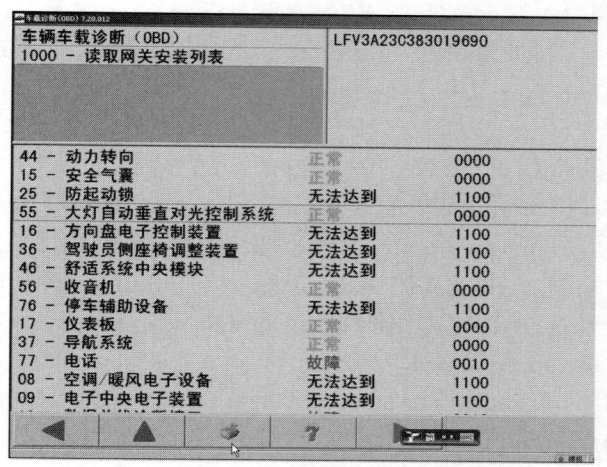

Figure 14-1 List of Gateway Control Unit

（3）Each control unit could be entered independently by the scan tool，but occasionally the control unit would have no response prompt；This phenomenon proved that the control unit could not be accessed occasionally because the scan tool would indicate that the control unit had no response in the event that it could not be accessed，consistent with the phenomenon seen in the gateway list.

（4）The scan tool was used to enter the gateway to read the fault code and the content appeared in the gateway：Fault code 00470 Combined comfort system data bus is in single wire mode Open circuit，as shown in Figure 14-2.

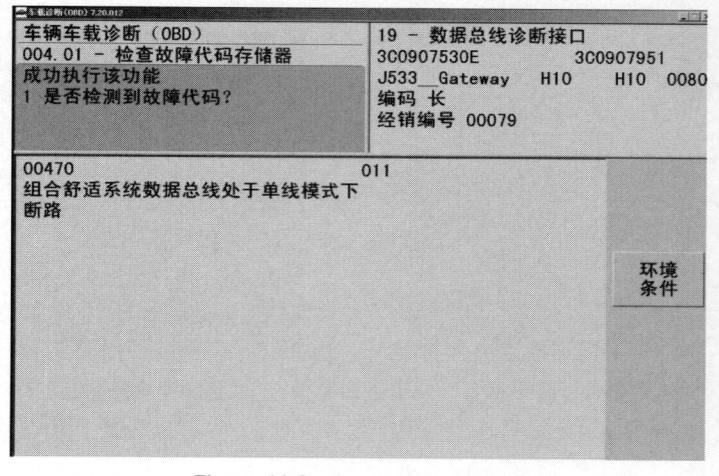

Figure 14-2 Gateway Fault Code

(5) It could be seen from the above data that the driver side door was in single wire mode. The left front door wiring harness plug was removed, the CAN bus between driver side door J386 and gateway J533 was measured with a multimeter. When measuring CAN-L, open circuit is found. After repairing CAN-L line and diagnosing with the scan tool, it was found that fault still remained, and single wire mode was still displayed in gateway.

(6) After removing the gateway plug and measuring the CAN bus between J533 and J386, and the wire connection was normal. The gateway plug was installed and the data flow was read again. The display was normal. When the gateway plug was shaken, the single wire mode appeared again, which indicated that the gateway plug or gateway had poor contact. There was no abnormality of the gateway plug upon inspection, it shall be judged as the gateway fault.

(7) After replacing the gateway, the fault was eliminated.

Summary: The fault of this car is combined with two faults, and the fault diagnosis shall be carried out according to the prompts given by the control unit. Because the comfort bus has a single wire mode, the owner did not feel any problem with the car. The failure to automatically locking occurred only if the gateway had poor contact and the comfort system could not receive the car speed signal.

[Typical Case Ⅱ] A Sagitar car stopped during driving and could not be started again.

Fault Description: A Sagitar car suddenly occurred airbag light, exhaust light and anti-slide light alarms during driving. Meanwhile, the engine shut down and could not be started after flameout.

Fault Diagnosis and Repair: The Volkswagen special scan tool was used to detect each control unit, and found that there were "01312 driveline data bus no signal/communication intermittent" and other fault codes stored in the 19-gateway, which could be cleared. After clearing, the car could be started, but the fault was repeated after driving for a period of time, and the car still could not be started; 01-engine computer had fault codes such as "28836 air conditioning control unit-J301 without communication, intermittent"; See Figure 14-3 and Figure 14-4.

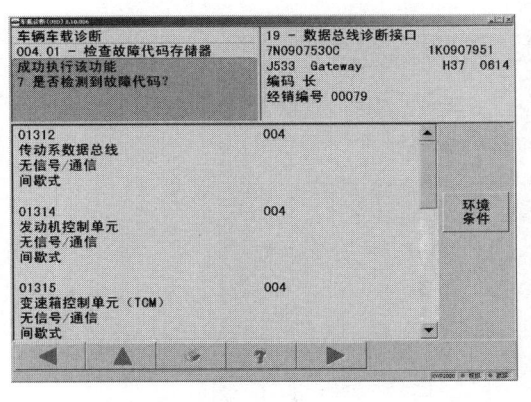

Figure 14-3　Fault Codes in Gateway

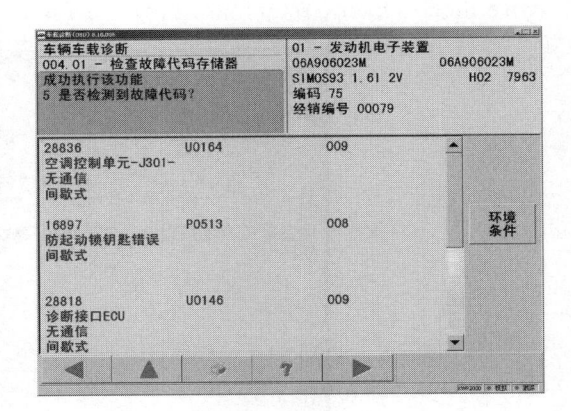

Figure 14-4　Fault Codes in Engine Electronic Control Unit

According to the meaning of fault codes, it could be seen that all the control units relat-

220　| Automobile Integrated Fault Diagnosis and Repair

ed to the power bus reported fault. It could be preliminarily judged that there may be the following.

reasons for the fault:

(1) A certain control unit on the drive CAN bus was damaged;

(2) Gateway failure;

(3) Drive CAN bus fault.

Combined with the fault displayed by the scan tool, according to the drive CAN network diagram, each control unit on the drive bus was disconnected and checked one by one. The fault display of the memory did not change, and then the gateway and instrument were replaced. The fault remained. Since the car was new, the probability of damage to the controller itself was small, and then the circuit of each controller on the power CAN bus was checked.

After further inspection, an open circuit was found in the circuit from the J533 controller T20/6 pin to drive CAN-L bus node B390.

After repairing the open-circuited part of CAN-L bus, a test run was conducted and the fault was eliminated.

Summary: The reason for this fault is that a wire was not pressed in the wiring harness node during manufacturing process, which was directly tied together with the node with adhesive tape. During driving, poor contact resulted in bus failure. Because the connection point was not completely disconnected, intermittent failure occurred.

For a bus fault, the effective method of disconnecting the control units on the relevant bus one by one is adopted to determine which control unit or wiring harness connected to the control unit is faulty.